Community Builders Handbook Series

SHOPPING CENTER
DEVELOPMENT HANDBOOK
Second Edition

Sponsored by the

Executive Group
of the
Commercial and Retail Development Council
of
ULI–the Urban Land Institute
1985

ULI–the Urban Land Institute, Washington, D.C.

About ULI–the Urban Land Institute

ULI–the Urban Land Institute is an independent, nonprofit research and educational organization incorporated in 1936 to improve the quality and standards of land use and development.

The Institute is committed to conducting practical research in the various fields of real estate knowledge; identifying and interpreting land use trends in relation to the changing economic, social, and civic needs of the people; and disseminating pertinent information leading to the orderly and more efficient use and development of land.

ULI receives its financial support from membership dues, sale of publications, and contributions for research and panel services.

Claude M. Ballard
President

ULI Staff for *Shopping Center Development Handbook*

Director of Publications	Frank H. Spink, Jr.
Project Director	John A. Casazza
Editor	Nancy H. Stewart
Staff Vice President, Operations	Robert L. Helms
Production Manager	Regina P. Agricola
Art Director	M. Elizabeth Van Buskirk
Artist	Christopher J. Dominiski
Artist	Helene E. Youstra

Second book, Second Edition, in a series of publications based on the philosophy of *The Community Builders Handbook*
First Edition and First Printing, 1947
Revised Printing, 1948
Second or J. C. Nichols Memorial Edition and Second Revised Printing, 1950
Third or The Members Edition and Third Revised Printing, 1954
Fourth Revised Printing, 1956
Fourth or The Executive Edition and Fifth Revised Printing, 1960
Sixth Printing, 1965
Fifth or Anniversary Edition and Seventh Revised Printing, 1968

Other books in the series:
Industrial Development Handbook, 1975
Shopping Center Development Handbook, 1977; Second Edition, 1985
Residential Development Handbook, 1978
Downtown Development Handbook, 1980
Recreational Development Handbook, 1981
Office Development Handbook, 1982

Recommended bibliographic listing:
Urban Land Institute. *Shopping Center Development Handbook*, Second Edition.
Washington: Urban Land Institute, 1985.
ULI Catalog Number S-27

Authors

John A. Casazza, Senior Associate, Urban Land Institute
Frank H. Spink, Jr.; Director, Commercial and Industrial Research; Urban Land Institute

Contributing Authors

Jerome Michael, President, Jerome Michael & Associates
Kelley S. Roark, Research Intern, Urban Land Institute
Cecil E. Sears, Senior Associate, Urban Land Institute
Richard M. Shapiro, Esquire, Pettit & Martin

with a Steering Committee
composed of the following
Urban Land Institute members

G. Smedes York, Chairman
President
York Properties, Inc.
Raleigh, North Carolina

Warren L. Beck
General Partner
Gabbert & Beck
Edina, Minnesota

Don M. Casto, III
Partner
Don M. Casto Organization
Columbus, Ohio

Cecil D. Conlee
President
The Conlee Company
Atlanta, Georgia

Donald R. Riehl
President
D. R. Riehl, Inc.
Pacific Grove, California

Robert M. Stanton
President
Goodman Segar Hogan, Inc.
Norfolk, Virginia

Phillip E. Stephens
Senior Vice President
EQK Partners
Bala Cynwyd, Pennsylvania

Acknowledgments

The preparation of the second edition of the *Shopping Center Development Handbook* required the time, effort, and cooperation of many individuals. Although it is impossible to mention everyone who participated in the project, a number of individuals deserve special thanks.

Appreciation is due first to J. Ross McKeever and to Nathaniel M. Griffin, principal authors of the first edition of the *Shopping Center Development Handbook*. The authors wish to thank those who assisted in the preparation of the case studies, particularly: Hope H. Dunlap, Director of Development, Kravco Company; Catherine Dunn, Director of Research and Communications, Goodman Segar Hogan, Inc.; Keith Koop, Associate, Henry S. Miller Company; J. Eric Smart, Senior Associate, Urban Land Institute; Phillip E. Stephens, Senior Vice President, EQK Partners; and Douglas M. Wrenn, former Associate, Urban Land Institute.

For their assistance and guidance in assembling graphics and in updating the book's section on architectural design, special thanks go to Chris Ramos, The Ramos Group, Architects, Kansas City; Charles Kober, Charles Kober Associates, Los Angeles; and Leonard Evantash, Leonard Evantash, Architects, King of Prussia, Pennsylvania. Thanks also go to Jack Gould, HSG/Gould Associates, Washington, D.C., for his review of the book's market analysis section; and to Leonard Borg, Jr., Hexalon Real Estate, Inc., Atlanta, for his assistance in revising part of the book's financial feasibiliity section.

Various ULI staff members have earned a note of thanks. Nancy Stewart edited the manuscript and assisted in the production process. Ann Benson, ULI's librarian, identified research materials. Tawanda Queen, Jane Lynas, and Louise Gant typed numerous drafts of the manuscript. Outside of ULI, Barbara Fishel of Editech is due appreciation for her proofreading support.

Finally, thanks to members of the Steering Committee, mentioned elsewhere, for assistance in identifying case studies and for their review of the manuscript.

About ULI Councils

Within the Urban Land Institute there are 14 councils: Commercial and Retail Development Blue Flight, Commercial and Retail Development Gold Flight, Urban Development/Mixed-Use Blue Flight, Urban Development/Mixed-Use Gold Flight, Industrial and Office Park Development Blue Flight, Industrial and Office Park Development Gold Flight, Community Development, Residential Development Blue Flight, Residential Development Gold Flight, Recreational Development, Small-Scale Development, Federal Policy, Development Regulations, and Development Services. Each council is composed of active members drawn from the ULI membership. Council appointment is based on knowledge, experience, and a willingness to share. Developers, consultants, public officials, and academicians are included on each of the councils to provide a broad perspective and to encourage interaction among various disciplines.

Commercial and Retail Development Council Executive Group 1984–1985

Chairmen

G. Smedes York*
York Properties, Inc.
Raleigh, NC

Kenneth W. Hubbard**
Gerald D. Hines Interests
New York, NY

Assistant Chairmen

Robert M. Stanton*
Goodman Segar Hogan, Inc.
Norfolk, VA

John W. McMahan**
John McMahan Associates, Inc.
San Francisco, CA

Bruce D. Alexander
The Rouse Company
Columbia, MD

Henri Alster
Alster International
New York, NY

A. Howard Amon, Jr.
J.C. Penney Company, Inc.
New York, NY

Mahlon Apgar, IV
Heritage Developments, Ltd.
Washington, DC

Jack A. Belz
Union Realty Company
Memphis, TN

Archie Bennett, Jr.
Mariner Corporation
Houston, TX

G. Peter Bidstrup
Doubletree, Inc.
Phoenix, AZ

Robert W. Bivens
Louisville Central Area, Inc.
Louisville, KY

Jeffrey A. Boughrum
Ramada Inns, Inc.
Phoenix, AZ

Michael P. Buckley
Halcyon, Ltd.
Hartford, CT

Temple Hoyne Buell
Buell Development Corporation
Denver, CO

Martin Bucksbaum
General Growth Companies, Inc.
Des Moines, IA

Franklin L. Burns
The D.C. Burns Realty & Trust Company
Denver, CO

Robert H. Carey
Robert H. Carey Real Estate Consultant
Birmingham, MI

Frank Carter
Carter & Associates, Inc.
Atlanta, GA

Ronald W. Case
Fredricks Development Corporation
Santa Ana, CA

Doug Casey
Homart Development Company
Chicago, IL

Don M. Casto, III
Don M. Casto Organization
Columbus, OH

David M. Childs
Skidmore, Owings & Merrill
Washington, DC

James A. Cloar
Central Business District Association
Dallas, TX

Cecil D. Conlee
The Conlee Company
Atlanta, GA

Dana H. Crawford
Larimer Square Associates
Denver, CO

George A. Devlin
National Planning, Inc.
Livonia, MI

David Donosky
Henry S. Miller Company
Dallas, TX

James B. Douglas
Seattle, WA

Roy P. Drachman
Roy Drachman Realty Company
Tucson, AZ

Fritz L. Duda
Fritz Duda Company
Dallas, TX

John M. Duncum
Dunshire Properties, Inc.
Houston, TX

Blake Eagle
Frank Russell Company
Tacoma, WA

Harold A. Ellis, Jr.
Grubb & Ellis Company
San Francisco, CA

Tommy Feagins
Parking Pros, Inc.
Houston, TX

James E. Foley, III
Jones Lang Wootton
Houston, TX

Laurence S. Geller
Safari Management, Inc.
Natchitoches, LA

Fredric Halperin
Coldwell Banker
Los Angeles, CA

G. Richard Hanor
Casto, Hanor & Associates
Ft. Lauderdale, FL

Antony Harbour
Gensler and Associates/Architects
Houston, TX

M. G. Herring, Jr.
The Herring Group, Inc.
Dallas, TX

Hunter A. Hogan, Jr.
Goodman Segar Hogan, Inc.
Norfolk, VA

Kenneth Howard Hughes
Kenneth J. Hughes Interests
Dallas, TX

Robert E. Hughes, Jr.
Hughes Real Estate, Inc.
Greenville, SC

Thomas J. Hutchison
Murdock Development Company
Los Angeles, CA

Allan Hutensky
The Bronson & Hutensky Company
Hartford, CT

Michael W. Jenkins
Goldman Sachs & Company
San Francisco, CA

Reverdy Johnson
Pettit & Martin
San Francisco, CA

Amy J. Jorgensen
First Winthrop Corporation
Boston, MA

Stephen R. Karp
New England Development & Management
Newton, MA

Michael Z. Kay
Portman Hotel Company
Atlanta, GA

Gordon Kennedy, Jr.
Gladstone Associates
Washington, DC

Claude John Klug
City of Commerce
Commerce, CA

Jim C. Kollaer
Henry S. Miller Company
Houston, TX

Robert C. Larson
The Taubman Company, Inc.
Troy, MI

Jerome F. Lipp
James J. Cordano Company
Sacramento, CA

Robert W. Lisle
The Travelers Insurance Company
Hartford, CT

Rodney M. Lockwood
Rodney Lockwood & Company
Birmingham, MI.

Daniel A. Lupiani
First National Bank of Chicago
Chicago, IL

Edward E. Mace
Lincoln Hotels
Dallas, TX

Philip J. McBride
McBride & Company
Denver, CO

Donald J. McNamara, Jr.
Bass Brothers Enterprises, Inc.
Ft. Worth, TX

Jerome J. Michael
Jerome Michael & Associates
Bethesda, MD

Henry S. Miller
Henry S. Miller Company
Dallas, TX

Harold W. Milner
Americana Hotels Corporation
Chicago, IL

John S. Minor, Jr.
Holiday Inns, Inc.
Memphis, TN

Dan M. Moody
Moody Oil Company/Moody Corporation
Houston, TX

Michael L. Morey
Madsen Corporation
Madison, WI

Robert T. Nahas
R.T. Nahas Company
Castro Valley, CA.

Raymond D. Nasher
Raymond D. Nasher Company
Dallas, TX

Daniel M. Neidich
Goldman Sachs & Company
New York, NY

Harry Newman, Jr.
Newman Brettin Properties
Long Beach, CA

James D. Noteware
Laventhol & Horwath
Philadelphia, PA

Jansen Noyes, III
Manufacturers Hanover Trust Company
New York, NY

Steven G. Nystrom
Connecticut National Bank
Hartford, CT

Jeremiah W. O'Connor, Jr.
J. W. O'Connor & Company, Inc.
New York, NY

T. W. Ohrbeck
Westin Hotels
Seattle, WA

James W. O'Keefe, Jr.
Morgan Stanley, Inc.
New York, NY

Richard M. Ortwein
The Koll Company
Newport Beach, CA

George R. Peacock
Equitable Real Estate Investment
Atlanta, GA

Charles S. Peck
Cushman Realty Corporation
Los Angeles, CA

Fredrick W. Petri
Wells Fargo Realty Advisors
Marina del Rey, CA

Ted Petrillo
Westage Development Group, Inc.
Somers, NY

Michael V. Prentiss
Cadillac Fairview Urban Development
Dallas, TX

Nicholas J. Pritzker
Hyatt Development Corporation
Chicago, IL

Raquel Ramati
Raquel Ramati & Associates
New York, NY

Richard M. Rosan
Real Estate Board of New York
New York, NY

Craig Ruth
Tooley & Company
Los Angeles, CA

John M. Ryan
Portman Properties
Atlanta, GA

Charles E. Sayres, Jr.
Metropolitan Life Insurance Company
Atlanta, GA

John G. Schreiber
JMB Realty Corporation
Chicago, IL

Charles J. Shaffer
Dayton Hudson Corporation
Minneapolis, MN

John A. Somers
Teachers Insurance & Annuity Association
New York, NY

Norman A. Spencer
Coldwell Banker
San Francisco, CA

Phillip E. Stephens
EQK Partners
Bala Cynwyd, PA

Gordon B. Swanson
Eastdil Realty, Inc.
San Francisco, CA

Oakleigh J. Thorne
Coldwell Banker Real Estate
  Consultation Services
Washington, DC

James M. Trucksess, Jr.
James M. Trucksess Real Estate
New York, NY

Frederick H. Trull
San Diego Unified Port District
San Diego, CA

Lawrence F. Walters
Dinwiddie Construction Company
San Francisco, CA

Michael J. Wechsler
Chemical Bank
New York, NY

J.A. Weinberg, Jr.
Washington, DC

Joseph B. Wilford
Trianon Mortgage Company
Altadena, CA

Lawrence A. Wilson
HCB Contractors
Dallas, TX

J.W. York
J.W. York & Company and York Construction Company
Raleigh, NC

*Commercial and Retail Development Council,
  Blue Flight
**Commercial and Retail Development Council,
  Gold Flight

Contents

List of Illustrations

A Brief History of the Community Builders
Handbook Series

The Community Builders Handbook Series came into being when the *Industrial Development Handbook* was published in 1975. This new series replaced *The Community Builders Handbook*, first published in 1947.

The original handbook was intended as a medium through which to share the experience and knowledge of developers and to encourage the improvement of land use and development practices. The handbook was sponsored by the Community Builders Council (now the Residential Council), which had been formed in 1944. Although the first edition contained only 205 pages and was sparsely illustrated, it represented a major achievement: for the first time, a book was available that described the development of residential communities and shopping centers.

The second edition, the J.C. Nichols Memorial Edition, published in 1950, was a modest revision and update of the original text. In 1954, the third or Members Edition, with 315 pages, significantly expanded the scope of the work. The fourth or Executive Edition, published in 1960, continued this expansion in response to the increasing complexity of development practices. With this edition, the handbook had grown to 476 pages, but it continued to focus on residential and shopping center development. The fifth or Anniversary Edition was published in 1968. The handbook had jumped to 526 pages and its coverage had once more been broadened. In addition to sections on residential and shopping center development, new material discussing a variety of special types of land development was included. Also added was a section on industrial development, drawing on the experience of ULI's Industrial Council, which had been formed in 1951. The Industrial Council had previously sponsored other ULI publications but the 1968 Anniversary Edition marked its first contribution to the handbook.

The Community Builders Handbook became widely recognized as a major reference source and textbook on land use and development practice based on the practical experience and accumulated knowledge of leading practitioners in the field. In 1965, as work on the 1968 edition was beginning, ULI was growing rapidly in membership and in areas of interest. The development industry was maturing and the Institute was examining new directions it might take. By 1970, the Institute decided to publish future editions of *The Community Builders Handbook* in separate volumes in order to provide expanded and more comprehensive coverage on each topic.

In 1972, the three original councils of the Institute—the Community Builders, Central City, and Industrial Councils—were reorganized into six councils to accommodate the growing diversity in development activities as well as in ULI's membership. Members of the Community Builders Council and the Central City Council formed the nucleus of the Commercial and Retail Development Council, under whose aegis the first edition of the *Shopping Center Development Handbook*—and now the second edition—were developed. The reorganization of the Institute itself represented one of the events that led to the multivolume Community Builders Handbook Series.

At present, there are six volumes in the Community Builders Handbook Series—the *Industrial Development Handbook* (1975), the *Shopping Center Development Handbook* (first edition, 1977), the *Residential Development Handbook* (1978), the *Downtown Development Handbook* (1980), the *Recreational Development Handbook* (1981), and the *Office Development Handbook* (1982). Other volumes focusing on a specific land use type may be added in the future.

This second edition of the *Shopping Center Development Handbook* marks the beginning of a new era for the Community Builders Handbook Series. As the currency of the first edition was evaluated during the planning of this edition, it was clear that while basic underlying principles had not changed, a simple update would not be enough. Thus, the second edition, while drawing upon the first, is essentially a new book—broader in scope and reflecting changes in concept and practice that have occurred since the first edition was written.

Frank H. Spink, Jr.
Managing Editor
Community Builders Handbook Series

Foreword

Shopping center development has reached a level of maturity and sophistication that would have been hard to imagine when *The Community Builders Handbook* first appeared in 1947. An even earlier ULI publication, *Mistakes We Have Made in Developing Shopping Centers*, written by J. C. Nichols and published in 1945, was the first publication to develop a body of practical knowledge about the evolving concept of shopping centers. The projects discussed represented the pioneering efforts out of which the contemporary shopping center evolved. The significance of these publications, however, lies as much in their approach as in their content. By emphasizing the recording and sharing of practical experience among leading shopping center developers, rather than theoretical concepts, *Mistakes We Have Made* became the guiding principle for *The Community Builders Handbook* in its first and all subsequent editions. This practical approach steered the preparation of the first edition of the *Shopping Center Development Handbook* as well as this, the second—and even more ambitious—edition. Throughout this book, the discussion focuses on recommended practices and standards of excellence.

As shopping centers have developed, several clearly identifiable types have been defined. We now recognize three major categories: neighborhood, community, and regional centers. The super regional center may reasonably be considered a fourth category, although it differs from the regional center only in magnitude. These categories are not precise, and patterns are still evolving. Typical tenant compositions for each of the basic types have changed: stores that might once have been found most often in one kind of center might now be found primarily in another. The sizes of centers have also changed dramatically: a center that might have been considered one of the giants 10 years ago is now simply another regional center, having been replaced in stature by the super regional center with as many as six department stores.

Special markets have stimulated increasing diversification and the development of a variety of special kinds of shopping centers that do not fit traditional definitions. This kind of evolution suggested the need to develop a second edition on shopping centers—a commitment the Steering Committee made over two years ago. Formed in the summer of 1982, the Steering Committee reviewed the first edition later that year and determined that it should be significantly revised and expanded to address fully current practices and trends in shopping center development.

Early in 1983, ULI staff identified appropriate changes and additions to the first edition, prepared a preliminary outline, and developed a research program and work schedule. Based on continuing research and on suggestions from the Steering Committee, the preliminary outline was modified and refined, and shopping centers were identified for potential case studies. In early 1984, the Steering Committee and the Commercial and Retail Development Council approved a final outline as work continued on the preparation of the manuscript for the second edition. The completed manuscript was presented to the Steering Committee in the fall of 1984 for its review and comments.

As an outcome of this review, the second edition of the *Shopping Center Development Handbook* incorporates throughout the book the knowledge and experience of committee members in the shopping center development field. We offer this volume of the Community Builders Handbook Series in the hope that it will prove a major contribution to the understanding of all facets of shopping center development.

G. Smedes York
Chairman
Commercial and Retail Development Council,
Blue Flight

Kenneth W. Hubbard
Chairman
Commercial and Retail Development Council,
Gold Flight

1.
Introduction

The shopping center is perhaps the most successful land use, development, real estate, and retail business concept of the 20th century. It is to the 20th century what the department store was to the 19th century. While the early 1900s had some prototypes, the shopping center is largely a post–World War II concept.

Shopping centers are a highly specialized development activity. The largest shopping centers are generally developed, owned, and managed by firms whose primary real estate activity is confined to shopping centers. Some of the larger national retailers—Sears, J.C. Penney, Dayton-Hudson, Federated, the May Company, and others—have created development subsidiaries. Although the dominance of large firms is less common in small centers, there are many examples of multiple development and ownership.

Definitions

The Shopping Center

To distinguish the shopping center from other forms of commercial retail development, it must first be defined. It is a specialized, commercial land use and building type, which today is found throughout the country but until the late 1970s thrived primarily in suburbia, occurring only rarely in urban downtowns or in rural areas. A later discussion of the evolution of the shopping center will describe its transformation from a suburban land use and development concept to one with much broader and varied applications. While the term "shopping center" is often used rather loosely, its definition and those of related terms have been standardized. When used accurately, a shopping center refers to:

> A group of architecturally unified commercial establishments built on a site that is planned, developed, owned, and managed as an operating unit related in its location, size, and type of shops to the trade area that it serves. The unit provides on-site parking in definite relationship to the types and total size of the stores.[1]

While seemingly broad in scope, this definition is quite restrictive and excludes much retail commercial development; for example, individual retail stores even when grouped side by side are excluded because they are not centrally managed. Thus, any number of small single-ownership strip commercial developments would not qualify as a shopping center,

---

[1] This definition was originated by the Community Builders Council of ULI–the Urban Land Institute. This council, established in 1944, formulated many planning and development principles and terms for the shopping center that are basic in the industry. The Commercial and Retail Development Council is the successor to the Community Builders Council as the ULI council concerned with shopping center development.

In 1947, under the chairmanship of Jesse Clyde Nichols of Kansas City, the Community Builders Council produced its first major publication, *The Community Builders Handbook*, which was divided into two sections—one on residential development, the other on shopping center development. The original *Community Builders Handbook* and its later editions were the forerunners of the present Community Builders Handbook Series, of which this handbook is a part.

and reasonably so, since a shopping center must have all the previously defined traits to be successful over time. Further, the definition given here for a shopping center distinguishes it as a land use and building type from miscellaneous collections of individual stores that stand on separate land parcels along streets and highways or that are clustered, forming a shopping district, with or without incidental off-street parking. Because of their preplanned layout and unified operation, shopping centers differ from these shopping districts or areas even though both represent commercial retail uses. In suburbia, a shopping center often forms the nucleus of a shopping area or district in an existing or emerging commercially zoned area, or it may represent the first project around which other commercial land uses are developed.

The following elements characterize the shopping center and set it apart from other commercial land uses:

- A unified architectural treatment for the building or buildings, providing space for tenants that are selected and managed as a unit for the benefit of all tenants. (A shopping center is not a miscellaneous or unplanned assemblage of separate or common-wall structures.)
- A unified site, suited to the type of center called for by the market. The site may permit building and parking expansion if trade area and other growth factors demand them.
- An easily accessible location within the trade area with adequate entrances and exits for vehicular and, where appropriate, pedestrian traffic.
- Sufficient on-site parking to meet the demands generated by the retail commercial uses. Parking should be arranged to distribute customer pedestrian traffic to the maximum advantage for retail shopping and to provide acceptable walking distances from parked cars to center entrances and to the individual stores.
- Service facilities (screened from customers) for the delivery of merchandise.
- Site improvements, such as landscaping, lighting, and signage, to create a desirable, attractive, and safe shopping environment.
- Tenant grouping that provides merchandising interplay among stores and the widest possible range and depth of merchandise appropriate for the trade area.
- Surroundings that are agreeable and comfortable for shopping and create a sense of identity and place.

These characteristics are not associated with the usual commercial district. An important point about shopping centers is that they create a single overall

1-1   The shopping center is characterized by its unified architectural design and by its central management system.

image for the individual tenants because they are under unified ownership and management and because the tenants and owner jointly promote the center.

Each element in a shopping center must be adapted to fit the circumstances peculiar to the site and its environs. Innovations and various interpretations of the basic features must be considered in planning, developing, and operating a successful shopping center. To succeed, each center must be not only profitable but also an asset to the community within which it is located.

Related Terms

The term "shopping center" is surrounded by a family of terms whose unique meanings contribute to a full understanding of the shopping center. Included are "GLA," "parking index," "trade area," and the names for the classes of goods a store or center may offer.

- **GLA.** In the shopping center industry, sizes of centers and tenant spaces are expressed in terms of *gross leasable area*, or *GLA*. Gross leasable area is the measurement used for uniform comparison and accurate measurement. It is an explicit unit of measure that is universally understood in the industry.

  GLA is the total floor area designed for the tenant's occupancy and exclusive use—including basements, mezzanines, or upper floors—expressed in square feet and measured from the centerline of joint partitions and from outside wall faces. It is the space for which tenants pay rent, including sales areas and integral stock areas.[2]

The difference between gross building area and gross leasable area is the enclosed common area not leasable to individual tenants. Gross leasable area does not include public or common areas such as public toilets, corridors, stairwells, elevators, machine and equipment rooms, lobbies, or enclosed mall areas. Gross building area would include these and other areas integral to the building function. The enclosed common area is typically less than 1 percent in open centers and 10 to 15 percent in centers with enclosed malls.[3] Because this percent varies with the design of the center, the GLA measurement was developed.

- **Parking index.** GLA is also used in calculations to determine the appropriate number of parking spaces for a shopping center because it affords a comparison between the shopping area and the parking demand of shoppers. Except for community rooms and management offices, common areas and storage areas in shopping centers do not generate parking demand. In defining the relationship between the demand for parking and the building area of a center, the shopping center industry developed a uniform standard by which to measure parking needs. The unit of measurement is known as the "parking index," which is the number of parking spaces per 1,000 square feet of GLA.

The currently recommended indices range from 4.0 spaces per 1,000 square feet of GLA to 5.0 spaces, depending on center size, and with additions required based on the quantitative presence of certain tenant categories and reductions based on the availability of transit. These standards were developed from the results of a major study in 1980 of parking demand conducted by Wilbur Smith and Associates, Inc., under the direction of ULI–the Urban Land Institute and sponsored by the International Council of Shopping Centers (ICSC).[4]

Before 1965, no empirical studies had been made on which the industry could base recommendations for parking spaces. In 1963 and 1964, however, ULI–the Urban Land Institute conducted a research project sponsored by the Research Foundation of the International Council of Shopping Centers, and in 1965, it published the first comprehensive study of parking requirements for shopping centers. This study recommended a standard of 5.5 spaces per 1,000 square feet of GLA. The standard was well received and widely adopted.[5]

By 1980, a series of changing demographic and behavioral factors, along with the findings of some interim studies, suggested that the single recommended standard needed restudy. In 1980, another major study was conducted, the findings of which led the industry to recommend the current standards—a series of indices based on center size and modified by the presence of certain tenants—rather than the single index previously recommended.

- **Trade area** is that area containing people who are likely to purchase a given class of goods or services from a particular firm or group of firms. The size of the trade area will vary based on the shopping center type and the tenant category.
- **Convenience goods** are those that are needed immediately and frequently and are therefore purchased where it is most convenient for the shopper. The shopper as a rule finds it most convenient to buy such goods near home, near work, or near a temporary residence when traveling.
- **Specialty goods** are those that shoppers will take more care and spend greater effort to purchase. Such merchandise has no clear trade area.
- **Shopping goods** are those on which shoppers spend the most effort, and for which they have the greatest desire to do comparison shopping. The trade area for shopping goods tends to be governed by this urge among shoppers for comparison shopping, and, therefore, its size will be affected by the availability of such goods.
- **Impulse goods** are those that shoppers do not actively or consciously seek. Within stores, impulse goods are positioned near entrances or exits or in carefully considered relationships to shopping goods. For example, a table of scarves or other accessories might be located between the entrance and the dress department in a women's store. Within a shopping center there are also stores that are primarily stocked with impulse goods—costume jewelry, accessories, snack food,

[2] This definition has been adopted by the shopping center industry as its standard for statistical comparison. It is the unit of measure used to establish recommended parking standards and is also the unit of measure used in the triennial study of receipts and expenses in shopping center operations in *Dollars & Cents of Shopping Centers* (Washington, D.C.: ULI–the Urban Land Institute).

[3] *Shopping Center Operating Cost Report* (New York: International Council of Shopping Centers, 1984), p. 95.

[4] Urban Land Institute, *Parking Requirements for Shopping Centers: Summary Recommendations and Research Study Report* (Washington, D.C.: ULI–the Urban Land Institute, 1982).

[5] Urban Land Institute, *Parking Requirements for Shopping Centers* (Washington, D.C.: ULI–the Urban Land Institute, 1965).

etc. These tenants need positions in a center where they can feed off the traffic generated by stores selling shopping, specialty, and convenience goods. Many of these types of stores could not exist outside a shopping center environment, which brings customers.

The Key Types of Shopping Centers

Shopping centers were originally divided into three principal categories—neighborhood, community, and regional—each with a clear and distinct function, trade area, and tenant mix. However, in actual practice, the distinction among the three types has not always been clear. Further, as specialized market opportunities have been identified, several subtypes of centers have evolved. These subtypes can themselves be considered distinct and basic categories or they can be considered subtypes of the three basic categories, with trade area characteristics used as the controlling factors in classification.

In all cases, even within the variations, the major tenant classification determines the type of shopping center. Tenant classifications and auxiliary facilities are in keeping with the territory from which the center draws customers. Neither the site area nor the building size determines the type of center.

The industry has often classified centers by size alone. In fact, a major survey of centers published biennially,[6] as well as much of the work of ICSC, has used size to classify centers. However, size alone is inadequate in defining shopping centers since it implies a direct correlation between center size and trade area, tenant characteristics and mix, and functions served in terms of categories of retail goods. This handbook classifies shopping center types by using all of these factors.

Neighborhood Shopping Center

The neighborhood center provides for the sale of convenience goods (food, drugs, and sundries) and personal services (those that meet the daily needs of an immediate neighborhood trade area).

A supermarket is the principal anchor tenant in the neighborhood center. Consumer shopping patterns show that geographical convenience is the most important factor determining the shopper's choice of supermarkets. A wide selection of merchandise and customer service are secondary considerations. Other principal tenants in the neighborhood center are the drugstore and the small variety store. Often centers not having a supermarket but similar in GLA to neighborhood centers are referred to as neighborhood centers; however, unless other food tenants can be aggregated as the equivalent to a supermarket, the center would probably be more appropriately classified as a small community center (since to be successful it would likely have to draw from a larger market area).

The neighborhood center has a typical gross leasable area of about 50,000 square feet in which to perform the functions ascribed to it; however, it may generally range from 30,000 to 100,000 square feet. In *Dollars & Cents of Shopping Centers: 1984*, the neighborhood center had a median size of 62,525 square feet in a sample of 388 centers.[7] Its site area requires from three to 10 acres; the neighborhood center normally serves a trade area population of 3,000 to 40,000 people within a five- to 10-minute drive. It has a parking index of approximately four spaces per 1,000 square feet of GLA.

Community Shopping Center

Initially, the community center was developed around a junior department store or large variety store as its anchor tenant, in addition to the supermarket. Of all the basic center types, the community center has undergone and is undergoing the most change in characteristics. The junior department store and variety store, while not extinct as anchor tenants, are less prevalent, having been supplanted as principal an-

1-2   The neighborhood center offers convenience goods and personal services.

[6] *Shopping Center World*, Communication Channels, Inc., New York. Since 1973 a census has been conducted every two years and reported in the January issue of the odd-numbered year.

[7] Urban Land Institute, *Dollars & Cents of Shopping Centers: 1984* (Washington, D.C.: ULI–the Urban Land Institute, 1984), p. 155.

1-3   The community center has a typical gross leasable area of about 150,000 square feet and often has a discount or off-price department store as the principal anchor tenant.

chor tenants by the discount or off-price department store, or by a strong specialty store such as a hardware/building/home improvement store or a combined drug/variety/garden center. Large-scale furniture warehouse stores and discount catalog display and pickup stores are other possible anchor tenants.

A community shopping center can largely be defined by what it does and does not have. It does not have a full-line department store, which would automatically categorize it as a regional shopping center. It does have a market area larger than a neighborhood center and thus draws customers from a longer distance. It offers greater depth and range of merchandise in shopping and specialty goods than the neighborhood center. It tends also to provide certain categories of goods that are less likely to be found in regional centers, such as furniture, hardware, and garden and building supplies.

The community center is the "in-between" center; some neighborhood centers have the potential to grow into community centers just as some community centers can expand into regional centers.

The community center has a typical gross leasable area of about 150,000 square feet but may range from 100,000 to 300,000 square feet. The median center size out of a sample of 243 centers in *Dollars & Cents of Shopping Centers: 1984* was 146,774 square feet.[8] The community center needs a site of 10 to 30 acres. It normally serves a trade area population of 40,000 to 150,000 people within a 10- to 20-minute drive and has a parking index that ranges from four to five spaces per 1,000 square feet of GLA.[9]

In the metropolitan area, a community center is vulnerable to competition. It is too large to thrive off its immediate neighborhood trade area and too small to make a strong impact on the whole community,

unless it is located in a smaller city with a population ranging from 50,000 to 100,000. The development of a strong regional center, with the pulling power of one or more department stores, may impinge on a community center's trade area. But in a normally strong market area, both can succeed, even if they are close to one another, because of the difference in the types of merchandise offered and because the community center is a shorter distance from its support market.

In cities with populations of 50,000 to 100,000, the community center, although lacking a full-line department store, may actually take on the stature of a regional center because of the center's local dominance and pulling power. An off-price or discount store may function as the leading tenant, substituting for a full-line department store.

Of all the centers, the community shopping center is the most difficult to estimate in terms of its market size and its drawing power. Because the community center offers some shopping goods and, in certain cases, special categories of goods, the market area is less predictable.

Regional Shopping Center

The regional center provides shopping goods, general merchandise, apparel, furniture, and home furnishings in full depth and variety. Its main attraction, around which the center is built, is the full-line department store, which as a rule has a minimum GLA of 100,000 square feet. While early regional centers typically had only one department store, that is no longer the case: two, three, and, in a few instances, up to five or six department stores have been placed in a single center. Whether several department stores located in a large regional center or only one store in a smaller regional center, department store sizes have over time both decreased and increased, and now often range from about 40,000 to more than 200,000 square feet.

For purposes of analyses, regional shopping centers have been subcategorized into the regional center and the super regional center. To qualify as super regional, a center must have three or more department stores. Thus, by definition, a regional center has one or two department stores. Regional and super regional centers are the largest types of shopping centers. They seek to reproduce shopping facilities once available only in central business districts.

The regional center contains a typical gross leasable area of 400,000 square feet and can range from

---

[8] Ibid., p. 109.

[9] *Parking Requirements for Shopping Centers* (1982), pp. 2, 17, 18.

1-4 Fairview Mall—a regional center in metropolitan Toronto. Regional and super regional centers offer shoppers a full range of shopping goods, general merchandise, apparel, furniture, and home furnishings.

300,000 to about 1 million square feet.[10] From a sample of 108 regional centers, *Dollars & Cents of Shopping Centers: 1984* found that the median size was 479,477 square feet.

A super regional center contains a typical gross leasable area of 800,000 square feet but can range from 500,000 to well over 1 million square feet with a few centers exceeding 1.5 million square feet. *Dollars & Cents of Shopping Centers: 1984* also showed a median of 855,454 square feet out of a sample of 93 super regional centers.[11]

The sites for regional and super regional centers vary dramatically—from 10 acres for a multilevel urban center to over 100 acres for a larger single-level super regional center. The regional center serves a population in excess of 150,000 people, who will often travel more than 25 to 30 minutes to reach the center.

Regional and super regional centers attract customers through their ability to offer full ranges of shopping facilities and goods, thereby extending their trade areas. Regional and super regionals do not differ in function—only in their range and strength in attracting customers.

Figure 1–5 compares the characteristics of the three major types of shopping centers. Numbers shown in the table must be regarded only as convenient indicators to define the various types of centers; the basic elements of any center may change should it need to adapt to the characteristics of the trade area, including the nature of the competition, population density, and income levels. The number of people needed to support a shopping center of any type, for example, cannot be fixed, because income level, disposable income, competition, and changing methods of merchandising as well as changing store sizes all enter

---

[10] *Dollars & Cents of Shopping Centers: 1984*, p. 61.

[11] Ibid., p. 19.

1-5   CHARACTERISTICS OF SHOPPING CENTERS

CENTER TYPE	LEADING TENANT (BASIS FOR CLASSIFICATION)	TYPICAL GLA (SQUARE FEET)	GENERAL RANGE IN GLA (SQUARE FEET)	USUAL MINIMUM SITE AREA (ACRES)	MINIMUM POPULATION SUPPORT REQUIRED
Neighborhood Centers	Supermarket	50,000	30,000– 100,000	3–10	3,000– 40,000
Community Centers	Junior Department Store, Large Variety, Discount, or Department Store	150,000	100,000– 300,000	10–30	40,000– 150,000
Regional Centers					
Regional Center	One or More Full-Line Department Store(s)	400,000	300,000– 900,000	10–60	150,000 or More
Super Regional Center	Three or More Full-Line Department Store(s)	800,000	500,000–1.5 million or more	15–100 or More	300,000 or More

into the calculations. Obviously, no rigid standard for size would be realistic. Local conditions within a trade area (number of households, income levels, existing retail outlets) are more important than any standard population data in estimating the purchasing power needed to support a center.

Once more it must be emphasized that tenant composition and the characteristics of the leading tenant define a shopping center type. Building area, site size, and population do not.

The Convenience Center and Strip Commercial

Two other types of retail commercial activity—the convenience center and the strip commercial—do not fit easily within the definition of shopping centers.

The convenience center is typified by the quick stop convenience store of which there are several national and many regional chains. They substitute today for the mom-and-pop grocery stores of yesterday. Frequently a convenience center is an adjunct to a neighborhood shopping center and, as such, is an integral part of that center. Or it may be a freestanding entity or combined with one or two other convenience uses, such as a coin-operated laundry, a cleaning pickup service, or a beauty or barber shop. The convenience retail cluster does not fall within the definition of neighborhood centers and is not discussed in detail in this handbook. However, the planning, design, and other concepts of center types presented in this handbook can be applied to it to some degree.

Strip commercial development, as distinguished from the "strip shopping center" (a frequently used physical description of a center with a linear configuration), is not a shopping center. Strip commercial can be a string of commercially zoned lots developed independently or a string of retail commercial stores on a single site where there is no anchor tenant and no central management, and where tenant mix results from leasing to available tenants with good credit, not from planning and executing a leasing program. While not condemning such retail development patterns out of hand, this handbook views such development as less likely to experience long-term success, to give concern to the needs of the consumer, and to be an asset to the community it serves. Again, however, much of the guidance and experience presented here can be applied to strip commercial development.

Variations of the Major Types

Shopping centers cannot be neatly confined to three principal categories. The typology of the shopping center is not that simplistic. Even early in its development, the shopping center form had its variations. However, specialization or subcategorization of shopping centers became a definite trend in the 1970s and has continued. The best analogy to this can be found in residential development. Beginning with two basic types—single-family detached houses and rental apartments—it has branched out into townhouses, garden apartments, condominiums, zero-lot-line units, and others. Each type developed in response to a segment of the housing market, just as variations of shopping center types have developed in response to segments of the retail market.

Specialty Centers

Perhaps the first subcategory classification of shopping center that evolved after the principal types were established was the "specialty shopping center." The term was applied to any center that failed to meet the traditional definitions. While the term is widely recognized in the shopping center industry as an appropriate classification for nontraditional shopping centers, the industry has never agreed on a clear definition of it. One salient characteristic that has often differentiated a specialty center from a conventional center has been the absence of a traditional anchor tenant. The role of the anchor tenant might be played by another type of tenant, or by a grouping of tenants that together might function as an anchor tenant, or by any number of other variations. For example, in a neighborhood shopping center, a combination of gourmet food shop, delicatessen, meat market, and green grocery might function in lieu of a supermarket. A food service cluster, several restaurants, and a cinema complex have also served as anchor tenants.

The term "theme center" was created to describe centers with a special architectural character or flavor. Most often such centers were also specialty centers, and thus the term "specialty/theme center" has been widely used. "Specialty center" is an inadequate description of several different subcategories of shopping centers and needs to be more precisely defined. Today, with so much specialization and market segmentation, the specialty center can be more exactly described by adding to it modifiers such as "fashion," "theme," "festival," "off-price," "outlet," "home improvement," and other qualifiers that could be targeted to a market segment.

Festival/Specialty Centers

The term "festival mall" came into being when The Rouse Company developed the concept for Faneuil

Hall Marketplace in Boston. As its name suggests, this type of shopping center is intended to create a special experience. It has a high percentage of GLA devoted to specialty restaurants and food vendors. Food vendors are typically concentrated as they are in a conventional food court, but a much greater emphasis is placed on ethnic authenticity, uniqueness of offerings, and frequently a blend of both on-site food service and specialty food retailing. Retail goods at a festival/specialty center tend to emphasize impulse and specialty items. There is often a strong entertainment theme with regular informal events featuring street mimes, jugglers, strolling musicians, and others. The trade area for a festival center must be quite large since a significant portion of its business activity will be from tourists. Thus, most festival centers would first be categorized as regional, and then subcategorized as festival/specialty centers. Typical of the festival center are its memorable architectural character and its relationship to other significant land uses—such as a waterfront or a historic area—both of which improve its market appeal.

This category of specialty centers encompasses many of the characteristics of centers that were previously called specialty centers and thus are referred to as festival/specialty centers.

Fashion Center

The fashion center is a concentration of apparel shops, boutiques, and custom quality shops carrying special merchandise usually of high quality and with high prices. It represents market segmentation by quality, taste, and price. Although not a necessary criterion, a fashion center may include one or more small specialty department stores; gourmet food and food service or a "gourmet" supermarket could be included. Fashion centers are most suitable for high-income areas. High-fashion centers can also draw on wide rather than limited trade areas when high-income areas are more broadly scattered. A fashion center could therefore have a market area scaled toward a neighborhood, community, or regional center. When it serves a neighborhood or community, it will be

1-6, 1-7   Located on the shore of Baltimore's Inner Harbor, Harborplace is a festival/specialty center containing 140,000 square feet of GLA. The festival/specialty center typically features a high percentage of GLA devoted to specialty restaurants and food vendors, a strong entertainment theme, and a memorable architectural character.

made up of small clothing and gift shops, and the traditional supermarket might instead be represented by a gourmet food shop, a butcher, and a green grocery. When such centers reach community and regional size, they will typically have as an "anchor tenant" a group of small specialty department stores; they also will probably have some tourist trade.

Generally, the fashion shopping center will be physically unique, sporting better quality architecture using high-cost finishes and materials. It will often have an architectural theme (occasionally as an adaptive use in a historical structure), special landscaping, or an unusual site configuration because of site restrictions. On average, the fashion center will have a smaller site area than its more traditional neighborhood, community, or regional counterpart. Parking requirements for the fashion center are usually below those typically required, since the dollar volume per sale at a fashion center will be higher than that at a conventional center and, therefore, the customer trips required for center success will be fewer in number but longer in duration. A fashion center will often provide amenities such as valet parking and reserved parking.[12]

Off-Price/Outlet Centers

Perhaps the most important retail development of the 1980s has been the advent of off-price and outlet centers. Although their growth has been dramatic, their place in the hierarchy of shopping facilities and their long-term success have yet to be determined. While this discussion combines off-price and outlet centers, developers of this retail type make significant distinctions—primarily related to tenancy and merchandising techniques—between off-price and outlet centers.

An outlet center is an aggregation of factory outlet stores. It has no specific anchor tenant although one or more of the larger tenants may perform this role. The outlet center is regional and enjoys a strong tourist trade.

The off-price center might be described as a fashion mall with discount (off-price) merchandising and with a commensurate design image. The goods sold in off-price stores are typically upper to high end, name brand merchandise that is sold significantly below the prices asked in full-price department stores and/or specialty stores. The size of the market area is between that of the community center and the regional center and has relatively little tourist orientation. The off-price/outlet center is a rapidly evolving shopping center type.

Discount Center

As noted earlier, the traditional anchor tenants of the community shopping center are fast being replaced by the discount department store. A discount center is a community-scale center anchored by a discount department store; it has become the most prevalent form of community shopping center.

Other Specialty Community Centers

The emergence of new anchor tenants (such as the home improvement store) has resulted in new special forms of community shopping centers. Evidence suggests that within a decade many of the commercial retail and semiwholesale uses that have traditionally remained independent of shopping center environments will be incorporated into various special forms of the community shopping center.

A current example is the "industrial shopping center," which emulates the shopping center concept. Rather than an anchor tenant, it typically has a grouping of special tenants who operate a retail/wholesale/manufacturing business dealing with such items as lighting and plumbing fixtures, mill work, security systems, catalog warehouse services, automobile specialty services, and others. Tenants are grouped in planned projects and provided with joint parking, building design features such as entrance canopies, sign control, and landscaping, and, sometimes, central management and promotional programs.

The specialization of community centers, though still in the beginning stages, appears to have merit in both retailing and in land use planning. It provides a home in the shopping center environment for retail/business uses that have historically been excluded.

Mixed-Use Development

A mixed-use development (MXD) has been defined by the Urban Land Institute as a larger-scale real estate project having the following characteristics:

- three or more significant revenue-producing uses (such as retail, office, residential, hotel/motel, and recreation), which, in well-planned projects, are mutually supporting;
- significant functional and physical integration of project components (and thus a highly intensive use of land), including uninterrupted pedestrian connections; and

---

[12] Pay parking is a unique feature of Bal Harbour Shops in Miami Beach, Florida, and is used to control and protect access to shopper parking that might otherwise be usurped by adjacent parking demands in a parking-scarce area.

- development conforming to a coherent plan (which frequently stipulates the type and scale of uses, permitted densities, and related items).[13]

The mixed-use development relies heavily on the synergistically related major uses within the project. The retail component in a mixed-use development may range from convenience retailing to serve the project's major land uses to a regional shopping center. The retail component could range in character from a traditional regional shopping center, in terms of both tenant mix and anchor tenants, to a specialty center type—most likely a fashion or festival/specialty center. The retail component of a mixed-use development will generally be multileveled and, of course, will be carefully integrated with the other land uses through interconnecting pedestrian pathways, shared parking, and uses specifically tailored to the needs of other land use components of the development.

The majority of mixed-use projects thus far have been developed in highly urbanized downtown locations—with some exceptions, particularly in the West and Southwest. As existing shopping centers are rehabilitated and expanded, many of them will likely evolve into mixed-use or multiuse developments. Many shopping centers today already represent multiuse developments in that the shopping center developer or other landowners controlling the surrounding parcels have constructed a variety of related land uses such as office buildings, high-density residential units, restaurants, cinema complexes, auto dealerships, and other uses that benefit from the attraction of customers to such a center. Clearly, the advantages of a mixed-use or multiuse development will be considered both in the development of new centers and in the remodeling and expansion of existing centers.

Downtown Retailing

While the shopping center was gaining momentum in the suburbs in the 1950s, downtown retailing, along with the downtowns of many cities, was in decline. When revitalization of core cities began, it was organized around new office development. For many years, it failed to include the shopping center concept even though those involved with core cities looked with envy upon the success of the shopping center in the suburbs and frequently saw it as a threat to the survival of downtown retailing. However, at the end of 1983, one study[14] identified over 100 downtown retail projects ranging from traditional shopping centers positioned in downtown—for example, the Central City Mall in San Bernardino, California; Glendale Galleria in Glendale, California; and Hawthorne Plaza in Hawthorne, California—to centers more carefully integrated into the fabric of downtown, like the Gallery at Market East in Philadelphia and Eaton Centre in Toronto, Canada. Some of the greatest successes have been festival/specialty centers: Faneuil Hall Marketplace in Boston always stands out in a list of such projects. While several earlier mixed-use developments might be mentioned at this point—the retail component of Water Tower Place in Chicago represents a good example of early design—the Horton Plaza project in San Diego, California, now under construction, illustrates how the retail component has increasingly been integrated into the surrounding fabric of the downtown.

Design Variations

As will be discussed later in the chapter on shopping center planning and design, the building design and configuration patterns associated with early shopping center development have changed dramatically in the last 10 years. For the most part, shopping centers were designed with single-level buildings for mall shops and multilevel buildings for department store tenants. They were clustered together as one

1-8 Plaza of the Americas is a mixed-use development in downtown Dallas containing a 100,000-square-foot specialty center together with office and hotel uses.

[13] Robert E. Witherspoon, John P. Abbett, and Robert M. Gladstone, *Mixed-Use Development: New Ways of Land Use* (Washington, D.C.: ULI–the Urban Land Institute, 1976), p. 6.

[14] J. Thomas Black, Libby Howland, and Stuart L. Rogel, *Downtown Retail Development: Conditions for Success and Project Profiles* (Washington, D.C.: ULI–the Urban Land Institute, 1983).

Frank H. Spink, Jr., "Downtown Malls: Prospects, Design, Constraints," *Shopping Centers: USA* (New Brunswick, New Jersey: Rutgers University, Center for Urban Policy Research, 1981), pp. 201–218.

group and surrounded by a large, surfaced parking lot with a few ancillary enterprises like auto accessories stores, service stations, banks, and cinemas. Malls began changing to multilevel centers because of site characteristics and because, as centers grew larger, the distance between anchors became too great and the single-level mall limited the sales activity of the anchor tenants on the second or third levels. The diversification of shopping center types led to the diversification of physical responses. Giving a center a theme, in which architectural design and landscape elements are used to differentiate one center from another, has become an important part of the segmentation of shopping center markets. Existing buildings were also adapted for use as shopping centers both in downtown and in the suburbs; prominent examples are Ghirardelli Square in San Francisco, Trolley Square in Salt Lake City, and Faneuil Hall Marketplace in Boston. The adaptability of the shopping center concept to changing design criteria, location criteria, and merchandising strategies appears limitless.

As noted earlier, the term "theme center" as used in the first edition of this handbook was considered synonymous with specialty center. Today, the theme for a center is more clearly understood to be a design strategy used to position a particular shopping center in the marketplace; it does not indicate a type of center. What remains important about "theme" is the idea that center identification and market attraction can be achieved through physical design and architectural character.

Evolution of the Shopping Center

Importance of the Automobile

The rise of automobiles, the rise of suburbs, and the rise of shopping centers are parts of a single phenomenon. When cities spread beyond established transportation lines, automobiles came into greater use to meet a variety of transportation needs. In pursuit of the shifting purchasing power, retailing moved into the suburbs; the present-day shopping center complex was launched.

As travel patterns and buying habits shifted with the advent of suburbs and shopping by car, new concentrations of stores bloomed away from established downtowns and business corridors. These new facilities were also built on new kinds of sites: the narrow and shallow strip commercial lots in business districts and along major streets could not readily ac-

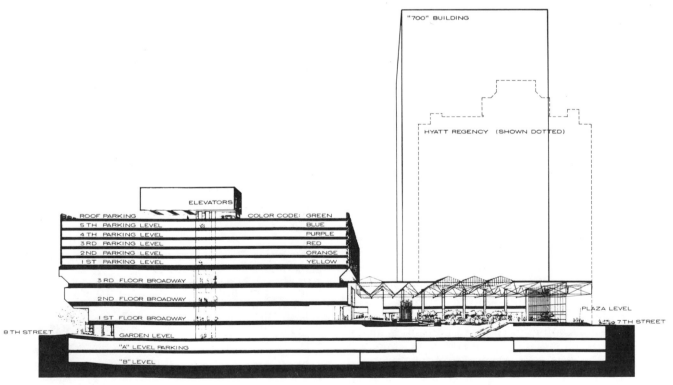

1-9   The retail component of Broadway Plaza, a 4.5-acre, mixed-use development in downtown Los Angeles, contains 100,000 square feet of specialty shops and a 250,000-square-foot Broadway department store.

commodate the on-site parking needed. Beginning in the 1920s, the provision of parking became a necessary adjunct of retail facilities.

Private enterprise responded to this need by devising a marketplace with its own built-in customer parking. Through a process of growth and innovation in response to the shifting nature of the market, early development on vacant sites unfolded from a strip of stores fronting on a street into the compact shopping center complex of today, identifiable by its planning principles, array of tenants, development procedures, and operational practices.

Early Experiments and Patterns

The shopping center concept grew out of early, freestanding Sears and Montgomery Ward stores and out of the innovative grocery outlets that were first built outside of downtown, on plots large enough to accommodate both the store and customer car parking spaces. From these experiments was developed a unified row of stores with display windows fronting on traffic streets and with parking for customers at the rear or side of the strip; the tenants usually comprised a food store, a drugstore, and several service shops. Gradually, the concept of grouping stores acquired the sophistication of site design, location, tenant selection, and operation found in today's shopping center.

The earliest "shopping center" venture predated even the advent of the large grocery markets that provided some on-lot customer parking. In 1907 in Baltimore, Edward H. Bouton, president of the Roland Park Company, constructed for several shops an architecturally unified building, which was set back from the street, at Roland Avenue and Upland Road. The site also provided space for horse-drawn carriages. Later, this space was easily converted to parking space for automobiles by paving the front grass and the carriage drive. In September 1975, when the Roland Park Company filed for a permit to tear down the building, local residents protested the action, viewing the demolition as the destruction of a historic landmark.

Bouton, also the developer of the prestigious residential community of Roland Park, pioneered in many other ways. He initiated the use of protective covenants, "zoning" for a specific use, setback requirements, architectural controls, flexible restrictions, wider lots, homeowners' maintenance funds, extensive landscaping, and civic responsibility on the part of the developer. He gathered other developers at his Roland Park home to discuss these advances in subdividing land as well as in integrating commercial facilities to serve nearby residential areas. At Bouton's home, community builders such as J.C. Nichols of

1-10   Country Club Plaza, Kansas City, Missouri. Developed in the 1920s, the project inaugurated stylized architecture, unified management policies, sign control, and landscaping amenities.

Kansas City and Hugh Potter[15] of Houston received inspiration and guidance.[16]

In the early 1920s, unified commercial ventures were often identified with high-quality residential communities fostered by forward-looking developers. J.C. Nichols led the way. It was during this period that he began his Country Club Plaza in what was then the outlying area of Kansas City. Nichols inaugurated stylized architecture (the first theme center) and unified management policies, sign control, and landscaping amenities. He provided customer parking in "parking stations." In the strictest sense, Country Club Plaza is not a shopping center but a shopping district; parking spaces are provided in parking garages and along public streets that cross the district. Still, the principles of a shopping center exist at Country Club Plaza in such areas as quality of management, tenant mix, and merchandising operations.

In 1931 in Dallas, Hugh Prather developed the first unified commercial project in which stores faced inward, away from the surrounding streets. Highland

[15] Past ULI president and chairman of the Community Builders Council.

[16] The following works discuss shopping center development during this period:

J.C. Nichols, *Mistakes We Have Made in Developing Shopping Centers*, ULI Technical Bulletin 4 (Washington, D.C.: ULI–the Urban Land Institute, 1945).

Seward H. Mott and Max S. Wehrly, eds., *Shopping Centers: An Analysis*, ULI Technical Bulletin 11 (Washington, D.C.: ULI–the Urban Land Institute, 1949).

J. Ross McKeever, *Shopping Centers: Planning Principles and Tested Policies*, ULI Technical Bulletin 20 (Washington, D.C.: ULI–the Urban Land Institute, 1953).

Shopping Centers Re-Studied: Part One—Emerging Patterns; Part Two—Practical Experiences, ULI Technical Bulletin 30 (Washington, D.C.: ULI–the Urban Land Institute, 1957).

1-11 Developed in 1931, Highland Park Shopping Village in Dallas was the first unified commercial project in which stores faced inward, away from the surrounding streets.

Park Shopping Village in Dallas can be called the prototype for today's planned shopping center: its site all in one piece unbisected by public streets, its individual stores unified under one image, built and managed as a unit under single ownership control, and its on-site parking determined by parking demand.

In 1937, Hugh Potter started a shopping center as an adjunct to his renowned Houston residential community, River Oaks. Potter used a then contemporary style of architecture that included cantilevered canopies along the storefronts. Although he violated an important current principle by allowing a major public street to bisect the center, River Oaks initiated many operational practices—for example, percentage leases and a merchants' association—that became standards in the industry.

These pioneers of the 1930s, each working to meet the needs of a particular area but without significant precedent to guide them, established the patterns of development that ultimately determined the merchandising concept of today's shopping center.

After World War II, suburban development boomed, fueled by 15 years of pent-up demand from the war and from the depression that preceded it. A wave of residential and commercial development swept through the country, forming "bedroom" suburbs—tract subdivisions lying outside the central city. Neighborhood shopping centers sprang up to accommodate these residential areas and to become ultimately a part of the new suburban scene.

In 1950, the next great shopping center innovation took place. On behalf of the Allied Stores Corporation of New York, James B. Douglas opened Northgate in Seattle—the first suburban regional shopping center built with a major full-line branch department store as the leading tenant. Northgate was also the first center to feature the central pedestrian mall with a service truck tunnel below. The open pedestrian mall and underground truck tunnel became an early building pattern for regional centers, although the truck tunnel soon proved to be too expensive to provide, and alternative loading docks were devised. Northgate has undergone several expansions and changes. It was expanded in 1963 and, in 1974, became an enclosed, air-conditioned mall. It now contains 1,153,762 square feet of GLA, and the original anchor tenant, The Bon, has been joined by J.C. Penney, Nordstrom, and Lamont.

During the 1950s, the spread of the suburbs gradually spurred the construction of shopping centers to serve the new market. That decade produced successful practices and innovations that led to proven procedures for shopping center planning; the shopping center became recognized as a distinct building and land use type.

Innovations began to come more quickly. The first regional shopping center to have an enclosed mall was planned in 1953 and opened in 1956. Southdale, near Minneapolis, instituted weatherproofed shopping on two levels surrounding a "garden court," all enclosed and under one roof.

In 1957, the shopping center as a new industry came of age. The International Council of Shopping Centers (ICSC), headquartered in New York City, was founded as a trade association to foster interest in and improve operating practices among shopping center developers, owners, managers, and tenants.

Shopping center development greatly increased in the 1960s. Planning and operating principles were tested and refined. Adjustments were made in response to changing conditions in financing, leasing, location, construction, and operational aspects of expanding markets. Variations in standard types began to appear.

The enclosed, heated, and air-conditioned mall became the dominant building form for regional centers. By adding two, three, and four full-line department stores, a regional complex gained strength in attracting customers. Such a broad range of shopping goods and other retail categories had once been found only in downtowns. By the second half of the 1960s, previously developed open mall centers were being converted to covered mall operations.

Diversification

While the 1960s experienced a rapid growth of shopping centers and a refinement of the basic concepts, the 1970s saw the emergence of specialization in regional markets. Coming into style was the fashion mall, a regional mall with an upper-end department store or a high-end limited department store as anchor tenant and with quality boutiques as mall tenants. The identification of market segments and therefore center type differentiation resulted. Most of the specialty types discussed earlier in this chapter were conceived either in the late 1960s or in the 1970s.

Also a new kind of market area was defined—the mid-market—which had several meanings, depending on the group of shopping center experts consulted. For some, it was a geographic concept—identifying site locations for regional shopping centers that fell between existing major markets. For others, it meant bringing the large regional shopping center into the environment of cities or clusters of cities that were in the middle-sized markets, as opposed to the major markets, in the United States—in other words, bringing the regional center to the smaller cities and metropolitan areas. This also included siting centers to serve a cluster of these smaller market areas.

In the 1970s, the mid-markets were defined as the growth opportunities for regional centers. This period also saw the growth of super regional shopping centers. Many regional centers expanded to become super regionals and many new super regionals were developed. By the end of the 1960s, the single-level mall was still the most popular concept, even for a large mall. By the end of the 1970s, most regional malls were multilevel and many began to have structured parking.

Diversification in uses was another major event of the 1970s. While the typical mall development of the 1960s was simply a shopping center, in the 1970s, the development community began to recognize the opportunities for peripheral development or for land uses on the shopping center site not directly related to retailing. Office buildings and ancillary commercial activities became part of shopping center development, although they were generally treated as separate development activities. In some cases, however, they were incorporated into the center itself; office buildings in particular became a more common component of shopping center development.

Up to this point, most shopping centers were freestanding, located on sites in rapidly growing areas. As fewer of these sites became available and communities began revitalizing downtowns through public policy initiatives, shopping centers began moving downtown. In the western part of the United States, the first downtown centers were often merely suburban mall designs with some modifications—most notably, structured parking—inserted into the down-

town of what was already an auto-oriented post–World War II suburban community. This was not the case, however, in eastern cities, where the shopping center was modified and reshaped to become a part of the urban downtown.

Perhaps the most significant innovation of the 1970s was that regional centers grew in stature from being simply locations for retail sales to becoming the focus of community activity, offering retail shopping, entertainment, food, theaters, and other forms of recreation or leisure time activity. The percentage of center GLA devoted to food service rose dramatically. Theaters were increasingly integrated into the mall singly or in clusters. Health spas, game rooms, and other new uses were introduced. The mall of the regional shopping center became downtown main street—a place to meet people, a place to see people.

The community shopping center began to diversify in various ways—the most obvious being a change in anchor tenants. The original junior department store or large variety store combined with a supermarket was replaced by the discount department store or by the super-super drug/junior department store/grocery store all under one roof. The community center further specialized by using as anchor tenants stores that had previously been freestanding—lumber, hardware, home improvements, warehouse furniture, and catalog warehouse stores, as well as the large women's specialty off-price (although in the 1970s that term was not yet coined) stores, depending on market opportunities. The minimall was a relatively short-lived concept that tried to capture the characteristics of the enclosed regional mall on a much smaller scale. (This concept was also tried on neighborhood centers in a

1-12　Fairlane Town Center—a super regional center in suburban Detroit containing more than 1.5 million square feet (GLA).

few cases.) Most of these new types of centers, which were first developed in the 1970s, require a market significantly larger than a neighborhood to survive but, because of specialization and the characteristics of the immediate market, do not need a regional market area.

In the 1970s, the neighborhood shopping center, on average, grew larger. Supermarkets expanded and the super drugstore (a combination of drug, sundry, variety, garden, and automotive supply goods) became popular. In some areas of the country where neighborhood centers were being developed in conjunction with rapidly growing residential areas, compatibility of design between the neighborhood center and its adjacent residential areas was emphasized. Higher densities and some office uses were often planned as transitional land uses between neighborhood centers and the adjoining community. Neighborhood centers also began to specialize as the tenant mix and the characteristics of even the grocery store were more carefully shaped and tailored to the demographics of the market area. Many large supermarket chains began to refine their product to incorporate delicatessens, bakeries, prepared food sections, gourmet wine and cheese shops, and a variety of other sections that could be mixed and matched to meet the demographics of the particular market. Compared to earlier years, the number of different types of tenants finding homes in neighborhood shopping centers grew considerably during the 1970s. This undoubtedly reflected the increasing number of centers and the growing differences of opinion within management as to what tenants were appropriate. Neighborhood shopping centers to a greater degree than either community or regional centers are managed by a more diverse group of owners and managers who may be less skillful in selecting appropriate tenants than managers of large regional centers, who tend to have permanent leasing and on-site management personnel.

From all the refinement, diversification, and innovation that went on with development in general in the 1970s, perhaps the most powerful new concept to emerge in the United States during that period was the mixed-use development—which frequently included a major retail component. First identified and defined by the Urban Land Institute in its 1976 publication, *Mixed-Use Development: New Ways of Land Use*, the mixed-use development has become a major development concept.[17] The intensity of development required to qualify as a *mixed-use* development is far stronger than that required for a *multiuse* development—a major concept, beginning in the late 1960s, that is also associated with suburban shopping center development.

Maturation

As will be noted later in a discussion of the shopping center and the economy, at the beginning of the 1980s, the national economy was suffering from inflation and a recession. To some extent, they slowed the growth of shopping center development. However, the shopping center industry had also reached maturity.

After rapid and vigorous efforts to meet demand for new regional and super regional shopping centers, many metropolitan areas had been overbuilt. At the same time, numerous shopping centers were beginning to age and needed major renovation and/or expansion in order to stay competitive with newer centers. Some of these older centers were in locations experiencing regrowth in other sectors. Conversion of garden apartments to condominiums created new demographic characteristics; infill development of offices, mid- and high-rise apartments, and other employment- and customer-generating projects around centers opened up redesign and expansion opportunities—all of which is expected to continue well into the 1980s.

In community and neighborhood centers, the economic situation of the early 1980s slowed the pace of new development required to support small centers. As they mature, small centers are less likely to be renovated or expanded; they will be maintained to the extent necessary to hold their market share unless significant deterioration of the centers or a declining or changing neighborhood dictates a more dramatic rehabilitation or the formation of a new image.

Another factor affecting neighborhood centers is the highly competitive nature of the grocery business and the narrow margins for profit that have led toward the gradually increasing size of the individual supermarket and to the introduction of various forms of discount stores; thus, store designs must be rethought for new centers and ways found to expand stores at existing centers. These changing characteristics have put pressure on the economic viability of some chains, causing sellouts and consolidations in the early 1980s.

While the main thrust of the 1980s will be to respond to the needs of a maturing industry, innovations in shopping centers will continue—one of the most recent and ballyhooed being the off-price and outlet centers. These centers began in the late 1970s/ early 1980s with relatively few, located primarily in manufacturing areas where factory outlets distribute second-grade and/or surplus goods. They have prolif-

---

[17] Witherspoon et al., *Mixed-Use Development: New Ways of Land Use.*

erated since then, and as many as 350 off-price/outlet malls are expected to exist in the United States by the end of 1985. While many participants in the development of these centers believe the centers constitute a trend that will continue well past the end of the decade, many leaders in the industry disagree, seeing this kind of merchandising as short-lived. Whether these forms of market segmentation will last may be a moot question. However, their existence demonstrates the likelihood that the 1980s and beyond will see continued refinement and segmentation of shopping center types.

Shopping Centers in the Economy

As an industry, shopping centers play an important role in the economy. The biennial census of shopping centers conducted by *Shopping Center World* since 1964 shows the dramatic growth in centers. Its most recent census of shopping centers set the number of centers at 23,304. Although the methods used to establish this number are quite sophisticated, the number is probably inaccurate. The census includes centers as small as 10,000 square feet, which would be disqualified under the definitional criteria used in this handbook. On the other hand, the census undoubtedly overlooks certain small centers since their ownership and management are more fragmented.

In 1950, according to records kept by the Urban Land Institute, only 100 centers in the neighborhood or community categories existed. By 1953, the number had tripled. But by 1984, an estimated 25,508 centers existed.[18] The *1984 Shopping Center Directory* lists 20,680 centers.[19] There are many reasons for an 18 percent disparity between the findings of these two major sources—the principal ones being poor reportage and double counting.

Since 1950 the percent of retail sales occurring in shopping centers has grown rapidly. By 1974, it was estimated that over 25 percent of all retail sales were made in shopping centers. By 1982, the percentage had risen to almost 42 percent, and, by 1985, it is expected to be 50 percent.[20] If sales of motor vehicles and gasoline had been excluded, the shopping center share of sales would have been 55.2 percent by the end of 1982.[21]

The 1970s

The 1970s began with bright prospects for the shopping center industry. But at mid-decade, a general economic softening showed that the period would be one of adjustments to new sets of conditions, particu-

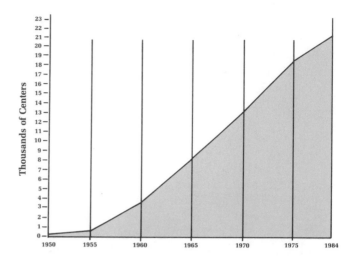

1-13   INCREASE IN NUMBER OF
          SHOPPING CENTERS, 1950-1984

larly for the land development industry. Severe restrictions and regulations were established. To protect the environment and to save energy, constraints were enacted that altered the pace of land development in all its forms.

Shopping center developers were not alone in having to face these limitations. Inflation complicated the general economic picture and contributed to high levels of unemployment and overall recessionary conditions in the economy.

The corollaries of undirected, rampant, nationwide urbanization have been land spoilage, ecological infringement, water pollution, landscape pollution, and lower air quality. The public began to react to flagrant abuses generated by uncontrolled urban growth at the beginning of the 1970s. Measures were taken to legislate national land use policy and to enact national and state controls over sensitive ecological areas such as wetlands, scenic areas, and coastal zones.[22]

[18] "Seventh Biennial Census of the Shopping Center Industry," *Shopping Center World*, January 1985, p. 55.

[19] The National Research Bureau, Inc., *1984 Shopping Center Directory* (Chicago: Automated Marketing Systems, Inc., 1983).

[20] Albert Sussman, "My View," *Shopping Center World*, May 1983, p. 342.

[21] S.O. Kaylin, "U.S. Shopping Centers Capture Increased Share of Nation's Retail Sales," *Shopping Center World*, May 1983, p. 151.

[22] J. Ross McKeever, *Shopping Center Zoning*, ULI Technical Bulletin 69 (Washington, D.C.: ULI–the Urban Land Institute, 1973). Discussed in the report are the Clean Air Act of 1970, establishment of the Environmental Protection Agency, and state and regional land use controls.

The EPA promulgated air quality regulations under the Clean Air Act of 1970. These regulations focused sharply on shopping centers as an "indirect source" of air quality deterioration. Although shopping centers are not themselves sources of air pollution, the EPA examined them because of the concentrations of automobile parking they created. Regulations based on evidence that parking concentrations induce air quality deterioration proved to be impractical, however, and on July 3, 1975, the EPA indefinitely suspended those portions of its indirect source regulations governing parking-related facilities.

In 1974, environmental considerations became complicated by supply shortages—the unprepared-for "energy crisis"—in organic fuels, particularly natural gas, oil, and gasoline. While this crisis has passed, the long-term prediction is that fuel costs will continue to rise, with the possibility of fuel shortages, either real or created by producing nations around the world.

Energy conservation had a dramatic impact on shopping centers, both those existing and those planned. When ULI conducted the *Dollars & Cents of Shopping Centers* studies in 1978 and 1981, a special questionnaire dealt with the response to rising energy costs. While the major response from centers in 1978 was to pass the energy cost escalations on to the tenant, centers were also retrofitting by increasing insulation, installing automatic controls, and altering HVAC systems. Operational changes were also made in temperature standards and in lighting levels. By the time the 1981 study was conducted, energy conservation practices had become so firmly ingrained in good shopping center design and operation that this special feature was dropped from the 1984 survey on the presumption that the industry had become fully responsive to energy conservation.[23]

The position of the shopping center was strengthened during the 1970s. Its ability to provide one-stop convenience and to combine trips gave it obvious advantages over scattered retail locations.

A major challenge to the shopping center and to its place in the economy occurred at the end of the dec-ade. In July 1979, the U.S. Department of Housing and Urban Development released a draft of "A Regional Shopping Center Policy." It was ultimately to be called "Community Conservation Guidance."[24] The principal objective of the policy was to control the development of regional shopping centers that would be detrimental to the retail areas of existing communities. The presumption was that urban revitalization objectives could not be achieved without restraining competition. The basic mechanism for assessing the potential effects of proposed centers was called a "community impact analysis." Only three or four of the analyses were ever completed, and these were released to mixed reactions concerning the possible impacts on existing retail activity from proposed new centers. This policy was discontinued with the change of federal administrations in 1980.

The 1980s and Beyond

The importance of the shopping center to the economy and its ability to respond positively to the challenges of economic recessions, energy shortages, environmental concerns, and economic management are clear measures of its staying power. It will continue to adapt to changing market opportunities during the 1980s while contributing to urban revitalization. The basic underlying principles of shopping center development, design, and operations set forth in this handbook have not changed over time.

---

[23] See Urban Land Institute, *Dollars & Cents of Shopping Centers: 1978* and *1981* (Washington, D.C.: ULI–the Urban Land Institute, 1978, 1981), pp. 260–263, 290–293.

[24] See Michael Morina, "Keeping Watch on the Fed's Community Conservation Guidance," *Urban Land*, September 1979, pp. 5–8. Also see Albert Sussman, "Community Conservation Guidelines: A Failure"; Marshall Kaplan, "Community Conservation Guidance: A Promising Initiative"; and "Community Conservation Guidance" in *Shopping Centers: USA* (New Brunswick, New Jersey: Rutgers University, Center for Urban Policy Research, 1981).

2.
Project Feasibility

The shopping center is a distinct commercial land use involving much more than a real estate venture. It is a retail merchandising complex that generates supplementary land uses and influences community values. In each of its several standard forms and variations, the shopping center is built on the concept of planned arrangement and development and unified management control. The whole undertaking goes through certain essential stages before arriving at the day when the project opens for business.

The development process comprises a series of complicated decisions, based on more than high hopes and good intentions. The procedure has moved from that of a few simple steps in site and tenant selection to one involving intricate studies in feasibility. Areas like market analysis, political climate, environmental impact evaluation, site planning, traffic analysis, tenant selection, lease negotiations, financial processing, architectural design, and public relations all require input from a team of experts under the guidance of an astute developer.

To solve the complexity of development problems, the developer draws on the teamwork of a group of professionals. Technical experts usually called upon include such professionals as the market analyst, land planner, architect, landscape architect, lawyer, engineering and construction specialist, accountant, financial adviser, and leasing agent. In some cases several or all of the disciplines are represented within the developer's own staff organization.

Team members must work together, meeting with the developer regularly to learn about collaborative assignments and the accomplishments and progress of each member of the team. The experienced developer knows that in decision making there is no substitute for informed judgment—his own, backed by the work of his development team. The experienced developer also recognizes that in the final analysis, he is responsible for all decisions made and the success or failure of the project.

The public approval process in many jurisdictions has become highly complex; in an era of growth management, environmental protection, and energy conservation, the team approach is necessary to coordinate and expedite the clearance and approval procedures in environmental impact and zoning matters as required by regulations at the state, regional, or local level.

In putting together any shopping center project, the development team must go through a number of preliminaries. At each stage, it should conduct a series of studies to aid in the decision-making process while proceeding toward construction. This series of steps making up the feasibility study must eventually provide the developer with his go or no-go decision.

The timetable for completion of tasks will change, usually growing longer. Snags invariably arise from local conditions and such contingencies as key tenant negotiations, financing commitments, permit approvals, and clearances.

Essential preliminaries of the feasibility study include:

- Market analysis, including an evaluation of existing competition as well as potential future competition.
- Economic analysis, including a careful study of the anticipated development costs and the income and expenses for the project.
- Site selection, evaluation, and control.
- Key tenant commitments.
- Leasing Plan.
- Financial negotiations.
- Zoning, environmental, and other public approvals.

The steps are detailed and depend on many variables and uncertainties. No precise how-to-do-it formula holds. Domino-like preliminaries precede any final decision. Ultimate site acquisition, for example, depends on zoning approval. In turn, leasing depends on site approvals and on securing key tenants, while financing depends on leasing. The full development process requires clearing a series of hurdles before construction can begin.

Market Analysis

Before embarking on any shopping center project, a developer must first identify and evaluate the market and then calculate its potential patronage for various categories of goods and services. This step should be taken before looking for suitable sites. A new regional shopping center can add the equivalent of the retail space of a small city to the existing retail structure. Where the population has not increased appreciably, the existing retail space in the trade area is probably adequate, at least quantitatively. In such situations, the entrepreneur building a new center must be sure the market can absorb an increase in retail space. This may require providing a new merchandising mix and/ or a stronger retail center.

A seasoned developer will clearly know the trade area characteristics that will suit the type of center he wants to build. But until he knows what key tenants are obtainable, the developer can only surmise the type or size of center that may be feasible.

Assume a neighborhood center is under consideration. Then, as James B. Douglas, a ULI member and early leader in shopping center development, once explained:

> If the top volume supermarket chain operating in the area is not represented in the vicinity of your proposed center, if the chain wants to expand its number of outlets, if its management traditionally makes reasonable deals with land developers, and if your real estate broker has a history of successful negotiations, then a certain pattern of success can be projected. On the other hand, if the major volume-producing chains have already established stores in the vicinity, leaving only poorer producers available for the proposed site, the size of the center, its success, and other factors will be evaluated differently. Only the person well versed in leasing will be able to resolve the selection of key tenants.
>
> For a regional shopping center proposal, the strength of the key tenants interested in the site selected determines the size, character, and success of the center—and even the price that can be paid for the land.

The type of center and its site character, drawing power, and ultimate success hinge strongly on such an investigation. The developer may have a hunch about what is feasible. But he must be equipped with hard data to interest prospective tenants, to identify the site, to sketch the proposed plan, to satisfy the community, to obtain zoning approval, and to secure financing.

Measurement of a project's possibilities becomes the first exploratory step in determining the feasibility of development:

> The developer's principal aim is to match the location, size, and composition of the center to the needs of the trade area. To do this, the developer usually tries to obtain an accurate economic analysis of the trade area, based on a market survey, from which he can derive a tentative plan for a shopping center.[1]

The market study is analogous to the situation of the chicken and the egg: A potential key tenant will not be interested in a center until a market analysis has been made, but a thorough analysis cannot be made until the kind of key tenant that the trade area will attract is known. As a consequence, two types of

---

[1] S. O. Kaylin, "Selecting the Best Site for a Shopping Center," *Shopping Center World*, Vol. 2, No. 5 (June 1973), p. 38; excerpted originally from S. O. Kaylin, *How to Create a Shopping Center* (New York: Communication Channels, Inc., 1973).

analyses must be made simultaneously: one is to interest potential key tenants in anchoring the prospective center; a second is to determine the number and types of customers who may be brought to the center. The customer draw influences the volume of business that can be expected by other major and supplementary tenants.

A specialist in the field should conduct the market analysis. The analysis does not take the place of a developer's sound judgment, but its measurements show quantitatively on paper whether or not the new center appears to be justified. With strong competition in the retail field, as well as the high cost of land development, building construction, and financing charges, a developer faces risks that leave little room for miscalculations, including miscalculations about the general tenor of community attitudes toward growth and development activity at the site or in its surroundings. In today's economic climate, a developer cannot afford to gamble on inflation bailing him out if he makes a bad decision.

The analysis tells the investor/developer whether a demand exists for shopping facilities. It also indicates whether new facilities are needed because of increased population and purchasing power, unmet demand, or as replacements for worn-out noncompetitive facilities.

The market study will also provide the information the developer most needs to "sell" his project to major tenants, local governments, and financial institutions. The analysis will help to determine how the project would serve the prospective market and whether it would generate a great enough sales volume to justify its development.

Further, based on the market analysis, the developer tries to decide on appropriate key tenants. Obtaining commitments from major tenants is fundamental in determining project types and size and in estimating project costs and framing leasing arrangements with other tenants. Such commitments are key to the economic feasibility of a project. Without key tenants, no shopping center—neither a small neighborhood center nor a regional giant—can materialize. Although specialty centers often do not have traditional anchor tenants, a cluster or group of tenants will function as the anchor tenant.

A shopping center cannot generate new business or create new buying power; it can only attract customers from existing businesses that may be obsolete, fulfill a need that has not been met within the market area, or capture the increase in purchasing power that accrues with population growth. It can cause a redistribution of business outlets and consumer patronage, but it cannot create new consumers. It can,

SALES POTENTIAL FOR A RETAIL CENTER:
ANALYTICAL PROCESS

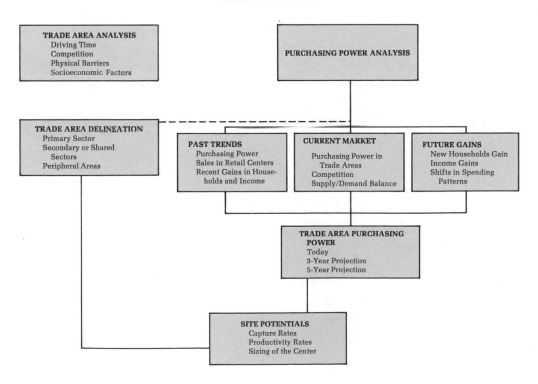

however, induce change in consumer purchasing behavior. Each new center must be justified by gauging the purchasing power available to it and the nature of the competition.

The required scope and degree of the market investigation will be suggested by population, income, purchasing power, competitive facilities, site access, proposed major tenants, and shoppers' buying habits and preferences. The number of potential customers living in a projected trade area will be counted. The territory from which customers will be drawn will be indicated by a study of access roads and will be limited by distance, travel time, and competition. A demographic study of the supporting population's income and composition will decide the type of retail outlets needed or wanted in the market area. The age groups and other characteristics of the trade area's population will strongly influence the tenant composition. Are major segments blue-collar workers, college-educated young people, or retirees? Accurately analyzing population traits and any changes in the composition of the population is of paramount importance in evaluating the feasibility of any retail location. The number, composition, density, growth rate, income, expenditures, buying habits, and lifestyles of the population can be translated into market potential. Much of this information can be extracted from census tract data, including metropolitan area supplements.

The total spendable income measured against the total volume of business done in existing retail areas shows whether excess purchasing power is available. Existing retail establishments that are unable to capture trade because of their shortcomings indicate that new centers might well be in order. Estimating the amount of this uncaptured trade that will be drawn to a new center will help to determine the size and type of the operation that should be planned. The character of the prospective trade area will shape the level of quality and thus the tone of the project.

Trade Area

The trade area is the geographic area that provides the majority of the steady customers necessary to support a shopping center. The boundaries of the trade area are determined by a number of factors, including the type of center, accessibility, physical barriers, location of competing facilities, and limitations of driving time and distance.[2]

As stated earlier, new shopping centers do not create new buying power; rather, they attract customers from existing districts or capture a portion of new purchasing power in a growing area. Hence, the extent of the area from which the center can be expected to draw customers must first be established.

Within a shopping center's trade area, customers closest to the site will affect the center most strongly, with customer influence diminishing gradually as the distance increases. Trade areas are usually divided into three categories or zones of influence, although the following general guidelines describing these categories will vary depending on the type of center and other factors.

- The primary trade area is the geographical area from which the center will derive its largest share of repeat sales. This area generally extends three to five miles from the site, is usually no more than a 10-minute drive, and draws 70 to 80 percent of the center's regular customers.
- The secondary trade area generates from 15 to 20 percent of the total sales of the average shopping center. Driving limits can be set at 15 to 20 minutes, or three to seven miles.
- The tertiary or fringe trade area forms the broadest area from which customers may be drawn.

[2] William J. McCollum, "Basic Research Procedures," *Market Research for Shopping Centers* (New York: International Council of Shopping Centers, 1980), p. 17.

2-2   PRIMARY TRADE AREA GENERAL GUIDELINES

TYPE OF CENTER	MINIMUM POPULATION SUPPORT NEEDED	RADIUS	DRIVING TIME
Super Regional	300,000 or More	12 Miles	30 Minutes
Regional	150,000 or More	8 Miles	20 Minutes
Community	40,000–150,000	3–5 Miles	10–20 Minutes
Neighborhood	2,500–40,000	1½ Miles	5–10 Minutes

Note: This table provides only general guidelines, which must be modified according to the characteristics of the specific shopping center that is being considered.

Although they must travel greater distances, customers may be attracted to the center because it is easily accessible and provides greater parking convenience and better merchandise than closer centers. Driving time from this area to the site can be set at roughly 25 to 30 minutes with the tertiary trade area extending 15 miles in major metropolitan markets. In smaller markets, however, it may extend as far as 50 miles.

Geographic distance and travel time must be differentiated. The competitive relationships of retail areas largely control the movement of shoppers in an urban area. Distance alone is therefore not a reliable criterion for establishing the extent of a trade area. However, it is influential: for example, the average person will travel one and one-half miles for food, three to five miles for apparel and household items when choice ranges are not important, and eight to 10 miles when choice ranges and prices are important. The late Larry Smith, eminent analyst and real estate consultant, believed that the population within seven to eight miles of the center probably accounts for 80 percent of the sales volume of a large regional center, and that a limited amount of business can be expected from shoppers farther away (within 15 to 18 miles of the center) who can use an expressway to reach the center in about 20 minutes.

The trade area may thus extend farther in one direction than in another. Natural barriers—such as lakes, rivers, hills, and parks that will remain as open space or undevelopable land for residential use—and artificial barriers also act as boundaries to the trade area. Travel times should be set by actual trial runs over access routes, with the runs made during off-peak times and under weather conditions typical of the area.

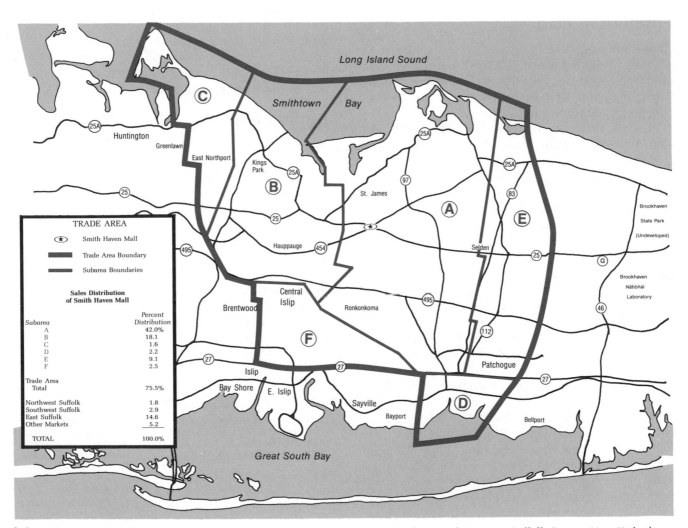

2-3 In an analysis of the expansion potential of Smith Haven Mall, an enclosed regional center in Suffolk County, New York, the trade area was divided into six subareas. This reflected the fact that various portions of the trade area possessed different demographic characteristics, travel patterns, and competitive shopping options. Source: HSG/Gould Associates.

The size of a trade area will depend on a site's accessibility from streets and highways—as well as from mass transit. Driving times, traffic lights, roadside hazards, and barriers such as steep slopes, stream valleys, parks, and railroads are all factors in the measurement of access. Allowance must be made for any proposed changes in existing routes.

A map of the trade area can be plotted based on geographic factors. Such a map puts into perspective current and proposed access routes, population density of developed areas, commercial locations and competitive facilities, and topography and land use features. Types of base maps useful for these purposes include ordinary route maps, such as those issued by service stations, topographic maps published by the U.S. Geological Survey, and aerial photos available from or specially prepared by commercial air mapping services.[3]

Population Data

Characteristics of the trade area's population must be studied, including the size of the present population and its potential for future growth, and the composition of the population according to age, income level, and family and household unit sizes.

The U.S. Census of Population and Housing (taken each decade) and the latest Census of Retail Trade (conducted every five years as part of the economic censuses) offer basic statistics. In mid-decade periods, such as between 1980 and 1985, population figures can be updated by special sample enumerations or by recourse to other survey sources. (See Figure 2-4, "Market Data Sources," for specific reference works and sources.) Projections for the trade area's population can be based on estimates for metropolitan area zones made by planning agencies.

Because the shopping center development industry has become more complex and centers are being targeted to specific market segments, the need for timely, accurate, and sophisticated demographic data has increased. In response to this need, a number of firms specializing in demographic data have emerged over the past 10 years. Many of them offer sophisticated demographic analyses, including the use of a statistical technique known as "cluster analysis." This technique divides the trade area's population into discrete socioeconomic groups or clusters, enabling users to determine quickly how many persons and households fit into a specific customer profile. For example, one firm offers data on 47 different demographic groups for any user-defined trade area and indicates the number of persons and households within each group as well as the proportion this group

represents of the entire trade area. These demographic groups are based on lifestyle information (as well as basic demographic data of age, sex, and income) in recognition of the fact that people with different lifestyles shop differently.[4]

Demographic data may also be obtained from a variety of sources. For example, if aerial photography is available for a census base year, current photographs will make it possible to identify growth activity and may even allow housing counts. Another source is building permit records showing the number of new dwelling units constructed in each census tract since the census year. Many metropolitan newspapers maintain updated census tract maps and regularly conduct buyer surveys. Utility companies can be checked for new meter installations, which increase in direct proportion to the increase in new dwelling units. Adjustments can be made to allow for known absorption of vacancies or demolitions. By such devices, fairly accurate estimates for population and households can be made in post-census years. In areas of rapid growth, state or local governments often conduct special censuses, since allocation of funds for roads, schools, health and welfare, etc., may be tied to population or to growth rates.

Buying Power

The income level within the trade area is important, not only in terms of total dollars available but also in relation to expendable income by retail categories. Income figures for households in the trade area can be derived from the census. In addition, the Bureau of Labor Statistics indicates how much families spend by income range for goods and service categories—such as food, general merchandise, apparel, furniture and home furnishings, and automotive parts and accessories. Consumer expenditures can be estimated from the purchasing power shown in each segment of the trade area. To approximate the total buying or purchasing power in a trade area, multiply the number of people by the average per capita expenditure for general merchandise and apparel. When the

---

[3] USGS maps can be purchased at public inquiry offices in Anchorage, Dallas, Denver, Los Angeles, Salt Lake City, San Francisco, Spokane, Washington, D.C., and Reston, Virginia. The two major public inquiry offices are located in Washington, D.C., and Reston, Virginia.

For information about sources and uses of USGS maps and commercial field instrument surveys and aerial surveys, see Donald C. Lochmoeller et al., *Industrial Development Handbook*, Community Builders Handbook Series (Washington, D.C.: ULI–the Urban Land Institute, 1975), pp. 98–99.

[4] Donald C. Wood and Mary Kay Healy, "Keeping the Data Up-to-Date," *National Mall Monitor*, September/October 1983, pp. 68–69.

General References

Bureau of the Census Catalog 1982–83. Information about census products issued from January 1980 to March 1983 on housing, business, population, etc.

Directory of Federal Statistics for Local Areas: A Guide to Sources, 1976 and *Directory of Federal Statistics for Local Areas: A Guide to Sources, Urban Update, 1977–1978.* Federal statistics sources for areas smaller than states.

Marketing Guides

Market Guide (annual). Market data for more than 1,500 U.S. and Canadian cities. Editor and Publisher, 575 Lexington Ave., New York, N.Y. 10022.

A Guide to Consumer Markets (annual). Compilation of U.S. statistics and graphs on consumers and their behavior in the marketplace. Conference Board, 845 Third Ave., New York, N.Y. 10022.

Marketing Economics Guide (annual). Estimates for population, households, income, and retail sales; ranks metropolitan areas. Marketing Economics Institute, 108 West 39th St., New York, N.Y. 10018.

"Survey of Buying Power," one of four statistical compilations in *Sales and Marketing Management* (16 issues/year). Gives current estimates of U.S. and Canadian geographic variations in population, income, and retail trade. Bill Communications, Inc., 633 Third Ave., New York, N.Y. 10017.

The following publications may be ordered from the Superintendent of Documents, U.S. Government Printing Office, Washington, D.C. 20402, from field offices maintained by the U.S. Department of Commerce in 48 large cities, or except where noted from the Customer Services Branch, Data Users Service Division, Bureau of the Census, Washington, D.C. 20233.

1982 Census of Retail Trade. In three parts:

- *Geographic Area Series.* Gives separate reports for the United States, each state, the District of Columbia, metropolitan areas, counties, and cities.

- *Major Retail Centers in SMSAs.* Gives details on number of establishments, sales, payroll, and employment for retail establishments.

- *Industry Series.* Includes "Merchandise Lines Sales" (U.S. summary data for 31 broad merchandise lines), "Miscellaneous Subjects," and "Establishments and Firm Size."

Current Business Reports. The Government Printing Office offers only the entire series; individual reports must be ordered from the Bureau of the Census.

- BR *Monthly Retail Trade—Sales and Inventories* with annual cumulation.

- BW *Monthly Wholesale Trade—Sales and Inventories* with annual cumulation.

- CB *Advance Monthly Retail Sales.*

Survey of Current Business. Current business statistics compiled by the Bureau of Economic Analysis, U.S. Department of Commerce, in 12 issues per year. Special reports on "Local Area Personal Income" (April), "National Income Issue" (July), "State and Regional Income" (twice a year). Order from GPO.

1980 Census of Population and Housing

- PC Reports: Population
  PC80-1-A: Number of Inhabitants
  PC80-1-B: General Population Characteristics
  PC80-S1-2: Population and Households by States and Counties: 1980.

- HC Reports: Housing
  HC 80-1-A: General Housing Characteristics
  HC 80-1-B: Detailed Housing Characteristics
  HC 80-1-C: Metropolitan Housing Characteristics

- PHC80-2: Census Tracts. A series of 372 reports and maps, one for each metropolitan area and one for each state that contains data for tracted areas outside of metropolitan areas.

Population Characteristics, Special Studies, and Income

- P-60, No. 132. *Money Income of Households, Families, and Persons in the United States: 1980.*

Bureau of Labor Statistics, U.S. Department of Labor, which publishes periodically the survey, *Consumer Expenditures and Income.*

number of expected customers is multiplied by the average annual expenditures for consumer items, the sales potential of the trade area comes into focus. The variation in expenditures of different income groups should also be taken into account.[5]

Income can be estimated by using a ratio of income to home value. The value of the owned home is usually rather closely related to family income. In the past, the customary amount that could be afforded for a house was 2 to 2½ times a family's annual income. Today, the amount commonly spent on housing in many markets is 2½ to 3 times a family's income. In the U.S. Census of Housing, the values (and rentals) of houses are available for each block in cities with a population of 50,000 or more. For suburban areas, the U.S. Bureau of the Census will furnish, at a reasonable cost, photostat sheets of unpublished data for census years, showing home values and rentals by enumerated districts. Where there is a state income tax, it may be possible to learn the distribution of families by income groups in a city or county.

As income declines, the proportion of total family income spent for food rapidly increases. Thus, in a trade area whose average family income is lower than the average for the city as a whole, the proportion of income spent in nonfood stores is much less than that in an area of medium-income or high-income families. Where all families within a given trade area have similar average incomes, the store composition will be quite different from that in a trade area with a large proportion of high-income families counterbalanced by a large proportion of low-income families.

Buying power and the number of families needed to support any shopping center are variables, particularly in a new development area. Developers of new communities in isolated areas must provide shopping facilities before a full market is justified to provide limited goods for families who move into the area.

Competition

A new shopping center will not, of course, attract all the business in its trade area. Basically, it will draw on three sources: the increase in population, patrons from existing stores in the trade area, and customers seeking goods and services not offered in the area.

A new center will not generate more purchasing power than already exists within the trade area, but it will bring about a redistribution of expenditures. For this reason, the market analysis should study the retail facilities that are or are not available. That portion of spendable income that is unsatisfied by local offerings must be determined. Often the study will reveal that potential sales are escaping to other communities.

With one exception, no formula exists for estimating the share of the buying power in a market area that can be attracted to a new center. The single exception is Reilly's Law of Retail Gravitation, formulated over 50 years ago by William J. Reilly at the University of Texas, Austin:

> When two cities compete for retail trade from the immediate rural areas, the breaking point for the attraction of such trade will be more or less in direct proportion to the population of the two cities and in inverse proportion to the square of the distance from the immediate area of each city.

In effect, all this law says is that people will travel to the largest place most easily reached. Reilly's Law cannot be used as the sole method by which to determine a shopping center's pull. Also, it should not be applied to market analyses for neighborhood centers. First employed to measure retail attraction between the central business districts of two cities, Reilly's Law was later adopted by a few analysts of early regional shopping centers to measure local attraction between different department stores. However, each case is different. Estimates for a proposed shopping center must allow for composite pulls from retail shopping areas. Some analysts believe a breaking point exists between competing retail districts when the natural pull of one is equal to that of the other. Proponents of a formula-judgment method sometimes find a revision of Reilly's Law useful in predicting the sales potential of a center, particularly if the center offers shopping goods like those found in a regional center.

In evaluating the feasibility of a new center, a developer should study other retail shopping facilities—both existing and proposed—with which his center would have to compete. These would consist of suburban shopping facilities within and beyond the trade area; retail facilities in the central business district, which might exercise a strong though varying influence on residents throughout the metropolitan area; and shopping facilities likely to be built in the future.

When the income of each segment of the trade area population has been determined, the amount can be calculated that households spend at shopping areas that would compete with a new center. The new cen-

[5] See *Survey of Consumer Expenditures*, issued periodically for total U.S. and urban and rural regions, with cross-classification of family characteristics; and current publications of the Bureau of Labor Statistics. These publications are available from the U.S. Department of Labor, Bureau of Labor Statistics, Washington, D.C. 20212.

Also see *Statistical Abstract of the United States* and *County and City Data Book: A Statistical Abstract Supplement*, both issued annually by the U.S. Bureau of the Census and available from the U.S. Government Printing Office, Washington, D.C. 20402.

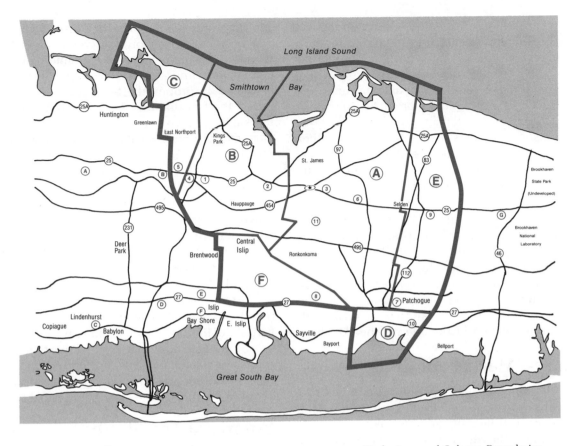

Trade Area Retailing

1 Gimbels
2 J.C. Penney
3 Discount Department Store
4 Discount Department Store
5 Discount Department Store
6 Discount Department Store
7 Discount Department Store
8 Times Square Stores
9 Two Guys
10 Discount Department Store
11 Discount Department Store

Competitive Framework

A Walt Whitman Mall
　　Abraham & Straus/Macy's
B Sears
C Great South Bay Center
　　Abraham & Straus/
　　J.C. Penney
D Gardiner Manor Shopping
　　Center
　　Sears/Gertz
E South Shore Mall
　　Macy's/J.C. Penney
F Gimbels
G Brookhaven Mall (proposed)

2-5　The competition within Smith Haven Mall's trade area. Source: HSG/Gould Associates.

Kind of Center

ter could accommodate any unused buying power, thus attracting a share of the trade area.

The anticipated volume of business and the appropriate merchandise mix for the new center will be determined by evaluating known data on the proportion of family income spent in each major category, such as food, clothing, furniture, and other retail. Proper tenant mix increases the pulling power of any shopping center. The function of tenant mix is to provide the greatest depth of selection across a wide range of consumer goods.

Future growth and its effect on a center must be taken into account with studies made on the community's economic base and on the direction that future growth may take.

After the trade area and the sales potential have been established, the kind of center that would be most feasible begins to take shape, particularly when leading or key tenants are known. When the market analysis is made, the names of probable tenants are compiled. In most areas, certain local merchants are stronger than others. For example, a majority of customers may prefer one supermarket over another; hence, the local standing of a merchant should be considered. Popular established merchants will draw more patronage to a new center, strengthening the center's appeal.

Identified market segments may suggest a special character for the proposed center, which would allow it to depart from the traditional neighborhood, community, or regional center tenant mix and to include special tenant categories that would be supported because of the presence (or absence) of a particular market segment. For example, if an area has few children and the child population is projected to remain low, there would be little demand for children's shopping goods (shoes, clothes, toys, etc.). On the other hand, there might be a greater demand for food-service tenants, since adults without children will be more prone to eat out. Further market analysis would quantify this potential.

Based on the estimated sales volume resulting from market analysis, the types of stores and the approximate square footage of building can be determined. After the building area and the types and sizes of stores have been established, parking needs can be estimated in relation to the gross leasable area. The total area required for the site can then be measured, and the planned layout of the site can be sketched.

Summary—Market Analysis

Although an expert in the field should conduct the market evaluation, the developer's judgment and common sense will temper the analysis.

To recapitulate, the rudiments of a market analysis include:

- Determining the trade area of the shopping center. The trade area is established based on population changes and estimated future growth in the area (which should be translated onto maps and displayed graphically); the area's basic employment and economy; and the proposed site's accessibility—present and future highway patterns, traffic counts, street capacities, and travel times (which should also be translated onto maps and other data displays).
- Estimating the purchasing power of primary, secondary, and remote trade areas. Disposable income can be estimated after federal income and local taxes, housing costs, and insurance, savings, and transportation costs have been deducted. The remaining dollars constitute net spendable income.
- Measuring competition.
- Gauging retail sales potential. This would include investigating total retail expenditures, the sales capacity of existing stores by types of merchandise, and the unused purchasing power available to the center.

While the fundamentals of market research are constant, different types of centers may need somewhat different market research approaches. For example, if a factory outlet center is being considered, the market analysis generally should survey a larger trade area than if an off-price center of the same size were being considered. Similarly, if a downtown festival/specialty center is proposed, the market analysis should reflect the fact that the size and buying power of the market for a downtown center depend on the size and character of a number of different markets, including close-in residents, metropolitan area residents, downtown office workers, and transient customers. Further, the market analysis for such a center should also review such factors as the drawing power of downtown and the character of the downtown environment (in terms of both appearance and safety), since these factors can directly affect the center's potential to succeed—or fail.

Finally, the assumptions made in any market study should be carefully chosen, clearly understood, and based on realizable goals. They are critical to the validity of the study. The primary purpose of a market survey is not to convince prospective tenants that the trade area needs and can support a proposed center, but to find out whether the area can support a new shopping center of the type being considered.

Financial Feasibility

Since it will draw upon and interpret the findings of the market study, the economic analysis should follow the market study. It will largely determine the financial feasibility of the center. The feasibility study will also begin to reveal the kind of center that might best be developed by analyzing factors such as total retail space (with space assigned to key tenants and supplementary stores) and by projecting rental income (by minimum rents, annual sales volume, and percentage rents).

Projections should be systematically developed into pro forma statements on the estimated cost of development, the income and expenses of the center, and the center's cash flow. The pro forma statement on development costs will indicate the estimated capital cost for the project. The capital cost represents the total investment in the project and may be broken down into the following major categories:

- Land and land improvements.
- Buildings and equipment.
- Overhead and development costs (sometimes called "soft costs") incurred before a center opens.

Composite items included in capital cost are:

- Land cost: the basic cost of land plus carrying charges until construction is completed.
- Off-site improvements, such as extending util-

SHOPPING CENTER ITEMS INCLUDED IN CAPITAL COSTS

LAND AND LAND IMPROVEMENTS	BUILDINGS AND EQUIPMENT	OVERHEAD AND DEVELOPMENT

Land or Leasehold Acquisition
Cost of Land
Good Faith Deposit
Broker's Fee
Escrow
Title Guarantee Policy
Standby Fee
Chattel Search
Legal Fee
Recording Fee

Off-Site and On-Site Land Improvements
Off-Site Streets and Sidewalks
Off-Site Sewers, Utilities, and Lights
Relocation of Power Lines
Traffic Controls
Surveys and Test Borings
Utilities
  Water Connection to Central System or On-Site Supply
  Storm Sewers
  Sanitary Sewer Connection to System or On-Site Disposal
  Gas Distribution Connection to Central System
  Primary Electrical Distribution
  Telephone Distribution
Parking Areas
  Curbs and Gutters
  Paving and Striping
  Pedestrian Walkways
  Traffic Controls and Signs
  Lighting
  Service Area Screens and Fences
Landscaping
  Grading
  Planting

Shell and Mall Building
Layout
Excavation
Footing and Foundations
Structural Frame
Exterior Walls
Roofing and Insulation
Subfloor
Sidewalk Canopy
Sidewalks and Mall Paving
Loading Docks and Service Courts
Truck and Service Tunnels
Equipment Rooms, Transformer Vaults, Cooling Towers
Heating and Cooling—Central Plants or Units
Incinerator
Community Halls
Offices for Central and Merchants' Association
Electric Wiring—Roughed In
Plumbing—Roughed In
Fire Sprinkler System
Public Toilets
Elevators, Escalators, Stairways
Contractor's Overhead and Profit
Pylons
Shopping Center Signs
Mall Furniture, Fountains, etc.
Maintenance Equipment and Tools
Office Furniture and Equipment

Tenant Improvements (paid for by developer)
Tenant Finish Allowance
Storefronts
Window Backs and Fronts
Finished Ceiling and Acoustical Tile
Finished Walls
Interior Painting
Floor Coverings—Tile and Terrazzo
Interior Partitioning
Lighting Fixtures
Plumbing Fixtures
Doors, Frames, and Hardware
Storefront Signs
Store Fixtures

Architecture and Engineering
Site Planning
Buildings and Improvements

Internal and Financing
Interest during Construction
Construction and Permanent Loan Fees
Loan Settlement Costs
Appraisal Costs
Legal Fees—Financing

Administrative Overhead and Construction Supervision
Construction Supervision
Field Office Expense
Bookkeeping
Home Office Expense
Travel and Entertainment
Salaries and Overhead of Staff
Printing and Stationery

Leasing Costs and Legal Fees
Leasing Fees Paid to Brokers
Salaries and Overhead of Staff
Scale Model, Brochures, etc.
Legal Fees—Leasing
Legal Fees—General

Other Overhead and Development
Market and Traffic Surveys
Zoning
Outside Accounting and Auditing
Real Estate Taxes
Other Taxes
Insurance
Advertising and Promotion of Opening
Landlord's Share of Formation and Assessments of Merchants
Miscellaneous Administrative Costs

Source: Urban Land Institute, *Dollars & Cents of Shopping Centers: 1984* (Washington, D.C.: ULI—the Urban Land Institute, 1984).

ities up to the site, and improving road or traffic access.

- On-site improvements in such areas as grading; underground utilities; storm drainage; parking lot paving, striping, and lighting; and—of major importance—landscaping.
- Building costs for construction of the basic building shell as well as the cost of tenant improvements paid by the landlord.
- Professional fees, including legal fees and fees for economic surveys, land planning, architecture, interior and graphic design, engineering, landscape architecture, and preparation of environmental impact statements and zoning approval applications.
- Lending commissions and financing fees for permanent financing.
- Leasing costs.
- Carrying charges during construction and until the project reaches the break-even point. These include interest and fees for construction financing, as well as taxes and insurance costs incurred during the construction period. Preopening expenses for publicity, public relations work, and the grand opening activities should also be provided for.

Figure 2-6 gives a detailed listing of items included in capital costs.

The income and expense (or operating) statement lists anticipated income and expenses and indicates the projected net operating income and cash flow for the center. Four major items provide income: minimum rents; percentage rents; reimbursements from tenants for operating expenses, taxes, and insurance; and miscellaneous income. Expenditures include management fees; on-site management costs; leasing costs; common area maintenance costs; heating, ventilation, and air conditioning (HVAC); tenant utilities; insurance; real estate taxes; marketing costs; and other miscellaneous items (see Figure 2-7).

The cash flow statement includes all quantifiable data in relation to time. It can help determine a project's profitability, the amount of debt financing needed, the ability of the project to carry the debt service, and the project's value.[6]

The income projections included in the pro forma statements are based on a leasing plan that represents the developer's estimate of the amounts of space to be rented to specific types of tenants. Thus, the allocation of space to the various types of tenants is a critical component of the financial feasibility analysis. Such a determination should be made only by an experienced economic analyst. Roy Drachman, a past president of ULI and of the International Council of Shopping Centers, has addressed the importance of the person who conducts such an analysis:

> The experience of a knowledgeable economic analyst is of great importance in relating the information in the survey to the merchandising plan for the center. In other words, he must correctly "analyze the market analysis" and interpret the "nose count" to create the end result . . . a shopping center containing stores offering the kind of merchandise at the proper prices and in sufficient quantity to satisfy the demand from the trade area.

For example, a qualified economist can point out to the developer the fact that the particular trade area has an unsatisfied purchasing demand for shoes (totaling approximately $1,320,000 per year). This may include $500,000 in medium-priced women's shoes, $250,000 in medium-priced men's shoes, and the balance in miscellaneous footwear. The analyst may further show that the center could feasibly contain a shoe store of 2,000 square feet offering medium-priced women's shoes, a shoe department of approximately 1,000 square feet within a high-fashion clothing store, a family shoe store of 3,000 to 3,500 square feet, and a store of approximately 1,500 square feet selling medium-priced men's shoes. These data might be summed up as follows:

SHOE TYPE	SALES VOLUME	STORE SIZE IN SQUARE FEET
Women's Medium-Priced	$ 500,000	2,000
Women's High-Priced	150,000	1,000
Family	350,000	3,000–3,500
Men's	250,000	1,500
Miscellaneous	70,000	–
	$1,320,000	7,500–8,000

This same type of analysis and recommended store size can be applied to the other lines of merchandise and can yield a close picture of what the tenant size and mix could be for all the stores in the center.

Even though feasibility studies are essential, they are not infallible. Often they have supported conclusions that ultimately were not valid and caused a project to fail. Developers may have seen them as necessary evils required only to secure financing and therefore wished them to render the most optimistic forecasts. The developer's analyst may have assumed

---

[6] A capitalization of the income stream can be used to compute the value of a new center that is leased at market rents. However, cost projections for the center must include leasing costs required to achieve a stabilized occupancy level. For centers that have been operating for several years and have leases that are below current market rents, capitalizing the current income stream can be misleading in determining the center's value. In order to determine the value of such a center, a multiyear discounted cash flow projection is needed to show the impact of below-market leases expiring and being replaced with leases written at estimated future market rents.

PRO FORMA OPERATING STATEMENT[1]
(GLA = 300,000 Square Feet)

INCOME		PER SQUARE FOOT OF GLA	TOTAL DOLLARS
Minimum Rent		$18.00	$5,400,000
Percentage Rent		1.00	300,000
Real Estate Taxes		1.25	375,000
Common Area Maintenance		4.00	1,200,000
Utilities		2.25	675,000
HVAC		2.00	600,000
Insurance		0.15	45,000
Other Income		0.15	45,000
GROSS POTENTIAL INCOME		28.80	8,640,000
Vacancy Allowance[2]	3.00%	−0.86	(259,200)
TOTAL INCOME		$27.94	$8,380,800
EXPENSES			
Management/Leasing Fee[3]	5.00%	$0.95	$285,000
General and Administrative		0.70	210,000
Common Area Maintenance		3.50	1,050,000
HVAC		1.40	420,000
Utilities		1.95	585,000
Insurance		0.15	45,000
Advertising and Promotion		0.25	75,000
Real Estate Taxes		1.25	375,000
Other Expenses		0.20	60,000
TOTAL EXPENSES		$10.35	$3,105,000
NET INCOME BEFORE DEBT SERVICE		$17.59	$5,275,800
Property Value			$58,000,000
Mortgage Amount			$43,500,000
Mortgage Constant[4]			11.00%
Annual Debt Service			$4,785,000

[1] For mall GLA only. Does not include department stores. Income and expenses for department stores are assumed to be on a break-even basis.

[2] Vacancy allowance at full occupancy, expected in year 3.

[3] Management and leasing fee based on 5 percent of minimum + percentage rent.

[4] Financing is a joint venture. Lender receives interest income as well as a share of the cash flow after debt service and a portion of the resale value of the property at the end of the holding period.

the role of the developer's advocate rather than that of an independent observer. And the mortgagee may not have had the staff available to evaluate the report properly and decide on its credibility. All this becomes especially crucial during a market downturn. The client should instruct his consultant on the precise nature of the study. The results should show a range of probable results and should not overstate growth projections.[7]

Site Selection, Evaluation, and Acquisition

Selecting the right site is crucial. Suitable sites for shopping center development are hard to find. In all

probability, when a site is discovered, the location will either not be zoned for commercial use or complications will develop in acquiring the property.

In site selection and evaluation, whether for a small neighborhood center or a regional giant, and whether or not the developer already owns the site, he must make sure that it has the best possible combination of the following characteristics: location and access,

[7] John R. White, "Nonfeasance with Feasibility = Failure: Improving Quality of Feasibility Studies," *Urban Land*, October 1976.

size, shape, topography, drainage, minimal subsoil complications, utilities, surroundings, zoning, and environmental impact.

If a site is already owned, it should be evaluated to justify its use for the proposed shopping center. Too often a developer will plan to build a shopping center simply because he owns a tract of land with highway frontage. His decision to build must be based on proof that the site qualifies according to the market and site analyses. If the site fails to qualify, the developer should acquire an appropriate site—or forget the development. Developing an inappropriate site merely because the developer owns it can result in over-development—because the best site will also be developed. And the center on the less desirable site will most likely suffer from the competition.

Location

Site location is of paramount importance in the success of all shopping center types. The site must qualify by virtue of its trade area characteristics, the income level of the households in the area, competition, highway access, and visual exposure.

Location and access are interrelated but separate aspects. The site must be easy to reach and its roads must have the extra capacity to avoid congestion during periods of high traffic volumes. The site must be easy to enter and safe to leave for customers and employees, or it must be able to be modified to make it so.

The site should represent an impregnable economic position. Its superior access, greater convenience, better merchant array, and improved services should make it impractical for another similar project to be developed nearby.

Recommended distances between shopping centers cannot be precisely established. After all, it is not distance between centers but customer convenience and availability of merchandise that count. For example, a convenience goods center can operate successfully next to or across the road from a regional center. Such coexistence is possible because the two types of centers offer different ranges of merchandise. Shoppers at a neighborhood center want convenience in buying everyday goods and services. Customers of the regional center are primarily comparative "shoppers" who are looking for and comparing general merchandise in terms of price, quality, size, color, and style.

But if one needs theoretical distances for site location, the indicators mentioned earlier in this chapter may be used as general guidelines:

- Neighborhood centers draw from a distance of approximately one and one-half miles, depend-ing on the density and character of the residential area. Walking distance is not a valid criterion, particularly in suburban locations. A mile and a half is too far per se to carry groceries. But in built-up areas where high-density, multifamily housing, and mixed use are part of the general development pattern, walking distances must be considered, as well as the site's location in relationship to other commercial areas and to mass transit.

- Community centers draw from an area within three to five miles of the site.

- Regional centers draw from distances of eight miles or more. Driving time rather than distance, however, better determines a center's area of influence. While the maximum driving time might be 20 minutes, this may entail a distance of as few as two to as many as 20 miles, depending on traffic and highway conditions to a site. Drawing power for regional centers in metropolitan areas suggests that five to 10 miles separate competing regional centers.

Neighborhood centers should be located to have access from collector streets and should avoid having minor residential service streets serve as their principal access.

If a neighborhood convenience type of center is justified in a new planned unit or residential cluster development, the center should be placed at an outer edge of the property where a major artery can serve the center, the outside territory, and the interior residential areas of the development.

Within a new, large-scale residential development such as a satellite community or new town on several thousand acres of land, the hierarchy of shopping center locations will be determined by land use allocation on the master development plan when the project is in its site planning stage. In these cases, site selection becomes part of the overall planning process, and the developer and his planning team will choose the most advantageous shopping center sites. A major commercial center can also incorporate civic facilities—offices, library, auditorium, and police and fire stations—as part of the planned center for the new community.

Community centers should be located for access from major thoroughfares. Because their array of stores represents limited lines of shopping goods, as well as convenience goods and services, these centers do not need to be accessible from an extended trade area via high-speed freeways.

Regional centers are customarily located on a site that is easily accessible from interchange points between expressways and freeways. If constraints are placed on energy use, easy access to mass transit may become equally or more important in regional centers. If a center is easily reached, travel distances will likely be short, and routes will allow customers, employees, and service vehicles to travel comfortably and easily. Distance from an interchange may range from one-half mile to a mile, depending on local circumstances.

When high-activity centers, such as busy regional shopping centers, have access points that are too close to freeway interchanges, traffic can become severely congested during peak travel hours. Shopper traffic interferes with the flow of through traffic, and the resulting congestion is intensified if stacking lanes (where cars wait to enter or exit from high-speed highways) are too short.

In theory, a cloverleaf-type separation between two intersecting traffic routes helps draw customers by giving the center high visibility and drivers the opportunity to change travel directions easily. But in reality,

a site at a cloverleaf grade separation offers poor access. The grade separation is complicated, confusing, and subject to traffic backups and accident hazards. Because of the high speeds of through traffic, it is often difficult to switch into lanes leading to off routes that would go to the center.

The only advantage a center has in fronting on a restricted access highway is that it has good visibility. Entrance and exit points to the site require special local access lanes so that the driver may avoid left turns and other traffic movement that might interfere with reaching the center easily.

If possible, the site for a regional center should offer ease of access and should be a reasonable distance from a radial highway leading to the city and from a circumferential highway that taps the urbanized residential periphery of the metropolitan area. The ideal site for a regional center would be ringed by major traffic routes having access points and traffic control devices carefully designed to disperse traffic over a

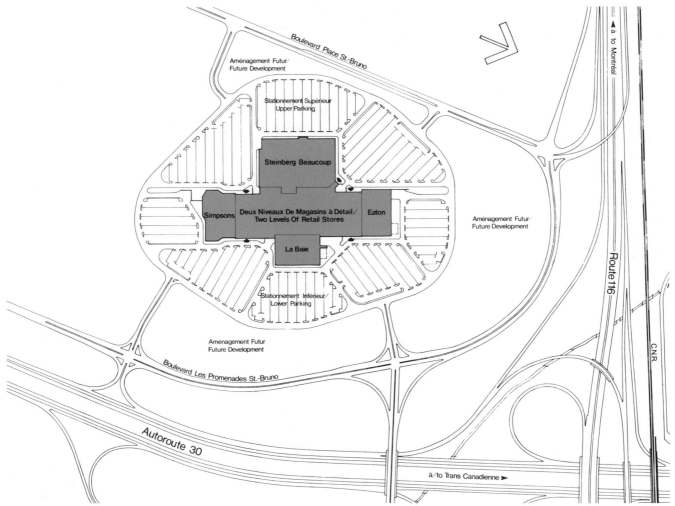

2-8   As illustrated by the site plan of Les Promenades–Saint Bruno near Montreal, a suburban regional center is customarily located on a site that is easily accessible from freeway interchanges.

major street system and to handle the peak loads generated by such centers.[8]

Access

Access is an integral part of site location. If a site is not easy to enter and safe to leave, it must have the potential to be made so. Traffic conditions should be free flowing as one drives toward and enters the site.

To achieve the best possible traffic access to any site, particularly to community and regional centers, the service of a professional traffic engineer is essential in the early site analysis stage.

Designing or redesigning traffic flow at entrances to centers requires the cooperation of both traffic engineers and local highway departments. If an access road cannot carry the additional traffic and turning movements generated by the center, the cost of necessary improvements should be investigated. A decision must then be made as to who will bear these costs—the highway construction authorities, the developer, or both—and, if the latter, in what proportion they will share the costs.

Left turns require specially constructed lanes or an "island" for turning movements. Right turns on heavily trafficked routes require deceleration lanes for easy entrance and acceleration lanes for easy exit. If cars moving into or out of a center create bottlenecks at entrances or backups on major traffic routes, customers can become annoyed.

Good visibility improves a center's accessibility. A shopper driving at local traffic speeds (35 miles per hour) can easily overshoot the parking area entrance if he has not seen the center from the road. Even though traffic flow attracts retail business, a site that fronts on a highway heavily built up with strings of competing distractions (including signs) is less accessible.[9]

As stated earlier, high-activity centers should be planned so that traffic originating at or destined for the center is separated from regional traffic. This can be done by locating access and exit points of major centers about one mile from regional freeways. Cars can then be directed by signs onto various arterial streets before feeding onto the freeway, thus avoiding congestion.[10]

Shape

The site should generally be regular in shape and should be all in one piece, undivided by highways or dedicated streets. Although a few successful centers exist whose sites are divided by dedicated streets, normally such sites should be avoided. A divided site is unworkable for an enclosed mall. Trafficways through a site impede the flow of pedestrians, complicate car movements within the parking area, and contradict the basic principle of a unified shopping facility.

Site depths cannot be standardized. They will depend on the type of centers to be built and the total acreage involved. The traditional strip commercial areas of the past are inappropriate design models for commercial developments. In order to accommodate parking and traffic circulation, shopping centers require much greater depth than did the old strip patterns.

A site with a regular shape—no acute angles, odd projections, or indentations—lends itself best to an efficient layout. If, however, an irregularly shaped site is used, it should still have adequate frontage in order for the center to be visible from access thoroughfares. Portions of an oddly shaped site may be unusable. On the other hand, oddly shaped parcels may accommodate to advantage freestanding auxiliary facilities—such as auto service centers; various types of convenience facilities or drive-in, fast food restaurants; dry cleaning establishments; or financial institutions.

Size

As a rule of thumb, each 40,000 square feet (about one acre) of site area will have roughly 10,000 square feet of building area and 30,000 square feet of surface parking area (including landscaping, circulation space, delivery area, etc.). For example, a 10-acre site will readily accommodate 100,000 square feet of building area for conventional shopping center development. A rough calculation of this sort is useful only for gauging the adequacy of a shopping center site in an outlying suburban location, however, and would not be applicable for determining the adequacy of a downtown site.

Today, shopping centers do not depend on vast site areas. Innovative planning for development of multiple uses within a single project enables a smaller amount of land to be used more intensively. Rising land costs may make a sprawling, single-level regional center economically unjustifiable.

Future land parcels will tend to be smaller, not only because of the limited number of sites available, but also because of zoning restrictions that are being en-

---

[8] See "Guidelines for Planning and Designing Access Systems for Shopping Centers," prepared by Technical Council Committee 5-DD, Institute of Traffic Engineers, Arlington, Virginia, 1976.

[9] William Applebaum, *Guide to Store Location Research: With Emphasis on Supermarkets* (Reading, Massachusetts: Addisonian Press, 1968).

[10] Ibid.

2-9 A regularly shaped property without acute angles, odd projections, or indentations is best for an efficient center layout, even though an irregular shape can be used.

acted in response to environmental concerns. Also, less land will be needed for parking since parking regulations are being revised to reflect more accurately parking demand. A horizontal center spreading over vast acreage destroys the intended benefit of a shopping center—to provide shopping convenience. With multilevel shopping in an enclosed mall and with structured parking, the development design goes vertical and requires less site area than horizontal development.

If the trade area of the proposed center stands a strong chance of growing, the developer would be wise to acquire a site large enough to allowing for future expansion. In suburban locations, the initial price of land for the site will normally be low enough to permit the developer to purchase extra land on which he could later provide additional facilities, including shops, offices, and parking spaces. However, initially he should construct no more retail space than is needed. To a great degree, future success

will depend on the strength of the original project location.

If a shopping center fully succeeds, reaching its projected sales volume by drawing a high proportion of the available purchasing power, others will inevitably try to tap into this success by building competitive facilities nearby—if land is available and if local zoning will allow it. (Open land zoned for residential use but located close to a shopping center may often be rezoned to permit additional commercial use.) The developer may therefore want to buy extra land in order to protect his location from subsequent undesirable encroachment. If the developer builds a center carefully conceived to fit its present trade area and allowing for its potential growth, the center may well be so successful that it will discourage any competition.

Land purchased when the center is first conceived but that is not used at the outset will likely increase in value. This land can be planned for compatible uses—

such as freestanding banks, restaurants, motels, and office and medical buildings—which should prove a feasible investment. However, because of high interest rates, taxes, and other carrying costs, developers are finding that holding land for extended periods is not as possible or as profitable as it once was.

The rising cost of land can become a dominant factor in the selection and development of a site. The high acquisition costs of a site may be offset if a multilevel, rather than a single-level, project is built—particularly if it is to be a large enclosed regional center. Such a vertical structure will also bring parking and walking distances within comfortable ranges. Walking distances between tenant stores are reduced, and if multilevel parking is used, walking distances between parking areas and stores are also reduced. In multilevel schemes, escalators should be strategically located in the enclosed mall, and each floor should have pedestrian and parking area entrances to the department stores to heighten the visibility of and interplay among stores and between levels.

Similarly, as a center matures and attracts a greater volume of sales and customers, additional leasable area may have to be provided. This will require additional parking areas, which could be double-decked to save space. When the cost of land for additional parking would equal or exceed the cost of constructing parking decks, or when the distance to additional land would be too great, decks should be constructed. A parking structure will not only provide parking closer to the stores but will also protect vehicles from the weather, an advantage in all but the mildest of climates. The design and placement of parking structures must be carefully evaluated; this requires the assistance of professionals who are sensitive to an appropriate relationship between the parking structure and the mall area.

Topography

Topography is an important factor in the selection and layout of a site and in the design and construction of the building(s). Fairly level or gently sloping ground is easily adaptable to shopping centers. With skill, a more steeply sloping site can be adapted to provide customer access at different levels. It can also be used to advantage in separating retail uses from office uses and in reducing competition from non-retail parkers for retail parking space. (This approach would be particularly applicable to multilevel regional centers and to mixed-use developments.)

Low-lying areas and poor drainage complicate the subsurface construction of any center. The ideal site—though hard to find—would have minimal subsoil complications and neither solid rock nor a high water table. Also, it would have a slope of less than 5 percent. If used for surface parking, a steeper slope must be cut and filled and may need sedimentation and detention or retention ponds to control surface water runoff.

Utilities

The availability of utilities is an asset to be considered in choosing a site. The cost of off-site improvements is a critical part of capital costs, and a location close or easily accessible to water, sewers, gas, and electricity will keep down the costs of such improvements. Off-site development costs can usually be shared with the municipality and the utility company. To minimize time-consuming negotiations with officials, the developer should make certain that the site is at least within easy reach of the required water supply and sewage disposal facilities.

Surroundings

Rarely can a site be found that is surrounded by major streets or trafficways. How land is used adjacent to or across the road from any site is important in evaluating the site's suitability for development. Whether this land is raw or developed, the local political climate may be opposed to any, or any further, development, especially that of an "intrusive" shopping center. The developer must first explore the local temper before he becomes too involved in selecting a site.

The public is not well versed in shopping center design. If the site, particularly that for a proposed neighborhood center, is adjacent to residential areas, any adverse impact on the livability of the houses nearby must be offset. The developer must be doubly sure that his project will meet the criteria for good shopping center design. He must be prepared to prevent visual, noise, or traffic "pollution." If he fails to provide access to the site by streets other than local residential streets or to separate commercial uses from single-family detached residences, his development proposal may well be killed.

A developer may deal with local objections to shopping centers by explaining the concept of a shopping center operation: it is not a miscellaneous aggregation of stores but an architecturally harmonious unit that uses less energy than freestanding stores, produces minimal air pollution, offers integrated parking for public benefit, and controls truck delivery, signing, lighting, and landscaping. Walls, solid fences, landscaped berms, or narrow but dense plantings of evergreens can buffer residential or other areas from the center's noise and night lighting.

Public agencies should express their interest in protecting the public benefit derived from comprehensively planned development by discouraging (through local planning and zoning policy) the tendency for parasitic commercial uses to spring up in strips near major shopping centers. In general, enlightened municipal planning bodies tend to look favorably on planned developments such as shopping centers. Because of a shopping center's planned site arrangement, including buffer provisions and screening, approval authorities find that the adverse effect a center has on streets, highways, and adjacent properties is far less than that of strip development.[11]

In rezoning an area from residential to commercial use, authorities should recognize that the total cost of providing public services such as police and fire protection, schools, streets, and utilities is much less for commercial facilities than for residential development. Commercial developments produce a sizable return in real estate and sales taxes—revenue that would be lost, or received by another municipality, if commercial use were not allowed.

Properly located, a center produces far more net income for the community than that produced from single-family residential development. The tax advantages available to the community should overcome many objections that may arise.[12]

A comprehensively planned shopping center development unquestionably increases the value of land adjacent to the center. If the developer controls the land, he should benefit directly from its increased value. Otherwise, he could benefit indirectly by encouraging development of compatible fringe uses, such as apartments, planned office parks, medical clinics, motels, restaurants, and other nonretail commercial uses that would not affect peak hour traffic

---

[11] J. Ross McKeever, *Shopping Center Zoning*, ULI Technical Bulletin 69 (Washington, D.C.: ULI–the Urban Land Institute, 1973).

[12] See Michael S. Levin, *Measuring the Fiscal Impact of a Shopping Center on Its Community* (New York: International Council of Shopping Centers, 1975).

2-10   Where land costs are extremely high, multilevel or vertical centers may result in a more economical land-to-building cost ratio.

flow to the center. Such fringe development would also concentrate shopper traffic within the vicinity of the center, rather than diluting and diverting potential customers to areas beyond the center's influence.

Apartments or office uses developed adjacent to a shopping center site make an excellent transition zone between a shopping center location and a single-family residential area. A site adjacent to high-density apartment developments benefits from receiving greater walk-in trade.

The shopping center can become a center of community life, with library, community center, and other public facilities located within the complex.

Site Acquisition

The cost of land counts heavily in the development of a shopping center. A single-level center requires approximately four square feet of land for each square foot of building area. This relationship allows one square foot of ground under the building and three square feet for roadways, parking spaces, malls, landscaping, and other nonbuilding uses. This means that if land is selling for $5 per square foot, $20 per square foot of building must be added to the cost of a single-level center. The economics of the project will determine what land cost can or cannot be supported.

As discussed earlier, high-priced sites may be feasible if they are developed with multilevel or vertical centers, resulting in a more economic land-to-building cost ratio. If centers incorporate mixed use and multifloor parking structures, the cost of the land must be compatible with the overall economics of the development.

Because land costs, building costs, and volume of sales vary greatly from one section of the country to another, no standard figures can be set for building sites. The fact that land costs are low in a certain location does not mean that a shopping center placed there will yield the best overall project economics. A strategic location, though more expensive, may enable a center to draw the full potential of sales from a trade area, spelling the difference between success and failure. The advantages and disadvantages of a site must be weighed. If several sites are being considered, the one selected should show from careful evaluation that it offers the strongest location for the particular project.

Several methods may be used for acquiring or gaining control of a site. Each offers varying advantages in financing and "leverage."

- Historic ownership—where the site has been owned and held for a number of years. The owner/developer may have no further acquisition

costs to pay, or, if so, such costs may constitute only a minimal part of the total capital outlay.

- Outright purchase—the least attractive, most costly method. Outright purchase entails heavy initial investment of equity or front-end funds. This approach is unappealing if development is uncertain, money markets are restricted, or interest rates are high—unless the developer is contemplating a subsequent sale and leaseback or land loan.

- Purchase contract with options—a favored method, since it allows the developer to run the hurdles of zoning and approval procedures without jeopardizing the bulk of his investment. The contract to purchase should provide other options subject to pertinent current conditions such as an acceptable land title report, an accurate property survey, zoning approval of the land use, investigation of any on-site and off-site easements, site conditions, stormwater runoff, site plan clearance, and any environmental clearances. The option period should allow the developer from nine months to two years before he must commit himself to purchase the land.

The developer should try not to conclude the purchase until he has obtained the building permits. If the developer can control the property by option until potentially adverse factors have been cleared away, he will risk less when he purchases the property.

- Deferred purchase with simultaneous sale and leaseback—an advantageous and commonly used technique by which the developer avoids heavy financial commitments. In effect, the developer induces the lender to buy the land and provide the money to build the center. The developer then leases the project from the lender but retains the option to buy back the development from the lending institution later.

- Ground lease—a popular approach that eliminates a major initial investment in land. The principle of land leasing is that it offers the landowner an alternative to direct sale and frees the developer from an initial investment in land. The financial arrangements of a ground lease are flexible and are well suited to shopping centers and other urban building types; the income tax laws have contributed to the popularity of this method of land control. A landowner who sells land that has increased in value must face a high capital gains tax. But by leasing for a long term (up to 99 years is common), the owner can spread the return to reduce the taxes. A ground lease will allow the owner to retain fee ownership while receiving, in effect, an annuity over the term of the lease. Inheritors or long-time owners of land may find ground leasing attractive, although they should first consider the many situations that could arise in the future. For example, as inflation occurs over the years, the fixed ground rent will cause a reduction in the sale value of the property until the lease term expires. Therefore, rent escalation provisions are important. The lessee benefits because the amount of capital required for land control is reduced. The annual ground rent payment is a deductible business expense. In order to maximize his possibilities for financing, the developer must insist on his right to place a mortgage on the fee title to the land he leases.

Under a ground lease, the developer becomes the middleman between the fee owner and the project's tenants, who produce income through rental payments. The annual ground rent is equivalent to a payment on a loan used to purchase land.

The lease can provide for readjustment of the ground rental at predetermined intervals. In addition, lessors often share in the equity income from projects developed on their land. They will receive annual rents running from 10 to 12 percent of the initial value of the land, plus benefits when tenants' rents are increased due to inflation. The landowners may even share in percentage rent payments from the tenants in lieu of other equity participation or escalation in ground rent.

There are two types of land leases:

—Subordinated—the preferred arrangement for the developer. The landowner submits the land to the lender as collateral should the developer default on mortgage payments. Lenders usually insist on subordination.

—Unsubordinated—the less risky arrangement for the landowner, whereby he does not agree to offer his land as collateral for the mortgage. However, because the developer will have difficulty securing a subsequent mortgage loan, the landowner may not be able to lease to the developer; thus, both would lose. Financing with an unsubordinated ground lease, if available, usually costs at least half a percent more per year than for a subordinated ground lease. Giving the mortgagee the right to purchase the land in case of default can sometimes substitute for subordination, although the mortgagee may deduct the price of the land from the loan.

Ground leasing frees capital and permits the developer to raise more capital through the mortgage medium. For example, if the land is worth $1 million and the owner can be persuaded to lease it, the developer is $1 million to the good in capital expenditures. When the land is leased with the right to mortgage the fee, $500,000 or more may be gained by borrowing on the land. Without the right to subordinate the fee on the land to a mortgage, the developer may not succeed in subsequent steps toward securing financing. If the developer obtains a ground lease that permits a mortgage on the fee, the financing takes the form of a straight first mortgage on land and building.

Summary—Site Selection, Evaluation, and Acquisition

Three principal factors weigh heavily in evaluating a location: size of the market; availability of key tenants for the selected site; and site characteristics, including access, size and shape, costs of land, site preparation, utilities, drainage, and favorable zoning and environmental considerations. The availability of adjacent vacant land that is suitable for later expansion and compatible uses will also influence site selection.

An accurate comparison of several alternative sites depends on an accurate economic appraisal of the project's income potential, measured against the costs of site acquisition, building construction, parking areas, and landscaping.

The site for a neighborhood shopping center must be easily accessible from the supporting residential area. In the case of an entirely new community, the site for a neighborhood center must not affect adjacent residential property adversely. Evaluating a site for a community center will be similar to that for a regional center, including considerations of the site's physical characteristics and surroundings. A well-planned regional center, with space allowances for various amenities or further expansion, will attract customers from greater distances.

Key Tenant Commitments

As a rule, a shopping center will not be built until the developer has secured commitments from key tenants.[13] The choice of key tenants will help determine site design, building design and layout, and financial negotiation. And as already noted, it is the key tenant or tenants, not the size of either the site or the center, that determines the type of center. The key tenants will also determine the image that the center will project.

---

[13] There are examples today of specialty, theme, off-price, and factory outlet centers that have been successfully developed without anchor tenants or with a cluster anchor such as a food court (as opposed to traditional anchor tenants).

2-11　The key tenant commitment is a form of partnership between the major store and the developer.

As stated earlier, the key or anchor tenants of a neighborhood center are the supermarket and the drugstore (with a single supermarket/drugstore combination having become more prevalent in recent years in some markets); the key tenants of a community center are the discount or off-price department store, the variety store, the hardware/building/home improvement store, or the combined drug/variety/garden center; and the key tenants of a regional center are full-line department stores (generally of at least 100,000 square feet each). Most highly successful regional centers include at least two department stores. If the type of center being considered is a variation of the major center types (such as one of the many already identified or emerging specialty center categories), the identification and commitment of key tenants are equally important. In this case, a group of tenants may function as the key tenant(s).

The commitment of the key tenant represents a form of partnership between the major store and the developer; for this reason the anchor tenant, whether a supermarket, discount store, or department store,

should be tied in closely with the developer in his land and building plans. The key tenants' requirements—often including firm ideas about the center's general arrangement and their locations—will influence the developer's decisions on leasing, financial negotiations, building treatment, architectural style, parking provisions, signing, and landscaping. Before site planning or further leasing occurs, key tenants should be committed to agreements for the total operation of the center.

In this stage, the project's form begins to adapt to the characteristics of the site and the potential of the trade area. For example, in a high-income area, two high-fashion stores may sign as tenants, thus creating a quality image for a proposed center. In this case, it is the quality of the market that determines the type of center suitable to the area. The image of the leading tenant in turn determines the type of satellite tenants that are suitable to the particular center. If a popular-priced store were the key tenant, all factors in tenant planning would be different. The wrong key tenant can complicate the problem of leasing to satellite tenants. On the other hand, leasing to a tenant mix that is too homogeneous, even in high-income areas, has proven a mistake.

In the early stages of development, the owner/developer or his leasing agent must determine what key tenants are available and must start negotiations with those tenants. A competent real estate leasing agent will recognize the characteristics of major key tenants in the area. He will know what their expansion goals are and what lease or occupancy provisions can be negotiated, because he will have had some experience in dealing with such major stores. He will also know of other commitments that the prospective key tenants have made, and he will know under what conditions these tenants will be available or unavailable, as well as what arrangements may make these tenants attract other tenants.

Because of the need to deal with these tenant selection subtleties, the leasing agent or real estate expert must be on the development team from the start and must work with the market analyst and guide the developer and his architect, engineer, and planner. Some developers have in-house leasing expertise. Successful developers who use outside agents know enough about the field so that they need not rely entirely on outside advice to resolve critical questions.

After the key tenants have been committed—preferably through a "letter of intent" or clear expression of interest, if not an actual lease or occupancy agreement—a building and site layout can be roughed out. Based on data from the market and economic analyses, supplementary tenant classifications can be used to produce a leasing plan.

In the discussion that follows, the term "lease" will often be used. However, the key tenant will often have purchased rather than leased the site. For the purpose of general discussion, the term "lease" is used in lieu of the term "occupancy agreement," even though the latter term might be more accurately applied in the case of some tenants.

In the book, *How to Create a Shopping Center*, S. O. Kaylin outlines the elements of a leasing plan as follows:

Type of tenant (by retail line); names of prospective tenants in each category; GLA assignable on basis of market study; the economic analysis, footnoted by characteristics of the prospects in each category; tentative location of each tenant on the building plan; and rate of percentage rent applicable to the tenant's sales in excess of a breakpoint, computed as

$$breakpoint = \frac{minimum\ rent}{rate\ of\ percentage\ rent}$$

Thus, if minimum rent is $20,000 per year and the rate of percentage rent is 5 percent, then

$$breakpoint = \frac{\$20,000}{.05} = \$400,000$$

The tenant would pay an annual rent of $20,000 until sales reached $400,000. If his sales totaled $500,000, he would pay $20,000 plus 5 percent of $100,000 (or $5,000) as overage rent, so that his total rent would reach $25,000. The list of tenants in the leasing plan shows each prospective tenant's breakpoint in total dollars and in dollars per square foot of GLA. Other listed data would include credit rating and length of lease.[14]

Leases with supplementary tenants are negotiated after major tenants have signed leases or made commitments. Commitments or expressions of interest from supplementary or satellite tenants precede the firming up of the financing plan and any preparation of construction details. In addition, developers do not start final plans or even complete the site acquisition until they have received zoning approval, which may impose economically infeasible conditions. Final commitments from major tenants will generally be subject to zoning approval.

A prospectus presented as an attractive brochure makes a useful exhibit in explaining to potential tenants market findings, site advantages, and the tentative arrangement of building and site. A rendering of the architectural treatment (showing, for example, whether a mall will be open, or enclosed and air conditioned) can also help with tenant negotiations.[15]

At this point, the developer should have a form lease to present to satellite tenants. Basic economic provisions should be made known to tenants early in the process. Matters should be discussed and resolved at the outset that involve the tenant's tax participation, contributions to common area maintenance, participation in a marketing fund or in a merchants' association, the rental scale, and the promotional program. Otherwise, misunderstandings can arise over the distribution of tenant and owner responsibilities, creating dissension and damaging the later operation of the center.

During the negotiation stage, a key tenant should make a firm commitment either to lease space in a

---

[14] S. O. Kaylin, *How to Create a Shopping Center*, Chapter 5.

[15] On a national basis, the process of leasing centers has become highly sophisticated. At its national convention each year, the ICSC has a leasing mall. Each of the major national shopping center development, leasing, and management firms along with many of the national chain tenants has an elaborate display booth and leasing suite.

building owned by the developer or to construct his own building. After key tenants have been tied down, the building layout can be planned. Supplementary tenants should be located so that pedestrian traffic is well distributed, thus encouraging impulse buying.

It is not always possible to have a key tenant committed to the project early in the development process. In major regional centers, for example, the developer must proceed (at his own risk) with certain planning efforts, such as obtaining zoning clearance, while he continues to negotiate with major department stores.

Leasing Plan

Since the leasing plan represents the center's investment potential, it is key in projecting the center's rental income. It should be prepared early in the development process and should address the following points:[16]

- The placement of tenants. Tenants should be located to draw the maximum pedestrian shopper flow past as much store frontage as possible.

- Building depths. Normally depths should not exceed 120 feet for mall shops or stores in an open center. Shops of small tenants in neighborhood centers are generally 60 to 100 feet deep. Malls should not exceed 40 feet in width except for courts and promotional areas. A balanced tenant mix should provide for both strong, credit-rated national firms and good local merchants in order to meet the financial credit requirements of lenders.

- The tenant mix. This should be predetermined by the merchandising plan, although not all goals of the original plan can be met. Tenant preferences and resistances will result in a number of compromises. Repositioning will require constant attention if the merchandising plan is to direct the leasing.

- "Pricing" each store space. Pricing will depend on the tenant's size, classification, location in the project, and the amount of tenant allowance.

---

[16] This list is taken from "The Developer's View of Shopping Center Finance," a paper presented by Harold R. Imus to ULI's Commercial and Retail Development Council.

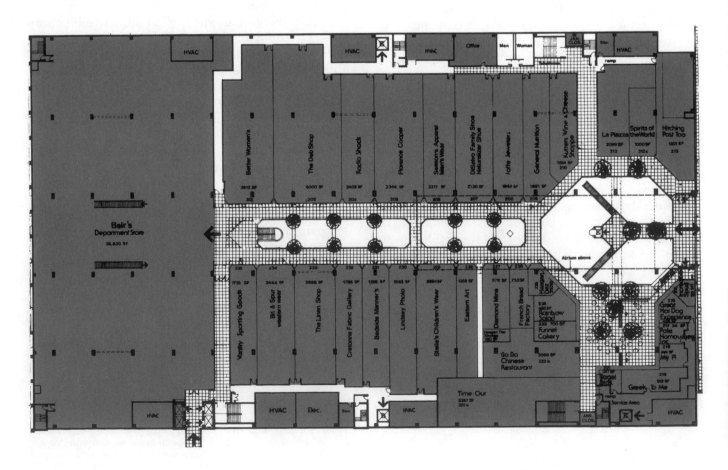

2-12   Upper-level leasing plan of the 220,000-square-foot Rainbow Centre, Niagara Falls, New York.

These prices should be constantly updated as the project moves from an essentially speculative paper exercise to a finalized program.

- Detailed rent schedules. Schedules should clearly indicate the tenant's name, classification, square footage allocation, minimum rent, and the rate of percentage rent. The tenant's share of costs for heating, ventilation, and air conditioning (HVAC) should be projected as a guide to those leasing the project. This schedule too should be continually updated.

- Method of handling tenant finish. The preferred approach is to provide shell space plus a finishing allowance to tenants. This method should be followed in all cases, even if a greater allowance is sometimes necessary to produce a "turnkey" solution for a particular tenant.

- The lease form. It should require a minimum of processing, with exhibits attached indicating landlord's work, tenant's work, HVAC rate schedules, other applicable rate schedules, and other related matters, including the site plan. The lease form can be modified (which is often necessary) most easily through an addendum. The addendum provides a ready reference for changes applicable to specific tenants.

The lease should provide for tenant payments for the costs of common area operation (including mall maintenance, insurance, and mall HVAC costs) as well as for real estate taxes. These charges should be prorated based on the GLA each tenant occupies. Commonly excepted are key tenants who are on other prearranged payment schedules.

In addition, the lease should clearly define responsibilities for the payment of HVAC and gas and electricity costs if separate metering has not been provided. Escalator clauses should provide for increased costs of labor, energy, administration, and replacement of parts. However, with today's high energy costs, separate metering is strongly recommended. (See Chapter 6 for a detailed discussion of the lease document.)

Lease provisions help define early on the landlord's fiscal obligations. They are well known to national tenants, but local tenants, who are unaccustomed to such provisions because of the limited scope of their operations, may resist them. The developer should nevertheless negotiate such costs with the tenants, explaining why their inclusion in the lease is essential. Obviously, owners of stronger centers can insist on reducing the fiscal uncertainty they must face, but the principles set forth above are useful in structuring any present-day shopping center.

The department store in a regional shopping center is treated differently from other tenants. The key department stores may build their own stores on land bought or leased from the developer. They usually do not build their own parking areas, but it is advisable that they contribute funds to the developer. The developer must have satisfactory reciprocal operating agreements that provide for handling of on-site and off-site construction costs, easements, operation of common areas, the marketing fund or merchants' association, the common "mall/department store" wall, and other areas of expense. Long-term cross-easements and agreements are extremely important to the permanent lender, the tenants, and the developer. Reciprocal easement agreements, or REAs, are necessary in any center with separate legal ownership or any type of site-sharing uses, such as freestanding banks, service stations, or restaurants.

To encourage department stores to enter the project on a buy/build basis, land can be sold to them at an appraised value, or it can be sold at or below cost. The amount of money involved, while substantial, represents a smaller subsidy than the amount that would result from a fairly favorable gross lease. Typically, the developer will sell to the department store not only a building pad but necessary improvements in parking as well. The sale price will, of course, be negotiated, but it rarely reflects the pro rata off-site and on-site improvement costs attributed to the land area sold.

Financing

Like the shopping center industry itself, development financing is undergoing considerable change. The process of creating a center's financial structure is more complex and individualized than it was during the decades of the 1960s and 1970s. Yet in the midst of these changes, a basic fact remains: a shopping center will attract debt and equity investment based on the anticipated return to all financial participants. Project economics, then, is still the foundation of project financing. Following are discussions of the elements that are shaping shopping center financing.

The Changing Financial Environment

Three factors are influencing shopping center financing in the 1980s: a growing concentration of the financial services industry, more interest-rate-sensitive capital in the market, and higher rates of interest.

Mergers and acquisitions among financial service firms have increased greatly. Retailers, such as Sears and J.C. Penney, are moving into financial services. Life insurance companies, savings and loans, com-

PRIME RATE CHANGES AND RATE SPREAD: 1950–1984

FIVE-YEAR PERIOD	CHANGES (NUMBER)	HIGH DURING PERIOD (PERCENT)	LOW DURING PERIOD (PERCENT)	PERCENTAGE SPREAD DURING PERIOD
1950–1954	11	3.25%	2.00%	1.25%
1955–1959	7	4.50	3.00	1.50
1960–1964	4	5.00	4.50	0.50
1965–1969	12	8.00	4.50	3.50
1970–1974	65	12.00	4.75	7.25
1975–1979	65	15.75	6.25	9.50
1980–1984	85	21.50	10.50	11.00

Source: Federal Reserve Board.

mercial banks, and Wall Street securities firms are expanding the financial services they offer. (The American Automobile Association was offering its members money market accounts and VISA credit cards by the middle of 1983.)

The relevance of such merger activity to the financing of shopping centers is twofold. First, as linkages develop between the real estate industry and the financial services industry, shopping center financing will more often be in the form of marketable securities. Secondly, because of the growing complexity of the financial markets and the critical importance of financing to shopping center developers, development organizations are forming that can raise at least part of their own financing, and financial groups are organizing that can develop projects. Thus, shopping center developers must be more attuned to the requirements for creating marketable securities such as bonds and syndication offerings. They also may find themselves competing for sites against financial institutions that were once their main sources of permanent funds. Successful shopping center developers in the 1980s are and will be those who not only are aware of the marketing and economic feasibility of a project, but are also strongly connected to reliable sources of development capital.

The second major factor in the changing financial environment is the increased sensitivity of capital to changing interest rates. One of the key ingredients fueling the growth of shopping centers during the 1970s was the availability of inexpensive, fixed-rate, long-term capital. The lending practices of the 1970s were based on the economic climate of the 1950s and 1960s. Yet the inflation rate accelerated and became more volatile, a condition that was soon mirrored in interest rates.

Figure 2-13 indicates the dramatic change in the financial markets that has been occurring. The highly sensitive commercial bank prime rate changed 34 times between 1950 and 1969. During the following 14 years, the rate jumped some 215 times. In 1980 alone the rate moved an incredible 39 times. Although inflation has slowed considerably, higher credit demands and federal deficits have kept interest rates volatile.

Because of this volatility, many lenders have been unable to offer traditional long-term loans to shopping center developers. They have shortened their loan maturities. For capital markets in general, this has produced an abundance of short-term funds and somewhat of a shortage of long-term funds. Consequently, shopping center developers may experience periods over the next few years when it is much easier to obtain construction loans than it is to obtain permanent mortgages.

High real interest rates constitute the third major factor in the financing picture. Figure 2-14 shows that real interest rates so far in the 1980s have been far higher than those of the 1970s. Some developers benefited from negative real interest rates during the 1970s, but today's rates make it highly unlikely that this will happen again. Further, the current high real rates, combined with lower rates of inflation, should result in higher returns to shopping center lenders in the 1980s than in the 1970s. Basically the imbalance of return between developer and lender that existed in previous decades is now being redressed. Finally, these high interest rates are making debt financing more expensive. The old practice of "mortgaging out" all development costs has become less feasible. As a result, more developers are examining the potential for raising additional equity capital to finance shopping center development.

The changing financial environment has, therefore, significantly altered old methods of financing shopping centers. Some developers are now issuing bonds to take advantage of the extensive investment sales networks in the securities industry. Larger developers

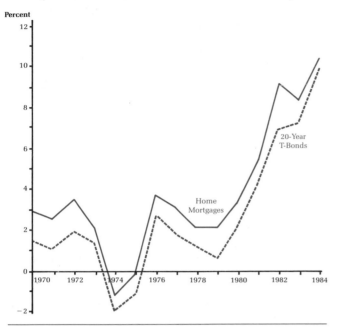

2-14 REAL INTEREST RATES: 1970–1984
(Nominal Rates Less GNP Price Deflator)

Sources: *Statistical Abstract of the U.S.* (Washington, D.C.: Government Printing Office, 1983); and *Federal Reserve Bulletin*, January 1985.

are exploring the acquisition or creation of financial operations. Several California developers, for example, have applied for permits to operate new state-chartered savings and loans. Interest rate volatility is producing shorter loan maturities and a decline in long-term funds. As a result, some shopping centers are using extended construction loans as the sole initial financial arrangement with no permanent "takeout" commitments in place. Higher interest rates also make equity financing more important than in previous decades. And government programs—such as industrial development bonds (IDBs) and Urban Development Action Grants (UDAGs)—offering lower interest rates are being widely used to finance new shopping centers.

Financing Sources

Experienced developers have long recognized the need to maintain close contact with lenders and financial consultants. Today, this need is stronger than ever. Some developers have full-time employees devoted to monitoring financial markets and initiating financing arrangements.

In today's changing capital markets, the source of financing for a particular shopping center can depend on the size of the developer, the size of the center, the tenants, the area of the country, and, in the case of government programs, even the location within a met-

ropolitan region. In any case, the financing being sought must be part of the project's overall financial plan. The project's financing must fit within the economic confines of the project's potential income, cash flow, tax benefits, and appreciation of value. In some cases, this will mean that more than one source of financing will be used.

At least nine major sources of financing are being used today: life insurance companies, pension funds, banks, savings and loans, credit companies, Wall Street securities firms, syndications, government funds, and foreign investors. Each of these sources has its own investment criteria. A shopping center proposal that is acceptable to one source may be of no interest to another. Further, as these sources change over time, deals they made two or three years ago may be totally unacceptable today. Contrarily, lenders may today be making deals they would not have made in the past. Developers need to remember that lenders are matching their loan types to their liabilities. These liabilities could involve consumer savings accounts, money market deposit accounts, trust and separate accounts, securities, and time deposits. As the sources of lenders' funds change, so too will the types of deals they are willing to make.

Life Insurance Companies (LICs)

Insurance companies represent an example of a lending group that is experiencing a change in its sources of funds. During the 1970s, most of the funds that LICs loaned were raised internally from insurance premiums. Today, less than half of their funds are generated in this way. LICs are becoming money managers for pension funds, trusts, endowments, and foundations. Virtually all major insurance companies manage property portfolios on behalf of these investors. They also issue guaranteed investment contracts (GICs) that are bought by pension funds.

GICs are fixed-rate securities with five- to seven-year maturities. Initially these funds were turned around only to finance existing properties. They have, however, financed some new shopping centers. The GIC can act as both a two-year construction loan and a three-year "mini-perm" loan. (A mini-perm loan functions as a permanent loan but must be repaid within a few years.) The developer also receives the security of a fixed-rate loan.

Life insurance companies are not, however, interested in all types of centers. They have specified minimum loans that will eliminate many small projects. Secondly, many LICs will provide financing only if they also participate in the project's cash flow and resale value. Developers must then be prepared to give up sizable equity interests. Also, because LICs are interested in properties for their pension fund clients, developers may find that they can even presell their center to the insurance company.

Pension Funds

Pension funds invest in real estate both directly and indirectly. Life insurance companies place large amounts of money in real estate for pension funds. Many analysts believe that pension funds will become the most significant source of real estate finance by the end of the 1980s.

Private funds and public funds represent the two major groups of pension funds. Private funds are those operated by corporations or unions and must conform to the investment guidelines of the Employee Retirement Income Security Act of 1974 (ERISA) and later amendments. Pension funds may make tax-free investments in leveraged real estate. However, the income and capital gains from these projects are tax-exempt only if the pension funds meet specific guidelines and conditions.

Public pension funds are those such as state employee or teacher retirement funds. They need not comply with ERISA. However, they may be limited in the types of investments they can make or in the size of any single investment. When investing in real estate, many public pension funds are required to focus primarily on in-state investments. Other funds may prefer residential mortgage debt, as opposed to commercial lending.

Most public and private pension fund managers attempt to achieve a balance of investment types. Real estate lending fits well into their longer-term investment plans. Again developers may find participating mortgages the dominant lending arrangement offered by many pension funds. Yet these will likely have longer loan maturities than mortgages offered by some LICs. Pension funds make direct loans primarily to prime shopping center projects. They are less likely to grant loans on smaller, more risky projects.

Banks

Commercial banks have become a funding source of growing importance. With the general shortening of maturities, commercial real estate loans now are a much better match with most banks' liability structures than they were in the 1970s. Further, the abundance of short-term money that evolved has made banks explore new lending opportunities.

Banks offer a wide range of loan types for shopping centers. Further, they are more willing to offer loans to the small- to medium-sized project, although this is not the case with large, money center banks. Among the types of financing banks provide for shopping centers are construction loans, interim loans, gap loans, and bullet loans.[17] Most bank real estate loans have floating interest rates. Banks often offer more favorable terms to developers whose other financing business they handle. Some projects have been financed, for example, through unsecured lines of credit at the developers' banks. In addition, banks often purchase IDBs for shopping center financing.

Savings and Loans (S&Ls) and Savings Banks (SBs)

The changing financial services industry is blurring the distinctions among banks, S&Ls, and savings banks. Many S&Ls have transformed themselves into savings banks over the last few years. The number of FSLIC-insured savings banks grew from six in January 1983 to over 200 by January 1984. Moreover, mergers between associations and the introduction of MMDAs (money market deposit accounts) and NOW (negotiable order of withdrawal) accounts have greatly increased the asset sizes of thrifts.

S&Ls have also been granted new asset powers by the Garn–St. Germaine bill of 1983 and state statutes such as California's Nolan bill. The result is that S&Ls and SBs now provide a wide range of financial services for shopping center developers. In addition to portfolio lending, S&Ls and banks alike often operate mortgage banking subsidiaries that will help developers obtain financing from other sources.

Finance and Credit Companies

Credit companies, such as General Electric Credit Corporation and Barclays American Business Credit, also provide sources of funds for shopping center development. They usually act as intermediaries between borrowers and other financial institutions. Therefore, their interest rates may be higher than those of other lenders. Yet because these firms also often provide construction and "mini-perm" loans on somewhat riskier shopping center projects, they serve an important function in the overall market for real estate credit.

Investment Banking and Securities Firms

Wall Street securities firms are in constant communication with investors of all types and sizes. As real

---

[17] These are all short-term loans (from three to seven years) with all or most of the loan amount paid at the end of the loan term. Developers use interim loans to pay off construction loans before securing permanent financing, while gap loans cover construction costs not included in the construction loans. Bullet loans basically serve as mini-perms.

estate financing involves more often the sale of securities, these firms will play an increasingly important role. For example, in 1983, shopping center developer Melvin Simon & Associates issued $110 million in unrated participating mortgage bonds through the firm of Drexel Burnham Lambert, Inc. Other large developers have also used securities firms to raise both real estate debt and equity funds. Merrill Lynch Hubbard raised the largest amount of real estate syndication funds in the first half of 1984.

New types of securities, such as collateralized mortgage obligations (CMOs), and the strides being made to provide a rating for commercial real estate debt portend an expanded role for Wall Street for the rest of this decade. Yet financing from Wall Street will be available only for the larger developers and projects. The cost to create a securities issue in mid-1984 was at least $200,000, regardless of the size of the issue. Thus, smaller developers must, for the present, continue to use local institutions and mortgage bankers. In the future, however, a consortium of developers and projects may be offered pooled access to Wall Street in a fashion similar to residential multibuilder bonds.

Syndications and Real Estate Investment Trusts (REITs)

The high cost of capital during the 1980s has led to a tremendous growth of equity financing, and favorable tax legislation in 1981 and 1982 increased the equity value of real estate overnight. Of the $14 billion raised by the public syndication firms between 1980 and 1984, over 80 percent was raised since 1981. REITs, which have been ignored for almost a decade, are also making a strong comeback, providing both debt and equity capital.

Most syndicators are interested in actual ownership of proposed properties. Since developers often become general partners in shopping center syndications, they receive many of the benefits of ownership along with project financing. Syndications can be created for small as well as large shopping centers. Because of the competition for investment-grade real estate projects, many syndicators are becoming more active in real estate development and construction.

Syndication has also provided the means for many developers to raise their own capital. The syndication is often formed while the developer has an option on the land. Thus, its proceeds can be used just like a construction loan—to acquire the land, develop the site, and construct the shopping center. In other situations, the developer can function as a contract builder to a syndicator.

REITs offer another source of funds. Unlike syndications, shares in REITs can be easily traded so that investors have added liquidity. Also, REITs can both make loans on and take equity positions in property. With such flexibility, REITs are well suited to finance shopping center development.

Government

Rarely will government financing be available for total project financing. However, when used with funds from other sources, government financing programs greatly enhance the feasibility of a project. To qualify for government financing, a project must serve a public purpose, stimulate economic growth, and conform to local planning and development guidelines. Shopping centers usually meet all three requirements. They provide goods and services to often underserved residential areas, offer employment opportunities, and meet all local zoning and building requirements.

The benefit of government programs is that they reduce the cost of financing shopping center development. The financing survey, *Dollars and Percents of Development Finance*, Fourth Quarter 1983, First Quarter 1984, conducted by the Urban Land Institute, shows that projects having some public financing had a mean construction loan interest rate of 9.58 percent. The mean rate for totally privately funded loans was 12.39 percent. This mean rate translates into a 22 percent lower interest expense. During periods of high interest rates, this lower expense can easily mean the difference between a feasible shopping center and just a dream.

Several government programs are currently available to help finance shopping centers. Government programs are subject to revision or termination, however. Therefore, part of the ensuing discussion applies to the programs funded through 1985.

- **Urban Development Action Grants (UDAGs).** This program, available through the Department of Housing and Urban Development, makes fund grants to local municipalities to assist in the financing of specific projects. The municipalities loan the funds to developers at highly attractive interest rates and with good terms. Some UDAGs provide an interest-free loan during construction with interest charged only upon completion. In addition, the interest rates have varied from 3 to 12 percent.
- **Industrial Revenue Bonds (IRBs).** This program provides tax-exempt bond funds for real estate development. Shopping centers of all sizes have benefited from the use of IRBs. Developers without a substantial credit rating have issued IRBs on

their projects backed with bank letters of credit. The authority to issue IRBs comes from the local jurisdiction in which the project will be built. However, the municipality in no way guarantees the repayment of the bonds. That is why other guarantees and the developer's credit rating are important to IRB financing.

- **Tax Abatement and Tax Increment Financing (TIF).** These are local programs that can assist in financing a project. Tax abatement reduces the property tax burden on a project, often postponing payment of the bulk of the taxes until after the first few years of a project's operation. Tax increment financing uses tax revenue from a specially created district to repay municipal bonds. The bonds can pay for land assembly or infrastructure improvement. A project that does not have to bear these costs becomes much more feasible.

Foreign Investors

Foreign investors are primarily attracted to existing centers with a proven operating history. They also prefer to purchase centers outright rather than provide loans for them. However, foreign lenders and investors do undertake joint ventures with U.S. developers on major commercial projects. With the elimination of the 30 percent tax withholding (part of the Deficit Reduction Act of 1984), an increasing number of foreign lenders may become more active in debt financing of U.S. real estate. The attractiveness of U.S. real estate is evidenced in a 1983 British pension fund survey shown in Figure 2-15.

2-15 SURVEY OF OVERSEAS REAL ESTATE INVESTMENT BY BRITISH PENSION FUNDS: 1983

COUNTRY	PER-CENT	PROPERTY TYPE	PER-CENT
United States	69%	Office Buildings	71%
Germany	6	Real Estate Separate Accounts[1]	15
Belgium	2	Shopping Centers	12
Holland	2	Industrial	1
Others	21	Residential	1
Totals	100%		100%

[1]Real estate portfolios managed by major U.S. institutions for pension fund clients.
Source: Debenham Tewson & Chinnocks, *Money into Property 1970–1983* (London, England: Debenham Tewson & Chinnocks, 1984).

Summary—Financing Sources

The source of financing depends on many variables. The developer must decide on the appropriate mix of debt and equity financing. The total amount of dollars needed will strongly influence where a developer seeks funding. Figure 2-16 provides one look at some of the differences that existed in the permanent financing terms offered from various sources in early 1984. Life insurance companies and commercial banks dominated the permanent loan market. However, much of their activity was due to their role as investors of pension fund money. As the decade progresses, the dominant position held by LICs will prob-

2-16   SURVEY OF TERMS ON PERMANENT LOANS BY LENDER: 1984

LENDER	LOAN AMOUNT	INTEREST RATE[1]	LOAN TERM (YEARS)[2]	LOAN-TO-VALUE RATIO[3]	NUMBER OF LOANS
Life Insurance Companies	$15,083,000	12.8%	9	76%	51
Pension Funds	15,668,000	13.1	23	71	12
Banks	16,753,000	12.7	6	77	44
Savings and Loans	13,037,000	12.6	8	80	37
Credit Companies	6,249,000	13.5	7	78	5
Mortgage Bankers	9,927,000	13.2	9	79	14
Public Financing[4]	5,397,000	9.6	19	80	23
Foreign Lenders	17,370,000	12.4	9	75	4

[1]Interest rate on nonparticipating loans.
[2]The loan term is not the same as the amortization period.
[3]The ratio between the amount of the loan and the total value of the project.
[4]Public financing applies to projects that were at least partially financed by IRBs, UDAGs, or other public programs.
Source: Urban Land Institute, *Dollars and Percents of Development Finance*, Fourth Quarter 1983, First Quarter 1984 (Washington, D.C.: ULI–the Urban Land Institute, 1984).

ably decline slightly as pension funds increasingly invest directly in shopping centers. Another factor revealed in Figure 2-16 is that only pension funds and public financing programs allowed developers loan terms over 10 years. Finally, the considerable advantage in interest rates resulting from public financing programs is readily apparent. As the 1980s move into the 1990s, developers must continue to monitor lenders because of the ongoing change that is expected throughout the financial services industry.

Techniques for Financing Shopping Centers

Financing depends on project economics. The developer may finance the entire construction costs through equity or through debt or through numerous combinations of the two. The developer must determine the appropriate mix of debt and equity as well as the ownership structure that will best fit the project's financial needs. Ownership could take the form of a corporation, a limited partnership, a general partnership, a real estate investment trust, or a sole proprietorship. Perhaps the key factor in deciding the ownership structure is the amount of equity to be placed in the project.

The following section identifies some of the debt and equity techniques used in shopping center financing. Among the common debt techniques are construction loans, construction loans with "miniperms," participating mortgages, land sale leasebacks, public financing programs, and convertible mortgages. Mechanisms used for equity financing are usually joint ventures, limited partnerships, or pre-sale agreements.

Debt Financing Options

Construction Loans. Construction loans are normally available from commercial banks, S&Ls, and, for larger projects, from life insurance companies. They contain floating interest rates that change with the lender's prime rate or cost of funds index. The loan covers the entire cost of construction, and most loans have reserves that pay the interest on the loans, freeing the developer of this obligation. Many lenders require that developers obtain a takeout commitment for a permanent loan before any construction funds are advanced.

Construction Loans with Mini-Perms. Recognizing the changing financial environment, banks, S&Ls, and life insurance companies are providing extended construction financing to developers. Rather than require a takeout commitment, these lenders provide both fixed-rate and floating-rate term loans that extend several years beyond the construction period. The developer is then able to secure more favorable permanent financing because he has both a fully operating center and the ability to better time his move to permanent financing.

Participating Mortgages. Participating mortgages have been a major debt instrument for almost two decades. In addition to receiving interest income at a stated rate, the lender receives a portion of the income from gross sales, a portion of the net income after debt service, and a share of the property's appreciation, or some combination of income and appreciation. A developer can usually obtain a takeout commitment for a participating mortgage either before construction begins or to refinance an extended construction loan. The lender's share of net income and appreciation varies with the interest rate charged. A common formula in the mid-1980s lowers the interest rate by 2 to 2.5 percentage points in return for 50 percent of the net income after debt service and 50 percent of the property's appreciated value. The loan term for participating mortgages may be 10 to 15 years.

Land Sale Leasebacks. While participating mortgages may be available on projects of all sizes, land sale leasebacks are generally available only on larger shopping center proposals. As noted earlier, a land sale leaseback involves the sale of the shopping center site to the lender or an investor. The developer then leases back the land on a long-term lease. The entire rent payment under the lease is tax deductible to the developer. Further, since the developer has all of his equity in the improvements, the entire value of his equity is eligible for depreciation. The lender/lessor receives rental income, a share in the project's profits, and unencumbered ownership of the land at the end of the lease term.

Leasehold Financing. To use this method the tenant must be a strong, nationally rated corporation or government, and the lease must be noncancelable without the lender's consent. Few neighborhood or community centers are thus able to use leasehold financing.

Public Financing Programs. Both UDAGs and IRBs are available to all sizes of shopping center developments. Both of these programs require that the developer meet the requirements of the respective agencies. IRBs may be used to finance 100 percent of the development costs and in a few cases may be advanced before construction, serving as both a construction and a permanent loan. UDAGs must be leveraged with private funding, generally at a ratio of better than $3 private to $1 UDAG. However, the very low interest rate on UDAGs, their use for construction, and their highly negotiable terms make them valuable tools in the total financing picture.

Developers considering the conversion of historic properties into specialty centers should be aware of the investment tax credits that are available. These credits are especially attractive to investors who purchase limited partnership shares as a tax shelter. Current pending legislation would, however, eliminate these credits.

Convertible Mortgages. A large shopping center project may also obtain financing through a convertible mortgage. The convertible mortgage is a loan that is converted into a specific equity interest in the property at a certain date. In exchange for this equity conversion feature, the lender provides a below-market interest rate to the developer. Further, the developer retains full ownership advantages, such as the benefits of depreciation during the loan period before the conversion date.

Equity Financing Options

Joint Ventures. A joint venture is the joint ownership of a project by the developer and a financial institution or a large investor. Financial institutions are primarily interested in large centers, whereas other strong financial partners may invest in projects of all sizes. The amount of equity the financing partner supplies to the project will vary. Institutional partners normally fund 100 percent of the development costs. Joint venture partners share in the proceeds from the development, and most joint ventures have a specified date of termination and sellout.

Limited Partnerships. The growth of the syndication industry has greatly expanded the ability of real estate to attract equity funds. Limited partnerships may be formed in all sizes. Private offerings are more expensive to issue and are therefore feasible only on larger projects. Some "blind pool" syndications exist that supply equity to several different projects, none of which has to be specified in the initial offering. Although the strength of the securities dealer and the issuing entity is of course crucial in attracting funds to blind pool syndications, it is also important in all limited partnerships. The developer may form the syndicate with his own project team, or he may employ a syndicator to arrange the offering. Developers not familiar with the intricacies of syndication packaging and marketing should not attempt to do this themselves.

Presale Agreement. A developer may find it advantageous to presell the entire project to an equity investor. The sales contract serves the same purpose as a takeout commitment in that it permits the developer to obtain construction financing. The developer receives a development profit at the sale without having to obtain it during the holding period of the investment.

Emerging Techniques. Real estate financing techniques are becoming more like those used in security sales. Already developers are issuing IRBs and unrated bonds, organizing real estate investment trusts, and making other "securitized" transactions. Within this decade methods will emerge enabling commercial mortgage debt to be transformed into rated bonds. This will expand the commercial debt market by opening it to new investors and improving its liquidity.

Preparing the Financing Package

In the development process, money is the most important ingredient. Therefore, the developer must exercise extreme care in creating the financing package. Whether preparing the package himself or using a consultant, the developer must disclose all project information clearly and accurately. The following items should be included in a loan package.

- A letter of transmittal that states the nature of the project and the amount of funds being requested.
- A market or feasibility study prepared by a recognized consulting firm. The study should discuss the trade area, population characteristics, competition, metropolitan growth, and all other factors that would affect the feasibility of the developer's proposal.
- A disclosure of all property characteristics, including a survey, site plan, building plans, photographs, and renderings.
- A detailed cash flow statement containing rent schedules, expenses, HVAC charges, common area maintenance costs, percentage rents, and all other items pertaining to the revenue and expenses of the proposed project.
- All legal documents, including the property deed or the sales contract, the title insurance policy, any letters of intent to lease, the lease forms, and all attachments and exhibits that are part of these documents.
- A detailed cost estimate of the project along with a projected construction schedule.
- A report on the developer's experience, including a description of other projects the developer has completed.

The above list describes the traditional requirements for a loan package. However, with the expanded use of limited partnerships and REITs, developers should be aware of certain basic elements of equity financing in these areas as well. All public syndications must be registered with the Securities and Exchange Commission (SEC) and with all state regulating agencies in which the offering will be sold. Small, private offerings do not have to register with the SEC. However, both public and private offerings must disclose information on the proposed syndication, including the following:

- Specific minimum income, net worth, and tax bracket standards that a "suitable" investor should possess as well as the minimum amounts each partner must invest.
- The promoter's or sponsor's compensation in all its forms, such as management fees, brokerage commissions, resale profit, interest income, and interests in the partnership.
- The rights of the limited partners, including the right to inspect partnership records and to take action against the promoters or sponsors in the event of fraud or negligence.
- The agreement to make periodic reports to the investors. For public offerings, these reports must be filed with the SEC and state commissions.

The nature of shopping center financing is changing. Both debt and equity financing are appearing in new forms. This discussion outlines only a few of the trends in this area. Developers should analyze their financing needs with the help of their lenders and consultants to derive the most appropriate financial structure for their particular projects.

Land Use Controls

Any shopping center site will require favorable zoning for a developer to be able to proceed. Thus, the zoning provisions in effect for a site must be carefully studied before a site is purchased. An early study should explore the attitudes of the local residents, zoning staff, and approval body toward a shopping center proposal. The feasibility of a project is affected by the zoning regulations in effect, as well as by the time and expense that will be required for the approval process.

Areas of fast growth that favor growth generally try to streamline the approval process and to allocate adequate land to new development. In areas of rapid growth where slow growth is advocated, permits may be difficult to obtain, restrictions profuse, and rezoning next to impossible, with little land available for new development. In moderate growth areas, the developer can expect any possible regulatory climate, depending on the size, staffing, and sophistication of the jurisdiction; on the availability of land and its geographic characteristics; and on a host of other variables. Each locality has to be approached as a new

experience, since procedures, time frames, and dispositions vary widely from area to area.[18]

In many cases, the site proposed for a shopping center is not zoned for commercial or mixed use when the development process begins. In the case of regional and super regional centers, the cost of accumulating large enough parcels of land on which to build a shopping center may be prohibitive if the land has already been zoned for commercial use. In other cases, a site may be zoned for commercial use, but the ordinance may have to be modified concerning provisions such as floor area ratio, building height, parking requirements, lot coverage, setbacks, or others.[19]

Avenues of Relief

If a developer is considering a project that is not consistent with the provisions of an ordinance, specific "avenues of relief" are delineated in the ordinance. Each of these avenues requires an application and approval process. A developer will usually hire a lawyer or employ the legal expertise of his own staff in working through a zoning relief process.

These avenues of relief fall into three main categories: rezoning, variances, and conditional use permits. The rezoning process typically involves filing of an application, a review process, an appearance before an appeals board or a zoning administrator, a public hearing, and final approval by a planning board or commission. A variance involves a request, in an area already zoned for commercial use, to build in a way that does not comply with the specific standards set forth in the text of the zoning ordinance. A conditional use permit is issued through a special provision in the zoning ordinance text. This provision will specify that, subject to review and approval by the local authority, special uses will be allowed that are not normally permitted in that zone. Typically, a conditional use provision will state certain requirements that must be met by the project (regarding setback, building height, parking, etc.) in order for the conditional use permit to be considered and granted. For both a variance and a conditional use permit, the developer goes through a similar review process, involving applications, review, and hearings before he does or does not receive approval.

Rezoning requests frequently deal with the issue of consistency with the community's comprehensive

---

[18] Frank J. Popper, *The Politics of Land Use Reform* (Madison, Wisconsin: The University of Wisconsin Press, 1981).

[19] American Society of Planning Officials, *Shopping Center Zoning* (Chicago: American Society of Planning Officials and Planning Advisory Service, 1959).

2-17   Pickering Wharf is a mixed-use development in Salem, Massachusetts, containing 71,000 square feet of retail space as well as office, residential, and entertainment uses. The project was subject to the review and approval of the Salem Redevelopment Authority, the Salem Planning Department, and the state's Department of Environmental Quality Engineering.

plan. If a site's zoning is consistent with the comprehensive plan, it is usually easier for a developer to petition for a zoning change. If a decision is made that is unfavorable and appears unreasonable, a developer may appeal to a zoning board of appeals that operates as a quasi-judicial review arm of the local government. By this point, the developer will probably have obtained legal counsel. If an appeal of the zoning board of appeals' decision is desired, the case would be heard at a lower court of the judicial system. Further appeal can be made through that system to the Supreme Court, if necessary. This process is, however, costly and time-consuming, and generally neither the developer nor the community wants to use it as the means to resolve a conflict.[20]

Site Plan Review

In addition to the zoning review and approval process, most communities have instituted a site plan review process for projects over a certain size. Site plan review involves a detailed evaluation of the project's design features such as signage, parking, landscaping, and structural characteristics. The probable effect the project will have on the surrounding area is also evaluated, based on environmental factors like topography and soil characteristics, infrastructure needs, and traffic generation. Social impacts are analyzed, especially on areas that are primarily residential. These are the considerations that frequently concern citizens the most, causing delays in the public hearings stage of the review process.

Municipalities have become more aware of the long-term effects of any soil erosion caused by the construction of a new shopping center. They also consider more carefully the effects of development on

[20] Urban Land Institute, *Shopping Center Zoning* (Washington, D.C.: ULI–the Urban Land Institute, 1973).

groundwater contamination and on potential storm-water runoff and flooding. This increased concern over environmental quality is reflected in the enactment of more specific standards and more careful review of these factors during site plan review. Typically, an outside consultant specializing in environmental matters prepares an environmental impact statement (EIS). Developers today thus consider more carefully during the early stages of planning the impact their projects will have on the environment.[21]

Historically, developers have found the specific standards included in the ordinance for commercial zones difficult to meet, requiring them frequently to request variances or special exceptions. Inferior site plan designs and a lack of innovation frequently resulted as developers and architects struggled to comply with often unnecessarily restrictive and outdated standards.[22]

Zoning Alternatives

Many communities have become aware of the problems inherent in designating a commercial zone that tries to regulate strip commercial development, independent retail operations, and planned shopping centers within the same framework. For this reason, special classifications known as "planned development districts" were devised, which provide much greater flexibility in shopping center design but require a mandatory site plan review. As already noted, comprehensive site plan review evaluates the project's compliance with certain criteria involving both physical and aesthetic standards. These evaluations require a sophisticated review staff, generally composed of engineers, architects, and planners, and also call for a high degree of cooperation among various government agencies. Agencies that typically become involved in site plan review include: the Office of Zoning, the Site Plan Review Branch, the Office of Planning, the Zoning Administration/Board of Appeals, the Department of Public Works, the Department of Transportation, and the Department of Environmental Protection. Other agencies may become involved, depending upon the issues that emerge in the process.[23]

Many communities now have planned development districts, recognizing the benefits that they can provide to the community by giving developers the flexibility to tailor development more closely to the unique qualities and characteristics of the area and the population being served.

Other communities have zoned to provide for shopping centers through the use of a "floating zone." A floating shopping center zone is described in detail in the zoning ordinance text but is not geographically located on the zoning map. The text specifies the types of development allowed and the standards that would usually be applied to a commercial district. The zone "floats" until a request is received to develop at a particular location. The merits of that location are then evaluated, and if it is approved, the approval process continues with a review of the site plan, after which the area under consideration is officially zoned for commercial use. Many communities still use this type of zoning.[24]

Zoning overlays represent a third zoning alternative for commercial development. These overlays specify areas in which a proposal for commercial development will be considered. Any development within the overlay district will be subject to certain conditions that do not exist outside the overlay zone.

Zoning overlays that are not specifically geared toward shopping center development can still affect the quality of a center developed within their areas. For instance, a downtown revitalization overlay may give density bonuses for the inclusion of residential units in the overall shopping center design. A floodplain overlay district may inhibit the types of permanent building that occur in the floodplain, which will decidedly affect design. An airport overlay district may have certain construction requirements related to sound insulation and building height.

With the growing urban shopping center market, municipalities are faced with the unique problems of approving site plans for enclosed malls that incorporate existing historic structures and include necessary parking areas. In such cases, municipalities are creating historic overlay districts with regulations to preserve historic structures and other urban features—adding another layer to the evaluation process.[25]

Federal, State, and Regional Regulation

Beginning in 1969 and continuing into the 1970s, the federal government became involved increasingly in environmental regulation with the passage of the Na-

[21] Frank J. Popper, *The Politics of Land Use Reform*.

[22] Ibid.

[23] Example taken from Fairfax County, Virginia, zoning ordinance.

[24] John A. Dawson, *Shopping Centre Development* (New York: Longman, Inc., 1983).

[25] Information on new zoning mechanisms was gathered in the fall of 1984 through interviews with developers, public officials, and land use lawyers from each region of the United States.

tional Environmental Policy Act, the Clean Air Act and Amendments, the Federal Water Pollution Control Act of 1972 as amended by the Clean Water Act of 1977, and the Noise Control Act and Amendments. Of these pieces of federal legislation, the Clean Air Act Amendments have had the greatest impact on shopping center development. This legislation makes localities more responsible for the regional and local impacts on air quality caused by traffic-generating development. The Clean Water Act involves the regulation of any development affecting water quality. In some cases, a larger regional shopping center can become affected by indirect source pollution regulations.

Concern about regional impacts of development on both the environment and on transportation systems has stimulated increasing state involvement in local land use regulation, as well as in the creation of regional authorities to oversee local activities. County governments also are playing an increasing role in land use regulation around the country, particularly in areas that are outside a municipal jurisdiction.

In some localities, the onus is still on the developer to know which regulations he must comply with and to make the appropriate applications. However, local regulations now often incorporate federal and state standards, and the locality oversees the review process to a larger degree, coordinating efforts between the various agencies and levels of government.

Development Agreements/Exactions

A major trend emerging in the development approval process in the 1980s is the use of development agreements. These are negotiated agreements between developers and local jurisdictions, often arbitrated by an attorney. The developer is given permission to build, in exchange for providing certain on- or off-site improvements for the local governing body. These improvements are known as exactions. Originally, development agreements were created to respond to the expenditures local communities had to make on additional improvements because of new developments. Municipalities began to require that developers instead pay for the off-site improvements that were necessitated by their projects. These improvements might include building and widening roads, adding traffic signals, running water and sewer lines to the project, and making other changes directly related to the development. In residential building this expanded in some cases to the provision of schools as well. In the fiscal crunch of the 1980s, many local

jurisdictions have found exactions to be a convenient way to finance municipal improvements and thus prevent new development from being an added burden on an already tight budget. In many areas, however, exactions are becoming less directly related to the needs caused by the development itself.

When a developer has already received permission to build, a development agreement may frequently involve other types of trade-offs: the developer negotiates for increased density or for other features such as a lower parking requirement, in exchange for providing or paying for a public improvement. These agreements, often called bonus agreements, involve careful arbitration to come up with a final proposal by which both parties feel they will benefit. Gaining popularity, bonuses are a frequently used technique in overlay or other special districts and are often incorporated in the text of the zoning ordinance.

Developers have successfully challenged unreasonable requests made by cities; courts determined that these requests were not sufficiently related to development-generated needs of the municipalities. In general, however, the use of exactions has become a legally accepted practice, and, in most instances, any disputes are resolved through negotiation between the developer and the community rather than through litigation.

Citizen Participation

Government at all levels is increasingly accommodating the desire of citizens to participate in shaping the development of their communities. For citizens with vastly diverging interests to reach a consensus on the direction and quality of development can sometimes be a frustrating and time-consuming process.

State law mandates that virtually every local jurisdiction meet certain requirements for public participation in the review process. When public hearings and other means of participation were first tried nationally, many developers experienced lengthy delays and enormous frustrations as citizens aired their views in unwieldy review procedures. Needless to say, public officials as well as citizens were equally frustrated with the newly evolving systems. Today, however, citizen participation has been largely formalized and now is handled as an orderly, routine part of the review and approval process. Indeed, the astute developer recognizes the important role that citizens play in obtaining project approval and works with them from the early stages of project planning. Citizens, along with public officials and developers, are also becoming more sophisticated in their involvement, recognizing that cooperative negotiation ultimately reaps benefits for all parties.

The Approval Process

The approval process customarily involves submitting proposals to and negotiating with the jurisdiction's planning staff, who ultimately recommend that a project be approved or denied. During this process, various agencies review the project, and public hearings are held. In the past, the developer obtained appropriate zoning for the site before he applied for permits. Today, as a rule, site plans must be reviewed and the project's compliance with parking and subdivision regulations considered before the developer can obtain any zoning approval.

Often a developer can first submit a basic concept plan, avoiding the expense of putting together a detailed site plan until the jurisdiction has indicated the project will likely be approved.

A developer beginning a project review process will usually select to represent his interests a local lawyer who knows the specifics of the local ordinance and procedures, as well as the local political climate. Also, a local lawyer will often receive more cooperation from officials than an "outsider." These lawyers often have their own engineers and other expert witnesses with good local credibility to testify for presentations. The lawyer helps the developer with myriad aspects of the approval process from rezoning to Adequate Public Facilities (APF) review. APF review involves the study of road, sewer, water, and fire service, and it is during this review process that negotiations regarding exactions are often conducted. The lawyer assists during the site plan review stage as well, negotiating optimal bonuses to be awarded based on meeting specified conditions. The attorney also represents the client in informal meetings with planning staff professionals and occasionally assists the developer with permit approval. The attorney will make formal presentations at hearings and other adjudicatory proceedings. The effectiveness of a developer's legal representative can cause a project to win or lose approval. Other factors that influence a project's approval are community attitudes toward the quality of the proposed development and/or the receptivity of the jurisdiction.

A well-planned, well-documented presentation at public hearings improves the developer's chances of obtaining community support. Use of photographs, statistical charts, drawings, and models makes presentations more vivid and comprehensible. An experienced land use lawyer will prepare an effective presentation, producing the required expert witnesses and supportive documents.

Community Concerns

In the past, many parts of the country allowed development to occur virtually unregulated. But by the 1970s and 1980s, many communities had become concerned about the social, environmental, and physical impacts of development and had begun to regulate it much more carefully.

A community will be primarily concerned with those elements of a shopping center that pertain to the general welfare of the community. Major considerations often have to do with the effects of competition on downtown retail operations, as well as on the everyday aspects of traffic, noise, infrastructure and utility requirements, and environmental impacts. Increasingly, communities also worry about the aesthetic qualities of a shopping center and how the center will affect the character of the surrounding community. If a developer is sensitive to these concerns and designs a center that is attractive and compatible with its surroundings, the approval process will be made much easier. Some developers make a point of contacting local residents and civic associations early in the planning process to explain the proposal. A developer may then avoid costly delays by entering the approval process with a plan that will not take the community by surprise and generate opposition.

During the approval process, the developer will want to promote good public relations. A community frequently needs reassurance when it is in the midst of transition to a more urban setting. The developer can provide this by alleviating community anxieties that were often caused by the negative consequences of past development practices.

Zoning favorable to shopping center development can also be in the public interest. Developers must carry the burden of proof in providing sound reasons for a project's approval, although numerous communities now recognize the benefits of a shopping center. A shopping center provides increases in net income from real estate and sales taxes in excess of the increased cost of the public services required by the center. Thus, a shopping center has a more favorable fiscal impact on a community than residential development. Centers also generate employment. Due to the nature of development agreements, communities receive many benefits from the development of shopping centers through exactions. These include road and infrastructure improvements and, in some cases,

2-18 In the design of Plaza Pasadena, Pasadena, California, special care was taken to create a strong formal entrance that would link the civic buildings of Pasadena, and to incorporate artistic elements into the center that would reflect the culture of the community.

community and transportation facilities. In addition, the community does not have the burden of underwriting the center's maintenance and security.

A developer needs to address specific community concerns. He must justify the need for an increase in the area's shopping facilities as well as the center's type of goods and services. The development team should also be prepared to discuss the issues of the center's architectural design, the lighting necessary for security, signage, traffic circulation, and the relationship with adjoining properties.

Developer Concerns

The developer will want to create a shopping environment that is popular with the community it serves. He will also want to develop a center with a tenant mix and operational costs that make it a feasible investment venture. For this reason, the private business aspects of a shopping center should remain the province of the developer, not the community. In addition, approval authorities should not set up specifications that inhibit design latitude and impose excessive costs or unusual burdens on the development. Overly

specific regulations often result in inflexible designs that are not as responsive as they should be to community needs. Shopping center types, sizes, and design will vary according to special tenant leasing needs and developer innovations. On-site parking and off-street loading are well-established principles of the shopping center concept providing adequate space for the convenience of customers and tenants. Because a shopping center's goal at the outset is to respond to its market, many community concerns regarding good shopping center design are also the developer's concerns. Allowing latitude for flexibility in design generally results in improved service to all parties.

An Atmosphere of Cooperation

Complicated ordinances and approval processes per se are not the chief problem developers or communities face. It is the adversary atmosphere that frequently envelopes these processes as officials, citizens, and developers are, in a sense, "pitted" against each other. If the jurisdiction regards the developer as an adversary, it may establish strict ordinance regulations as leverage in negotiating with the developer. Obviously, this will not be conducive to the resolution of differences. If developers and community officials first establish an atmosphere of cooperation and mutual trust between them, they will be far better equipped to negotiate with each other to their mutual satisfaction. A community should understand the development business, and the developer should understand the community. Through this understanding, reasonable compromises can be reached.

Development agreements represent a common method of facilitating negotiation. They allow developers and officials to negotiate aspects of the project or the surrounding area that are of critical concern and to reach agreements on acceptable levels of development. While leading to better overall development, development agreements also reassure citizen opponents that community concerns are being addressed.

In Virginia, a system of proffers has been established through state legislation. This makes it possible for developers and communities to negotiate trade-offs that normally could not be achieved through a development agreement. Other states may adopt the proffer system in the near future.

Both development agreements and proffers can be useful tools when implemented in an atmosphere of mutual cooperation and respect by developers and officials who are knowledgeable and wise. But an inexperienced developer or local official may agree to inappropriate terms because of misinformation or a lack of information.

Summary—Land Use Controls

In general, both developers and communities will agree that sophisticated land use control processes are good for the community in the long run. Changes and advances are occurring in the quality and characteristics of shopping center development. In many cases, traditional commercial zoning regulations are not equipped to respond appropriately to these changes. For this reason, land use regulations are incorporating more flexibility in order to better meet the needs of the community, the developer, the shopping center, and the market.

3.
Planning and Design

Once the feasibility of development has been determined and the "go" decision has been made, serious site planning and architectural and structural design can begin.

The planning and design of the center will be a challenge for the design team. The structure must house the business of retailing; the site must accommodate the parking of automobiles; and the building and site treatment must appeal to and be convenient to customers while satisfying tenants, compensating the owner, and accommodating community interests and values. In addition, the center must be designed within ever tighter restraints involving environmental concerns, energy conservation, and more difficult land use controls. The whole concept calls for an architectural quality compatible with the type and location of the center, the topography of the site, and the configuration of the building(s). Achieving this also requires melding the principles of good planning, landscaping, architectural design, and engineering with skillful merchandising, public relations, and management. Compromises will be made between what can be afforded and what may be left out, but the finished center must be an appealing and convenient marketplace in which to shop, and it must

meet the needs of its trade area. Only then can it be profitable for the community, the tenants, and the owner.

The design team's task therefore is special. The design must achieve an overall harmony of style while permitting reasonable variations among tenants to give them identity. The architect and planner must coordinate their skills with those of other experts on the developer's team. This coordination is necessary in designing a regional mall, but it is even more important for the smaller center, where an absence of good planning has often resulted in a poor or mediocre appearance. The public understandably considers many smaller centers unsightly. A hodgepodge of materials, poor taste in signage, and inferior architecture have often been combined to produce a center that visually pollutes an area.

Before a shopping center can be designed, the type of center, its key tenant types, and the general array of space for the tenants must be known. The developer's decisions and commitments affect the structural framework, particularly when an enclosed mall or special building cluster is intended . Just as the exterior design treatment is dictated by the size, shape, and location of the property, so the placement and grouping of tenants within the structure are based on the leasing or merchandising plan. Decisions about mall configuration, structural framing, and mechanical equipment alternatives within the limits of cost should be made before exterior architecture is determined.

Unless the center is to have a basement, the foundation requires only simple excavations in order to lay column footings and grade beams to support load-bearing walls. A flat built-up roof over a long-spanning joist roof allows load-bearing columns to be spaced widely apart, providing maximum flexibility in designing widths and depths of individual stores. Building depths, which previously ran from 125 to 150 feet, now typically run from 80 to 120 feet, largely because the increased cost of construction has forced tenants into smaller spaces, and, rather than give up frontage, the stores have become shallower. Smaller shops now may be as shallow as 30 feet, with mall stalls against otherwise blank department store walls as shallow as 12 feet. Many shops may be no more than 30 to 60 feet deep, with the rear space designed to serve either as storage area or as overlap area for deeper adjacent units.

In addition to the structural and interior design controls imposed on the designer by the character and tenant makeup of the particular project, external controls are imposed by public reactions to current general conditions. For example, the public's growing concern with environmental and ecological matters has led to buildings and site designs that harmonize more than ever before with the character of the community. And in the long run, the need for energy efficiency to control operating costs may influence shopping center design as much as site location. Energy-saving measures are being incorporated in the enclosed mall. For example, rooftop air conditioners for each tenant can be replaced with a system using chilled water circulated from a central plant or with a hybrid system. Instead of untreated glass over central areas, translucent double Plexiglass sandwich panels and north clerestory lighting are being used. Display windows on exterior walls are being eliminated or are being installed only where they face north or east. Other recent changes include increased insulation to reduce loss or gain of heat through walls and roofs, automatic cycle lighting, and a decreased use of intensive heat-producing lighting systems with a corresponding increase in the use of paired-up sodium lamps rather than metal arc lamps of the same wattage. Graphics are being improved: illuminated identification signs with black letters silhouetted on a light background are being used instead of brilliant self-lighted lettering. Energy-saving devices and inno-

vative design techniques are limited only by the ingenuity and resourcefulness of architects, designers, and engineers.

Today's center must be designed so that it is accessible to the handicapped and complies with accessibility codes and standards. Laws mandating accessibility in privately owned public buildings (including shopping centers) exist at the federal, state, and local levels. These laws are incorporated into building codes and in general require that buildings be free of barriers to handicapped individuals. The developer and his design team must be aware of all accessibility codes and must make certain that these requirements are incorporated in the center's design. Failure to do so will add costs to the project, since installed features that fail to provide access to the handicapped according to codes will have to be replaced with components that do. Such changes will also take time and may delay the occupancy permit for the center. There are many accessibility standards, and requirements obviously differ at the state and local levels. However, the design features covered by these codes are essentially the same and include arrival and parking areas, walkways, ramps, entrances and doorways, corridors, stairs, elevators, toilet facilities, drinking fountains, public telephones, and signs.[1]

Shopping center developers and designers must deal with inflation as a force that is changing the "traditional" pattern of shopping center development. An attractive material or a construction technique requiring a good deal of specialized labor may become too expensive. The architect's job will be to find new materials and new methods that will create an equally attractive appearance at affordable costs.

Building efficiency has always been important, but today's costs make it essential. Design solutions should maximize the leasable space and minimize the nonleasable spaces that are not required for customer use. With rising land costs, an inefficient parking layout is intolerable. With labor costs rising faster than income, an interior or exterior that requires high maintenance cannot be allowed.

However, maximum space at minimum cost is not the only goal. To be successful, a shopping center must be attractive and pleasant for the customer. A lack of quality in the finished appearance will be projected to the customer, reducing the appeal and thus the earning capacity of the center. However, at the other extreme, an ostentatious, overdesigned center may frighten away customers in a mid- or off-price mall.

[1] David J. Fishman, *Shopping Centers and the Accessibility Codes* (New York: International Council of Shopping Centers, 1979).

Exterior Features

Building Configurations

Determining the building configuration is an important part of the site planning process for both developer and tenant. The developer's main consideration in the building pattern should be placement of the key or anchor tenants. These tenants must be positioned so that they draw shopper traffic between them and other tenants.

Building configurations have steadily evolved. The original shopping center concept started as a linear building with parking in the rear, at the sides, or in front. The L, U, and T were variations designed to fit restricted site and special locations with respect to adjacent streets. Then, in larger centers, stores courageously turned their backs on the public street, with two strip buildings facing each other separated by parking. Later, this intervening parking space was contracted and transformed into an open and then enclosed landscaped mall. The mall structure, with its shop frontages, became an island surrounded by parking space.

The Linear Center and Variations

The linear layout is basically a straight line of stores, tied together by a canopy over a pedestrian walk that

3-1   SHOPPING CENTER BUILDING
              CONFIGURATIONS

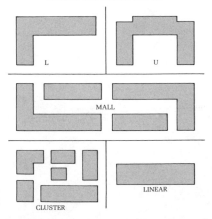

Linear—a line of stores tied together by a canopy over the sidewalk, which runs along the fronts of the stores. Economical for small centers, but must be kept within a reasonable length to avoid excessive walking distances and difficult merchandising.

The L—basically a linear layout, but with one end turned. Good for corner locations.

The U—basically a linear layout with both ends turned in the same direction.

The mall—essentially a pedestrian way between two facing linear buildings. The mall may also take other shapes—an L, for example.

The cluster—a group of retail buildings separated by small pedestrian malls or courts.

goes along the storefronts. The linear building is normally set back from the access street, and most of the parking is placed between the street and the building. This center design is often referred to as a "strip center." Although this term describes a particular physical arrangement that can be used for shopping centers, it is also a term that (when used in combination, as in "strip development" and "strip commercial") does not include all of the factors that qualify a development as a shopping center.

The linear arrangement is most commonly applied to the neighborhood center. The most successful configuration places two major units—usually a supermarket and a drugstore—at the ends of the center. A linear center is generally the least expensive structure to build and is easily adapted to most site conditions. With strong sign control and good architectural treatment, the linear center can be an attractive and successful merchandising unit.

The linear center should not be too long to accommodate comfortable walking distances. About 400 feet is standard, although centers 750 feet long, and longer, have been successful. People are apparently willing to walk farther in a shopping center than they are downtown. Also, if adequate parking is provided, customers can drive around within a center to various sections of the center. However, this can impair vehicular circulation within the center's parking area and/or reduce the parking capacity. Therefore, if a long linear center is planned, alternative building configurations should be carefully considered.

The L-shaped linear center basically has one end turned; the U-shaped center has both ends turned in the same direction. The major reason for using the L or U shape is to restrict the length of a center that would, if laid out in a straight line, be too long. The L can be turned in either direction according to the necessary site orientation. The L or U shape will also make the fullest use of a site that is nearly square; a linear development on such a site would waste space (site capacity) and provide unnecessary parking. In general, the L is suitable for larger neighborhood and smaller community centers, the U for larger community centers.

Early shopping centers provided canopies or colonnaded roof projections along the storefronts to protect pedestrians from weather conditions. The front sidewalk of a neighborhood linear center can be glass-enclosed and air-conditioned to make it more comfortable for and appealing to shoppers.

The Mall

Essentially a pedestrianway between two facing linear buildings, the mall becomes a pedestrian street for back-and-forth shopping movement. It has become the standard pattern for the regional center and is being applied to community-size centers.

The mall may be either open to the sky or roofed over with glass or plastic skylights to allow natural lighting. Also, many existing open malls are being enclosed with tension-supported fabric roofs (which are generally made of Teflon-coated fiber glass). The weather-protected area is usually heated and cooled according to the season. The enclosed mall, equipped with heating and air conditioning, has become the dominant design for regional centers, regardless of climate. Under current practices of mall construction, the enclosed mall is consistent with goals of energy conservation; it is designed with an efficient, centralized plant or rooftop units, low wattage lighting, and complete insulation.

The Cluster

The cluster is an extension of the mall concept, but often with more buildings freestanding. In a regional center, the cluster varies in shape, using forms of the letters X and Y, as well as the dumbbell. In addition, an offset design with "meandering" mall streets may be used in lieu of the straight mall. The cluster is a design that has been applied to the one-department-store regional center. The department store is placed in the center of the complex, surrounded by smaller stores, rather than at one end of a mall, which would leave the other end with no anchor or a weak anchor. The X and Y forms represent the kinds of design solutions that have been developed for centers with three or four department stores.

Other Building Configurations

Although there is a tendency to classify building configurations according to easily identifiable shapes, a center's building configuration will actually be determined by the characteristics of the particular site and by market and economic considerations. A particular site for a neighborhood center, for example, might be better suited to a bent linear configuration rather than a full L shape. Larger and therefore more complex centers will have many more variations, particularly when they are used to create a special image or character. Also, when shopping centers are located in existing buildings through adaptive use or are integral elements of mixed-use developments, the adaptation of basic configurations can be substantial.

The stacking of levels in a regional center reduces walking distances and creates a more compact shopping area. The double-level or triple-level treatment is a solution called for by certain design limitations caused by site size and configuration.

3-2   A linear center should be no longer than a comfortable walking distance.

3-3 Stacking levels in a regional center reduces walking distances and creates a more compact shopping area.

In addition, a freestanding building has become an accepted feature of both open and enclosed regional centers for those tenants that provide convenience shopping. Such tenants include supermarkets, drive-in banks, dry cleaners and laundries, barber and beauty shops, coin-operated laundries, specialized carryout fast-food services, shoe repair shops, and others. Restaurants and theaters may also be placed in freestanding buildings. These buildings provide for the kind of shops that require close-by parking, quick turnover, and fast customer service.

Freestanding buildings, when skillfully positioned, create flexibility in tenant locations, providing greater customer convenience and making possible one-trip shopping. The customary sea of parking is avoided with each building having its own area of convenient parking. Tenants who prefer customer parking at their front door can thus be included in the regional center complex.

Summary—Building Configurations

With any building configuration, there are basic design principles that the experienced developer and architect understand but that the inexperienced overlook. For example, if an enclosed mall is too wide, it is expensive to operate and discourages the back-and-forth movement created by impulse buying. If a mall is too narrow, it becomes crowded, hard to keep clean, and difficult to use for promotional activities. Thirty to forty feet is the typical mall width. A mall can be widened into a court at one or two spots, both for the design and as areas for promotional activities.

Common design errors, found in all building patterns, include unvarying widths or depths of all stores, no matter what their type; smaller stores being positioned so that they are difficult to service without interfering with pedestrian or auto traffic; and dead spaces that are hard to lease because of their indirect pedestrian access. Multiple corners, setbacks, odd angles, and the like should be avoided in most small centers. In regional malls, however, these special treatments may be used to avoid a tunnel effect in the mall and to spark interest and visual excitement. In any case, the mall is the central feature of the center and therefore must possess individuality and character of design. In the linear center and its variations, the pedestrian arcade is also central, and its design characteristics are crucial to the center's image.

Parking

The act of parking will mark the customer's first contact with the shopping center. The experience should be pleasant. The parking area should support the center's prime role—that of providing an attractive and convenient marketplace.

Although parking is not a commercial use in itself, it is essential to the commercial uses within the center. It also, as a rule, takes up more space than any other physical component of the center. And whether the parking is surface or structure, it must be carefully planned. Parking design requirements—parking area, driveway layout, access aisles, individual stall dimensions and arrangements, pedestrian movements from the parking area to the center, and the grading, paving, landscaping, and lighting of the parking surface—are major elements of the site planning process.

The chief concerns in providing the indispensable parking area are the number of spaces needed and their best arrangement. The problem is complicated when the off-street parking requirements of a local zoning ordinance are not reasonably related to actual parking demand in the shopping center. When the off-street parking area required by ordinance exceeds the demand, it becomes clear to center owners and tenants that the actual demand for spaces is a more suitable basis for determining the number of spaces that should be established. Excessive zoning require-

3-4 Parking ordinarily takes up more area than any other physical component of the center. Northridge Fashion Center in Los Angeles's San Fernando Valley contains both surface and structured parking.

ments also result in a wasteland of unused pavement, causing both a poor appearance and a needless expense to the developer and the tenants. Some communities have enacted regulations to limit the amount of parking provided, causing a shortfall. Although the objective of these regulations is often to control air quality or to encourage transit use, they most likely result in traffic congestion, consumer frustration, and damage to the success of the center. A successful shopping center depends on adequate parking—not too much but also not too little. For this reason, parking requirements at shopping centers have received considerable attention over the years.

Parking Standards and Demand

Parking demand at a shopping center, as compared with that of a freestanding store, is lightened by the fact that a customer visits several stores during a single shopping trip. Characteristics of multipurpose shopping, shared spaces, and rate of parking space turnover distinguish the parking requirements of shopping centers from those of freestanding commercial enterprises—a distinction generally not accounted for in zoning ordinances that establish fixed ratios of number of parking spaces to amount of building area for each commercial use.

The following factors affect parking demand and parking provision:

- Vehicle miles traveled to reach the center.
- Cost of fuel.
- Government regulations.
- Mass transit availability and cost.
- Walk-in trade.
- Size and type of center.
- Tenant mix.
- Total GLA.
- Character and income level of the trade area.
- Cost of land.

Two terms are used to describe the relationship of parking provision to the shopping center structure:

Parking area ratio is the site area assigned to parking use in relation to building area.

Parking index is the actual number of parking spaces per 1,000 square feet of GLA in a shopping center.

For planning purposes and preliminary site evaluation, the parking area ratio serves merely as a useful tool for estimating the area needed for parking; it is not a suitable measurement for establishing parking standards. Parking area ratio, when stated as 2:1 or 3:1, for example, only makes a preliminary estimate of the site's building and parking capacity; the number of spaces that will actually occupy this parking area depends on such variables as angle and size of car stalls, width of moving aisles and access drives, and the arrangement of other parking appurtenances.

The amount of retail selling space depends on tenant type; display of goods; method of selling; the number, size, and variety of items; and other variables. For this reason, selling space is an unsuitable unit to use for statistical comparisons of building area to parking provisions. But the gross leasable area (GLA) is measurable. Furthermore, each tenant's GLA is stated in the lease; GLA is thus a known and realistic factor for measuring the adequacy of parking provision in relation to retail use.

Based on a comprehensive study of parking requirements for shopping centers conducted by ULI under the auspices of the International Council of Shopping Centers, the following base parking standards are recommended for a typical shopping center today:[2]

- 4.0 spaces per 1,000 square feet of gross leasable area (GLA) for centers having a GLA of 25,000 to 400,000 square feet;
- from 4.0 to 5.0 spaces in a linear progression, with an average of 4.5 spaces per 1,000 square feet of GLA, for centers having from 400,000 to 600,000 square feet; and
- 5.0 spaces per 1,000 square feet of GLA for centers having a GLA of over 600,000 square feet.

These new standards recognize differences in center size and the impact of certain uses. They are therefore somewhat more complex than the single index of 5.5 spaces per 1,000 square feet of GLA previously recommended. To understand fully and apply correctly the recommended standards, one should read the complete ULI report.

The provision of parking based on these standards will serve patron and employee needs at the 20th busiest hour of the year, and allow a surplus during all but 19 hours of the remainder of the more than 3,000 hours during which a typical center is open annually. During 19 hours of each year, which are distributed over 10 peak shopping days, some patrons will not be able to find vacant spaces when they first enter the center. However, these standards will need to be adjusted depending on the quantitative presence of certain land uses.[3]

Within the full range of tenants found in shopping centers, offices, cinemas, and food services require additional consideration.

- **Offices.** Office space amounting up to 10 percent of the total GLA can be accommodated without providing parking in addition to that imposed by the application of the overall parking indices. Office space in excess of 10 percent of the center's GLA requires additional parking, although it requires less than a freestanding office building because of the availability of parking for dual purposes. Office entrances should be located so that office tenants do not use the best retail park-

ing spaces. Mixed-use developments where the primary use in building area is other than retail selling were not addressed in this study and therefore the standards set forth here may not be applied.[4]

- **Cinemas.** At centers with 100,000 to 200,000 square feet of GLA having cinemas with up to 450 seats, and at centers with over 200,000 square feet of GLA having cinemas with up to 750 seats, patrons can be accommodated without the provision of parking spaces in addition to the overall recommended standard. Cinemas having more than this number of seats, or cinemas located at smaller centers, however, require a nominal three additional spaces per 100 seats, as set forth in the full study report.[5]
- **Food Services.** The amount of center GLA devoted to food service tenants influences the number of required parking spaces. The number of spaces to be added (or subtracted) from the amount of parking otherwise required can be calculated (using procedures presented in the study report) for centers in which up to 5 percent of center GLA is devoted to food service.[6]

Several key factors that had been considered likely to cause variances in demand were not supported by the study. No differences were found in demand because of regional location at centers located in the United States as opposed to Canada, or at centers located in small as opposed to large cities. The findings concerning suburban location versus downtown location were less firm. While comparison did not show statistically significant differences in peak demand between suburban centers and those located in established retail areas, this conclusion could not be made for centers in the CBDs of major cities where tenant service and high walk-in trade must be considered.

According to the ULI study, a center will generate on a Saturday an average of eight peak hour trips per 1,000 square feet of GLA. A trip is defined as one car driving in and one car driving out, with the peak trip period coinciding with the peak shopping period (noon to 5:00 p.m.). For a given center, the peak hour

[2] Urban Land Institute, *Parking Requirements for Shopping Centers: Summary Recommendations and Research Study Report* (Washington, D.C.: ULI–the Urban Land Institute, 1982).

[3] Ibid., p. 2.

[4] Ibid., p. 16.

[5] Ibid., p. 17.

[6] Ibid., pp. 17, 18.

trip rate could be as much as 50 percent higher or lower than this average generation rate. Figure 3-5 presents a typical parking demand accumulation pattern for a peak Saturday. This curve represents the parking trend for an average center during a Saturday before Christmas. Even during the busiest day of the year, the peak parking demands at a typical center occur for only about a two-hour period.[7]

The findings of the ULI study led to the conclusions that shopping center developers, lenders, and tenants have overestimated the demand for off-street parking, and that most zoning ordinance regulations for shopping center parking call for a substantially greater number of parking spaces than is actually necessary.[8]

Shared Parking

Parking demand for a shopping center that is part of a mixed-use/multiuse project or for a center that has nonretail uses will be influenced by the parking accumulation characteristics of all of the land uses con-

tained in the project. Different land uses experience their peak parking demands at different hours of the day, days of the week, and seasons of the year. In addition, the "captive market" effect of a mixed-use/ multiuse project influences parking demand; that is, in a mixed-use/multiuse project, customers may be attracted to two or more land uses on a single auto trip to the project. Because of these characteristics, less demand is generated for parking space in mixed-use/ multiuse projects than in separate freestanding developments of similar size and character; two or more land uses may also share a parking facility without conflict or encroachment. For this reason, parking demand estimates for a shopping center that is part of a mixed-use/multiuse development or for a center

---

[7] Ibid., pp. 39, 40.

[8] Until the ULI study in 1981, an earlier study conducted in 1963 had recommended a parking ratio of 5.5 spaces per 1,000 square feet of GLA. See Urban Land Institute, *Parking Requirements for Shopping Centers* (Washington, D.C.: ULI–the Urban Land Institute, 1963).

3-5   TYPICAL PEAK SATURDAY SHOPPING CENTER PARKING ACCUMULATION PATTERNS

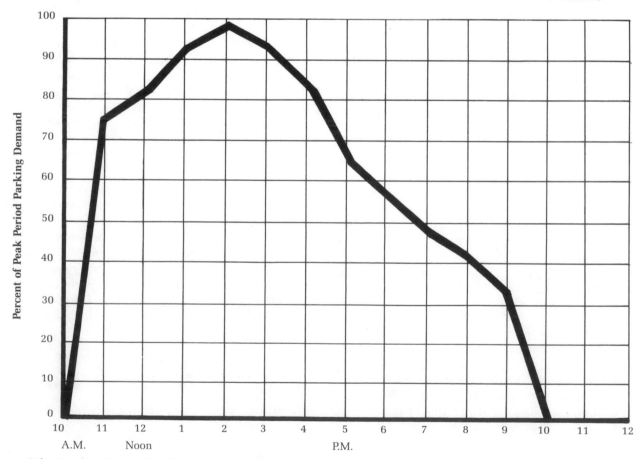

Source: Urban Land Institute, *Parking Requirements for Shopping Centers: Summary Recommendations and Research Study Report* (Washington, D.C.: ULI–the Urban Land Institute, 1982).

that has nonretail uses should be based on an estimate of shared parking demand for the entire project.[9]

Small Cars

The size of cars is in a state of flux. At the beginning of the 1980s, it was easy to assume that compact and subcompact cars would be dominant in the future, and that the principles of parking space and layout should be restudied. In 1981, 64 percent of all new cars sold in the United States were either compacts or subcompacts.[10] A 1980 study by the United States Department of Transportation indicated that, by 1990, depending on fuel availability and prices, the percent of all compact automobiles in the United States could reach a high of 95 percent, with the most likely proportion being somewhere between 70 and 80 percent.[11] This will not happen. Prompting that forecast was not the public's preference for small cars, but the public's desire to economize on gasoline. Manufacturers quickly found ways to reduce weight, not always by reduced size, and engine performance improved. Thus, in 1983, small car sales fell to 47 percent of all U.S. automobile sales. This trend continued in 1984.[12]

Responses to changing car sizes have been the subject of much discussion. The following summary of findings comes from a year-long study conducted in 1983 (sponsored by the International Council of Shopping Centers with participation from the National Retail Merchants Association and the American Planning Association):

- In almost all cases, it is extremely difficult to plan for the use of small car parking spaces at shopping centers. A wide range of factors must be considered, including the mix of large and small cars in a particular market, physical conditions and limitations of the parking lot, a profile of the center's customers, and the specific needs of the center's tenants.

- Small or compact cars may not be the dominant factor in the U.S. automobile population in the years ahead. Technological advances may make larger cars feasible, and popular trends may dictate increased demand for them. If that is the case, parking lots designed for a vehicle mix dominated by small cars would be inadequate to handle a center's traffic, especially at peak shopping periods.

- Most local parking ordinances relating to small cars are focused on compact or subcompact cars, usually in segregated parking areas. In general, this format does not work well for shopping centers because of the high turnover rate and lack of effective parking lot control measures.

- Newly designed and redesigned parking lots hold promise for increasing the number of parking spaces that can be made available in a given amount of area. Maximizing the available land to get more parking spaces or the same number in a smaller area—thus freeing land for expansion of retail space—can be achieved in a number of ways. They include changing parking angles, downsizing parking modules, restriping lots to use available areas more effectively, and mixing small and large parking spaces.

- Certain key factors must be considered when planning a new or redesigned parking lot in order to make the most effective use of an available area:

  —*Environment and Specific Conditions:* The state or locality in which the center is located and all attendant parking ordinances, annual climatic conditions, aspects relating to the terrain of the parking lot site, the local highway network, and access roadways.

  —*Shopping Center Site:* The site plan, ground contours, landscaping, placement of light stanchions, plans for both surface and deck parking, plans for controlled or noncontrolled parking and free or metered/charged parking.

  —*Vehicle Mix:* The composition of car sizes in the vehicle population of a shopping center's immediate trade area, and technical and performance standards of those vehicles.

  —*Customer Profile:* Areas of the parking lot where the greatest turnover will occur, evaluation of traffic patterns and their impact on the parking lot areas adjacent to department stores and the general retail areas.

  —*Tenant Categories:* The kinds of businesses located within a center can influence parking patterns dramatically. Some tenants require parking for their customers that will provide for rapid turnover, while others require parking for a longer term.

- The method used to design or redesign a shopping center parking lot to maximize available

[9] Urban Land Institute, *Shared Parking* (Washington, D.C.: ULI–the Urban Land Institute, 1983).

[10] From Richard F. Roti, "On Changing Automobile and Parking Stall Sizes," *Urban Land*, Vol. 42, No. 1, January 1983.

[11] "The U.S. Automobile Industry, 1980." Report to the President from the Secretary of Transportation, Office of the Assistant Secretary for Policy and International Affairs, January 1981.

[12] International Council of Shopping Centers, *Shopping Center Parking: The Influence of Changing Car Sizes* (New York: ICSC, 1984), p. 40.

CHANGES IN DIMENSIONS OF THE PARKING DESIGN VEHICLE

DIMENSION	1948[2]	1957[3]	1970[4]	LARGE CAR DESIGN VEHICLE		SMALL CAR DESIGN VEHICLE	
				CURRENT	FUTURE	CURRENT	FUTURE
Overall Width	76″	78″	80″	72″– 80″	72″– 77″	66″– 69″	66″– 69″
Overall Length	216″	216″	225″	192″–216″	192″–204″	180″–187″	180″–187″
Turning Radius Outside Point, Front Bumper (R)	25.25′	23.25′	24.5′	20.5′ ±		18.0′ ±	

[1]Dimensional range of design vehicles currently being used by various parking consultants and designers.
[2]Edmund R. Ricker, *The Traffic Design of Parking Garages* (Saugatuck, Connecticut: The Eno Foundation for Highway Traffic Control, 1948).
[3]Edmund R. Ricker, *The Traffic Design of Parking Garages*, Revised Edition (Saugatuck, Connecticut: The Eno Foundation for Highway Traffic Control, 1957).
[4]G. E. Kanaan and D. K. Witheford, "Parking Lot Design Standards," *Traffic Quarterly*, Vol. 27, No. 3, July 1973.
Source: International Council of Shopping Centers, *Shopping Center Parking: The Influence of Changing Car Sizes* (New York: ICSC, 1984).

areas and provide adequate parking must be selected on a case-by-case basis. No standard formula exists. The project should be carefully evaluated with the assistance of a professional consultant on parking lot design.[13]

While it appears that the mixture of car sizes in 1990 will not vary greatly from that of 1984–1985, the shopping center developer should be prepared for change, since the fleet in operation today is significantly different in size from what it was in the 1970s. The changes that have occurred are illustrated in Figure 3-6.

If the proportion of small cars that will park at the center can be determined, they can be accommodated in several ways:

- By providing separate parking bays designed for small vehicles. Many centers currently allocate 20 percent or fewer spaces for small vehicles. For compact cars, parking bay widths of 54 feet are suggested. These widths will accommodate compact cars parked at 90 degrees on both sides of the aisles, with stalls 15 to 17 feet in length and 7.5 to eight feet in width. This system of measurements can always be used in new centers, and, depending on conditions, might also be adapted to existing centers. It will accommodate full-size cars angle-parked, allowing a gradual transition to compact car space over time without redesigning the parking lot.

- By cross-aisle separation, with compact cars parked perpendicularly on one side and full-size vehicles parked at an angle on the other side. The Drachman System of parking—which also uses the 54-foot bay width—or comparable systems may be implemented (see Figure 3-7).

- In existing centers, by generally reducing stall widths to 8.5 feet. Because of the proportion of small vehicles, two large vehicles may be less likely to park adjacent to one another; thus, space for opening doors (which governs the required distance between adjacently parked vehicles) and stall width can be reduced.

Rearranging a surface parking area to accommodate compact vehicles can improve capacity, resulting in additional spaces in the same area or the same number of spaces in less area to serve the same demand. Surface parking facilities, used by most shopping centers, are easier to redesign to serve compact vehicles than are parking structures in which physical conditions such as columns and ramps may restrain the conversion.[14]

Layout

Ease of parking should be the guiding criterion for parking layout at any center. Parking at a shopping center must be simple, trouble-free, and safe. The shopper should be able to move confidently through the parking area without ever having been there before or knowing the layout in advance.

A parking bay or parking module in a surface parking lot includes the driving aisle and the stalls on both sides. Aisles can also serve as pedestrian pathways leading to the stores. Raised walks between the bays are unnecessary and expensive. In addition, they interfere with sweeping and snow removal. Wheel stops also complicate mechanical cleaning operations and

---

[13] Ibid., pp. 4, 5.

[14] *Parking Requirements for Shopping Centers* (1982), p. 21.

DRACHMAN SYSTEM OF PARKING
(SMALL AND LARGE CARS IN ONE BAY)

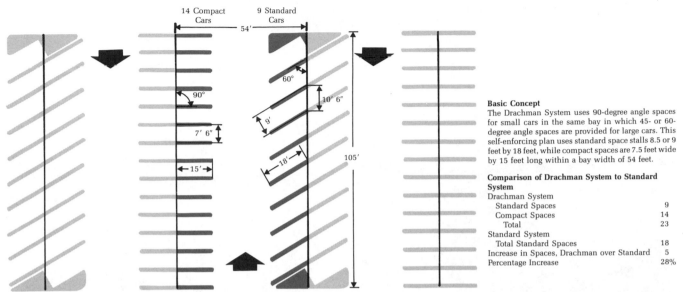

Source: Urban Land Institute, *Parking Requirements for Shopping Centers: Summary Recommendations and Research Study Report* (Washington, D.C.: ULI–the Urban Land Institute, 1982).

should be used only where parking spaces are adjacent to access driveways or where there are landscaped areas.

Access aisles should allow the shopper to walk directly toward, rather than parallel to, the building front. The maximum walking distance from a car to the stores should be 400 feet and should preferably be limited to 300 to 350 feet, except for employee parking areas.

Circulation for cars within the center should be continuous, preferably one-way and counterclockwise. Drivers should also be able to maneuver within the site without entering a public highway. In a regional center, parking area circulation requires a belt roadway around the edge of the site and another around the building cluster. The inner belt allows for fire and emergency access and also for delivery and customer dropoff and pickup.

Main traffic aisles are of two types—entrance and exit lanes, and belt lanes. Major aisles may allow for two-way movement. Minor aisles are one-way but require directional indicators, often a combination of arrows painted on the pavement and standing indicator signs.

Where there are several thousand car spaces, parking stalls should not be provided along the main aisles leading to the stores; this restriction prevents congestion of the main access aisles to the center. A very large surface parking facility should be divided into sections so that customers may easily identify their parking location. Each of the divisions should contain a maximum of about 800 to 1,000 spaces.

For the convenience or neighborhood center, parking along the storefronts makes a good arrangement. This design accommodates quick visits to the stores and fast turnover of prime spaces. Wheel stops, front bumper guards, or extended curb lines are required to prevent car fronts from jutting over into the canopied walkway.

At one time, truck tunnels were commonly used at regional centers to separate shoppers from freight delivery. The economics of constructing and maintaining a truck tunnel, however, are now prohibitive. Instead, the enclosed regional center either schedules most deliveries for nonshopping hours or provides a screened or walled truck delivery court from which a group of stores can be serviced.[15]

As a rule, achieving smooth traffic circulation at a shopping center requires the advice of a qualified parking or traffic consultant.

---

[15] See "Guidelines for Planning and Designing Access Systems for Shopping Centers," prepared by Technical Council Committee 5-DD, Institute of Traffic Engineers, Arlington, Virginia, 1976.

3-8, 3-9 Parking area circulation in a regional center requires a belt roadway around the edge of the site and another around the building cluster.

Patterns

There are two patterns for surface parking layouts: perpendicular and angular. Perpendicular or 90-degree parking economizes on space and facilitates circulation. It also offers the advantage of two-way traffic through the aisle, as well as the safety of better sight lines, greater parking capacity, and shorter cruising distances. By contrast, angular parking spaces, with either 45-degree or 60-degree angles, are easier for the driver to swing into with one motion. Single parking requires one-way circulation—which is safer though perhaps less convenient than two-way traffic—and allows a narrower parking module to be used.

The dilemma over perpendicular or diagonal parking is best solved by using the pattern that generally prevails in the community and that is best adapted to the particular site considerations. Each surface parking layout must be evaluated for circulation of pedestrians between the parked cars and the stores, for circulation of drivers moving in and out of the parking area or looking for a vacant space, and for use of space. Angle parking is more widely used across the nation than is perpendicular parking.

For perpendicular parking, the standard bay for full-size cars has been 65 feet deep, comprising two

stalls, each 20 feet deep, and a center aisle of 25 feet to allow for two-way circulation. The standard stall has a width of nine feet. It is likely that most new centers will reduce these measurements with stall widths ranging from 8.5 to nine feet and stall lengths ranging from 17 to 18 feet. The module will be narrow with 90-degree parking layouts having modules of 58 to 62 feet. Figure 3-10 illustrates current thinking based on two design-vehicle sizes that might reasonably represent car sizes in the future.

Recognizing the uncertainties of car sizes and the difficulties in managing variable stall sizes in a center, Donald O'Hara of Barton-Aschman Associates, Inc., has suggested downgrading the size of the stall in relationship to its distance from the center's buildings. That is, the spaces closest to the center's buildings would be the largest, since they are used most often (in off-peak hours those spaces farthest from the buildings are rarely used) and therefore customer convenience is maximized. Spaces farther away would be reduced in size to an adequate but somewhat tighter set of dimensions and would be used at peak hours. During peak hours, shoppers will value the presence of a vacant space more than the generousness of its size. This approach will create a greater number of spaces in a given area of land, or less land covered by a given number of spaces. It would appear to have merit also when viewed from the perspective of customer service. This idea, like many of those for accommodating small cars, remains untested.

Stalls

In some areas of a center, stall widths should not be reduced. High turnover calls for parking stalls with ample width to park easily, to avoid straddling spaces, and to allow car doors to be opened without bumping the adjacent car. The nine-foot width accommodates these needs. A nine-foot stall width, for example, is still best for the area close to a supermarket. A customer laden with groceries would have difficulty loading them into a car parked with less room. This recommendation may be less applicable, however, if the practice at the center is for cars to pick up groceries at the curb rather than for groceries to be taken to the parked vehicle.

With an 8.5-foot stall, two-door cars are more likely to bump the next car unless care is taken in opening and closing the doors. While a nine-foot stall width is preferred, an 8.75-foot width might be an acceptable compromise. Any shopper would prefer having the convenience of an available parking space to the ease of loading provided by a large space.

Where the nine-foot stall width is used, a four-inch-striped hairpin or looped line painted on the pavement surface makes a good space indicator. The hairpin or looped line (16 inches between lines) is preferred over straight-line striping because it acts as a psychological aid in keeping spaces equal between cars. In any case, all space markers should be painted; a button divider system is difficult to change if the parking pattern needs alteration. The length of parking stalls is less important to operations than width, since aisle width can compensate for a short stall and since customers parking tend not to pull all the way into the stall. Nevertheless, stall length must be determined in order to calculate space requirements.

3-10 DIMENSIONS OF POSSIBLE PARKING DESIGN VEHICLES

	WIDTH (W)	LENGTH (L)	WALL-TO-WALL FRONT RADIUS (R)	CURB-TO-CURB REAR RADIUS (r)	REAR WIDTH (t_r)	BODY OVERHANG FROM REAR TIRE (O_s)	WALL-TO-WALL REAR RADIUS (R′)
Large Cars							
	80″	218″	20.75′	12.25′	5.08′	0.75′	17.5′
DESIGN VEHICLE	77″	215″	20.50′	12.00′	5.10′	0.63′	17.4′
	74″	208″	20.40′	11.90′	5.00′	0.67′	17.3′
	72″	202″	20.30′	11.85′	4.90′	0.65′	17.1′
	71″	196″	20.00′	11.60′	4.80′	0.60′	17.0′
Small Cars							
	69″	187″	19.37′	10.70′	4.71′	0.50′	16.2′
	68″	182″	18.70′	10.70′	4.75′	0.54′	15.8′
DESIGN VEHICLE	66″	175″	18.00′	9.60′	4.60′	0.46′	15.0′
	64″	169″	17.40′	8.20′	4.67′	0.44′	13.6′
	63″	164″	17.00′	8.00′	4.46′	0.44′	13.3′

W = Overall width
L = Overall length
O_s = Body side overhang from center of rear tire
t_r = Width from center of rear tires

Minimum Turning Radius:
r = Inside rear wheel
R = Outside point, front bumper
R′ = Outside point, rear bumper

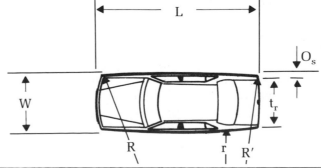

Source: International Council of Shopping Centers, *Shopping Center Parking: The Influence of Changing Car Sizes* (New York: ICSC, 1984), p. 15.

Stalls for the handicapped should be located close to center entrances, and should relate to a pedestrian pathway that is level or ramped and to entrance doors that are accessible for the handicapped. These spaces should be wider than normal to accommodate special vehicles, a full door swing, and wheelchairs. The currently recommended stall width is 12 feet.

Appearance and Construction

Surface parking areas must have a substantial subbase (5.5 to six inches) and be well drained and paved. (Blacktop is the most common paving material.) Parking areas need such amenities as screening, landscaping, and lighting. They must be maintained to prevent potholes from developing and to keep litter from accumulating. Stalls must be clearly marked.

Where there is enough land or where land cost is not prohibitive, trees can be planted in wells to avoid an otherwise barren appearance. However, trees must then be protected from cars and from accumulations of salt and snow in colder climates. Landscaping intermediate spots in the parking area not only requires an expenditure up front but also adds extra maintenance costs to the shopping center management and thus increases the common area charges the tenants must pay. The aesthetic benefits, however, can be immeasurable.

Since the surface parking area is part of the open space at a shopping center, when landscaped, it can become one of the center's amenities. Shopping center open space includes the parking area, malls, pedestrian pathways, buffer areas, and all other portions of the site not covered by buildings, except for the access drives and uncovered service courts. The landscaping of parking areas and of shopping center open space in general should be designed to be both tasteful and durable. Ground cover, shrubs, and bushes, massed at appropriate places on the site, and occasional trees planted in wells or clusters are suitable. Landscape components should be designed not to interfere with parking, parking area maintenance, or snow removal. Plantings should be hardy, easily maintained, and capable of thriving in the local climate.[16]

Depressing the parking area by about two feet, so that the tops of cars are below eye level when viewed from adjacent public streets, will increase the feeling of openness by allowing views directly from the streets to the store fronts. Berms constructed at the perimeter of the parking area can also improve the center's appearance from adjacent streets and properties. These berms, either along public streets or between the various parking sections, can also serve as landscaping features.

Proper maintenance of the parking area is essential. Management must attend to matters of policing, cleanup, night lighting, orderly use, and other maintenance. Tenants pay for maintenance costs, based on the proportion of space they occupy.

Employee Parking

Because employees park all day, they may be allotted parking spaces with stall widths of eight feet. They should not be allowed to occupy prime spaces needed for customers. By doing so, they could prevent customer spaces from turning over four or five times during a shopping day.

At best, employee parking is hard to control. Regulations are usually covered in the lease, which should provide that the landlord has the right to:

- Designate number and location of employee parking places.
- Receive, on request, the car license numbers of tenants' employees.
- Cancel the lease if the tenant does not cooperate.
- Charge the tenant a specified amount per day for each employee car parked outside the designated area.

In practice, it may be difficult to achieve such ideal provisions.

In a linear convenience center, employee parking is best placed at the rear of the stores. A minimum width of 40 feet will be required for a combined rear service and employee parking area. This will allow one row of cars and a driveway along the rear property line. A better arrangement can be made with a width of 60 feet, which would permit the rear service area to function better as a truck delivery drive and parking area. The rear setback must be increased when plantings are needed along the back property line as a buffer between the stores and adjacent residences. Or, if land is at a premium, a screening wall can be placed on the property line.

In other types of centers, a special employee parking area should be assigned and the requirements for employee parking enforced. In these centers, employee parking areas should be placed at the outer edge of the site, where they will not interfere with the more desirable parking spaces closer to the stores. A center that fails to designate special employee parking areas may find its employees' cars habitually occupying the spaces closest to the stores or filling the surrounding

---

[16] See J. Ross McKeever, *Shopping Center Zoning*, ULI Technical Bulletin 69 (Washington, D.C.: ULI–the Urban Land Institute, 1973). Also see International Council of Shopping Centers, *Maintenance and Repair of Asphalt Paved Parking Lots* (New York: ICSC, 1975).

streets, to the annoyance of neighbors. In some cities an ordinance permits the landlord, on signed complaint, to have the police ticket such cars for a substantial fine or haul the car to a police impounding lot, causing the car owner to pay an even larger fine.

Value of a Parking Stall

Placing a value on each parking stall can indicate its relationship to the sales volume of the center once the center is in operation and parking demand has reached the capacity of the center's parking area. The value of a parking space can be determined by dividing the total annual sales volume of all tenants by the number of parking spaces. To illustrate, in a regional center with total sales of $139 million and 5,000 parking spaces, the value of a parking space is equal to approximately $28,000 in annual sales.

If employees park their cars in the most convenient spaces, they are holding up stalls that should be used for generating retail sales. Employee parking at a neighborhood center, for example, can be analyzed as follows: If each parking space is known to generate $37,250 in annual sales and if 60 spaces are needed for employees, the sales loss—when employees occupy prime spaces and thereby drive away trade—would be $2,235,000. The employee parking problem can also be analyzed as follows: At an average rent percentage of 4 percent, an additional $89,400 in net rent would be produced from these spaces. At 8 percent return, this would produce $1,117,500. Each employee car space, capitalized at 8 percent, can be valued at $18,625.

These calculations must be used carefully. It is easy to conclude that adding spaces will guarantee added income or that subtracting spaces will cause sales to decrease. As stated earlier, a successful center needs enough parking but not too much. "Enough" parking is determined by measuring or predicting parking demand. The standards previously recommended will provide enough parking if adjustments are made to the special circumstances of a given center. It is only when this balance has been achieved that misuse of spaces, particularly during peak periods, has an imputed value.

Commuter Parking

As mass transit reaches more shopping centers, thus reducing parking demand, the strong possibility arises of commuters parking in shopping center spaces. Such a situation will be more likely to develop where the bus routes that serve the center also serve employment centers. The figures just given for the value of a parking space clearly indicate the economic issues. Private shopping center developers should not be expected to provide public parking lots for commuters. Like employee parking, this will be difficult to police and will require the cooperation of the community.

Where local laws will allow police ticketing, parking lots in centers can be given time limits and tickets can be issued. Where this is not possible, private policing or closing of the lots during the morning rush hour period may be the only solution. At the same time, the shopping center developer needs to be perceived as a good neighbor in the community; hardline control of commuter parking may result in negative feelings in the community toward the center in general, which may in turn result in loss of business for the center. Where excess land is available and a parking conflict exists, it may be possible to lease a designated portion of the site to the transit authority for transit parking for at least the cost of maintenance and repair. Requests for tax abatement may also be possible. In the final analysis, parking in shopping centers represents private parking for customers, and the developer must protect this right when other uses would be detrimental to the center's operations.

Parking and Taxes

In some cities, the assessor values land used exclusively for parking purposes at the same rate as land used for business. In these cities, shopping center parking bears an inequitable tax load. Where commitments are made for the continued use of designated areas for parking, such as at shopping centers, the calculation of land value for tax purposes should be adjusted to the restricted use of the parking area.

While parking areas contribute substantially to the success of a center, this success is also reflected in the higher taxable value of the land and structures occupied by the business use, as well as in the value of the business itself. Because the shopping center's parking area is not itself a direct revenue producer, its valuation for tax purposes should be based on its use as parking, not on its business use. Municipalities can follow this practice with good results. The valuation can also be based on acreage rather than on square feet. However, where real estate taxes on parking areas are included in common area maintenance charges paid by tenants, loading the taxes on the buildings to relieve the tax load on the parking area may actually impose an undue burden on the owner, rather than relieving him of an economic inequity. In addition, some jurisdictions approach the value of a property on the basis of its income; land and building are not valued separately but as parts of a single package.

Structured Parking

To avoid excessive walking distances between the parked car and the stores in regional centers and to solve parking space problems that may be created by a shopping center's development or by its later expansion, a self-operated parking structure can be built.

At many centers, adjacent land for parking area expansion either is not available or has become so costly that building a parking structure or deck may be the most economical means of providing additional parking spaces. A parking structure can be built closer to the stores, and it can be depreciated, whereas land cannot.

A parking structure has further advantages. When small cars enter the facility, they can be more effectively channeled to small car spaces. Less space per car can be assigned because islands and other aesthetic appurtenances are eliminated. However, a parking garage also requires a ramp system (which should be as unintimidating as possible to poor drivers), overhead clearances, column spacing, and ventilation for those parts of the structure that are below grade. An entrance magazine—a temporary storage area for cars waiting to be parked—is not needed in a self-operating parking structure.

The multideck parking structure is particularly adaptable to sloping sites, where direct entrance to each level of the stores can be provided. For double-level or triple-level shopping centers, entrances can also lead from each level of the parking deck to the center.

Parking structures will often spring up around shopping centers because of the increased value of the land. Surface parking may no longer be the highest and best use for expanses of ground near larger retail centers. Other uses, such as hotels, office buildings, clinics, additional department stores, and commercial recreational facilities may replace surface parking, making it necessary to provide structures for existing and any additional parking.

The point at which a developer determines that he should build a structure for additional parking rather than buy more ground is the point at which the value of the land he would have to acquire exceeds what it would cost to construct a parking facility. Present (1984) construction costs for a three-level structure are somewhere around $20 per square foot, depending on the section of the country, building costs, and other factors. (In 1976, such costs averaged $8 per square foot.) Construction costs are affected by the size and shape of the usable land area, the perimeter wall-to-floor area ratio, the parking bay span ratio, and the elevated versus on-grade ratio (with the cost per square foot increasing with each additional park-

3-11 A pedestrian bridge connects structured parking to the center at Bellevue Square, Bellevue, Washington.

ing level).[17] Should land prices and construction costs rise to a point where the provision of free parking at a shopping center is no longer economical, developers may be forced either to charge customers a fee for parking or to turn parking areas over to the municipality, which will install parking meters and maintain the areas.

The security of parking structures should be considered. Misfortunes to patrons range from vandalism and car theft to mugging and rape. While these same crimes can and do occur in surface parking areas, particularly in those areas most isolated from the shopping center, customers tend to perceive structured parking as potentially more risky than surface parking. Television monitoring equipment, sound communication systems, and adequate lighting can help improve safety.

Summary—Parking

The factors that must be considered in providing parking for the shopping center vary in degree and extent according to the type of center, its location, its tenancy, and its trade area characteristics. In general,

[17] Richard F. Roti, "Construction and Development Costs," *The Dimensions of Parking*, second edition (Washington, D.C.: ULI–the Urban Land Institute, 1983), pp. 26–28.

the parking arrangement depends on such amenity and convenience factors as the following:

- Site potential or parking spaces needed in relation to the GLA of the retail structure (see page 65 for standards established in a 1981 ULI study).
- Shape of the site and position of the buildings. These factors determine the necessary layout.
- Direction of traffic flow to the site, and volume in each direction, as well as any outside treatment needed for left turns or acceleration or deceleration lanes for entering and leaving a large center.
- Entrance and exit points; stacking lanes of adequate length to avoid congestion of periphery streets or on-site parking aisles. Exits should parallel entrances wherever possible, with exit lanes separated from entrance lanes by dividers or planters.
- Circulation within the site—outer perimeter and along the storefronts—for pedestrians, automobiles, buses, and emergency vehicles.
- Separation of customer and truck service traffic, when possible.
- A reasonable walking distance from the parking stall to the store (400 feet is the recommended maximum).
- Balanced parking area distribution according to individual tenant requirements.
- Adequate storm drainage allowance; a 3 percent grade assures good drainage into catch basins. A high quality of surface and seal coat should be applied over a well-compacted subgrade.
- Width and angle of the parking stall; direction of movement through the aisles; ease of parking. Rely on painted lines and arrows and standing signs to control parking. Looped lines are preferred as stall indicators.
- Landscaping to break up the sea of asphalt paving and, in general, to improve the center's appearance.
- Economic factors, such as land cost, real estate taxes, operating costs, and escalator provisions in tenant leases to provide for maintenance of the parking area through common area charges to tenants.
- Lighting using standards of moderate height, with perimeter lights (which might disturb neighbors) deflected from any nearby residences.
- Use of bumpers or wheel stops only where unavoidable, in order to ease cleaning and snow removal operations.
- A straight driving lane of at least 100 feet at all important entrances of a larger center. Arriving drivers can then avoid turns and will not block entrances. The straight lanes can also serve as stacking lanes for cars leaving the center.

Stormwater Management

The proper handling of stormwater runoff has become a major issue in shopping center design. The strategy used to handle stormwater runoff should be developed in the preliminary stage of development planning. Peak stormwater flows and total runoff increase dramatically after a site has been partly covered by buildings and parking areas. Reducing or delaying this runoff is an important design issue with significant cost implications. Communities not having excess storm system capacities—and few do have them—are or will be examining such concepts as rooftop ponding, temporary detention basins (in portions of the parking area, for example), detention or retention ponds, and other mechanisms for reducing the runoff rate and total runoff after development. Likewise, potential water pollution may be another problem that will need to be addressed.

Therefore, it is important that the developer investigate the methods of managing stormwater runoff in the community in which he wants to develop. The stormwater management system for a center should be based on the following principles:

- The design of the system must take into account the convenience and safety of the project as well as the overall safety of the drainage basin as the area becomes fully developed.
- The design of permanent and temporary ponding storage should be an integral part of the overall development planning process.
- The design of permanent storage facilities should consider safety and visual appearance in addition to the primary function of storage, and opportunities for temporary storage should be considered and planned for in the design of the system.
- Stormwater runoff systems should facilitate aquifer recharge when it is necessary to compensate for groundwater removal.
- Some communities have a blanket per-acre storm sewer charge. The developer designing an on-site stormwater retention system should receive a credit from the community against the stormwater assessment charge.
- The use of overland flows and open channels and swales should blend into the natural features of the site, and they should be designed to minimize safety hazards.
- Stormwater management systems, parking layout, and the location of curbs and gutters should be planned simultaneously, whenever possible.
- The maximum flow in the deepest part of a gutter should not exceed 10 cubic feet per second.

- The number and spacing of stormwater inlets should be carefully regulated, and their design should incorporate factors of safety and efficiency.
- Any enclosed portion of a system should be designed to manage stormwater, not just to dispose of it or disperse it.
- Energy dissipaters should be designed and installed for the outfall of enclosed systems when stormwater is discharged onto highly erodible soils.
- Pipe sizes used in the enclosed system should be based on computed hydraulic data for the system.
- The use of enclosed components in a system should be minimized, based on the ability of the existing natural systems to accommodate stormwater runoff.
- Maintenance costs and construction should be minimized.[18]

Over the past decade, stormwater management has depended increasingly on the use of retention and detention ponds (see case study on University Mall). Retention ponds are generally used to treat stormwater by removing suspended materials and by providing extended contact with aquatic vegetation for removal of nutrients. By definition, retention is the impoundment of runoff (in many states usually the first inch), which is either percolated into the soil or released to the atmosphere through a combination of evaporation and plant transpiration.

However, this concept in its purest form is difficult to implement in high-water-table areas that do not allow rapid percolation. During the rainy season in such areas, retention ponds can remain overburdened, and pollutants can bypass the pond and go directly into other waters. To prevent this, a well-designed retention pond usually contains a bleed-off device that will release retained water downstream over a period of five to 10 days. In this way, the process of retention is actually being transformed into long-term detention.

Many local regulations stipulate that peak discharge rates for the design storm after development should not exceed peak rates that occurred before development. This is typically accomplished through detention ponds that store floodwaters temporarily and release them downstream at a slower rate. Detention periods typically last several hours as opposed to retention periods of five to 10 days.

Topography

If a site has a slope that corresponds to grades on surrounding roads, an opportunity may exist for a two-level arrangement of buildings and parking. Sloping site conditions offer the possibility of innovative two-level development solutions in larger projects. Smaller neighborhood and community projects are more readily arranged on a single level.

Shops on both levels must be equally accessible; concentrating the "best" stores on either level is a disadvantage to both merchants and customers. With two levels of merchandising, parking must be divided to provide equal accessibility to upper and lower malls. Neither level should dominate the center; both should be equally important.

Sensitive use of a site's topography can produce a compatibility between the shopping center and the site's natural characteristics (see the case study on Montgomery Village Off-Price Center). A sloping site with specimen trees that need to be preserved can be skillfully reshaped to accommodate a stepped but single-level center.

Landscaping

The image of the shopping center has been badly damaged by some past performances. By exposing a barren expanse of parking lot to the public's view, some centers appear to be a sea of asphalt, which has been universally criticized. As mentioned earlier, a surface parking lot is part of the shopping center's

3-12   The use of retention or detention ponds can control stormwater runoff.

[18] ULI, NAHB, and ASCE, *Residential Storm Water Management* (Washington, D.C.: ULI, NAHB, and ASCE, 1975).

open space, and, when properly designed and landscaped, it can become one of the center's amenity features.

Landscaping within a parking area should generally be confined to trees and massed plantings in wells or in clearly delineated areas. Plantings should be located where they will not interfere with parking, parking area maintenance, or snow removal. In the provisions of site plan approval, under the zoning and building permit clearance documents, landscaping and specifications for it should be discussed as optional rather than mandatory matters. Nevertheless, a total landscaping expenditure of 3 to 5 percent of the total building costs—depending on the size and character of the center—might be recommended. Presenting performance standards will allow creative design, whereas if developers are required to spend a certain amount on landscaping they must shoulder a cost burden that will not necessarily result in well-conceived landscaping. Zoning requirements typically call for landscaping of parking lot boundaries and property line buffer strips. Zoning provisions that specify a percentage of total site area for landscape treatment, however, or that specify the placement, type, or diameter of trees are often going too far in protecting the public welfare. Landscaping should be used to meet design objectives and not simply to cover the site area. Although the initial cost of such requirements may seem insignificant, the developer must also consider the long-term maintenance costs of any landscaped areas.

When a shopping center—generally a neighborhood center—is to be located close to a residential area, more substantial buffers can be introduced to insulate the nearby residences. High, dense foliage can be planted in a strip some 20 feet wide or, where plants are not practical, masonry walls or attractive fences may be provided.

3-13, 3-14, 3-15   Exterior landscaping is an important design consideration.

Effective landscaping along the border provides an environmental amenity.[19] However, neither the location nor the height of landscaping features should block the vision of drivers. As discussed earlier, hardy ground covers, shrubs, and bushes concentrated at appropriate places within the buffers are appropriate landscaping features, as are trees in wells.

Landscaping and its installation and maintenance are part of the expense of shopping center operation. Lighting will play an important role in the selection of interior mall landscaping. Plantings and seasonal floral displays appropriately placed inside the center make the center much more appealing to customers. In a mall layout, plantings, water displays, and sculptures can transform an interior pedestrian space into a focal point for the community and a gathering place for suitable community events. In addition, quite often the interior mall area can be included in the total landscaped area, if such an area is required by zoning.

Building Materials

The center's exterior facing materials strongly contribute to the center's visual image and special identity. The image created should be one of harmony tempered by tasteful variation in selected details. Although the center obviously should not look a hodgepodge, an attractive unified exterior need not exclude the use of more than one major material to create a distinct image. Materials should be locally available (if possible), capable of being speedily assembled and erected, durable, and easily maintained. They should provide waterproofing and insulation and, of course, an attractive appearance.

Masonry is an excellent external material. It offers the greatest flexibility in the variety of ways it can be treated and designed. The use of precast concrete wall panels—provided the production plant is within reasonable hauling distance of the site and enough lead time is allowed—can speed up the construction.

Metal panels are constantly being improved and are becoming more and more practicable for projects such as the shopping center. In some areas, wood that has been treated for weather exposure can readily be adapted to neighborhood and convenience centers. A great many centers have resorted to metal stud enclosures with insulating plaster type materials such as Dryvit. These can be given a variety of textures, plans, and shapes.

Consistency of exterior materials is more important to department stores than similarity of design or detail. Since department stores are not always designed by the mall architect, they tend to call for a more distinctive look. This often entails the use of totally different materials that, while making the department

3-16 Exterior building materials help to establish a center's identity.

store stand out, may, in the case of three or four stores, tend to create a mishmash. Charles Kober, president of Charles Kober Associates, points out that to a large extent the exterior appearance of a regional center is affected by how much control the developer is willing to exert over the major tenants. Some developers seek to provide more neutral spaces between the strong architecture of the major stores, while other developers first decide on a design theme for the mall's exterior and then work with the anchor tenants to make certain that their architecture and materials are compatible with the rest of the mall. Charles Kober notes that regardless of the design method, the mall's exterior appearance must be cohesive, welcoming, and friendly. It also must reflect the identity of the merchandise inside and "must make the customer want to come inside and stay."[20]

Building Entrances

In an enclosed mall, entrances to the center should be prominent design features. A change of material or

---

[19] Gary O. Robinette, *Plants, People, and Environmental Quality* (Washington, D.C.: National Park Service, U.S. Department of the Interior, 1972).

[20] David Goldman, "Storefront Systems, Fascia Create Important First Impression," *Shopping Center World*, March 1983.

3-17, 3-18, 3-19 Entrances to an enclosed mall should be prominent design features and inviting to the shopper.

roof height, or a wall extension or indention, may be introduced to identify the entrances and to give them a certain distinction. Attractive exterior lighting can also highlight entrances. For example, Chris Ramos, president of The Ramos Group, Kansas City, points out: "The peak hours for shopping are in dusk and darkness. If an entrance has wonderful architectural form but is not sufficiently illuminated, customers will head for the department store entrances, not the main mall entrances where they should be going. With sufficient illumination to make it bright and attractive, a center will convey to customers the sense that they are entering an exciting theatrical event."

Entrances to the retail component of a mixed-use development should be distinctive and inviting, since many potential customers may be office workers or hotel guests who are already on the site and must be enticed into the retail area. E. Eddie Henson, president of Williams Realty Corporation, Tulsa, notes that in designing entrances for the retail component of a mixed-use project, "You should spend more attention than usual to signal people and make them aware that they are leaving the office environment or the hotel lobby and entering the excitement of the retail area. You do this through floor coverings, wall coverings, color, and ceiling treatments."

Though they should look inviting, too many entrances to an enclosed mall will make it difficult to concentrate shopper traffic within the mall. An exception to this would be the downtown mall where it is essential that the center function as an integral component of the downtown, not turn its back on the surrounding environment.

Canopies

For nonenclosed malls, the colonnaded walk or arcade is the traditional means of sheltering customers and protecting storefronts from weathering. In such conventional shopping centers, covered walkways are essential not only for protection from inclement weather but also for enjoyable shopping in any kind of weather. Experience has shown that 12 to 15 feet is a good width for the walkway.

Canopies may be either cantilevered from the building wall or supported by freestanding columns or pillars. Their widths and heights will be determined by the proportions appropriate to the architectural style. With a canopy higher than 12 feet, the building wall below provides an ideal surface on which to place signs. Such a design supports the architectural quality of the center and helps in an overall program to control signs. The style and mate-

3-20 Attractive exterior lighting can be used to highlight entrances.

3-21 Canopies may either be cantilevered from the building wall or supported by freestanding columns or pillars.

rials of the canopy may be dictated or influenced by that of the region—for instance, roofing tiles in the Southwest, slate in New England, and cedar shakes in the West.

When canopies are placed along building facades in unenclosed malls, window shopping and window displays become important inducements to impulse buying while allowing shoppers to compare prices. Furthermore, customers are free to view the merchandise displays without having to explain that they are "just looking." Canopies increase the attractiveness of wide window displays. Windows also may be scaled to feature spot displays suited to certain kinds of shops. Mullion windows are suitable only when they are part of the center's architectural style.

Signage

Good signage should be an integral part of the building design. The shopping center's graphics are the province of the architect whose design must prevent visual pollution. Even though a graphic designer is commonly brought in, the architect is still responsible for creating a building design that provides well-planned locations for signage. These two professionals must work closely together from the early design preliminaries.

Sign regulation constitutes an important part of shopping center management policy. In fact, the

shopping center industry has led the way in sign control. Sign approval is one of the conditions included in the tenant's lease, and the developer's private control of the style and size of signs is often more severe than municipal regulations would be. Insisting on uniformity of scale, size, and placement is a worthwhile and important practice. However, currently tenants are being given more freedom in designing tasteful attractive signs that fit into a total image, rather than a rigid format.

Offenders in shopping centers where signage lacks taste or restraint include not only local tenants but also the national and local chain merchants who use individual trademark signs. Department stores also have logos and other special lettering forms, which, like those of the chains, must be coordinated with the overall design of exterior graphics.

Shopping center signage is typically subject to a municipality's sign control ordinance, which also governs conventional business and commercial districts. Unfortunately, such regulations—geared primarily toward individual business properties—are rarely suitable for shopping centers. Sign regulations are among the most controversial aspects of zoning law, and there are those who would argue that the legal basis for such regulation is debatable, since sign design has to do with aesthetics. Nevertheless, signage regulations that include design as well as size and locational criteria have been upheld in the courts and must be taken into account when establishing a center's program of graphic design.[21]

When signage has been developed as a special element of the architectural design, the developer may find the zoning authorities receptive to a carefully prepared signage program that deviates from the sign control ordinance—especially if the ordinance was written to control the signage for single-purpose structures rather than shopping centers. The city can assist the developer by enforcing the approved program, thus relieving the developer of the need to negotiate with tenants having ideas about signage that

may be inconsistent with the developer's overall sign concept.

Shopkeepers want to be easily identified by customers in the shopping center environment, and each wants to be as readily identified as his competitors. Finally, each wants that which identifies his goods and services to be uniquely his own. However, it has been found that when all signs in a center are required

---

[21] William R. Ewald, Jr., and Daniel R. Mandelker, *Street Graphics: A Concept and a System* (Washington, D.C.: American Society of Landscape Architects Foundation, 1971). *Street Graphics* is the most useful available guide to the appropriate provisions and administration of sign control ordinances.

3-22, 3-23, 3-24 Effective sign control requires uniformity of scale, size, and placement of signs, but not necessarily uniformity of typography.

to conform to the same guidelines of size and style, each tenant is more amenable to restrictions on his signage. The conclusion to be drawn is that when graphic controls are uniformly applied, shopkeepers no longer feel the need of erecting signs that are larger or more dazzling than those of their neighbors and competitors. In fact, proprietors in well-controlled shopping centers often find that their sales actually increase while their expenditures for signs are considerably reduced. They discover that they are able not only to retain their individual identities within the framework of such controls, but also that they become identified with the shopping center as a whole—an entity that is larger and more memorable than any of the individual stores composing it.

In this respect, the shopping center has a great advantage over a single store on a downtown street or in a detached commercial strip because the developer of a well-managed center can insist on his own design and sign control. The shopping center normally does not need an illuminated pylon sign in order to be identified. Commonly found in older centers, such signs often do not conform in taste to the shopping center concept, whereas a well-designed sign is more acceptable and identifies the center equally well.

Developers provide for sign control by a declaration of permitted and prohibited signage as well as an approval clause in each tenant's lease. Such declarations forbid roof signs and larger projecting signs and favor placement at a certain level on, above, or below a canopy, depending on the architectural treatment. Both public and private sign controls commonly prohibit moving or flashing parts.

Experience with sign control has shown that it is appreciated immediately by the public and eventually by the merchants (who may at first be reluctant to accept it) in a center. As mentioned, the enforcement of uniformity is more difficult when trademark signs are involved, but a compromise can usually be reached that is compatible with the center's own specifications for color and lighting.

The problem of sign control is minimized when the architectural design of the center incorporates the details of size, style, location, and lighting of signs. Effectiveness of design depends on the designer's skill in achieving uniformity in character without necessarily requiring uniformity in typography. Center management should establish specifications, and the allowed placement of signs should be spelled out in the lease. If neon is permitted, it is recommended that the color of the neon signs be uniform. This will not necessarily apply in the case of food courts, which seek a more frivolous, even carnival-like, atmosphere.

Developers may go so far—and many do—as to prohibit the use of paper or paste-on window signs.

Many developers control all signs, permanent or temporary, that are visible either through show windows or through store entrances. It is important to recognize that signage that is improperly handled can negate an otherwise carefully developed center image.

Night Lighting

Because a greater percentage of retail business is now being conducted during the evening, exterior night lighting has become an important safety as well as design feature. It helps to protect the public, and it can be used to create an image and character for the center.

Lighting in parking areas should provide about 1.5 footcandles at the pavement surface. Strong lighting—approximately five footcandles—should be provided in structured parking to assure safety. In the parking areas, poles should be placed in islands at the ends of parking bays. The level of intensity of outside lighting is a private management concern, not one for zoning specifications, although the developer could reasonably be required to ensure that the height of the standards and the direction of the lighting prevent adjacent properties from being bothered by glare.

The latest available nonglare and high-intensity lighting should be used to provide adequate illumination, to reduce spillover lighting, and to avoid excessive electricity costs. Lighting levels can be reduced

3-25 In addition to safeguarding the public, night lighting can create an image and character for the center.

half an hour after closing time, except in areas where employee security and safety are a problem.

To design an effective lighting system, decisions must be made regarding light sources, mounting height, spacing, and light control. Light sources should be evaluated based on their efficiency, durability, and color. Light sources vary in light output (lumens), depending on the characteristics of the light. Higher wattage lamps are more efficient than lower wattage lights (see Figure 3-26). However, it may sometimes be more efficient to use a number of smaller units in order to light an area without wasting energy.[22]

Truck Service Facility

The delivery court has become the principal truck service facility for the loading and unloading of goods. It must be screened and placed out of the customer's view.

Small soft-line shops can be served by rear corridors leading from a service court. In a neighborhood or community nonmall center, occasional box deliveries from light express or parcel post vehicles can be made across the canopy walkway without distracting the shoppers. Regional centers also successfully use over-the-sidewalk delivery by regulating delivery hours. Department stores generally have separate control of their deliveries at their own service docks, and, by masonry screening, at their truck service entries.

Early regional centers were designed with truck tunnels under the mall to serve all tenants. Though tunnels offered the great advantage of complete separation of truck delivery traffic from pedestrian and customer traffic, tunnels were expensive to build, operate, and manage. The costs involved now have made truck service tunnels infeasible in most shopping center development. The exception may be in mixed-use or multiuse centers or on constricted sites where land costs are high.

Interior Features

Tenant Spaces

The space a tenant has leased typically contains a certain frontage on the mall, unfinished party walls separating the space from that of retail neighbors, an unfinished floor, and exposed joists for roof support. A rear door and utilities have usually been indicated within the space.

Most developers use an allowance system for finishing the tenant space. The developer/landlord lists a maximum dollar amount per square foot of GLA for specific tenant work such as storefronts, finished floors, walls, and ceilings, primary electrical conduits, secondary wiring, and so on; interior finishing and fixturing are not installed except as part of a specially negotiated turnkey agreement. The allowance may include floors and floor coverings, but tenants pay for all light fixtures, counters, shelves, painting, and other custom fixtures and finishing. In essence, the owner furnishes the bare space. The work that the landlord is to do and the work that is the tenant's responsibility are plainly shown on working drawings and specifications and are spelled out in the lease. After the stipulated amount for an item has been reached, it is up to the tenant to pay for the rest. This system protects developers against excessive tenant demands that can upset construction cost estimates.

Some developers assist tenants in certain phases of store planning, particularly in the area of storefront design, signs, and even the color coordination of sales areas. They have recognized the importance of reasonably harmonious store interiors in creating a pleasing and exciting retail image for the center as a whole.

[22] Center for Design Planning, *Streetscape Equipment Sourcebook 2* (Washington, D.C.: ULI–the Urban Land Institute, 1979), pp. 22–23.

3-26   LIFE AND LUMEN/WATT FOR TYPICAL LIGHT SOURCES

SOURCE	HOURS AVERAGE LIFE	INITIAL LUMENS/WATT INCLUDING BALLAST
Incandescent (100–1,500 W)	1,000–3,000	17–23 (No Ballast)
Fluorescent (30–215 W)	20,000	62–63
Mercury (100–1,000 W)	24,000	35–59
Metal Halide (175–1,000 W)	15,000	67–116
High-Pressure Sodium (70–1,000 W)	20,000	64–130
Low-Pressure Sodium (35–180 W)	18,000	80–150

Source: Center for Design Planning, *Streetscape Equipment Handbook 2* (Washington, D.C.: ULI–the Urban Land Institute, 1979).

3-27 Delivery areas should be screened from the customer's view.

Some developers have provided an "improved shell" rather than a "bare shell" in certain situations. Conversely, other developers are now making tenant spaces more barren (with dirt floors, no demising walls, etc.) and no finishing allowances.

Tenant allowances depend primarily on the type of center and type of tenant. Allowances can range from nothing to a full turnkey job. Typical regional center allowances range from $4 to $7 per square foot. In smaller centers, developers may have to provide fully finished tenant space. Highly desirable tenants will demand allowance concessions.

Building Flexibility

Whatever the structural column spacings used in any type of center, the design should allow for a measure of flexibility in store partitioning.

Except for intervening fire walls, the spacing of which is governed by local fire protection codes, partitions between tenant spaces should not be used as bearing walls. Tenant partitions should be built of materials and by methods that allow for their easy removal. The design should provide for future reallocation of store space and for readjustments in fixtures needed as tenants expand or shift their locations in the center. To allow for flexibility in operations, structural elements such as plumbing and heating

stacks, air-conditioning ducts, toilets, and stairways should be placed on end walls or on the walls least likely to be removed in enlarging a store or redividing the spaces, rather than on side partitions between tenants.

After construction begins, changes in tenancy may require an altering of the tenant arrangement in order to improve the groupings of related shops, to accommodate tenant needs, or to free the "hot spot" locations for higher rental shops or more intensive use. Flexibility in design as well as non-load-bearing walls allows tenant spaces to be enlarged or decreased. Good locations can be created, and a plan can be devised that will remain workable throughout the full leasing program.

In one-story neighborhood centers, heavy masonry piers between storefronts should be avoided. Such piers are expensive to install and difficult to remove, and they reduce window frontage. (Of course, such advice is impractical if the center is to have a traditional exterior architectural treatment.) Small steel columns with curtain walls of gypsum wallboard or exposed concrete block are used for interior partitions. To install quickly and to save labor costs and provide an incombustible and vermin-proof structure, developers building one-story buildings can use steel beam and column construction with steel truss or bar joist roof members carrying an insulated steel roof deck and monolithic concrete floor. Often, even the concrete floor slab is provided by the tenant.

Malls

The desire to separate foot traffic from motor traffic and the increased emphasis on amenities led to the open pedestrian mall in shopping centers.

The early mall offered the attraction of a central open space, which was improved tremendously by a gardenlike treatment. Canopied walks, specimen trees, flowers, sculptures, and fountains created a parklike atmosphere where customers could rest on benches and generally relax and enjoy the surroundings. Later the appeal of this pedestrian "street" was increased by enclosing and weather conditioning it.

A shopping center with a mall has no "best side of the street." The pattern encourages shoppers to move back and forth from one side of the mall to the other. For this reason, the mall is an asset in merchandising and a stimulus for impulse buying, as well as a pleasant and convenient place for shoppers.

Pedestrian flow along the mall is encouraged by careful placement of the tenants to sustain the interest of shoppers. The usual arrangement of a mall center with more than one major tenant is to place one at each end of the mall. A department store that is the single principal magnet is usually placed midway on one side of the mall, and the next strongest tenants are placed at the ends. Such a pattern can become a cluster in which the department store magnet is surrounded by small stores, with short pedestrian malls leading from them to the stores of secondary pulling power; this strengthens customer circulation to the smaller intervening units.

In the current generation of centers, the open mall is a rarity. Exceptions are found in places such as Hawaii where the climate is conducive to year-round outdoor living, and in specialty, community, or neighborhood centers. The enclosed mall has become a nearly universal pattern except in small centers.

The fully weather-conditioned enclosed mall has assets not found in open mall centers, many of which can lead to increased sales volume. The design also permits open storefronts, which save in display window expense. The entire mall frontage of a store can, in effect, become open "window" area. When benches, plants, ornamental "spectaculars," and other mall furnishings are provided, the mall creates a setting for even greater merchandising vitality and centerwide promotion. Because of such advantages and because of the continuing popularity of enclosed malls, open malls are being converted to enclosed malls—if increased sales volumes justify the capital expense of conversion. An open mall can be roofed over by a "sky shield" or can be converted to a com-

3-28 Anchor tenants are usually placed at the ends of the mall.

3-29 Many open malls are being enclosed, using tension-supported fabric roofs (most often made of Teflon-coated fiberglass). Shown here is The Mall at 163rd Street in Miami.

pletely enclosed and weather-conditioned space to increase the comfort and circulation of customers.

A straight-line mall is likely to produce an unattractive and monotonous tunnel effect if its length is too great in relation to its width. To improve the visual effect and provide shorter sight distances, the pattern may assume such alphabetical shapes as the H, T, Y, Z, or L. A meandering traffic pattern creates more interesting movement and brings shoppers closer to storefronts. Pedestrian flow within the mall can also be directed by the strategic placement of seating areas, planters, kiosks, and other physical barriers as well as by changes in floor covering materials, colors, and patterns. The use of mirrors and other reflective surfaces, particularly on escalator channels and along portions of the concourse walls, can provide a more dramatic feeling within the mall area. Shapes within the mall can also be varied to create a design theme. At Bannister Mall in Kansas City, for example, the emphasis is on curvilinear lines rather than on straight lines and sharp edges.

Where a change occurs in the direction of customer flow between anchor tenants, a court or widened area can be introduced. Such an area can be architecturally dramatic, and adjacent leasable space can command premium rents. It can also serve as a setting for special promotional events and displays—antique shows, for example, or Christmas or Easter displays—

and should be designed to accommodate large assemblies of people and large vehicles. This can often be done by designing the space in the style of an amphitheater. Fountains, sitting areas, escalators, and sculptures can be featured attractions of the court.

Although mall widths generally range from 30 to 40 feet, the width may be increased to 60 feet or more for courts and other special areas, depending on the height and treatment of the ceiling. In multilevel malls, courts offer even greater opportunities for dramatic treatment. The ceilings can be up to 50 feet higher than in the adjacent mall area. Thirteen feet is an attractive and practical ceiling height, which will keep heating and air-conditioning costs within reasonable limits; the mall in a small regional center (one with approximately 300,000 square feet of GLA) may have a lower ceiling. In larger regional centers, a mall ceiling height of 15 feet has worked well. The height can be varied to avoid long straight sight lines and to provide a more interesting and pleasing appearance than that of the single-height hallway. It is also important to consider acoustics; the mall should have no echo effect.

Because the mall customarily runs a sizable distance between major retail tenants—either the department stores, or a department store and a larger variety store or food store—the architect's problem is to design this distance to seem short while it still provides

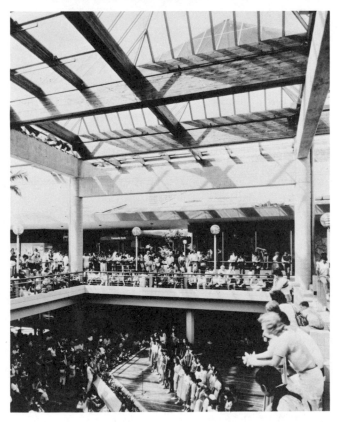

3-30, 3-31, 3-32, 3-33 The court area offers the opportunity for dramatic architectural treatment and makes a good setting for promotional events and displays. Fountains, sitting areas, escalators, and sculptures may be featured in this area.

enough length for an array of tenants. If storefronts are appealing and varied, shoppers will tend to become interested and involved with their surroundings and will not mind the walk. Occasional storefronts intruding into the mall two or three feet will give an undulating storefront line and make the mall more interesting. As an inexpensive solution to linearity, some developers hang banners across the mall to break up sight distances.

The desire of developers to provide enough retailing area for the stores that are part of the shopping complex—while keeping the mall length within a comfortable walking distance—bears directly on the depth of the stores. A hypothetical example: If a developer feels that his center requires 300,000 square feet of retail area, and if he divides this footage equally on both sides of a two-story mall, establishing 700 feet as the desired length between the leading stores, the average depth of stores on both sides of the mall might be 100 to 110 feet.

The GLA of enclosed malls normally equals about 84 to 89 percent of the gross building area, the remaining space being malls, courts, entrances, corridors, toilet facilities, and management facilities. In some cases, additional leasable space may be provided by designating special areas (other than kiosks) within the mall.

Kiosks

The kiosk, a freestanding booth, represents a retailing innovation in enclosed malls. It encourages impulse buying and allows the flexibility of including very small tenant spaces—those of 100 square feet or so. Kiosks must be low enough not to interfere with the view across the mall or with the view of tenant signs or lighting. If they are too high, they will appear to be separate stores, will separate traffic along the mall, and will deprive the tenants nearby from being seen from across the mall.

The addition to a mall of carefully selected kiosks, placed in areas of heavy traffic, greatly helps to create a gay, bustling marketplace atmosphere. Low counter-height kiosks are suitable for a variety of retail and service uses—such as candy, card, key, costume jewelry, and giftware sales, and travel agencies, ticket counters, newsstands, insurance agencies, and other outlets.

Although in lease negotiations some of the major tenants may seek to restrict kiosks, some smaller mall tenants may wish to augment their sales by operating kiosks in front of or near their stores. The owner or developer can receive substantial additional rental income from kiosks at little extra cost to himself.

Often, particularly when older malls are being renovated or enclosed, lean-to or similar style kiosks can be used to cover blank masonry wall space or unwanted department store show windows. They can add excitement to previously dull and dark areas of the mall, as well as generate substantial new income at a minimum investment to the developer. Normally, these kiosks are not roofed and require no air conditioning, heating, or sprinklers.

Developers must use discretion in introducing kiosks, making certain they meet established design guidelines. Food service outlets that require on-site cooking or that emit odors of any kind should not be permitted.

Multiple Levels

Vertical merchandising is being used increasingly as the solution to restricted sites and to the need to bring stores closer together for the convenience of shoppers. The multilevel mall reduces site coverage and walking distances between stores and between the parking areas and the stores. Multilevels also allow the regional center to include a mix of uses in compact buildings on restricted-area, high-cost sites.

Multilevel centers challenge architects, since their design requires a complex evaluation of site use, traffic movement, graphics, and amenities. This complexity is increased by the need to provide escalators, elevators, and stairways for vertical circulation. Still, the savings in required site area can help balance the greater capital costs of multilevel design.

Multilevel centers have distinct marketing benefits, provided the tenants are distributed to best advantage for interplay among the shopping levels. It is important for the developer to maintain careful control over tenant location when leasing a two-level center. Most mall tenants believe that their customer drawing power depends on a well-designed connection between the smaller tenants and the major stores. Therefore, the department store should have entrances from each level. Access to parking facilities from each level is also desirable and can be readily accomplished on a site with a natural or artificial slope or in a center with structured parking.

Visibility of the various levels is a very important aspect of multilevel design. The use of dramatic two-story design elements, including shops floating between levels, is a technique that has been used to prevent isolation of one level from another. The placement and prominence of vertical transportation must also be carefully considered. End courts or central courts can feature stairways, elevators, or escalators, that lead to a second gallery on the upper level and provide additional visual exposure for stores in the

3-34, 3-35   An important aspect of multilevel design is that the levels be visible to customers.

gallery area. Cross bridges may be used to connect both sides of the upper level and to offer dramatic views of activity on both levels.

Areas of vertical circulation between levels can be integrated into the overall design of the multilevel center. Architect Chris Ramos notes that necessities such as escalators and stairs can be designed to serve as attractive amenities. For example, at Rockaway Town Square, Rockaway, New Jersey, the landing on the stairs between the first and second levels was oversized (14 feet wide), and benches, chairs, and planters were added, allowing it to function as a plaza or "perch" from which to people-watch. Similarly, the space under stairways can be turned into a strong design feature, with recessed seating and carpeting installed to create an attractive area. As Ramos explains, "The stairs, the landing, the space underneath, even the railings, are all designed as an articulated amenity of the mall. It doesn't just look like a way to get from one level to another. It looks like an assembly of artistic components." However, if not designed carefully, escalators and stairs can obscure tenants from view and create difficult areas to lease, especially in the department store courts.

It is seldom advisable for neighborhood centers to have two stories. Second floors do not necessarily increase earnings, and extra costs are involved for construction, plumbing, heating, and maintenance. It is uneconomical to provide elevators or escalators to reach the second floor. If they are included in small centers, second floors are usually occupied by office rather than retail tenants. Office employees are all-day parkers, and office visitors are generally long-time, nonshopping parkers. Doctors and dentists make poor tenants for the second floor of a neighborhood center because of the special plumbing, wiring, and maintenance they require. Such tenants are better located in a separate medical building.

A small two-story center is likely to succeed only in an area of limited and high-cost commercial land, high population density, and a high level of disposable income. Suitable second-floor tenants are those that pull people to the center regularly and frequently, have visitors who will not park longer than an hour during shopping hours, and require no display space on the ground floor. Some service tenants, such as beauty shops, photographers, dance studios, and the like, are appropriate for second-floor locations. Stairs to second floors should be easy to climb, with intermediate landings—another reason for designing low ceilings on the first floor. Ideally, site topography will allow a design that provides at-grade access to the second level. An old real estate adage applies to most small shopping centers: Ground floor areas are

3-36, 3-37 Areas of vertical circulation can be integrated into the design of a multilevel center. At City Center Square in Kansas City, vinyl murals on the outer side of each of the escalators depict Kansas City in the 1920s and 1930s.

rented. Basements and second floors are "given away."

An exception to the above predicament of the small center is the current trend to convert "downtown" buildings, often historically certified and housing offices or warehouses, into multilevel shopping malls. These buildings are often tourist attractions and usually house a disproportionate number of restaurants and other food concessions.

Food Courts

Over the last 10 to 15 years, the food court has become a major component of many regional malls and specialty centers. It consists of a cluster of quick service food stands grouped around a common or public seating area. The design of the food court should provide a theme and a festive ambience. A high-quality design together with a proper tenant mix can often allow the food court to function as an anchor for the center (see Chapter 5 for information on food court tenants).

In order to create the desired festive setting, the design of the food court should pay close attention to features like natural lighting, the decor of public areas, design criteria for tenants, and the configuration and design of seating areas. Amenities such as terraces, water features, and landscaping are important, particularly to temper the visual impact of the

seating area in a large-scale food court. Among the most successful food courts, seating encourages the pleasure of seeing and being seen. Thus, seating often borders circulation routes or overlooks a multilevel public environment. Some newer food courts feature light-menu cafes with open kitchens, creating additional opportunities for seeing and being seen.

The location of the food court is vital. If the food court is, in fact, an anchor, then it should be a destination, in a location designed to draw people past other shops. On the other hand, if it is a convenience or an "oasis," it should be located to attract the greatest number of people going from "anchor" to "anchor"— that is, in the most heavily trafficked area. Another important factor to consider is whether the food court's location will allow it to remain open beyond the center's normal hours of operation and to be accessible to customers of various late night entertainment uses located within the center (such as cinemas) without creating a security problem for the center.

Whether a food court is to have fixed or movable tables and seats is an important choice to make. Fixing them avoids the need for continually restraightening the tables and chairs and reduces the risk of loss. But fixing the distance between tables and chairs means that those who are either very small (for example, children) or obese can never be completely com-

3-38   The food court at the Glendale Galleria, Glendale, California.

fortable. A frequent compromise is to fix the tables and leave the chairs movable. The amount of space that should be allotted to seating is debatable, but as a rule of thumb, one square foot of seating area should be allowed for each square foot of food court GLA—or approximately 35 seats for each food court tenant.

The food court uses a central air-conditioning system and, in a way, it is treated like a major tenant. Each of its individual tenants is in a stall, usually pre-designed, with its own exhaust system and plumbing. A variable air volume (VAV) system lends itself very well to this type of operation. Central systems for trash and garbage removal and for deliveries are essential. Sometimes, if the developer supplies trays, a common tray-washing area is necessary, and in some cases, a refrigerated garbage room may be used. Normally, restroom and telephone facilities are centrally located for the use of employees and customers.

Storefronts

Enclosed malls accommodate the widest possible display of merchandise for those stores fronting on pedestrian malls. Storefronts must be both architecturally integrated with the mall and reflective of the store's merchandise and image. They may be completely or partially open; merchandise may be placed before the public without the barrier of glass. With no doors to open, customers may enter sales areas under the most favorable circumstances. The full width of a store becomes the entrance. Shoplifting can become a problem, however, if store space layouts are not designed so that personnel at front sales locations can control them.

Devices for closing the storefronts in enclosed malls range from sliding glass doors to open grilles that drop from overhead. The variety of attractive display possibilities for storefronts is virtually limitless. Storefronts in an enclosed mall are often less expensive to merchandise because tenants are able to do away with window backs and other expensive display materials.

Store Size

There is a saying in the shopping center industry: Any store size is all right if it is not too big. The leasing program will include plans for store sizes. A merchant on a long-term lease may want the biggest store possible to accommodate possible expansion in the future. The developer/owner should have structural flexibility and, if possible, a flexible leasing agreement that allows a tenant to be moved if the need for a larger (or smaller) space is demonstrated.

3-39   Three-dimensional storefronts allow shoppers to see lower-level shops from upper levels.

Small stores add character to the center. Plans for small stores must provide suitable depths; this usually entails overlapping a large store in an L shape behind the small store.

The following advice is important in planning store sizes:

- Each tenant should be held to the minimum space needed, as it is better for the tenant to be a little tight on space than to be rattling around in too much room with insufficient sales to justify the rent, especially in light of today's higher building and operating costs, which are reflected in higher rents. Most tenants will recognize the prudence of gauging their space to the projected volume of sales.
- If possible, frontages for major tenants should be limited to permit exposure of as many different merchants as possible to the mall or pedestrian traffic.
- Variety in retail tenant mix is more important than the size of any particular store. There is evidence that centers with a variety of retail tenants are considerably more successful than those with only a few large stores.[23]

Store Width

A standard store width cannot be given for any particular type of tenant. Chain store companies have studied the matter for years and have employed the best talent in the store planning field to ascertain the proper width for their stores. Merchants generally have their own ideas about store size, based on their experience and study, and will usually advise the developer of their needs. Unfortunately, the merchants' ideas often do not coincide with the developer's need to restrict mall store widths in order to keep the mall to reasonable length and to allow frontage on the mall to as many tenants as possible.

In most present-day centers, the architectural design calls for structures with wide spans between the structural columns. Stores are fitted into these structural steel frames without much regard for column locations. With clever layout, columns are disguised as part of the fixtures and often can be used as part of the store's decorative features.

Developers should keep in mind that they have only so much frontage "for sale." Usually the amount of available frontage in a center is limited. The developer should prevent a merchant from using too much of this valuable commodity for a wide but shallow store if the merchant can achieve as high a sales volume in the same square footage with a greater store depth.

Store Depth

The ability to provide stores of varying depths is an asset to any center. A range of depths from 40 to 120 feet is often both required and feasible. Where buildings must have uniform depths, small stores may be "carved out" of deeper space, leaving rear overlap areas for the neighboring larger stores.

The developer must avoid creating excessive depths from which neither he nor the tenant can obtain an adequate return. If shopper traffic moves on two frontages, if delivery is at the back of the store and ground-level storage facilities have to be provided, or if the center has no basements, greater store depth is needed. Less depth is needed if storage and service facilities are in the basement and if pedestrian traffic passes on only one side of the store. Greater store depths in regional centers are generally a product of specifically planned uses, such as large high-quality stores, multiscreen theaters, and the like.

In small stores that may be deepened later, electric panels and equipment should be placed on the side walls so that they will not have to be relocated if the rear wall is moved.

Store Ceiling Height

The appropriate ceiling height for a store depends somewhat on the exterior architectural treatment and certainly on the total area of the store. Lower ceilings are the trend, encouraged partly because they save in energy consumption in the use of heating, air conditioning, and lighting, and they are less expensive to build and maintain. However, they require architectural "breaks" to produce a pleasing appearance.

The distance from the floor slab to the underside of the bar joists holding the roof may vary from 10 to 14 feet, depending on the architectural style of the building, the depth of the stores, and the type of tenants. The air space between the finished ceiling and the roof usually contains air-conditioning ducts, electrical wires, recessed lighting boxes and panels, telephone wires, plumbing lines, and other utility hardware; such equipment requires from two to three feet of space between the finished ceiling and the structure. Developers have found that the installation of T-bars and lay-in acoustical finished ceilings makes it easy to reach the utility lines.

Although many stores have 11-foot finished ceilings, some small stores may have ceilings as low as nine feet. Certain specialized tenants using more space, such as variety stores and supermarkets, require finished ceilings as high as 13 feet. Ceilings in

---

[23] For median store sizes (in GLA) by tenant classification, see Urban Land Institute, *Dollars & Cents of Shopping Centers* (Washington, D.C.: ULI–the Urban Land Institute, triennial).

93

storage areas out of customers' view need not be finished, but many fire codes require that they have lay-in panels or other materials with a two-hour fire-resistant rating. Mezzanines used for either sales or storage space will obviously require different ceiling heights.

Basements

At one time, large regional centers needed basements to accommodate their truck service tunnels. Basements were fairly easy to provide, because they could be scooped out at the same time the tunnel was dug. Today, however, with truck service courts and service delivery areas built level with the main building, basements are no longer needed and are generally considered too costly to construct when they are not providing income-producing space.

Although the new generation of shopping centers does not require them, basements have been used in some areas for storage and heating equipment, for office space, and for store expansion space. The original cost of providing basement space is relatively low, especially in colder sections of the country where foundation footings four or five feet below grade are necessary. However, the basement is still an added capital cost and generally is a low-income producer.

Cost-saving features in basement construction include the use of concrete block foundations where subsurface conditions permit, with transverse beams providing the first floor support. This construction method eliminates the need for basement stair headers and permits basement stairs to be relocated and widened without undue expense when store spaces and tenant arrangements are revised.

Stairways leading to a basement should be constructed of concrete or steel, and if the basement is to be used for merchandising, the stairways should be five feet wide. Some stores, such as furniture and variety chains, specifically request basement areas for merchandising and may require elevators.

Interior Walls

Party walls between retail stores in enclosed mall centers can be constructed of any of a variety of materials, depending on the local building and fire codes. Some codes require fire walls that extend to the underside of the roof. Sometimes concrete block is used; sometimes metal stud partitions with gypsum wallboard are used. The latter provides maximum flexibility for future changes in store sizes.

Partitioning between the sales and the storage areas of a store generally consists of stud and gypsum wallboard construction. The wall finish may be anything from paint to wallpaper to painted decoration to a vinyl cover. Most fire codes require that this partitioning extend to the underside of the roof.

Plumbing

Since plumbing lines often must run under the floor slab, they are best installed while subfloors are exposed during construction. Stores that do not have special plumbing requirements usually confine plumbing fixtures to small toilet areas and washbasins, but restaurants, beauty and barber shops, and other stores with more complex needs find plumbing a major improvement cost.

Plumbing requirements for a shopping center are essentially the same as those for freestanding stores. The tenant customarily provides any water heating equipment needed. Restaurants and major stores provide restrooms for customers. Where permitted, a group of small tenants can be served by shared restrooms provided by the developer and maintained by the group through common area charges.

Leases should specify the developer's responsibility for providing vents and drains for tenants, such as supermarkets, restaurants, and dry cleaners, who require large plumbing installations. If a center has no basement, floor installations should be deferred until the tenant spaces are leased, because the formulation of the tenants' underfloor requirements will lag behind the developer's construction schedule.

Because the tenants' plumbing requirements will lag behind construction, the tenant slab is often part of the tenants' responsibility, not that of the developer. In a multilevel mall, this can create a problem for plumbing stacks and vent locations, and must be taken into account.

Sprinklers must be installed in enclosed malls and in other mall buildings. The system required depends on local fire insurance rates and building codes and on available water supplies. In many instances, a sprinkler connection is brought to the tenant's lease line, and the tenant hooks up the sprinkler and does any other work within the tenant space needed for the system to conform to the layout. Even if a mall is allowed by code to go without a sprinkler system (common in one-level malls), obtaining insurance without fire protection is virtually impossible.

Lighting

Generally, a developer provides a source of electricity at a panel, and each tenant is required to provide his own lighting and other electrical needs; all, of course, require the landlord's approval. Since ceilings are also usually a tenant's responsibility, the tenant—not the developer—must coordinate ceiling work with lighting installation.

3-40 Sandwiched between parking above and below, the two-level, 300,000-square-foot ZCMI Center shopping mall is without natural light. However, lighted glass ceilings, fascias, and soffits give shoppers the feeling of being in a translucent glass tent flooded with daylight.

Ceilings in the enclosed mall space are frequently skylighted. As mentioned earlier, side wall clerestories save energy but are not nearly as appealing aesthetically as skylights. Also, clerestories often create problems with sun glare, depending, of course, on their orientation. However, they allow natural daylight to filter in, thus benefiting both the mall atmosphere and the specimen plantings customarily found in enclosed malls.

Lighting of enclosed mall areas is usually designed not to detract from the light intensity of the store windows while providing a pleasing, natural overall effect. Combinations of fluorescent and incandescent lighting plus indirect lighting may be used. Incandescent lighting requires more fixtures, more wiring, and greater wattage than fluorescent lighting to produce the same number of footcandles. In addition, it generates greater heat. In recent years, incandescent lighting has been largely replaced by high-intensity discharge (HID) lighting, which provides more lumens per watt and generates less heat.

Too much attention is often given to lighting store interiors rather than to lighting the merchandise. To reduce consumption of electricity, light colors could be used to eliminate the need for floodlighting. Store interiors can be designed with fewer outlets and shorter wiring runs to reduce installation and operating costs. By using high lumen output lights, fewer fixtures are needed.

Flooring

Special floor covering is usually put over the concrete slab in tenant sales areas, although it is often omitted in storage areas. Floor coverings range from various tile materials to carpeting. Wood flooring is not recommended for stores unless the whole decorative scheme calls for it. Stores often vary the floor coverings in different parts of the sales area, depending on the character of the merchandise and the way in which the merchandise is presented. Tenants are almost always responsible for the flooring in their spaces, done in accordance with criteria established by the owner and incorporated into the lease.

Floor surfaces of enclosed malls consist of a wide variety of materials—polished concrete, carpets, various kinds of tile pavers, treated wood parquet (particularly on upper floors), terrazzo, and either poured-in-place or precast tiles. The developer should be careful in choosing the surface material; it must be durable and easy to clean and maintain. The floor must not be slippery, yet it must not be so rough that it

3-41 Flooring should be durable and easy to clean and maintain.

Heating and Air Conditioning

A shopping center can be heated and cooled either by individual units for each store or by a central plant for the entire center. Tenants are responsible for their own individual units; the shopping center's management is responsible for a central plant, which offers the greatest centerwide convenience. Hybrid systems, employing large, multitenant rooftop units, are also available. One of these systems—the variable air volume system (VAV)—increases or decreases the amount or volume of air to each space according to the demands of the space. A thermostat controls a VAV terminal that controls the amount of air—usually cooling air—admitted into the space. Either a central plant or rooftop package senses the system pressure requirements and maintains a constant temperature and pressure while varying the volume. In a conventional system, the volume is constant and the temperature varies.

With energy savings an essential criterion of HVAC systems, the mechanical engineer must evaluate all possible systems and the availability of various fuels. Good judgment, based on thorough analysis, is necessary not only in the development of new projects but also in the improvements of operating centers. Solutions are complicated by the differences in needs and requirements of the various tenant classifications.

Developers can reduce air-conditioning loads by using extra building insulation and a heat-reflective coating on the roof. In enclosed malls, engineers should be employed to check each tenant's air-conditioning system to assure proper balance so that stores do not "bleed off" conditioned air from the mall area.

In many areas, substantial additional income is available to owners through the submetering of energy from the local utility company; in other words, the owner buys from the company at wholesale rates and sells to tenants at retail rates. Because state and local utility laws vary greatly, as do the practices and policies of electric companies, the legality of submetering must be investigated. For this reason, both legal counsel and the advice of a heating engineer should be sought.

interferes with cleaning. Quality ceramic tile floors are serviceable and economical. Flooring with a small-pattern design will be easier to replace if cracks appear in some sections from heavy use.

The floor of enclosed malls can be made more attractive and warmer in appearance if a carefully designed variety of materials is used, rather than unvarying, dead-white terrazzo. The entryway of most stores can be made more dramatic and appealing if their floor materials are noticeably different from those of the mall. Floor designs help break up the monotony of lengthy malls or walkways.

4.
Expansion and Renovation of Existing Centers

One of the leading trends in the shopping center development industry today is the expansion and renovation of existing centers. This trend is related to the physical and functional aging of centers as well as to the declining opportunities for the development of new centers. An existing center may suffer from an obsolete design, from physical neglect, from an inappropriate tenant mix due to a changing market and new competition, or from the loss of its status as a tax shelter. For this reason, many owners of older, existing centers have had to decide whether to expand or renovate or both.

Feasibility Analysis

In deciding whether to undertake the expansion/renovation of an existing center, the owner must determine if the expansion/renovation program is justified in terms of the potential return on investment. To determine this, he must examine a number of factors, both internal and external. Internal factors to be analyzed include data on the center's tenant mix and lease terms, the sales performance of individual tenants, the center's market share, the relative position of the center vis-à-vis its market, the existing management, and the availability of land for expansion. External factors include the market area coverage, the composition of the market, the overall retail potential reflected in the expenditures of the area's residents,

4-1, 4-2   An existing center may suffer from an obsolete design, physical neglect, or an inappropriate tenant mix.

the competition and its impact on the center, potential new developments, the availability of new tenants to improve or expand the center's tenant mix, and an estimate of the size and timing of the proposed expansion. These internal and external factors in combination can be evaluated in terms of investment criteria to test a proposed renovation/expansion.

Analysis of Sales Performance

Unlike the developer of a new center who has to work with estimates, the "redeveloper" of an existing center already knows the sales performance of the tenants, the rents, the lease terms, and the individual tenant management capabilities. In diagnosing the need for renovation, the redeveloper may begin with sales performance figures. A five- to seven-year history is adequate, since the detection of trends is the primary goal. Total center sales and their relationship to those of similar retailing in the region are usually the first indicators of whether and to what degree to renovate and/or expand. For example, if the growth rate of sales for a center equals or surpasses that of its competitors, the center could probably benefit from an expansion, with the prospect of updating antiquated rents. If the growth rate is lower than that of the market or if sales are declining, the center's owners should investigate the causes; a renovation may be appropriate. Sales rates in a center thus serve as a barometer to indicate whether a renovation and/or expansion is in order.

Sales for individual tenants, classified into retail categories, are significant not only in terms of relative growth but also as a percentage of total sales within respective categories. Tenants can be classified initially as good, fair, and poor performers. Good performers may serve as a standard; poor ones may be scrutinized and possibly given assistance in management and marketing, or they may be put on a list of tenants who might be replaced.

Analysis of Leases

Leases must be carefully reviewed with regard to the following items:

- The degree of approval rights and control vested in any one tenant.
- Duration of leases and any options.
- Rents (both minimum and percentage) as compared to the current fair market value and percentage rents.
- Flexibility of the lease provisions with regard to assignments, subleases, and use.
- The type and value of existing tenant improvements and who has control of such improvements at the end of the lease term.

- Real property tax questions.
- Contributions to operating expenses.
- Common areas.
- Signage.

Owners should give special attention to tenants whose terms expire in the near future, within say two to three years, with no options to renew. The rents of these tenants could most easily be raised to current market rates, provided the tenants' sales levels are satisfactory. Even tenants with options to renew in the near future are usually willing to renegotiate their positions when centers are renovated. Tenants whose performances are poor and whose leases are soon to expire will head the list of potential eliminations. The opportunity to upgrade rent and lease terms is a major signal in favor of renovation.

In anticipation of renovation, landlords may have leases drawn to provide for stipulated increases in minimum rent should certain events occur, such as the addition of another anchor or the enclosure of an open center. Leases for open malls should require tenants to pay for common area maintenance (CAM) and for HVAC costs if the mall is enclosed. The landlord in a strong negotiating posture may also include a provision for tenants to remodel their storefronts if the mall is enclosed. Leases should clearly allow the landlord to change the center without the tenants' approval. Some landlords insist on using only short-term leases, with the view toward later incorporating such clauses when they are ready to renovate and/or enclose a center.

Tenant Mix Analysis

A tenant's percentage of the floor area and a tenant's sales in each retail category compared with the total center sales make up the "tenant profile." Ideally, the tenant sales profile should correspond to the trade area's expenditure profile for identical categories, but the mathematical relation between floor area profile and sales profile is not directly proportionate.

For example, department stores in a regional center may represent 60 to 65 percent of the total floor area of the center. Yet department store sales may represent 46 percent of the center's total sales, with the balance of the center's stores representing 54 percent. If the expenditure profile of the trade area residents indicates a 50–50 ratio, the center is somewhat under-merchandised in terms of department stores. Similarly, overmerchandising may be strongly indicated in a category—for example, shoes—when the center's sales profile corresponds to the trade area's expenditure profile and sales per square foot of its shoe stores are static or below those of shoe stores in other parts of the trade area. Such a tenant group, however, may not necessarily be marked for elimination or redirection; if the center is expanded and an anchor store added, numerous shoe stores may well be in demand.

An analysis of the tenant mix therefore serves as an additional indicator for renovation/expansion. The larger the disparity between center sales and trade area expenditures, the greater the need for renovation. The tenant mix should also be analyzed as to how consistent it would be with the center's new image and identity resulting from renovation.

Customer Surveys

An existing center provides the opportunity to conduct direct market interviews. Customer interviews can reveal the public's reaction to such matters as image, the general design of the center, the quality/volume of individual tenants in the center, and the center's strengths and weaknesses in terms of customer conveniences. Such interviews will also reveal how responsive the customers are to marketing efforts, and who the center's competitors are. Data obtained from customer interviews, particularly when related to social and economic characteristics of the trade area in general, provide information on trade area delineation, market penetration, and market shares and their distribution—both geographically and by economic groups—as well as data on customer habits, preferences, and likes and dislikes. Properly structured and conducted, customer interviews can either reaffirm or refute the need for a renovation.

Analysis of Expansion Potential

The last but not the least of the internal factors that should be considered is the center's potential to expand. Generally, three approaches exist for expanding a center and creating additional revenue-producing space: developing outparcels; developing a portion of the existing parking area; and creating leasable space from part of the common areas in the existing mall. Creating additional leasable space can offset the center's remodeling costs significantly. In addition, many center renovations involve subdividing larger stores into smaller ones.

Because of the opportunities for shared parking, developing outparcels with nonretail uses (such as office or cinema uses) may make it possible to create additional leasable space without an accompanying demand for additional parking. Since these nonretail uses tend to experience their peak parking demand at hours of the day and days of the week that differ from the peak demand periods for retail, such uses could share parking space with retail uses without conflict,

thus eliminating the need to provide more parking area to accommodate the new revenue-producing uses.[1]

By restriping an existing parking lot and reducing stall sizes or changing parking angles, it may also be possible to provide the same or a greater number of stalls within a smaller land area, thus freeing a portion of the existing parking area for the development of additional leasable space. Further, inappropriate parking standards were used for many older centers, resulting in a surplus of parking space even during the busiest hours of the year and creating opportunities for the development of additional revenue-producing space.

Blank department store walls can be lined with small but high-rent "wall shops" and tenant spaces can be reconfigured to increase the number of spaces and thus allow a greater number of tenants. Large common areas in older centers also present opportunities for expansion. Early open malls were usually much wider than necessary for convenient pedestrian circulation; many were as wide as 60 to 80 feet. By comparison, most malls today are 30 to 40 feet in width. However, an important factor to consider is that narrowing mall width often means deepening existing shops that are already far deeper than needed today.

Market Analysis

The decision to renovate or expand rests ultimately on an analysis of external factors related to the nature of the market. For instance, the locational value of the center should be reassessed, basing the assessment on highway improvements, residential expansion, and commercial developments. Qualitative changes in neighborhood composition should be examined for both positive and negative signs. Trade areas are in constant change, growing or shrinking both vertically and horizontally. The geographical limits of a trade area should be tested before a new department store is added to a center. Can the area support another store? Also, is the economic level of the residents compatible with the quality of the center and its proposed expansion? If a department store is added to a center, other companion retail tenants will usually be added, in a proportion related to the expenditure profile of the area market. This factor would indicate the extent of expansion needed. The geographical distribution of specific income groups indicates the quality as well as the quantity of nondepartment store tenants needed in the center.

---

[1] See Barton-Aschman Associates, Inc., *Shared Parking* (Washington, D.C.: ULI–the Urban Land Institute, 1984).

The effect of existing and proposed competition is measured both qualitatively and quantitatively, since an area market can support only so much of any retail category. A market analysis will provide information on customer income groups in the area and on those groups that go elsewhere to do their shopping. The latter information would suggest the type and quality of stores that are lacking in the center. If 30 percent of the families in a trade area have higher incomes, but only 5 percent of them are represented in an on-site interview sample at the center, most of them probably shop elsewhere.

Based on a thorough market analysis to determine the needs of the customers compared with what the center, as well as its competitors, offers, a number of expansion/renovation hypotheses can be developed. If the market analysis reveals that the addition of a department store would benefit the center, and land for it is available, this expansion alternative can be explored. Adding a new anchor, which in turn attracts other minor tenants, reduces the chance of customers' going elsewhere in the trade area. When a major store is not available or the market cannot support it, opportunities may still exist to expand the nondepartment store portion of the center, and thus possibly

make the center more competitive with the market at large. Inadequate or only moderate market support will most likely rule out a decision to renovate the center. An example of correlating external and internal factors relative to renovation is shown in Figure 4-3.

Once the market factors are understood, various renovation alternatives can be evaluated. This requires preliminary sketches and tentative estimates of the cost of the planned renovation/expansion. Cost estimates developed for the proposed alternatives provide the basis for a financial pro forma statement.

Financial Analysis

The preparation of a financial analysis is the final step one must take in making a decision whether to renovate, expand, or take another course of action. The pro forma financial analysis should include the following elements:

- Capital costs of all renovation alternatives: a full expansion to market limits, including structured parking or the acquisition of more land if necessary; a less ambitious expansion, ruling out the addition of a major store; no expansion but a

4-3   TRADE AREA (TA) ANALYSIS AND CENTER CORRELATION TO DETERMINE EXTENT OF RENOVATION/EXPANSION

STORE CLASSIFICATION	TA POTENTIAL[1] TOTAL PROFILE ($000)		EXISTING CENTER SALES PROFILE ($000)		CENTER SHARE[3] EXISTING	CENTER SHARE[3] POTENTIAL	SALES PROFILE ($000)		POTENTIAL VOLUME AND FLOOR AREA[4,5] SALES PER SQUARE FOOT	FLOOR AREA (SQUARE FEET)	EXISTING FLOOR (SQUARE FEET)	NET ADD (SQUARE FEET)
Department	$120,000	54.25%	$31,130	69.52%	25.94%	35.00%	$42,000	62.41%	$120	350,000	286,000	64,000
Variety	5,000	2.26	1,300	2.90	26.00	25.00	1,250	1.86	85	14,706	20,000	−5,294[6]
Women's	22,000	9.95	2,752	6.15	12.51	25.00	5,500	8.17	165	33,333	18,500	14,833
Men's	13,000	5.88	1,092	2.44	8.40	25.00	3,250	4.83	140	23,214	9,500	13,714
Family	5,000	2.26	1,274	2.85	25.48	25.00	1,250	1.86	110	11,364	13,000	−1,636
Children's	1,400	0.63	420	0.94	30.00	25.00	350	0.52	110	3,182	4,500	−1,318
Accessories	1,200	0.54	588	1.31	49.00	25.00	300	0.45	145	2,069	4,000	−1,931
Shoes	11,000	4.97	4,085	9.12	37.14	25.00	2,750	4.09	185	14,865	25,500	−10,635[6]
Furniture	17,400	N.A.[2]	881	N.A.	N.A.	N.A.	N.A.	N.A.	N.A.	8,000	8,000	0
Furnishings	7,000	3.16	588	1.31	8.40	25.00	1,750	2.60	175	10,000	4,000	6,000
Pictures/Frames	800	0.36	291	0.65	36.38	25.00	200	0.30	105	1,905	2,500	−595
Music	2,400	1.08	550	1.23	22.92	25.00	600	0.89	165	3,636	3,600	36
Radio, TV	7,000	3.16	0	0.00	0.00	25.00	1,750	2.60	135	12,963	0	12,963
Luggage	800	0.36	190	0.42	23.75	25.00	200	0.30	110	1,818	2,000	−182
Photo	1,600	0.72	105	0.23	6.56	25.00	400	0.59	165	2,424	1,800	624
Cards/Gifts	2,800	1.27	195	0.44	6.96	25.00	700	1.04	185	3,784	3,500	284
Jewelry	7,000	3.16	217	0.48	3.10	25.00	1,750	2.60	215	8,140	5,000	3,140
Sporting Goods	5,000	2.26	0	0.00	0.00	25.00	1,250	1.86	135	9,259	0	9,259
Books	2,400	1.08	0	0.00	0.00	25.00	600	0.89	195	3,077	0	3,077
Hobbies, Toys	4,000	1.81	0	0.00	0.00	25.00	1,000	1.49	145	6,897	0	6,897
Sewing	1,800	0.81	0	0.00	0.00	25.00	450	0.67	145	3,103	0	3,103
Total	238,600		45,658		19.14%					536,920	419,400	
Total Excluding Furniture	221,200	100.00%	44,777	100.00%	20.24%		67,300	100.00%		527,739	411,400	116,339

[1]As per market analysis.
[2]Not included in profile calculations; tenancy optional.
[3]Existing market share = center sales/trade area potential; potential shares based on market analysis and impact of competition (not shown).
[4]Estimated sales = trade area potential times potential center share.
[5]Floor area based on breakeven sales per square foot (estimated sales/sales per square foot).
[6]Tenants to be replaced if feasible.

4-4 COMPARATIVE PRO FORMA FINANCIAL ANALYSIS: BEFORE AND AFTER RENOVATION
(Dollars in Thousands)

	EXIST-ING	RENOVA-TION	REFI-NANCE
Net Operating Income	$ 1,563	$ 2,637	$ 2,637
Capitalization			
Rate	9.00%	10.50%	10.50%
Value	$17,367	$25,114	$25,114
Financing			
Mortgage (Outstanding)	4,500	7,060	17,580
Equity—Buildup	10,670	11,310	7,534
Equity—Initial Cash	3,000	3,640	7,534
Total Funding	15,170	18,370	25,114
Debt Service			
Amortization	1,154	1,474	2,198
Principal Outstanding	4,500	7,060	0
Cash Equity Buildup, Cumulative	10,670	11,310	7,534
Cash Flow	409	1,163	440
Cash Flow as Percent of Equity Buildup	3.83%	10.28%	5.83%
Cash Flow as Percent of Initial Cash Equity	13.62%	31.94%	5.83%

renovation of the existing structure; or some simple form of practical modification.

- Projected sales for all tenants in the center, existing and new. These should include estimates indicating how a renovation would affect marginal existing tenants; this information would help in screening tenants for possible elimination and replacement. Screening could be a highly subjective process; usually an existing tenant with a poor performance is not eliminated unless a proven merchandiser is found to replace it. The main purpose of sales projections is budgetary—that is, to estimate potential overage rents.

- Rent schedules, reflecting current terms as well as anticipated gross income from new tenants, along with pass-throughs.

- Estimated operating expenses.

- Capitalization, for purposes of evaluating financing alternatives.

- Mortgage and equity requirements, which will help to determine whether to refinance, wholly or in part.

- Cash flow analysis to determine present property value estimates or other investment criteria (cash or cash return, return on market equity, or internal rate of return if property is eventually sold).

A pro forma financial analysis developed along these lines provides the ultimate framework in which to make a decision on whether or not to renovate, how to renovate, and to what extent to renovate. (See Figure 4-4.)

Physical Design Changes

If the developer decides to go ahead, detailed plans will be required for the center's physical renovation and expansion. In preparing these plans, the developer and his design team should consider the following key areas.

Parking Lot Design

As noted earlier, parking lot design can be a critical factor in the success of a renovation/expansion project. In considering the possibilities for modifying the existing parking area, a developer should analyze the following factors: ingress and egress; pedestrian and vehicular conflicts; and the overall configuration and appearance of the parking area.

Poorly designed entrances and exits not only present a traffic hazard but also cause congestion that can create a negative image of the center. Vehicular access to the center can often be improved and congestion minimized on adjacent roadways by redesigning entrances so that they penetrate farther into the site, thus providing stacking space within the parking area. Deeper entrances will also allow traffic counters to be placed farther in. With this arrangement, both front car wheels hit the counters simultaneously, and bogus counts are avoided. Exiting may be improved by establishing double left-turn lanes out of the center or by providing more sophisticated traffic signals. The possibilities for reducing the number of existing exits and entrances should also be considered. Many older centers have too many curb cuts, making it difficult to control traffic flow. By eliminating some of the existing exits and entrances and limiting access points to strategic locations, traffic flow can be more easily controlled. Reducing the number of exits and entrances can also create space for more parking stalls.

Conflicts between vehicles and pedestrians must be minimized. Ideally, the parking area should be designed so that pedestrians are walking parallel to moving cars; thus, visibility is better for both drivers and pedestrians. Whenever feasible, walkways should also be provided within parking lots. Because the greatest pedestrian/vehicular conflict occurs in the "cruising" or fire lane located immediately adjacent to storefront walkways, this lane must be carefully designed to discourage fast-moving vehicles as well as vehicular movements through the center using this lane. Speed bumps or narrowed lanes may serve this purpose. Vehicular circulation through the site must be directed away from the fire lane to the outer edge of the parking lot where there is less pedestrian traffic.

The possibilities for changing the configuration and appearance of the existing parking lot must also be examined. Typically, the parking lot is the foreground of the center and, thus, must be made an integral part of the center's overall design concept. Obviously, an ugly parking lot detracts considerably from the center's "curb appeal." One of the most logical ways to improve the appearance as well as the functioning of the parking area is to break up the "sea of asphalt" by the installation of strategically placed plantings and berming. This might include landscaping and berming along the perimeter of the site as well as landscaped islands within the parking area.

In most older centers, parking lots need to be restriped and/or repaved. This offers the chance to change stall sizes and angles as well as bay widths to make more efficient use of the parking area. Rearranging an existing parking area to accommodate compacts can also improve capacity, adding spaces in the same area or maintaining the same number of spaces in less area. However, as noted in Chapter 3, it is difficult to plan for the use of small car parking spaces at shopping centers.

Landscaping and Mall Furniture

In the renovation of an existing center, landscaping improvements may range from a simple refurbishment of existing landscaping to its total replacement. Plant materials must be carefully selected and placed to soften the center's appearance while not blocking views of signage and storefronts, and to allow adequate sight distance within parking areas and at vehicular entrances and exits. Landscaping, both exterior and interior, should provide as much permanent, year-round greenery as possible, as well as seasonal color (with flowering plants).

Mall furniture (benches, planters, and trash receptacles) should be selected according to design and durability. Mall furniture in an older center will usually need to be replaced: it will most likely be worn, and its design will date the center. Designs selected should obviously be compatible with the overall design concept for the renovated center. If common areas are downsized in the renovation, modular furniture might lend more flexibility in the use of common areas. While the cost of new mall furniture is generally small compared with the total project cost (1 percent or less is typical), the effect of mall furniture on the center's overall appearance is significant.

Lighting

Because lighting is an important factor in terms of the center's appearance, security, and energy consumption, both the exterior and interior lighting systems should be carefully inspected and evaluated. Lighting of common areas must be adequate, with glare kept to a minimum. Special consideration, of course, must be given to the lighting of parking lots, mall entrances, and areas of pedestrian circulation. Lighting can also

be used for aesthetic reasons and to attract shoppers to the center at night. However, in a specialty or theme center where period lighting may be used, care must be taken to balance aesthetics with the need for adequate illumination.

In an enclosed mall, interior lighting levels must be carefully balanced, and any modifications to it should, of course, be evaluated in terms of energy consumption. Lighting in mall interiors should not be so bright that it detracts from lighted storefronts, but it should be adequate to light interior mall landscaping. Since interior lighting should provide a pleasant, natural effect, opportunities to increase natural lighting by means of skylights and clerestories should be considered. Finally, the design of light standards must be compatible with the center's overall design.

Buildings and Walkways

The condition of existing buildings must first be studied to determine the amount of renovation needed. Deficiencies in maintenance obviously should be corrected, and buildings should comply with building codes. A developer considering the acquisition of an older center for renovation and expansion might do well to meet with the local building inspector to obtain some idea of the extent of renovation that may be required to correct existing problems. It would also be helpful to prepare a checklist of items that should be examined, such as the overall structural condition, the HVAC, flooring, plumbing (including sprinkler systems), sound systems, security systems, restrooms, mall entrances and exits (including door hardware), trash systems, access for the handicapped, storefronts, and signage.

In addition to determining essential functional renovation, the development team must determine the extent and nature of cosmetic renovation needed to improve the center's overall appearance and "curb appeal." The alteration of building facades is one of the easiest ways to change dramatically a center's character and appearance. If the buildings are structurally sound, it may be possible to construct new facades (generally of lightweight materials) around them, thus avoiding demolition and rebuilding and significantly reducing renovation costs. Constructing new facades around the existing structures will also make it easier for tenants to remain in operation during the renovation. For example, in the renovation of Pacific Plaza in San Diego, new storefronts were developed to encase the existing storefronts and a variety of forms and materials were used to provide individual character and identity for tenants. In the renovation of an older strip center's facade, the opportunities to reduce the visual impact of the cen-

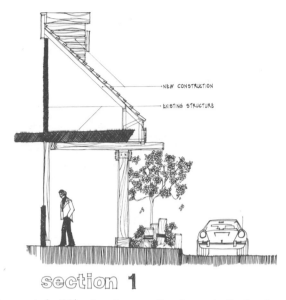

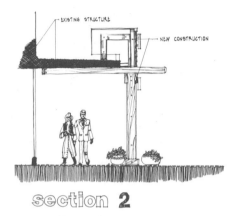

section 1   section 2

4-5   Changes to building facades can alter dramatically the character and appearance of both the buildings and the center as a whole. If the buildings are structurally sound, it may be possible to construct new facades around them.

ter's length must be examined. Vertical design details (such as clock towers) can provide visual diversity and minimize the effect of the center's horizontal form.

With an older open center, it might be advisable to cover parts of existing walkways with arcades or canopies to provide a pedestrian character and also to protect shoppers from the weather. However, the decision whether or not to enclose a regional center must be based on a thorough analysis of the competition, the climate, and the cost. In a market with a mild climate and little competition from enclosed malls, a center may not need to be enclosed.

Finally, walkways should be considered. Are they adequate for efficient pedestrian circulation through-

out the center? In older open strip centers, walkways need to be widened or repaired. If so, or if new walkways are needed, interesting and decorative materials should be investigated. Although concrete in its ordinary application has a rather uninteresting appearance, its visual appeal can be enhanced through the use of wood expansion joints, patterned stamped concrete, or exposed aggregate concrete. Other masonry materials should also be considered.

Signage

Since coordinated signage is essential, this will mean that in most renovations all signs will have to be replaced. New signage must be compatible with the overall design of the renovation. Although signage needs to be large enough to convey information from appropriate distances, it must not be so large that it overpowers the design of the buildings. Sizes obviously will vary, depending on whether signs are meant to be read from streets or highways adjacent to the center, the parking area, or the storefronts. While graphics must be controlled, they must strike a balance between aesthetic coordination and adequate tenant identification. Because of retailers' concerns with maintaining their own identities, some opposition to a coordinated signage program can be expected from tenants.

Tenant Coordination

The renovation and expansion of an older center generally involves more than physical changes to the center. The renovation and expansion must be coordinated with the tenants. Because the tenant mix must

4-6   The addition of vertical design details can minimize the visual impact of the linear center.

103

4-7, 4-8   Coordinated signage is essential in the renovation of a center.

be consistent with the new image and identity being created for the center, it may be necessary to change or upgrade the mix.

Successfully undertaking a renovation/expansion will require the enthusiastic support and cooperation of tenants, which will depend on the developer's frequent communication and coordination with tenants. The developer should not announce the renovation to tenants without first undertaking a thorough review and analysis of the existing tenant mix and the status of all leases in order to locate possible obstacles to the renovation. Leases must be carefully reviewed with regard to a number of items, including the control vested in any one tenant, terms of leases (option periods), rents as compared to the current fair market value and percentage rent, real property tax questions, common areas, and signage.

Following this, the developer can best inform the tenants of a renovation/expansion by convening a meeting with them in which the development team reviews the rationale for the renovation/expansion, the planned architectural design and other physical renovation (including changes to signage), the construction schedule, the period of time that the tenants will be without identification signage, and the steps that will be taken to minimize the inconvenience to tenants and shoppers. In addition, the developer should address what is expected of the tenants (with regard to increased common area maintenance and operation costs, additional merchants' association assessments to pay for the "grand reopening," sign removal and new sign acquisition, and similar items). Most importantly, the developer must convince tenants at this meeting that he is looking after their best interests, by reviewing for them the advantages that they can expect as a result of the renovation. Tenants must be convinced that their increased costs following the renovation will be more than offset by increased shopper traffic and sales volumes.

After this initial meeting, the developer is in a position to renegotiate leases with individual tenants, keeping in mind the fact that the existing tenants can be an excellent source for referrals who might lease any vacant space. While the lease renegotiation process will vary from tenant to tenant, several items typically will be discussed. Tenants generally will seek the following during renegotiation: additional renewal options; an extended term in which to amortize store interior improvements; a developer contribution to the cost of new signage; opportunities for store expansion or relocation; and a construction allowance for leasehold improvements and/or a new storefront. The developer will usually seek: a capital contribution from the tenant to the cost of renovation; a rent increase; the conversion of gross leases to net leases; extensions of lease terms from key tenants (an important factor in obtaining new financing for the renovation); an increased common area maintenance contribution; the modification of restrictive covenants; tenant renovation of storefronts and store interiors; and the possible expansion of key tenants where space is available.[2]

Scheduling and Logistics

The renovation/expansion should be carefully planned and scheduled to allow the center to remain fully operational during the construction period. In-

[2] Don M. Casto III and Richard W. Trott, "Renovating a Small Center," *Shopping Center Report* (New York: International Council of Shopping Centers, 1983).

terference with shopper traffic must be minimized to avoid the loss of sales revenue and to protect against potential liability. Center entrances and exits (both vehicular and pedestrian) should not be blocked during construction, and it is essential that the site be kept as clean as possible (with daily cleanups made by the general contractor). Arrangements should also be made for temporary services needed to provide a convenient as well as safe atmosphere (temporary lighting, warning signs, barricades, security guards, and so forth).

Building materials should not be delivered during peak shopping hours. In addition, construction ideally should not occur during the peak retail season: if possible, construction should start after Easter and be completed before Thanksgiving.

Finally, it is imperative that the developer explain the renovation/expansion objectives to all members of the development team. Team rapport must be established and team members must agree on the project's critical path and meet the required deadlines. A tenant coordinator is a key member of the team and should be on board before and during the construction period to assist tenants.

Promotion

A complete promotional campaign should be developed for the renovation/expansion, consisting of pre-construction announcements, promotion during the renovation, promotion for the grand reopening, and, finally, the grand reopening. A well-executed promotional campaign, capitalizing on the excitement of the renovation, can actually increase sales activity during the construction period. In renegotiating leases, the developer/owner should make certain that a grand reopening assessment is included in all new leases.

Summary—Expansion/Renovation

In summary, the successful expansion/renovation is one that improves the financial performance of the center—both in terms of the owner's return and the center's share of the market. Achieving such success will require a thorough market analysis, a detailed pro forma financial analysis, and a carefully planned and executed renovation/expansion program that addresses the physical aspects of renovation and expansion, tenant/developer coordination, tenant compatibility and changes in tenant mix, scheduling, and promotional activities.

Case Studies

As with so many aspects of the development process, there are no hard-and-fast rules governing the renovation and expansion of shopping centers. For example, there is no unvarying formula with which to determine the time, cost, and scope of a remodeling job; no foolproof way to predict the amount of increase (if any) in tenant sales as the result of an expansion; and no rigid step-by-step method of planning, designing, and constructing a center renovation.

Each center is unique and requires its own carefully planned and orchestrated renovation and expansion program. The following case studies illustrate successful renovation and expansion strategies for a variety of centers.

Town & Country
Whitehall, Ohio

Like many other older, suburban shopping centers, Town & Country Shopping Center had become unattractive and outdated. A renovation, directly affecting 380,300 square feet of gross leasable area, offered the developer the opportunity to change the center's image and to increase its sales and rents. In some cases, leases were renegotiated; in other cases, new tenants were found who were geared to accommodate affluent suburban shoppers. As a result, sales increased by 33 percent, and the developer's cash flow increased by 75 percent. The renovation also increased the size of the shopping center: when a national chain supermarket tenant relocated and expanded within Town & Country, the center's total GLA increased to 500,024 square feet from its original GLA of 466,000 square feet. The developer also widened and landscaped sidewalks, installed new canopies and signs, and improved the parking area.

Town & Country is a community specialty center with a linear building configuration. Built in 1948, it was one of the first outlying retail locations for stores like J.C. Penney, S.S. Kresge, and Richman Brothers. By the mid-1970s, however, its preeminent position in the trade area had been eroded by the opening of an enclosed mall center (with over 1 million square feet of GLA) several miles away, the construction of freeways and interstate highways not easily accessible from Town & Country, and a more sophisticated buying public. Still, the center had been well maintained, a reasonably strong demand existed for retail space in its trade area, the location was still good, and the surrounding population possessed the favorable characteristics of stability and density. A solid foundation existed for physical and economic improvement.

The Site

Town & Country is located in Whitehall—a suburb on the east side of Columbus—about four miles from downtown Columbus and about two miles inside I-270, which encircles the metropolitan area. The site itself is flat and has 2,900 feet of frontage on East Broad Street, a major east/west thoroughfare in Columbus with traffic volumes averaging 19,200 vehicles per day. This extensive frontage, combined with the narrowness of the property, was the greatest design limitation of the original development. An established trade area of middle-class and upper-middle-class neighborhoods borders the site on the east, south, and west. Residential areas to the north do not contribute significantly to Town & Country's trade, since a large federal supply depot and the Columbus airport separate them from the center.

The Renovation Process

Planning and design for the renovation initially included only those stores north of East Broad Street. The work was accomplished in seven distinct construction projects. As a result of the first, which took five months and was considered a test for further renovation, a number of prospective tenants expressed interest in locating in Town & Country. Therefore, the developer decided to proceed with the remaining renovation projects.

The first project involved the Kroger supermarket, which wanted to expand its space at Town & Country from 17,500 to 32,000 square feet. The developer built

4-9, 4-10 Before and after renovation.

106

4-11, 4-12   Two types of canopies were used (wood frame and stucco) to help break up the length of the center. Stucco canopies identify the storefronts of most of the major tenants.

the larger unit for Kroger on a four-acre parcel nearby. The rezoning required for the new area, as well as other requests for variances, received the cooperation of municipal authorities because the project promised a significant improvement to the community.

In each construction project, tenants were informed ahead of time of the renovation and its schedule. All subcontracts were awarded and all major materials were accumulated at or near the site before construction began. First, signs were removed and the canopy demolished as far as the storefronts; next, the ground was excavated for footing placements for the new canopy and, usually on the same day, the footings were poured. Stores were typically without signs for 30 days.

During construction, a concerted effort was made to avoid disrupting business. Trusses and heavy timber framing for the new canopy were fabricated at the rear of the site and at an off-site warehouse. Storage space on the site was kept to a minimum to avoid infringing on the parking area. Wood was stained off site and was only touched up after being put in place. Landscaping, widening, and other upgrading of the sidewalk took place when business would be least disrupted.

The average renovation of a section took three and one-half to four months. In the summer of 1977, the final piece of work was completed: the many old light standards in the parking area were replaced with fewer, 60-foot standards with mercury vapor lights.

Design Features

Renovation design was guided by three objectives the developer wished to achieve: a new canopy that would better protect shoppers from the weather and better define the walkway; an architectural character

that would appeal to the shopper; and a system of store identification signs that would be understandable to the customer but still subordinate to the overall center design. Limits were imposed on these objectives by the existing lease obligations and by the need to keep sales from suffering during construction. Improvements in on-site circulation of vehicles was limited by the narrowness of the site and the location of the original buildings. Nevertheless, some renovation was possible in the parking area: besides the installation of new lights and light standards, concrete islands were taken out to make snow removal easier, several landscaped islands were added, and the fire lane in front of the stores was reduced in width from 35 to 29 feet. Reducing the fire lane created space for more convenient pickups, or for landscaped areas to

4-13   Attractive canopies protect shoppers from the weather.

107

4-14 Towers provide vertical relief and are part of the center's overall sign system.

4-15 Signs are designed to be easily replaced.

separate pedestrian and vehicular traffic. The new design also decreased the traffic area shoppers have to cross while walking between the stores and their cars.

Canopies were designed to have one of two profiles. One is a framework of cedar posts and beams, cedar panels, and canvas sections; it is open and light and intricately detailed. The other consists of stuccoed, blocklike forms that rest on round concrete columns; this type has a simpler but more solid appearance and identifies the storefronts of most of the major tenants. Alternating the two canopy forms helped the scheduling of construction, and using two designs helped visually break up the length of the shopping center. In addition to the canopy work, the sidewalk was increased from a width of 8 to 10 feet to a width of 14 to 15 feet. Since these improvements were made, store owners have noticed an increase in pedestrian flow along the storefronts, a noticeable departure from the prerenovation pattern in which nearly all pedestrian movement was back and forth between the car and a particular store.

Signs at Town & Country carry only the stores' names and are styled in one of the two canopy profiles. Stucco canopy sections feature individual signs with backlighted letters up to 60 inches high. Wood frame sections have smaller plastic backlighted signs. Signs vary in size and placement according to whether they are meant to be read from the highway, the parking area, or the storefront, and store owners have the option of mounting a plastic sign on the face of a tower. These towers, in addition to being part of the overall sign system, provide vertical relief to the

otherwise entirely horizontal canopies. All signs are designed to be easily replaced.

Market and Merchants' Association

Town & Country is in the Columbus metropolitan area, which has a population of slightly over 1 million. The center's trade area comprises approximately 390,000 people and an average per capita income of $8,028. Town & Country has increased its market share considerably since the renovation: merchants at the center report that there has been an influx of new customers, and that sales between 1973 and 1976 increased from $63.66 to $84.52 per square foot of GLA. Sales for 1983 were $133.46 per square foot of GLA.

Town & Country has a nonprofit merchants' association, funded by merchants' contributions. The association promotes the center in general and sponsors seasonal promotional events, such as back-to-school sales. An important part of the renovation project was the renegotiation of leases to increase this contribution to better promote the center. Dues, which ran between $0.05 and $0.10 per square foot before the renovation, have gradually been increased to $0.25 to $0.30 per square foot. Common area charges have also been increased.

Experience Gained

● During construction, the developer must be sensitive to the needs of operating retailers. Unlike

4-16 Stucco canopy sections feature individual signs with backlighted letters.

4-17 Some storefronts underwent few changes.

that of conventional construction, the work area of a center under renovation must be shared with employees, customers, and deliverymen. Failure to preserve easy access can seriously damage the businesses.

- When possible, major construction components should be assembled away from the site.
- Rigid control of graphics is essential. The developer must stand his ground by persuading new and old tenants to buy signs that conform to the design guidelines.
- Important to renovation is the renegotiation of leases. When possible, the developer should increase minimum rents, common area charges, and merchants' association contributions, and should include lease provisions for store expansions and interior and storefront renovations. Financing of the center will be easier to obtain if the

developer has extended-term leases with the major tenants.

- The public should be informed that the center will remain open throughout construction, and the merchants should participate in a promotions program that emphasizes the "new" center or its "grand reopening."
- Heavy construction should be avoided in peak retail periods, such as the back-to-school and Christmas seasons. Ideally, construction would begin in early spring and end before September.
- A center can be remodeled in stages to test the design as well as the response of shoppers and prospective tenants.
- Store identification signs should be left in place as long as possible; work should be coordinated with fabricators of the new signs so that the signs may be installed as soon as construction permits.

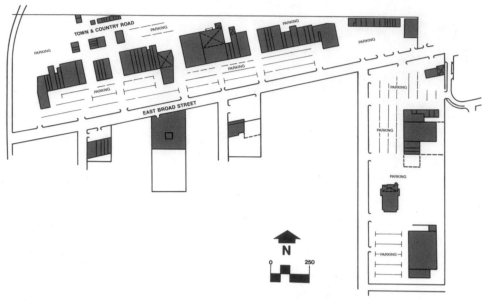

4-18

PROJECT DATA—TOWN & COUNTRY

Land Use Information:

Total Site Area: 45.7 acres (18.51 hectares)
Renovation Site Area: 28.0 acres (11.34 hectares)
Total Gross Leasable Area:[1] 500,024 square feet
Renovation GLA:[1] 380,317 square feet
Floor Area Ratio:[2] 0.25
Parking Spaces: 2,100
Parking Index: 4.2 spaces per 1,000 square feet of GLA

Land Use Plan:

	Acres	Percent of Project
Building Coverage	11.4	24.9
Parking, Loading, and Paving	33.4	73.1
Sidewalks and Landscaping	0.9	2.0
Total Site Area	45.7	100.0

Economic Information:

Site Improvements:[3] $50,000
Canopy Construction:
Range: $125 to $500 per front foot
Average: $241.67 per front foot

Total Renovation Cost: $570,120[4]

Pro Forma Statement:

	Before Renovation	After Renovation
Income:		
Rent Minimum	$678,681	$1,106,405
Rent Overage	175,431	193,254
Common Area Charges	20,147	46,282
Total Income	$874,259	$1,345,941
Expenses:		
Taxes	$ 77,450	$ 91,900
Insurance	19,400	29,250
Maintenance and Repairs	74,770 ($0.15/ square foot)	124,617 ($0.25/ square foot)
Legal, Accounting, and Miscellaneous	3,000	6,000
Total Expenses	$174,620	$ 251,767
Net Operating Profit	$699,639	$1,094,174
Debt Service:		
Original Loan No. 1	$ 27,420	$ 27,420
Original Loan No. 2	49,000	–
Original Loan No. 3	144,000	–
New Loan ($1,250,000 at 9.5% for 20 years)	–	139,825
New Loan (Kroger $700,000)	–	71,936
Amortize Remodel Expense (New Leases—$441,000 at 9% for 12 years)	–	61,600
Total Debt Service	$220,420	$ 300,781
CASH FLOW	$479,219	$ 793,393

Sales and Operation:

	Before Renovation (1973)	After Renovation (1976)	After Renovation (1983)
Sales per Square Foot of GLA	$63.66	$84.52	$133.46
Tenant Lease Rates			
Percent of Gross Sales	1%–6%	1%–6%	1%–6%
Minimum Guarantee per Square Foot of GLA[5]	$1.25–$2.50	$3.00–$5.00	$5.00–$7.00
Merchants' Association Dues per Square Foot of GLA	$0.05–$0.10	$0.20–$0.25	$0.25–$0.30
Common Area Charges per Square Foot of GLA[6]	$0.15	$0.25	$0.25

Tenant Information:

Classification[7]	Number of Stores	Percent of Total Tenants	Square Feet of GLA	Percent of GLA	Average Percent of GLA in Community Centers[7]
General Merchandise	4	4.5	54,384	10.8	38.5
Food	3	3.4	59,950	12.0	14.1
Food Service	10	11.2	19,242	3.8	5.2
Clothing	16	18.0	126,359	25.3	7.4
Shoes	2	2.2	7,640	1.5	2.2
Home Furnishings	2	2.2	6,250	1.2	2.5
Home Appliances/Music	–	–	–	–	2.4
Building Materials/Garden	2	2.2	17,500	3.5	2.2
Automotive Supplies/Service Station	1	1.1	9,186	1.8	1.1
Hobby/Special Interest	2	2.2	18,000	3.6	2.1
Gifts/Specialty	1	1.1	16,500	3.3	2.1
Jewelry and Cosmetics	3	3.4	3,345	.7	.9
Liquor	1	1.1	5,000	1.0	.6
Drugs	2	2.2	15,500	3.1	5.2
Other Retail	12	13.5	36,109	7.2	3.1
Personal Services	15	16.9	32,002	6.4	2.9
Recreation/Community	–	–	–	–	3.2
Financial	3	3.4	9,383	1.9	2.5
Offices (other than financial)	1	1.1	2,300	.5	1.8
Other	1	1.1	17,287	3.5	–
Vacant	8	9.0	44,087	8.8	–
Total	89	100.0	500,024	100.0	100.0

Notes:

[1] In this project, gross building area equals gross leasable area (GLA).

[2] FAR equals total GLA divided by total site area.

[3] Includes new mercury vapor lighting and removal of concrete dividers.

[4] Includes architectural and engineering fees and direct costs such as field supervision and landscaping, but no developer overhead.

[5] Lower figures are medians for stores with 10,000 to 15,000 square feet; higher figures are medians for stores with 3,000 square feet.

[6] For maintenance of blacktop, concrete, and landscaping and for removal of snow and debris.

[7] Dollars & Cents of Shopping Centers: 1984 (Washington, D.C.: ULI–the Urban Land Institute, 1984), p. 272.

Developer/Management:
Don M. Casto Organization
209 East State Street
Columbus, Ohio 43215

Architecture/Planning:
Trott and Bean Associates
50 West Broad Street
Columbus, Ohio 43215

Pacific Plaza
Pacific Beach, California

Pacific Plaza is a 17-year-old community shopping center located in the center of Pacific Beach, a community that is a part of the city of San Diego. The developer purchased the center in 1974. Like many other linear centers of its era, Pacific Plaza had little landscaping, stark architectural features, and haphazard sign control.

The center has since undergone an extensive renovation that was designed not only to improve its physical appearance but also to replace its nondescript linear quality with the diversity and vitality of a downtown streetscape environment. Buildings have been given new exteriors constructed with a variety of materials; the site has been attractively landscaped; walkways and benches have been provided; and a nearly inaccessible courtyard has been converted to an outdoor eating area and the project's focal point.

The renovation is being undertaken in three phases—the first two of which have been completed. Phase I involved the renovation of 126,911 square feet. Phase II involved the conversion of a 24,750-square-foot Newberry's (which is located within Phase I) to nine shops containing 19,445 square feet. The final phase of the renovation, still to be undertaken, will involve the remodeling of approximately 69,000 square feet.

Before renovation, the center had been moderately successful. Although rents were relatively low, sales volumes were comparable to other centers in the area.

4-20   A nearly inaccessible courtyard was converted to an outdoor eating area and the project's focal point.

Since the renovation, however, the overall value of the project has increased significantly. The average sales revenue of those tenants who remained after the renovation has increased by more than 33 percent, and the rental return to the developer has increased by more than 40 percent.

The Site

The project occupies 12.75 acres in the commercial area of Pacific Beach at the northeast corner of the intersection of two major streets, Garnet Avenue, one of the two main streets in Pacific Beach, and Jewell Street, which serves the community's residential area and continues through to the well-known community of La Jolla. Traffic on Grant Avenue, the frontage street, averages 25,000 vehicles per day. At the rear of the site is a high- to medium-density residential area. The remaining development in the vicinity of the site is primarily strip commercial.

This section of the community's commercial area had been declining for some time. However, the renovation of Pacific Plaza has had a positive effect on the area. A substantial number of buildings in the immediate area have been either completely renovated or have been torn down and replaced by new buildings. A five-acre shopping center immediately adjacent to Pacific Plaza, across Jewell Street, was also completely renovated to maintain a competitive position. The cumulative effect of these renovations has been to change completely the visual appearance and the commercial vitality of a major portion of the Pacific Beach shopping area.

Renovation Strategy

The development and planning approach to the renovation and upgrading of the center included the following goals:

- to increase the use of the land;
- to upgrade the physical appearance of the site and the buildings;
- to increase the use of the existing buildings; and
- to upgrade the types of tenants and the tenant mix.

In order to accomplish these goals and to ensure the project's economic viability, it was necessary to establish an extremely intricate, phased construction program, which enabled all of the major tenants as well as the shop tenants to remain in business during renovation.

The initial planning studies indicated that the site was underused. In particular, the corner of the site, at the intersection of Garnet Avenue and Jewell Street, was totally vacant. The existing zoning on the site and the exhibits attached to the major tenant leases prevented the addition of any building area. The developer used planning and design studies for the renovation of the site and the buildings—including a proposal to construct a bank building at the corner—in negotiations with both the city and the major tenants. By presenting an overall development proposal, the developer obtained rezoning approval from the city of San Diego and the major tenant approvals that enabled the project to go forward. The developer also had to obtain parking and setback variances, as well as a Coastal Commission Permit from the state of California in accordance with its Coastal Plan. The process of obtaining the necessary permits, rezoning, and major tenant approvals took approximately one year. Constructing the bank building at the corner was important to the project's success. This building made the project economically feasible by providing the initial cash flow needed to underwrite the renovation program.

Because the existing site contained little landscaping (about 100 square feet) and the buildings, although structurally sound, were unattractive, even a minor renovation would have been somewhat dramatic. However, because of the center's strategic location and its high long-term value, it was decided that both the site and the buildings should be completely renovated, altering drastically not only the appearance but also the character of the center. As a result, a monotonous linear commercial development has taken on the flavor and diversity of a downtown streetscape.

Since the buildings were structurally sound, the developer could build around the existing structures, thus avoiding demolition and rebuilding and significantly reducing renovation costs. Tenants could also remain in operation throughout the entire renovation. New storefronts were developed to encase the existing storefronts, and a variety of forms and materials were used (including clay and Mexican tiles, wood shingles, ship-lay siding, and colored canvas awnings) in order to establish each tenant's identity. These varied materials provided texture, warmth, color, and contrast and created a higher-quality image for the project, which has attracted higher-quality tenants. Wood shingle and tile roofs were used in varying shapes to break up the roof masses. Arcades were constructed under the original canopies using wood columns, trellises, and vines, helping to orient the center toward pedestrians. Unique signage and graphics were adopted using wood-carved signs in a compatible variety of designs and colors, thus further identifying tenants.

The project was substantially landscaped on the perimeter of the site, in the parking lot, and adjacent to the buildings. Landscaped islands with vertical structures in the parking lot greatly improved the appearance of the parking area. Landscaping was also used to separate pedestrian and parking areas. Berms were created containing mature trees, grass, and a variety of plantings, and giving variety to the topography. Trees were sited so that they did not block storefronts and signs from view. A pedestrian atmosphere was created by providing walkways with decorative cobblestone paving, seating areas, carved wood directional signs, and low-level lighting.

The original design of the center had created a nearly inaccessible courtyard. The 14,000 square feet of space adjacent to the courtyard was either not

4-21, 4-22   The renovation has given a distinctively fresh character to the center.

leased or leased at extremely low rents. This problem was solved by enlarging the entrance to the courtyard, building additional leasable space with a visually striking exterior design, and developing a landscaped courtyard with a large outdoor eating area. The key to the success of this concept was finding a delicatessen and wine shop that would encourage the use of the outdoor eating area and stimulate pedestrian movement and interest. The entire courtyard area has been completely re-leased to specialty tenants.

The renovated courtyard serves as the focal point of the center. Landscaped berms, trees, planters, built-in benches, and tables provide a pleasant and visually exciting outdoor eating environment. Extending the building fronts and front doors into the courtyard area and providing awnings and canopies have made the various shops more visible and accessible and have increased their rental values. The wider courtyard entrance and the entrance signs have also drawn attention to the various shops.

The Phase II renovation—in which the developer, responding to strong demand from the Pacific Beach area for small shops, remodeled Newberry's space into nine shops—was intended to achieve higher rents and to further enhance the courtyard, attracting shoppers and creating a natural pedestrian flow into the area. The shops created in Phase II range in size from 600 to 1,300 square feet (with the exception of one 11,455-square-foot food store). Rents average approximately $14 per square foot.

Tenants

An aggressive leasing and "unleasing" program was pursued to upgrade the center's tenant mix. Tenants whose leases were expiring or were short term were

4-23 New facades encase the existing storefronts and a variety of forms and materials were used to give each tenant its own character and identity.

discouraged from staying. After nearly a year of tenant negotiations, although major tenants were retained (with the exception of Newberry's in Phase II), approximately 60 percent of the shop tenants were replaced. Many of the new tenants were basically mall-oriented but were attracted to the project because of the revitalization of the center and the neighborhood. During the lease negotiations, many of the existing tenants became actively involved in the renovation of the center, remodeling and refurbishing their own interiors. For example, one of the major tenants, a drugstore, spent $100,000 remodeling its interior.

Experience Gained

- Quality renovation of an existing community shopping center can attract higher-quality, soft-goods tenants who normally locate in a regional mall.
- The timing of leases is crucial to the success of a renovation project. The renovation must occur at the same time that leases are up for termination or renegotiation. This will provide maximum flexibility, allowing the developer to obtain the best tenants at the highest rents and to eliminate those tenants who are not compatible with the renovation plans.
- The developer decided against tenants' participating financially in the renovation of the center. Although this increased the developer's costs significantly, the developer could then request higher rents when renegotiating leases, thereby increasing the project's long-term profitability.
- When renovating structurally sound buildings, demolition costs can be avoided by burying the existing structures inside the new construction. This will also allow tenants to continue operating during renovation, an essential factor in assuring the project's economic viability.
- The key to dramatically changing the image of an older, linear shopping center is to create a downtown streetscape character. This can be accomplished by replacing the center's uniformity with diversity of form and materials. Such diversity will provide individual tenants with their own identities and will enable the center to serve as a focal point for the community.
- Unexpected problems will frequently arise during the actual renovation, sometimes resulting in significantly higher costs than originally estimated. For example, in the renovation of Pacific Plaza, the developer underestimated the cost of roof and HVAC repairs. The use of scaled photos of previous conditions can help save design time and estimate construction costs.

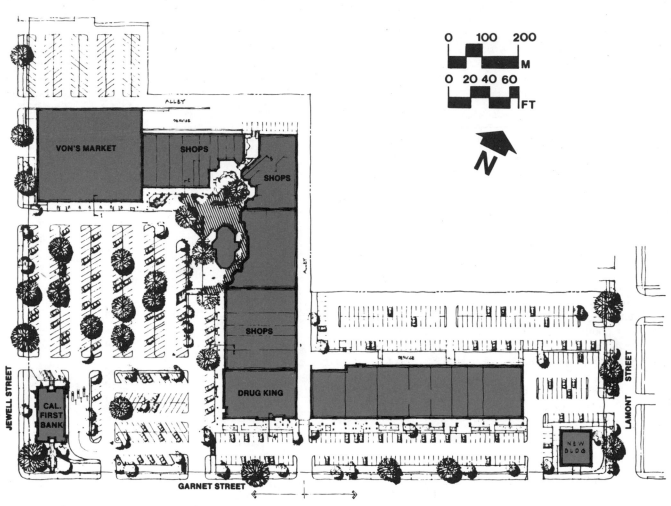

4-24

4-25

PROJECT DATA—PACIFIC PLAZA

Land Use Information:

Site Area: 12.75 acres (5.16 hectares)

Gross Building Area (GBA):[1] 121,606 square feet

Gross Leasable Area (GLA):[2] 191,095 square feet

Parking Spaces:[3] 741

Parking Index: 3.8 spaces per 1,000 square feet of GLA

Land Use Plan:

	Acres	Percent
Buildings	2.90	34.0
Parking	4.35	51.0
Landscaping	.68	8.0
Courtyard and Circulation	.60	7.0
Total	8.53[4]	100.0

Economic Information:

Site Acquisition Cost: $4.4 million (1974)

Site Improvement Cost:

Phase I:[5] $320,000

Phase II:[6] $89,000

Renovation Cost:

Phase I: $815,000

Phase II:[7] $729,000

New Construction Cost:[8] $310,000

Lease Information:

Sales: $148.50 per square foot

Rents:[9] $5.52 per square foot

Term: 2 to 5 years

Provisions: triple net

Merchants' Association Dues: $0.07 to $0.14 per square foot of GLA

Tenant Information:

Classification[10]	Number of Stores	Percent of Total Tenants	Square Feet of GLA	Percent of GLA	Average Percent of GLA in Community Centers[10]
General Merchandise	–	–	–	–	38.5
Food	2	5.0	37,400	19.5	14.1
Food Service	7	17.0	17,170	8.9	5.2
Clothing	5	12.0	14,967	7.8	7.4
Shoes	2	5.0	1,620	0.8	2.2
Home Furnishings	1	3.0	11,455	5.9	2.5
Home Appliances/Music	–	–	–	–	2.4
Building Materials/Garden	–	–	–	–	2.2
Automotive Supplies/Service Station	–	–	–	–	1.1
Hobby/Special Interest	1	3.0	7,000	3.6	2.1
Gifts/Specialty	2	5.0	6,145	3.2	2.1
Jewelry and Cosmetics	2	5.0	3,005	1.5	.9
Liquor	–	–	–	–	.6
Drugs	1	3.0	13,020	6.8	5.2
Other Retail	6	14.0	17,663	9.2	3.1
Personal Services	6	14.0	8,700	4.5	2.9
Recreation/Community	1	3.0	6,000	3.1	3.2
Financial	3	7.0	12,920	6.7	2.5
Offices (other than financial)	–	–	–	–	1.8
Other	2	5.0	34,030	17.8	–
Total	41	100.0	191,095	100.0	100.0

Notes:
[1] Total GBA for Phases I and II. The remodeling/conversion of Newberry's to nine shops in Phase II reduced the original Phase I GBA by 5,305 square feet (from 126,911 to 121,606 square feet).
[2] Total GLA for Phases I, II, and III.
[3] Includes 446 spaces in Phases I and II and 295 spaces in Phase III.
[4] Phases I and II only.
[5] Includes cost for landscaping, paving, lighting, courtyard, and amenities.
[6] Includes cost for excavation, sewer/water, curbs/sidewalks, landscaping, electrical/masonry, and miscellaneous.
[7] Cost for renovation/conversion of Newberry's. Equals $37.50 per square foot.
[8] Construction cost for 5,710-square-foot (GBA) bank building.
[9] Average minimum rent. Average rent including percentage rents is $6.83 per square foot.
[10] *Dollars & Cents of Shopping Centers: 1984* (Washington, D.C.: ULI—the Urban Land Institute, 1984), p. 272.

Developer:
La Jolla Development Company
P.O. Box 2388
La Jolla, California 92038

Architecture:
SGPA Planning and Architecture
P.O. Box 33326
San Diego, California 92103

Landscape Architecture:
J.J.J. Kennedy
3755 Ocean Front Walk
San Diego, California 92109

Green Acres Mall
Valley Stream, New York

When The Equitable Life Assurance Society of the United States and Kravco Company assumed control of the 19-year-old Green Acres Mall on Long Island in 1977, they inherited a regional shopping center in a prime location in a strong market area. They also inherited 1,363,000 square feet of physically decayed property with poorly designed mall space, a Korvette's store on the edge of bankruptcy, poor relations with the neighboring Alexander's department store, and competition from other malls that had significantly cut into Green Acres's market. Sales volumes were decent, but they had stabilized while competitive area mall sales had grown. By undertaking an innovative renovation, expansion, and remarketing effort in 1982, Kravco boosted the center's net operating income by 197 percent. Per square foot rents jumped 140 percent. Mean expenditure levels of shoppers were up 30 percent to 42 percent above the Benchmark national average.[3] Gross sales increased 50 percent, pushing up market share as well. Based on a 10 percent cap rate, which is conservative in today's active market, the $29 million investment immediately increased Green Acres's value to at least $60 million more than its original purchase price of $30 million. Its value continues to grow.

With The Equitable as an active owner and with Kravco as owner, developer, and managing agent, Green Acres Mall underwent multiple improvements: Korvette was replaced by Sterns; a new 144,377-square-foot Sears "Store of the Future" was introduced; a 276,188-square-foot, two-level mall housing an international food court and 70 additional shops was added; approximately 73 existing mall shops were converted into 96 shops; 150,000 square feet of space was abandoned; and a new parking structure and more on-site parking were built. At the same time, Kravco instituted modern mall management and marketing techniques aimed at encouraging, and, in fact, requiring, tenants to act together for advertising, promotions, and seasonal sales.

Location and Trade Area

Green Acres Mall is located both in the village of Valley Stream and in the township of Hempstead on Long Island, New York. Situated in Nassau County, Green Acres Mall is approximately 1,000 feet east of Queens, a borough of New York City. When the property was acquired in 1977, Hempstead was the largest township in the United States with a total population of approximately 851,000 and a land area of 142.6 square miles. During the 1950s, Hempstead grew 71 percent, and Levittown, Hempstead's largest community, became a synonym for rapid suburban growth. Hempstead's land area was almost completely developed by 1960 and, since then, its population has remained fairly constant, its slight growth averaging 0.34 percent annually.

---

[3]Kravco Company uses the Jones Report Benchmark, which represents the nationwide average for various shopping center characteristics. It is based on the last 20,000 consumer interviews during the most recent one-year period.

4-26, 4-27   Aerial view of Green Acres Mall before and after expansion and renovation.

The trade area for Green Acres has an irregular radius of four to six miles, or a maximum drive of 15 to 20 minutes, and contains approximately 1,300,000 people. The trade area spans Queens and Nassau Counties, both of which are noted for numerous densely arranged modest single-family homes and a high degree of owner occupancy. The area can be characterized as strongly middle-income with pockets of upper-middle-income households. Mean annual household income is $30,757, more than $5,000 higher than the national average of approximately $25,000. Although household income in Queens and Nassau ranked a healthy 108th and 45th respectively among the nation's counties in 1975, the major strength of the market area lies in the extreme density of the residential population. In 1975, Queens and Nassau Counties also ranked fourth and ninth nationally in total personal income. Within the two counties, approximately $4 billion was spent in 1983 on retail merchandise; retail sales growth has been strong—at over 11 percent annually during the early 1980s—despite the general nationwide recession.

Queens ranked among the 15 most important industrial areas in the United States in the late 1970s, with John F. Kennedy International and LaGuardia Airports being the primary employers. Waterfront commerce, principally petroleum-related, is another major source of employment. Grumman Aerospace is Nassau's single largest employer; Cutler-Hammer, Sperry Rand, and Singer also have divisions in the county. Nassau's industrial base has shifted from defense (in the 1950s) to a broader electronics base much more independent of cyclical economic swings in defense procurements. Unemployment in Nassau County is generally less than the national average, while in Queens it is about the same as the national average.

The Green Acres trade area mean age is 36.5, with the population of Queens somewhat younger than that of Nassau. The population comprises 64 percent whites, 29 percent blacks, and 7 percent other. Although the trade area population is expected to decline slightly in the future, the number of households with incomes ranging from $25,000 to $75,000 annually will increase 11 percent over the next five years. Since 84 percent of mall sales are made to this group, the center's already excellent performance is expected to improve even more in the near future.

Green Acres Mall is readily accessible through public and private transportation facilities. A Long Island railroad station serving local commuter traffic is one block north of the site, and the mall is visible from the train route. Green Acres Mall stands on the south side of Sunrise Highway, a major seven-lane divided high-

4-28　The open air mall before it was enclosed.

way that travels the length of Long Island and connects to New York City. The site has four entrances and exits—equipped with traffic signals—to and from Sunrise Highway. Southern State Parkway, a six-lane, limited-access, east/west highway is located one-half mile north of the site. The six-lane, limited-access Cross Island Parkway and the Laurelton Parkway one-quarter mile west of Green Acres connect the mall to the northerly sections of Queens and Nassau Counties. Local access is provided by Mill Road and Central Avenue, major north/south roads that converge at Sunrise Highway less than one-quarter mile east of Green Acres. South Terrace Place to the north of Sunrise Highway and numerous small roads connecting with the Green Acres perimeter loop road also provide local access to the site.

The Valley Stream neighborhood immediately surrounding Green Acres is considerably more affluent than the trade area as a whole. A large number of residents commute daily to their jobs in New York City. Southeast of the center are 200 garden apartment units that were developed at the same time as the original mall. Alexander's department store fronts on Sunrise Highway and is surrounded by the center on three sides. In addition, Green Acres Mall itself includes several retail outparcels. Single-family homes surround the rest of the site.

Project History

Green Acres Shopping Center was built in 1955–1956 and formally opened in 1958 as one of the first regional shopping centers in the United States. The Chanin Organization in New York City, headed by Irwin S. Chanin, designed and constructed the development and managed it until The Equitable purchased it in 1977. Gimbels, J.C. Penney, Woolworth, Grand Union and First National food stores, and Walgreen represent some of the nationally known major retail chains that had been tenants since 1957. There were 96 original tenants in all, and, in succeeding years, turnover was low with the shopping center virtually 100 percent occupied.

When Green Acres first opened, the open air mall was 70 feet wide with shops on each side and 10-foot-wide canopies projecting out over the storefronts. The mall was at grade level. The full basement below included a truck tunnel the full length of the mall, loading areas, storage, and sales space for J.C. Penney, Bonds, F.W. Woolworth, Gleicher, and Newberry's. The mall was enclosed and climate-controlled in 1970, although these structural changes were made with little sophistication and without major alterations to the canopy. The landlord invited store owners to move their storefronts forward to the edge of the canopy and occupy that space rent-free. Most of them did so, but the stores remained enclosed by glass storefronts as if they were in an open mall, and the signage remained the same. Storefronts were not uniform in design, and mall finish materials were low in quality.

Over the years the mall aged, maintenance became almost nonexistent, and no improvements were made. In 1977, swallows nested behind J.C. Penney and flew throughout the 35-foot-high mall space. The

original management perceived Alexander's as a threat to mall business, rather than a potential magnet, and built a 10-foot-tall fence separating it from the Green Acres parking lot. The mix of stores—with a significant lack of women's apparel shops—did not serve the market well. Many stores were too large, and sales volumes per square foot were lower than they should have been for the strong market area. Other shopping areas, including King's Plaza, the "Miracle Mile," Roosevelt Field, downtown Garden City, and Sunrise Mall, provided better tenant mixes and more attractive shopping facilities. Shoppers from the affluent area surrounding Green Acres stopped going to the center and were replaced by lower-income customers. By the late 1970s, the other competing shopping areas had significantly eroded Green Acres's market share.

The Equitable purchased the mall in 1977, when Gimbels, J.C. Penney, and Korvette's were the major anchors. Shortly thereafter, Kravco became an owner and assumed management and development responsibilities. At the time, the center also had 18 satellite stores, including Macy's Tire/Battery/Accessory, three restaurants, a theater, a bowling alley, the Grand Union and Finast (originally First National) food stores, a carpet store, and miscellaneous other retail stores.

Expansion and Renovation Process

The expansion and renovation program aimed to revitalize the antiquated shopping center and to enhance its sales, rents, and market share. Participants in the Equitable/Kravco joint venture wanted to bring back the affluent customers of the immediate and surrounding areas. They wanted to renovate and expand the dingy center into a modern shopping environment that both they and the community would be proud of and enjoy. They also wanted to keep the shopping center open during construction to maintain tenants, customers, and revenues.

The permit process for the renovation proved to be complex. Because Green Acres was located both in the village of Valley Stream and in the township of Hempstead, all major permits had to be secured from both governments. Regulations governing site development and the permit process itself varied between the entities. To ease the filing process, both governing bodies agreed that Hempstead would function as the leading agency. Thus, permits would first be filed in Hempstead, and adjustments required by Valley Stream, if any, would then be filed in Valley Stream. In spite of this difficulty with the permit process, construction began only six months after the first permit was filed.

4-29   The original mall enclosure in 1970 left stores enclosed by their individual glass storefronts and made no changes in the signage.

4-30, 4-31, 4-32, 4-33   The new two-level mall is anchored by Sears and contains 276,188 square feet of leasable space, including a food court.

Providing parking for the expansion presented a major problem. Existing parking stalls were uncomfortably narrow in width, varying from 7.5 to eight feet. They were restriped with widths of nine feet when the parking lot was resurfaced. To accommodate the expanded retail area and to make up for spaces lost in the restriping, additional parking spaces had to be provided. An old landfill site across the perimeter loop road from the shopping center was acquired to provide overflow parking for 2,322 cars. A new two-level parking structure adjacent to the new Sears provided another 393 spaces.

The parking expansion was so expensive that the joint venture elected to abandon 150,000 square feet of marginally productive leasable area in order to minimize the parking requirement. Space was abandoned in the basement and at the rear of the 185-foot-deep stores on the main level. Originally used for storage and secondary sales area, this space commanded very low rents. Its continued operation was infeasible since it would have required as much parking as prime retail sales space. In addition, major changes had occurred in retail marketing techniques during the 1960s and 1970s. By the late 1970s, mer-

120

chants could move the same volume of merchandise in 50 percent less sales space than was needed in the 1950s. Store sizes throughout the existing mall were trimmed to maximize sales per square foot while adding 31 percent more tenants.

The new two-level mall addition includes skylights, interior trees, fountains, tile flooring, oak benches, a glass-enclosed elevator, and 48-inch escalators. The contemporary design creates a handsome, glittering space full of light to enhance the shopping experience. The new mall, which is anchored by Sears, runs north/south and bisects the existing east/west mall. The old grade-level mall was renovated to complement the modern look of the expansion. Its 23-foot-high ceilings were lowered to 14 feet, and landscaped skylit courts were provided at intervals. The aging canopy, dating from the structure's open-air days, was removed, and unsightly storefronts and signs were also demolished and replaced. New lighting, flooring, planting, seating, and fountains were added to the renovated space.

Tenants were carefully selected to target better the needs of the trade area population. In particular, the original center had too few women's apparel stores, and those were directed at an older clientele. Women's apparel, particularly for young working women, is the lifeblood of the regional mall; this deficiency was corrected by bringing in several new stores. Average shopping trips to the old mall had been short, partly because of a lack of food concessions. The new food court was designed to lengthen overall shopping trips as well as to draw customers through the new section of the mall. For legal reasons, it was impossible to connect the new mall addition to the existing Alexander's department store, but the fence was removed. Ninety-three new shops were added to expand the array of choices available, based on the belief that shoppers will choose the largest mall, all other factors being equal. Anchoring the renovated and expanded center are Gimbels, J.C. Penney, Sterns, and Sears.

Management and Promotion

Immediately after The Equitable and Kravco became responsible for managing Green Acres Mall, they streamlined procedures for leasing and managing the center and for tracking and reporting mall sales. A comprehensive marketing program was begun, and a stronger merchants' association was activated. Tenant cooperation on sales events, promotion, advertising, and market research was encouraged, and then required, as leases were renewed. Poorly performing retail stores were shifted or replaced with more successful stores. Now tenants contribute $0.50 per square foot annually to the merchants' association,

with the mall owners contributing one-third of the annual budget. The merchants' association advertises in the print media 10 times a year, and tenants are required to advertise a specified number of times annually. Cooperative sales are organized nine times during the year, and in-mall promotional activities are held each month.

The grand opening for Green Acres Mall was held over a six-week period in October 1983 after 14 months of construction. The objective of the six-week gala was to introduce the shiny new expansion and renovation to old and new customers. It marked the kickoff of an energetic assault on the Nassau/Queens retail market. The grand opening promotion used television, radio, and print media as well as promotional events consisting of a ribbon cutting, live radio broadcasts from the mall, fashion shows, music, celebrity autograph signings, puppet shows, and special merchandising sales. This promotion was organized by Kravco management and the merchants' association, with the new and existing tenants contributing $0.40 and $0.20 per square foot respectively on a special one-time basis and the mall owners also contributing a substantial sum. Traffic and sales were overwhelming, and stores exceeded sales projections for the six-week period by 25 to 50 percent. The program was effective, and customers continued to shop at Green Acres Mall as stores reported increasing earnings. In addition to The Equitable and Kravco ongoing marketing and management programs, the expansion and renovation provided the final competitive edge Green Acres needed to maintain its marketing strength in the decade ahead.

4-34   The existing grade-level mall was renovated to complement the new mall.

Experience Gained

- Important to the renovation and expansion program was upgrading the tenant mix so that the center would appeal to all segments of the market. This included the addition of a Sears "Store of the Future," women's fashion stores, fashion accessories stores, a furniture store, and an international food court. Although the current tenant mix comprises approximately 80 percent chain stores and 20 percent local merchants, the developer believes that having the right local tenants will attract customers who might be unfamiliar with some of the national chain tenants just entering the market.

- The developer believes that the success of the expansion and renovation program can be attributed in part to the strict enforcement of design criteria established for tenant spaces to assure their compatibility with the overall mall design. Old signs were replaced and all existing storefronts were modernized.

- Many of the original stores were oversized. By reducing tenant spaces and adding new stores, the developer improved the tenant mix and maximized the center's rental income per square foot.

- Customers continued to shop at the center during the construction period, despite the inevitable inconveniences. Sales continued at a steady pace throughout this period.

- The large truck tunnel running beneath the mall was maintained and provides an efficient delivery operation.

- Because customers of the existing center had shown concern about safety measures, security was upgraded: new closed circuit cameras were installed in parking areas to provide continuous surveillance; the intensity of lighting in the parking area was doubled; paging and fire detection systems were installed throughout the mall; and new mobile communications equipment was provided.

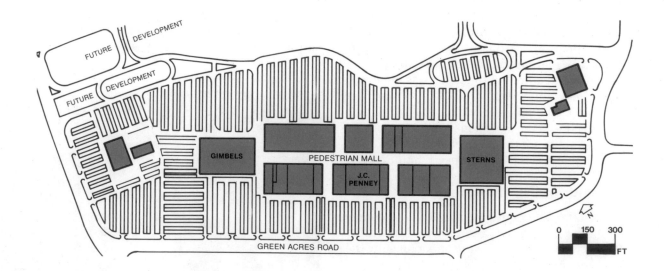

ORIGINAL GREEN ACRES PLAN—1956

4-35

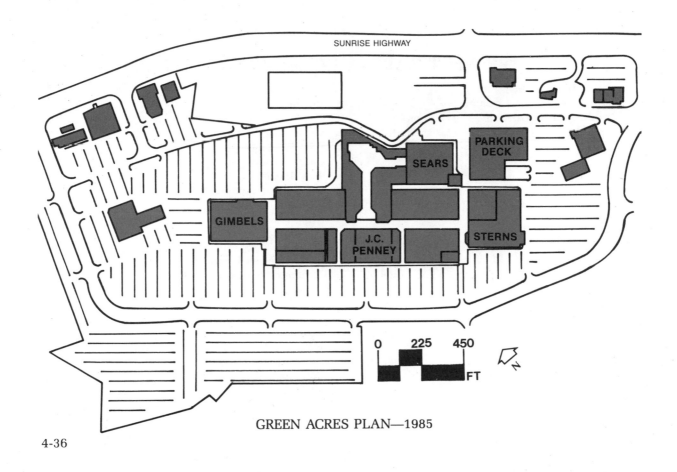

GREEN ACRES PLAN—1985

4-36

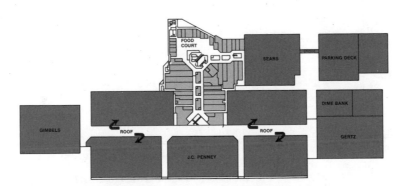

SECOND FLOOR LEASING PLAN—1985

4-37

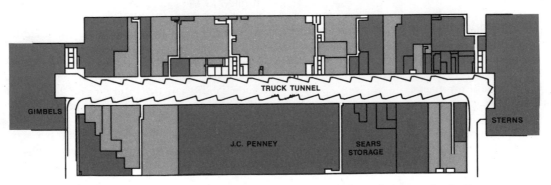

4-38   BASEMENT LEASING PLAN—1985 (abandoned space shaded)

PROJECT DATA—GREEN ACRES MALL

Land Use Information:

Site Area: 88.7 acres (37.9 hectares)
Gross Building Area (GBA): 1,792,677 square feet
Gross Leasable Area (GLA): 1,366,727 square feet
Parking:
Total Spaces: 7,407
Surface Spaces: 7,014
Structural Spaces: 393
Parking Index: 5.42 spaces per 1,000 square feet GLA

Economic Information:

Shopping Center Acquisition Cost:[1] $29,280,000
Hard Construction Costs:

Off-site Improvements	$ 284,573
On-site Improvements	2,185,896
Sears Parking Deck	2,168,768
S.W. Parking and Bulova Access	774,717
Electrical Distribution System	2,359,176
HVAC (New Mall)	1,335,669
HVAC (Existing Mall)	380,795
Shell Construction (New Mall)	6,463,995
Shell Construction (Existing Mall)	1,551,839
Tenant Work	105,286
New Mall Finishes	2,202,028
Existing Mall Finishes	1,329,848
Food Court	117,250
Office's Restrooms	79,306
General Conditions and Fees	2,464,350
Construction Management Fee	339,800
Total General Construction	$24,143,296
Additional Leasing Requirements	96,500
Permits	26,341
Offset S.W. Parking and Bulova	(193,217)
Site Utilities	361,704
Development Fee	100,000
Miscellaneous Finishing Cost	282,870
Common Area Equipment	155,257
Tenant Relocation Costs	1,082,735
Tenant Allowance—Net	(325,727)
Contingency	31,126
Total Hard Construction Costs	$25,760,885

Soft Costs:

Legal, Title, and Other	$ 688,051
Architectural and Engineering	2,059,615
Real Estate Taxes during Construction	400,000
Interest	1,041,449
Working Capital and Contingency	50,000
Total Soft Costs	$ 4,239,115
Total Project Cost	$30,000,000
Less Sears Recovery	1,000,000
Net Project Cost	$29,000,000

1984 Projected Statement of Operations:

Income:

Minimum Rent	$ 9,037,000
Percentage Rent	1,531,000
HVAC Net Income	198,000
Miscellaneous	50,000
Total Income	$10,816,000
Operating Expenses	1,842,000
Cash Flow from Operations	8,974,000
Other Receipts (or Disbursements)	(17,000)
Cash Flow	$ 8,957,000

1984 Projected Operating Expenses:

Common Area Expenses (Income):

Payroll	$ 419,000
Electricity	499,000
Repairs	133,000
Janitorial	47,000
Insurance	74,000
Security	321,000
Snow Removal	70,000
Others	59,000
Total Expenses	$ 1,622,000
(Income)	($ 1,519,000)

Total Operating Expenses:

Net Common Area Expenses	$ 103,000
Food Court—Net	(46,000)
Administrative Expenses	103,000
Repairs and Maintenance	55,000
Insurance	16,000
Professional Fees	25,000
Advertising—Contribution to Merchants' Association	71,000
Realty Tax	1,076,000
Management Fees	434,000
Miscellaneous	5,000
Total Operating Expenses	$ 1,842,000

Lease Information:

Sales:[2] $267 per square foot
Rents:[3] $24.65 per square foot
Term: 5 to 15 years
Provisions: All new mall leases are net (excluding taxes). All existing mall leases are to be converted to absolute net at or before lease expiration. Common area maintenance costs plus service and administration charges are allocated among mall tenants. Common area costs include liability and fire insurance on the mall. The cost of HVAC for common areas is included in common area maintenance.
Merchants' Association Dues:[4] $0.50 per square foot
Tenant Finishing Allowance: $5.08 per square foot (average)

Tenant Information:

Classification[5]	Number of Stores	Percent of Total Tenants	Square Feet of GLA	Percent of GLA	Average Percent of GLA in Super Regional Centers[5]
General Merchandise	3	1.5	143,284	18.5	7.3
Food	9	4.4	32,508	4.2	4.3
Food Service	28	14.0	84,169	10.9	9.0
Clothing	47	23.2	137,318	17.7	30.8
Shoes	22	10.8	51,578	6.7	9.3
Home Furnishings	13	6.4	46,477	6.0	2.3
Home Appliances/Music	9	4.4	23,799	3.1	3.8
Building Materials/Garden	1	.5	3,800	.5	.4
Automotive Supplies/Service Station	2	1.0	1,980	.3	.5
Hobby/Special Interest	8	3.9	33,853	4.4	4.9
Gifts/Specialty	9	4.4	26,808	3.5	6.6
Jewelry and Cosmetics	12	5.9	9,215	1.2	3.5
Liquor	1	.5	3,728	.5	.2
Drugs	1	.5	9,450	1.2	2.7
Other Retail	11	5.4	6,647	.8	3.9
Personal Services	6	2.9	8,282	1.1	2.1
Recreation/Community	3	1.5	18,351	2.4	4.2
Financial	4	1.9	105,398	13.6	2.2
Offices (other than financial)	3	1.5	4,711	.6	2.1
Other (vacant)	11	5.4	22,763	2.8	—
Total	203	100.0	774,119[6]	100.0	100.0

Notes:

[1] Including mortgage of $3,280,000.

[2] 1983 sales. Expansion and renovation opened in October 1983. The 1984 sales projection exceeds $300 per square foot.

[3] Average minimum rent.

[4] Mall tenants also paid a grand opening charge of $0.40 per square foot.

[5] *Dollars & Cents of Shopping Centers: 1984* (Washington, D.C.: ULI–the Urban Land Institute, 1984), p. 271.

[6] Total mall GLA. Excludes anchor tenants.

Developer/Owner/Manager:
Kravco Company
234 Goddard Boulevard
King of Prussia, Pennsylvania 19406

Owner:
The Equitable Life Assurance Society of the United States
1285 Avenue of the Americas
New York, New York 10019

Architecture:
GSGS&D
Clarks Summit, Pennsylvania 18411

Traffic Consultant/Civil Engineer:
Raymond Keyes Engineers, PC
Elmsford, New York 10523

General Contractor:
E.W. Howell Company, Inc.
Babylon, New York 11702

Soil Consultant:
Woodward Clyde Consultants
Plymouth Meeting, Pennsylvania 19462

Parking Deck Consultant:
Michael Dimitri
Ramp Engineering
Manhasset, New York 11030

Environmental Consultant:
Steven Gordan, Esquire
Tenafly, New Jersey 07670

Landscape Architecture:
McCloskey and Faber
Gibralter Road
Horsham, Pennsylvania 19044

Mazza Gallerie
Washington, D.C.

Mazza Gallerie, a 272,735-square-foot (GLA) enclosed, four-level center that opened in 1977, originally positioned itself as one of the finest collections of shops and boutiques in Washington, D.C. From its inception, the center was assured of a unique role in the market. Not only was it anchored by the area's sole Neiman-Marcus store, but the tenant list also included some of the most prestigious local and international retailers on the East Coast. Furthermore, the center's location in the Washington, D.C., metropolitan area featured excellent access and proximity to top residential neighborhoods. With ample indoor parking and a prime site at the intersection of Wisconsin and Western Avenues, the center was strategically located to serve a trade area of approximately 290,000 people with a median household income of more than $39,000. Finally, Mazza Gallerie's distinctive white marble facade and four-level atrium combined to make a bold architectural statement. It seemed that the interdependent elements of location, tenant mix, and physical appearance would guarantee the success of the center.

Unfortunately, the project was not an immediate success. In spite of the inherent drawing power of Neiman-Marcus, the center did not attract an acceptable customer volume, nor did the stores prosper. Competing prestigious retailers in the surrounding area continued to capture shoppers and sales dollars.

In 1981, the original developer sold Mazza Gallerie to 5300 Wisconsin Avenue Joint Venture, whose managing partner is the Prudential Insurance Company of America. Shortly thereafter, Prudential selected Goodman Segar Hogan, Inc., as the leasing, property management, and development firm to emphasize the center's unique characteristics and to maximize the value of the property for the owner.

Several problems were diagnosed, especially in the tenant and merchandise mix and physical plan of the center. The initial leasing effort resulted in a mix that only partially reflected the image of Mazza Gallerie and the needs of the affluent trade area. Of equal importance, the travertine-clad structure appeared as a giant, uninviting "abstract sculpture" with poorly defined entrances. The bright white interior spaces were stark and not conducive to a pleasant shopping environment, while interior and exterior signs and graphics were confusing. The first floor was barren and underused. The center was inefficient for all concerned—landlord, merchants, and customers alike—and it represented a special opportunity for change. Correcting this multifaceted problem required a development program that would create the appropriate environment to re-lease space to the right mix of retail tenants and to draw shoppers.

The physical renovation of Mazza Gallerie began in August 1982 and was substantially completed before the Christmas season, on schedule and under budget. The revision of the center's tenant mix, which required more time, was largely accomplished by the spring of 1984.

4-40, 4-41 The center's renovation was designed to create a new architectural theme that would "soften" the center's appearance. A turn-of-the-century Viennese design was used, featuring black and white ceramic tile accents.

4-42, 4-43 The main entrance was enlarged and enclosed with a 47-foot-high glass curtain wall—enabling passersby to see retail activity inside the building.

The Site and Trade Area

Mazza Gallerie occupies an 83,294-square-foot site at the southwest corner of Wisconsin Avenue and Western Avenue near the Washington, D.C./Maryland boundary. Wisconsin Avenue, a major retail corridor, provides direct access to downtown Washington and Georgetown to the south as well as to Interstate 495 (the Capital Beltway) to the north. The center is also easily reached by subway. Approximately 25,000 riders each day use the nearby Friendship Heights Metro station, which opened in August 1984.

The center's trade area encompasses a major part of northwest Washington, D.C., south central Montgomery County, Maryland, northern Arlington County, Virginia, and northeastern Fairfax County, Virginia. It included 120,700 households in 1980 with an estimated average household income of $39,000. More than 25 percent of the homes in the trade area had annual incomes exceeding $50,000 in 1980, while 59 percent had incomes in excess of $25,000. The trade area extends 10 miles from its southeastern corner to its northern and western extremities, and its population in 1980 was 288,289. Major competitive shopping centers include Georgetown Park (177,000 square feet) in Washington, D.C., White Flint Mall (800,000 square feet) in Kensington, Maryland, and Tysons Corner (1 million square feet) in McLean, Virginia.

Physical Renovation

The center's physical renovation evolved around the need for a distinctive new architectural theme that would simultaneously "soften" the appearance of the center and reinforce the image of retail sophistication while increasing the center's overall productivity. A turn-of-the-century Viennese design was selected in which the bold lines of the building were accented by a black and white ceramic tile pattern placed at eye level along the exterior facade, at each entrance, and on interior columns at major points of circulation. The tiles provide a visual bridge between the outside and inside areas of the building, and they lead shoppers to elevators and escalators to make circulation easier and more apparent.

The atrium was painted beige, and custom wall sconces were installed at all levels in the atrium. The skylight, which was originally the source of a distracting glare, was fitted with a special screen to diffuse sunlight. Glass balustrades with brass highlights were installed around the atrium. Once a forgotten area, the top floor—newly carpeted, lighted, and sporting other finishes—has become an attractive destination.

The final transformation involved the first floor of the atrium, where a restaurant on an elevated platform was added, providing a central meeting place. The new tile motif was used on the platform, maintaining design continuity.

4-44 The atrium was painted beige and custom-made wall sconces were installed at all levels.

The development team undertook an extensive landscaping and streetscaping program—relocating utility lines underground; building new sidewalks; installing benches and special street lights; and planting trees. Because trees were spaced in conformance with local standards and traditional District of Columbia street lights were used, the center could become an integral part of the Wisconsin Avenue corridor. At the same time, replacing the solid concrete sidewalks and curbs with concrete aggregate, brick pavers, and granite curbing, subtly enhanced the center's individuality.

Exterior signs were revamped and incorporated into the design of the facade, and entrances were flanked with brass logotypes. The main entrance on Wisconsin Avenue, formerly a dark, recessed opening with no focus, was enlarged and enclosed by a glass curtain wall 47 feet high. This expanse of glass served the twofold purpose of creating an attractive two-story vestibule as well as enabling passersby to see retail activity inside the building. A custom-woven tapestry decorates the vestibule. The new entrances feature tile-faced canopies.

New signage inside the center has improved customer circulation. Brass-framed directories have replaced mall signs, and access to the underground parking garage is now clearly marked with simple, bold signs. Lighting levels within the garage were also increased, and the garage was color-coded so that customers can easily locate their cars.

To assure continuity in the mall's design, tenants must comply with strict sign controls. However, other design elements (such as the use of spherical glass and pop-out entries) allow tenants some flexibility within certain limits.

Tenant Mix

In addition to the extensive changes in the center's physical appearance, the renovation concentrated on dramatically improving the tenant mix. The main objective was to improve the center's image in order to attract new tenants and strengthen the relationship among existing tenants. Neiman-Marcus continues to anchor the Mazza Gallerie (it is the only Neiman-Marcus store between New York and Georgia), which features a mix of high-end fashion and specialty stores, including local and international retailers, as well as quality restaurants. In order to optimize sales volumes, some existing tenants were relocated. For example, the Pleasant Peasant, an Atlanta-based restaurant, was moved to the central atrium, and the center's third floor was made a fashion level, including a skin and beauty care center and four women's couturier shops. Some of the other tenants at the Mazza Gallerie include a gourmet cookware and cut-

4-45 An extensive landscaping and streetscaping program added trees, special street lights, benches, and new sidewalks. Utility lines were relocated underground.

lery shop, an upscale toy retailer, a men's clothier, and a home furnishings and fabric retailer.

Marketing

The objectives of the marketing program are to reflect the center's desired high-quality cosmopolitan image; showcase the stores; make shoppers more aware of the location and services of the center; and increase the center's market share within the trade area, its affluent out-of-town customer traffic, and the length of time shoppers spend in the Mazza Gallerie.

Promotions involve the participation of the center's merchants, high-quality performing and visual artists, media, and/or media-sponsored community groups. Promotional events include store merchandise presentations, concerts, art shows, theatrical performances, and black-tie fundraisers for worthy nonprofit organizations. All promotions are publicized by the advertising and invitations of participants, and by television, radio, and/or print media.

The center's advertising includes the use of radio, in-house signage, and local publications. All advertising is produced in-house to guarantee quality control, to reduce merchants' association costs, and to generate free advertising through the negotiations of advertising trades with the media and with major corporations.

The affairs and activities of the merchants' association are conducted and managed by its board of directors, the members of which are elected at an annual meeting of the association. The association employs a director of marketing and public relations to design and produce promotions, advertising, and publicity, and to plan the annual budget spending.

The board of directors meets monthly to report on customer response to the Mazza Gallerie and the center's promotional events and advertising; to share concepts and strategies on how to better serve Mazza Gallerie customers, increase the center's image, its customer traffic, and ultimately its gross sales; to review and approve the scheduling and production of the center's promotional events and advertising; and to review and approve the budgeting of the association's funds.

The association's income is derived from merchants' monthly dues ($0.50 per square foot of store space, with the exception of Neiman-Marcus), a Neiman-Marcus voluntary contribution, the landlord's required matching funds (25 percent of the total merchants' dues and contributions), and the landlord's voluntary contribution. The association's 1984 budget was approximately $176,000.

4-46 Lighting levels within the garage were increased and the garage was color-coded so that customers could easily identify their parking areas.

Experience Gained

- The physical appearance and design impact of a center may be altered dramatically by introducing high-quality materials and finishes. However, a well-conceived and integrated program of individual components (such as lighting, graphics, project theme, landscape materials, and signage) is essential.
- The budget and schedule for a renovation should be sufficiently flexible to allow for unexpected conditions encountered in the field.
- The renovation work must be carefully planned so that it will not disturb operations of existing stores. In this regard, the redevelopment team should establish a strong personal liaison with all existing tenants affected by the renovation work. In particular, the construction contractor must recognize the importance of maintaining good relations with tenants and respond to the developer's requests to accommodate existing tenants.
- The mall management staff should be involved in all planning and construction decisions. This will ensure smoother progress toward completion of the renovation.
- In order to reposition and remerchandise the center successfully, the Mazza Gallerie team had to improve the tenant mix not only by attracting new tenants but also by relocating existing tenants to strengthen their synergetic relationship.
- The developer must define precisely the objectives of the physical renovation and remerchandising of the center and carefully review these goals with the architect. Design review meetings should be held regularly with cost estimates provided by the construction manager to keep the design within the construction budget.

MAZZA GALLERIE FLOOR PLANS

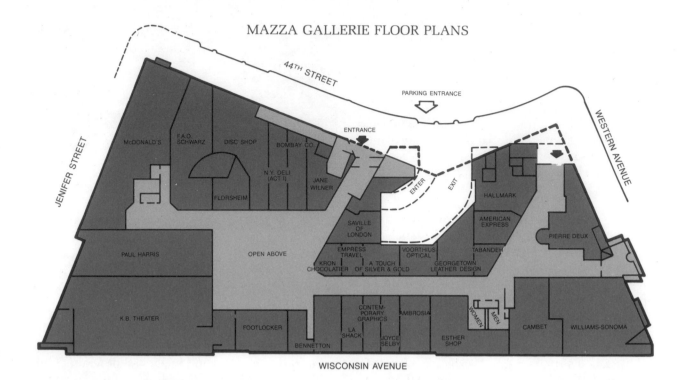

GARDEN LEVEL

4-47

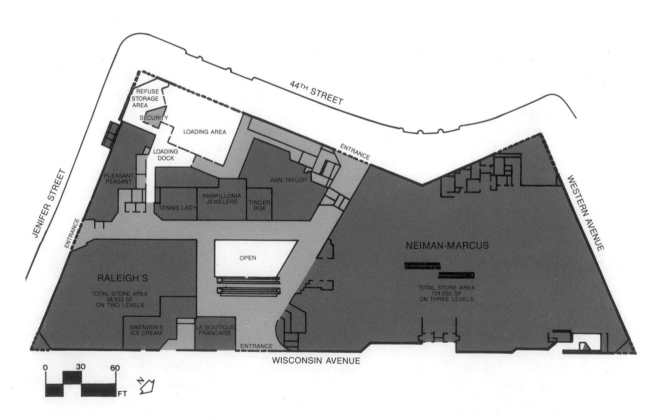

FIRST LEVEL

4-48

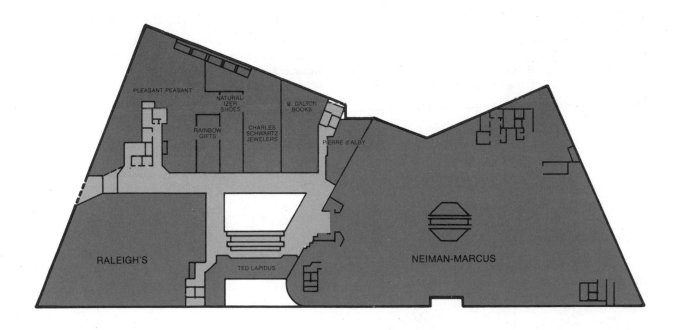

SECOND LEVEL

4-49

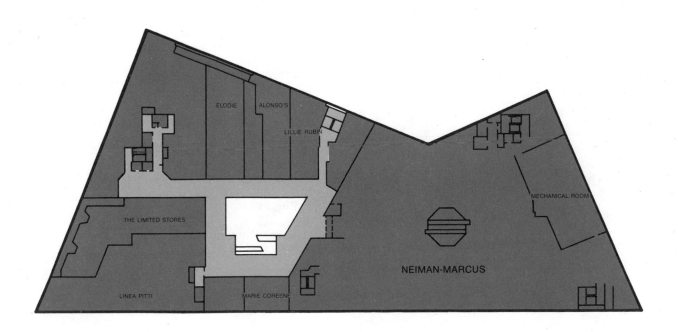

THIRD LEVEL

4-50

PROJECT DATA—MAZZA GALLERIE

Land Use Information:
Site Area: 1.91 acres (.77 hectares)
Gross Building Area (GBA): 320,748 square feet
Gross Leasable Area (GLA): 272,735 square feet
Parking Spaces: 865

Merchants' Association Budget (1984):

Merchants' Dues	$ 54,000
Neiman-Marcus Voluntary Contribution ...	9,996
Landlord 25 Percent Matching Funds	15,999
Landlord Voluntary Contribution	96,000
Total	$ 175,995

Lease Information:

Sales:[2] $151.32 per square foot
Minimum Rents:[3] $14.55 per square foot
Percentage Rents: 4.5 percent of gross sales
Term: 5 years (average)
Provisions: Net; all leases have escalator clauses.

Economic Information:
Total Renovation Cost:[1] $2,700,000
Income (1983):

Minimum Rents	$2,561,040
Percentage Rents	148,156
Common Area Charges	588,456
Advance Payments	108
Miscellaneous Income	170,766
Tenant Paid Expense	5,364
Amortization	1,014
Storage Charge	4,213
Parking	63,788
Security Deposit	2,250
Total Income	$3,545,155

Expenses (1983):

Contract Cleaning	$ 77,291
Cleaning Supplies and Materials	3,085
Waste Removal	21,675
Electricity	246,047
Water-Sewer	17,108
Grading, Landscaping/Grounds Conditioning	30,967
Gardening, Landscaping, and Grounds	4,375
Parking and Garage	20,793
Security Contract Service	138,410
R&M Labor	63,010
R&M Electrical	27,873
R&M Plumbing	8,351
R&M HVAC	23,152
R&M Elevator and Escalator	57,136
R&M Structural and Roof	7,130
R&M Parking and Garage	4,190
R&M Other Building Maintenance	27,413
Administrative Labor	23,170
Office Expenses	16,633
Advertising and Promotion	65,656
Management Fees	121,267
Other Professional Fees and Licenses	67,685
Association Dues	78,028
Other Administrative Expenses	18,198
Capital Improvements	35,068
Total Expenses	$1,203,711

Total Operating Profit (1983): $2,341,444

Tenant Information:

Classification[4]	Number of Stores	Percent of Total Tenants	Square Feet of GLA	Percent of GLA	Average Percent of GLA in Regional Centers[4]
General Merchandise..............	1	1.8	124,000	45.4	14.1
Food...........................	2	3.5	1,947	0.7	8.8
Food Service	5	8.8	19,756	7.2	7.0
Clothing	18	31.6	65,914	24.2	24.9
Shoes..........................	4	7.0	4,880	1.8	6.8
Home Furnishings	3	5.3	6,734	2.5	1.8
Home Appliances/Music	2	3.5	3,162	1.2	2.9
Building Materials/Garden..........	–	–	–	–	1.6
Automotive Supplies/Service Station	–	–	–	–	1.0
Hobby/Special Interest	1	1.8	3,512	1.3	3.8
Gifts/Specialty	5	8.8	10,727	4.0	5.2
Jewelry and Cosmetics	3	5.3	5,758	2.1	2.8
Liquor	–	–	–	–	.4
Drugs..........................	1	1.8	775	0.3	3.7
Other Retail	1	1.8	587	0.2	4.1
Personal Services	4	7.0	5,224	1.9	2.3
Recreation.......................	1	1.8	7,579	2.8	3.8
Financial........................	–	–	–	–	3.0
Offices (other than financial)........	1	1.8	803	0.3	2.1
Other (available)	5	8.8	11,377	4.2	–
Total...........................	57	100.0	272,735	100.0	100.0

Notes:
[1] Includes hard and soft renovation costs.
[2] Average estimated sales for 1983.
[3] Average minimum rents as of January 1984.
[4] *Dollars & Cents of Shopping Centers: 1984* (Washington, D.C.: ULI–the Urban Land Institute, 1984), p. 271.

Development Director:
Goodman Segar Hogan, Inc.
P.O. Box 2700
Norfolk, Virginia 23501

Owner:
5300 Wisconsin Avenue Joint Venture/Prudential Life
  Insurance Company of America
Prudential Plaza
Newark, New Jersey 07101

Architecture:
RTKL Associates, Inc.
400 East Pratt
Baltimore, Maryland 21202

King of Prussia Shopping Complex Upper Merion Township, Pennsylvania

The King of Prussia Shopping Complex is located in Upper Merion Township, Pennsylvania, approximately 18 miles, or a 30-minute drive northwest of the center city area of Philadelphia. In its present configuration, the complex consists of two separate enclosed malls, King of Prussia Plaza and The Court at King of Prussia, totaling approximately 2,460,000 square feet of GLA and including seven department stores and on-site parking for over 12,000 cars. The malls are physically separated by a public street, Goddard Boulevard, although the developer constructed a bridge over the street to make the two malls easily accessible to one another.

Currently, the Kravco Company and The Equitable Life Assurance Society of the United States jointly own the two centers. Both properties were originally developed by two predecessors of the Kravco Company—The Plaza by the M. A. Kravitz Company, Inc., and The Court by Kravco, Inc.

The development of the King of Prussia complex was originally conceived in 1959 and took place in five phases over the next quarter of a century, with the final phase of the current development being completed in the fall of 1983. The developer at first planned the project as a discount community shopping center. It was originally developed as an open mall with two department stores, a Woolworth variety store, and a supermarket as anchor tenants, and, after four successive expansion programs undertaken by its owners, grew into a super regional shopping complex with seven department stores and approximately 325 malls shops and service businesses, thereby offering its customers the broadest possible range of merchandise available at a single location in a suburban setting. In fact, the number of retail stores and the diversity of merchandise offered to customers exceed the amount of retailing available in the downtown of all but the largest cities in the United States.

The evolution of this complex took place over 25 years and represents a unique success story in the history of the shopping center development industry in America. Moreover, to a great extent, King of Prussia's development embodies the entire spectrum of both the problems and the opportunities that a developer often encounters in the process of planning, construction, leasing, marketing, and managing shopping centers. The original development and four subsequent renovations/expansions of the complex took place over such a protracted period of time that virtually all the architectural and design standards,

construction practices, and merchandising concepts that were characteristic of shopping center development during a given "generation" in the evolution of the industry are represented by one of the five phases of King of Prussia's development. The original buildings are representative of early shopping center design and leasing practices; however, as the state-of-the-art grew more sophisticated over the next two decades, subsequent phases progressively reflected more contemporary design and leasing standards.

4-52   EXPANSION AND RENOVATION CHRONOLOGY

Phase I: Original Development (1959–1963)
- Construction of 725,000-square-foot (GLA) open mall (King of Prussia Plaza) anchored by E.J. Korvette and J.C. Penney.

Phase II: Expansion of The Plaza (1963–1966)
- Addition of two department stores—John Wanamaker and Gimbels.
- Construction of two-level enclosed mall to increase The Plaza to approximately 1.3 million square feet (GLA) with 140 stores.

Phase III: The Court at King of Prussia (1976–1981)
- Construction of 963,000-square-foot (total GLA) fashion mall—anchored by Bambergers, Bloomingdale's, and Abraham and Straus and containing 250,000 square feet (GLA) of mall shops (approximately 123 stores).
- Construction of three-level parking structure with approximately 3,000 spaces.
- Construction of bridge between The Court and The Plaza.

Phase IV: Renovation of The Plaza (1979–1980)
- Enclosure of original 725,000-square-foot open mall.
- Redesign of tenants' storefronts.
- Reconstruction of four mall entrances.
- Construction of 23,000 square feet of new GLA.
- Removal/renovation of three auto accessory stores.
- Conversion of office areas to retail space.

Phase V: Expansion of The Plaza (1980–1983)
- Termination of E.J. Korvette lease.
- Addition of 215,000-square-foot Sears store.
- Addition of 140,000 square feet (GLA) of mall shops, including 25,000-square-foot food court.

4-53 The complex contains approximately 2,460,000 square feet of GLA, including seven department stores and on-site parking for over 12,000 cars.

The developer undertook each renovation and expansion phase in response to four prevailing circumstances:

- The population growth in suburban communities located west and northwest of Philadelphia;
- The impact of competitive retail developments (both existing and proposed) in King of Prussia's primary or secondary trading areas;
- Changes in consumer shopping habits or merchandise preferences (observed by the developer over an extended period of time); and
- The opportunities presented when three full-line quality department stores decided to enter the Philadelphia market, as well as other leasing opportunities made possible by the growth in the number of successful mall tenants (many being chains) over a long period of time.

The Site

King of Prussia is a post office address, not a governmental jurisdiction. It is located in Upper Merion Township, Montgomery County, Pennsylvania—approximately three miles east of the Valley Forge National Historical Park. Local legend has it that the center was named in honor of Fredrick Von Steuben, who was the king of Prussia when that country lent military support to General Washington and the American patriots who were camped at Valley Forge during the winter of 1777–1778. Upper Merion Township has a current population of 31,000.

The economic viability of King of Prussia as a hub for successful retailing was made possible from the beginning and through four redevelopment and expansion programs by the site's excellent access to the highway system and to a broad market of shoppers.

Specifically, the King of Prussia shopping complex is located at the junction of three of the most important highways in southeastern Pennsylvania—the Pennsylvania Turnpike (I-476), the Schuylkill Expressway (I-76), and U.S. Route 202. The Pennsylvania Turnpike is a four-lane, divided toll road crossing the entire state of Pennsylvania in an east/west direction from New Jersey to the Ohio state line near Pittsburgh. The Schuylkill Expressway is the major limited-access highway connecting Center City Philadelphia with all the affluent suburban residential areas northwest of Philadelphia. It intersects with the Pennsylvania Turnpike at the King of Prussia/Valley Forge exit, which is the busiest interchange in the turnpike system. U.S. Route 202 and Pennsylvania Route 363 provide primary access to the site. The King of Prussia Plaza fronts on Route 363, and The Court at King of Prussia fronts on Route 202. Route 202 extends southwestward from King of Prussia through Chester County and into Wilmington, Delaware, approximately 30 miles southwest of King of Prussia. Running northeast, U.S. Route 202 carries traffic past the King of Prussia shopping complex through Norristown and through other areas of Montgomery County. Route 202 is especially important to King of Prussia because it bisects the growth areas of Chester County, southwest of the shopping centers, where new office buildings, new research and development facilities, and high-quality residential development are concentrated. Route 363 is a feeder road providing primary access from several of the suburban communities in the immediate vicinity of King of Prussia to the shopping complex. This excellent highway network was directly responsible for creating a location in which retailing and other commercial activity in and around the King of Prussia/Valley Forge area could thrive.

The site consists of two parcels of land, with The Plaza built on one parcel of approximately 92 acres and The Court on a second parcel of about 34 acres. Soil conditions on both sites posed a problem for the developer: a limestone belt and numerous "sink holes" underlay the surface, requiring extraordinary foundation design. In addition, two natural streams were located on The Plaza site. The developer relocated one stream, placing it at the perimeter of the site, and enclosed the second stream, which runs beneath a portion of the building areas. The land on which The Court was built was a natural floodplain and required extensive soil replacement and the relocation and enclosure of a stream flowing through the property.

The Trade Area

The primary trade area supporting the shopping centers has a total population of some 500,000, with

4-54   John Wanamaker opened in The Plaza in 1965.

approximately 160,000 households. Shoppers who live in King of Prussia's primary market can reach the malls in less than 20 minutes' driving time. Families having all levels of disposable income characterize this market. The towns of Bridgeport and Norristown northeast of the center are made up largely of middle-class or working-class households. Similarly, Conshohocken, to the east of the complex, is primarily a working-class residential and industrial community.

To the south, southeast, and southwest of King of Prussia are a number of communities known collectively as the "Main Line," a generic expression describing those communities that grew up around station stops along the "main line" of the Pennsylvania Railroad, which extends from its main station in Center City Philadelphia through the western suburbs of Philadelphia, and through Lancaster, Harrisburg, and beyond. The Pennsylvania Railroad (now operated by the Southeastern Pennsylvania Transportation Authority, "SEPTA") always offered commuter service to and from the city of Philadelphia, and the communities with station stops on the main line grew into affluent suburban areas. These communities include Bala Cynwyd, Wynnewood, Merion, Ardmore, Haverford, Bryn Mawr, Rosemont, Villanova, Radnor, St. Davids, Wayne, Strafford, Devon, Berwyn, and Paoli. Many of these names are famous throughout the country, conveying an image of gracious living. Household incomes in these communities average from $40,000 to $50,000, with many substantially higher. Similarly, housing values traditionally range from $125,000 to $250,000, with many houses costing much more.

Commercial development in the King of Prussia/ Valley Forge area has been an important influence on the long-term success of the shopping centers, as well as on the character of the area in general. Over 5 million square feet of office space, numerous industrial buildings, and approximately 1,500 hotel rooms are currently located in the King of Prussia/Valley Forge area. Occupancy levels of both the offices and lodging facilities have always been excellent. Many companies have established their headquarters or main regional offices in King of Prussia/Valley Forge. Little land is currently available for future development in the immediate vicinity of King of Prussia, and most new development is now taking place along Route 202, five miles or more west of the shopping complex.

The Development and Expansion Process

Phase I: Original Development (1959–1963). In 1959, the Kravco Company, then known as the M. A. Kravitz Company, Inc., began planning a discount community shopping center on a site of approximately 30 acres at the northeast corner of U.S. 202 and Goddard Boulevard. The Court at King of Prussia now stands on this parcel. The Kravitz Company secured a commitment from E.J. Korvette to lease approximately 190,000 square feet for a discount department store (including a 30,000-square-foot furniture and carpet division) and from a regional supermarket to lease 30,000 square feet. At that time, both of these stores were successful retailers (although both have since gone out of business). The development was designed as a typical linear shopping center.

Zoning approval was obtained to support the project; however, a competitive supermarket, Acme Stores, owned approximately 96 acres on the other side of Goddard Boulevard. The developer arranged to trade the original 30 acres to Acme for a parcel of like size owned by Acme; at the same time, the developer purchased an additional 30 acres from Acme. Finally, the Kravitz Company secured an option to buy the 36 acres remaining in Acme's original 96-acre property.

With all land parcels under control, the developer relocated the shopping center to the former Acme parcel and redesigned the architectural plans to include a combination convenience shopping center and an open mall. The development concept allowed for three department stores, including E.J. Korvette and J.C. Penney (with provisions for a third department store at a later date).

The Equitable Life Assurance Society of the United States provided the permanent mortgage financing. Construction began in early 1961, and E.J. Korvette opened in September 1962, J.C. Penney opened in November 1962, and the open mall was completed in August 1963. Phase I, containing some 725,000 square feet, was largely finished. The mall was substantially landscaped and other outdoor amenities were added, including an eight-sided concrete amphitheater for outdoor performances as well as various fountains and gazebos. The open mall created a pleasant shopping environment and was an instant success.

Customers frequented the center from a broad regional geographic area, constituting the center's secondary trading area. Many shoppers traveled to King of Prussia from distances as great as 75 to 100 miles, and from rural areas, small towns, and larger cities in southeastern Pennsylvania, including Allentown, Bethlehem, Reading, Lancaster, and Harrisburg. Shoppers also came from Wilmington, Delaware, and from other areas of northern Delaware, as well as from the city of Philadelphia and from communities in southern New Jersey. Customers traveled to The Plaza not only by automobile, but also in bus tours, many of which were organized by groups from communities in the secondary market. King of Prussia became a destination in itself. As time went by, however, new enclosed shopping malls were developed in the secondary trade area, as well as in the greater Philadelphia metropolitan area, and, as a consequence, the size of the center's primary and secondary trade areas was reduced.

Phase II: Expansion of The Plaza (1963–1966). In 1963, planning began on the Plymouth Meeting Mall, a new two-level enclosed mall that The Rouse Company developed approximately seven miles east of King of Prussia at the intersection of the Pennsylvania Turnpike and the northeast extension of the turnpike that connects with Allentown, some 40 miles north. The Kravitz Company began to realize that enclosed shopping malls represented the preferred shopping environment for the future. It secured a commitment from the John Wanamaker Company, one of Philadelphia's three major department stores, to locate in King of Prussia. In 1965, the new Wanamaker store opened in The Plaza in an attractive, octagonally shaped, freestanding building and became King of Prussia's first anchor tenant offering a full line of department store merchandise.

Wanamaker's entry into King of Prussia allowed the developer to plan a new two-level, enclosed mall to be constructed around the J.C. Penney department store, and by 1965, the developer was able to attract Gimbels to the center. The new two-level mall connecting Wanamaker and Gimbels, with entrances to both Penney and Korvette, opened in 1966. Wanamaker agreed

to allow an entrance from its store into the mall only on the upper level and, for the next 18 years, the enclosed mall existed without an entrance from the Wanamaker store on the ground-floor level. This phase of the development was also unique in that the new two-level mall was built in front of the Penney store, removing the entrance to Penney directly from the center's parking lot.

By 1967, King of Prussia Plaza had grown into a true regional-sized shopping center with both open and enclosed mall areas and a total GLA of about 1,300,000 square feet, including some 140 stores offering a full complement of merchandise and services. For many years, sales volumes of the stores fronting on the open mall exceeded the volumes of the stores in the enclosed mall. The Plaza remained essentially in this configuration until 1980.

Phase III: The Court at King of Prussia (1976–1981). In 1973, Bambergers, a division of the R.H. Macy Company, entered the Philadelphia metropolitan market. The developer began plans to accommodate Bambergers as a fifth department store anchor in The Plaza, exploring a number of alternative configurations. None, however, were acceptable to Bambergers, primarily because of difficulties with merchandising considerations and problems associated with loading merchandise going to Bambergers and to other mall shops in the area of the proposed new store.

The original 30 acres of unimproved land that was conveyed to Acme in 1961 had remained vacant on the opposite side of Goddard Boulevard, the road surrounding King of Prussia Plaza. In 1976, Bambergers agreed to the development of a freestanding store opposite Goddard Boulevard on this parcel. Kravco acquired the parcel from Acme and planned to develop it as a two-level enclosed mall with Bambergers and a second department store as anchors.

Kravco began negotiations with Bloomingdale's, a division of Federated Department Stores, which was interested in locating one or more stores in the greater Philadelphia area. Ultimately, Bloomingdale's agreed to join Bambergers in the proposed new mall sponsored by the Kravco organization. At the same time, Federated decided to locate one or more units of its Abraham & Straus division in the Philadelphia area and selected King of Prussia as the first location.

Kravco revised its plans to provide for a three-department-store mall with approximately 250,000 square feet of mall shops on two levels in a complex totaling some 963,000 square feet. A large parking structure would also have to be built to meet the parking ratios required by the local township as well as by the department store merchants. Fortunately,

4-55 The Court is anchored by Bloomingdale's, Bambergers, and Abraham & Straus.

the site elevations sloped downward toward the rear of the site from the grade along the Route 202 frontage, accommodating a three-level parking structure with approximately 3,000 spaces. The facility was built in front of the center along Route 202, with the upper deck level with Route 202. Thus, it did not hide the three-story department store buildings and the two-level mall. Moreover, the garage was designed so that its lower level matched the lower level of both the mall and the department stores. Similarly, the upper level of the garage matched the upper level of the mall and the middle or "fashion" level of the three department stores.

The three-department-store mall also required the relocation of Goddard Boulevard (in an easterly direction and on land that was a paved surface parking area for The Plaza), in order to fit the mall buildings on the relatively small site and thereby provide for more parking and land area for the new mall. After a long period of physical planning, traffic analysis, and other engineering studies with the township, state highway officials, and the department store merchants, the developer relocated Goddard Boulevard, also obtaining the approvals needed to construct a bridge over the relocated road to connect the two malls, thereby greatly facilitating the flow of automobile traffic. The developer also constructed an outdoor canopy over a sidewalk connecting the two centers, making it more comfortable for pedestrians.

King of Prussia Plaza had always been merchandised toward a broad spectrum of shopper groups; in fact, by the late 1970s, both the department stores and the mall shops were oriented toward more popular priced merchandise. King of Prussia Plaza did not offer a wide selection of merchandise to the more affluent shopper. Recognizing this and the fact that nearly 1 million square feet of additional retail space aimed toward a wide market could have a detrimental effect on sales of the existing merchants in King of Prussia Plaza, the developer pursued a leasing strategy for the new development geared toward higher-priced or more "fashion-oriented" stores that would fit comfortably with the high-fashion image of Bloomingdale's and the other two department stores. In addition, the developer took great care to avoid leasing space in The Court to chain stores that were already established in The Plaza—except in special cases. Out of approximately 125 stores in The Court, only 10 merchants also have units in The Plaza.

Construction on the new mall, which was named The Court at King of Prussia, began early in 1980 and the mall opened in August 1981. Total project costs amounted to more than $70 million, including the costs of the department store buildings and the parking garage. Each department store built its own store on land that it had either purchased or leased from the developer. The garage cost over $11 million and represents one of the largest parking structures in the eastern United States financed exclusively by private capital. Each of the department stores shared in the cost of the parking structure and other site improvements.

The Court was an instant success. At its opening, it was over 80 percent leased to a well-balanced collection of fashion-oriented stores, and sales volumes were excellent from the beginning. More important, however, was the fact that The Court attracted a class of shoppers that had not previously visited King of Prussia Plaza with any regularity. Historically, the more affluent shopper from the Main Line communities had shopped in freestanding "boutiques" located along Lancaster Avenue (U.S. Route 30), a commercial thoroughfare bisecting the Main Line, in Center City Philadelphia, or in New York City. The addition of the new fashion-oriented stores in The Court succeeded in attracting many of these shoppers. Moreover, it brought back many shoppers from the broad secondary trade area (extending up to 75 miles from the mall) that had been lost to malls built in or near their own communities.

Phase IV: Renovation of The Plaza (1979–1980). In planning the new Court at King of Prussia, the developer was concerned that the merchants in The Plaza would inevitably be subject to intense competition. During the last half of the 1970s, The Plaza began to suffer from a number of design and merchandising problems. It obviously needed to be redeveloped into a more contemporary shopping environment in order to remain attractive to shoppers and to maintain its market presence. By the late 1970s, sales volumes of the stores fronting along the original open mall area had begun to soften compared to sales of tenants in the enclosed mall. Moreover, the financial difficulties of one of The Plaza's anchor tenants, E. J. Korvette, were reflected in its store, which further tarnished The Plaza's image. For several years before its closing, the Korvette store was poorly stocked and was generally not well merchandised for its customer base; as a result, its sales volume had been declining.

The developer planned a comprehensive renovation of the 725,000 square feet of GLA that had constituted Phase I of the original development. This program consisted of six interrelated projects: (1) the enclosure of the open mall area; (2) the redesign and modernization of a number of the tenants' storefronts; (3) the reconstruction and modernization of four mall entrances; (4) the construction of some 23,000 square feet of new GLA within the newly enclosed mall area; (5) the removal and/or renovation of three auto accessory stores that had been leased to the department store merchants; and (6) the conversion of certain office areas to retail space.

The developer began the renovation in the spring of 1980 by first enclosing all open mall areas. In order to acquaint shoppers with the scope of the project, signs were erected at various locations, which carried the phrase "We're crowning the king" as well as a brief description of the improvements that were underway. New construction and additions included roofs with a number of skylights over the open areas of the mall,

4-56   The ceiling in The Court consists of layered drywall reinforcing the fan-shaped design.

a concrete floor base finished in quarry tile, a fountain set in a court at the entrance to the Wanamaker store, interior landscaping and other decorative ornaments, and mall entrances. Most of the construction took place during daytime shopping hours, and all stores remained open during the construction process.

To help pay for the project, the developer persuaded J.C. Penney and John Wanamaker to build several mall shops against blank exterior walls of their stores. These kiosklike structures proved successful: they not only enlivened the once "dead" wall space but could also be rented at attractive rates per square foot compared to their relatively low construction cost.

To proceed with the project, various approvals were needed from the existing department store merchants. The developer agreed, among other things, to build and/or pay for new storefront entrances for Penney, Woolworth, and several other stores. Moreover, it was deemed to be in the best interest of both the landlord and the tenants for the developer to modernize the storefronts and interiors of as many of the tenants as possible along the new mall. The developer worked with each tenant to accomplish this objective. The large majority of tenants responded favorably, and the result was a totally renovated "like new" one-level shopping mall.

Korvette, Penney, and Wanamaker all had automobile accessory stores located on parcels fronting along Goddard Boulevard, which encircles The Plaza. By the late 1970s, sales volumes of these auto stores had declined and the developer negotiated to acquire each tenant's interest in each of the stores. The Wanamaker auto center was demolished to accommodate additional parking area; the Korvette auto store was leased to a restaurant; and the Penney auto store was leased to the operator of a discotheque. Sales volumes of the latter two units have been outstanding.

Finally, approximately 20,000 square feet of office space was located on the second level of a building situated next to the new mall entrance adjacent to the Wanamaker store. The offices of Kravco, Inc., had been located in a portion of this space for about 10 years. Office employees were using parking areas that were important to the retail merchants' businesses. In 1980, Kravco, Inc., began constructing a new office building on Goddard Boulevard opposite the mall and, upon its completion in April 1981, relocated the company's headquarters to the new building. The developer was able to relocate several stores on the ground floor beneath the offices and to re-lease the entire area to Conrans, an English furniture store with several new stores in the United States. Despite many problems in keeping stores affected by the renovation open for business during construction, the program was completed on schedule. Most of the renovation was finished in time for the 1980 Christmas season, about four months before the opening of the new Bambergers store in The Court at King of Prussia. Costing approximately $4.5 million, the renovation has been a great success. Sales volumes of the stores fronting the mall have increased substantially since the mall was enclosed and the project modernized.

Phase V: Expansion of The Plaza (1980–1983). During the late 1970s, E. J. Korvette was experiencing severe financial difficulties. The developer negotiated an agreement to purchase the remaining term of the Korvette lease, before the tenant filed for bankruptcy. Three other discount department stores were willing to take over the Korvette store on an "as is" basis and at a substantial profit to the owners of the King of Prussia complex. However, the developer took a longer view and began negotiations with Sears to combine and move two of its older stores on either side of the King of Prussia area into a new store in King of Prussia Plaza. One of the Sears stores was located in Norristown, about six miles north of King of Prussia, and the second store was a freestanding unit located in St. Davids, one of the communities in the heart of the Main Line, about four miles south of King of Prussia. Both stores were successful units for the company; however, with The Court under construction, King of Prussia would inevitably become the dominant retail location in northwestern Philadelphia and would hold that position well into the 21st century. Sears elected to be a part of the complex. It began planning a new 215,000-square-foot store that became the prototype for Sears's "Store of the Future," a concept involving a completely new merchandising scheme with a more upscale interior design. The new Sears store also included a Sears Financial Services Center, with offices of Allstate Insurance, a Coldwell Banker residential real estate brokerage, and a Dean Witter Reynolds Securities brokerage operation—the latter two operations being recent acquisitions of Sears, which were intended to move Sears headlong into the financial services industry.

With Sears's entry into The Plaza, the developer made plans to expand the center by adding approximately 140,000 square feet of new mall shops, including a new 25,000-square-foot food court. Although part of the two-level Korvette store was demolished, the remainder was completely renovated as part of the development program. The lower level was turned into the new Garden Food Court, a 34,000-square-foot toy store, and a new restaurant with an entrance on the parking lot. The upper level was converted into a combination of retail and office uses. The project also involved substantial new construction, including 50 new stores. The Plaza now contains a total of some 1.3 million square feet of retail GLA, including more than 200 mall shops occupying over 600,000 square feet, plus approximately 45,000 square feet of office space. The entire project cost a total of about $9.5 million.

The most recent activity following the opening of Sears and the expansion associated with it was a renovation of the two-level mall area (Phase II of the expansion program) that opened in 1965–1966. The developer's objective was to upgrade this portion of the mall to make it visually compatible with the new mall expansion and thereby give the entire mall a unified appearance. New quarry tile floors were installed on the lower level, and new wood parquet tile flooring was installed on the upper level. In addition, high-intensity lighting fixtures and new ceiling tiles were put in, and other ceiling areas were repainted. As was the case in the enclosure of the single-level areas of The Plaza, which were originally in an open mall, the developer worked with the mall tenants to modernize their stores. Many stores have been recently remodeled, including new storefronts and signage.

Financing during the 1980s

The Court, the enclosure of The Plaza, and the Sears expansion (Phases III, IV, and V) were all built between 1980 and 1983. The owner's total cost for the three phases was approximately $52 million. By 1980, interest rates on conventional loans for quality real estate projects had risen to a range of 13 to 16 percent, depending upon the precise moment at which the loan was secured. Loans made during this period also usually had much shorter terms (from five to 15 years) than had previously been common when mortgages had terms of 25 to 35 years. Loans written during the early 1980s often included provisions for the lender to share in the growth in rentals and/or the value of the property over the term of the loan. In 1982, the owners of King of Prussia secured the total project cost for Phases III, IV, and V in a complex transaction that included the sale of a 50 percent interest in the total King of Prussia complex to The Equitable Life Assurance Society of the United States, the institution that had provided the original permanent financing for Phases I and II of King of Prussia Plaza in the early and mid-1960s.

Architectural Concepts

The design of The Court, by Cope Linder Associates of Philadelphia, was intentionally different from that of The Plaza. The developer, the architect, and the department stores all agreed that The Court should be finished with higher-quality materials and should have a more sophisticated appearance than The Plaza. This decision, however, was largely dictated by the developer's plan that The Plaza and The Court attract somewhat different classes of shoppers, yet simultaneously complement each other in appealing to the broadest possible segments of the retail market.

The Court is designed as a two-level, "fanlike" configuration built primarily around the rear of the new Bloomingdale's store. The mall has three fountain courts at the entrances to each of the department stores. Clerestory skylights provide natural light throughout the day along the north elevation of the mall area, and the ceiling consists of a series of layered drywall elements reinforcing the fan-shaped design. Full-grown plants on the lower level give the mall a warm, natural atmosphere.

All phases of The Plaza, including the plans that were drawn for the original discount community center (on the site that The Court now occupies), were designed by the architectural firm of Evantash–Friedman Associates (and two subsequent firms sponsored by its main principal, Leonard Evantash, RA). In all renovations of The Plaza, beginning with the enclosure of the open mall in 1980, the architect was careful to select materials that would give the center a unified appearance. For example, the same floor tiles, ceiling tiles, lighting fixtures, and interior landscaping and seating elements were used throughout The Plaza. Decorative banners and paint finishes were coordinated. The original brick exterior walls of The Plaza buildings were painted to match the brick walls along the new mall.

Leasing Practices

Written during Phase I, the original leases with The Plaza's mall stores provided that the tenants pay a fixed minimum annual rental plus a stipulated percentage of their gross sales over a given level of annual sales. In addition, the early leases generally required that tenants pay increases in real estate taxes and common area maintenance (CAM) expenses over a stipulated base amount per square foot. Several of the original leases also provided for tenant contributions to CAM and taxes to offset percentage rental payments. Rooftop units installed by the landlord provided heating and air conditioning for the stores along the original open mall. Tenants paid for the operating costs of the units as well as the costs of other utilities serving the stores.

As The Plaza was expanded during Phase II, leases were negotiated on a "net" basis; however, in many instances the landlord agreed to contribute a stipulated amount per square foot toward the cost of CAM.

Leases in The Court are on a completely net basis, as are new leases in the Sears expansion (Phase V). As the original leases in The Plaza have expired, they have been converted to a net basis.

The developer constructed the buildings occupied by all the original major tenants in The Plaza (J.C. Penney, Korvette, Gimbels, John Wanamaker, Acme, and Woolworth) and leased the buildings to the stores. As was typical in lease arrangements with anchor tenants during this period, leases to the major tenants in The Plaza have a wide variety of clauses for the payment of percentage rents, as well as a variety of formulas by which anchor stores contribute to taxes, CAM, and the cost of utilities. In some cases, leases with the anchor stores provide for offsets against percentage rents. Additionally, anchor stores typically do not pay a full pro rata share of common area expenses and taxes.

Each of the department stores in The Court, as well as the Sears store in The Plaza, own their own buildings on land that was either purchased or leased by the store from the owner.

Sales, Marketing, and Promotional Activities

During 1979 and 1980, the developer undertook a series of studies concerning the viability of building and leasing the additional mall space that was planned for The Court and the Sears expansion. The studies concluded that in order to sustain the total King of Prussia complex, sales volumes for both malls (including the department stores) would have to exceed an annual rate of $350 million by the end of 1984, the first full calendar year after the opening of the expanded complex. The developer's projections of sales volumes have already been exceeded. In fact, sales volumes for the entire complex approached $400 million by the end of 1984.

Separate merchants' associations, both of which are supported by the services of a professional marketing firm, handle the marketing, promotional, and media advertising for The Court and The Plaza. Each center has an on-site marketing director who coordinates marketing activities with the director of marketing and sales at the Kravco Company headquarters. The marketing budgets for both centers total over $500,000 a year. At monthly meetings, the board of trustees of each merchants' association plans programs designed to stimulate sales at each mall.

Following are the objectives of each merchants' association:

4-57, 4-58, 4-59 The expansion of The Plaza (Phase V of the expansion and renovation program) added a 215,000-square-foot Sears store and 140,000 square feet of mall shops, including a 25,000-square-foot food court.

- To position each mall as a dominant, exciting retail shopping facility.
- To increase customer traffic during major merchandising periods.
- To sustain community goodwill, build customer loyalty, and augment repeat shopping patterns.
- To maximize retailer participation in merchants' association activities, including sales events, special events, and cooperative advertising.
- To unify the image of the entire King of Prussia complex so that the complex will benefit from the cross-shopping potential at The Plaza and The Court.
- To conduct market research surveys to provide information on target marketing efforts, specifically in the area of media placement and tabloid distribution.

Major marketing strategies are designed to enhance joint promotional and advertising opportunities during peak retail seasons. For example, "The Court and The Plaza Together," an advertising "tag line" used recently, promotes combined merchandising events, joint media buys, and copy for tabloids whose distribution dates are coordinated to benefit both malls.

A joint committee of merchants' association members from The Court and The Plaza meets quarterly to evaluate the results of promotional and advertising programs for the entire complex.

The advertising and promotional activities of both centers consist of advertising via printed media, radio and television spots, and planned promotional activities and other special events.

To target the King of Prussia complex's large and expanding market, advertisements promoting key merchandising events are placed in seven community newspapers and in *The Philadelphia Inquirer*, the dominant morning newspaper in the area. In addition, 10 newspaper tabloids are published yearly, paralleling major merchandising and sales seasons. Approximately 125,000 newspaper tabloid inserts are distributed at each printing, and 40,000 tabloids are mailed directly to selected households in the primary trade area. Lease agreements stipulate that merchants advertise in the tabloids four to 10 times per year. Both malls are entitled to free editorial space in the tabloids to promote specific merchants, focusing on new store openings and promoting merchandising seasons and other special events.

Radio spots are also used to support major merchandising seasons and events. The current radio buy penetrates over 45 percent of the primary target demographic market. The Court and The Plaza combine funds to maximize the frequency of radio spots. Radio stations are also invited to participate in community or charitable functions at each of the malls, thereby providing "free" radio time. As the most expensive medium, television advertising is reserved for primary retail merchandising periods. The Plaza and The

Court purchase television ad time at least four times each year. Use of network-affiliated stations during key prime time viewing periods provides maximum television ratings.

Press releases are prepared for each special event in each mall and are distributed to local weekly papers, to major metropolitan daily papers, and to radio and television stations. Notices of events specifically geared toward community interest or fundraising activities also appear on cable stations.

Finally, community events featuring area schools, charities, and other civic organizations, are routinely held in each mall. Examples of events have included a flower show ("Orchids to You") and an exhibit featuring selected art from area museums ("Museums-on-Mall"). These events are designed to increase shopper momentum during nonpeak sales periods. Monies collected from fountains in the malls are contributed to local charitable organizations.

Experience Gained

Almost every conceivable problem that could confront the builder/developer of a retail facility was encountered in the development of the King of Prussia complex. These problems included the bankruptcy of two major tenants; changes in consumer buying habits (the steady growth in suburban mall shopping, in the popularity of "fashion" merchandise, and, more recently, in factory outlet and off-price retail facilities); adverse soil conditions; difficulties with stormwater management and sewer moratoria; the lack of state and local funds to support highway improvements; and fluctuations in financial markets resulting in both the periodic shortage of capital and in the high cost of investment capital that was available. The developer gained a wealth of knowledge in dealing with these problems. Among the lessons learned were:

- A good working relationship with township, county, and state public authorities can help turn the developer's dream—which often appears impossible—into a reality. During the development of the King of Prussia complex, many public officials, both elected and appointed, as well as paid staff employees, participated in decisions affecting the project. During the project's 25 years in development, the composition of the local planning board, the board of supervisors, and officials at the Pennsylvania Department of Transportation changed many times.
- The developer learned that, with perseverance, a solution can always be found to any given problem. Recognizing the needs of other parties, addressing these needs, and accepting necessary compromises are highly important in the land development process.
- Anticipating potential competition and reinvesting capital in real property at the right time can prevent possible competition from materializing.
- The developer learned the advantages of building retail facilities to a "human" scale. Overly extravagant or wasted space can result in adverse economic conditions in both the short and long term.
- A large critical mass of stores can be beneficial in retailing if the quantity or supply of goods and services can be supported by the size of the population and buying power of the trade areas, and if the highway patterns can adequately handle the amount of automobile traffic that must frequent the center in order to support it.
- A development of this magnitude was made possible by the property's excellent location. King of Prussia has once again become a shopping environment that can draw customers from great distances. This is due primarily to a superior highway system, which makes the King of Prussia complex highly accessible, and to the immense diversity of merchandise the center offers its customers. Stores range from the original supermarket, "strip stores," and other mall shops offering more popular-priced products and services in The Plaza, to Bloomingdale's, Bambergers, and 123 mall shops offering higher-priced, more upscale merchandise in The Court.
- The owners of the King of Prussia complex envision further intense development taking place in the years to come—and to support it, more structured parking.

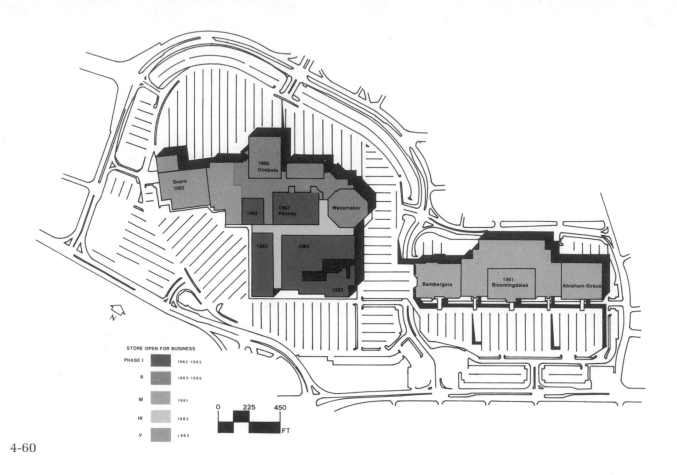

4-61 PROJECT DATA—KING OF PRUSSIA SHOPPING COMPLEX

Land Use Information:

Site Area: 125.46 acres (50.81 hectares)[1]

Gross Leasable Area (GLA):

The Plaza	1,495,000[2]
The Court	963,000
Total	2,458,000

The Plaza Department Stores:

	Square Feet
Gimbels	217,000
J.C. Penney	203,000
Sears	215,000
John Wanamaker	197,000
Total	832,000

The Court Department Stores:

Abraham & Straus	230,000
Bambergers	252,000
Bloomingdale's	230,000
Total	712,000
Grand Total Department Stores	1,544,000

Parking:

Total Spaces: 12,200[3]
Surface Spaces: 9,200
Structured Spaces: 3,000

Economic Information:

	Approximate Total Cost
Phase I—The Plaza (1959–1963)	$10,800,000[4]
Phase II—The Plaza Expansion (1963–1966)	11,150,000[5]
Phase III—The Court (1976–1981)	37,700,000[6]
Phase IV—Enclosure of The Plaza (1980–1981)	4,500,000
Phase V—Expansion of The Plaza (1980–1983)	9,500,000[7]
Total	$73,650,000

Sales:

The Plaza	Actual 1983 Sales Total	Per Square Foot	Projected Sales 1984[8] Total	Per Square Foot	1985 Total	Per Square Foot
Department Stores	$ 97,194,000	$117	$106,000,000	$128	$111,000,000	$133
Mall Stores[9]	78,745,000	134	102,000,000	175	109,000,000	186
Total	$175,939,000		$208,000,000		$220,000,000	
The Court						
Department Stores[10]	$101,000,000	$142	$117,000,000	$164	$124,000,000	$175
Mall Stores[9]	53,656,000	239	59,000,000	263	62,000,000	276
Total	$154,656,000		$176,000,000		$186,000,000	
Grand Total	$330,595,000		$384,000,000		$406,000,000	

Rents:

The Plaza: $14.50 per square foot[11]
The Court: $18.25 per square foot[12]

The Plaza Tenant Information:[13]

Classification[14]	Number of Stores	Square Feet of GLA	Percent of GLA	Average Percent of GLA in Super Regional Centers[14]
General Merchandise	1	49,446	7.0	7.3
Food	12	44,359	6.8	4.3
Food Service	35	84,472	12.8	9.0
Clothing	34	108,123	16.4	30.0
Shoes	19	41,919	6.4	9.3
Home Furnishings	9	36,621	5.6	2.3
Home Appliances/Music	13	24,682	3.8	3.8
Building Materials/Garden	–	–	–	.4
Automotive Supplies/Service Station	1	4,500	.7	.5
Hobby/Special Interest	11	63,190	9.5	4.9
Gifts/Specialty	22	28,836	4.4	6.6
Jewelry and Cosmetics	10	7,577	1.1	3.5
Liquor	–	–	–	.2
Drugs	1	9,250	1.4	2.7
Other Retail	12	58,109	8.8	3.9
Personal Services	12	12,735	1.9	2.1
Recreation/Community	9	36,130	5.5	4.2
Financial	–	–	–	2.2
Offices (other than financial)	16	45,388	6.8	2.1
Other (vacancy)	–	7,552	1.1	–
Total	217	662,889	100.0	100.0

The Court Tenant Information:[13]

Classification[14]	Number of Stores	Square Feet of GLA	Percent of GLA	Average Percent of GLA in Super Regional Centers[14]
General Merchandise	–	–	–	7.3
Food	5	3,640	1.5	4.3
Food Service	15	35,257	14.0	9.0
Clothing	35	98,819	39.4	30.8
Shoes	18	25,765	10.3	9.3
Home Furnishings	5	6,856	2.7	2.3
Home Appliances/Music	5	11,970	4.8	3.8
Building Materials/Garden	–	–	–	.4
Automotive Supplies/Service Station	–	–	–	.5
Hobby/Special Interest	6	7,205	2.9	4.9
Gifts/Specialty	10	19,415	7.7	6.6
Jewelry and Cosmetics	7	9,187	3.7	3.5
Liquor	–	–	–	.2
Drugs	1	5,600	2.2	2.7
Other Retail	5	6,495	2.6	3.9
Personal Services	7	10,962	4.4	2.1
Recreation/Community	3	1,350	.5	4.2
Financial	–	–	–	2.2
Offices (other than financial)	1	100	.0	2.1
Other (vacancy)	–	8,315	3.3	–
Total	123	250,936	100.0	100.0

Notes:

[1] The Plaza occupies 91.62 acres; The Court occupies 33.84 acres (including 3.93 acres owned by Federated Department Stores).

[2] Includes some 45,000 square feet of office space.

[3] Includes 7,400 spaces at The Plaza and 4,800 at The Court. Approximate total.

[4] Including Penney and Korvette department stores.

[5] Including Gimbels and Wanamaker department stores.

[6] Excluding Bambergers, Bloomingdale's, and Abraham & Straus department stores.

[7] Excluding the Sears, Roebuck department store.

[8] Based on six-month actual sales.

[9] Sales per square foot are based on GLA, excluding space occupied by tenants who do not pay percentage rent.

[10] Based on reliable estimates. Department stores in The Court are not required to report sales.

[11] Average base rent for new mall stores in the Phase V expansion. Leases are on a net basis.

[12] Average base rent. Leases are on a net basis.

[13] Excluding department stores.

[14] *Dollars & Cents of Shopping Centers: 1984* (Washington, D.C.: ULI–the Urban Land Institute, 1984), p. 272.

Developer/Owner/Manager:
Kravco Company
234 Goddard Boulevard
King of Prussia, Pennsylvania 19406

Owner:
The Equitable Life Assurance Society of the United States
1285 Avenue of the Americas
New York, New York 10019

Architecture/Planning (The Plaza):
Evantash Associates
234 Goddard Boulevard
King of Prussia, Pennsylvania 19406

Architecture/Planning (The Court):
Cope Linder Associates
Reading Terminal
1 North 12th Street
Philadelphia, Pennsylvania 19107

5.
Tenants

The retail tenants of a shopping center make it viable. The developer merely melds the components of a center—its tenants, its building structure, and its site attributes—into the ambience of a particular development.

Despite the importance of the preliminaries in planning for the type and size of a center, site and building construction cannot begin until anchor tenants are identified, selected, and committed. The need to secure key tenants cannot be overemphasized. At the beginning, reliable commitments rather than agreements to precise lease provisions are sufficient. Specific terms can later be negotiated. Whether or not key tenants are to lease space in a shell or in a finished building or are to lease independently or to buy land, binding overall commitments should be obtained before building and final site layouts are begun.

The key tenants—whether a supermarket, discount store, or full-line department store—should be tied in closely with the development team in the building and site planning. They will influence the developer's decisions on building treatment and architectural style and even parking, lighting, signing, and landscaping. Furthermore, at this point in the planning, the key tenants should be committed to agreements for ultimate centerwide operations, such as common area maintenance, tax participation, and participation in the center's promotional programs.

Key Tenants

A center's tenant mix cannot be decided by a formula; each community and each shopping center are different. Any list of the tenant classifications most frequently found in a given type of center can serve only as a guide in making selections. Based on market and feasibility studies, a shopping center's composition will ultimately be determined by the developer's search for and negotiation with tenants. It will also obviously depend on the type of center to be built. Once a developer knows the characteristics of the market his center will serve, he can decide first on the anchor tenant classifications and then on the supplementary array.

5-1　The supermarket or giant supermarket/drug combination is the neighborhood center's key tenant.

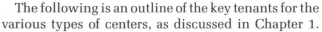

5-2　The anchor tenant in the community center is usually a discount or off-price department store, a specialty store (such as a hardware/building/home improvement store), or a combined drug/variety/garden store.

The following is an outline of the key tenants for the various types of centers, as discussed in Chapter 1.

In a *neighborhood center*, a supermarket or a giant supermarket/drugstore combination is the key tenant. Other principal tenants may be a drugstore and/or a small variety store. These centers also usually have personal services, food service, and convenience goods tenants. In lieu of a supermarket as the anchor tenant, some neighborhood centers may have a combination of food tenants that are equivalent to a supermarket.

The anchor tenant for a *community center* is most often a discount or off-price department store, a specialty store (such as a hardware/building/home improvement store), or a combined drug/variety/garden store. A junior department store or a large variety store may also serve as the anchor tenant in the community center, although this is not a common practice today, as it was in past years. Supplementary tenants include those that might be found in a neighborhood center, with added representation in shopping goods, particularly in the categories of apparel and home furnishings. A community center may also include banking and professional services, and recreational facilities, as well as tenants that are unlikely to be found in a regional center, such as hardware, and garden and building supplies. As noted earlier, a community center does not have a full-line department store as an anchor tenant.

At least one full-line department store of 100,000 square feet GLA is essential for *regional centers*. A majority of regional centers include two or more such department stores. For the supplementary tenant roster, all tenant classifications are drawn upon. Custom-arily, there are several stores from the same category, allowing the final tenant composition to represent as closely as possible the ranges in price and merchandise once found only in downtowns.

Super regional centers require by definition three or more full-line department stores of generally not less than 100,000 square feet each and a total center GLA of at least 500,000 square feet. Some super regional centers may have up to five or six department stores and a gross leasable area of more than 1.5 million square feet.

Specialty centers do not need a key tenant from the traditional categories. The grouping of tenants is determined by the special nature of the trade area or according to the tenants' suitability to a unique structure, such as a rehabilitated historic structure. In some specialty centers a group of tenants, such as a food-service cluster of a number of restaurants, or a cinema complex, may effectively serve as an anchor tenant.

The gross leasable area of specialty centers may range from as small as 40,000 square feet to as large as 300,000 square feet. Although center size and market area are not directly related, a specialty center's market—neighborhood, community, or regional (including tourists)—will be a guide to center size. A variety of tenants—boutiques, import shops, high-fashion or specialty apparel shops, arts and crafts stores, hobby shops or other specialty stores, food stores, and food-service outlets—may be considered suitable to the character, quality, and drawing power of the location. A festival/specialty center, such as The Waterside in Norfolk, Virginia, or South Street Seaport in New York City, typically has a high percentage of GLA devoted to specialty restaurants and food vendors. Retail goods at a festival/specialty center also tend to emphasize strongly impulse and specialty items.

Any specialty center, whether located in a new structure or in a landmark structure or other building newly converted for retail use, must have at least one prime or anchor tenant (or a group of tenants that serve as a "cluster" anchor, such as the food-service and food tenants in a food court). The key tenant will vary with the type of specialty center and its market.

In all types of centers, the developer needs to be flexible in selecting tenants and negotiating with them. Numerous adjustments will be made in interior arrangements and tenant leases. Under normal conditions, key tenants will have committed themselves to a substantial percentage of the center's planned GLA before final construction drawings are made; otherwise, the development will take on aspects of a speculative enterprise.

Classification

Tenants are classified in several ways: by lines of business in which they are principally engaged; by overall credit rating; and by ownership. Some definitions adopted by the Urban Land Institute are useful in describing prospective tenants by ownership classification:

- National chain store: a business operating in four or more metropolitan areas in three or more states.
- Independent store: a business having not more than two outlets in only one metropolitan area.
- Local chain store: a business that does not fall into either of the preceding categories.

The tenant classifications by lines of business, as presented in Figure 5-5, are those established for *Dollars & Cents of Shopping Centers: 1984.* The principal groupings are generally related to major standard industrial classification (SIC) codes.[1]

Placement

Tenant placement follows a simple guideline: locate major or anchor tenants so that to reach them shoppers must walk past the storefronts of supplementary tenants. Separate the key tenants. Place one at each end of a strip or mall, for example, rather than side by side near the center of the building. Arrange parking and major entrances and exits of the building so that customers may move to and from the key tenants

---

[1] The two works in which these codes are set forth are the Urban Land Institute's *Dollars & Cents of Shopping Centers: 1984* (Washington, D.C.: ULI–the Urban Land Institute, 1984); and *The Standard Industrial Classification Manual,* prepared by the Statistical Policy Division of the Executive Office of the President, Office of Management and Budget. Definitions and classifications found in the SIC manual are used by government, industry, and trade associations in gathering statistics.

5-4   South Street Seaport, New York City.

5-3   Most regional centers include two or more department stores as anchor tenants.

TENANT CLASSIFICATIONS AND CODE NUMBERS

	SIC CODE	TENANT CLASS		SIC CODE	TENANT CLASS
General Merchandise			**Home Appliances/Music**		
Department Store	5311	A-01	Appliances	5722	G-01
Junior Department Store	5311	A-02	Radio, Video, Stereo	5732	G-02
Variety Store	5311	A-03	Sewing Machines	5722	G-03
Discount Department Store	5311	A-04	Records and Tapes	5733	G-04
Showroom/Catalog Store	5399	A-05	Musical Instruments	5733	G-05
			Gourmet Cookware	5719	G-06
Food			Computer/Calculator		
Supermarket	5411	B-01	(retail)	5999	G-07
Convenience Market	5411	B-02			
Meat, Poultry, and Fish	5423	B-03	**Building Materials/Garden**		
Specialty Food	5499	B-04	Paint and Wallpaper	5231	H-02
Delicatessen	5411	B-05	Hardware	5251	H-03
Bakery	5463	B-06	Home Improvements	5211	H-04
Candy and Nuts	5441	B-07			
Dairy Products	5451	B-08	**Automotive Supplies/Service Station**		
Health Food	5499	B-09	Automotive (TBA)	5531	K-01
			Service Station	5541	K-03
Food Service					
Restaurant without Liquor	5812	C-01	**Hobby/Special Interest**		
Restaurant with Liquor	5812	C-02	Sporting Goods—General	5941	M-01
Cafeteria	5812	C-03	Hobby	5945	M-02
Fast Food/Carryout	5812	C-04	Art Gallery	5999	M-03
Cocktail Lounge	5813	C-05	Cameras	5946	M-04
Doughnut Shop	5812	C-06	Toys	5945	M-05
Ice Cream Parlor	5812	C-07	Bike Shop	5941	M-06
Pretzel Shop	5812	C-09	Arts and Crafts	5999	M-07
Cookie Shop	5812	C-10	Coin Shop	5999	M-08
			Outfitters	5941	M-09
Clothing			Game Store	5945	M-10
Ladies' Specialty	5631	D-01			
Ladies' Ready-to-Wear	5621	D-02	**Gifts/Specialty**		
Bridal Shop	5621	D-03	Imports	5999	N-01
Maternity	5621	D-04	Luggage and Leather	5948	N-02
Hosiery	5631	D-05	Cards and Gifts	5947	N-03
Childrens Wear	5641	D-07	Candle	5999	N-04
Menswear	5611	D-08	Books and Stationery	5942/3	N-05
Family Wear	5651	D-09	Decorative Accessories		
Unisex/Jean Shop	5699	D-11	(including hardware		
Leather Shop	5699	D-12	and collectible gifts)	5947/5719	N-06
Uniform Shop	5699	D-13			
Special Apparel—Unisex	5699	D-14	**Jewelry and Cosmetics**		
			Credit Jewelry	5944	P-01
Shoes			Costume Jewelry	5999	P-02
Family Shoes	5661	E-01	Jewelry	5944	P-03
Ladies' Shoes	5661	E-02	Cosmetics	5999	P-04
Men's and Boys' Shoes	5661	E-03			
Children's Shoes	5661	E-04	**Liquor**		
Athletic Footwear	5661/5941	E-05	Liquor and Wine	5921	Q-01
			Wine and Cheese	5921/5451	Q-02
Home Furnishings					
Furniture	5712	F-01	**Drugs**		
Lamps	5719	F-02	Super Drug		
Floor Coverings	5713	F-03	(over 10,000 square feet)	5912	R-01
Curtains and Drapes	5714	F-04	Drugs	5912	R-02
China and Glassware	5719	F-06			
Fireplace Equipment	5719	F-07			
Bath Shop	5719	F-08			
Contemporary Home					
Accessories	5719	F-09			
Cutlery	5719	F-10			

	SIC CODE	TENANT CLASS
Other Retail		
Fabric Shop	5949	S-01
Tobacco	5993	S-02
Pet Shop	5999	S-03
Flowers	5992	S-04
Plant Store	5992	S-05
Other Retail	5999	S-06
Telephone Store	5999	S-07
Eyeglasses—Optician	5999/8042	S-08
Personal Services		
Beauty	7231	T-01
Barber	7241	T-02
Shoe Repair	7251	T-03
Cleaner and Dyers	7212	T-04
Laundry	7212	T-05
Health Spa/Figure Salon	7299	T-06
Photographer	7221	T-07
Formal Wear/Rental	7299	T-08
Interior Decorator	7399	T-09
Travel Agent	4722	T-10
Key Shop	7699	T-11
Unisex Hair	7231/8299	T-12
Film Processing	7395	T-13
Photocopy/Fast Print	7332	T-14
Recreation/Community		
Post Office	7399	W-01
Music Studio and Dance	7911/8299	W-02
Bowling Alley	7933	W-03
Cinemas	7832	W-04
Ice/Roller Skating	7999	W-05
Community Hall	—	W-06
Arcade, Amusement	7993	W-07
Day Care and Nursery	8351	W-08

	SIC CODE	TENANT CLASS
Financial		
Banks	602	X-01
Savings and Loan	612	X-02
Finance Company	6145	X-03
Brokerage	6211	X-05
Insurance	6411	X-06
Real Estate	6531	X-07
Automatic Teller Machine	6059	X-08
Offices (other than financial)		
Optometrist	8042	Y-01
Medical and Dental	8011/8021/8031	Y-02
Legal	8111	Y-03
Accounting	8931	Y-04
Employment Agency	7361	Y-06
Other Offices	—	Y-07
Other		
Vacant Space	—	Z-01
Miscellaneous Income	—	Z-02
Warehouse	—	Z-03

(Tenant class numbers not in sequence indicate classifications not repeated from previous *Dollars & Cents of Shopping Centers* studies.)

Source: SIC codes are from *The Standard Industrial Classification Manual* (Washington, D.C.: U.S. Office of Management and Budget). Tenant classes are from *Dollars & Cents of Shopping Centers: 1984* (Washington, D.C.: ULI–the Urban Land Institute, 1984).

conveniently while also being exposed to as many other tenants as possible.

Tenants may have strong and sometimes apparently arbitrary views about where they will or will not locate within a center. The developer must seriously consider these views if he wishes to have particular tenants in the center.

A location that is advantageous for one type of business may be entirely wrong for another. Placement within the tenant composition is important and complex. Grouping of tenants in the center may follow either the "mix" or the "match" principles as long as it sustains the interest of customers and draws shoppers through the entire center. Although stores may be arranged in affinity groupings, mixing is desirable. Logical clusters may include service and re-

pair shops; food and food services; and variety, hardware, appliance, and home furnishings stores. The merchandising principles involved in determining tenant array in a shopping center are similar to those used by successful full-line department stores to determine locations for their various departments within the store.

Stores offering convenience goods or personal services should be easily accessible from the parking area. In fact, developers of regional centers often find it preferable to locate supermarkets and certain "pickup" personal service stores, such as dry cleaners, laundries, and carryouts, in a separate building at the edge of a parking area, allowing customers immediate access with quick, in-and-out parking. A long walk into a mall to reach a convenience store will be

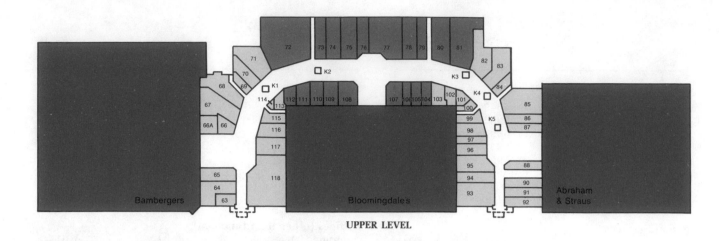

UPPER LEVEL

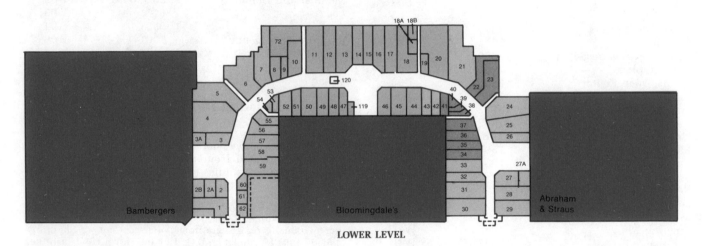

LOWER LEVEL

Department stores.

High-fashion tenants carefully selected to help establish The Court's image as a fashion center and to complement the high-fashion merchandise offered by Bloomingdale's, Bambergers, and Abraham & Straus on the second level.

Tenants offering quality merchandise at lower prices than the high-fashion tenants.

Tenants that were selected to offer a mix of general merchandise, food service, and personal services. Houlihan's and The Magic Pan restaurants flank the second-level entrances, giving the center the ambience of high quality associated with sit-down, full-menu dining and complementing the department stores' restaurants.

Cluster of food-service tenants.

Tenants providing a mix of general merchandise, food, and personal services.

Department Stores

    Abraham & Straus
    Bambergers
    Bloomingdale's

Banks and Financial Sevices

  2A American Bank and Trust Company of
      Pennsylvania

Books, Cards, and Gifts

 106 Affections
  19 Art Explosion
   6 B. Dalton

  71 Brookstone Company
   7 Card-O-Rama
 105 Dandelion
   9 Fluf N Stuf
 113 Hoffritz for Cutlery
  53 Scrimshaw
  84 The Spectrum Showcase
  K2 The Wee Cottage
  63 Wadsworth Gallery
  52 Wicks N Sticks

Children's Clothing

  76 The Children's Boutique

Family Clothing

  20 Designs
  56 The Lodge at Harvard Square
 27A Wild Tops

Men's Clothing

  72 Brooks Brothers
 111 Custom Shop, Shirtmakers
  98 Jeans West
  44 Oaktree

5-6 Tenant mix and placement at The Court at King of Prussia.

Women's Clothing

75 Ann Taylor
26 Benetton
74 Caché
18 Canadian's
13 Casual Corner
50 G & G
4 The Gap
70 Gaspari
69 Joan Bari
67 J. Putnam
17 Ladybug
85 Lane Bryant
81 The Limited
15 Narragansett
99 Neena
48 Page Boy Maternity
65 Paraphernalia
73 Peck and Peck
78 T. Edwards
112 Tennis Lady
59 Ups & Downs

Drugstore/Variety

21 CVS

Health Foods, Vitamins

32 General Nutrition
K4 The Vitamin Health Center

Home Furnishings/Specialty Shops

64 The Batherie
25 Lechter's
10 Printways
95 Showcase of Fine Fabrics
103 Taj Mahal
100 This End Up
86 Wicker Imports

Jewelry

108 Caldwell II
88 Christian Bernard
2 Gordon's Jewelers
80 J.E. Caldwell
46 Littman Jewelers
K3 Nomad's Treasure
K1 Plumb Gold
3A Village Silver

Luggage

45 Philadelphia Trunk Company

Personal Services

117 American Vision Center
1 Beaux Gens Salon
90 Command Performance Hair Salon
54 i Natural
91,92 IBM Product Center
61 Ma & Pa Bell
K5 Metropolitan Life Insurance

Photography

96 Camerart
29 Express Photo

Radio, Television

30 Granada T.V.
5 Video Concepts

Records, Tapes, Music

97 Grand Records
24 Listening Booth

Restaurants

37 Everything Yogurt
40 Famous Chocolate Chip
38 Frontier Fruit and Nut
35 Hilary's Ice Cream
55 Hoffert's Candy
118 Houlihan's
101 La Croissanterie
93 The Magic Pan
34 Magic Wok
60 Morrow's Nut House
41 MMMuffins
39 The Nectar Tree
68 Olga's Kitchen
83 Roy Rogers
23 Sbarro
12 Skolnik's Bagel Bakery
36 Tater Junction
28 Vie De France

Children's Shoes

8 Joy Buster Brown

Family Shoes

22 Footlocker

Men's Shoes

110 Church's Shoes
107 Florsheim
16 Florsheim Thayer–McNeil
3 Harwyn Shoes
49 Houston Hat and Boot Company
47 Johnston and Murphy
87 Peter Lord

Women's Shoes

14 Ansonia
79 Chandler Shoes
66A Chorus Line
43 Connie Shoes
16 Florsheim Thayer–McNeil
66 Joyce Selby
51 Naturalizer Shoes
104 Palter Shoes
109 Pappagallo
102 Red Cross Shoes
116 Wild Pair

Sporting Goods

11 Athleisure
77 Eddie Bauer
57 Open Country
58 Philadelphia Sport Specialties

Toys and Hobbies

42 Games and Gadgets
82 Kay-Bee Toy and Hobby

Tobacco

115 The Tinder Box

Miscellaneous

119 Elevator
120 Information and Stroller Rental
18A Management Office
18B Restrooms

---

neither welcomed by the customer nor appropriate for the tenant. In addition, a buying trip to a supermarket serves a purpose far different from that of a shopping trip for general merchandise and apparel, and the rent structure of a regional center may be difficult for a supermarket or other low-margin tenants. (In fact, the trade area for a supermarket is so narrow that supermarkets may not belong in regional centers to begin with.)

In locating tenants, the developer should consider the following aspects:

- Suitability of the tenant for the location, as well as the amount of rent a tenant is able to pay.
- Local preferences for certain tenants.
- Compatibility and complementary status among adjoining stores.
- Compatibility of the tenant's merchandising practices with those of adjoining stores.
- Parking needs generated by the tenant.
- Customer convenience.

TENANT CLASSIFICATION	RANK	MEDIAN GLA	MEDIAN SALES VOLUME PER SQUARE FOOT GLA	MEDIAN TOTAL RENT PER SQUARE FOOT GLA
Food				
Supermarket	2	25,500	$271.46	$3.44
Food Service				
Restaurant without Liquor	8	2,250	105.32	6.93
Restaurant with Liquor	4	3,200	117.05	8.00
Fast Food/Carryout	9	1,500	150.59	9.00
Clothing				
Ladies' Specialty	17	1,440	112.54	7.37
Ladies' Ready-to-Wear	10	1,700	103.15	7.00
Home Appliances/Music				
Radio, Video, Stereo	13	1,800	93.49	5.93
Gifts/Specialty				
Cards and Gifts	14	2,250	71.75	7.00
Jewelry and Cosmetics				
Jewelry	19	1,000	128.20	7.79
Liquor				
Liquor and Wine	16	2,450	177.89	6.00
Drugs				
Drugs	12	5,800	113.60	3.84
Other Retail				
Other Retail	5	1,320	77.14	6.75
Personal Services				
Beauty	1	1,200	70.47	7.00
Barber	11	615	59.19	6.00
Cleaner and Dyers	6	1,500	75.86	6.75
Financial				
Banks	18	3,188	–	6.65
Savings and Loan	20	2,048	–	8.50
Real Estate	15	1,200	–	7.73
Offices (other than financial)				
Medical and Dental	7	1,200	–	7.48
Other Offices	3	1,135	–	6.81

Tenant Mix

Tenant classifications by kind of center are listed only to suggest a common tenant mix. The mix will naturally be affected by circumstances of leasing, financing, and tenant availability for a particular trade area. In addition, a tenant appropriate for one center could be a mistake in another. Selection of store types must be left to the individual developer, who will base his choices on varying income ranges and other characteristics of the tributary population, inducements to impulse buying, local buying habits, store sizes, and merchandising practices in different site conditions and various geographic areas. However, certain store types tend to be prevalent in particular center types, apart from the definition of center type by key tenant classifications. Nearly every neighborhood center, for example, except for the new specialty or high-fashion center, will contain a drugstore as well as a food-service store and supermarket.

Seasoned leasing brokers, appraisers, landlords, and shopping center operators have learned the following about grouping certain kinds of businesses:

TENANT CLASSIFICATION	RANK	MEDIAN GLA	MEDIAN SALES VOLUME PER SQUARE FOOT GLA	MEDIAN TOTAL RENT PER SQUARE FOOT GLA
General Merchandise				
Junior Department Store	13	30,552	$ 83.67	$2.48
Discount Department Store	18	60,000	85.11	2.25
Food				
Supermarket	5	25,368	265.13	3.23
Food Service				
Restaurant without Liquor	10	2,780	107.38	6.71
Restaurant with Liquor	7	3,600	115.84	7.09
Fast Food/Carryout	9	1,750	146.04	8.80
Clothing				
Ladies' Specialty	12	2,000	110.41	6.84
Ladies' Ready-to-Wear	1	3,000	98.62	5.80
Shoes				
Family Shoes	4	3,073	74.28	5.04
Home Appliances/Music				
Radio, Video, Stereo	8	2,000	126.26	5.71
Gifts/Specialty				
Cards and Gifts	11	2,440	73.64	5.82
Books and Stationery	16	2,000	99.23	6.48
Jewelry and Cosmetics				
Jewelry	14	1,335	185.35	9.11
Drugs				
Drugs	20	7,500	122.13	3.83
Other Retail				
Other Retail	3	1,360	98.21	6.50
Personal Services				
Beauty	6	1,235	81.21	6.31
Cleaner and Dyers	17	1,680	61.62	6.00
Financial				
Banks	19	3,027	–	5.00
Offices (other than financial)				
Medical and Dental	15	1,000	–	6.31
Other Offices	2	1,000	–	5.35

- Men's stores—shoes, clothing, haberdashery, and sporting goods—tend to swell each other's volume.
- Similarly, women's apparel, shoes, and millinery, and children's clothes and toys—the soft lines—do better if located close to one another.
- Food product businesses—groceries, meat and fish markets, delicatessens, bakeries, doughnut shops, and confectioners—do well when grouped together.
- Stores selling personal services and conveniences are naturally compatible.

Even though surveys have been made of the store types and groupings suitable for shopping centers,[2] these studies have not included the effect of proper groupings on the prosperity of the whole center. Another immeasurable factor is the ability of a particular merchant to work as a member of the merchandising team—the team that ultimately becomes the shopping center.

---

[2] For a discussion of the principles of compatibility among retail businesses in selecting tenants, see Richard L. Nelson, *The Selection of Retail Locations* (New York: McGraw-Hill, 1966).

TENANT CLASSIFICATION	RANK	AVERAGE NUMBER OF STORES	MEDIAN GLA	MEDIAN SALES VOLUME PER SQUARE FOOT GLA	MEDIAN TOTAL RENT PER SQUARE FOOT GLA
General Merchandise					
Department Store	14	1.0	105,644	$ 89.77	$ 2.18
Food					
Candy and Nuts	16	1.0	700	204.22	18.88
Food Service					
Restaurant without Liquor	20	.9	2,768	122.00	8.50
Restaurant with Liquor	12	1.1	4,236	120.17	7.52
Fast Food/Carryout	2	3.0	900	201.99	17.66
Clothing					
Ladies' Specialty	6	2.0	2,376	136.62	8.60
Ladies' Ready-to-Wear	1	6.5	3,750	110.30	7.72
Menswear	4	2.6	3,257	131.55	8.00
Unisex/Jean Shop	11	1.4	2,616	160.10	10.00
Special Apparel—Unisex	17	1.0	1,102	170.00	15.00
Shoes					
Family Shoes	3	2.9	3,290	112.43	9.00
Ladies' Shoes	8	1.9	1,840	135.34	13.00
Men's and Boys' Shoes	15	1.0	1,359	165.71	13.67
Home Appliances/Music					
Radio, Video, Stereo	13	1.1	2,312	191.71	10.00
Gifts/Specialty					
Cards and Gifts	7	2.0	2,485	112.60	9.02
Books and Stationery	9	1.5	3,160	149.79	10.00
Jewelry and Cosmetics					
Jewelry	5	2.6	1,438	264.19	17.55
Other Retail					
Other Retail	10	1.4	1,125	129.91	10.00
Financial					
Banks	18	1.0	2,300	—	7.64
Offices (other than financial)					
Other Offices	19	1.0	1,200	—	7.90

In a well-laid-out shopping center, all locations will be good. Each tenant's location carries equal advantage for high-volume retailing. The long-established retail theory of the "100 percent location" that was once applied to downtowns should not be reflected in well-designed shopping centers. Certain types of tenants do not in fact require locations on a main mall; they will be sought out. Banks, travel agencies, restaurants, and service shops are suited to side malls or other locations that have less pedestrian traffic.

In choosing stores for a center in a new growth area, the developer must secure shops that can render a service to the trade area and that have the financial stamina to weather a pioneering period. Other special points to consider are the tenant's credit rating, his profit and loss experience, his advertising policy, his type of merchandise, his class of customers, his housekeeping practices, his long-term operational record and merchandising policy, and his integrity.

Certain axioms about store grouping have grown out of shopping center experience: Arrange tenants to provide the greatest amount of interplay among the stores. Choose carefully the location of a supermarket because of its heavy demand for parking spaces; if there is no convenient parking for the supermarket, or for a theater, there will be no customers.

As discussed earlier, a neighborhood center typically has a supermarket as its major tenant with a

TENANT CLASSIFICATION	RANK	AVERAGE NUMBER OF STORES	MEDIAN GLA	MEDIAN SALES VOLUME PER SQUARE FOOT GLA	MEDIAN TOTAL RENT PER SQUARE FOOT GLA
General Merchandise					
Department Store (unowned)	10	2.3	153,182	$109.34	$ .40
Food					
Candy and Nuts	14	1.8	714	239.97	22.50
Food Service					
Restaurant with Liquor	15	1.7	4,683	132.10	8.08
Fast Food/Carryout	2	5.2	760	205.79	20.50
Clothing					
Ladies' Specialty	9	2.4	1,920	152.95	10.00
Ladies' Ready-to-Wear	1	10.9	3,743	119.85	8.28
Menswear	3	4.6	3,215	134.51	8.75
Unisex/Jean Shop	8	2.6	3,087	169.14	11.45
Special Apparel—Unisex	13	1.8	1,491	171.25	14.00
Shoes					
Family Shoes	4	4.2	3,256	129.58	10.00
Ladies' Shoes	5	4.1	1,844	168.92	13.00
Men's and Boys' Shoes	11	2.3	1,264	171.93	15.00
Home Appliances/Music					
Radio, Video, Stereo	16	1.6	2,457	243.26	10.99
Records and Tapes	20	1.4	2,750	188.59	11.99
Gifts/Specialty					
Cards and Gifts	7	3.0	2,516	136.85	12.00
Books and Stationery	12	2.0	3,466	163.16	11.74
Jewelry and Cosmetics					
Jewelry	6	3.8	1,467	343.56	20.59
Other Retail					
Other Retail	17	1.5	1,000	161.38	14.00
Offices (other than financial)					
Medical and Dental	19	1.4	951	—	8.44
Other Offices	18	1.4	788	—	8.22

drugstore often occupying the second highest percentage of total GLA. Figure 5-7 is offered as a guide for tenant composition.[3] Community centers, the "in-between" centers, provide a greater array of tenant classifications than do neighborhood centers. See Figure 5-8.

Tenant classifications for regional and super regional centers (see Figures 5-9 and 5-10) depend somewhat on lease negotiations with the department stores. As mentioned before, a regional center must have at least one full-line department store. Proper tenant location, though complicated, is essential. In super regional centers, the merchandising plan requires even greater care to place small tenants in the path of pedestrian circulation among the larger magnets—department stores, junior department stores, specialty stores, and quality restaurants.

A regional center must be all-inclusive and self-sufficient, suggesting the importance of grouping stores. To be self-sufficient, the center must have not only stores with big drawing power but also a full range of merchandise available to shoppers, including nearly every retail offering (with the growing exception of a variety store) once found downtown.

Completeness also means competition within the center. Competition among merchants is good for the center and good for the merchants. It keeps merchants

[3] This list of tenants in neighborhood centers, as well as the lists that follow for community, regional, and super regional centers, are taken from *Dollars & Cents of Shopping Centers: 1984*, published by the Urban Land Institute. The ranking shown in the lists, as well as the median sales volumes and median rents were current in 1984 but obviously will change.

SALES PER SQUARE FOOT, AND TOTAL CHARGES FOR SELECTED TENANTS: 1975–1984

	1975			1978			1981			1984		
	MEDIAN SQ. FT. GLA	MEDIAN SALES/ SQ. FT. GLA[1]	TOTAL CHARGES/ SQ. FT. GLA[1]	MEDIAN SQ. FT. GLA	MEDIAN SALES/ SQ. FT. GLA[1]	TOTAL CHARGES/ SQ. FT. GLA[1]	MEDIAN SQ. FT. GLA	MEDIAN SALES/ SQ. FT. GLA[1]	TOTAL CHARGES/ SQ. FT. GLA[1]	MEDIAN SQ. FT. GLA	MEDIAN SALES/ SQ. FT. GLA[1]	TOTAL CHARGES/ SQ. FT. GLA[1]
Super Regional Centers												
Department Store	180,000	$ 75.03	$ 1.91	163,086	$ 67.43	$ 2.22	165,364	$ 81.79	$ 3.02	127,082	$ 93.00	$ 2.43
Unowned Department Store	176,057	—	—	173,064	—	—	164,694	—	—	153,182	—	—
Candy and Nuts	818	102.83	13.70	750	149.41	19.32	662	200.39	25.28	714	239.97	28.66
Fast Food/Carryout	1,073	175.09	14.87	1,099	127.25	15.33	950	155.70	22.15	760	205.79	29.89
Ladies' Specialty	1,732	87.85	7.38	1,672	105.27	10.38	1,857	133.30	13.74	1,920	152.95	15.25
Ladies' Ready-to-Wear	3,638	87.43	6.95	3,840	102.47	8.23	3,705	117.86	11.31	3,743	119.85	12.98
Menswear	3,435	100.89	7.81	3,158	103.73	9.15	3,109	115.16	11.90	3,215	134.51	12.79
Family Shoes	4,230	73.11	6.93	3,377	101.94	9.73	3,350	130.98	13.31	3,256	129.58	14.44
Ladies' Shoes	3,633	68.21	6.32	2,915	94.51	10.29	2,400	148.76	14.66	1,844	168.92	18.46
Men's and Boys' Shoes	1,500	120.50	10.34	1,418	123.68	14.31	1,270	160.93	18.67	1,264	171.93	19.70
Radio, Video, Stereo	2,533	97.34	5.73	2,367	160.21	8.50	2,196	185.62	11.95	2,457	243.26	15.29
Sporting Goods	4,569	89.27	5.48	4,003	111.56	8.73	5,250	126.23	9.10	4,270	145.47	12.03
Cards and Gifts	2,100	78.16	8.85	2,416	89.91	10.20	2,487	117.78	14.63	2,516	136.85	16.85
Jewelry	2,220	185.11	11.31	1,924	189.65	14.37	1,531	321.13	23.43	1,467	343.56	26.40
Drugs	11,806	85.65	4.43	5,392	119.74	9.00	5,661	130.43	11.26	6,408	145.77	12.92
Super Drug (over 10,000 sq. ft.)[2]	—	—	—	13,661	98.43	5.11	15,000	114.15	5.60	15,990	135.61	6.15
Beauty Shop	1,316	70.25	6.73	1,351	73.49	9.00	1,382	112.26	13.64	1,322	134.47	17.32
Banks	4,608	—	5.67	4,279	—	8.35	3,773	—	10.75	2,762	—	11.62
Regional Centers												
Department Store	122,621	$ 61.42	$ 1.69	131,000	$ 65.65	$ 1.87	100,000	$ 83.48	$ 2.38	105,644	$ 89.77	$ 2.55
Unowned Department Store	189,118	—	—	184,065	—	—	147,427	—	—	155,686	—	—
Candy and Nuts	800	87.37	10.73	732	121.55	14.67	700	151.30	19.10	700	204.22	25.06
Fast Food/Carryout	1,057	113.50	11.43	1,100	125.17	13.15	1,000	161.75	15.94	900	201.99	23.78
Ladies' Specialty	1,742	81.50	6.81	2,038	100.13	8.53	2,462	110.24	9.05	2,376	136.62	11.65
Ladies' Ready-to-Wear	4,005	85.76	5.74	4,003	91.10	7.17	3,706	112.67	8.37	3,750	110.30	10.98
Menswear	3,288	96.19	6.58	3,417	99.18	7.59	3,173	116.43	8.75	3,257	131.55	11.57
Family Shoes	3,840	67.75	5.66	3,663	88.29	7.16	3,360	103.57	8.90	3,290	112.43	12.17
Ladies' Shoes	4,000	67.46	6.36	3,164	82.99	7.96	2,500	110.56	9.80	1,840	135.34	17.09
Men's and Boys' Shoes	1,500	107.88	8.76	1,492	117.65	11.00	1,460	141.65	11.73	1,359	165.71	16.98
Radio, Video, Stereo	2,474	120.22	6.05	2,361	127.90	7.01	2,200	165.37	8.53	2,312	191.71	12.92
Sporting Goods	4,970	80.38	4.55	3,600	113.32	6.58	3,000	119.35	8.47	4,000	138.10	11.06
Cards and Gifts	1,950	71.00	7.42	2,265	76.92	8.46	2,500	95.78	9.88	2,485	112.60	12.61
Jewelry	2,079	141.22	8.52	1,792	180.32	12.48	1,607	271.59	16.55	1,438	264.19	21.77
Drugs	10,116	79.84	3.28	7,450	107.95	4.59	7,332	150.19	5.33	7,076	157.71	7.21
Super Drug (over 10,000 sq. ft.)[2]	—	—	—	15,000	90.06	3.48	15,300	124.65	4.16	15,200	131.11	4.84
Beauty Shop	1,422	61.38	5.60	1,280	68.13	7.15	1,162	83.43	9.35	1,281	109.68	10.70
Banks	3,600	—	5.15	3,370	—	6.14	2,582	—	7.81	2,300	—	9.77

on their toes (aggressive) and gives customers the comparison shopping they want.

The amount of sales space should be based on the estimated sales volume determined in the market analysis. It is also important to consider the number of people required to support a center of the proposed size.

Tenant Variety in All Categories of Shopping Centers

When discussing key tenants and other tenants most frequently associated with a certain shopping center type, one tends to assume the absence of all other tenant types. One could then conclude that certain tenants cannot successfully locate in a certain type of shopping center and/or that certain tenants should be excluded. However, a careful analysis of *Dollars & Cents of Shopping Centers: 1984* suggests otherwise. Each of the 128 categories of tenants identified is found in every type of center. But each occurs at different frequencies in different centers. For example, a cookie shop, a relatively new tenant category (having first been included in the study in 1981), is most commonly found in regional and super regional centers but occasionally appears operating successfully in community and neighborhood centers. In contrast, a coin-operated laundry is rarely found in large centers but is a common tenant in neighborhood centers, even though it does not appear in the top 20 shown in the tables. The success of a shopping center's tenant mix lies not in including or excluding a specific tenant type, but rather in selecting and com-

	1975			1978			1981			1984		
	MEDIAN SQ. FT. GLA	MEDIAN SALES/ SQ. FT. GLA[1]	TOTAL CHARGES/ SQ. FT. GLA[1]	MEDIAN SQ. FT. GLA	MEDIAN SALES/ SQ. FT. GLA[1]	TOTAL CHARGES/ SQ. FT. GLA[1]	MEDIAN SQ. FT. GLA	MEDIAN SALES/ SQ. FT. GLA[1]	TOTAL CHARGES/ SQ. FT. GLA[1]	MEDIAN SQ. FT. GLA	MEDIAN SALES/ SQ. FT. GLA[1]	TOTAL CHARGES/ SQ. FT. GLA[1]
Community Centers												
Jr. Department Store	30,000	$ 51.97	$1.79	37,500	$ 60.49	$1.93	48,613	$ 83.63	$ 2.25	30,552	$ 83.67	$ 2.68
Discount Department Store	72,500	57.56	1.83	64,726	62.98	1.90	57,826	70.51	2.12	60,000	85.11	2.60
Supermarket	20,519	135.23	1.93	22,384	200.98	2.47	24,360	248.95	3.14	25,368	265.13	3.59
Restaurant with Liquor	3,938	62.00	3.95	4,150	75.86	4.99	3,279	115.13	7.65	3,600	115.84	8.27
Fast Food/Carryout	1,306	78.89	6.02	1,323	115.51	7.63	1,300	161.64	10.59	1,750	146.04	9.84
Ladies' Ready-to-Wear	2,940	61.83	3.99	2,969	76.84	4.78	3,190	94.62	6.13	3,000	98.62	6.94
Menswear	3,000	65.55	4.10	3,040	79.10	4.70	3,000	105.03	6.30	2,704	101.96	7.22
Family Shoes	3,200	52.37	3.15	3,024	62.27	4.00	3,120	76.44	5.48	3,073	74.82	5.89
Radio, Video, Stereo	2,000	67.45	3.30	2,000	98.14	3.97	1,953	116.17	5.51	2,000	126.26	6.14
Cards and Gifts	2,000	48.90	3.96	2,000	50.04	4.71	2,129	66.17	6.51	2,440	73.64	6.94
Jewelry	1,806	77.94	4.76	1,500	129.68	6.37	1,400	166.93	8.92	1,335	185.35	10.84
Beauty Shop	1,200	50.55	3.99	1,200	47.05	4.65	1,212	62.33	5.86	1,235	81.21	7.12
Banks	2,864	—	3.78	3,200	—	4.52	2,937	—	5.54	3,027	—	6.11
Neighborhood Centers												
Supermarket	20,000	$133.19	$2.08	22,648	$178.73	$2.62	24,650	$228.57	$ 3.38	25,500	$271.46	$ 3.89
Restaurant with Liquor	3,161	55.03	3.43	3,600	75.65	5.27	3,260	105.79	7.36	3,200	117.05	8.97
Fast Food/Carryout	1,600	50.06	4.28	1,410	96.29	6.17	1,500	101.20	7.49	1,500	150.59	10.18
Ice Cream Parlor	1,110	53.70	4.21	1,160	89.46	4.98	1,200	96.45	8.08	1,100	129.44	9.24
Ladies' Ready-to-Wear	2,000	63.05	3.95	1,680	50.04	4.42	1,800	81.56	6.00	1,700	103.15	8.03
Radio, Video, Stereo	2,100	49.66	3.32	2,000	98.14	4.04	2,000	85.33	4.94	1,800	93.49	7.22
Cards and Gifts	1,800	37.29	4.05	1,810	39.98	4.14	2,000	44.82	5.96	2,250	71.75	8.04
Liquor and Wine	2,400	79.50	3.73	2,300	130.72	4.49	2,400	202.45	6.02	2,450	177.89	7.01
Drugs	7,305	64.82	2.35	4,900	78.31	3.05	5,631	110.30	3.84	5,800	113.60	4.34
Super Drug (over 10,000 sq. ft.)[2]	—	—	—	15,000	89.33	2.80	15,000	93.20	3.00	15,702	121.77	3.75[2]
Beauty Shop	1,200	49.85	4.00	1,200	47.65	4.16	1,145	63.88	5.74	1,200	70.47	7.77
Barber	620	38.88	3.80	640	36.97	4.12	656	51.22	5.50	615	59.17	6.44
Cleaner and Dyers	1,600	33.81	3.47	1,600	33.14	3.81	1,500	49.42	5.40	1,500	75.86	7.77
Laundry	1,578	16.29	3.03	1,500	16.77	3.57	1,500	27.69	4.75	1,650	34.91	5.09
Banks	2,594	—	3.41	2,539	—	4.30	2,594	—	6.12	3,188	—	7.94

[1]All dollar figures are in current dollars.
[2]All drug stores were combined in the 1975 study.
Source: Urban Land Institute, *Dollars & Cents of Shopping Centers: 1975, 1978, 1981,* and *1984.*

bining a group of mutually reinforcing tenants that will serve the needs of the particular market.

Tenant Evaluation

Shopping center operators must watch carefully and evaluate tenant performance. If tenant sales volumes are low, the tenants can be replaced, provided they are on short-term leases; otherwise, problems may be corrected through negotiations. Operators of new centers must monitor and encourage tenant performance, particularly the performance of any tenants that are first-time entrants into a shopping center.

If a developer/owner decides to reduce the proportion of triple-A credit-rated national chains and to increase the number of local chains and independent merchants (who have built-in customer appeal, merchandising expertise, and operational performance capabilities), he must continuously evaluate perfor-

mance and assist the independent merchants in merchandising.

In enclosed malls, the ability of tenants to pull customer traffic into and along the mall may be a greater test of productivity than are the clauses of a lease. An anchor tenant, particularly, is expected to deliver a sizable number of customers to the rest of the tenants.

In any center, certain tenants will need to be relocated. Some tenants will outgrow their original spaces; others will require smaller spaces. Still others may need to be shifted to strengthen the overall operations of a center.

Many merchants fail because they start with too much space and must carry its additional overhead. It is essential to have the flexibility to adapt space to the changing needs of tenants. Some tenant classifications continue to move toward smaller tenant spaces to encourage higher productivity and more intensive use of the space. In other cases, tenant spaces have been growing (see Figures 5-12 and 5-14).

Developers seeking tenants must consider not only the services that a center is to offer a community but also current trends in tenant classifications and merchandising. They must avoid fads, yet they must take into account the effects of current economic conditions. Current surveys can help determine these effects. In order to select a tenant mix that is on target for the center's trade area, a developer must also remember that his leasing strategy will need to be carefully fine tuned; for example, it is not enough to know that the tenant mix should include two sit-down res-

taurants of so many seats—further study must be done to determine the specific types of restaurants that would be most appropriate (based on detailed demographics for the center's trade area).

In calculating the rental income stream to be achieved, the developer must remember that all types of stores cannot and should not pay the same rents per square foot. Each tenant should be aware that his rent is based on the probable volume and profit level in his particular business. Certain types of service establishments may pay comparatively low rents and may even be loss leaders for their centers. Such tenants, however, are valuable to high-rent tenants for their draw-

5-12

CHANGING STORE SIZE[1]
(Percentage Change in Median Store Sizes)

	1981–1984				1975–1984			
	SUPER REGIONAL	REGIONAL	COMMUNITY	NEIGHBOR-HOOD	SUPER REGIONAL	REGIONAL	COMMUNITY	NEIGHBOR-HOOD
Department Store	−23	6	[2]	[2]	−29	−14	[2]	[2]
Unowned Department Store	−7	6	[2]	[2]	−13	−18	[2]	[2]
Junior Department Store	−19	7	−37	[2]	−20	73	[2]	[2]
Variety Store	−8	16	11	6	−7	−11	11	23
Discount Department Store	[2]	[2]	4	[2]	[2]	[2]	−17	[2]
Supermarket	−16	18	4	4	−10	16	24	28
Specialty Food	7	−6	16	−3	7	−10	−34	−47
Candy and Nuts	8	0	24	[2]	−13	−13	−16	[2]
Restaurant without Liquor	−16	−2	0	−1	−13	0	−18	−2
Restaurant with Liquor	−3	−4	10	−2	−22	−22	−8	1
Fast Food/Carryout	−20	−10	35	0	−29	−15	34	−6
Ice Cream Parlor	−7	−11	−1	−8	−15	−23	3	−1
Ladies' Specialty	3	4	3	20	11	37	24	−13
Ladies' Ready-to-Wear	1	1	−6	−6	3	−6	2	−19
Menswear	4	3	−10	14	−6	−1	−10	20
Unisex/Jean Shop	24	14	13	17	62	57	45	67
Family Shoes	−3	−2	−2	11	−23	−14	−4	1
Ladies' Shoes	−23	−26	−11	[2]	−49	−50	−52	[2]
Men's and Boys' Shoes	−1	−7	[2]	[2]	−16	−9	[2]	[2]
Furniture	17	0	12	31	−7	−53	−44	−36
Radio, Video, Stereo	12	5	3	−10	−3	−7	0	−14
Records and Tapes	12	0	2	[2]	43	45	12	[2]
Hardware	[2]	[2]	−1	17	[2]	[2]	22	9
Sporting Goods—General	−19	33	−13	38	−7	−20	4	2
Cards and Gifts	1	−1	15	13	20	27	22	25
Books and Stationery	−1	2	−1	9	−9	13	11	11
Jewelry	−4	−10	−46	[2]	−34	−31	−26	[2]
Liquor and Wine	[2]	[2]	0	2	[2]	[2]	7	2
Super Drug (over 10,000 square feet)	7	−1	−13	5	[3]	[3]	[3]	[3]
Drugs	13	−4	0	3	[3]	[3]	[3]	[3]
Fabric Shop	1	−5	0	−2	13	29	15	−20
Beauty Shop	−4	10	2	5	1	−10	3	0
Barber Shop	[2]	7	13	−6	[2]	11	6	−1
Cleaner and Dyers	[2]	[2]	5	0	[2]	[2]	−15	−6
Banks	−27	−11	3	23	−40	−36	6	−23
Number Shrinking	17	14	11	8	20	19	11	11
Number Getting Larger	13	14	17	16	8	9	18	10

[1]Because of the variables in samples between studies, percentage changes of less than 5 percent probably have no significance.
[2]The sample was too small to report (under 50 stores).
[3]Before 1978, super drugs and drugs were combined into one category.
Source: Urban Land Institute, *Dollars & Cents of Shopping Centers: 1975, 1981,* and *1984.*

ing power and for rounding out a center's services to the community, which is essential in maintaining continued patronage and goodwill.

Food and Food Service

Supermarkets

A supermarket is the anchor tenant in a traditional neighborhood center, a key tenant in community centers, and an optional tenant in a regional center, not now customary unless placed in a separate structure to which customers drive directly.

Today, the term "supermarket" is applied to a number of distinct store types, ranging from a conventional supermarket to a food warehouse. *Chain Store Guide* defines a conventional supermarket as "a complete full-line, self-service market operating in a sales area of more than 6,000 square feet with an annual sales volume of at least $2 million." A super store is defined as one with more than 30,000 square feet of sales area and an annual sales volume of at least $5 million. A superette has a sales area of less than 6,000 square feet and an annual sales volume of less than $2 million. A food warehouse offers cut-rate prices and minimal ambience. In 1983, warehouse stores had a median sales area of 23,500 square feet, while super warehouse stores were sometimes as large as 60,000 to 75,000 square feet. Finally, combination supermarket/drugstores often are as large as 60,000 square

5-13 A food warehouse offers cut-rate prices and minimal ambience.

feet (and in 1983 had a median sales area of 49,457 square feet).[4]

In choosing from among these possibilities, the developer may also have to decide whether to build one or more than one supermarket in a strong location. He must take into account the fact that rates for percentage rents on food items are between 1 and 1.75 percent of sales, whereas rates on nonfood items could be roughly 6 percent if sold by stores other than the supermarket. Because of the differences in percentage

---

[4] Food Marketing Institute, *Facts About Store Development* (Washington, D.C.: Food Marketing Institute (FMI), 1983).

5-14   CHANGING STORE SIZE—COMPARISON OF EXISTING STORES BY SELECTED TYPE WITH NEW STORES OPENED IN 1981/1983
(Square Feet)

Store Type	Existing Stores	New Stores	Size Trend
Department Store			
Full	100,000–179,000	100,000–170,000	Diminishing
Junior	42,500– 50,000	25,000– 65,000	Enlarging
Discount Department Store			
Large	70,000–100,000	70,000–100,000	Remaining
Small	40,000– 50,000	43,000– 65,000	Enlarging
Variety Store	13,000– 42,000	15,000– 50,000	Enlarging
Supermarket	22,000– 36,000	30,000– 48,000	Enlarging
Drugstore	10,000– 15,000	9,000– 13,000	Diminishing
Specialty Store	2,500– 6,000	2,900– 7,500	Enlarging
Home Center	10,000– 60,000	35,000– 60,000	Enlarging

Source: *Chain Store Age*, July 1982.

FOOD STORE FORMATS AND REAL ESTATE CHARACTERISTICS
FOR THE 1980s

CHARACTERISTIC	FOOD/DRUG COMBINATION	SUPER STORE	CONVENTIONAL SUPERMARKET	WAREHOUSE STORE
Median Store Size (square feet of sales area)[1]	49,457	38,000	22,000	23,500
Weekly Sales ($000)	$250–400	$150–350	$75–250	$75–400
Nonfood Sales (percentage)	30–35%	20–25%	10–15%	0
Trade Area:				
Size (miles)	3–5	3	2–3	5–10
Population	60,000	50,000	40–50,000	150,000
Market Share (percentage)	15%	15%	10–15%	2–5%
Preferred Location	Freestanding	NSC[2]	NSC[2]	Freestanding or NSC[2]
Type of Real Estate	Build-to-Suit or Recycled Discount Stores	Build-to-Suit or Recycled Discount Stores	Recycled Stores	Recycled Stores
Number of Stores	500	9,000	30,000	1,750
Growth for the 1980s	Major Thrust	Major Thrust	Limited to Specific Markets and Segments	Limited to Specific Markets and Segments

[1]1983 median store size.
[2]Neighborhood shopping center.
Source: Howard L. Green & Assoc., Inc., 1025 East Maple, Suite 200, Birmingham, Michigan 48011; and *1983 Facts About Store Development* (Washington, D.C.: Food Marketing Institute (FMI), 1983).

rates for various classes of merchandise, it is important to have a clear understanding of the specific internal characteristics of a supermarket. The fact that food items are sold at low markups is well known. The proportion of nonfood sales to total GLA varies widely and changes somewhat each year. However, in general, supermarkets today are increasingly selling a larger proportion of nonfood items. In addition, most supermarket chains are targeting each store to the demographics of its specific trade area, in terms of both the store's design and the merchandise mix.[5]

Supermarkets need adequate parking for heavy customer turnover and direct entrances from the parking areas. They require loading docks for trucks, truck turning areas, and special trash storage and pickup spaces. The best architectural treatment for these areas is a court, screened from the view of customers.

In general, supermarkets are not big customer attractions within the larger regional or super regional center. The smaller the center, the more important they become. In those centers where the supermarket is a preferred tenant, its *drawing* power is its greatest contribution to the center as a whole.

Other Food Stores

Small food specialty shops—delicatessens and stores that offer meats, fish, and poultry, candy and nuts, baked goods, or dairy products—when effectively merchandised, are valued tenants in any shopping center.

Restaurants

Every shopping center needs eating facilities. Even a small neighborhood center should have at least a counter or fountain operation. In a regional center, eating places of every type are important. A quality restaurant operation can draw patrons from throughout a trade area. The good restaurant takes a skillful operator with special know-how.

A freestanding location on the shopping center site permits drive-to service and specially assigned parking spaces. Since a good restaurant may do much of its business on Sundays or during evening hours, it

---

[5] For complete information about supermarket sales volume, store size, extent of competition, lease terms, customer count, departments within the store, etc., see *Facts About Store Development* and *Food Marketing Industry Speaks*. Both are published annually by the Food Marketing Institute (FMI), Washington, D.C.

should be easily accessible and readily identified, and it should provide adequate parking. It may also be located so that it is accessible from a mall or plaza, thus drawing traffic to an area that might otherwise receive light pedestrian traffic.

Restaurants vary greatly as to classification and type of operation: they may be independent or belong to a national chain. They may range from the small, quick-order, limited-menu counter or table service operation to the distinctively decorated, high-quality, high-price gourmet table service establishment, with or without liquor.

All types have both succeeded and failed in regional, community, and specialty centers. Because the rate of failure is notoriously high, a carefully selected operator is essential.

All regional centers need at least one *quality* restaurant and, if the law allows, liquor service. However, high-priced restaurants often do poorly in regional centers. If a developer can lease restaurant space only by providing fixtures and furniture, he should select the best locally known successful proprietor and ad- vance the necessary funds, based on the assumption that he will eventually recover his investment.

Food Courts

As mentioned earlier, the food court has become a major component of many regional malls and special- ty centers. It consists of a cluster of food-service (and, occasionally, food-related) tenants grouped around a common or public eating area. The goal in the design and leasing of the food court is to create a festive atmosphere that will result in a high volume of sales and customer traffic for the center (see Chapter 3 for information on the design of food courts).

The need for a strong thematic organization of as many elements as possible has led to a mix of tenant categories, from an exclusive food-service mix to a food-related retail program, such as cleverly packaged and merchandised gourmet items, coffees and spices, or cookware and kitchen gadgetry. Mixing tenant cate- gories can expand the drawing power of a food court

5-16   PRINCIPAL FOOD LINES MOST FREQUENTLY FOUND IN FOOD COURTS

	NUMBER IN SAMPLE	MEDIAN GLA (SQUARE FEET)	MEDIAN SALES PER SQUARE FOOT OF GLA	MEDIAN TOTAL RENT PER SQUARE FOOT OF GLA
Super Regional Centers:				
Sample Size—191				
Hot Dogs	22	500	$317.72	$33.18
Hamburgers	15	687	221.70	30.00
Potatoes	15	544	264.56	31.99
European	15	617	205.81	25.55
Mexican	15	740	234.15	25.55
Pizza	14	760	281.56	24.00
Oriental	13	596	233.81	29.98
Ice Cream	13	678	187.85	23.25
Pastries/Croissants	11	682	156.53	23.78
Chicken	10	730	212.29	18.88
Cookies	8	526	311.97	40.00
Sandwiches	6	538	221.97	25.00
Regional Centers:				
Sample Size—78				
Hot Dogs	10	530	260.04	32.99
Mexican	8	574	313.00	34.51
Pizza	7	672	265.69	30.48
Ice Cream	7	436	—	—
Oriental	5	480	—	—

Source: Urban Land Institute, *Dollars & Cents of Shopping Centers: 1984* (Washington, D.C.: ULI–the Urban Land Institute, 1984).

as well as reinforce a chosen theme. A successfully implemented theme may have numerous benefits:

- The center's marketing potential will be strengthened.
- Participants can share marketing, overhead, and direct expenses.
- By having unified theme elements, the project will be more identifiable and memorable to customers.
- Tenants will be more easily encouraged to strive for individual quality in the preparation and presentation of their foods.

The objective of a food court should be to obtain a variety of tenants while at the same time protecting the food cluster concept. Complementary, not competitive, menus should be available, although foods should offer some variety (see Figure 5-16). If space is leased to operators who offer unique local specialties, several potential problems must be avoided or dealt with:

- Because of the individuality and aspirations of local operators, menu control may be difficult.
- Disputes must be settled for the good of the collective entity; management thus needs to be strong and decisive.
- The developer will probably face higher tenant allowances among potentially undercapitalized local entrepreneurs, in contrast to the fast food chains or franchise operations.

- "Spin-offs" can easily become "step-children." The successful skills of the parent operation must be recreated by a dedicated operator. Absentee management should be avoided.

The successful food court makes the most of competition among its various operations, keeping quality, performance, and aspirations high. Occasionally, food courts may have a single operator behind a facade of differing menus, giving only the illusion of diversity. Having only one operator simplifies lease negotiations: one lease assures fewer duplications of equipment—with one master kitchen, central supplies, etc.—and even simplifies solutions to the space-consuming problems of access. But quality typically suffers. The theme food court, in food preparation and presentation, requires more than one kitchen.[6]

In addition to kitchens, the food court will require washing and cold storage facilities. All food court tenants are on separate percentage leases, and therefore pay a higher overall rent than a single restaurant tenant. Management must carefully evaluate problems of maintenance, cleanliness, and placement within the center. Other details it must work out include whether to use china, silverware, and glasses or whether to rely on disposable items; whether these items will be separately or commonly owned by the food service tenants; what the practical and financial arrangements will be for procuring, stocking, and washing or disposing of these items; what arrangements it will make for providing condiments and paying cleanup costs; and so forth.

Fast Food Outlets

In a regional center the chain fast food outlet will most likely be treated like any other mall tenant. In community and neighborhood centers, however, this will not be the case. Most fast food chains have distinctive building designs and specific on-site circulation and parking patterns related to their method of operation. While the building design of such outlets has improved considerably over the prevailing design of the 1950s and early 1960s, the general appearance of fast food stores is still the target of public criticism. A shopping center developer planning to include such tenants should apply the same standards of design control he would apply to any other freestanding tenant. The developer's ability and willingness to help modify the unacceptable characteristics of these uses will be important in obtaining necessary public approvals.

5-17 The food court at Charleston Town Center, a 930,000-square-foot center in downtown Charleston, West Virginia.

6 David Lemonds, "Food Courts: A Legacy Meets Today's Market," *Urban Land*, March 1983.

5-18 The same standards of design control should be applied to fast food tenants as to any other freestanding tenants.

General Merchandise and Apparel

Department Stores

One full-line department store (and more commonly two such stores) containing at least 100,000 square feet of GLA will function as the key or anchor tenant(s) in a regional center. If the center has three or more department stores and at least 500,000 square feet of GLA, it becomes a super regional center.

As the dominant tenants of regional shopping centers, department stores are the main generators of customer traffic. With more than one department store, the center's configuration must be designed to separate them. Supplementary tenants will then be positioned to benefit from the flow of customers between the anchor stores. The department stores will need balanced parking directly accessible to them. Providing for a safe and convenient customer flow between the parking areas and the building entrances while drawing pedestrians through the mall is the crux of good site planning and building design in regional centers.

In negotiating for a department store tenant, developers should be aware of customer loyalties, the segment of the market the tenant serves, the store's policies in price lines, and its merchandising image. One or more department stores will usually serve each market area. These stores may already be operating in the area, and the success of a new regional center may depend on whether the developer can pull the stores into the center. Other department store chains that wish to establish new market outlets will generally prefer to be associated with established stores.

Before adding another department store to an existing center, a developer must be sure that the additional anchor will increase the center's drawing power, that the deal to be struck with the anchor is economically feasible, and that the trade area can support another department store.

Over time, there has been a noticeable movement away from the traditional arrangement in which a department store leases GLA from the shopping center owner in much the same way as other stores in the center. Today each department store typically buys its own land (including a portion of the parking areas) from the shopping center developer/owner. In such cases, however, customers see no physical evidence of a difference in ownership between the department stores and between the rest of the center; the department stores remain an integral part of the center's design. In smaller markets, a gross lease may be preferred for department stores.

When anchor department stores build and own their units, a complex set of legal operating arrangements and cross easements becomes necessary. Various agreements between the department stores and the shopping center owner must cover such items as the type of department store to be operated, the hours of operation, the continuation of store operations, participation in the operation and maintenance of the common area, including the parking area, and participation in the merchants' association (if one exists) and advertising and promotional programs. The content and thoroughness of these agreements are particularly significant to lending institutions.

Since full-line stores are such major attractors, the quality of the architectural design must be closely related to the character of the trade area. Each department store, with its own standards in merchandising techniques and quality, should complement the other stores but should also help set the tone for the entire center.

Off-Price and Discount Stores

Once an anathema to the shopping center, the off-price store and the discount store are now commonly found in community centers. As noted earlier, the off-price store or the discount store is often a principal anchor tenant in a community center, filling the role that the junior department store or the variety store had in past years. Both off-price and discount stores are self-service operations, which keeps down overhead and allows consumers to make purchases at lower prices, often at discounts of 20 percent or more. These stores also keep down prices by buying in volume, working with lower profit margins, receiving merchandise directly from manufacturers, and using sales areas as storage areas (thus reducing storage space to as little as 10 percent of the gross leasable area). In contrast, traditional department stores generally use from 20 to 40 percent of their floor area for storage and other nonselling purposes.

Although the off-price store and the discount store both offer merchandise at a significant cost savings to consumers, they typically differ in other ways. The off-price store caters to white-collar, middle-, and upper-middle-income buyers who are price sensitive and seeking quality, brand-name merchandise at a discount. The discount store usually caters to blue-collar, middle-income, lower-middle-income, and lower-income buyers who are cost conscious and will buy lesser-quality merchandise at a discount.

If an off-price store or a discount store is to be a key tenant in a community center, its practices of merchandising, advertising, and sign control must be compatible with those of satellite tenants and shopping center management. The developer should also bear in mind that off-price and discount tenants typically will not pay percentage rents that are as high as those paid by traditional retailers. Most off-price and discount retailers pay percentage rents that are approximately 1 percent below those paid by traditional retailers for comparable locations. However, sales per square foot for off-price and discount tenants are often much higher than those generated by traditional retailers.

Apparel Stores

Tenants in the apparel category cover a full range of store types, quality, style, and price. In a neighborhood center, an apparel store usually offers goods that are a convenience to the local market. Apparel stores represent the lifeblood of community and regional centers. Men's, women's, children's, and family clothing lines strongly attract comparison shopping. Independent merchants, local chains, national chains, custom clothing shops, ready-to-wear outlets, and accessories are all represented. Store area, sales, and rents based on productivity are important factors to the developer who is seeking such tenants.

Community and regional centers may contain groups of selected high-price, high-fashion, and other specialized apparel stores. In the right trade area, such stores can strengthen a center's drawing power. For example, women's stores with attractive clothing and prices can provide the impetus for special-purpose shopping trips.

Men's stores with complete clothing lines have become more important in regional centers and less important in community and neighborhood centers. A selected range of haberdashery can be appropriate in a neighborhood center.

Shoe Stores

While a neighborhood center may or may not have a shoe store, community and regional centers include a number of them, usually chain stores. Because competition within the lines bolsters sales volumes, it may be feasible to include several women's and family shoe stores. The stores must, of course, be carefully selected. There should be fewer stores for men than for women and children, because men buy fewer pairs of shoes per season.

Furniture and Home Furnishings

A furniture store produces little traffic and a low sales volume per square foot of GLA. The average household purchases furniture infrequently and makes a special shopping trip for it. Furniture stores fit into suburban locations and the pattern of evening shopping. But they usually require larger display and storage areas while paying low rents per square foot.

Full-line furniture stores are more suitable to freestanding locations than to shopping centers. If a furniture store is to be placed in a center, it will probably be located in a low-rent basement or other space away from the principal shopping area. A full-line furniture store is rarely found in a neighborhood center.

An interior decorator shop may substitute for a full-line furniture store in any center. Such a shop may offer a token selection of home furnishings, functioning like a specialized boutique. As with the furniture store, a decorator shop need not be located in a high-traffic area.

The size of a furniture store may range from 700 square feet upward. A freestanding, full-line furniture store can occupy 50,000 square feet or more.

Other Retail Goods and Services

Hardware and Home Improvement Centers

These centers use self-service supermarket merchandising techniques to sell ranges of selected household wares. Furthermore, the do-it-yourself market has transformed the traditional hardware store into a building equipment and materials and home repair center. Display racks occupy space once used by the clerk's aisle. The hardware store appears most often in neighborhood and community centers. Large home improvement centers have become major tenants in community centers. In regional centers, such home centers can be placed on the periphery of the site, similar to the location afforded a freestanding supermarket.

5-19 Because they offer opportunities for comparison shopping, apparel stores are important tenants in community and regional centers.

5-20 Freestanding tire, battery, and accessory (TBA) stores usually occupy secondary locations.

Wallpaper and Paint Stores

Wallpaper and paint stores are a special version of the hardware store classification and can be found in every type of center.

Garden Shops and Plant Stores

Garden shops require space for outdoor sales and displays. The display area must be adjacent to the store itself, necessitating special attention in site arrangement. During certain seasons, department stores may add a special garden shop that may be converted to other uses during the rest of the year. Today, garden shop and plant merchandise is often offered in a combined drug/variety/garden center that may serve as the principal anchor tenant for a community center. A plant store may be defined as a form of florist and is frequently combined with a florist shop. It can be found in any center type.

Auto Supply Stores

An auto accessory store customarily does not belong in the main unit of a shopping center, unless it is associated with a department store. This store, known as a tire, battery, and accessory (TBA) store, should be placed in a secondary or freestanding location, where parking and car service will not interfere with the center's general customer parking.

Some chain department stores have their own TBA stores to supplement customer services. If a TBA store is not placed in a freestanding building, it can be attached to its department store. Most department stores have a firm preference for one approach or the other.

Auto supply stores are found in community and neighborhood centers, although until recently they were considered a heavy commercial use and therefore not appropriate tenants. Changing store design

and merchandising techniques have upgraded this category so that the auto supply store has become an acceptable tenant.

Drugstores

A good drugstore is a key tenant in a neighborhood center. It is also a desirable tenant in any other type of center, except a high-fashion or other specialty center. Community and regional centers may have two drugstores; these may be prescription pharmacies, traditional drugstores with or without fountain service, or the super or merchandising drugstore, usually of the chain type.

A prescription pharmacy usually contains 650 to 1,200 square feet of GLA; a traditional drugstore contains 3,000 to 5,000 square feet; and a super drugstore has over 10,000 square feet (with some having 25,000 to 30,000 square feet). Developers must generally choose between a chain drugstore and a strong independent merchant. Because of its size, a super drugstore may fill the center's variety store needs. It is also frequently in direct competition with the nonfood areas of supermarkets. Therefore, in neighborhood and community centers it is important to maintain a careful balance among the super drugstore, the supermarket, and the variety store tenants.

Service Shops

Tenants providing personal services are common to all types and sizes of shopping centers, although they occupy a much higher percentage of total GLA in neighborhood centers than they do in regionals.

Barber shops or men's hair stylists, unisex hair salons, beauty salons, laundries and dry cleaning services, shoe repair shops, key makers, health spas, travel agents, and other service shops are all important for the convenience of shoppers. Service tenants are usually independent merchants who pay high rents per square foot of store area. Since the gross sales of service shops are difficult to ascertain, such tenants may pay a higher minimum guaranteed rent per square foot instead of a sales percentage.

Service shops are traffic builders in a neighborhood center and traffic users in a larger center. They need locations that provide direct access to customer parking, because much of their trade is the "run-in, run-out" kind. In an enclosed mall center, most of the service shops are usually placed in either a secondary location or apart from the mall in a freestanding building or in another separate convenience facility on the property.

Recreational/Community Facilities

Recreational/community facilities aid in the public relations efforts of a regional center. The community room is usually placed in a secondary location. As a center becomes the focal point of a suburban community, the community room can become a place in which to hold civic meetings, club gatherings, and social affairs. If a community room can be located next to a restaurant, the room can be used for banquets, luncheon meetings, and receptions. Other recreational/community facilities include post offices, music and dance studios, bowling alleys, cinemas, ice or roller skating rinks, arcade/amusement centers, and day-care/nursery centers.

Day-care facilities and nurseries were once considered an asset to a center; they attracted mothers who while shopping could leave their children in a supervised activity area. However, because liability insurance requirements and the public attitude toward child care have changed, nurseries need be considered only as an adjunct of a larger-scale multiuse development. Today, most successful day-care/nursery facilities are located in freestanding structures unrelated to shopping centers.

The amusement/video center has become the current version of the penny arcade. Such tenants have been successfully introduced into regional centers when they were given secondary locations and special architectural treatment. However, the issue of whether to include amusement/video centers should be carefully considered, since they can have a number of adverse effects—contributing to loitering, noise, litter, and vandalism—if they are not properly controlled. In addition, amusement/video centers are often considered undesirable by the local community and, thus, if included may have a negative impact on the community's perception and image of the center. If an amusement/video center is brought in, only tenants who can demonstrate an ability to control and police their premises should be selected. Such tenants have also appeared in community and neighborhood centers, although in neighborhood centers they tend to appear as a cluster of video game machines set up in an existing store. If center management is unable to pay consistent attention to such tenants and provide necessary controls, as might be the case in smaller shopping centers, it would be advisable not to include amusement/video tenants. The unsteady economic performance of many game rooms is another factor to consider in deciding whether or not to include such tenants.

Facilities for Special Tenants

Office Buildings

Office buildings for a single corporation or for multiple tenants bring more people to a center. Usually, offices in a shopping center are located in freestanding buildings; however, they have also been successfully integrated into the shopping center building complex. Certainly, this is true of mixed-use developments: the Galleria in Houston is a hallmark example. Because offices generate business for shops and restaurants, the construction of office buildings on regional shopping center properties has become a natural trend. But, if an office building is provided, the site area must be adequate to handle the parking and traffic that offices generate, and it must be able to accommodate all-day parkers. Even so, the combined parking demand for office space and retail uses will be less than the demand generated by each of these uses individually. Such shared parking must be carefully evaluated.[7]

Office parking demand (which peaks on weekdays between 9 a.m. and 5 p.m.) normally does not conflict

[7] See Barton-Aschman Associates, Inc., *Shared Parking* (Washington, D.C.: ULI–the Urban Land Institute, 1983).

5-21 Service tenants need locations that provide direct access to customer parking.

with peak shopping hours. For this reason, the parking standard for shopping centers will accommodate office tenants until the net rentable area (NRA) of the offices reaches 10 percent of the centers' GLA (see Chapter 3). When this point is reached, additional parking space should be constructed.

To determine whether a well-planned office building will help the center, the following factors should be evaluated:

- The need for and desirability of offices in the area.
- The experience of other office buildings in the area.
- The possibility of locating an office building in a section of the shopping center where high-density retail facilities or other facilities of greater benefit to the project would not be feasible.

If a market does exist for an office building within the shopping center complex, the developer must first determine the costs of construction and the economics of including an office component. It might be preferable to develop a completely separate office park in the vicinity of the center. Office park employees, like employees of an on-site office tenant, can use the shopping center for dining and noontime shopping, particularly if convenient pedestrian access can be provided to reduce or eliminate vehicular traffic between the two land uses.

Second-Floor Offices

Although office tenants in a shopping complex enjoy working where they can also shop and eat nearby during the lunch hour, offices placed above retail stores in shopping centers typically do not make good rental properties. Office space on a second level of an enclosed mall center does not lease as rapidly as the retail space. If the shopping center management

5-22   A high-rise office building is part of Sharpstown Center, Houston.

places enough emphasis on office leasing, most second-story office spaces will eventually be filled, but rental rates may well be lower than expected. Elevators and stairs will also be required between the two floors, increasing the expense. Taken together, the difficulties of renting second-floor offices and the problems involved in vertical circulation and service may justify the exclusion of this type of rental space above a ground floor of retail space.

Medical Offices

As with other kinds of offices, doctors' and dentists' offices are probably best placed in freestanding clinic-type buildings either on the site or on an adjacent property. A one-story clinic building eliminates the cost of running elevators and extensive plumbing to a second level. Even so, a limited number of medical offices may feasibly be located within neighborhood or community center buildings, particularly where the site configuration and topography would allow some separation of uses.

If a medical building is included on the site, special parking must be provided. Unlike general office parking, medical building parking may interfere with shopping center parking; medical buildings should therefore have separate parking areas.

Banks

In states where branch banking is permitted, banks are common tenants in shopping centers. They are frequently located in a freestanding building so that they can offer the convenience of drive-in service. Drive-in facilities must be carefully placed on the site in order to achieve good visibility while assuring easy traffic movement and adequate stacking areas for bank customers waiting to use the drive-up windows. Circulation must be arranged so that it does not block walk-in entrances or shopping center traffic. The appropriate number of windows and stacking spaces depends on the volume of customers expected.

Banks and savings and loan institutions often enter the center on ground leases and pay their own construction and outfitting costs. If placed in the center on other than a ground lease, these tenants pay relatively high rents per square foot. A percentage lease based on deposit values is rare.

Net leases are quite common in freestanding buildings. If a ground lease is executed with a bank that will construct its own facility, the bank must become party to cross easements and operating agreements.

The advent of the automatic teller machine may change dramatically the way in which banking services are provided. Placed in kiosks, these machines

5-23 Banks are frequently placed in a freestanding building so that drive-in facilities can be provided without blocking traffic circulation of the shopping center.

can eliminate the need for branch banks; thus, they may appear less frequently in shopping centers.

Bowling Alleys

The popularity of bowling has waned. Like the furniture store, a bowling center is a large space user, and rental rates do not justify its inclusion, even in a regional center. Bowling facilities should be built in freestanding, single-tenant structures or in entertainment complexes outside the shopping center property.

Cinemas

The multiscreen theater has become common in regional or community shopping centers. Each auditorium has a seating capacity of 250, 350, or 400, and all theaters share a common lobby, projection booth, and vending machines. Such theaters may be freestanding or part of the shopping center structure. Security problems may arise after retail closing hours if a theater lobby opens directly onto the main pedestrian mall. But because theaters have operating hours that often differ from those of retail stores, they do not require additional parking spaces in a center. A multiscreen theater complex sometimes functions in community centers as a key tenant, typically tied to other "entertainment" uses—restaurants/cocktail lounges, family restaurants, and specialty food-service uses.

The risk of overkill from too many theaters in shopping centers is reduced because successful centers are located within established market areas. The drawing power of the shopping center can provide a good yardstick for the potential success of the cinema. Theaters also generate customer traffic through the shopping center before and sometimes after movies have been shown. Good bookings and active promotion are major factors in successful cinema operation. Reve-

nue percentages from the theater's vending machines help to determine the rents theaters pay to the center. Theater companies that both own a cinema in a freestanding building and lease a theater a few miles away in a shopping center sometimes funnel assured movie hits to the freestanding cinema in order to limit percentage rents they must pay for the leased cinema.

Service Stations

Building a new service station within a shopping center is likely to be only marginally profitable. However, if a service station site is sold before a center is developed, the station will most likely become part of a neighborhood center or be located on a corner site that has been developed independently of the shopping center. This is why service stations, although ubiquitous, do not appear in listings of the top 20 tenants in neighborhood and community centers. Until 1974, most community and regional shopping centers encouraged service stations to join the complex as a freestanding facility, either through an independent franchise operation or through a direct oil company land ownership or ground lease. This was done to provide an added convenience to shoppers and store employees. In fact, some department stores have ventured into gasoline service, either as a part of their TBA facilities or as a separate operation within a regional center.

Two types of lease agreements are commonly used for service stations: fixed payment and variable payment agreements. The fixed payment arrangement involves a flat monthly rent, whereas the variable payment is based on the monthly volume of gasoline sales. A developer should keep in mind that gasoline sales at a shopping center station typically represent a higher proportion of gross service station revenues than they do at a station in an isolated commercial neighborhood where services account for a larger share of total revenues.

Like other leases, a variable payment lease provides that the tenant must pay a minimum rate even if his gas sales should drop. But with today's rapid changes in gasoline prices, a developer should insist on a lease that provides for a percentage of total sales rather than a fixed rate per gallon. Because most gas station operators lease their stations from the oil company, most developers' leases are made directly with the oil company.

The location and design of a service station in relationship to a shopping center have become important issues, especially in neighborhood and community centers, where oil companies have customarily sought corner locations so that the shopping center

5-24 The service station is most often found in the neighborhood center or on a corner site owned and developed independently of the shopping center.

site is often wrapped around the stations. It is particularly important that the shopping center developer maintain design control to keep the station design compatible with that of the main building mass. Cross easements for joint access are also important. Since the design and location of service stations have received a great deal of criticism, the developer may find that public approval for a shopping center will hinge on proper design and location. When a service station site has been sold before a shopping center has been developed, design control and joint access may be difficult to obtain. This is a situation to be avoided, since it may require compromises in center design to overcome adverse effects.

Other Establishments

Other possible nonretail uses are health spas, indoor tennis, ice skating, and other commercial/recreational enterprises. Such establishments within a center are possible if market conditions and planned arrangement of land uses justify multiuse installations. Both freestanding and integrated examples of these uses can be found.

Summary—Tenants

The proper tenant mix is crucial to a center's success. While certain tenant classifications are commonly found in different types of centers, universally applicable standards as to tenant mix cannot be established. Each community and each shopping center are different. Therefore, tenants should be selected by means of a sound leasing strategy formulated from the findings of the market and feasibility studies for the specific center.

Placement of tenants within the center is also important and complex. Anchor tenants should be placed so that to reach them pedestrian shoppers must pass by storefronts of supplementary tenants. Other factors to consider in developing a strategy for tenant placement include the drawing power of the tenant, the tenant's need to be easily accessible, the tenant's compatibility with adjacent tenants, and the parking demand generated by the tenant.

6.
Operation and Management

The Lease as an Operational Tool

The lease document provides the foundation for the successful operation of the shopping center. The lease and its provisions establish the level of income that the developer/landlord anticipates from his enterprise. The shopping center lease varies extensively from a standard commercial lease.

A lease is a contract by which a landlord gives a tenant the use and possession of designated premises for a specified period of time in exchange for payments of specified amounts. Leasing refers to such conveyance. The conveying party is the lessor, and the party to whom the terminable use right is conveyed is the lessee. In real estate, the terminable use right conveyed to the lessee is a leasehold. Rents are based on estimates of the value of the leased premise. Although they are not discussed here, many possible and probable causes might be identified that separately or in combination can increase or decrease the value of future uses for a particular premise.

The area of tenant leasing must be carefully studied at the outset of the development venture, as mentioned earlier in this book; regardless of the type or location of the center, leasing must be part of the preliminary investigation and planning process. The lease shapes, draws together, and controls the various tangible and intangible elements that will attract shoppers. The lease document's treatment of details and its handling of the many facets of the shopping center will in large measure determine the center's final atmosphere, customer appeal, and degree of financial success. Because the lease is a legal instrument, a lawyer informed in the field should draft it. No universal leasing document can be made that will apply to all shopping centers, all tenant types, and all jurisdictions.[1]

This section discusses the practices currently employed in shopping center leasing to balance landlord risk with tenant performance, including the use of percentage devices established in the provisions of participating lease agreements.

---

[1] See the sample lease in Appendix D. This lease is presented only as an example and is not intended as a definitive or universally applicable document.

Percentage Leases

A shopping center developer/owner is confronted with two basic economic needs that his leasing must meet. First, he must be assured of an adequate income stream to meet his fixed expenses. Second, he must receive a return on his equity that reflects the value of his property. If properly structured, the combination of minimum guaranteed rent plus percentage rent, or rent as a percentage of sales, can answer both needs.

Besides providing a basic return on the investment, minimum rents should cover the fixed expenses of shopping center operation—principal and interest on the mortgage, real estate taxes, insurance, maintenance, housekeeping, and other expenses. The percentage rent, when added to the minimum guaranteed rent, should provide for the potential of an increasing return on investment. The adequacy of the minimum rent structure is assured by special lease provisions, such as escalator clauses and the establishment of a formula for shared common area charges and real estate taxes, which protect the landlord against inflation.

In the retail field, the percentage lease has become the most widely used kind of rental contract for both tenant and landlord. In its simplest form, the percentage lease is an instrument wherein the tenant agrees to pay a rental equal to a stipulated percentage of the gross dollar volume of the tenant's sales. In shopping centers, the most common type of percentage lease is one in which the tenant agrees to pay a specified minimum rent even if the negotiated percentage of gross sales is less than the agreed-upon minimum. This combination of minimum rent and percentage rent takes the needs of both landlord and tenant into account; the guaranteed minimum protects the shopping center owner if the tenant's sales are not high enough to produce the necessary rental income. But the owner receives less when times are rough, and more as the tenant's business prospers, since total rent charges fluctuate with the volume of business.

Percentage lease rates and the amount of the minimum rental should be based on the kind of business, the volume of business per square foot of leased space, the markup on merchandise, the business value of the tenant space and of the shopping center location, the amount of competition, and other factors.[2]

Of the several types of percentage leases, the most commonly used lease, as noted, provides for a minimum guaranteed rental from which the owner will derive enough income to cover amortization and operating costs, plus a basic return on his investment. This protects the owner during the early years of a development and during periods of recession. During periods of normal business activity, both parties participate in the high level of trade.

As discussed in Chapter 2, the breakpoint in gross sales volume—under which the minimum rent applies, and over which the percentage rent applies—can be determined mathematically once the minimum rental and the rate of percentage rent are established. To illustrate: if the owner knows his minimum rental should be $6,000, and if the agreed-upon percentage rate is 6 percent, gross sales of $100,000 would be the breakpoint. But if gross sales fell below this figure, say to $50,000, the owner would still be paid $6,000; with a straight percentage lease, he would receive only $3,000 in this instance. When sales exceed the $100,000 level, the rate of percentage applies to the overage. For this reason, the landlord strives to obtain overage rents for both the tenant's operations and his own. The overage offers the cushion in shopping centers, the "balance after operating expenses."

Because of its balancing of tenant and landlord interests, the percentage lease with a minimum guarantee is used for almost all types of tenants in shopping centers. As with every rule, however, there are exceptions; these exceptions are likely to be financial institutions and nonretail tenants such as banks, savings and loans, and small loan companies; service shops; and offices for such tenants as insurance agencies, doctors, and dentists. Where only fixed guarantees are involved, the developer would be wise to consider short-term leases or leases that escalate based either on a series of specified steps or on the consumer price index (CPI). With fixed rentals, the owner is at a disadvantage. He is not properly provided with incentive income as he proceeds to develop and promote his center. With short-term leases, he is better able to adjust rental incomes in line with the rising value of the center location, higher operating costs, and other changing circumstances.

The Lease Document

An attorney will draft the lease, but the developer should establish the business terms upon which the document is based. A well-constructed and well-drawn lease is also a management tool, as it sets down the rules and regulations of conduct for both tenant and landlord.

Any sample lease form for a shopping center should be used carefully. The developer must avoid any legal form based on another jurisdiction. Many factors prevent a rigid leasing formula from being

[2] Median and ranges of percentage rents by tenant classification and by type of shopping center are detailed in Urban Land Institute, *Dollars & Cents of Shopping Centers* (Washington, D.C.: ULI–the Urban Land Institute, triennial).

applicable to all parts of the United States. Lease provisions must also conform to the circumstances and requirements of the particular shopping center type. Above all, it is unwise to enter into any important transaction, such as a long-term lease for a commercial property, without the counsel of an attorney who resides in the city where the center is located and who is familiar with statutes, ordinances, and court decisions applicable to the development and operation of a shopping center in that jurisdiction.

Besides establishing obligations, responsibilities, and leasehold arrangements, the lease incorporates the means of preserving the shopping center's character and appearance as a merchandising complex over a long period of time. When drafted properly, lease provisions establish beneficial relationships between the developer and tenant.

For a well-planned operation, the lease should cover these items, which are then discussed in sections following:

- Description of the premises.
- Lease term.
- Rental terms: the minimum guaranteed rent and the rate of percentage rent based on gross sales (including a definition of gross sales).
- Tenant's share of operating expenses, property taxes, and other expenses.
- Permitted use of the premises, including hours of operation.
- Alterations and improvements of the premises.
- Issues related to financing of the center.
- Assignment and subletting.
- Landlord's lien.
- Indemnification and insurance.
- Rights of landlord to enter the premises.
- Damage or destruction to the premises, building, or common area.
- Condemnation.
- Default.
- Surrender of the premises.
- Membership and participation in the merchants' association or payments to the marketing fund.
- Miscellaneous provisions.
- A plan of the site and building layout indicating the demised premises, as an appended exhibit to the document.

Form and Use

Although anchor tenants or national chains may sometimes have the economic power to insist upon the use of their own lease forms, if possible all tenant leases in a shopping center should be written on the landlord's form. The form should take into account the particular operational or physical characteristics of the center—market trends and competition as well as the relative economic strength of the center owner. A major regional shopping center developer can probably impose a more extensive lease form than can the owner of a small neighborhood center. The longer form may contain provisions for a merchants' association or promotional fund, restrictions upon hours and methods of operation, use of common areas, tenant improvements and alterations, and a radius clause. The lease form must also reflect the requirements of state law as well as any imposed by municipal ordinances, deed restrictions or covenants, and conditions and restrictions. The landlord will usually need a different lease form for the first tenants in a center in order to address such issues as the tenant's initial improvements and participation in a grand opening, as well as the initial basis on which the tenant's share of taxes and operating expenses is calculated.

Once the lease form has been developed by the developer/owner and his attorney and reviewed by knowledgeable leasing brokers, it should be printed in a format that permits all variable data—such as the name of the tenant, the term, the rent, the use, hours of operation and address for notices—to be inserted on a separate sheet (called the "Basic Lease Information" or "Fundamental Lease Provisions") that can be reviewed at a glance. The designation of the tenant on the signature page of the lease form should also be added. Use of a printed form presents a psychological impediment to amendments, which, if any are made, should be set forth in a separately prepared addendum to the lease. This approach helps the landlord or other parties to review individual leases: the economic terms of each lease and any departures from the basic form or additional terms may quickly be noted by reviewing the basic lease information and any addenda.

Description of the Premises

The area and general location of the premises should be described in the lease. A lease for a new center may need to describe the area of the premises as built. A floor plan attached to the lease should describe the exact area, location, and configuration of the space the tenant will occupy. If the landlord gives the tenant exclusive responsibility for maintenance of a certain area or allows the tenant to use additional space—for example, part of the common area in front of a shop—such responsibility or use should be granted as a license. If the premises are described to include common areas or portions of the structure and the landlord or other tenants interferes with the use of these areas, the tenant could have cause to demand an abatement of rent based on constructive eviction.

Tenants will want confirmations that their premises include the use of parking areas and malls. Such a confirmation should be granted as a nonexclusive license: areas used for these purposes should not be described as part of the premises. The landlord should reserve the right to grant similar nonexclusive use to other tenants, to promulgate rules and regulations regarding the use of such facilities, to designate specific parking areas for employees or for the use of any tenant, to make changes in the parking layout and perhaps to withdraw property from parking use, and to close temporarily and/or redesign all or any portion of the common areas. The right to close and/or redesign common areas can be quite important in leases for older centers where a remodeling or refurbishing program is being considered.

Term of Lease

The appropriate term depends on the market; the size, strength, and credit of a tenant; and the landlord's desire to protect future options. As a rule, economically weaker tenants and smaller spaces warrant shorter lease terms. Typically, shop tenants, even national chains, will be given leases with only three- to five-year terms, with the limit on rental increases during that term depending upon market conditions at the time of leasing. Shorter leases allow the landlord to renegotiate with the majority of smaller tenants more frequently, and also to weed out tenants with poor performance. Certain tenants, such as restaurants, require longer lease terms in order to finance their furnishings, fixtures, and equipment; the landlord's primary incentive in accepting longer terms derives from having lease provisions that require rents to be periodically readjusted to market value. If an option to renew is granted a small tenant, not only should the rent be readjusted to the market, but it may be advisable to condition the right of renewal upon the tenant's achievement of a certain level of gross sales.

The lease term may begin at a different date from that of rental payments. Tenants may be granted a free rent period during which to install fixtures on their premises, and major tenants may be able to insist that their rental obligations will not begin until certain other designated major tenants and perhaps a specified number of shop tenants are also open for business. In those leases where certain events are tied to anniversaries of the commencement of rental payment rather than to the commencement of the term, the landlord and tenant may need to execute, and sometimes to record, a memorandum documenting the relevant date.

Rent

Most shopping center leases require monthly payments of minimum rents and percentage rents based upon gross sales. Gross sales should be defined as broadly as possible and should always include receipts for merchandise and services sold in or from the premises by the tenant and the tenant's subtenants, licensees, and concessionaires, as well as gross receipts from merchandise and services sold as a result of orders received at the premises by mail, telephone, video, or other electronic, mechanical, or automated means, whether such orders are filled on the premises or elsewhere.

Typically excluded from gross sales are the sales amounts or excise taxes collected from customers and the amounts of any refunds or credits made for returned merchandise—but only if the receipts for such merchandise were included in an earlier calculation of gross sales.

Finally, gross sales should be reported monthly within a fairly short period—perhaps 10 days—after the end of each month. Ideally, the tenant's report should show daily sales as well as sales broken down among the tenant and each of its subtenants, licensees, and concessionaires, as well as an itemization of all deductions from gross sales. An independent certified public accountant should audit tenant sales once a year.

It may be unrealistic to expect smaller tenants to produce monthly reports even though the landlord must receive monthly payments of percentage rents. One compromise is to require the tenant to make monthly payments equal to the monthly average of the percentage rents paid the previous year, with an adjustment at the end of the year. The auditing and reporting requirements are particularly important for a tenant who has other stores whose gross sales are not yet sufficient to require payment of percentage rents or whose percentage rents are lower.

The lease should designate the location where the tenant will maintain account books and records relating to gross sales, should require that these records be retained for at least three years, and should permit the landlord and his representatives to audit such books at any time after giving reasonable notice. Some leases now call for the tenant to adopt and maintain a procedure to keep adequate daily records of sales and to provide the landlord access to any records or reports relating to sales or excise taxes as well as to the results of an audit of the tenant's business by a certified public accountant. The tenant should pay for the audit if the audit indicates that statements of gross sales previously made by the tenant fall short of the amount of actual gross sales by more than 2 percent.

Tenant's Share of Operating Expenses, Property Taxes, and Other Expenses

From the landlord's point of view, the preferred lease arrangement requires the tenant to pay his share of all property taxes and assessments as well as all operating expenses incurred in connection with the project. In new projects, because first-year taxes and expenses will be artificially low, tenants may be reluctant to pay increases in operating expenses and property taxes thereafter. To ward off this problem, the landlord can calculate base year taxes and operating expenses as if the building were 90 or 95 percent occupied. In mixed-use projects, another issue concerns the allocation of property taxes and operating expenses among parking, office, and retail areas. To preserve flexibility with respect to operating expenses, the lease should simply state that such allocations will be based on generally acceptable accounting practices. Property taxes may be handled most directly by allocating to each project component explicit percentages for the payment of the taxes.

Both taxes and assessments and operating expenses should be defined to include standard and special assessments as well as any governmental impositions—for example, for special transit service, street improvements, or contributions in lieu of providing housing or parkland. In states such as California, where assessed values may be readjusted to reflect the sales price when property changes hands, tenants may ask for a provision that protects them from tax increases resulting from the reassessments. The landlord would obviously wish to avoid this provision and might argue that until reassessment following a sale of the center, tenants enjoy artificially small increases in property taxes because assessments are not regularly increased to reflect increases in the market value of the shopping center.

Common area expenses or operating expenses should also be broadly defined to include costs incurred in connection with the operation of the particular building in which the tenants are located as well as all related areas including parking, service roads, malls, and any expenses that may be incurred under a reciprocal easement agreement. Operating expenses should include the obvious expenses of repair, maintenance, utilities, and insurance, as well as the depreciation of machinery and equipment used to maintain the premises, and reasonable replacement reserves. Operating expenses should also cover the cost of capital improvements made to the building after the lease goes into effect if these improvements are reasonably anticipated to reduce other operating expenses or are required under a law not applicable to the building at the time the lease was executed, amortized over the reasonable useful life of such improvements. In addition, operating expenses should include the landlord's interest cost on funds borrowed to pay for the cost of such capital improvements. Operating expenses can be defined to include management fees or a specific percentage, anywhere from 5 to 15 percent, for administrative and overhead expenses, calculated on the basis of all the other specific operating expenses.

The pass-through of operating expenses and property taxes is always based upon the tenant's "percentage share" of the total area to which the particular operating expenses or property taxes are applied. This pass-through should be drafted to reflect an agreed-upon number of initial total square feet of such improvements with a provision that permits an adjustment in the percentage share if there is a change in the rentable area of the improvements to which such expenses relate. In mixed-use projects, the lease should recognize that certain expenses may be allocated to an office or residential portion and certain expenses allocated to all portions of the project, and that the allocation among such portions shall be made by the landlord's accountant. Similar apportionment is required when particular tenants pay directly all of certain expenses that would otherwise be included in operating expenses. An example might be heat and air conditioning within the shop spaces themselves.

The lease should always permit the landlord to estimate property taxes and operating expenses that are to be incurred during the calendar year and require the tenant to pay these estimated amounts monthly. The landlord should have the right to revise his share of the estimate and adjust the lessee's payments if he determines the estimate will be significantly off.

The lease should provide that the tenant pay on time for all utilities used in the premises, as well as for all taxes and assessments on the lessee's inventory, furnishings, fixtures, and equipment, and any gross receipts taxes or other taxes chargeable to rentals paid under the lease. This provision gives the landlord grounds for eviction or other action should a tenant attempt to continue business on a marginal basis.

Use

Use clauses are of critical importance in maintaining a proper tenant mix and the enforceability of restrictions upon assignment and subletting. The permitted use should be described with the greatest possible specificity. If a tenant is to sell women's clothing, the permitted use can be described in terms of articles of clothing, price range, and sometimes even primary lines to be carried. Restaurant leases can describe the types of meals served as well as items to be included, or sometimes excluded, from the menu.

For the landlord's protection, some leases include a radius clause that restricts the tenant from owning or operating another store within a specified distance from the premises. The distance will depend on the type of business involved. This provision can be coupled with one that gives the landlord the option of permitting the operation of the nearby store but requiring that all or a portion of gross sales from that store be included in the calculation of gross sales from the leased premises in order to determine the tenant's percentage rent.

In the past, major tenants were able to insist that lease provisions be included that granted them exclusives in price and merchandise lines. The enforcement activities of the Federal Trade Commission in the 1970s resulted in a series of consent decrees, preventing major tenants from using their bargaining power to require landlords:

- to allow major tenants to control advertising by other tenants;
- to prohibit discount selling in the center;
- to prevent the inclusion of certain other tenants in the center; or
- to limit the amount of space leased to other tenants.

Major tenants do, however, retain the right to negotiate lease clauses that will protect the location of their stores and establish a reasonable range of categories of uses from which the landlord may select tenants to be located near the major tenants. Restrictions on shop tenants' activities should be aimed toward preserving the quality of the center rather than stifling competition in pricing. Any exclusives provided in the bases should be reviewed with counsel, as federal law in this area is in flux and the landlord's activities may also be subject to scrutiny under state antitrust law. In addition, the fact that a major tenant is a joint venturer with the landlord may lead to greater antitrust exposure.

Use clauses should also contain general language that prohibits the tenant from using the premises in a manner that is illegal, that affects the rate of insurance on the building or premises, and that interferes with or annoys other tenants. Specific limitations may be necessary for uses such as restaurants, which might introduce undesirable noises or odors.

A clause specifying certain minimum hours of operation is essential, particularly when tenants are located in malls. Requirements may also be needed concerning the lighting of window displays and interiors during night operations and after closing hours in order to maintain or enhance the attractiveness of the center.

Alterations and Improvements of Premises

The lease should tightly control the tenant's ability to alter the interior or exterior of the tenant's premises without the landlord's consent. The landlord should also fully control the initial improvement of the premises. The lease should prevent the tenant from placing any sign, awning, canopy, advertising matter, or any other material on the glass at the exterior of the premises or on any other portion of the exterior of the premises without the landlord's consent, and should also prevent the tenant from placing any merchandise, equipment, or furniture outside the premises. These restrictions are clearly necessary to control the appearance of the center and should be strictly enforced. The restrictions on alterations should also prevent the installation of radio or television antennas, loudspeakers, or any other devices on the exterior of the premises.

Additional language in the lease should describe the means and methods by which the tenant may carry out alterations, including a requirement that the premises and the building be kept free from liens arising out of work performed on the premises. In some states, the law provides that mechanics' liens will not attach to the landlord's interest in property if the landlord posts or files a notice of nonresponsibility before the tenant's construction begins. In such cases, the lease should stipulate that even after the landlord has consented to tenant improvements, the tenant should notify the landlord of the work before it begins.

In some states, even the posting of a notice of nonresponsibility may not protect the landlord from liens arising out of tenant improvements if the landlord contributed to the cost of the improvements or, as provided in many leases, the landlord is given ownership of the improvements after they are completed. If the landlord lacks protection from liens, the lease should require the tenant to provide labor and materials and completion bonds before starting work.

Financing the Shopping Center

A lease may address a number of issues that might arise in connection with the financing or refinancing of a shopping center. Occasionally the lease is made contingent upon the landlord's obtaining financing for the property: if the landlord is unable to obtain acceptable financing within a specified time, the tenants are released from their commitments and the landlord from further obligations. In this situation, additional language should be inserted, if possible, calling for the tenant to consent to nonmaterial modifications in the language of the lease if required by the lender. If the tenant refuses to consent to such a modification, as well as to other possible remedies, the landlord should have the right to cancel the lease. To be fair, the landlord should no longer be able to request lender-oriented lease modifications after delivering possession of the premises to the tenant.

The lease must always require the tenant to execute and deliver an estoppel certificate to the landlord within a certain period after the landlord's request for such a certificate. In connection with such a certificate, the tenant should provide any reasonable information requested concerning the status of the lease and the premises. Ideally, this provision should also oblige the tenant to deliver its most recent financial statement if requested by a lender.

The lease should also contain a provision stating that, unless a mortgagee, trustee, or ground lessor elects otherwise, the lease is subject and subordinate to any ground lease, deed of trust, or mortgage placed upon the building and to any and all advances made in security thereof. This provision is subject to negotiation with major tenants, who will usually insist that their subordination be conditioned upon the execution and delivery of an explicit nondisturbance agreement from a ground lessor or lender providing generally that, even if a lessor's ground lease is terminated or the building is foreclosed and sold under a trust deed or mortgage, as long as the tenant is performing his obligations under the lease, he will not be disturbed.

Assignment and Subletting

For the tenant to sublet the premises or assign the lease should always require the landlord's consent. This restriction, together with the use clause, gives the landlord control over the use and occupancy of the premises. The landlord's consent to such subletting or assignment is, as a general rule, not unreasonably withheld; in fact, in some states, this condition is legally implied. It is a matter to be determined with local counsel. In some states, a lease provision imposing a "reasonableness" requirement upon the landlord's refusal to consent to assignment or subletting may leave the landlord wide latitude, while in other states, the basis for withholding consent is limited to the proposed subtenant's or assignee's credit or business experience. These provisions should be carefully considered in light of local law.

Even if a reasonableness limitation is imposed upon the landlord or implied by law, it is not always clear whether the limitation extends to subletting part of the premises as well as the entire premises. Situations may arise, particularly with regard to large stores, in which the landlord does not want to permit a "Balkanization" of the premises with multiple subtenancies.

The definition of "assignment" should be drafted to recognize the transfer of various interests in the entity that is the tenant, as for example, a sale of partnership interests or the controlling stock of a corporate tenant. A restricted assignment should also be defined to include those that occur "by operation of law" as well as assignments for the benefit of creditors or in connection with voluntary or involuntary bankruptcy or reorganization, although the latter provision may, in fact, be unenforceable.

If any tenant has been given a lease without a percentage rent provision, the landlord should be compensated with a provision calling for the tenant to pay some portion or all of the consideration he receives in connection with the transfer of his leasehold interest. The landlord may then share in the tenant's profit from a bargain lease.

Landlord's Lien

The furnishings and fixtures that a tenant installs may be an asset to the landlord in re-leasing the premises should the tenant default and the landlord terminate the lease. For that reason, the lease should contain language creating a lien on furnishings and fixtures to secure payment of the tenant's obligations under the lease.

As a practical matter, however, many tenants either lease furniture and equipment or finance its acquisition. For this reason, the landlord should be prepared, either in the lease form or in an addendum, to subordinate the lien to that of any bona fide lessor, supplier, or lender, and to execute and deliver any documents that may reasonably be required as evidence of this subordination.

Indemnification and Insurance

All leases should contain a provision by which the tenant waives any claims against the landlord for damage to property or injury to persons in, on, or about the premises arising from any cause other than from the negligence or willful act of the landlord. The exact wording of this provision should reflect state law negligence doctrines. The lease should also protect the landlord from liability for any damage to the property of the tenant or others located on the premises caused by theft or resulting from fire, explosion, water leakage, or the failure of utilities. In other words, the tenant will maintain coverage for any damage to his property or interruption of his business. In addition, the tenant's coverage should include a provision that holds the landlord harmless from any claims or expenses incurred by the landlord in connection with the tenant's use of the premises, unless the landlord caused such expenses or claims. The landlord will maintain insurance to protect himself against tenants' claims; however, the indemnification language of the lease establishes the primary responsibilities for such indemnification and insurance coverage.

The tenant should be required to obtain and maintain at his expense insurance coverage for general public liability naming the landlord as additionally insured, as well as coverage for the cost of full replacement of the tenant's improvements to its premises. The exact language of the insurance requirements should be drafted with the help of an experienced insurance adviser with an eye toward special situations, such as liability for the storage or use of hazardous materials.

Occasionally, a tenant that is a major national corporation will prefer to insure itself rather than purchase insurance. This may be acceptable if the tenant is likely to retain adequate financial resources.

Insurance provisions should always contain a waiver of subrogation as well as a requirement for both the landlord and tenant to seek these waivers from their respective property and liability insurers. Such waivers tend to speed the settlement of claims.

Entry by Landlord

The landlord should have explicit rights to enter the tenant's premises during normal business hours to inspect, repair, or reconstruct any part of the building; to install or repair improvements to or within parts of the building adjacent to the tenant; to perform any work required because the tenant has defaulted under the lease; to post notices of nonresponsibility; and to show the premises to prospective lenders, purchasers, and replacement tenants. Without the right of entry to repair or improve the building and adjacent premises, the landlord may be stymied in preparing adjacent spaces for other tenants. In emergencies, the landlord should have the right to enter the premises at any time and without notice. The tenant should be required at all times to provide the landlord with keys to all areas of the premises except that of the tenant's safe or other similar designated areas.

Damage or Destruction

The exact drafting of this provision will depend, to some extent, on the relative bargaining power of the landlord and tenant. Several combinations of damage may be considered involving partial or complete damage to the premises and partial or complete damage to the building or the common area. Each party will want the option to treat damage or destruction as an opportunity unilaterally to decide whether or not to continue the particular lease. While the language of this provision in leases with major tenants may be subject to considerable negotiation, the lease form for other tenants should contain certain provisions. Typically, if only the tenant's area is damaged, the tenant will receive no rent abatement and must reconstruct the damaged section as soon as possible. This arrangement presumes that the tenant maintains adequate insurance. If the damage is to a portion of the building beyond the exterior boundary of the tenant's premises but necessary for the tenant's occupancy, the landlord will usually agree to repair it if the repairs can be made within a reasonable period, perhaps 90 days. If the landlord is committed to make the repair, the lease will remain in effect. Even if the repair will require more than the stated length of time, the landlord will want the right to keep the lease in effect if he has notified the tenant within a shorter period after the damage occurred, say 30 days, of his commitment to make the repair. Any abatement in minimum rent related to damage extending beyond the tenant's area should be in the proportion that the damaged area of the premises bears to the total premises. No abatement should be allowed if the damage resulted from the acts or negligence of the tenant or his employees. Some tenants may justifiably insist upon a rent abatement if damage to the building or common area affects their sales volumes. Before agreeing to this provision, the landlord should be satisfied that his insurance or rental losses will cover revenues lost for this reason.

Condemnation

Even though the exercise of eminent domain is uncommon, it provides another area in which substantial negotiation can occur between the landlord and a major tenant. (However, it does not affect the other tenants, with whom the landlord should still use the unmodified lease form.) The condemnation provision should address at least two situations—a total or "material" taking, and a partial taking. When any portion of the tenant's premises is taken in a manner that interferes with the tenant's use, either the landlord or tenant should have the right—after giving notice to the other within a reasonably short period after the taking (perhaps 30 days)—to terminate the lease as of the date of the notice. In addition, the landlord may want the right to terminate the lease if any major tenant—for example, one occupying more than 10,000 square feet—terminates his lease or abandons his premises as a result of the taking, or if more than half of the area of the shopping center or more than 20 percent of the area of the premises is taken.

In the case of a partial taking of the premises that does not result in terminating the whole lease, that part of the lease applying to the taking should terminate and the rent should be adjusted equitably. If the building or premises must be repaired because of the partial taking, the landlord's responsibility for the repair should be limited to the condemnation monies awarded for this purpose.

The lease should provide that, in any event, all awards for condemnation be payable to the landlord. The tenant will only be entitled to awards—up to the point that they do not diminish the awards otherwise due to the landlord—for the taking of his fixtures and personal property and for relocation expenses.

Default

There are two major aspects of a default provision: a definition of the default and a description of the landlord's remedies. Typically, a tenant will be in default when any of the following events occurs:

- The tenant fails to pay rent for more than a short period after the time due, typically five to 10 days. This provision may be modified to provide that the grace period will not apply if a tenant has failed more than two or three times in any 12-month period to pay rent when due. Tenants often request that an event of default not occur until a specified period after receipt from the landlord of a notice that rent is unpaid. This provision puts an additional administrative burden upon the landlord and extends the notice periods that generally are already provided by law before an eviction proceeding can begin. For this reason, lenders regard the provision with disfavor.

- The tenant fails to perform any other obligations under the lease, including paying other amounts that may be due, for as long as 10 days or some other reasonable period after notice.

- The tenant goes bankrupt or becomes insolvent; or engages in any fraudulent transfer of assets to protect them from creditors, or in an assignment in connection with a general assignment for the benefit of creditors; or initiates or is subject to the commencement of proceedings under the provisions of the Federal Bankruptcy Act unless such proceedings are discharged within a specified period, customarily 30 or 60 days. This last is a common provision that has been made generally unenforceable by the Bankruptcy Reform Act of

1978, except in rare instances when an insolvent tenant is liquidated with the consent of all of his creditors, and does not, therefore, seek protection under the Bankruptcy Act. The Bankruptcy Act prohibits termination of a lease after proceedings begin under the act. In addition, under most lease forms a transfer of the tenant's leasehold to defraud creditors or a general assignment to benefit creditors, without the landlord's previous consent, would be events of default anyway. They would be defined as such because they would be probable indicators of incipient bankruptcy and might provide an opportunity for the landlord to terminate the lease and regain the use of the premises before the tenant files for bankruptcy protection.

- A receiver is appointed for a substantial portion of the assets of the tenant or the levy upon the lease or any estate of the tenant by attachment or execution, and the tenant fails to have the attachment or execution "vacated" within a specified period, typically 30 days. A receiver is likely to be appointed at the request of creditors, again, typically in the context of a bankruptcy. A levy by attachment will be ordered by a court upon the request of a party who has initiated a suit against the tenant and has convinced the court that the tenant is likely to dissipate his assets before they can be used to pay a judgment. The levy of execution then occurs when someone has won a judgment against the tenant. Either of such events may indicate a tenant's weak financial state and both are included as events of default because the landlord will likely not want a receiver or judgment creditor as tenant.

- The tenant abandons the premises.

Leases are basically contracts and the remedies available to a landlord upon a tenant's default are normal contractual remedies, subject in some states to statutory constraints. As a basic concept, if the tenant defaults, the landlord is entitled to the benefit of his bargain. This includes, first of all, the right to treat the lease as terminated. Until the landlord has declared the lease terminated, however, the landlord is entitled to the rent accruing under the lease, together with interest at the rate provided in the lease, or otherwise at the legal rate. If the landlord finds a new tenant before terminating the lease, the landlord will be entitled to brokerage commissions and some or all of the remodeling expenses incurred in connection with the new tenant. After the lease is terminated, the landlord should be entitled to the benefit of his bargain, measured by the present value of the lease payments he would otherwise have received, less any loss he could have avoided by re-letting the premises. Typically, the tenant bears the burden of providing the amount of loss the landlord should have avoided. If the lease rate when the tenant defaulted was significantly below market, the landlord will want to find a new tenant and terminate the lease as soon as possible. If the market is soft, and the defaulting tenant or his guarantor has substantial assets, the landlord may refrain from terminating the lease and permit unpaid rent to accrue, pending trial.

Of course, there may be many other reasons for not permitting a space to remain vacant during this period. If, on the other hand, it is clear that the tenant is insolvent and may file for bankruptcy, the landlord may be wise to terminate the lease as soon as possible in order to regain possession of the premises before the tenant is protected by a "stay" in bankruptcy. Once the tenant has come under the protection of the Bankruptcy Act, the landlord becomes a general unsecured creditor with respect to amounts owed and, if the trustee in bankruptcy rejects the lease, a limit is placed on the landlord's recovery for "benefit of the bargain" damages related to future rents. Strategies for dealing with defaulting tenants who may go bankrupt, or have already sought protection under the statute, should be reviewed with counsel expert in this area of the law.

When a tenant files for protection under the Bankruptcy Act, he can seek to liquidate, or make an arrangement with his creditors, perhaps in connection with a reorganization. Once the tenant files for protection under the Act, his trustee in bankruptcy, or the tenant himself as debtor in possession, must decide within 60 days to "assume" or reject the lease, and during that period he must perform the tenant's obligations under the lease. Of course, trustees in bankruptcy and debtors in possession may not have the funds with which to perform such obligations. In addition, there may be delays in surrendering possession of the premises upon rejection of a lease while fixtures, equipment, and inventory on the premises are moved to storage or are sold.

Shopping center owners are provided with certain particularly explicit protections when the bankrupt tenant or his trustee wants to assume the lease. In order to assume the lease, the bankrupt tenant or his trustee must provide "adequate assurance" with regard to curing existing defaults and performing under the lease provisions. Adequate assurance must be given regarding the source of rent. The tenant or his trustee must also assure that the percentage rent due under the lease will not decline substantially; that assumption or assignment of the lease will not breach any provision relating to radius, location, use, or ex-

clusivity; and that assumption or assignment will not disrupt the tenant mix or balance. If such assurance can be given, the tenant or his trustee can assign the lease to a third party unless there is a provision that would prohibit or condition the assignment.

The lease should also contain language explicitly permitting the landlord to pay any amount, other than rental, on behalf of the tenant, or to perform any other act that the tenant has failed to perform on his own behalf. The landlord could then consider these expenditures as additional rent due under the lease.

Surrender of Premises

Typically, the tenant will be obligated to surrender the premises in good condition and repair and to remove his property upon the expiration or earlier termination of the lease. The lease will also contain a provision that permits the landlord to remove any personal property that he finds on the premises upon lease termination or expiration and eventually to sell such property in behalf of the tenant's account. If the landlord comes into possession of the tenant's personal property, the landlord cannot dispose of the property freely but must follow legal requirements and be prepared to provide an accounting for the proceeds of any sale.

Merchants' Association or Marketing Fund

The merchants' association can be an essential factor in the successful operation of a shopping center. The lease should contain a paragraph giving the landlord the option to establish a merchants' association and requiring the tenant to join and make contributions. The tenant usually contributes to the merchants' association a specific amount per square foot of rentable area, with a guaranteed minimum (for example, $500 a year) subject to escalation related to inflation. An alternative arrangement requires the tenant to contribute on the basis of gross sales, but this may not benefit the association because shops with the lowest gross sales typically require the greatest assistance from the merchants' association.

Many developers with substantial shopping center experience prefer to use a marketing fund as an alternative to the merchants' association. The developer, subject to advice from a tenants' advisory board, controls expenditures from the fund. This arrangement is a natural outgrowth of the grand opening promotional assessment that is often included in leases for new shopping centers.

In addition to the foregoing requirements, or sometimes as an alternative, some leases require each tenant to spend a stated percentage of gross sales for advertising.

Miscellaneous Provisions

Some of what are often referred to as "miscellaneous" provisions may in fact be of great significance in determining the outcome of disputes with tenants. For example:

- **Additional Rent.** Some jurisdictions may require leases to state that any sums that may be payable to the landlord are additional rent. This is because the statute providing a summary proceeding for eviction will do so only for nonpayment of "rent."
- **Attorneys' Fees.** This provision is necessary to enable the landlord to recover attorneys' fees spent in bringing actions against the tenant and should be worded carefully so that reimbursement is not conditioned upon bringing such actions to final judgment.
- **Sale of the Premises.** This provides that upon sale of the premises, the landlord is released from any further lease obligations accruing or attributable to any period after the landlord's ownership is terminated.
- **Notices.** This provision states that a notice is effective upon the earlier of (1) its delivery to a responsible employee of the tenant at the premises or (2) a specified period after the notice has been mailed, addressed as set forth in the basic lease information and with postage prepaid.
- **Waiver.** The waiver is needed to make clear the fact that the landlord's failure to enforce a provision of the lease on one occasion does not necessarily jeopardize the landlord's right to enforce that provision later.
- **Complete Agreement.** The lease must state that no oral agreements exist between the landlord and the tenant affecting the premises and that the lease incorporates and supersedes any and all previous writings, such as letters of intent, between the parties.

Management

Thus, many of the details of shopping center operation and management are established in the lease. Through the lease provisions the shopping center management establishes control of the tenant mix and the assessments for common area operation and maintenance, and provides for the enforcement of sign control, hours of operation, employee parking, tenant housekeeping, and maintenance of interior

premises. Furthermore, through the organization and operation of the merchants' association or marketing fund, as detailed in the lease, the center management helps foster and strengthen an image for the center that is attractive to shoppers in the trade area.

The lease provides for smooth center operation and management by clearly dividing responsibility between the landlord and the tenant; it describes what the tenant is obliged to maintain and what the landlord is required to perform. Structural maintenance and capital improvement of the buildings, for example, are the owner's responsibility, as is the repair of outside walls, roofs, sidewalks, and canopies, subject to tenant reimbursements. The owner, with tenant contributions, also maintains and repairs parking lots and landscaped areas, whereas the tenants are responsible for the repair and maintenance of the tenant spaces.

In addition to allocating work responsibilities to the tenant and the landlord, the lease establishes who will pay for the upkeep and operation of the various areas of the center. In most centers, this distribution of financial support is simplified by separating each tenant's rental payment from the tenant's contribution to common area operation. The lease then describes which expenses the owner will cover and which will be considered common area expenses. Lighting of the parking area, for example, is considered a maintenance cost and is therefore charged to the tenants through a provision in the lease. The distribution of air-conditioning charges depends on whether the system involves a central plant or individual package units. In either case, capital costs and operating charges are divided between landlord and tenant and, as in all other areas of center operation and maintenance, the chosen arrangement must be made legally enforceable through inclusion in the lease.

The lease can also be seen as the second of three steps that help assure the center's proper operation and management and its ultimate success as a business venture. The first of these steps involves the consideration of such development criteria as a strong location with respect to access from the trade area, proper site planning, good tenant mix, and appropriateness of store sizes and building layout for the individual tenant's merchandising abilities and for the needs of the trade area. The second step includes the leasing program and the many operational arrangements that are set forth in the tenant lease. The third step is the ongoing operation and management of the center. Only so much groundwork can be laid; after that point, it is up to the center management, in its day-to-day decisions and policies, to guide the center toward success for both the owner and the merchants.

For a center to succeed, it must have strong and enthusiastic merchants, a general manager who is given a free hand and who possesses promotional skills and a knowledge of merchandising, and a developer/owner who is keenly interested in promoting the center. For a promotional campaign to succeed, the market must be known and the various techniques of marketing—buying, inventorying, displaying, pricing, selling to please customers, promoting, and advertising—must be understood by the developer and employed by the merchants. The shopping center is no longer simply a real estate operation; it is a business—a complex for merchandising.

Although no one has yet found a way to measure the energy, the know-how, or the capability of management, the intangible qualities of managerial efficiency and effectiveness are important in making a center profitable or unprofitable. The shopping center manager and his staff can contribute only so much to the success of the center, however. The mechanics of management and the decisions made by the manager cannot assure a thriving marketplace. Likewise, the developer can provide only the setting for success, because it is largely the merchants who determine the customer draw and who cause the center to succeed or fail. For this reason, the most important responsibility of the shopping center's management is to stimulate the merchants to create a marketplace that is above the commonplace. The merchants must be encouraged to tailor their array of goods and services and their ranges of colors, sizes, prices, and styles of merchandise to the current and changing demands of the buying public. Only by responding sensitively to the market can the center become the place to shop.

Management Arrangements

Since a shopping center must be treated as an ongoing merchandising operation rather than as a straightforward real estate venture, center management must be carefully arranged to be most responsive to the center's needs. The owner, whether or not he is also the manager, must provide leadership and drive. The shopping center manager preferably should be experienced in either retailing or real estate management.[3]

Depending on the size of the center and the arrangements for operation worked out earlier in the lease negotiations, the shopping center owner/developer provides for maintenance and management in one of the following ways:

- He acts as or employs his own manager to supervise the maintenance and management force, including the supervision of promotion and advertising, whether this work is handled by outside contract or by the center's management staff. The owner also retains the promotion director as a key member of the management staff. In some arrangements, the owner pays the promotion director's salary as part of his contribution to the merchants' association or marketing fund.
- He turns over the center's operations to a management firm, if he does not have this capacity in his own organization. This is a common practice in neighborhood centers.

When a management firm handles a center's operations, the fee paid to the firm is usually determined by negotiation. The fee of course depends on the extent of services rendered; the firm would charge a higher fee if the contract called for it to be responsible for advertising, promotion, and coordination of the merchants' association.

A leasing and management contract should be considered as two separate agreements. If a management firm is only to secure leases and perform no other management functions, the prevailing rates in the area for real estate management may be used as a guide. In shopping center leasing, commissions paid to the broker who secures a tenant lease vary little from those paid for securing commercial leases downtown, even though the clauses in a shopping center lease vary from those in other commercial leases. For management alone, fees are generally based on a percentage of the gross rentals collected.[4]

Special Management Concerns

In addition to maintenance and other areas of shopping center operation, a number of management concerns may be troublesome and require the landlord's special attention. These include matters of sign control, enforcement of parking regulations, evening and Sunday operation, and the whole area of real estate taxes.[5]

---

[3] For a complete reference source for shopping center management, see Robert J. Flynn, ed., *Carpenter's Shopping Center Management: Principles and Practices* (New York: International Council of Shopping Centers, 1984).

[4] The International Council of Shopping Centers offers its members the "Shopping Center Management Agreement" form, containing recommended language for operating contracts. The form can be a valuable aid to developers, management brokers, and attorneys in concluding shopping center management contracts. Also available to ICSC members is "Auditing Tenants' Gross Sales," Shopping Center Report 11, by Roger S. Smith (New York: International Council of Shopping Centers, 1966).

[5] ICSC members are referred to the "Shopping Center Maintenance Schedule Checklist," available from ICSC.

Sign Control

As discussed earlier, the owner and manager must maintain rigid control over the size, location, and design of all signs and other graphics. If management directives are to succeed in preventing poor or incompatible signage, controls must be incorporated into the lease in a form that is strongly enforceable. Lease clauses should limit the amount of space that the tenants' signs may occupy, require that no signs be placed on the roof, and provide that any lettering to be placed on glass be approved by the landlord.[6]

The shopping center management should not offer concessions in matters of sign control. In today's merchandising, many tenants, such as chain drugstores, favor the placement of paper signs on display windows to promote certain merchandise or to announce sales. But the practice is probably not effective and can give the center as a whole a shabby appearance. The careful management of any center involves rigid control over exterior paper signs.

Where the renovation of an existing center involves a new signage program, the owner would do well to "give a little and take a little" by offering to pay a portion of the cost of new signs. Whatever policy is adopted, all tenants must be offered the same arrangement.

Parking Enforcement

A considerable number of employee cars must be accommodated at any center. In fact, parking standards typically include an allotment of between 15 and 20 percent of the total parking area to accommodate employee parking (in those cases where separate off-site employee parking has not been provided).

Regulations designating certain portions of the parking area for employee parking are included in the lease; the lease further provides that flagrant violations can lead to cancellation of the lease. These provisions are necessary since the center's parking areas are private property and thus the parking regulations cannot be enforced by the local police. At any rate, the center management must continually check to see whether regulations are observed and must work with individual tenants and through the merchants' association (if one exists) to enforce these regulations. Otherwise, employees will occupy prime parking spaces best used for customer parking.

Parking violations by the public are another matter. Since persons who misuse parking spaces may also be customers of the center, diplomacy and finesse must be used in dealing with violations. The greatest problem arises when commuters find the shopping center a convenient place to leave their cars all day.

These parkers either work nearby or park their cars at the center and take another form of transportation to their place of employment. Such a situation calls for a municipal ordinance, such as that already in effect in Kansas City, Missouri, which permits police enforcement of parking regulations on private lots.

With real estate assessments continuing to cause problems for shopping center and other business owners, the time may come when center owner/developers will be forced, in effect, to turn their parking areas over to the municipality for maintenance and enforcement. The municipalities in turn would have to support these operations by installing parking meters on the lot or otherwise by charging for customer parking.

Evening and Sunday Operation

Evening shopping has become a major force in retailing. The practice has shifted the peak hours of trade and the traditional shopping schedules to such a point that most centers now stay open six nights a week. Evening sales now typically account for 30 to 40 percent of a center's trade.

Late afternoon and evening shopping interferes less with evening rush hour traffic. It also results in merchants' opening their stores later on weekday mornings. This affects the center's operations, particularly the morning demand on the parking area. The challenge then faced by management is to achieve greater trade volumes in off-peak hours through effective advertising and promotion.

Operation after dark also requires better lighting of walks and parking areas and greater attention to store illumination for both interior and exterior design. Incandescent and fluorescent lights should be mixed to get a balance between warm and cold light. Lighting also adds glamour to the centers at night, but it must not consume excessive energy. Holding down the costs of lighting and heating or air conditioning the center while expanding the hours of evening operation calls for skillful planning and design by the center management and the tenants.

Many centers today are open on Sunday. Shopping center operators report that weekend shopping accounts for an even greater proportion of the sales volume than it traditionally did in central business districts. Business activity starts building on Thursday and reaches its peak in the afternoon on Saturday, the heaviest shopping day. In some areas, however, Sunday openings produce the highest sales volumes *per hour* of the week.

---

[6] See the sample sign agreement under Appendix D (Exhibit C, Part II).

OPERATING HOURS PER WEEK OF LINEAR CENTERS AND ENCLOSED MALLS

	UNDER 100,000 SQUARE FEET	100,000 PLUS SQUARE FEET	UNDER 250,000 SQUARE FEET	250,000– 499,999 SQUARE FEET	500,000– 1,000,000 SQUARE FEET	OVER 1,000,000 SQUARE FEET	LINEAR AGE TOTALS	ENCLOSED AGE TOTALS
Under 3 Years	65.00	53.29[1]	70.00	70.46	70.32	67.50[1]	61.10	70.16
3–10 Years	68.13	71.96	71.69	67.59	69.60	71.55	69.53	69.80
Over 10 Years	67.48	67.75	69.52	68.91	72.30	72.33	67.61	70.79
Size Totals	67.44	67.91	70.29	68.71	70.74	71.77	67.64	70.29

[1]A sample of fewer than 10 responses was used. The statistic may not be significant.

Linear Centers

Enclosed Malls

Source: International Council of Shopping Centers, *ICSC Shopping Center Operating Cost Report 1984* (New York: ICSC, 1984).

Store hours can be regulated by agreement or by specification in the lease. However, the lease should explicitly prohibit the independent action of a tenant who chooses not to remain open during regular daytime, evening, or Sunday hours. Most centers are open six nights per week and a limited number of hours on Sunday. The hours of small tenants should be tied to the hours established by the major tenants.

Real Estate Taxes

Real estate taxes and assessments create another special problem for the shopping center owner, because real estate taxes represent one of the landlord's greatest exposures to operational expense. As reported in the Urban Land Institute's 1984 edition of *Dollars & Cents of Shopping Centers*, real estate taxes in 1984 accounted for 19 percent of total operating expenses in super regional centers, 20 percent in regional centers, 27 percent in community centers, and 29 percent in neighborhood centers.

To protect the owner from increases in real estate taxes, a lease clause should provide that tenants pay for tax hikes through rent increases. Tenants will therefore be concerned about local assessment practices and may help in finding tax relief.

Future taxes are often underestimated. To be on the safe side, taxes should be figured at the local rate and at the full assessed value based on whatever assessment method the local assessor uses. Centers are reassessed frequently but the trend is ever upward, as shown in Figure 6-2.

The difference in value between land used for building and land used for parking should be reflected in the tax assessment of the shopping center property. The land used for parking should be valued

6-2   REAL ESTATE TAXES PER SQUARE FOOT OF GLA

TYPE OF CENTER	1975	1984
Neighborhood	$.32	$.41
Community	.30	.32
Regional	.36	.65
Super Regional	.63	.90

Source: Urban Land Institute, *Dollars & Cents of Shopping Centers* (Washington, D.C.: ULI–the Urban Land Institute, 1975, 1984).

as parking area, not as commercial property similar to that occupied by the commercial structure. Shopping center parking area used to the public benefit supports the thesis that more reasonable valuations are needed for shopping centers. Standard factors used to assess downtown properties—front footage values, corner influences, standards of depths, and so on—should not be applied to the shopping center, where roughly 25 percent of the land is used for building and 75 percent for free parking.

Accounting

Many references have been made to ULI's triennial publication, *Dollars & Cents of Shopping Centers*. This study analyzes the balance left in shopping center operations after operating expenses are subtracted from gross receipts. From this balance must be subtracted depreciation, debt service, and income taxes in order to arrive at an actual return on investment. *Dollars & Cents* presents current data on the various components of shopping center income and expense as well as other data on centers in the United States and Canada. Its purpose, then, is to provide a reference source for finding and evaluating levels of performance in shopping center operations.

The categories of measurement used in *Dollars & Cents* and the accounting methods that the presentation of data reflects are based on another ULI publication, the *Standard Manual of Accounting for Shopping Center Operations.*[7] Whereas *Dollars & Cents* is intended as neither a directive nor a manual but rather as a reference work on current levels of shopping center performance, the *Standard Manual* was developed by a special ULI committee because of the need for uniformity in shopping center accounting methods to provide consistent presentations and meaningful comparisons of operating results. Special accounting methods were not required for asset and liability accounting, since methods are much the same for shopping centers as for other businesses. Rather, the area of income and expense accounting needed special and standardized methods. Income accounting in shopping centers is largely a reflection of the revenue received through provisions in the tenant lease, including rental income from tenants, income from common area services, income from the sale of utilities to tenants (where submetering is involved), and income from miscellaneous sources. Expense accounting in shopping centers, on the other hand, must be tailored to provide center owners, developers, and managers with useful data for budget projections and for comparison within the industry. The *Standard Manual* was designed to meet these accounting needs and to facilitate the sharing of information in order to improve the practices and performance of shopping center management and operation. Much of the information that follows is based on the *Standard Manual.*

Income Accounting

The total income or total operating receipts are derived from all money received from rent, common area charges, and other income. Total rent is the income from tenants for the leased space, including the minimum guaranteed yearly rent (or the straight percentage rent when no minimum guarantee is set) and the overage rent received as a percentage of sales above the established breakpoint. Because of the many different rental arrangements commonly used, only the figures contributing to the total rent are useful for rental comparisons (including those found in *Dollars & Cents of Shopping Centers*) across the industry. But in income accounting in the individual shopping center, the records should show readily the

data in each of the following categories as established in each tenant's lease:

- GLA in square feet.
- Sales—annual volume and per square foot of GLA.
- Rate of percentage rent.
- Percentage rent when no minimum guarantee is established.
- Minimum guaranteed yearly rent.
- Overage rent earned for the year.
- Charges to tenants for common area services, including charges for heating and air conditioning an enclosed mall.
- Charges under the escalator clauses, accounted separately for each type of charge.
- Utility charges for the year, where applicable.
- Miscellaneous income, including revenue from such facilities as public telephones, pay toilets, and vending machines.
- Total rent and total charges.

Expense Accounting

The standard system of expense accounting is based on two objectives. The first and more important is the need to classify and present accounting data according to the accounting and information needs of the shopping center management. The second objective is to provide accounting methods that facilitate the industrywide gathering and analysis of operating expense data. To accommodate these two objectives, shopping center expenses are categorized in two ways: by using a system of functional categories, and by using a system of natural categories. The functional categories can be applied to all centers; they provide the framework for comparison across the industry. The natural division of expenses, on the other hand, ties the functional expenses with the primary objectives of expenditure. The following is a breakdown of expenses according to these two systems:

Functional Expense Categories

- Building maintenance.
- Parking lot, mall, and other public areas.
- Central utility systems.
- Office area services.
- Advertising and promotion.
- Finance expenses.
- Depreciation and amortization of deferred costs.
- Real estate taxes.
- Insurance.
- General and administrative.

---

[7] Urban Land Institute, *Standard Manual of Accounting for Shopping Center Operations* (Washington, D.C.: ULI–the Urban Land Institute, 1971).

Natural Expense Categories

- Payroll and supplementary benefits.
- Management fees.
- Contractual services.
- Professional services.
- Leasing fees and commissions.
- Materials and supplies.
- Equipment expenses.
- Utilities.
- Travel and entertainment.
- Communication.
- Taxes and licenses.
- Contributions to merchants' association.
- Insurance.
- Losses from bad debts.
- Interest.
- Depreciation.
- Amortization of deferred costs.
- Ground rent.

Taken together, the two groups of categories provide a logical basis for analytical comparisons of individual shopping center results with industry data as well as day-to-day information for management purposes. The standard system is designed to serve as the expense classification for a complete system of accounting, with two exceptions—financing costs and depreciation of the structures (real and appurtenances).

Depreciation procedures—or the spreading of a capital expense over a period of years—have changed significantly in recent years, beginning with the enactment of the Economic Recovery Tax Act (ERTA) in 1981. ERTA set forth Accelerated Cost Recovery System (ACRS) provisions, which reduced the depreciation period for structures placed in service after December 31, 1980, from a polyglot of periods determined by facts and circumstances to 15 years. The Deficit Reduction Act (DRA) of 1984 has since increased the depreciation period from 15 to 18 years for property placed in service after March 15, 1984. It should be noted that depreciation regulations are being changed with increasing frequency in the 1980s and, thus, the procedures described here may soon be out of date. Because of the impact of these changes on a center's taxable income, it is essential that the shopping center developer and his accountant be totally familiar with current tax laws.

Because regional, community, and neighborhood centers differ substantially in size and complexity, their management needs for accounting information will also vary. If a large shopping center wants to use the standard system of expense accounting as a tool for financial planning and budgetary control, it should also establish for internal use a subdivision of functional categories or an expansion of natural divisions with assignments of responsibility and supervisory personnel.

Marketing and Promotion

A successful center is a promoted center. Promotion is important to owners of both large and small centers. By building shopper traffic and increasing sales for all tenants in the center, effective promotion affects the level of percentage rents and thus plays a major role in determining the rate of return to the developer/owner. For this reason, promotion is essential for all sizes and types of shopping centers and should be a well-conceived program.

The successful marketing of a shopping center is a complex task that must follow a careful plan. Reduced to its simplest common denominator, the goal of the plan is to produce profit for the center's tenants and owner. And profit, for a retail entity like a shopping center, comes from the sale of merchandise.

All of the elements of the plan must be thought out well in advance. They should represent a coordinated effort among all of the center's merchants, and be directed specifically at the customers in the center's trade area. A good plan goes beyond advertising, sales promotion, and presenting a series of special events. It avoids "backing into" a program using a trial and error approach. Instead, it is a deliberate series of actions taken to bring a center to its potential volume and beyond.

The concept of positioning is at the foundation of a successful marketing plan. Positioning means more than creating a favorable image of a center in its customers' minds, although this is a key ingredient. The marketing/promotion director must carefully analyze the center's strengths and weaknesses (including in the assessment such factors as location, tenant mix, architecture, and ease of accessibility) and devote the same care to determining competitors' strengths and weaknesses. To be successful, the marketing program must capitalize on the center's strengths and the competitors' weaknesses.[8]

The amount and type of promotion for a center will obviously depend on the size and nature of the development, and, therefore, a promotional program that is effective for one center should not be blindly copied and used for another center. However, a number of basic guidelines should be followed in order to plan and implement a center's promotional program successfully.[9]

- Financial participation in the center's promotional activities should be mandatory for all tenants, and a clause to this effect should be included in the lease.

[8] S. Albert Wenner, *Promotion and Marketing for Shopping Centers* (New York: International Council of Shopping Centers, 1980), p. xi.

[9] Ibid., p. xii.

- At least six months before the center's opening (or reopening in the case of a renovation/expansion), an aggressive publicity program should be instituted.
- Preferably six months to a year before opening (but no later than three months), the center should have operating a merchants' association or a steering committee of merchants structured as a marketing fund (see below for information on the distinction between a merchants' association and a marketing fund).
- All promotion for the center should be developed and implemented by the center's marketing director or advertising agency.
- The center and its stores should be promoted as a single, cohesive unit. In this regard, all print advertising for the center should appear as a unit with a cohesive theme. Similarly, radio and/or television advertising must promote all stores as a unit and use an identical theme.
- The promotion of merchandise should be supported by and coordinated with an event that is designed to further attract the public to the center. And vice versa: major promotional events should be coordinated with some type of merchandise promotion.
- The center should be involved in community affairs in order to help the community, build good will, and increase traffic to the center. For example, the center might give financial support to major community endeavors, share the use of shopping center facilities, plan and participate in civic events, and so forth.
- The center's promotional unit and the merchants should always be in communication with each other.

Merchants' Association

A merchants' association has traditionally been responsible for the promotion of a shopping center. It acts as a clearinghouse for suggestions, ideas, and programming of promotional events. A lease clause is the recommended vehicle by which to establish a merchants' association. Most lease agreements stipulate that an association will be formed, that the tenants will pay a specified rate per square foot to the association, and that the developer will pay a certain percentage of the annual costs. Generally, the lease will further stipulate that the developer and tenants will pay a specified amount of the center's preopening and opening costs and that bylaws, personnel, and detailed programs and budgets will be developed at a later date (before the first organizational meeting of

the association).[10] Preferably, the association should be operating six months or more (and definitely no less than three months) before the center opens.

Bylaws establish the specific purposes, organization, and requirements of the association and should be programmed by an individual or an agency with experience in the operation and promotion of shopping centers. They should be reviewed and approved by lawyers before they are printed and should be available before the association's first meeting.

Bylaws set forth all pertinent information and rules, including rules governing election of officers, duties of officers, a quorum, order of business for monthly meetings, date of annual meeting, appointment of committees, and, usually, the establishment of a board of directors consisting of a president, vice president, secretary, and treasurer. The usual standing committees cover the areas of finance, advertising, special events, and publicity. The authority to assess dues and fees for advertising, promotion, seasonal decoration, and other activities is spelled out in the formal lease document. In joining the association as required in the lease, the tenant also agrees to abide by the association's charter and bylaws.

The owner can rely on either of two operational policies with respect to the merchants' association. He can act merely as the agent for the association, relying on the members' interests to guide the operation of the center, in which case an executive secretary or professional promotions director will be hired and paid by the association; or he can actively run the association, relying on the officer/members and committees to cooperate in the advertising and promotional programs.

The owner must recognize his responsibility for promoting the center. The association members should approve a comprehensive promotions program, and a promotions director will execute the program. When the owner pays the salary of the director, the owner maintains control of promotion, even in small centers. Associations have trouble when the landlord leaves the center's merchants to their own devices; in general, tenants are slow to appreciate what an association can do for them.

An association may be organized as a for-profit corporation with a charter and bylaws. Although a nonprofit corporation has tax advantages, its activities are limited. The for-profit organization operates more broadly and can escape taxes at the end of the year by investing all its tenant assessments in promotional events and other activities.

_____

[10] Ibid., p. 2.

A part-time or full-time paid secretary is essential for successful operation. No member alone can assume the multiple responsibilities of correspondence, newsletter preparation, notices, billings, and other duties; members must always spend their main efforts on making their own stores pay. In small centers, the association cannot always maintain a staff; staff work must then be handled as part of the owner's contribution.

If the association does not employ a full- or part-time promotions manager, it can contract the services of a local public relations firm. Even though a large agency that is not locally based can be used, the representative who handles the center's work should be local. In general, the more local the management responsibility, the better the operation.

The merchants' association can be charged with a wide range of activities—joint advertising of the center, including the use of the center's name on advertising mastheads, letterheads, bill heads, and statements; special centerwide promotion; seasonal events and decorations; enforcement of parking lot regulations, particularly those regarding employee parking; business referrals and credit systems; store hours and night openings; merchant directory; and centerwide news bulletins or special newspapers for trade area distribution. The importance of involving the merchants cannot be overstressed; unless they are actively involved, merchants will merely accept what is offered.

The basis of assessment for contributions to the cost of the association's activities varies widely. The most equitable method is that all tenants contribute to the advertising fund, most often, according to each tenant's GLA. Though done less often, contributions can also be based on a straight percentage of gross sales; a formula combining the percentage of sales volume and the number of square feet occupied; front footage occupied; a percentage of the tenant's annual rent in relation to the total annual rent of the center; individually negotiated assessments unrelated to the merchant's size or volume; and combinations of these methods, although formulas that combine several of these methods may be difficult to administer. Tenants, such as banks, whose leases do not include percentage clauses, should contribute to the promotion fund on the basis of square feet occupied. A lease can also specify the amount to be contributed for preopening and grand opening promotion and for the first year of operation. The developer generally pays one-quarter to one-third of the annual association budget. As a rule of thumb, most grand opening budgets range from 50 to 100 percent of the annual assessment and budget.

If a tenant does not pay his dues, he is violating the lease and the landlord must take action. Terminating the lease is preferable to a lawsuit, which neither the tenant nor the landlord wants.

The owner/developer must not only organize the merchants' association but must also participate in and guide its activities. He must contribute to the operating fund, as mentioned earlier. An active association needs an active and energetic owner who will stimulate interest, originate and launch promotions, prepare budgets, and coordinate all activities of the association.

To stimulate the merchants, the tenants can be sent a monthly association bulletin that includes sales volume increases and decreases from the previous month and year. This information can be presented by tenant classification—shoes, ladies' wear, and so forth. Tenants will report to management their sales monthly; management can then incorporate these figures to formulate and report overall sales volumes and trends without revealing the sales volumes of individual tenants. The monthly bulletin, as part of the educational program for the merchants, will also contain other news and information about future programs of interest to the merchants.

Marketing Fund

An alternative to the establishment of a merchants' association is the use of a marketing fund to promote the center. The use of the marketing fund instead of a merchants' association is a relatively new technique (beginning in the mid-1970s), but one that is now widely used. Tenants are still assessed to provide funds to promote the center. However, unlike the merchants' association, the marketing fund is totally controlled and administered by the developer/owner of the center. The fund is administered by a marketing director, who reports to the developer/owner rather than to a merchants' association.

The underlying reason for using a marketing fund instead of a merchants' association is that the elected directors of a merchants' association may be viewed as lacking the expertise in marketing, promotion, and publicity that a professional has and, therefore, they should not be responsible for the promotional activities for the center. Many new centers include provisions for a marketing fund (rather than a merchants' association) in their leases (see Figure 6-3), and some older centers are converting to a marketing fund.[11] A key advantage of the marketing fund is that it frees the marketing director from the many organizational de-

---

[11] Robert J. Flynn, *Carpenter's Shopping Center Management*, pp. 91 and 92.

35. MARKETING FUND: (i) Landlord will promptly establish a Marketing Fund for the Shopping Center. Tenant agrees to pay to Landlord the Marketing Charge, payable in advance on the first day of each month, as Tenant's contribution toward the advertising, promotion, public relations, and administrative expenses related thereto. The Marketing Charge payable by Tenant to Landlord will be subject to adjustment by a percentage equal to the percentage of increase or decrease from the base period (as hereafter defined) of the "Consumer's Price Index for Urban Wage Earners and Clerical Workers, U.S. City Average All Items, Series A (1967 = 100)," issued by the Bureau of Labor Statistics of The United States Department of Labor in the Current Labor Statistics Section of the Monthly Labor Review (final publication only), provided that said index has increased or decreased by at least ten percent (10%) or more from the base period. The term "base period" as used herein shall refer to the date on which said index is published, which is closest to the date immediately preceding the formation of said Fund. In any event, however, and notwithstanding any decrease in such index, the Marketing Charge payable by Tenant to Landlord shall at no time be less than the amount set forth under Paragraph 1 (t) hereof. (ii) If Tenant shall open or be required under the terms of this Lease to open for business in the Demised Premises at any time before or within ninety (90) days after the date of the grand opening of the Shopping Center, Tenant also agrees to pay to Landlord in addition to the foregoing Marketing Charge, an initial contribution in the amount of the Grand Opening Charge, for the purpose of defraying the advertising, promotion, and public relations expenses to be incurred by Landlord (or to reimburse Landlord for advancing such expenses) in connection with the preopening and grand opening promotion of the Shopping Center; such Grand Opening Charge shall be paid to Landlord by Tenant within ten (10) days following the presentation of a bill to Tenant therefor. (iii) Tenant also agrees to advertise Tenant's business in the Demised Premises in special Shopping Center newspaper sections or tabloids sponsored by Landlord for advertising by merchants of the Shopping Center; and in connection therewith, Tenant agrees to purchase, not less than but limited to six (6) times during each Lease Year, advertising space hereinafter specified. Tenant agrees to purchase in each instance advertising space in minimum amounts based upon the Gross Leasable Area of the demised premises as follows: (a) six hundred (600) square feet or less of Gross Leasable Area—sixteen (16) column inches; (b) Between 601 and 2,000 square feet of Gross Leasable Area—forty-eight (48) column inches; (c) Between 2,001 and 3,000 square feet of Gross Leasable Area—eighty (80) column inches; and (d) 3,001 square feet or more of Gross Leasable Area—one hundred sixty-eight (168) column inches. If Tenant shall refuse or neglect to timely submit its copy of such advertising, Landlord, at its election, shall have the right (but not the obligation) to submit copy consisting of Tenant's Trade Name and address to the printer for inclusion in such printed advertising media on behalf of and for the account of Tenant. If Tenant shall refuse or neglect to pay for such advertising, Landlord may pay such sum or sums of money by reason of the failure or neglect of Tenant to perform; and in such event, Tenant agrees to reimburse and pay Landlord upon demand, all such sums so expended, which shall be deemed to be additional rent for the purposes of enforcement and collection. (iv) Landlord agrees to contribute not less than twenty-five percent (25%) of the total amount of promotional charges paid to said Marketing Fund by the tenants of the Shopping Center, provided, however, that Landlord's contribution will in no event exceed Ten Thousand Dollars ($10,000) during any Lease Year. However, Landlord, at its option, may elect to contribute all or part of the services of a Marketing Director and/or Secretary and their respective offices, as a part of such cash contribution. The Promotion Director shall be under the exclusive control and supervision of Landlord and Landlord shall have the sole right and exclusive authority to employ and discharge such Marketing Director. In lieu and instead of the Marketing Fund, Landlord shall have the right and option to form a Merchants' Association; and in such case, Tenant shall become a member in good standing of said Association and Landlord agrees to promptly pay to said Association Tenant's Marketing Charge and/or the Grand Opening Charge, as and when actually paid to Landlord by Tenant.

Source: Doral Chenoweth, *The Answers to Every Question You Wanted to Ask about Conversion from Associations to Marketing Funds* (Columbus, Ohio: Marketing/Media Enterprises, Inc., 1984).

tails and internal politics of the merchants' association, allowing him to concentrate on marketing and promotion rather than on association details. In addition, the marketing fund enables long-term promotional goals and programs to be established (which is difficult to do under a merchants' association with its frequent change of leaders).

When a marketing fund is used, tenants pay fees directly to the developer/owner and, thus, do not play an active role in the development of the promotional program (although a steering committee of tenants is sometimes appointed to operate in an advisory capacity). Therefore, it is particularly important for the developer and the marketing director to establish and maintain clear lines of communication with tenants in order to obtain their strong cooperation.

If a center has an existing merchants' association, a number of factors should be carefully examined before deciding whether or not to convert from an association to a marketing fund. For example, the existing association should be retained if:

- Merchants are working well together and participating strongly in group promotional/advertising activities.
- Association leadership is consistent and strong, tending to the business of marketing the center, while not interfering with operational matters.
- The association board acts as a creative input and advisory body, allowing a professional marketing director to do an effective long-term marketing job with well-defined programs.
- The association maintains tight financial controls, not subjecting its membership to the liabilities of a deficit or to taxes on a profit.
- The association is an effective two-way communication mechanism, and the leadership uses peer pressure to encourage good merchandising and participation for the benefit of the entire center.
- The shopping center owner is getting a satisfactory return on his investment in the activities of the merchants' association.
- The shopping center owner does not wish to be responsible for marketing the center.
- The shopping center owner is not sufficiently knowledgeable about retailing and marketing and is not able to guide a strong marketing program.
- The center's finances, leasing record, and/or operations are too weak to take the steps necessary to convert to a marketing fund.[12]

On the other hand, conversion to a marketing fund is appropriate if:

- Merchants are apathetic and not participating in group promotion and advertising activities.
- Association leadership allows merchants' meetings to turn into operational grievance sessions with little discussion of marketing.
- The turnover of store managers is high, resulting in frequent changes in association leadership and in the marketing program.
- The association board continually acts in the interest of a few merchants rather than for the good of the entire center.
- The association funds are spent on nonproductive activities or are continually overspent, causing deficits.

- The decision-making process is so cumbersome, illogical, or political that only mediocre or short-term marketing programs result.
- The center is unable to attract or to keep professional marketing talent because of the frustration of working with an association.
- Meetings and administration take up so much time that little is left for marketing the center.
- The center owner is better able than an association to guide and administer the marketing effort and is willing to accept this responsibility.[13]

If a decision is made to convert to a marketing fund, the following steps should be taken:

- An attorney should prepare an amendment to the lease (see Figure 6-4) providing for the marketing fund.
- Agreements should be obtained from major tenants stating that they will resign from the merchants' association, will continue funding the promotion of the center through a marketing fund, and will participate on an advisory committee.
- Tenants agreeing to the change should sign lease amendments redirecting payments from the association to the marketing fund.
- For those tenants who do not agree to convert, the merchants' association should continue to operate—on a token basis. Meetings should be held, officers elected, contributions collected, and all lease obligations and legal requirements of the merchants' association satisfied. Those tenants wishing to remain members of the association should assume administrative responsibilities.
- The marketing fund should be operated independently of the merchants' association, should one still exist. Only marketing fund contributors should be included in promotional activities paid for by the fund.
- Marketing fund conversion should be included as a condition in lease renewals, lease modifications, and operational requests by hold-out tenants.
- When the last tenant has converted to the fund, the merchants' association should be legally dissolved.[14]

Finally, it should be remembered that the process of conversion may take several years and may result in acrimony between the owner and tenants.

---

[12] "Jones Report for Shopping Center Marketing," April 1980, Vol. 11, No. 7.

[13] Ibid.

[14] Ibid.

6-4   SUGGESTED LEASE AMENDMENT FOR CONVERSION TO MARKETING FUND

To convert existing lease provisions from the merchants' association to the marketing fund concept, the following lease amendment is suggested.

First Lease Amendment

This Agreement, made and entered into this _____ day of 198____, by and between (developer), hereinafter referred to as Landlord, and _____ _____, hereinafter referred to as Tenant:

Witnesseth:

That whereas, Landlord and Tenant did on _____, 198____, enter into a lease agreement for certain premises located at _____ _____ Mall, _____ (city), hereinafter referred to as "the lease," and incorporated herein by reference thereafter, and _____ _____ that whereas, Landlord and Tenant are desirous of modifying "the lease" as follows:

Now, therefore, in consideration of the mutual covenants hereinafter set forth, the Parties agree that "the lease" shall be amended and modified as follows:

Merchants' Association

1. Article XX, Section 20.01 Membership shall be deemed deleted and of no force or effect and substituted therefor shall be the following provisions: (Substitute the Marketing Fund clause described in Figure 6-3.)

Source: Doral Chenoweth, *The Answers to Every Question You Wanted to Ask about Conversion from Associations to Marketing Funds* (Columbus, Ohio: Marketing/Media Enterprises, Inc., 1984).

Finally, it should be remembered that the process of conversion may take several years and may result in acrimony between the owner and tenants.

Type of Promotion

Whether a center's promotion is handled by a merchants' association or a marketing fund, important decisions must be made concerning the type of promotion to be undertaken. Promotional and special events can be used successfully to make a community more aware of a center and to attract shoppers. Promotional events may take any number of forms. Whatever form they take, they must be aimed at attracting customers, not just curious crowds. "Pack the stores, not the parking lots" is a maxim that applies to promotional events. Carnival-type promotions are of limited benefit and should only be used to offer attractive merchandise and sound values.

Developers emphasize that promotions for a center should be planned around a major tenant's individual promotion. Timing and merchandise offerings should not be duplicated. Most developers have found it helpful to focus on five or six major promotions during the year and supplement these with appropriate minor events. Promotional events and activities should be set up and budgeted a year in advance, and association members should be given a full description of the program and budget. A record should be kept of each promotional event so that the owner or promotions director can review completed promotions to see why they were or were not successful.

Christmas, Easter, Halloween, and other holidays provide occasions for special promotions and seasonal decorations of the center. Other worthwhile promotional schemes include "giveaways," children's attractions, and special sales on holidays or other occasions. For example, a "suburban living fair" or an "urban living fair" can replace the traditional mid-summer clearance sale. Special promotional events always benefit from the use of live models to illustrate such activities as patio cooking, urban living, and the use of children's play equipment. For all promotional activities, the developer/owner must replace and refurbish display materials as needed.

In addition to promotional events, the center can be promoted through advertising, which should help the public to associate the individual shops within the center with the image of the center itself. The market area of the media selected as most effective to promote the center should match that of the center as closely as possible. For example, it would not seem logical for a neighborhood center to use television to advertise to an area that is 40 or 50 times larger than its market. Newspaper (often full-page ads) and radio advertising are most frequently used. Newspaper ads are relatively inexpensive and can be widely distributed. Radio is considered one of the most effective forms of advertising in today's market, and because of the size of the market that it reaches, it can also be inexpensive. However, it reaches only certain market segments, depending on the nature of the radio stations. Television is the most persuasive and powerful advertising medium, but it can be extremely costly. Other advertising possibilities include direct mail, billboards, and mass transit advertising. There are no hard-and-fast rules as to the advertising mix that should be implemented. Advertising will vary widely from center to center, depending on the center's needs and the funds available.

7.
Case Studies

This chapter comprises case studies of 14 shopping centers. Its intent is to present representative examples of the major types of shopping centers and variations of these types, and to communicate the direction of contemporary development.

To be included among these studies, a project had to be economically viable and its developer willing to share experiences with a wider audience. Further, each development had to be of superior quality, with features worth emulating. The profiles, however, are not presented as necessarily the best examples of their respective types. Such judgments would be difficult to make, and many other projects would have served equally well.

The narrative is based on lengthy interviews with the developers of the centers and with other project professionals. Economic data have been treated as uniformly as possible to permit comparisons; these data have also been generalized to protect developer confidences. Readers interested in profiles of shopping center economic performance are referred to *Dollars & Cents of Shopping Centers*, mentioned earlier in this book.

Some conclusions suggested by individual projects may appear inconsistent with the overall perspective of the industry. This is to be expected; shopping center development is not so much a science as an art. Special concepts that succeed in one situation may be limited in their application elsewhere. Rules of thumb have a way of becoming quickly outmoded.

The following projects, grouped by center type, are featured:

Major Center Types

Neighborhood Centers
Wheatley Plaza
Greenvale, New York

University Mall
Fairfax County, Virginia

Community Centers
Vermont-Slauson Shopping Center
Los Angeles, California

Trinity Valley
Carrollton, Texas

Regional/Super Regional Centers
The Grand Avenue
Milwaukee, Wisconsin

Coquitlam Centre
Vancouver, British Columbia

Prestonwood Town Center
Dallas, Texas

Variations of Major Center Types

Community/Specialty Center
Danville Livery and Mercantile
Danville, California

Regional/Specialty Center
The Bell Tower
Lee County, Florida

Festival/Specialty Centers
The Waterside
Norfolk, Virginia

The Pavilion
Washington, D.C.

Off-Price/Outlet Centers
Montgomery Village Off-Price Center
Gaithersburg, Maryland

Liberty Village
Flemington, New Jersey

Mixed-Use Development
Town Square
St. Paul, Minnesota

Major Center Types

As noted in Chapter 1, the **neighborhood center** provides primarily for the daily shopping needs of an immediate neighborhood trade area. It has a tenant mix that emphasizes the sale of convenience goods (food, drugs, and sundries) and personal services, and has a supermarket as its principal tenant. The definition of a neighborhood center (like that of other center types) is based on the characteristics of the center's trade area and its tenants; the size of the center does not determine its type. For this reason, examples may be found of correctly classified neighborhood centers (based on their trade area and tenant mix) that are larger than some community centers.

Often described as the "in-between" center, the **community center** has a trade area that is larger than a neighborhood center but smaller than a regional center. While it offers a greater range of tenants and merchandise than the neighborhood center, it lacks a full-line department store (which is present only in the

regional and super regional centers). It does, however, typically offer certain types of merchandise (such as furniture, hardware, and garden and building supplies) that are less likely to be found in regional centers. Today's community center will most often have a discount or off-price department store or a strong specialty store (such as a hardware/building/home improvement store or a combined drug/variety/garden center) as the principal anchor tenant. While the junior department store or larger variety store still functions as the anchor tenant in some community centers, it does so less frequently than in the past. Other leading tenants that are appearing more often are the large combination supermarket/drugstore or the superwarehouse store, the large-scale furniture warehouse store, and the discount catalog display and pickup store.

Regional and super regional centers provide a full range of shopping goods, general merchandise, apparel, furniture, and home furnishings, and are built around the full-line department store. The regional center has one or two department stores as anchor tenants (most often two), a typical gross leasable area of 400,000 square feet, and can range in size from 300,000 to 1 million square feet. The super regional center has three or more department stores, a typical gross leasable area of 800,000 square feet, and can range from 500,000 to well over 1 million square feet. Both centers have large trade areas and serve populations of more than 150,000, often drawing shoppers who must go distances requiring over 25 to 30 minutes of travel time to reach the center.

Variations of Major Center Types

The term "specialty center" has been used for some time to describe any center that represents a departure from traditional shopping center development concepts and cannot be accurately described as a neighborhood, community, or regional/super regional center. Today, the specialty center is defined more precisely to reflect the differences among the many existing and emerging types of specialty centers. These differences, for example, include tenant mix of various centers and the market segments and trade area to which a center is targeted. Using this refined typology, a number of specialty center types may be identified, including community/specialty; regional/specialty; festival/specialty; fashion; discount; off-price; factory outlet; and home improvement centers.

197

WHEATLEY PLAZA (Neighborhood Center)
Greenvale, New York

7-1   Although the center is in a traditional L-shaped configuration often used for "linear" shopping centers, it deviates from the typical pattern. Stores line the perimeter of the site and parking is on the interior.

Wheatley Plaza is a 113,345-square-foot (GLA) neighborhood shopping center located in Greenvale, Long Island, New York. The center is targeted to an upper-middle-income market, with a primary trade area of 287,000. The median household income within a one- to two-mile radius ranges from $45,000 to $50,000. Wheatley Plaza has a 53,000-square-foot Pathmark supercenter as its chief anchor tenant and a 9,000-square-foot restaurant as a secondary anchor. Although classified as a neighborhood center because it has a supermarket as its principal anchor tenant, the center's tenant mix is targeted to the special needs and tastes of higher-income customers as well as to the everyday needs of the local neighborhood. Tenants are primarily upscale specialty shops, with 50 percent of these being national chains such as Record World and Haagen Dazs. Specialty tenants include sporting goods, men's and women's wear, hairdressing, health food and toy stores, and other types of boutiques.

Although the center is in a traditional L-shaped configuration often associated with "linear" shopping centers, it deviates from the typical pattern in that its 580 parking spaces are on the interior of the lot, while the stores themselves line the adjacent streets. This was done for a variety of reasons, both practical and aesthetic. The center was designed to appeal to automobile passersby through extensive landscaping and design amenities on the street side, including show windows and attractive awnings. At the same time, shoppers entering the mall-like center from the parking lot are met with glass-covered walkways and an outdoor courtyard and dining area.

Originally, the site was used for a large garden shop and greenhouse business (at that time, the city permitted no commercial development beyond 100 feet of the roadway in order to protect local residents from the disruption of commercial activity). The planning process for the center began in 1974 and 1975 and included a zoning change in the area to allow commercial uses to extend beyond 100 feet from the street. The developer held meetings with local civic associations during the planning process and offered a design compromise that eliminated much of the negative side effects of development at the chosen location. After conducting public hearings and completing the review process, the town of North Hempstead approved the zoning change, and construction began in the spring of 1979. Completed in the fall of 1980, the project is currently 100 percent leased. Many of the small tenants began paying percentage rents the first year, and sales for the Pathmark anchor store are at present 50 percent above its national average.

The Site

Wheatley Plaza occupies a 9.5-acre site at the intersection of Northern Boulevard and Glen Cove Road, the second most trafficked intersection in Long Island. Northern Boulevard is a major east/west commuter corridor to New York City, and Glen Cove Road is one of the few through north/south streets on Long Island and is one mile from the Long Island Expressway. The shopping center services an area within a five-mile radius from Manhasset to Huntington. The historic town of Roslyn is one mile to the west; C.W. Post University and the New York Institute of Technology, the Village of Brookline, Locust Valley, and Muttontown are to the east; and the North Shore towns of Glen Cove and Oyster Bay are to the north. Commercial uses are found on adjacent streets north and west, and residential uses, including new homes and established residences, are found south and east.

Planning and Design

Wheatley Plaza was designed to appeal to an upscale market in an affluent area of Long Island. The goal of the architect and developer was to create a controlled shopping environment at a heavily trafficked intersection that would provide for the trade area's shopping needs, attract quality tenants, and retain the scale and character of its suburban surroundings. To accomplish this objective, they planned the center to face the interior of the lot. Access to shops is through a glass-covered walkway, which provides the ambience of an indoor mall when complemented by a dining courtyard and colonnades. Storefronts consist of white aluminum frames with woodfill and glass panels. Brick facades and brick paving on all sides, attractive awnings, lanterns, and extensive landscape treatments contribute further to the atmosphere of the center. Additional landscaping, offset walls, and show windows on the street side provide an interesting architectural setting that is highly visible and presents an attractive front to the public. All signs are three-dimensional, have white faces with bronze aluminum sides, and lighted letters. Individual letters are all the same size but have varying letter styles.

All small tenants have a store depth of 84 feet, with widths ranging from 12 to 24 feet and averaging 20 feet. Tenants agreed in their leases to design store interiors to be consistent with the quality and style of the exterior design of the center. However, the amount of interior finishing provided by the developer varied widely from tenant to tenant. Approximately 50 percent of the tenants leased shell space and were responsible for all interior design. Because many tenants could no longer afford to finish the shells when interest rates rose, the developer gave allowances for finishing work.

Obtaining a strong anchor tenant was crucial to the initial planning of the shopping center. The developer had already allocated 30,000 square feet of space for an upscale supermarket tenant. A Pathmark located down the street badly needed additional space; its volume of business was creating a congestion problem that was threatening to discourage customers. Even though the Pathmark was looking for 53,000 square feet to accommodate its "supercenter" design, it was also interested in the Wheatley Plaza location. By moving there, it would prevent a competitor from taking the anchor spot.

The developer negotiated an agreement with Pathmark, with both sides making concessions. The devel-

oper agreed to allocate to Pathmark the 53,000 square feet needed, taking the additional footage from allocations to several small stores. Pathmark, in exchange, agreed to modify its design to include a truck bay with room for two trailers (to comply with the city's wish to screen unattractive truck activity) and to alter the shape of its standard storage area to fit the building configuration. It also agreed not to have window signs, to install "clerestory" window and ceiling drops, and to use the landlord's architect for interior design. Because the cost of these elements, in addition to Pathmark's own supercenter design, would exceed the amount that Pathmark would typically spend, the developer agreed to pay part of the difference. (Pathmark had already installed indirect and accent lighting and other upscale interior design features.)

7-2 Designed to appeal to automobile passersby, the center's street side features extensive landscaping, display windows, and attractive awnings.

Tenant Mix

The center was designed with a supermarket as the major anchor at one end of the "L," along Northern Boulevard. At the other end along Glen Cove Road and serving as an additional anchor is a large restaurant, with a brass roof and other outstanding design features. The 53,000-square-foot Pathmark supercenter—with its own deluxe design features—supplies more than the typical grocery products. The 9,000-square-foot anchor restaurant is complemented by a large kosher deli restaurant. The center also leases office space on the second level, and the remainder of the businesses include small specialty shops of approximately 1,500 to 2,000 square feet. Less than 10 percent of Wheatley Plaza's tenants are first-time operations. As a result of careful selection, the developer was able to lease to a variety of national chains and local businesses. The large chains include Walden Books, Record World, and Haagen Dazs, for example, while local operations include the Little Doll House, Mansouri Men's Shop, Mansouri Women's Shop, London Jewelers, Jeanery, and other similar stores.

Marketing

The developer's management company arranges the advertising, which is financed through a promotional fund subsidized by the developer for special projects. Tenants pay a standard fee of approximately $0.50 per square foot for advertising, and, in addition, pay a certain amount per line of advertising in the *New York Times*. This amount varies by store size, type, and number of lines. The center runs continuing ads in the Sunday edition of *The New York Times*.

During the opening year, the center sponsored a number of promotions to draw customers. The promotions had light entertainment themes and promoted a community atmosphere. They included wine and cheese events, live guitar music, a parrot show, and other events designed to draw a crowd. At this point, the center relies primarily on newspaper advertising.

Experienced Gained

- The biggest difficulty was drawing traffic off the street into the project's interior. Leasing to a successful restaurant as a secondary anchor tenant solved this problem.
- An additional problem involved the need to build

a linear shopping center in an affluent neighborhood. By inverting the design, placing traffic on the interior, and adding amenities, the developer was able to make the center appeal to an upscale crowd.

- The traditional problem of rigid zoning restrictions was resolved creatively through both negotiations and construction design. As mentioned, the community's policy restricted commercial development to within 100 feet of the roadway, in order to separate residential areas from loading and other commercial activities. The developer limited truck loading to two locations at either extreme of the center, far from residences, and, by locating the shopping center on the street edge of the site, he used parking lots and landscaping to buffer residences from commercial activity.

- The city was concerned with the potential for excessive congestion at an already heavily congested intersection. The developer addressed this concern by providing an additional traffic lane, which extended from beyond his property line to the intersection. He also agreed to purchase two traffic signals to assist in traffic regulation. The total cost for signals and the additional lane was $250,000.

- The need for a dual facade, both facing street traffic and on the interior, raised construction costs above those typical for a linear center. The use of projections, ornamental lighting, special signing, heavy landscaping, and other aesthetic extras also added $350,000 to building costs.

- After the chief anchor store was secured, leasing went smoothly until the national economy took a turn for the worse. Although the center was almost fully leased when interest rates rose to 20 percent, many of the signed leases were returned. It took nine months for the developer to regain the position he had had in leasing space. As a result of this setback, the Pathmark grand opening occurred six months before that of the rest of the center. However, by October of 1980, the rest of the center was leased, and there is now a waiting list of prospective tenants.

- Tenants for the Wheatley Plaza center were difficult to find because they had to fit the high tone that the developer was looking for, and they had to be willing to pay for interior design work that was of the same caliber as the facade work. However, rent rates presented no obstacle; at $20 to $23 per square foot, they were competitive with local rates. In order to assure consistency of design, many tenants were required by lease to hire

7-3, 7-4   Design amenities on the parking lot side include glass-covered walkways and an outdoor courtyard and dining area.

the developer's architect to design their interiors. All architectural plans had to be approved by the developer.

- By providing the atmosphere of an enclosed mall through the center's various amenities, the development team has successfully combined an upscale center in an affluent market with a linear shopping design. By locating the buildings along the road and having them open into the interior of the site, the center offers a viable alternative to the traditional linear design. Wheatley Plaza also comfortably blended commercial use with nearby residential uses, showing what negotiation and compromise in design can achieve in dealing with local government regulation. Relying on public contacts and creative thinking, the developer and architect carefully engineered a successful shopping center design that is practical, profitable, and serves the needs of its trade area.

- Wheatley Plaza has been a marked success in meeting its objective of providing an upscale shopping facility along a busy intersection, while also providing the area with a strong, community-oriented mix of stores and acting as an architectural landmark and focus to a previously chaotic main intersection. The inverted design of the traditional linear center, with the shopping facilities along the street and parking in the interior, serves several purposes. First, it accommodates the city's desire to keep housing as far away as possible from commercial activity; the landscaping and parking arrangement act as an additional buffer. Second, it prevents parking from becoming the major focus of the suburban streetscape—a problem that many suburban communities suffer from. Third, it brings show windows closer to passing traffic, giving stores better visibility and thus attracting business.

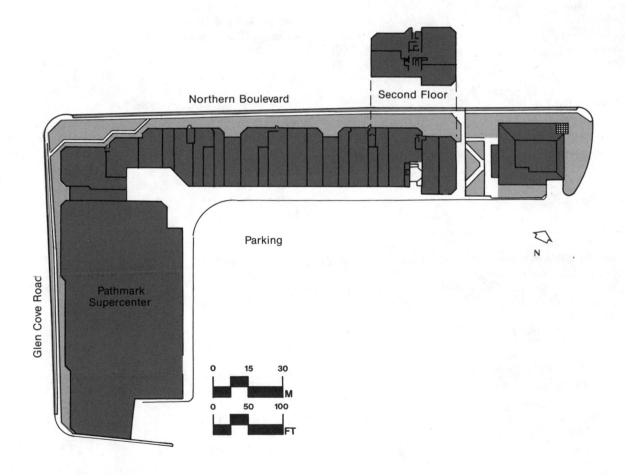

7-5

PROJECT DATA—WHEATLEY PLAZA

Land Use Information:
Site Area: 9.5 acres (3.8 hectares)
Gross Building Area (GBA): 120,000 square feet
Gross Leasable Area (GLA): 113,345 square feet
Parking Spaces: 580
Parking Index: 5 spaces per 1,000 square feet of GLA

Land Use Plan:

	Acres	Percent
Building Coverage	3.0	31.6
Streets and Parking	4.0	42.1
Open Space/Landscaping	2.5	26.3
Total	9.5	100.0

Economic Information:
Site Acquisition Cost: N.A. (leasehold for 99 years)
Off-Site Improvement Cost: $250,000
On-Site Improvement Cost:

Excavation	$ 40,000
Grading	10,000
Sewer/Water	150,000
Paving	200,000
Curbs/Sidewalks	100,000
Landscaping	100,000
Total	$600,000

Total Construction Cost: $7.2 million[1]
Construction Cost per Gross Square Foot: $60
Operating Expenses:

Taxes	$200,000
Insurance	40,000
Services	10,000
Maintenance	25,000
Janitorial	25,000
Utilities	40,000
Legal	10,000
Management	60,000
Miscellaneous	20,000
Total	$430,000

Lease Information:
Sales: $250 per square foot (not including supermarket)
Rents: $20 to $23 per square foot
Term: 7 to 10 years
Provisions: All leases are net. Percentage rent is fixed at 6 percent of gross sales.
Average Sales Volume: $250,000 to $300,000 per year (for small businesses)

Tenant Information:

Classification[2]	Number of Stores	Percent of Total Tenants	Square Feet of GLA	Percent of GLA	Average Percent of GLA in Neighborhood Centers[2]
General Merchandise	–	–	–	–	5.6
Food	3	10.3	58,903	51.4	30.8
Food Service	2	6.9	11,400	9.9	8.8
Clothing	4	13.8	8,406	7.6	5.0
Shoes	1	3.5	1,344	1.4	1.3
Home Furnishings	–	–	–	–	2.6
Home Appliances/Music[3]	1	3.5	2,000	1.8	2.4
Building Materials/Garden	–	–	–	–	3.4
Automotive Supplies/Service Station	–	–	–	–	1.7
Hobby/Special Interest	1	3.5	780	0.8	2.7
Gifts/Specialty	3	10.3	4,972	4.4	2.5
Jewelry and Cosmetics	1	3.5	1,928	1.7	.7
Liquor	1	3.5	3,226	2.9	1.5
Drugs[3]	–	–	–	–	8.5
Other Retail	5	17.1	6,352	5.6	4.4
Personal Services	5	17.1	10,130	8.9	6.5
Recreation/Community	–	–	–	–	3.5
Financial	1	3.5	2,350	2.2	4.2
Offices (other than financial)	1	3.5	1,554	1.4	4.0
Total	29	100.0	113,345	100.0	100.0

Notes:
[1] Includes building construction and site improvement costs.
[2] *Dollars & Cents of Shopping Centers: 1984* (Washington, D.C.: ULI–the Urban Land Institute, 1984), p. 272.
[3] Separate department at Pathmark.

Developer:

Frank Castagna
Frank Castagna & Son
2110 Northern Boulevard
Manhasset, New York 11030

Architecture/Planning:

Stephen Sanders and Associates
1447 Northern Boulevard
Manhasset, New York 11030

Landscape Architecture:

William Schmitt, P.E., R.L.A.
199 East Main Street
Smithtown, New York

Management:

Wheatley Plaza Associates
2110 Northern Boulevard
Manhasset, New York 11030

UNIVERSITY MALL (Neighborhood Center)
Fairfax County, Virginia

7-7   The lower-level shops have convenient parking.

University Mall is a two-level neighborhood shopping center with a gross leasable area of 116,061 square feet and space for approximately 38 tenants. The mall opened in May 1977, by early 1978 was about 80 percent leased, and presently is 100 percent leased. Future plans call for the construction of two freestanding bank buildings and office condominiums.

The planning and execution of University Mall were carried out with considerable sensitivity to environmental, aesthetic, and community concerns. For example, several elements of the project—including the dedication of an open space buffer between the project and its residential surroundings, and the solicitation of certain types of tenants—evolved from suggestions made by nearby residents. Entrances to the parking area were placed to conform with road plans of the state university across the highway. Fairfax County's strict requirements for development projects account for some of the environmental sensitivity shown in the project. But the developer's own preferences and his reading of the market's demand for better quality helped create a design that exceeds the mandated standards of environmental and aesthetic quality.

The shopping center is built in four sections. The major tenant—a 38,050-square-foot chain food and drugstore—anchors the western end of the mall. An upper level centers around an open interior mall, from which all stores (including the supermarket) are entered; and an enclosed minimall—containing stores, offices, and a restaurant with bar—anchors the eastern end of this upper level. The lower level has stores laid out in a single strip, easily accessible by automobile. A service station stands some distance away on the north/central portion of the site.

The property is part of a land grant made in 1729 by Lord Fairfax to an ancestor of its current owner. Since that time, the parcel has changed hands only through inheritance, and today it is being developed as a joint venture of the landowner and a general partner. The land is leased to the general partner for 75 years, after which it and the buildings on it will revert to the owner. The general partner is responsible for developing and managing the retail mall and the office buildings.

The Site

University Mall is located at the intersection of two important highways of Fairfax County—Ox Road (Route 123) and Braddock Road (Route 620). The site lies just south of the city of Fairfax, about 20 miles from downtown Washington. Besides George Mason University, a rapidly growing commuter university immediately to the north, the vicinity consists primarily of single-family-home subdivisions, many of recent vintage. Rapid residential growth characterizes the area. When the project was conceived, both Braddock and Ox Roads were two-lane highways, but at the county's request, the developer added two lanes and a median strip to Braddock Road, comprising 2,100 feet along the site, which was then dedicated to Fairfax County. The county is widening Ox Road to four lanes. The triangular, 28-acre site is highest at its northern apex, dropping 40 feet from that point to the southern base of the triangle. Before development the site was heavily wooded.

Design and Architecture

The upper level is designed so that customers must go into the mall to enter any of the stores. The 220-foot open interior mall contains trees in brick planters, brick benches, and trash receptacles. Overhanging mansard roofs along the stores protect customers from rain and snow. The stores along this mall have the smallest amount of GLA and generally handle merchandise in the categories of clothing, gifts, hobbies, books, and specialty foods. A three-cinema theater is on the lower level, which is accessible by car. Two staircases lead from it to the upper level. Service doors for the stores are located at the buildings' peripheries behind brick screens, in keeping with the overall architectural character.

The four-part complex consists of brick and block structures combined with structural concrete and steel. The design follows a colonial architectural theme; most stores, for example, have small-paned windows with redwood frames.

Tenants lease unfinished spaces, then finish them under comprehensive controls relating to color, design, lighting, fixtures, and signs. Signs that identify stores are brown with white lettering chosen from a limited number of styles. Signs on the building facades are 30 inches high and 15 to 25 feet long; those under the canopy of the interior mall are one foot high and four feet long. All finishing that the tenants do also requires the landlord's approval.

Considerable care went into the 6.5 acres of landscaping and open space. A 3.5-acre tract, ranging in width from 50 to 75 feet, stretches across the southern end and will be kept in its natural state (through dedication) for 25 years. A chain link fence was erected at the parking lot edge of this natural buffer instead of at the property line. The dedicated open space could then be freely used by University Mall's neighbors to the south without diminishing its usefulness as a buffer for nearby homeowners or as a visual

7-8   Stairs to the open mall on the upper level.

amenity for the complex in general. Another 4,200-square-foot area has been reserved as permanent open space in the southeast corner of the site, near the future office complex. The third and final element consists of 2.9 acres of landscaped borders and parking lot islands. Grassed berms screen the project from the north on Route 123; only the tops of the lighting standards tell that the site has been developed.

Water Management

The developer took a number of steps to prevent erosion and siltation during construction. The site was first cleared at the highest, northernmost point and then in stages down the slope. Exposed soil was covered with loose straw and was seeded as soon as the area was no longer needed for construction traffic. No soil was left exposed longer than 10 days. Older trees were left standing when possible, and grading was generally avoided. The buildings were configured in an open V to take advantage of the natural contours of the site.

The developer instigated certain erosion control measures at the construction site, which are among those spelled out in county regulations. County law

also stipulates that the peak discharge on a site may not exceed the predevelopment flow of the 10-year storm. To accommodate the increased runoff caused by extensive paving, University Mall's parking areas are contoured and designed (with barrier islands) to funnel water into two pipes leading to a retention pond at the center of the southern boundary. These inflow pipes can accept water at the rate of 50 cubic feet per second. A 24-inch pipe that permits a flow of 32 cubic feet per second regulates outflow from the pond (which has a 12-foot bank on the downstream side) into the county's sewer system. The collection and retention system handles water from all paved areas except a small portion in the southwest corner, from which the water is channeled directly into storm sewer pipes across Ox Road. The overall system was engineered to handle the 100-year storm and was built at a cost of $100,000.

Market and Tenants

University Mall's trade area population is young and affluent. George Mason University, the neighbor to the north, has an enrollment of 14,500 students, mostly commuters. The project is located in one of the 10 highest-income counties (based on median family income) in the country.

Although University Mall is classified as a neighborhood shopping center, it is larger than most neighborhood centers, which typically range from 30,000 to 100,000 square feet of GLA, and offers a greater scale and variety of merchandise than do most neighborhood centers. It also has a multicinema theater complex, which is common in regional and community centers but unusual in a neighborhood center. While the wide range of tenant types is intended to increase the strength of University Mall's drawing power, the project is nevertheless classified as a neighborhood center because it has a supermarket as its anchor tenant and provides primarily for the daily shopping needs of the local area.

Merchants' Association and Zoning

The merchants' association is responsible for advertising, promotion, and public relations. The landlord guides and assists the association's board but does not determine its operation. The association establishes dues—based on the size of each tenant's space—which are supplemented by a contribution from the landlord.

Seventy percent of the site is zoned as a commercial design shopping center, which permits the retail, of-

7-9   Customers must enter the upper-level stores from the mall.

7-10   The stormwater retention pond.

fice, and service station uses already in place. Eighteen percent is zoned for commercial office low-rise use, which prohibits retail uses and limits the building height to 40 feet. The remaining 12 percent has been dedicated for 25 years as undisturbed open space.

Experience Gained

- Consultation with neighbors and local citizens' associations pays off. Residents of the surrounding subdivisions were at first opposed to any development and might have delayed the project or even caused the county to deny the developer's proposal. The developer met with citizens' associations, however, asked for their suggestions, described his plans, and explained that holding the land idle caused a tax burden and that some type of development was virtually inevitable. Opposition faded, and neighbors of the project generally came to regard the developer as a responsible member of the community.

- In an attempt to beat a county environmental study program to be required in the future, which

might have added $15,000 to $20,000 to the project's cost, the developer began construction before design and contracting decisions could be carefully worked out. But the problems and delays caused by the premature start cost more than the money saved.

- The developer should review all contracts—the architect's, the general contractor's, and all subcontractors'—before starting the project. He should investigate the qualifications of subcontractors and should have a voice in selecting subcontractors. All contracts should be completed before construction begins, and penalties should be set for delays in construction. Nonperformers should be replaced.

- Modifying design in the field does not work. Potential problems must be carefully considered and solutions prepared in the planning stage.

- Several merchants lost interest in leasing space because of delays in construction. Had they been assured of a well-planned timetable with definite dates of completion, this probably could have been avoided.

7-11   Existing trees were left standing where possible.

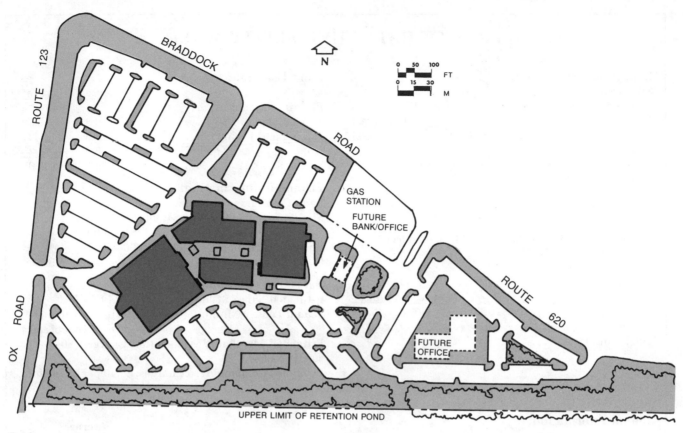

UPPER LIMIT OF RETENTION POND

7-12

PROJECT DATA—UNIVERSITY MALL

Land Use Information:
Site Area:
Shopping Center .... 21.5 acres (8.7 hectares)
Future Office .... 6.5 acres (2.6 hectares)
Total Project .... 28.0 acres (11.3 hectares)

Gross Building Area (GBA in Square Feet):[1]
Shopping Center[2] 116,061
Future Office 60,000
Total Project[3] 176,061

Open Mall and Public Area:[4] 17,235 square feet
Floor Area Ratio (FAR):[5] 14.4

Parking:

	Spaces	Index[6]
Shopping	860	7.2
Office	250	4.2
Total Project	1,110[7]	6.1

Land Use Plan:

	Acres	Percent
Building Coverage[8]	4.1	14.8
Service Station Area	0.8	2.8
Parking and Paving	16.6	59.2
Landscaping and Open Space	6.5	23.2
Total	28.0	100.0

Economic Information:
Land Cost:[9] none
Site Improvement Cost:[10] $1,880,125
Retention/Drainage System Cost: $100,000
Road Construction Cost:[11] $175,000
Construction Cost:[12] $25.46 per square foot of GBA

Sales and Operation:
Estimated Sales: $178 per square foot of GLA
Tenant Leases: Minimum—$8 to $10 per square foot
Overage—2 percent to 8 percent of sales
Estimated Merchants' Association Charges: $0.25 per square foot of GLA
Estimated Common Area Charges: $0.40 per square foot of GLA

Tenant Information:

Classification[13]	Number of Stores	Square Feet of GLA	Percent of GLA	Average Percent of GLA in Neighborhood Centers[13]
General Merchandise	–	–	–	5.6
Food	2[14]	38,050	32.8	30.8
Food Service	2	9,970	8.6	8.8
Clothing	3	4,420	3.8	5.0
Shoes	2	5,370	4.6	1.3
Home Furnishings	3	8,660	7.5	2.6
Home Appliances/Music	2	2,620	2.3	2.4
Building Materials/Garden	–	–	–	3.4
Automotive Supplies/Service Station	1[15]	(2,500)[15]	–	1.7
Hobby/Special Interest	3	3,370	2.9	2.7
Gifts/Specialty	1	2,650	2.3	2.5
Jewelry and Cosmetics	–	–	–	.7
Liquor	–	–	–	1.5
Drugs	–[14]	–	–	8.5
Other Retail	1	1,310	1.1	4.4
Personal Services	4	5,987	5.2	6.5
Recreation/Community	4	16,760	14.4	3.5
Financial	1	1,240	1.1	4.2
Offices (other than financial)	9	15,654	13.4	4.0
Total	38	116,061	100.0	100.0

Notes:

[1] In this project, shopping center GBA is equal to gross leasable area (GLA).

[2] Shopping center GLA plus freestanding bank/office GBA.

[3] Does not include service station building.

[4] Public area consists of mall court, minimall corridor, and walkways along lower-level stores.

[5] FAR = GBA divided by total site area.

[6] Parking index: number of spaces per 1,000 square feet of GLA.

[7] Parking area construction has been completed for both present and future elements of project.

[8] Includes open court in shopping center.

[9] Land owned by developer's family since 1729. Leased for 75 years to general partner, who is developer and manager of project.

[10] Includes clearing, grading, utilities, and parking area construction.

[11] For 2,100 feet of Route 620, dedicated to county after construction.

[12] For four building sections of retail center.

[13] *Dollars & Cents of Shopping Centers: 1984* (Washington, D.C.: ULI—the Urban Land Institute, 1984), p. 272.

[14] The major tenant is a combined food and drug store, listed here under the food classification.

[15] Freestanding service station.

Developer:

Collegetown Associates
1403 North Courthouse Road
Arlington, Virginia 22201

Architecture/Planning:

Dewberry and Davis
8411 Arlington Boulevard
Fairfax, Virginia 22030

Management:

Rucker Enterprises, Inc.
1403 North Courthouse Road
Arlington, Virginia 22201

VERMONT-SLAUSON SHOPPING CENTER (Community Center)
Los Angeles, California

7-14, 7-15   Security was a primary concern in the design of the center. A six-foot-high, wrought-iron fence surrounds the center and access is limited to two entrances and exits.

Vermont-Slauson Shopping Center is a 148,284-square-foot (GLA) community center that was developed as a joint venture between the public and the private sectors. The project occupies a 9.7-acre site in north central Los Angeles, a high-density, inner-city area characterized by low incomes and high crime. With the help of exceptional security measures, the center has operated very successfully since its opening in the fall of 1981. Sales averaged $253 per square foot in 1983, the center's second full year of operation. Three major tenants anchor the development—a discount department store (Zodys), a drug chain (Sav-On), and a supermarket (Boys). Public funding for the $8.2 million project totaled approximately $5 million, including a $1.5 million Economic Development Administration Grant (EDA), a $2.5 million Urban Development Action Grant (UDAG), and $1 million from the city of Los Angeles. Private investment amounted to approximately $2.2 million. In addition, Sears, Roebuck and Co. donated a portion of the site, which was valued at $1.2 million.

The Site

The site lies at the intersection of Vermont and Slauson Avenues, two major arterials with high traffic volumes. These streets are lined primarily with storefront retail and service businesses. The predominantly single-family detached homes in the area are old but maintained with pride. However, the community has a high rate of unemployment and is known for its gangs and high crime rate, all of which presented special problems in designing the project and in attracting tenants to the center.

The site was relatively flat and had no unusual physical characteristics before it was acquired for development. Several buildings, including an old Sears department store, had to be demolished. In addition, a street that bisected the parcel had to be vacated and a portion of the site required rezoning.

Background and Development Agreements

Since the 1920s, the Sears store had served as the anchor for retail activities in the community. However, in 1977, following a number of unprofitable years, Sears abandoned this location.

Local merchants were concerned about the negative impact that the Sears closing would have on retailing in the area and approached the city of Los Angeles regarding possible solutions. Sears indicated a willingness to donate the property to a nonprofit group, and, in 1979, the city established the Vermont-Slauson Economic Development Corporation (VSEDC), to which Sears donated the property and building.

The city commissioned economic and architectural studies on the development potential of the site. These studies focused on the reuse of the Sears building. In 1978, city officials approached a private developer, Alexander Haagen Development, who determined that the Sears building, though structurally sound, was obsolete as a retail facility. Haagen Development recommended that the structure be demolished, together with several other buildings, and an entirely new retail center be created on the site.

A limited partnership was then formed between Haagen Development (as general partner) and VSEDC (as limited partner) for the purpose of developing a new community shopping center. The VSEDC received the federal and city grants and also holds title to the property; Haagen Development holds a 90-year ground lease. City block grant funds were used to acquire the property needed in addition to that donated by Sears. Haagen Development negotiated the various deals to complete the land assembly and the use of eminent domain was not required. Sixty percent of the center's profits (following the return on investment of private sector money) goes to the VSEDC; 40 percent of the center's profits goes to the private developer, who operates the center. The money allocated to the VSEDC will be used for further development of the local community.

Design and Security

The primary concern in the planning and design of the project was to provide adequate security. The site is surrounded by a six-foot-high wrought-iron fence and can be entered at only two gates (one on Vermont Avenue and one on Slauson Avenue). The gates are locked at 11 p.m. and reopened at 5 a.m. Each entrance/exit has a gatehouse for security personnel. The wrought-iron fence was selected instead of a concrete wall to allow passers-by to see the project from the street, to eliminate the possibility of the wall's being covered with graffiti, to avoid areas where litter could collect, and to minimize potential hiding places for criminals. Within the center, a uniformed, armed security force is on duty 24 hours a day, seven days a week. Supplementing this 17-man force is a two-man patrol provided eight hours a day by the Los Angeles police department. Buildings were designed so that tenants could easily install alarm systems. Annual security costs for the center run approximately $2.07 per square foot.

7-16   The center is anchored by three major tenants—Boys (a supermarket), Zodys (a discount department store), and Sav-On (part of a drugstore chain).

The center consists of four adjoining buildings, each with approximately 160,000 square feet (GBA) and two small freestanding buildings of 4,200 and 1,500 square feet (GBA). The one-story buildings have an "early California" design theme and blend mission-tile canopy roofs, light-colored textured plaster, heavy wood trim, and split-face concrete masonry. Creeping vines were planted along the buildings' exteriors to minimize problems with graffiti. Additional landscaping includes landscaped areas of approximately three to 20 feet wide, which run along the perimeter of the site adjacent to the wrought-iron fence and landscaped islands within the parking area. Masonry walls and plantings screen trash receptacles, and the site is cleaned and swept daily.

Market and Leasing

The center serves an area of about 10 square miles containing a population of approximately 160,000. Several other community shopping centers in the trade area are old and unattractive with little or no security. No discount department stores are located near the site. The developer structured rents to attract the three major tenants and to make it possible for the local merchants already located on the site to remain.

Experience Gained

- The extra security measures taken for the project have been crucial to its success. However, while heavy security strongly attracted tenants, it incurred unusually high common area expenses, which had to be offset by rents below the market rate. Even so, the project's public funds assured its economic viability.

- For a public/private partnership to operate smoothly and efficiently, the elected public officials must clearly document at the outset of the project what they want to accomplish and make certain that all public agency staff members are aware of and adhere to these objectives. This will expedite the government review and approval process, so that the private developer can avoid major delays and cost overruns.

- Before making a commitment to a joint venture with the public sector, the private developer should confirm that the public sector will obtain approvals for rezoning, street vacations (voiding previously dedicated streets), or other similar actions that may be required. The developer will then not have to participate in the time-consuming and costly process of obtaining such approvals.

- The community should be represented on the board of directors of a local economic development corporation that is to participate as a limited partner with a private developer. However, all members of the board must be familiar with the role of a limited partner and understand what is equitable in a limited partner relationship.
- So that local merchants already on the site could remain in business while the project was under development, it was necessary to demolish the existing buildings in three phases. This increased the cost of the project.
- Decisions regarding what appeared to be comparatively simple items—such as the type of fence to be provided around the perimeter of the site—required lengthy procedures. For example, the private developer believed that a wrought-iron fence would be best for security reasons. The city, on the other hand, believing that such a fence would present a negative image of the center and the community, recommended instead a low concrete block wall. After considerable debate, the private developer convinced the city that a wrought-iron fence was needed for security and that rather than detracting from the center's image, it would give the center an air of exclusivity similar to that of a gated residential community.
- In a high-crime area, fencing a retail center and providing a security force around the clock are highly preferable to installing grill gates on windows and doors. Grill gates present a negative image and make it impossible for tenants to display their merchandise in a manner that has style and quality.
- A project of this type requires that the private developer know and be involved in the local area; therefore, a local developer can best undertake it.
- From the perspective of the private developer, working in partnership with the public sector

7-17, 7-18 Buildings have an "early California" design theme and blend mission-tile canopy roofs, light-colored textured plaster, heavy wood trim, and split-face concrete masonry.

may present a number of drawbacks, including delays in funding, extensive contractual and sign-off requirements, frequent progress reporting, and complex bidding procedures.

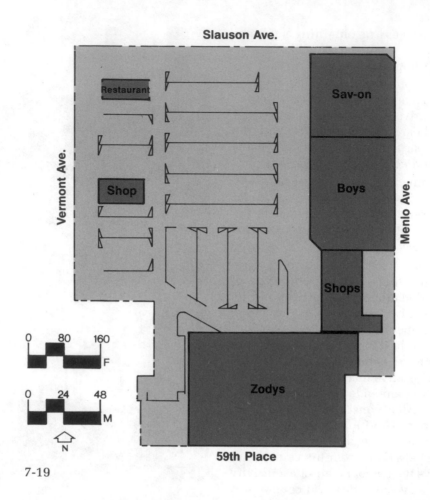

Slauson Ave.

Restaurant

Sav-on

Vermont Ave.

Shop

Boys

Menlo Ave.

Shops

0   80   160
F

0   24   48
M

N

Zodys

59th Place

7-19

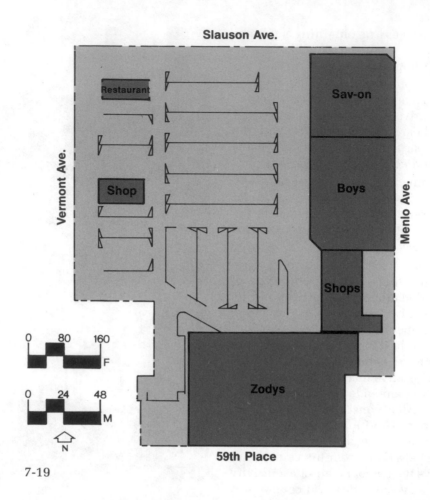

7-20 PROJECT DATA—VERMONT-SLAUSON SHOPPING CENTER

Land Use Information:
Site Area: 9.66 acres (3.91 hectares)
Gross Building Area (GBA): 165,768 square feet
Gross Leasable Area (GLA): 148,284 square feet
Floor Area Ratio (FAR):[1] .39
Parking Spaces: 699
Parking Index: 4 spaces per 1,000 square feet

Land Use Plan:

	Acres	Percent
Buildings	3.39	35.0
Parking, Landscaping, Circulation	6.27	65.0
Total	9.66	100.0

Economic Information:
Site Acquisition Cost: $1,932,000[2]
On-Site Improvement Cost:

Fine Grading and Paving	$320,463
Electrical	86,253
Plumbing	73,844
Landscaping	70,776
Fencing	78,276
Gate Houses	14,073
Total	$643,685

Off-Site Improvement Cost: $156,795
Construction Cost: $4,252,000[3]
Soft Costs:

Architectural and Engineering Fees	$220,000
Construction Supervision and Inspection	25,000
Fees and Permits	15,000
Interim Financing	113,500
Interim Loan Fee	20,000
Legal, Title, and Other Professional Fees	10,000
Contingency	10,000
Other	75,485
Total	$488,985

Total Project Cost:
Private Developer $2,220,000
Economic Administration Grant 1,520,000
Urban Development Action Grant 2,520,000
City of Los Angeles 1,000,000
Sears[4] 1,200,000
Total $8,460,000

Rents: $5 to $12 per square foot[5]
Sales: $253 per square foot (1983)

Annual Operating Expenses:[6]
Total $477,000
Per Square Foot[7] $2.94

Tenant Information:

Classification[8]	Number of Stores	Square Feet of GLA	Percent of GLA	Average Percent of GLA in Community Centers[8]
General Merchandise[9]	1	66,096	44.6	38.5
Food	1	33,600	22.7	14.1
Food Service	1	4,000	2.7	5.2
Clothing	5	10,685	7.2	7.4
Shoes	1	1,680	1.1	2.2
Home Furnishings	–	–	–	2.5
Home Appliances/Music	1	2,226	1.5	2.4
Building Materials/Garden	–	–	–	2.2
Automotive Supplies/Service Station	–	–	–	1.1
Hobby/Special Interest	–	–	–	2.1
Gifts/Specialty	1	920	.6	2.1
Jewelry and Cosmetics	–	–	–	.9
Liquor	–	–	–	.6
Drugs	1	25,487	17.2	5.2
Other Retail	4	3,590	2.4	3.1
Personal Services	–	–	–	2.9
Recreation/Community	–	–	–	3.2
Financial	–	–	–	2.5
Offices (other than financial)	–	–	–	1.8
Total	16	148,284	100.0	100.0

Notes:
[1] FAR = GBA divided by total site area.
[2] Includes property donated by Sears to the city, which had a value of $1.2 million.
[3] Hard costs only.
[4] Donation of Sears property to the city.
[5] Net rents. Common area expenses are not included.

[6] Operating expenses for 1983.
[7] Includes security cost of approximately $2.07 per square foot.
[8] *Dollars & Cents of Shopping Centers: 1984* (Washington, D.C.: ULI–the Urban Land Institute, 1984), p. 272.
[9] Zodys department store.

Developers:

Alexander Haagen Development
3500 Sepulveda Boulevard
Manhattan Beach, California 90266

Mayor's City Economic Development Office
Los Angeles, California 90012

Vermont-Slauson Economic Development Corporation
5918 South Vermont Avenue
Los Angeles, California 90044

Architecture:

Maxwell Starkman & Associates
9420 Wilshire Boulevard
Beverly Hills, California 90212

Planning:

Lester Paley & Associates
Suite 200
12410 Burbank Boulevard
North Hollywood, California

Landscape Architecture:

Molner-Ormenyi & Associates
2014 South Sepulveda Boulevard
Los Angeles, California 90025

TRINITY VALLEY (Community Center)
Carrollton, Texas

7-21 Triangular columns of uneven heights and canopies of different widths were used to break up the visual impact of the center's length.

Trinity Valley contains 264,488 square feet of gross leasable area (GLA) in Carrollton, Texas, a suburb of Dallas. It is a community center being developed in four phases, which currently has completed two phases with approximately 219,349 square feet of GLA. The center was over 65 percent leased at its opening in December 1980 and is now 97.5 percent leased. The final two phases are expected to include 19,639 and 25,500 square feet of leasable space, respectively.

In a linear configuration, the center is approximately 1,500 feet long. Target, a major 100,836-square-foot off-price department store, anchors the south end of the center. Extending north from Target to the second anchor tenant, Kroger, is 41,134 square feet of leasable space with an average depth of 80 feet. Part of a major supermarket chain, Kroger's 43,456-square-foot store anchors the north end of Phase I. Extending north from Kroger is Phase II—34,123 square feet of space with a depth of 80 feet. All stores can be easily reached by automobile.

In order to assure the development of a quality center, the planning and construction of Trinity Valley were well coordinated with careful attention given to the best use of the land, the aesthetics of the center, and the concerns of the community. The developer worked with surrounding residents and the city to obtain suitable zoning for the project and to provide an acceptable buffer between the project and its residential surroundings. Several elements of the project, such as site preparation and layout of the center, required coordination between Dayton-Hudson's development team (the developer of the Target department store) and the Henry S. Miller Company (the developer for the remainder of the center). Together, the two teams provided a layout that would work for all of the tenants while making maximum use of the land and providing an attractive end product.

The commercial/retail division of the Henry S. Miller Company has handled the land brokerage, development, and management of the project. The company acquired the property in two pieces. The first was the southernmost 20 acres, which the company bought in 1973, eight acres off the south end of which it sold to Target in 1978. In 1979, the company purchased an additional eight acres contiguous to the north end of the original tract.

The Site

Trinity Valley stands at the northeast corner of two important thoroughfares in north Carrollton. Josey Lane is a six-lane north/south highway on which approximately 30,000 cars travel each day, while Trinity Mills Road is an east/west street carrying approxi-

mately 21,500 cars a day. The developer has dedicated a 300-foot right-of-way between the south side of the property and the north side of Trinity Mills road for the construction of Highway 190, a major freeway through the north Dallas area. The site lies approximately 25 miles north of downtown Dallas. Smaller shopping center development is located at the southeast and southwest corners of the Josey Lane/Trinity Mills Road intersection. A bank building is located at the northwest corner surrounded by undeveloped land that is zoned for commercial use. The surrounding area consists mostly of single-family-home subdivisions with strong residential growth some four miles to the north. The site covers approximately 28 acres; from its highest point at the northern end, the terrain gradually slopes to the southern end.

Site Engineering

The development of Trinity Valley required extensive site work before construction could begin. Since Target owned its site separately, both parties had to agree upon the site work they wanted. Both development teams then hired a mutually acceptable civil engineer who certified site work costs and routinely inspected the project to maintain quality control. This arrangement worked well for both parties. The back side of the property had to be heavily excavated, and because of the grading, measures were taken to prevent erosion.

Problems with the site have stemmed from its soil, which basically consists of highly changeable clays that expand when wet and contract when dry. Underneath the parking surface, the top soil was mixed with lime to form a "water barrier" to prevent soaking of the soils underneath. Beneath the slabs of the shopping center, a select fill technique was used: the bad soil was excavated from the slab site and an acceptable (nonexpanding) soil was substituted. Unfortunately, the soil still continued to expand and contract somewhat, causing some slabs to buckle. In Phase II lime was pressure-injected seven feet down into the soil to help prevent this problem. They also used French drains to keep rains away from expansive soil near building slabs.

Planning and Architecture

The positioning of the Target department store and the length and slope of the site were major considerations in the planning and design of the center. With Target's store facing Josey Lane, it was decided to set the center at the back of the property. The gradual slope of the property also posed a problem: the slab breaks and canopy drops had to be placed at uneven

7-22 A supermarket and an off-price department store anchor the center.

intervals. The architect used triangular columns of uneven heights placed at the slab breaks and canopies of varying widths to detract from the unevenness and to break up the monotonous length of the center. At the same time, to give the center uniformity, the architect had the fascia constructed of material matching Target's building exterior.

The 1,500 feet of sidewalk is heavily bordered with trees, shrubs, and flowers. (The parking lot is also landscaped.) Wooden benches and trash receptacles are placed along the sidewalk for the customers' convenience. The roof extends over the sidewalk to protect pedestrians from rain and snow, and all stores have front entrances opening to the sidewalk. Service doors for the stores are located behind the building.

Construction basically comprises concrete slab floors, tilt-up walls, tar and gravel built-up roof, and an asphalt parking lot. All store fronts are glass. Tenants lease unfinished spaces, which they finish with the landlord's approval. The landlord also controls signage, which must be in the form of illuminated box signs. At Trinity Valley, signs are multicolored to give the center added flair.

In a good-will effort directed at neighboring residential property owners, the developers donated trees for each owner's backyard, the purpose being to build a natural screen between the residential and commercial areas. If homeowners already had a protective screen of trees, the developers donated the trees to the public park system.

Zoning

The first 20 acres of the Trinity Valley development were zoned for retail use; however, the eight acres acquired at the north end were zoned for residential use and therefore had to be rezoned. The proposal for the entire project was submitted with provisions for the tree donations and dedication of the Highway 190 right-of-way discussed earlier. Upon approval of the plan, building began immediately.

Market, Tenants, and Marketing

Trinity Valley's trade area population is large, young, and relatively affluent. Approximately 11,000 people live within a one-mile radius; 106,000 live within a five-mile radius. The average age is 29, and the average income is about $44,000.

Tenants have been selected to offer a variety of convenience and shopper goods. Kroger, Target, and the personal service stores fulfill the basic needs of

7-23 The sidewalk space is landscaped and has wooden benches and trash receptacles.

7-24   All tenants must have illuminated box signs. Multicolored signs give the center added flair.

the community, while the large variety of other tenants offers the opportunity for specialty shopping. Phases I and II currently provide space for 38 tenants.

The center has been marketed through the use of a number of techniques since its opening. Free hot dogs, popcorn, and soft drinks attracted community interest at the center's grand opening. After the opening, most of the marketing was left up to the tenants. Although no formal merchants' association exists, the developer has been successful in marketing the center through a cooperative advertising program with the tenants. The Henry Miller Company contributes 20 percent of the cost for any advertising program in which at least one-third of the tenants participate. The tenants now run full-page advertisements monthly in the *Dallas Times Herald*.

Experience Gained

- A column-type architectural design used with varying canopy widths was highly effective in breaking up the length of the center and in drawing attention away from the canopy drops.
- Building on highly expansive soil causes problems and increases the cost of the site work, a factor that should be considered before developing.
- It is important that the developer/owner show a continued interest in the project. Trinity Valley's cooperative advertising program, whereby the developer contributes 20 percent, has been highly successful.

- Coordination of the site work package between Target and the developer was simplified by the use of a mutually agreed upon third party acting as engineer.
- In a project this large, the benefits of using concrete tilt-up wall construction rather than concrete block construction are significant. The technique is less expensive and less time-consuming.
- In a phased development, it is important for the developer to maintain financial flexibility when securing funding for the project as a whole and for each development phase. Although only one lender was used on this project, alternative sources were available.
- The use of perimeter French drain systems to route subsurface water around pad sites with highly expansive soils has worked well.
- Past experience of the developer has shown and the project at Trinity Valley has again proven that the commitment of an anchor tenant gives a tremendous boost in starting a large project; it helps secure financing and draws small tenants into the center. The developer recommends against beginning any larger development without such a commitment.
- Including neighborhood residents in plans for land use and applications for rezoning will minimize opposition. In the development of Trinity Valley, the donation of trees to form a natural screen between the project and neighboring sites was effective in helping the developer obtain project approval.

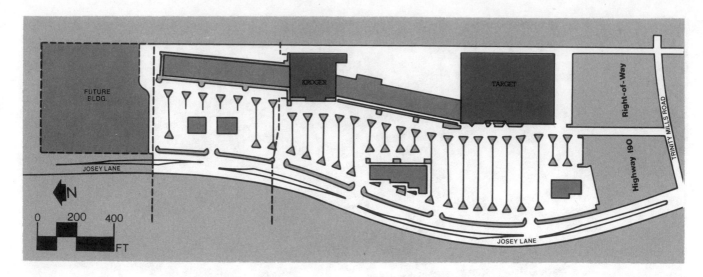

7-25

7-26 PROJECT DATA—TRINITY VALLEY

Land Use Information:
Site Area: 27.86 acres (11.28 hectares)
Gross Building Area (GBA):[1] 264,488 square feet
Gross Leasable Area (GLA):[2] 118,513 square feet
Parking Spaces: 1,446
Parking Index: 5.5 spaces per 1,000 square feet of GBA

Land Use Plan:

	Acres	Percent
Building Coverage	6.9	24.7
Streets and Parking	19.0	68.1
Open Space/Landscaping	2.0	7.2
	27.9	100.0

Economic Information:
Site Acquisition Cost:[3] $2,851,456
On-Site Improvement Cost:

Excavation and Grading[4]	$ 794,064
Sewer/Water[5]	529,376
Paving[6]	1,323,440
Curbs/Sidewalk[7]	264,488
Landscaping[8]	529,376
Total	$3,440,744

Construction Cost:[9] $3,196,760

Operating Expenses:[10]

Taxes	$ 86,000
Insurance	7,500
Maintenance	102,000
Management	35,000
Total	$230,500

Lease Information:

Sales: $179.24 per square foot
Rents: $9 to $14.76 per square foot[11]
Percentage Rents: 4 to 7 percent of gross sales
Term: 3 to 10 years with options for 2 to 5 years

Tenant Information:

Classification[12]	Number of Stores	Percent of Total Tenants	Square Feet of GLA	Percent of GLA	Average Percent of GLA in Community Centers[12]
General Merchandise	1	2.63	100,836	45.93	38.5
Food	1	2.63	43,456	19.79	14.1
Food Service	5	13.16	10,500	4.78	5.2
Clothing	2	5.26	4,196	1.91	7.4
Shoes	3	7.89	8,080	3.68	2.2
Home Furnishings	4	10.53	11,860	5.40	2.5
Home Appliances/Music	1	2.63	3,200	1.46	2.4
Building Materials/Garden	–	–	–	–	2.2
Automotive Supplies/Service Station	–	–	–	–	1.1
Hobby/Special Interest	1	2.63	340	.25	2.1
Gifts/Specialty	–	–	–	–	2.1
Jewelry and Cosmetics	1	2.63	1,200	.55	.9
Liquor	–	–	–	–	.6
Drugs	–	–	–	–	5.2
Other Retail	5	13.16	8,893	4.05	3.1
Personal Services	4	10.53	5,440	2.48	2.9
Recreation/Community	2	5.26	7,600	3.46	3.2
Financial	–	–	–	–	2.5
Offices (other than financial)	5	13.16	8,180	3.73	1.8
Other	3	7.89	5,568	2.54	—
Total	38	100.00	219,349	100.00	100.0

Notes:

[1] Gross building area for all four phases.
[2] Gross leasable area for Phases I and II, excluding Target.
[3] Land cost was approximately $2.35 per square foot.
[4] Excavation and grading costs are figured at $3.00 per square foot of gross building area.
[5] Sewer/water costs are figured at $2.00 per square foot of gross building area.
[6] Paving is figured at $5.00 per square foot of gross building area.
[7] Curbs/sidewalks are figured at $1.00 per square foot of gross building area.

[8] Landscaping is figured at $2.00 per square foot of gross building area.
[9] Construction cost for Phases I and II, excluding Target. Equals $27 per square foot of gross building area.
[10] Operating expenses for 118,513 square feet of GLA in Phases I and II, excluding Target.
[11] Minimum rents. Do not include tax and insurance payments by tenants. All leases are net.
[12] *Dollars & Cents of Shopping Centers: 1984* (Washington, D.C.: ULI—the Urban Land Institute, 1984), p. 272.

Developer:

Herbert D. Weitzman
Henry S. Miller Company
Commercial/Retail Division
2001 Bryan Tower
30th Floor
Dallas, Texas 75231

Architecture:

Aguirre, Hastings, Rojas
1349 Empire Central
Suite 300
Dallas, Texas 75247

Landscape Architecture:

Linda Tycher
11333 N. Central Expressway
Suite 101
Dallas, Texas 75243

Management:

Henry S. Miller Management
2001 Bryan Tower
29th Floor
Dallas, Texas 75231

THE GRAND AVENUE (Regional Center)
Milwaukee, Wisconsin

7-27   The Plankinton Arcade was built in 1916 and features terrazzo floors, white-glazed terra cotta columns and walls, an ornamental plaza, ornamental grillwork, a skylight, chandeliers, and a glass-domed rotunda with a pool and fountain.

Setting a significant development trend in recent years has been the dramatic increase in downtown retail development. This may be attributed to a number of factors, including:

- growth in CBD office employment;
- the public's growing appreciation of urban life-styles and festival and specialty retailing;
- a more aggressive public sector, armed with sophisticated tools for encouraging private investment and participating in private real estate development;
- a dramatic reduction in "easy" opportunities for retail projects in suburban markets, causing the retail investor to look elsewhere, including downtown;
- scores of successful pioneering projects in downtowns, large and small; and
- a resurgence of demand from relatively affluent households for housing in and near downtowns.

A 1983 ULI study identified over 100 downtown retail projects, including traditional shopping centers located in downtown, festival/specialty centers, retail components of larger mixed-use projects, and retail restructuring (that is, creating a fundamentally different retail environment by combining new and refurbished older elements).[1]

The Grand Avenue represents one example of a highly successful retail project in a downtown setting. This multilevel regional center spans four blocks in the heart of downtown Milwaukee and combines new construction with old. Skywalks and two shopping arcades (one new and one old) connect six historic office and retail structures, forming a continuous and enclosed pedestrian concourse. Two previously existing major department stores—a 350,000-square-foot Gimbels and a 250,000-square-foot Boston Store—anchor opposite ends of the center, while smaller shops and an F.W. Woolworth store line the skylit arcades. All six historic buildings (Gimbels, Boston Store, the Plankinton Building, the First Bank headquarters, the Majestic Building, and the F.W. Woolworth Building) date from the turn of the century. All but the First Bank headquarters building are eligible for the National Register of Historic Places.

Two large central areas, one in each arcade, provide plantings, fountains, natural light, and seating. Approximately 125 shops occupy the 245,000 square feet of retail space in the two arcades between the major department stores. An 18-restaurant food court, known as the Speisegarten, occupies 27,000 square feet of space on the third level of the new arcade and offers a variety of ethnic and fast foods as well as a central seating area. The project provides 2,400 parking spaces, including 1,050 spaces located in two existing department store garages and 1,350 spaces in two newly constructed public garages that have direct access to both arcades.

The project resulted from a collaboration of the Milwaukee Redevelopment Corporation (MRC), a private limited-profit redevelopment corporation, the city of Milwaukee, and The Rouse Company. The total cost of the project was approximately $70 million, excluding the costs incurred in the renovation of the two department stores and the First Bank and Majestic Buildings. Private and public sector costs each totaled some $35 million. Ground was broken in December 1980 and the complex opened in August 1982.

The Site

The project occupies four blocks in the center of downtown Milwaukee. It fronts on west Wisconsin Avenue, Milwaukee's main street, between the Milwaukee River on the east and Fourth Street on the west. The site is part of the city's downtown revitalization area and is within easy walking distance of the Hyatt Regency Hotel, the convention center complex, the Marc Plaza Hotel, the Performing Arts Center, city hall, and the new Federal Office Building. These developments and The Grand Avenue are being linked by skywalks. Access to Milwaukee's freeway system is one block south of The Grand Avenue.

Downtown Milwaukee comprises about 700 acres bounded by Lake Michigan on the east and a nearly completed loop of freeways on the remaining three sides. Over 450 stores, 6 million square feet of office space, and 25,000 parking spaces are contained in this 160-block area. The city of Milwaukee has 650,000 inhabitants, and the metropolitan area has approximately 1.4 million.

The Grand Avenue site is essentially flat with significant subsurface hazards, including poor soil conditions.

Development Strategy and Financing

As early as 1957, Milwaukee's public and private sectors recognized that the downtown was deteriorating and in need of rejuvenation. Milwaukee's business and civic community has long been active in planning and development; thus, in 1973, when the Milwaukee Redevelopment Corporation (MRC) was con-

---

[1] See Urban Land Institute, *Downtown Retail Development* (Washington, D.C.: ULI–the Urban Land Institute, 1983).

7-28 The new arcade is highlighted by a food court and a centrally located grand court.

ceived as a mechanism to spur growth downtown, 35 private companies were willing to purchase approximately $2.5 million in stock to establish it. An additional $500,000 was contributed to an existing non-profit, business-supported organization to provide funds for downtown study and research. The MRC is a limited-profit corporation that can acquire land, work with consultants and city officials, and, like any other private developer, become directly involved in downtown project implementation. MRC took the lead in developing The Grand Avenue, from conceptualization and planning in the mid-1970s to final negotiations and contracts with the city, The Rouse Company, and federal officials. The MRC developed the project and was responsible for all design contracts and construction of the retail shell, the completed public arcade, and the F.W. Woolworth store.

Public/private cooperation was instrumental in arranging a financing package suitable to all parties. A tax increment financing district was created to fund public improvements, including the construction of all public concourses and skyways, 1,350 new parking spaces, and some underground utility improvements. Proceeds from the tax increment financing district are being used to repay $23 million in general

obligation bonds. A $12.6 million Urban Development Action Grant (UDAG) covered the shortfall in public funding. The UDAG funds paid for site acquisition, demolition, business relocation, additional underground utility improvements, and some public street improvements. MRC stockholders provided over $16 million in cash to pay for the construction of the building shell and for the land and buildings that MRC owns. The Rouse Company raised $18 million to finance all tenant improvements, interior leasehold improvements, and soft costs associated with leasing and operations.

In exchange for the large public investment, the city and MRC receive lease revenue, a portion of the project's net cash flow, and increased property tax revenues from the project. MRC leases the 245,000-square-foot retail space to Rouse–Milwaukee, Inc., and the city leases the parking garages and the public arcade to Rouse–Milwaukee Garage Maintenance, Inc. MRC has agreed to pay the city a portion of its net cash flow. Tax revenues from the project are expected to average $1 million annually. Increased property tax values from buildings surrounding The Grand Avenue that are in the designated tax increment district will be used to repay the city's $23 million bond issue and to make further public improvements in downtown. Three additional skywalks have been built in downtown to link The Grand Avenue with adjoining blocks, financed in part by the city.

Planning and Architecture

The plan for The Grand Avenue represents an unusual, physically interdependent combination of new and existing buildings. It has concentrated on the preservation and renovation of existing buildings with a modest amount of new construction. Demolition of existing structures was kept to a minimum. The project's most dramatic design feature is the continuous enclosed pedestrian concourse that stretches 1,100 feet from Gimbels to Boston Store and includes a series of retail skywalks, the new arcade, and the historic Plankinton arcade. Two vehicular skybridges link the two public parking garages. As the city's main retail street, Wisconsin Avenue was used as an exterior focus for the project and the location of the project's primary entrances. In addition to the main entrance at Third Street, the complex has over a dozen entries from adjoining streets. The two parking structures were built along the south edge of the site where obsolete buildings had been demolished.

Set in the historic Plankinton Building, the Plankinton Arcade was built in 1916 of reinforced concrete and pan-formed concrete decks. Its architectural style is 15th century Italian Gothic. It features terrazzo floors, white-glazed terra cotta columns and walls, an ornamental plaza and grillwork, a skylight, chandeliers, and a glass-domed rotunda with a pool and fountain. Restoring the arcade to its original appearance required considerable renovation. This included the removal of a second-level floor, the reglazing of the skylight with insulated glass, and the replacement and/or cleaning of the terrazzo floors, the terra cotta columns and walls, the decorative plaster, the grillwork, the chandeliers, and the brass handrails.

Framed in structural steel with lightweight reinforced concrete slab, the new arcade is highlighted by the third-level food court and a centrally located grand court containing a pool with cascading water, plants, trees, and seating. Skylights extend its full length from east to west. In both this arcade and the Plankinton Arcade, decorative lighting accents the exposed overhead steel skylight framing. A glass-enclosed elevator in the grand court and sets of escalators provide access from the street level to the second and third floors. Handrails in the new arcade are polished brass.

The project's entrances include decorative lighting and directories. A circular stairway creates a focus at

7-29   Skylights extend the full length of the new arcade. Skylights in both arcades are accented with decorative lighting.

the west end of the new arcade near Boston Store's entrance; an existing decorative stairway at the east end of the Plankinton Arcade has been restored. Second-level skywalks connect the new arcade to the Plankinton Arcade and the Plankinton Arcade to Gimbels. One skywalk features retailers operating from pushcarts and the other contains a restaurant.

Engineering

A central water plant with three electric centrifugal chillers supplies water chilled to 45 degrees to an individual air handler for each tenant, and to seven air handlers serving the mall areas. Systems serving tenant areas maintain a temperature of 76 degrees and a relative humidity of 50 percent in summer. Auxiliary electric heaters serving tenant areas maintain a temperature of 68 degrees in winter. The public areas maintain a temperature of 78 degrees in summer and 65 degrees in winter and a humidity of 50 percent in the summer. Hot water coils in the arcade air-handling units and perimeter baseboard along the outside walls receive their heat from the local electric utility's district steam system. All air handlers have full outside air capabilities and economizer controls to minimize energy use for cooling in mild weather. They also have setback thermostats to minimize energy use at night.

Market and Tenants

Initial market research indicated that The Grand Avenue had the strong potential to attract suburban shoppers if the proper theme and tenant mix were established. The project's primary trade area is within five miles of the center, while the secondary trade area is within a 30-minute drive of the site. By linking the two major department stores downtown, the developers capitalized on the existing retail patterns of Milwaukee's traditional shopping street.

Tenants were carefully chosen to create a "festival" atmosphere, while also offering a variety of general merchandise, home furnishings, apparel, and specialty goods that appeal to a largely suburban shopping crowd. At the project's opening, the tenant mix was 48 percent local merchants, 12 percent regional merchants, and 40 percent national merchants.

Experience Gained

- The development team concept formed the basis for the successful design, construction, and operation of The Grand Avenue. The resourceful public and private funding formula—including an Urban Development Action Grant, tax increment financing, local private corporation stockholder equity, and leasehold improvements by The Rouse Company—provided the essential financial components of the project.

- The involvement of Milwaukee's public and private sectors in a joint task force, cochaired by the city's mayor and one of its most prominent businessmen, resulted in the development of a plan that was acceptable to both the public and private sectors. Having the backing of the city's private and public sector leadership was instrumental in the project's implementation.

- Integrating the project with the existing community by retaining multiple entrances to the department stores, to the Plankinton Building, and to the new construction and rehabilitated buildings along the way resulted in a project that reaches out to the main shopping street, while using the

7-30   Second-level skywalks connect the new arcade to the Plankinton Arcade and the Plankinton Arcade to Gimbels.

7-31 The 18-tenant food court occupies 27,000 square feet on the third level of the new arcade.

internal public mall (concourse) as a contemporary shopping environment.

- A project of this complexity must have comprehensive management to operate smoothly. For this reason, The Rouse Company was given overall management responsibility for both the public and the private spaces (including the public parking garages).

- The project was completed on schedule and close to the original budget, in part because the development team was on site during construction and made frequent day-to-day decisions. Undertaking a project of this nature requires considerable flexibility and the ability to anticipate problems.

- Important to the project's design is that it provides direct access from the parking garages into the mall. In addition, parking rates are structured to discourage long-term parking, thus assuring adequate parking for customers. Shoppers receive three hours of free parking with any purchase and free parking after 5:00 p.m. and on weekends.

- Virtually every technique of land assembly was used. Acquisition of existing buildings, the relocation of occupants, and the city's demolition of structures were coupled with the MRC's purchase of the F.W. Woolworth Building, the Plankinton Building, and the First Bank property. Several Plankinton Building retail tenants remained in business throughout the construction period.

- The construction of the new arcade and the skybridges adjoining existing buildings presented a significant engineering problem. Old foundation walls tended to shift when pile driving and excavation occurred nearby; some of the adjoining foundation walls had to be repaired or rebuilt during construction.

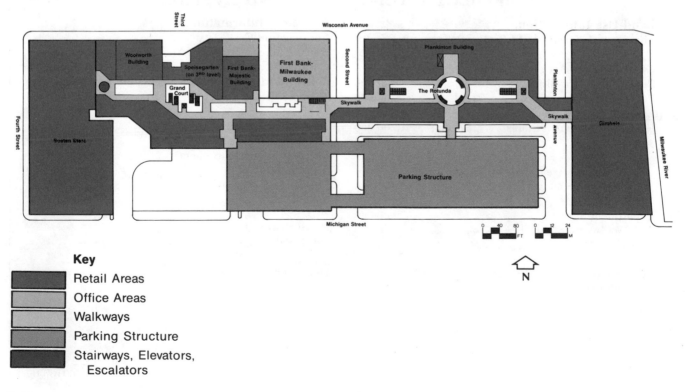

Key

- Retail Areas
- Office Areas
- Walkways
- Parking Structure
- Stairways, Elevators, Escalators

7-32

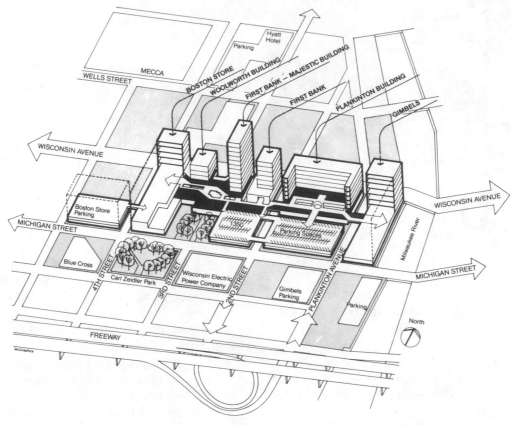

7-33

7-34

PROJECT DATA—THE GRAND AVENUE

Land Use Information:
Site Area: 7.75 acres (3.14 hectares)

Gross Building Area (GBA in Square Feet):

Retail Space (arcades)	300,000
Public Concourse	100,000
Existing Office Space	500,000
Existing Department Stores	1,200,000
Total	2,100,000

Gross Leasable Area (GLA in Square Feet):

Retail Space (arcades)	245,000
Office Space	400,000
Department Stores	600,000
F.W. Woolworth Store	50,000
Total	1,295,000

Floor Area Ratio (FAR):[1] 6.2
Parking Spaces: 2,400[2]

Economic Information:
Construction Cost:

New Parking Garages and Vehicular Bridges	$ 7,000,000
Retail Arcades and Public Concourse[3]	23,000,000
Total	$30,000,000

Total Project Cost:

City of Milwaukee[4]	$35,600,000
Milwaukee Redevelopment Corporation	16,000,000
The Rouse Company	18,000,000
Total	$69,600,000

Retail Rents: $5 to $45 per square foot[5]
Retail Sales: $209 per square foot

Operating Expenses:

Taxes	$ 483,000
Insurance	30,000
Services/Maintenance/Janitorial	1,500,000
Utilities	550,000
Legal	30,000
Management	425,000
Total	$3,018,000

Tenant Information:

Classification[6]	Number of Stores	Percent of Total Tenants	Square Feet of GLA	Percent of GLA	Average Percent of GLA in Regional Centers[6]
General Merchandise	–	–	–	–	14.1
Food	–	–	–	–	8.8
Food Service	34	23	39,300	16	7.0
Clothing	28	19	80,800	33	24.9
Shoes	15	10	31,800	13	6.8
Home Furnishings	6	4	9,800	4	1.8
Home Appliances/Music	–	–	–	–	2.9
Building Materials/Garden	–	–	–	–	1.6
Automotive Supplies/Service Station	–	–	–	–	1.0
Hobby/Special Interest	–	–	–	–	3.8
Gifts/Specialty[7]	27	18	34,300	14	5.2
Jewelry and Cosmetics	–	–	–	–	2.8
Liquor	–	–	–	–	.4
Drugs	4	2	9,800	4	3.7
Other Retail	22	14	27,000	11	4.1
Personal Services	12	8	12,200	5	2.3
Recreation/Community	–	–	–	–	3.8
Financial	–	–	–	–	3.0
Offices (other than financial)	–	–	–	–	2.1
Other	–	–	–	–	–
Total	148	100	245,000	100	100.0

Notes:

[1] FAR equals GBA divided by total site area.

[2] Includes 1,350 spaces in two new garages, 750 existing spaces in the Boston Store garage, and 300 existing spaces in the Gimbels garage.

[3] Construction cost for 245,000 square feet (GLA) of retail arcades and for the 100,000-square-foot public concourse.

[4] Includes a $12.6 million Urban Development Action Grant. The remainder was provided by general obligation bonds.

[5] Rents for retail space range from $5 per square foot for larger spaces with limited mall frontage to $45 per square foot for smaller spaces with high visibility and for higher volume food court tenants.

[6] *Dollars & Cents of Shopping Centers: 1984* (Washington, D.C.: ULI–the Urban Land Institute, 1984), p. 271.

[7] Includes gifts/specialty and jewelry and cosmetics.

Developers:

Milwaukee Redevelopment Corporation
Milwaukee, Wisconsin 53203

City of Milwaukee
Department of City Development
Milwaukee, Wisconsin 53233

Rouse–Milwaukee, Inc.,
  a subsidiary of The Rouse Company
Columbia, Maryland 21044

Architecture:

Elbasani, Logan & Severin Design Group
Berkeley, California

Graphics:

Sussman/Prejza
Santa Monica, California

COQUITLAM CENTRE (Super Regional Center)
Vancouver, British Columbia

7-35 The center court. The mall design features steeply pitched roofs, skylights with stained glass accents, hemlock siding, and landscaping.

The Coquitlam Centre—a super regional shopping center having 925,000 square feet of gross building area (GBA)—is the focus of a planned regional town center in the burgeoning suburbs east of Vancouver. Placed on a compact 53.4-acre site, the two-level project was made possible through the cooperation of a private developer working with local municipal authorities to create and implement the town center concept. Special consideration for local rainy weather, energy efficiency, and art combine to produce a highly attractive and functional design.

Opened in 1979, the Coquitlam Centre is anchored by three national department stores, Eaton's, The Bay, and Woodwards, the largest retailer based in western Canada. Each of these stores occupies an average of 135,000 square feet of gross leasable area (GLA). Woodwards also has a 46,602-square-foot supermarket, part of a food complex serving as a fourth anchor for the project. One hundred forty-nine shops and food facilities occupy the 265,712 square feet of leasable space along the four arms of the mall. The center has 4,400 parking spaces and is serviced by numerous bus lines. A commuter train park-and-ride terminal is being built across one of the bordering streets.

Project History

In the early 1970s, suburban growth was obviously heading farther east of Vancouver, up the Frazer River Valley. The Greater Vancouver Regional District, a senior umbrella planning organization established a long-term goal of containing undesired sprawl by creating seven satellite towns around the urban core, each with its own commercial, residential, and industrial functions.

The Coquitlam district was identified as one of the surrounding regions with no urban focus, inadequate shopping, and rapid growth. The president of the Praxis Group had seen the potential for a major regional center and was assembling land under ownership and option. However, firm plans for locating the regional town center were slow in coming.

In 1976, as others were still waiting to see what would happen, the district of Coquitlam teamed up with Praxis to take the lead in establishing a 1,000-acre, multiuse town center. With two department stores committed during the early planning stages, the Vancouver-based Daon Corporation approached the Praxis Group. A 50/50 joint venture was subsequently established to build the Coquitlam Centre.

In conceiving the mall as part of the town center, the developers negotiated a land use contract with the municipal government, which combined the zoning bylaws and a development agreement recorded on the title. Included were municipal requirements that the developers help build a water system to provide excess capacity for the area and widen and upgrade the major arteries that border the project on three sides. The street improvements were valuable for enhancing access and visibility. The developers also agreed to incorporate a 4,000-square-foot public auditorium into the center.

The developers began preparations in 1977 by clearing the land and preloading the site with up to 12 feet of sandfill to help compress the loose subsoils. Construction commenced in the fall of 1977, and two years later the project opened in one phase on schedule and within budget.

The Site

With a natural slope of 17 feet, the site required minimal cut and fill to accommodate the two-level mall, affording each mall level direct access to on-grade parking. The square shape of the site lent itself well to a centrally placed building with parking divided into quadrants of roughly equal parking capacity. Future mall expansion would require building a parking structure. However, in order to protect a nearby salmon spawning creek, a stormwater retention system capable of handling a 10-year peak was required. Because of heavy rainfalls in the area, a retention system built on the parking lot surface might have caused flooding in the parking lot; therefore, an underground basin was constructed to handle parking lot runoff. Water flow from the 10 acres of roof is controlled for gradual release.

Landscaped walkways cross the parking lots. The Coquitlam Centre has a total of five acres of plantings, comprising 900 trees and 12,000 shrubs.

Planning and Design

The developers began designing Coquitlam by studying similar contemporary centers in the western United States. Having built and leased shopping malls across Canada, they believed the key planning goals to be shopper convenience, overall attractiveness, and operational efficiency.

Important to convenience was keeping walking distances to a minimum and simplifying navigation. The mall is shaped like a cruciform, with the two-level department stores at three of the ends and food services anchoring the fourth leg. Considerable care was taken to ensure equal vertical and horizontal pedestrian flow. The maximum distance between department stores is 544 feet. The concept of two levels, with

7-36 Stained glass is used in the center court and in front of each department store.

an open second level connected by bridges and the lower-level storefronts extending farther into the mall area, gives shoppers maximum views of mall stores on both levels. The second-level mall stores are 56 feet apart; the stores in the lower court are only 32 feet apart. Escalators and walkways have tempered glass side enclosures to minimize obstruction of view in the courts.

The developers were especially interested in creating a spacious, attractive environment to offset the weather typical of this coastal area of British Columbia—overcast days and 75 inches of rainfall a year. The mall design and choice of material represented a conscious effort to compensate for gray days. The center was designed with 72-foot-high steeply pitched roofs, extensive skylights, integral plantings, and 8,000 square feet of stained glass accents. The overall mall area occupies 115,000 square feet and includes a 100-foot-square center court and smaller courts in front of each department store.

Warm earth tone materials were chosen as the finish, consistent with the "West Coast" environment. Hemlock siding is used extensively inside, giving ever-changing effects when struck by shadows from the stained glass windows. The mall floor combines light colored travertine marble and darker brick pavers. Trees and other interior plantings complement the mall design. Scattered throughout are sculptures by 26 different artists. Three different artists created different treatments of the stained glass components in the central court and in front of each department store.

The building's exterior has a uniform veneer of brown earth tone brick, although the anchor stores were allowed a limited choice of trims. Each department store has exposure on the main highway to passing traffic. Reflective glass panels and decorative light fixtures emphasize the four mall entrance canopies. Loading ramps for each of the mall's four quadrants are screened from view. Each quadrant has a

7-37　Glass canopies identify mall entrances.

service corridor that includes freight elevators and trash compactors.

Energy System

The Coquitlam Centre achieved economies in its operations by setting goals to hold down energy consumption, spread peak demands, and justify any increased capital costs with savings in operational costs. The heart of the system at Coquitlam is a computer-controlled heat storage and exchange system, made up of a series of storage tanks containing 350,000 gallons of water processed through a chiller and cooling tower. The computer also controls the lighting and mechanical systems.

Heating requirements are met primarily by lighting in the stores and by heat scavenged from the chiller system, which, due to the mild west coast climate, operates year round. There is an auxiliary electrically heated boiler for extremely cold weather. Abundant hydroelectric resources, standard in British Columbia, provide the primary source of power.

The cooling system is operated at night, when most of the other heat-producing functions in the building are shut down. The cooling capacity, spread over a period of time, allows chillers to be about 40 percent smaller than otherwise necessary, and by operating without interruption for long periods at full load, the system maximizes efficiency and minimizes the cost of and need for maintenance. The cooler night air also enables the cooling tower to operate more effectively.

Mall lighting is maintained at deliberately low levels of 25 to 30 footcandles per square foot in order to contrast with tenant lighting and create an inviting appearance for the stores. When natural light levels are strong enough, certain lights can be shut off by means of multiple staged circuits. All skylights are double glazed, and the need to insulate was carefully analyzed. The HVAC system can be converted to solar energy should future conditions warrant it. To make

7-38 Brown earth tone brick was used for the exterior.

7-39 Sculptures are scattered throughout the mall.

certain that all tenants do their share to conserve energy, the lease agreement establishes a design standard for energy consumption at six watts per square foot. Cost penalties kick in if this load is exceeded.

Market

The Coquitlam Centre trade area encompasses suburban, semirural, and rural residential neighborhoods with a conservative population projection of 180,000 by the year 1986 (165,000 in 1984). The trade area is one of the two remaining areas in the Vancouver area physically capable of accepting major housing development and population growth. Growth in all other sectors of the region is hindered by physical impediments such as unsuitable terrain, lack of servicing capacity, and the legal barrier of the Provincial Agricultural Land Reserve.

The nearest major competitive retail facility is over seven miles to the southwest, and none presently exists to the east of the site. While Coquitlam is well positioned to benefit from expected trade area growth and is serving as a catalyst to development in the new town center, the project was not built to depend on future markets for its economic viability.

Tenants and Management

A balanced and attractive tenant mix was carefully established at Coquitlam. The project was 82 percent leased at opening and was fully occupied soon after. Only four stores changed in the first two years of operation.

Food operations are concentrated in a 54,000-square-foot food court, which contains 10 fast food outlets and a 450-seat plaza featuring handsome and durable travertine marble tables and oak benches. An 11,000-square-foot restaurant is adjacent; the department stores also serve food.

Architectural controls specify storefront and sign design criteria, emphasizing the continuity of finishing materials, light intrusion, and overall quality. No specific controls are placed on the design of store interiors, but design consultants and the developers' staffs are in close touch.

The Coquitlam Centre is promoted by means of a marketing fund, which is administered by the center marketing director. All tenants contribute on the same basis as they would to a merchants' association. As per the lease agreement, the mall tenants contribute 4 percent of minimum and percentage rents to the fund. The department stores contribute flat sums each year, and the landlord contributes 25 percent of the total.

In addition to the $25 minimum rent per square foot, mall tenants contribute $7.50 per square foot for the maintenance of common areas. Coquitlam Centre has an in-house staff handling all functions except security and landscaping, which are subcontracted.

The Coquitlam Centre incorporated the use of a privately operated day-care center for shoppers, which has proven remarkably successful. A bank was difficult to attract; mall banks typically earn little in relation to the high service costs incurred due to shoppers changing money. Profitable mall kiosks are scheduled as the center's activity grows.

Experience Gained

- The floor plan is very important to a shopping mall's success. Easy access and orientation to facilities, with a balance between levels and anchors, translates into more shopper traffic.

- The capital expense in energy conservation can be more than offset by savings in operations, though the initial cost must somehow be recouped from the tenants.

- An attractive and interesting environment, while difficult to quantify in terms of a return, is often well worth the added investment. Not only do the extra touches help give personality to a center that will draw people from afar, but also the use of quality materials, for instance, can in the long run save money because they are more durable.

- A small private developer can respond quickly and innovatively to unique market opportunities. Moreover, ownership and operations under one compact organization can sustain the personal attention to details that make a project more distinctive.

7-40   The center was designed to make navigation simple and keep walking distances to a minimum.

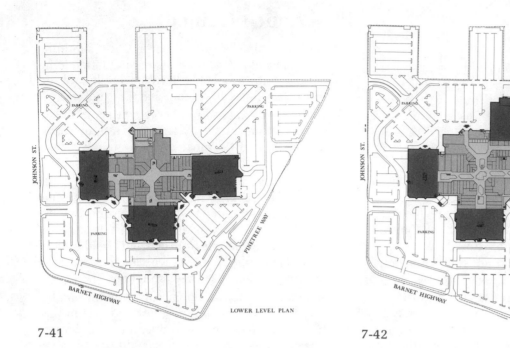

7-41

7-42

THE COQUITLAM CENTRE

LOWER LEVEL PLAN

UPPER LEVEL PLAN

7-43 PROJECT DATA—COQUITLAM CENTRE

Land Use Information:
Site Area: 53.4 acres (21.6 hectares)
Gross Building Area (GBA): 925,000 square feet

Gross Leasable Area (GLA in Square Feet):

Mall Space	265,712
Woodward's	151,455
Eaton's	134,241
The Bay	120,527
Woodward's Bargain Store	8,883
Supermarket	46,602
Total	727,420

Floor Area Ratio (FAR):[1] .40
Parking Spaces: 4,400
Parking Index: 5.5 per 1,000 square feet of GLA

Land Use Plan:

	Acres	Percent
Buildings	11.5	21.5
Parking and Paving	36.9	69.0
Landscaping	5.0	9.5
Total	53.4	100.0

Economic Information (Canadian Dollars):
Total Project Cost: $60 million (1979)
Sales: $210 per square foot
Minimum Rents from Mall Tenants: $25 per square foot
Percentage Rents: 1.5 to 10 percent of gross sales
Terms: Rental escalation, average 5 years
Dues for Center Promotion: 4 percent of rent, majors pay flat annual sum
Common Area Charges: $7.50 per square foot of GLA[2]

Operating Expenses:

Taxes	$1,249,800
Insurance	41,000
Maintenance[3]	640,000
Janitorial	168,000
Utilities	252,000
Management	220,000
Miscellaneous	148,000
Total	$2,718,800

Tenant Information:

Classification[4]	Number of Stores	Percent of Total Tenants	Square Feet of GLA	Percent of GLA	Average Percent of GLA in Super Regional Centers[4]
General Merchandise	2	1.3	26,459	10.0	7.3
Food	11	7.2	9,848	3.7	4.3
Food Service	11	7.2	3,010	1.1	9.0
Clothing	30	19.7	75,601	28.4	30.8
Shoes	11	7.2	22,416	8.4	9.3
Home Furnishings	2	1.3	2,485	.9	2.3
Home Appliances/Music	20	13.2	23,277	8.8	3.8
Building Materials/Garden	–	–	–	–	.4
Automotive Supplies/Service Station	–	–	–	–	.5
Hobby/Special Interest	5	3.3	5,256	2.0	4.9
Gifts/Specialty	24	15.8	31,307	11.8	6.6
Jewelry and Cosmetics	10	6.6	13,144	5.0	3.5
Liquor	–	–	–	–	.2
Drugs	1	.7	8,797	3.3	2.7
Other Retail	1	.7	11,075	4.2	3.9
Personal Services	11	7.2	7,936	3.0	2.1
Recreation/Community	–	–	–	–	4.2
Financial	2	1.3	6,832	2.6	2.2
Offices (other than financial)	3	2.0	6,162	2.3	2.1
Other	5	3.3	12,107	4.5	–
Total	149	100.0	265,712	100.0	100.0

Notes:
[1] FAR = GBA divided by total site area.
[2] Includes property taxes and insurance.
[3] Includes wages.
[4] *Dollars & Cents of Shopping Centers: 1984* (Washington, D.C.:
ULI–the Urban Land Institute, 1984), p. 271.

Owner/Manager:

Morguard Investments Limited
6 Crescent Road
Toronto, Ontario, Canada M4W 3K9

Developers:

Praxis Group Ltd.
300-545 Clyde Avenue
West Vancouver, B.C., Canada V7T 1C5

Daon Development Corporation
999 West Hastings Street
Vancouver, B.C., Canada V6C 2W7

Architecture:

B. James Wensley & Associates Architects Ltd.
14727-87 Avenue
Edmonton, Alberta, Canada T5R 4E5

Landscape Architecture:

Don Vaughan & Associates Ltd.
1152 Mainland Street, Suite 210
Vancouver, B.C., Canada V6B 2T9

PRESTONWOOD TOWN CENTER
(Super Regional Center)
Dallas, Texas

7-44, 7-45   Five department stores anchor the center.

Occupying 92 acres in Dallas, Prestonwood Town Center is an enclosed super regional mall offering 1,133,848 square feet of gross leasable area. The project contains five major department stores, a 25,000-square-foot ice rink, over 155 shops and restaurants, an 18-tenant food court, and parking for 6,424 automobiles. The center creates a gardenlike atmosphere, and is architecturally acclaimed for its use of natural daylight, for its extensive landscaping both inside and outside, and for its design that is broken up into "neighborhood" areas with works of art in major courts, a play yard for children, and other attractions. The two-level project also features four sit-down restaurants (in addition to the food court), a movie complex with five theaters, and two banks.

History

As a major regional mall of this type, Prestonwood has an unusual history. Originally, Ernest Hahn, the developer, was approached by Pollard Simmons, a major landowner and developer in the Dallas community to develop jointly a mall at a north Dallas location. Simmons had selected the site, which was near a residential area and zoned residential. Through an 8- to 10-month process of municipal review of the application, citizen opposition ran high. In the meantime, Hahn persuaded Simmons that land he owned one and one-fourth miles west of the original site and adjacent to the Dallas Toll Road (Parkway) would make a more desirable location for a regional center. Simmons agreed to change the site, and, thus, the planning process began again. J.C. Penney and Neiman-Marcus, both of whom had already made a commitment to the center, agreed to the change of location.

The new location, along the Dallas Parkway and Arapaho and Beltline roads, also required rezoning. Although public participation was required at both the planning commission and city council level, there was little opposition, and the rezoning was approved after one and one-half years of processing time. In order to obtain city agreement to the rezoning, Hahn agreed to provide major off-site improvements, primarily relating to traffic circulation. He added two lanes to the parkway, built a bridge on Arapaho and extended it to the center, widened Beltline Road, and built an additional street on the center's fourth side.

During the planning process, Montgomery Ward and Joske's also made a commitment to the new center, and Lord & Taylor was invited but preferred to go to Valley View, a center nearby and within the same general trade area. A lawsuit developed because that location conflicted with the terms of a radius clause

for a Lord & Taylor at a nearby location. The radius clause was contested for two years without success, and finally Lord & Taylor decided to move to Prestonwood instead because it was located outside the radius.

Prestonwood Town Center was the first regional center in the far-north section of Dallas. Since its construction, millions of square feet of office, commercial, and residential space have been built in the area surrounding the center, and four more regional centers have been built to the north. Prestonwood is doing well, however, commanding a large share of the market, and it is gaining popularity.

The Site

Prestonwood Town Center is located in the heart of what is referred to as the "North Dallas retail corridor." This corridor contains over 4.5 million square feet of retail GLA within a 2.5-mile radius. When the center was built, the area was almost entirely open, undeveloped fields. As the area became more developed, the center was surrounded. It is now bounded on the north by retail and residential development (including single- and multifamily housing). On the south, the center is bordered by retail, office, and restaurant uses. On the east, a private golf course, retail space, and multiunit housing are located, with the west containing high-rise office, hotel, retail, and restaurant uses. The frontage onto the Dallas Parkway was sold to another developer and made into an office complex located on the perimeter of the site and integrated into the overall Prestonwood development.

Prestonwood has access to three major highways and one secondary road. Located in the most affluent part of the Dallas marketplace and in the newest growth area, the center is complemented by what has been described as the best roadway access of any regional center in Dallas.

The project site was originally on a limestone base with a level surface and little vegetation. The developer landscaped extensively, using screening and creating varied parking levels. This scale of landscaping was unusual for the Dallas marketplace at that time, with costs running close to $1 million. Underground drainage for Prestonwood connects with a natural creek located to the east, which handles the center's drainage needs adequately.

Planning and Design

Prestonwood was designed to be informal, comfortable, and "noninstitutional." Its landscaping and masonry walls with earth tones contrast sharply with the marble, chrome, and glass of other centers nearby. In the interior, sand-colored tile floors are used, with wooden parklike benches, "woodsy" tree landscaping, and natural lighting. Storefront designs are individualized, and make use of woods, mirrors, and glass. In general, the center was designed to keep all components at a human scale.

The center is broken up into courtyard areas, each designed to be the focal point of a distinct little "neighborhood," with unique characteristics to appeal to different types of shoppers. The courtyards are located at the entrances to each major department store, and were designed around $200,000 worth of sculptures that were selected for the center. The large central court contains a 30-foot-high, four-faced antique clock that was moved from the Goodyear Building in Los Angeles to Prestonwood. The clock chimes the melody of the Westminster chimes on the hour, and has become a major attraction. The clock court also includes a carpeted children's play yard, with wooden sculptures used for climbing and seating. Other courtyard attractions include a brass sculpture, a brightly colored kite arrangement, and an acrylic prism sculpture that deflects rainbow-colored light around the Montgomery Ward courtyard.

The center also features a 25,000-square-foot (the size for official competition) ice skating rink that draws skaters for lessons, hockey tournaments, and even international competitions. On the second level, above the rink, is the 18-tenant food court, with tables on two tiers overlooking the rink. The court seating surrounds the rink on three sides, with food merchants lining the seating area. Food court shops provide a variety of American and international foods, and sport a festive air partially created by the use of brightly colored awnings over each of the tenant shops. The skating rink also is covered (above the food court level) with a scalloped orange and red canopy with backlighting.

Prestonwood's interior landscaping is extensive, including 30-foot Ficus trees and other plants in planting wells, and low planters containing bright seasonal flowers. Trees in planters on the lower level extend into the upper level through large openings, providing a natural amenity to both levels.

The lighting at Prestonwood is unique. Lamp posts light the second level, with warm light directed toward the ceiling and reflected onto shoppers indirectly. The stores and the upper level light the lower level. The lighting is designed to make stores the focal point, although bridges and court areas are spotlighted. Extensive skylighting floods the center with natural light. This, combined with the landscaping, contributes to the center's comfortable atmosphere.

7-46   The project is broken up into courtyard areas, each designed to be the focal point of a distinct little "neighborhood."

At Prestonwood, a unique storefront design, called "pop-out" storefronts, was used. Tenants were allowed to design three-dimensional storefronts that extend two and one-half to three feet from the planning wall. These storefronts, "popping out" in varying degrees, allow tenants greater flexibility and creativity in their design and provide the atmosphere of a village street with interesting angles and contrasts among individual stores. Because of the narrow mall (35 feet wide), this design reduces the center's common area maintenance requirements. It also allows passersby to see lower-level shops from the upper level.

Mall entrances were designed to make a strong statement with bright lighting and landscaping, and thus to attract customers. Prestonwood's parking area was graded so that 50 percent of the parking spaces are accessible from the lower level and 50 percent from the upper level. The parking lot was carefully landscaped, with a total of 1,608,000 square feet devoted to exterior plantings, at a cost of $956,000. The open space design appeals to passersby, helping to attract customers.

Market Considerations

Dallas is characterized by a growing population and an increasing amount of disposable income. Its market is one of the nation's fastest growing with 43 percent of the county's population under the age of 35, and an effective buying income exceeding $14 billion. The North Dallas retail corridor has developed rapidly in recent years, with new construction including condominiums, hotels, convention facilities, high-rise office buildings, and other retail facilities. The rate of residential growth in the zip code areas immediately surrounding Prestonwood is the fastest in the area.

Prestonwood's primary trade area has a population of more than 250,000. North Dallas residents are primarily affluent young professionals ranging from 25 to 44 years of age with average yearly incomes of over $30,000 and homes valued at $100,000 or more. The market not only is growing but is also becoming younger and more affluent. In addition, the local market is transient, with over 16 percent living at their present address for less than two years.

Although the market is strong, competition is increasing and, thus, Prestonwood has to work to continue its successful sales record. Research has demonstrated that customers frequent the center more because of its excellent tenant mix than because of

promotional events. For this reason, the center concentrates on 12 major merchandising events each year, and primarily uses printed advertising (as well as some radio advertising).

Handling promotion is a merchants' association, headed by an 11-member board of directors, including the developer. The board meets monthly to provide guidance and input into the marketing strategy of the center. The current promotional and advertising budget is $300,000, with merchants assessed yearly dues of $1.25 per square foot. The association maintains the objective of promoting the center as a whole, rather than highlighting individual merchants.

New hotels in the area have increased the potential to attract tourist and convention traffic. Prestonwood responds to this market through a "tour bag" program for new visitors. New office development has also increased the luncheon and noontime traffic. Prestonwood's primary marketing objectives at this time relate to maintaining a strong position in an increasingly competitive market in "the golden corridor."

Tenants

As noted earlier, Prestonwood is anchored by five department stores (J.C. Penney, Montgomery Ward, Neiman-Marcus, Joske's, and Lord & Taylor), and has

7-47   The 25,000-square-foot ice skating rink.

7-48 The food court is located on the second level and the seating area overlooks the skating rink.

over 155 shops, including four sit-down restaurants, an 18-tenant food court, a movie complex with five theaters, and two banks.

Most small shops sell specialty items such as clothing, cards, shoes, cosmetics, sports supplies, nuts, or toys. The tenant mix emphasizes fashion and soft goods retailing, although the center tries to appeal to a broad spectrum of prospective shoppers. It responds to changes in the market it serves with adjustments in its mix, and annual market surveys indicate that the center is frequented primarily because of its selection of stores.

Only 2.5 percent of Prestonwood's tenants are first-time operators and 45 percent belong to national chains. Typical leases are for five years. Rents average $22 to $25 per square foot but range from $12 to $100 per square foot, depending on the location and size of store. For instance, a store paying $100 per square foot would be small, located on the lower level with mall frontage on three sides, and have high traffic. Tenants pay percentage rents of 3 to 10 percent, with the food court tenants paying 10 percent. In 1983, 47 tenants paid percentage rents.

All Prestonwood shops are irregular in shape, with average dimensions of 30 by 75 feet, or 2,250 square feet. The depth of stores varies considerably, from very shallow (with shops located along department store walls) to as deep as 120 feet. This variety in shop sizes, along with the diversity in pop-out storefront design, adds to the neighborhood character of the center.

Tenants are arranged in areas of major interest, centered around the various courts. The skating rink, for instance, is surrounded by stores that attract children, such as toy and cookie stores, a video arcade, and a pizza parlor. The court at Montgomery Ward is surrounded by moderately priced, family-oriented stores for the value-conscious shopper. The court at Neiman-Marcus contains stores that appeal to a higher-income crowd, such as specialty shops, travel centers, and high fashion clothing stores. This arrangement of shops by type of buyer maximizes the exposure of those stores. Shoppers arriving for a specific purpose are more likely because of this arrangement to be attracted to the merchandise and price range of other stores they encounter in the same area.

Experience Gained

- Rather than experience further delays in trying to obtain an unpopular zoning change, the developer changed the project's site to a more favorable location. This proved sensible, although one year's planning for the original center was sacrificed.

- The developer planned Prestonwood to be "ahead of its time," spending additional funds to achieve more pleasing interior and exterior designs, and to experiment with untried design styles. These innovations have paid off, keeping Prestonwood competitive in a market that now includes the latest in shopping center design.

- Accommodating the city's requests to improve roadways on the center's periphery, the developer also benefited: his project received good access from all sides.

- Selling part of the acreage for office towers has created a new market potential among the daily noontime shoppers.

- The food court initially had tables primarily for parties of four. However, lunch customers typically are single or in parties of two. For this reason, many of the original tables are being replaced with smaller ones.

- Stores placed at either end of the project are difficult to see, attract little traffic, and therefore are hard to lease. Prestonwood is working on a plan to locate restaurants with a sidewalk cafe atmosphere at these locations, where they should attract traffic.

- Because sales of designer-label merchandise have grown, the center has increased the number of high fashion shops.

- Trees planted at the main entrances of the anchor stores have grown so that they block visibility of the stores. Since these trees would lose their shape if pruned, they will be replaced with smaller ones.

- The increase in hotel and convention traffic has given Prestonwood the opportunity to adjust its marketing strategy to a new clientele. This responsiveness to demand has helped the center to maintain its position in a competitive market.

- Management surveys indicate that the average shopper visits the center for 90 minutes, entering a total of three shops during the visit. Prestonwood management has found that its tenant location strategy—whereby shops with similar appeal are grouped together—works well in maximizing the benefits of this shopping pattern.

- Additional surveys indicate that the most heavily trafficked mall entrance is the skating rink court—probably because parents first drop off their children at this court before shopping.

- Attention to special details gives Prestonwood Town Center its charm and popularity. The developer personally selected the sculpture for each court, chose types of plants used, and selected various other accents, from the brick color to the wooden animals in the children's play yard.

7-49 "Pop-out" storefronts were used.

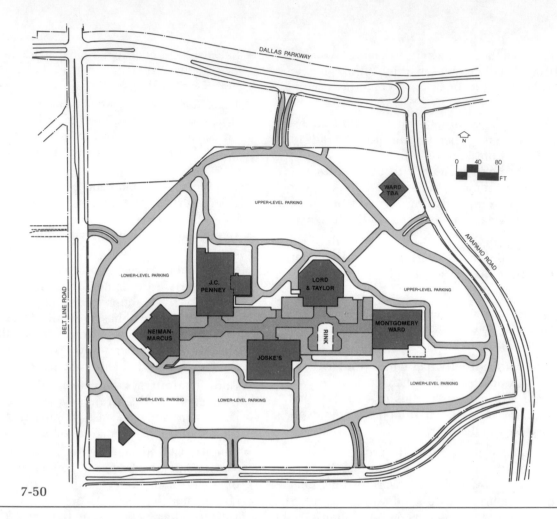

7-50

7-51

PROJECT DATA—PRESTONWOOD TOWN CENTER

Land Use Information:
Site Area: 91.5 acres (37.1 hectares)
Gross Building Area (GBA): 1,357,364 square feet
Gross Leasable Area (GLA): 1,133,848 square feet
Parking Spaces: 6,424
Parking Index: 5.79 spaces per 1,000 square feet of GLA

Land Use Plan:

	Acres	Percent
Building Coverage	31.1	34.0
Circulating Streets and Parking	49.4	54.0
Open Space/Landscaping	11.0	12.0
Total	91.5	100.0

Economic Information:
Site Acquisition Cost: $2,996,044
Off-Site Improvement Cost: $2,340,545
On-Site Improvement Cost: $3,228,822[1]
Exterior Landscaping: $956,682

Construction Cost:[2]

Superstructure	$ 5,205,949
HVAC	1,018,163
Electrical	693,000
Plumbing	306,714
Elevators and Escalators	324,424
Fees	899,498
Finishes	3,545,479
Graphics	150,000
Total	$12,143,227

Construction Cost per Gross Square Foot: $30.80

Operating Expenses:

Taxes	$ 612,888
Insurance	26,676
Services–Gross Rent	761,045
Maintenance	1,385,964
Office	24,716
Utilities	851,127
Legal	20,000
Management	322,015
Miscellaneous	88,539
Total	$4,092,970

Lease Information:
Minimum Rents: $22 to $25 per square foot (average)[3]
Percentage Rents: 3 to 10 percent of gross sales
Term: 5 years

Tenant Information:

Classification[4]	Number of Stores	Percent of Total Tenants	Square Feet of GLA	Percent of GLA	Average Percent of GLA in Super Regional Centers[4]
General Merchandise	14	8.9	43,849	11.1	7.3
Food	6	3.9	7,568	1.9	4.3
Food Service	23	14.8	35,434	9.0	9.0
Clothing	51	32.7	136,183	34.6	30.8
Shoes	18	11.5	35,798	9.1	9.3
Home Furnishings	11	7.0	29,733	7.6	2.3
Home Appliances/Music	6	3.8	19,598	5.0	3.8
Building Materials/Garden	–	–	–	–	.4
Automotive Supplies/Service Station	–	–	–	–	.5
Hobby/Special Interest	–	–	–	–	4.9
Gifts/Specialty	9	5.8	15,279	3.9	6.6
Jewelry and Cosmetics	15	9.7	21,532	5.5	3.5
Liquor	–	–	–	–	.2
Drugs	–	–	–	–	2.7
Other Retail	–	–	–	–	3.9
Personal Services	–	–	–	–	2.1
Recreation/Community	3	1.9	48,455	12.3	4.2
Financial	–	–	–	–	2.2
Offices (other than financial)	–	–	–	–	2.1
Total	156	100.0	393,429[5]	100.0	100.0

Notes:
[1] On-site improvement cost includes landscaping.
[2] Construction cost for enclosed mall not including department stores.
[3] Minimum rents range from $12 to $100 per square foot, depending on size and location of store.
[4] *Dollars & Cents of Shopping Centers: 1984* (Washington, D.C.: ULI–the Urban Land Institute, 1984), p. 271.
[5] Excluding department store space.

Developer:

Ernest W. Hahn, Inc.
3666 Kearny Villa Road
San Diego, California 92123

Management:

Ernest W. Hahn, Inc.
Property Management
Management Office
Space 1149, 5301 Beltline Road
Dallas, Texas 75240

Architecture:

Charles Kober Associates
2706 Wilshire Boulevard
Los Angeles, California 90057

Interior Landscaping:

North Haven Gardens
9152 Forest Lane
Dallas, Texas

Landscape Architecture:

Carter and Burgess, Inc.
P.O. Box 2973
Fort Worth, Texas 76113

DANVILLE LIVERY AND MERCANTILE
(Community/Specialty Center)
Danville, California

7-52, 7-53 Buildings have either an early downtown village or rural ranch design theme.

Danville Livery and Mercantile is a community/specialty center sited on 13.5 acres in Danville, California. The project offers 126,167 square feet of gross leasable area divided among a variety of specialty shops, restaurants, offices, and financial institutions. It features an early "downtown" village and rural ranch architectural design theme that is compatible with the architecture of local historic buildings while providing for the practicalities of contemporary merchandising. The center also uniquely blends the convenience of the typical neighborhood or community center with the recreational shopping environment present in most types of specialty centers. Contrasting with the inward orientation and mall design of many specialty centers whose parking is located in large areas at the perimeter of the site, Danville Livery and Mercantile offers the convenience and high visibility of storefront parking. At the same time, the center's tenant mix, architectural design, casual outdoor sitting and eating areas, attractive landscaping, and rustic character invite recreational shopping. The center's primary trade area is similar in size to that of a community center.

Planning for the Danville Livery and Mercantile began in March 1977, and construction was started in June 1980, following a lengthy review and approval process. The developer was required to make a number of major off-site improvements: widening existing roadways, placing signals at two intersections, constructing a new street, and reconstructing a freeway exit ramp. Leasing began in January 1981 and the center was officially opened in October 1982. By March 1984, 109,025 square feet (GBA) were completed, with four freestanding buildings still to be constructed.

The Site

The project is located in the San Ramon Valley area of Contra Costa County in the city of Danville. Interstate 680, a short distance east of the site, provides direct access north to Walnut Creek and Concord and south to Fremont and San Jose. Highway 24 to the north provides freeway access to Oakland and San Francisco. In driving time, the center is approximately 45 minutes southeast of San Francisco, 35 minutes east of Oakland, and 45 minutes north of San Jose.

Standing at the southern end of downtown Danville, the site is bordered on the east by San Ramon Valley Boulevard (downtown Danville's main street). Commercial and residential land uses surround the project. Immediately to the north is a neighborhood shopping center anchored by a Safeway supermarket; across the street to the east is another neighborhood center anchored by a Lucky Market and Longs Drugstore; bordering the site on the south and west are single-family detached homes ranging in price from $250,000 to $300,000. Bishop Ranch, a 585-acre office and industrial park, is located approximately three miles south of the site.

The site slopes gently from west to east. Existing vegetation included mature redwood, cedar, and walnut trees, many of which were incorporated into the landscaping of the center, including several 50-foot-tall redwoods. Portions of the site contain expansive clay soils. The site offers picturesque views of grass-covered rolling hills to both the east and west, including a view of Mt. Diablo to the east.

Planning and Design

The overall planning and design objective was to combine the convenience typically found in a neighborhood or community center with the attractive and interesting design required for a high-quality specialty center. The site plan offers storefront parking while also providing a parklike setting that invites pedestrians to meander throughout the center and its retail shops. Instead of being located along the perimeter of the site with shops oriented toward an interior mall, parking areas have been dispersed throughout the center, attractively landscaped, and integrated into the center's overall design.

The center's seven freestanding buildings sit at the front of the site along San Ramon Valley Boulevard or along Sycamore Valley Road (which crosses the site in an east/west direction) and, accordingly, have an early downtown village design that complements the design of other structures in downtown Danville. These buildings feature painted, finished wood exteriors with refined detailing. Designed for multiple tenancy, they are occupied by financial institutions and related office uses requiring the visibility and accessibility of a main street location.

In contrast to the freestanding buildings, the specialty retail and office buildings at the interior of the site feature a rural ranch theme characterized by rough-sawn, stained wood exteriors, wood shake roofs, and open exposed trusses, beams, and rafters. They are designed to provide maximum flexibility for leasing purposes, and have 40- to 60-foot depths and full frontages. Office tenants occupy buildings south of Sycamore Valley Road while specialty retail shops and restaurants and a limited number of second-floor office tenants occupy buildings north of the road. All retail space is at ground level. Dark green trim and signage differentiate office buildings from the rust-trimmed retail buildings.

7-54, 7-55 The center offers the convenience of storefront parking. Parking areas are dispersed throughout the center, attractively landscaped, and integrated into the overall design.

Extensive landscaping, outdoor sitting and eating areas, and meandering walkways create a parklike environment. Landscaping includes major existing trees together with complementary new plantings, much of which has been set in raised wood planters. The northern portion of the center has been designed around a stand of mature redwood trees. Also providing a strong visual image for the center is the use of berming, heavy timber retaining walls, wood curbs and stairways, wood and textured concrete walkways, small brick courtyards, low-scale lighting, and coordinated signage. Outdoor sitting areas vary in size from single wood benches to small courtyards and large wood decks and porches. Solid wood fencing and plantings buffer the center from adjacent residential development.

Market Considerations

The center's primary market consists of the relatively affluent San Ramon Valley communities of Alamo, Diablo, Danville, San Ramon, and Blackhawk. This market extends about five miles to the north and five miles to the south and has a population of approximately 57,000 people whose average annual household income is $50,000. During 1983, average home prices in the market area ranged from $150,000 to $343,000. With the ongoing development of Bishop Ranch—which alone will employ 23,000 people—employment within the trade area is expected to increase dramatically during the next 10 years. The project's secondary market consists of affluent shoppers throughout the San Francisco Bay Area, who enjoy traveling to the scenic community of Danville for a day of shopping and relaxation.

The primary marketing objective is to keep local shoppers in the area. Before the center was developed, local residents had to leave the area to find quality merchandise in a quality setting. Most local residents were traveling to downtown Walnut Creek (approximately eight miles to the north) or to two regional centers (the Sun Valley Mall, which is located in Concord, approximately five miles north of Walnut Creek, and the Stoneridge Mall, which is located in Pleasanton, approximately eight miles south of Danville) to do their shopping. By providing easy access and good surroundings and merchandise, the center has been able to keep the local discretionary income in Danville.

A series of events have been used to promote the project. In conjunction with local charities and civic groups, the center has hosted a number of civic events, including the local chili "cook-off," a major

7-56 Many existing trees, including several large redwoods, were saved.

7-57, 7-58, 7-59, 7-60   Extensive landscaping and berming, outdoor seating and eating areas, and meandering walkways create a parklike setting.

Fourth of July picnic, and a local 10-kilometer race that attracted 5,000 participants. The developer has also participated in functions sponsored by the local Chamber of Commerce. While advertising to date has centered around promotions and related newspaper ads, a direct mail campaign to local households is being implemented. The developer paid 100 percent of the cost of the promotion for the grand opening and for the first Christmas. The center is promoted by a merchants' association. An annual promotional budget of $50,000 has been established, with the developer paying one-fourth. In addition to their share of the advertising budget, tenants pay annual association dues of $75.

Tenants

The retail tenant mix has been geared to attract upper-income female shoppers who are seeking quality merchandise. Although the center has no anchor tenant, the food-service tenants function as the primary draw to shoppers. Along with the specialty gift stores, they attract the recreational shopper. Most tenant spaces range in size from 600 to 2,500 square feet. Occupying the largest tenant space (approximately 12,000 square feet) is an antiques collective that attracts both local shoppers and those from outside the primary market area. Tenants have been carefully placed within the center. Spaces in buildings closest to the perimeter of the site have been leased to tenants selling impulse or convenience items (such as candy, cards, ice cream, yogurt, fresh pasta, and flowers); spaces in buildings in the interior of the site have been leased primarily to tenants selling more expensive merchandise (such as antiques, clothing, and expensive gifts). Roughly 50 percent of the tenants are first-time merchants.

Experience Gained

- Attention to detail is essential in carrying out a general design theme and in creating the proper merchandising atmosphere that is vital to the success of a specialty center. The development team spent many hours on specifics such as landscaping, signage, storefront design, colors, materials, traffic flow, pedestrian flow, accent lighting, and other items.
- To make a nonanchored center like Danville Livery and Mercantile work requires a design that offers the convenience of a linear center together with the architectural interest and relaxed atmosphere of a specialty center.
- In three years of meetings with local planning groups ranging from adjacent homeowners to the local Board of Supervisors, the virtues of patience and compromise were often reestablished. Being from out of town, the developer had to have a local contact to monitor Danville's political climate.
- In order to endure the lengthy review and approval process that is often required today, a developer must have an excellent working relationship with his bank and/or joint venture partner.
- Obtaining the proper tenant mix was crucial to the center's success. By controlling the leasing through the use of an in-house leasing team, the developer was able to obtain a tenant mix that works well and is appropriate for a high-quality specialty center.
- The initial success of a nonanchored specialty center will depend on whether a "critical mass" of quality, high-draw tenants will commit themselves to the project at the outset. In this regard, major food-service tenants ideally should be in place when the project opens. Ironically, the center may find it difficult to attract such tenants until it has opened and become established.
- Preferably, a specialty center should be located adjacent to a major freeway interchange to assure maximum visibility and accessibility. However, it can succeed without this prime setting if it is located in an established shopping area. Danville Livery and Mercantile's position next to several established neighborhood centers was an important factor in the center's success.

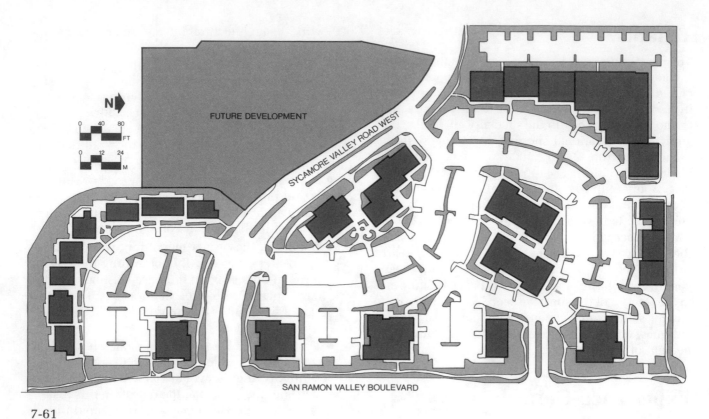

FUTURE DEVELOPMENT

SYCAMORE VALLEY ROAD WEST

SAN RAMON VALLEY BOULEVARD

7-61

7-62   PROJECT DATA—DANVILLE LIVERY AND MERCANTILE

Land Use Information:
Site Area: 13.5 acres (5.5 hectares)[1]
Gross Building Area (GBA): 132,808 square feet[2]
Gross Leasable Area (GLA): 126,167 square feet
Floor Area Ratio (FAR): .23[3]
Parking:
Total Spaces: 651
Index: 4.9 spaces per 1,000 square feet of GLA
Compact Spaces: 70

Land Use Plan:

	Acres	Percent
Building Coverage	2.76	20.0
Streets and Parking	6.05	45.0
Open Space/Landscaping	4.69	35.0
Total	13.50	100.0

Economic Information:
Site Acquisition Cost: $3,961,000
Off-Site Improvement Cost: $923,000
On-Site Improvement Cost: $1,793,000

Soft Costs:

Architectural and Engineering	$1,149,000
Fees and Permits	436,000
Legal, Title, and Other Professional Fees	157,000
Interim Financing and Other Fees	1,360,000
Leasing Commissions	265,000
Other	64,000
Total	$3,431,000

Construction Cost: $8,395,000[4]
Annual Operating Expenses:

Management	$ 91,900
Advertising and Promotion	22,000
Legal, Accounting, and Professional Services	15,000
Repairs and Maintenance	15,000
Insurance[5]	15,100
Taxes[5]	136,300
Common Area Maintenance[5]	140,000
Other	15,000
Total Operating Expenses	$450,300

Lease Information:

Sales: $143 per square foot (not including antiques store)

Rents:[6]

  In-Line Office: $15.60 to $18 per square foot

  In-Line Retail:

    600 to 900 square feet; $15 to $19.20 per square foot

    900 to 2,500 square feet; $13.80 to $15 per square foot

    12,000 square feet; $12 per square foot

  Freestanding Buildings:

    Financial; $24 to $29 per square foot

Term: 2 to 3 years [7]

Tenant Information:

Classification[8]	Number of Stores	Percent of GLA	Square Feet of GLA	Percent of GLA
General Merchandise	—	—	—	—
Food	2	3.4	1,967	2.4
Food Service	5	8.6	5,744	7.1
Clothing	4	6.9	3,128	3.9
Shoes	—	—	—	—
Home Furnishings	3	5.2	14,011	17.4
Home Appliances/Music	2	3.4	3,025	3.8
Building Materials/Garden	—	—	—	—
Automotive Supplies/Service Station	—	—	—	—
Hobby/Special Interest	4	6.9	4,457	5.5
Gifts/Specialty	7	12.1	10,491	13.0
Jewelry and Cosmetics	1	1.7	822	1.0
Liquor	—	—	—	—
Drugs	—	—	—	—
Other Retail	2	3.4	1,427	1.8
Personal Services	4	6.9	5,621	7.0
Recreation/Community	—	—	—	—
Financial	10	17.3	13,901	17.2
Offices (other than financial)	14	24.2	16,069	19.9
Total	58	100.0	80,663[9]	100.0

Notes:

[1] Retail and office site only. The project also includes two undeveloped parcels (containing 2.95 and 2.41 acres) that are currently zoned for residential use.

[2] Retail and office buildings only.

[3] FAR equals GBA divided by total site area.

[4] $63.21 per square foot. Hard costs only.

[5] Reimbursable from tenants.

[6] These rents do not include common area maintenance, utilities, taxes, and insurance charges of $1.80 to $2.40 per square foot. Most tenants also pay percentage rents ranging from 1.5 to 6.0 percent of gross sales. All leases are adjusted annually for changes in the cost of living.

[7] Average lease term. Does not include pad buildings. Leases for pad buildings are for 20 years with rents negotiated every five years.

[8] *Dollars & Cents of Shopping Centers: 1984*, (Washington, D.C.: ULI–the Urban Land Institute, 1984), p. 271.

[9] GLA Leased as of March 1984.

Developer:

La Jolla Development Company
P.O. Box 2388
La Jolla, California 92038

Architecture/Planning:

SGPA Planning and Architecture
P.O. Box 33326
San Diego, California 92103

Landscape Architecture:

Arbegast, Newton, and Griffith
1647 Hopkins Street
Berkeley, California 94707

Management:

Asset Management Group
(A division of La Jolla Development Company and Collins Development Company)
430 Sycamore Valley Road West
Danville, California 94526

THE BELL TOWER (Regional/Specialty Center)
Lee County, Florida

7-63   Spanish mission–style architecture has established a strong visual image and identity for the center.

Containing 184,000 square feet of GLA, The Bell Tower is a regional specialty shopping center set in southwest Florida in the rapidly growing Fort Myers area. The open-air center responds to a growing customer preference for leisurely shopping in an intimate, relaxed environment. Its design emulates Florida's Spanish colonial period and features stone fountains, courtyards, waterfalls and streams, meandering walkways, wooden footbridges, and dense tropical foliage.

Jacobson's department store (containing 51,616 square feet of GLA) and three high-quality restaurants anchor the $20 million project. Plans call for a second department store. In addition, the center houses a variety of high-end boutiques and specialty stores, most of which are operated by local merchants. Because the project's unique design and tenant mix have made it a shopping destination for a large regional market, it is classified as a regional/specialty center.

Construction of The Bell Tower began in May 1981, and the project opened in October 1982. The Bell Tower represents the first phase of a larger mixed-use development that is expected to include office and hotel uses.

The Site

The 35-acre site is located approximately six miles south of Fort Myers, Florida, in Lee County. The Fort Myers area has been experiencing dramatic population growth in recent years, with the Fort Myers metropolitan area among the fastest growing in the country. Since most of this growth has been occurring south of Fort Myers in the area encompassing The Bell Tower, the site is ideally located. Also bolstering the center's market is the area's year-round population, which roughly doubles during the peak tourist season from December through April. The site is convenient to Fort Myers and also to Sanibel Island and Captiva Island, two major resort islands located west of the project in the Gulf of Mexico. Collier County and the affluent city of Naples are to the south and within convenient driving distance.

U.S. Highway 41 borders the project on the west and Daniels Road borders it on the south. The original "Tamiami Trail," U.S. 41 is a heavily traveled four-lane highway and is one of two major north/south routes through Fort Myers. Daniels Road provides direct access to the Southwest Florida Regional Airport, which is located approximately seven miles east of the site. Interstate 75 is located immediately east of the airport.

Development in the vicinity of the site along U.S. 41 is primarily strip commercial. The site was flat, sandy, and sparsely vegetated, but had no unusual development constraints.

Architecture and Planning

The primary design goal was to establish a strong visual image and identity for the center by providing a setting that would be distinct from other shopping centers in the area. The center is designed in the style of a Spanish mission and presents an aura of tradition, durability, and quality. Design features include light-colored stucco walls, barrel tile roofs, clay paver tiles, timber details, and graceful arches. Deep colonnades, wood trellises, and louvered screens protect shoppers from the sun and rain while allowing breezes to circulate through the center. These design elements are compatible with the subtropical climate of the Fort Myers area.

Although the center is not an enclosed mall, it was planned with an inward orientation to protect it from the parking area and the traffic and noise of U.S. 41, and to create a more exclusive setting. A 50-foot-tall bell tower was built as a landmark for the center and can be easily spotted from U.S. 41. It also helps customers find their way within the complex. Bells in the tower strike the quarter hours and provide carillon music.

The center was designed to provide a sense of intimacy and discovery, which the typical mall often lacks. The floor plan is meandering and reminiscent of a European village. Walkways wind through covered colonnades, providing shoppers with a variety of spatial experiences and unexpected vistas that beckon them to explore the whole complex. Small courtyards open up to large extensively landscaped gardens with winding streams, ponds, and waterfalls. Wooden footbridges that cross the water enable shoppers to walk from one colonnade to another. The focal point of the complex is a large, formal, open-air courtyard located adjacent to the center's major tenant (Jacobson's department store) and featuring a multilevel, hand-carved, stone fountain from Mexico. The central courtyard serves as a backdrop for various promotional events and community displays.

Storefronts are designed in the style of Spanish missions. Tenants may choose from three different storefronts, thus giving the center some visual diversity. Coordinated, carved, and hand-painted wood signs help to unify the overall design of the storefronts. The developer finished the interiors for tenants except for painting and installing carpets and light fixtures, for which an allowance was provided.

The complex has one entrance from U.S. 41 and a second entrance from Daniels Road. They feed into a

7-64   A large, formal courtyard with a hand-carved stone fountain serves as the center's focal point.

loop roadway leading to four interior drives within the 1,150-space parking area. Plum trees border the roadway, and a 200-foot-wide landscaped space abuts Daniels Road. A stormwater detention area was created next to the complex.

Marketing and Tenants

Marketing and leasing of The Bell Tower have been geared toward affluent shoppers residing within a 50-minute drive of the center (extending as far south as Marco Island and as far north as Sarasota). The center's mix of high-end, fashion-oriented tenants, its quality restaurants, and its unique design have drawn customers from a large regional market as well as from the Fort Myers vicinity. Two marketing plans are used: one for the tourist season and the other for the year-round market.

Tenants are required to pay $0.75 per square foot of leasable space to help finance the center's promotional campaign. The developer contributes 25 percent of the tenants' total contributions. The promotional program offers a variety of activities held at the center: fashion shows, musical concerts, art shows, and various community exhibits are given in the central courtyard; individual performances and displays are given in three wooden gazebos located along the center's walkways. Television advertising supplements promotional events.

Experience Gained

- To help smooth the local review and approval process, it is important that the developer be re-

garded as part of the community and not as an "outsider" by local officials and residents. The developer can strengthen his relationship with the community by relying on local consultants and contractors wherever possible and by hiring a local project manager and staff.

- Even in a resort area like South Florida, tenants should not be selected solely on the basis of the tourist trade. The center's tenant mix should be able to attract serious local shoppers year-round.

- Short-term leases are advisable except in the case of major tenants. The developer will then have more frequent opportunities to replace tenants who are performing poorly.

- The selection of restaurant tenants has been important to the success of the center. Having high-quality restaurants (as opposed to fast food tenants) has encouraged people to drive longer distances to the center and to spend more time there. These restaurants have also attracted a more affluent customer whose needs and wants are compatible with the merchandise mix offered by the center's other tenants.

- To attract local, independent merchants to the center, the developer had to finish the interior spaces rather than provide only shell spaces with finishing allowances to tenants. Typically, local merchants are not accustomed to "building a store." Although finishing interior space proved to be a leasing advantage and was more cost-effective in the long run, it required that many risky front-end decisions be made regarding the

7-65   Wide, covered colonnades protect shoppers from the sun and rain.

7-66, 7-67   The center features lush tropical foliage, wooden footbridges, and ponds and streams.

size of tenant spaces (since in most instances tenant spaces were allocated before tenants were secured).

- A strong management is needed to deal with local merchants. They require considerable advice and "hand-holding" concerning issues such as the display of merchandise and the effective use of advertising. This special care, while requiring considerable time and effort, will assure that the center presents a consistent, high-quality image. A store planner is useful in advising local merchants.

- It is unrealistic to expect to prelease space to local merchants. As a rule, they will not begin signing leases until construction is underway and until numerous (one is generally not enough to convince them the center will succeed) well-known tenants have signed leases.

- The greatest demand came from potential tenants seeking 1,000 to 1,600 square feet of space. There was little demand for stores ranging from 3,000 to 5,000 square feet.

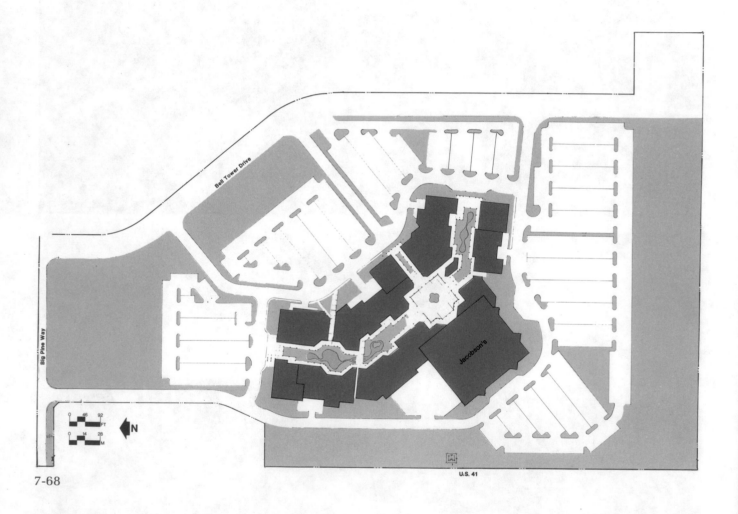

7-68

PROJECT DATA—THE BELL TOWER

Land Use Information:
Site Area: 35 acres (14.2 hectares)
Gross Building Area (GBA): 200,000 square feet
Gross Leasable Area (GLA): 184,000 square feet
Floor Area Ratio (FAR):[1] .13
Parking Spaces: 1,150
Parking Index: 6.2 spaces per 1,000 square feet of GLA

Economic Information:
Site Acquisition Cost: $3.2 million
Site Improvement Cost: $1.5 million
Construction Cost: $12 million
Total Project Cost: $20 million
Rents: $12 to $16 per square foot[2]
Sales: $175 to $200 per square foot

Land Use Plan:

	Acres	Percent
Buildings	4.59	13.12
Parking	2.88	8.21
Landscaping/Circulation	27.53	78.67
Total	35.00	100.00

Tenant Information:

Classification[3]	Number of Stores	Percent of Total Tenants	Square Feet of GLA	Percent of Total GLA	Average Percent of GLA in Regional Centers[3]
General Merchandise	1	2.38	51,616	35.04	14.1
Food	2	4.76	15,132	10.30	8.8
Food Services	3	7.14	3,963	2.70	7.0
Clothing	11	26.19	14,944	10.17	24.9
Shoes	1	2.38	1,010	.69	6.8
Home Furnishings	5	11.90	9,484	6.46	1.8
Home Appliances/Music	–	–	–	–	2.9
Building Materials/Garden	–	–	–	–	1.6
Automotive Supplies/Service Station	–	–	–	–	1.0
Hobby/Special Interest	3	7.14	6,683	4.55	3.8
Gifts/Specialty	6	14.29	11,033	7.51	5.2
Jewelry and Cosmetics	2	4.76	2,521	1.72	2.8
Liquor	–	–	–	–	.4
Drugs	–	–	–	–	3.7
Other Retail	1	2.38	1,622	1.10	4.1
Personal Services	4	9.54	6,420	4.37	2.3
Recreation/Community	1	2.38	18,000	12.25	3.8
Financial	2	4.76	4,599	3.14	3.0
Offices (other than financial)	–	–	–	–	2.1
Other	–	–	–	–	–
Total	42	100.00	147,027[4]	100.00	100.0

Notes:
[1] FAR = GBA divided by the total site area.
[2] Net rents (1983 data). These do not include common area charges, utilities, and additional charges totaling $5 per square foot. All leases contain percentage rent clauses.
[3] *Dollars & Cents of Shopping Centers: 1984* (Washington, D.C.: ULI—the Urban Land Institute, 1984), p. 271.
[4] GLA leased as of May 1983.

Developer:

Oxford Development Company
Suite 4500
One Oxford Centre
Pittsburgh, Pennsylvania 15219

Architecture:

Burt Hill Kosar Rittelmann Associates
Suite 200, Sunrise Office Center
8800 South Tamiami Trail
Fort Myers, Florida 33907

Engineering:

Johnson Engineering
P.O. Box 1550
Fort Myers, Florida

Landscape Architecture:

Turnberry Corporation
P.O. Box 630815
Miami, Florida 33153

THE WATERSIDE (Festival/Specialty Center)
Norfolk, Virginia

7-70 The pavilion is oriented so that dining terraces, walkways, and sitting areas focus on the river.

The festival/specialty center first attracted major attention in the mid-1970s with The Rouse Company's successful development of Faneuil Hall Marketplace in Boston. The festival/specialty center is intended to make shopping a recreational and entertainment activity. It is characterized by a distinctive architectural design (including the adaptive use of historic structures), a unique location, and an unusual tenant mix emphasizing food service and specialty shops. Typically, the trade area for this type of center equals that of a regional center. The festival mall is also strongly oriented toward tourists. For example, The Rouse Company has reported that tourists account for approximately 45 percent of the sales at Harborplace in Baltimore.

Although the festival retailing concept has proven successful in a number of large cities like Baltimore, Boston, New York, and San Diego, medium-sized cities have few successful examples to show. The Waterside in Norfolk, Virginia, is one notable exception. Situated in a waterfront redevelopment area along the Elizabeth River, this festival/specialty center contains 79,000 square feet of GLA and consists of a two-level steel and glass pavilion with a second-level, glass-enclosed pedestrian bridge connecting a new 627-space parking garage, a promenade and small amphitheater along the water's edge, a small boat marina, and berthings for character ships (ships having historical or cultural significance) and tour boats. The pavilion is positioned so that dining terraces, walkways, and sitting areas have river views of passing barges, tugboats, and luxury yachts entering the Intercoastal Waterway.

The Waterside contains five sit-down restaurants, 22 fast food booths, and 35 specialty retail and market produce shops, as well as 34 kiosks and 18 pushcarts with short-term leases. The project attracts tourists and residents from the Tidewater region of Virginia, including the market areas of Virginia Beach, Portsmouth, Newport News, Suffolk, Chesapeake, Hampton, Norfolk, and Williamsburg. Cultural events, both planned and spontaneous, are staged regularly to create a festive ambience and establish The Waterside as a shopping, eating, and entertainment destination.

Completed in June 1983 and containing 130,000 square feet of gross building area (GBA), the pavilion represents Phase I of the project development plan. The plan calls for a GBA of 100,000 square feet of commercial space to be added in the second phase. The parking garage will also be expanded. Implementation of the final phase is subject to market demand, economic conditions, and other development factors.

The Site

The 4.5-acre waterfront site is bordered by the Elizabeth River to the south and Waterside Drive (previously Waterfront Drive) to the north. Immediately east is the Omni International Hotel. The western edge of the site borders Town Point Park, a 6.5-acre public open space with two berths for character vessels and tour boats, a waterfront promenade, an open-air amphitheater, accommodations for exhibits and festivals, a small boat harbor, and diverse seasonal plantings. Waterfront Drive was converted to Waterside Drive, a landscaped six-lane divided boulevard. New street level pedestrian crossings connect the project area and Town Point Park to Norfolk's financial district and government center. A pedestrian bridge links The Waterside to a 627-space parking garage located on the northern side of Waterside Drive.

The site lies within the 100-year flood level (elevation 109.25 feet) and is covered by an amalgamation of fill material ranging from chunks of discarded concrete and assorted other refuse to compacted gravel. Stormwater drains either directly into the river by overland flow or is channeled through storm sewers to a pumping station. Underlying the fill is 3,000 feet of unconsolidated sands, silts, and clays resting on a base of pre-Cambrian rock. Consequently, the developer had to go 60 to 90 feet below the ground surface to find suitable soil for building foundations or pilings.

Development Strategy

The Waterside is one element of a massive waterfront redevelopment program initiated by the city and directed by the Norfolk Redevelopment and Housing Authority. The basic revitalization strategy is to coordinate public improvements that would stimulate private investment and development. This public/private development approach was described in the "Downtown Strategy Plan" prepared for the city by Wallace Roberts & Todd in 1981.

The plan pinpointed Norfolk's waterfront as the key to encouraging private development. It identified the harbor as the city's major natural asset and noted that the annual Harborfest celebration—a city-sponsored, three-day waterfront festival—clearly demonstrated that large numbers of people could be attracted to the downtown waterfront. Harborfest started with 10,000 people celebrating the visit of the tall ships during the 1976 national bicentennial celebration and since then has become a major East Coast event. Last year, it brought 750,000 people.

7-71　The pavilion's design is reminiscent of a Victorian-style park building.

Subsequent to the "Downtown Strategy Plan," Wallace Roberts & Todd prepared a "Waterfront Master Plan" for the city calling for a festival market, a waterfront park at Town Point, and waterfront promenades, as well as outlining the public improvements necessary for project development. Of major importance in the plan was the construction of Town Point Park—which stabilized the edge of the waterfront—and alterations to both the functional and physical characteristics of Waterside Drive. These improvements would provide pedestrian access to the waterfront and create a major public open space in the downtown.

The city selected James W. Rouse's Enterprise Development Company to develop the plan's festival market. Rouse established Waterside Associates—a joint venture between Norfolk Marketplace, Inc. (a subsidiary of the Enterprise Development Company) and Waterfront Enterprises, Inc. (a subsidiary of Harvey Lindsay & Company)—to develop the project in partnership with the city of Norfolk and the Norfolk Redevelopment and Housing Authority.

The city contributed $9.8 million in federal redevelopment funds toward construction of The Water-

side, which had a total cost of $13.8 million; loans from local private banks to the Norfolk Redevelopment and Housing Authority financed the difference between the city's contribution and the total cost. Waterside Associates obtained the $13.8 million loan for 30 years at $11\frac{5}{8}$ percent interest. In addition, the Norfolk city council authorized $14.5 million for capital improvements on the waterfront around the marketplace, including Town Point Park and the parking garage.

In return, the city receives 50 percent of the net cash flow generated by the project after deducting operating expenses, development and management fees, and debt service. Waterside Associates entered into a long-term ground lease with the Norfolk Redevelopment and Housing Authority. The lease is for 44 years with three 15-year renewal options.

Design and Engineering

Inspired by the ferry terminal market building that once occupied the site, the pavilion's design is reminiscent of a Victorian park building. The steel and glass structure is light and airy. Its Victorian-style

details are reflected in the floor tile patterns, roof brackets, overhangs, fan windows, and light fixtures.

The interior of the building is composed of three distinct skylight areas: the central court containing a figurehead centerpiece and raised performance stage; the east court, featuring a model of the clipper ship *Comet* and a fish aquarium; and the west court, where an elevator with a pilot house motif and a mariners' museum are located. These various components provide important points of interest and visually interconnect shops on the first and second floors. To facilitate vertical circulation and take full advantage of river views, the sit-down restaurants are all located on the side of the building facing the water's edge. Three second-level floor openings were included to improve views from either level and to create an open marketplace atmosphere.

While increasing and improving views of the river were important design objectives, it was also important to provide new opportunities for water-oriented recreation. Fulfilling this goal necessitated many site improvements. The shoreline was stabilized to accommodate a pedestrian promenade and boat mooring. New bulkheads were constructed and Otter Berth

7-72, 7-73, 7-74   The interior of the building has three distinct skylight areas.

267

widened. An area was dredged and a wave screen installed to create a small boat harbor, making the project much more accessible to the many boaters in the region.

As with most urban waterfront projects, The Waterside was subjected to a complex development approval process. The Virginia Department of State Highways had to approve the alterations involving the pedestrian bridge and Waterside Drive. The U.S. Army Corps of Engineers had to approve the shoreline improvements. Zoning had to be approved within special public interest codes, and the city's Architectural Review Board had to approve the center's design. In addition, project financing depended on the city council's approval of the development lease, bonds, and grants. The plan and its implementation involved the joint effort of the Norfolk Redevelopment and Housing Authority, the Mayor's Ad Hoc Committee, and the consultant team.

Tenants and Marketing

Probably the most distinctive aspects of the project are its theme—that of a festival marketplace with a heavy emphasis on food service and specialty retail—and its location in a medium-sized southeastern city. Because of its location in a smaller market area, the project is marketed as a unique regional destination for shopping, eating, and being entertained. The festival programs and special events are an important part of the marketing program. The project managers and merchants' association work with a group called Festevents, Ltd., which the city formed to promote events on the waterfront. Tenants are assessed $2 per square foot to support the merchants' association.

The project's waterfront location and recreational aspects make it highly popular on weekends. Although fewer families visit The Waterside during the week, it is crowded with downtown office workers at lunchtime and after work.

Many of the tenants are small independent businesses operated by local people, many of whom are new to the business. To accommodate artisans and craft merchants, pushcarts and kiosks can be leased for short terms. Pushcarts (seven feet by three feet) can be leased for a week or a month, and kiosks (100 to 250 square feet) are leased for six months. The fast food tenants are grouped by type of cuisine: the ethnic foods are located on one side of the marketplace and the American foods on the opposite side.

7-75   A pedestrian bridge links the project directly to a 627-space parking garage.

7-76   The waterfront promenade provides access to Town Point Park.

Experience Gained

- The concentration of development responsibility and control within one public agency—the Norfolk Redevelopment and Housing Authority—was necessary to facilitate a viable public/private development approach.

- Because Wallace Roberts & Todd prepared both the plan for the city's waterfront and the design for The Waterside, the site plan and building design were completely integrated.

- Public/private development partnerships are particularly appropriate and useful for the development of downtown retail projects as well as for the development of urban waterfront sites.

- The festival programming sponsored by the city attracts people to the waterfront and enhances the market for retail development.

- This type of project requires early solutions to ongoing interior and exterior maintenance needs, as well as a highly operative maintenance and management program set up at the outset.

- Parking is perceived as a problem because of the peak demand periods created by the food vendors and restaurants and by the location and schedule of the tour boats. In addition, shoppers who are accustomed to close-in parking at suburban centers feel inconvenienced when they cannot park in the garage across the street from the project (despite the availability of other parking within easy walking distance).

- It was important to recognize financial limitations and defer dealing with certain project elements until a later stage of development.

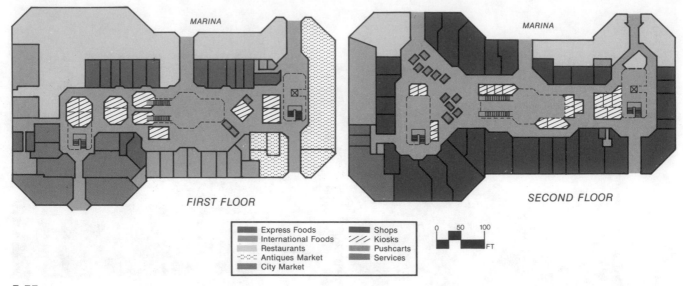

FIRST FLOOR

SECOND FLOOR

■ Express Foods		■ Shops	
■ International Foods		▨ Kiosks	
■ Restaurants		▥ Pushcarts	
▦ Antiques Market		■ Services	
■ City Market			

0   50   100
FT

7-77

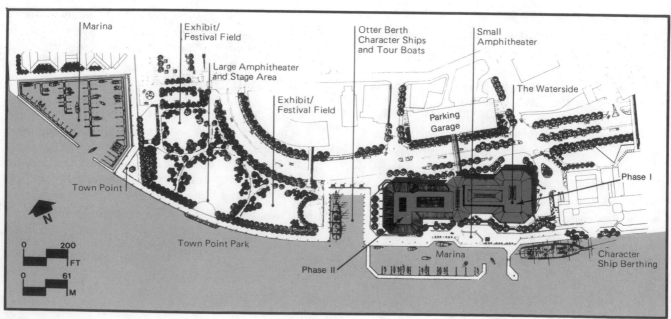

7-78

PROJECT DATA—THE WATERSIDE

Land Use Information:
Site Area: 4.5 acres (1.8 hectares)
Gross Buiding Area (GBA): 130,000 square feet
Gross Leasable Area (GLA): 79,000 square feet
Floor Area Ratio (FAR): 61[1]
Parking Spaces: 627
Parking Index: 5.7 spaces per 1,000 square feet of GLA

Economic Information:
Site Acquisition Cost: N.A.[2]
Site Improvement Cost: $8,900,000[3]
Construction Cost:
Total: $8,300,000
Per Gross Square Foot: $63.85
Per Net Square Foot: $105.06
Total Project Cost: $13,800,000[4]
Rents: $12 to $80 per square foot
Sales: approximately $300 per square foot

Tenant Information:

Classification[5]	Number of Stores	Percent of Total Tenants	Square Feet of GLA	Percent of Total GLA
General Merchandise	–	–	–	–
Food	12	9.8	8,145	10.3
Food Services	30	24.5	34,314	43.4
Clothing	5	4.0	6,246	7.9
Shoes	1	0.9	2,217	2.8
Home Furnishings[6]	7	5.7	3,756	4.7
Home Appliances/Music	–	–	–	–
Building Materials/Garden	–	–	–	–
Automotive Supplies/Service Station	–	–	–	–
Hobby/Special Interest	–	–	–	–
Gifts/Specialty	44	36.0	19,607	24.8
Jewelry and Cosmetics	1	0.9	306	0.4
Liquor	–	–	–	–
Drugs	–	–	–	–
Other Retail	1	0.9	1,529	1.9
Personal Services	1	0.9	50	0.1
Recreation/Community	1	0.9	1,852	2.4
Financial	3	2.4	283	0.4
Offices (other than financial)	1	0.9	380	0.5
Other[7]	15	12.2	315	0.4
Total	122	100.0	79,000	100.0

Notes:
[1] FAR equals gross building area divided by total site area.
[2] The city owns the property and leases it to the developer.
[3] The Norfolk Redevelopment and Housing Authority made all site improvements.
[4] Loaned to the private developer by the Norfolk Redevelopment and Housing Authority for 30 years at 11⅝ percent interest.
[5] *Dollars & Cents of Shopping Centers: 1984* (Washington, D.C.: ULI–the Urban Land Institute, 1984), p. 271.
[6] Antique shops.
[7] Pushcarts.

Developer:
Waterside Associates, Inc., a joint venture of
    Enterprise Development Company and Harvey
    Lindsay & Company
710 American City Building
Columbia, Maryland 21044

Architecture/Planning:
Wallace Roberts & Todd
1737 Chestnut Street
Philadelphia, Pennsylvania 19103

Management:
Harvey Lindsay & Company
749 Boush Street
Norfolk, Virginia 23510

THE PAVILION (Festival/Specialty Center)
Washington, D.C.

7-80   The project is located in the heart of Washington, D.C.'s Federal Triangle.

Over much of its 84-year history, the Old Post Office Building in Washington, D.C., was perceived by many as an eyesore that should be demolished because its architecture clashed with the other Neo-Classical government buildings along Pennsylvania Avenue. Just 15 years after its opening in 1899, the building was abandoned by the U.S. Post Office for newer quarters. Over the ensuing years it was occupied by a variety of federal government agencies, most recently by the FBI's wire-tapping division, and was allowed to deteriorate badly. Several times it narrowly escaped demolition.

Today, however, the building is a highly successful adaptive use project containing a mix of festival retail, office, and cultural and entertainment uses. It is the first project in the United States to be developed under the Cooperative Use Act of 1976, which allows the private development and use of federally owned buildings.

The Pavilion is a 52,939-square-foot (GLA) festival/specialty center that occupies the building's lower three levels and features 45 specialty shops and restaurants, a performing arts stage, a tourist information center, and an observation deck (operated by the National Park Service) within the building's clock tower (which also contains the Ditchley bells, a bicentennial gift to the U.S. Congress from Great Britain). The building's seven upper floors house the offices of several federal agencies, including those of the National Endowment for the Arts and the National Endowment for the Humanities.

The lower three floors were renovated and converted to retail use by the Evans Development Company of Baltimore under a 55-year lease from the General Services Administration (GSA). Private sources financed the $9.5 million retail project. The federal government used $30 million in federal funds to renovate the building's base and upper floors. The lease for the building was executed in October 1982, having taken approximately two years to negotiate with the federal government. Evans pays a minimum rent to the federal government, which also shares in the center's income and profits, receiving a base rent plus 10 percent of the increase in minimum rents and 10 percent of the percentage rents paid by retail tenants. Retail tenants pay minimum rents ranging from $25 to $60 per square foot and percentage rents ranging from 6 to 10 percent of gross sales. The developer is responsible for the security and maintenance of both the retail and public portions of the building. With sales averaging $500 per square foot since The Pavilion's opening in September 1983, the project is proving profitable to both the private developer and the federal government as landlord.

Because the building is federally owned and is designated as a historic landmark, plans for The Pavilion went through a detailed, multilevel review and approval process. Approvals were required from all GSA departments, the Fine Arts Commission, the National Capital Planning Commission, the State Historic Preservation Office, the U.S. Department of the Interior, the Pennsylvania Avenue Development Corporation, and various city agencies.

The Site

The Old Post Office Building occupies one block in downtown Washington on the south side of Pennsylvania Avenue between 11th and 12th Streets. It is conveniently located in the center of the Federal Triangle between the White House (four blocks to the west) and the Capitol (10 blocks to the east), and between the F Street corridor to the north (Washington's traditional retail core) and the Mall to the south (in which are concentrated Washington's primary tourist attractions, including the Smithsonian Institution's 11 separate museums and galleries). In addition, government and privately occupied office space (which will total more than 7.6 million square feet by 1985) surrounds the Old Post Office. The Federal Triangle Metro (subway) station is located less than 100 feet away, directly across 12th Street.

The Pavilion is accessible to the greater Washington metropolitan area by major routes and interstate highways. It is within minutes of Interstates 395 and 295, the George Washington Parkway, the Baltimore–Washington Parkway, and New York, Constitution, and Connecticut Avenues.

Architecture and Renovation

The building was designed by Willoughby J. Edbrooke in the Richardsonian Romanesque style popularized by Henry Hobson Richardson in the late 19th century. It is built of Maine granite and its exterior features arched entrances and fenestration, turrets, and a 315-foot clock tower (making it second only to the Washington Monument as Washington's tallest structure). Because the building had been designated a historic landmark, changes to the basic exterior were not permitted (with the exception of green awnings placed around the base of the building and bronze letters mounted on the outside arches).

The building's interior was originally designed to accommodate the operations of the post office. It included a high, skylit atrium space with a solid-floor, mail-sorting room measuring 99 feet by 184 feet. Suspended 30 feet above the floor was a glass-enclosed metal truss supporting a series of catwalks from

273

7-81 The Old Post Office Building is built of Maine granite and features arched entrances and fenestration, turrets, and a 315-foot clock tower.

which postal workers could observe activity below. Over the years, the atrium's skylight had been covered by metal sheets to reduce water leakage. Arthur Cotton Moore, the architect responsible for renovating the base and the office portion of the building, restored the skylight by replacing the metal with one-inch-thick tempered, reflective glass. Other preliminary improvements to the interior in preparation for its conversion included cutting through the building's main floor to the boiler room basement and creating a small stage.

Benjamin Thompson & Associates, responsible for the design of The Pavilion, enlarged and improved the stage to serve as a focal point for the project where dancers, musicians, puppeteers, and other entertainers could perform daily. The stage is portable and can be moved if necessary. The retail shops and restaurants flank the stage on three levels: the stage floor, the cutaway main floor, and a newly constructed balcony floor. A large stairway leading from the stage area to the main floor and a second stairway from the main floor to the balcony floor were added to provide additional access between levels. The three levels are also linked by a series of elevators. The metal truss located 30 feet above the main floor, with its glass removed, was retained for its historical significance, as a frame for lighting and design elements and as a buffer between the retail and the office space. The skylight is located 215 feet above the stage level. The original wrought-iron railing from a catwalk in the metal grid was saved and shaped to enclose the balcony level. Other pieces of the building's original granite, which were discovered in storage, were used for benches and planters in The Pavilion's public space.

Interior materials were selected to create a compatible motif and include brass fittings, red oak woodwork, frosted glass, ceramic tile, and marble. All

274

flooring throughout The Pavilion is new. The stage level, which contains the main public seating for shoppers patronizing the fast food tenants, is covered by ceramic tile laid in a pattern that reflects the building's arches and curves. Polished marble tiles of dark green, peach, and off-white cover the floor on the main level. The architect designed all the storefronts, which consist of flat glass panels arranged in a curve and trimmed with brass and wood. A sign zone was also established for tenants. The developer had to approve the designs, colors, and materials with which the tenants finished store interiors.

The developer improved the building's mechanical and electrical systems, replacing steam radiators with water-to-air heat pumps. The additional cooling load made it necessary to increase the building's facilities. However, since there was no good location to construct a cooling tower, a tower in the IRS Building adjacent to the Old Post Office was used. Exhaust ducts required for the food-service tenants were not allowed at or near street level and, therefore, were designed to penetrate the roof above the ninth floor. The original mercury vapor lamps were replaced with soft incandescent lights suspended from the metal grid. In addition, recessed troughs were provided along the storefronts for indirect lighting effects, and strings of miniature lights were placed in trees and potted plants.

Market Considerations

The Pavilion serves three distinct markets: residents of the Washington metropolitan area (with a population of 3.1 million); downtown office employees (with 115,000 workers within a 15-minute walk); and tourists (with 20 million annual visitors). Approximately 35 percent of the visitors to The Pavilion are tourists, with the balance evenly divided between area residents and downtown office workers. Accordingly, the objective of the marketing plan has been to reach all three markets. It was believed, and has been confirmed, that once people made the trip to The Pavilion, they would return with their friends and tell others about the project.

To obtain national publicity directed at attracting the tourist market, the delivery of mail by the pony express was reenacted, starting in New England two months before the project's grand opening and culminating in the delivery of an invitation to the President at the White House. Press releases were sent to every newspaper, television, and radio station along the route (resulting in over 300 newspaper articles, and both local and national radio and television coverage). The area's residents and employees were reached by newspaper, television, and radio cam-

7-82 The building's skylight was restored and the metal truss above the main floor was retained.

paigns started several weeks before and continued through the grand opening. Daily free entertainment events are also an integral part of The Pavilion's marketing program, with an average of 80 events held each month.

A developer-controlled marketing fund with an annual budget of $240,000 is used to promote The Pavilion. The developer's contribution makes up 25 percent of the fund, and tenants are assessed $4 per square foot. Roughly one-half of the budget goes toward the funding of entertainment. The developer holds monthly meetings with tenants to keep them informed of the marketing program.

Tenants

The tenant mix is made up of approximately 73 percent food-service tenants and 27 percent retail shops and was selected to appeal to the three target markets.

275

7-83 The stage (lower) level contains the performing arts stage and the main public seating area for shoppers patronizing the fast food tenants.

7-84 Polished marble tiles of dark green, peach, and off-white cover the floor on the main level.

7-85 Storefronts consist of flat glass panels arranged in a curve and trimmed with brass and wood.

Food-service tenants include five sit-down restaurants occupying the main and balcony levels and 14 fast food operations located on the stage level in an area known as The Cookery. Within The Cookery, fast food tenants are grouped in one of two areas—Main Street, U.S.A., or Embassy Row. The 26 specialty shops are located on the main and stage levels and include women's apparel, men's apparel, jewelry, a flower stand, a candy store, card and stationery stores, and gift shops.

Experience Gained

- The need to coordinate renovation work with the GSA, the general contractor, and the tenants made the project's construction manager a key member of the development team. The construction manager also played an important role in assisting retail tenants in the design and construction of their stores. A food merchandiser proved to be instrumental in helping food-service tenants in the design and operation of their space and in familiarizing them with the food court concept.
- The developer should expect to encounter some difficulty in obtaining private financing for a project with a leasehold interest in a federal building. The length of the lease term will be a major concern of the lender. In addition, the lender must be sophisticated enough to recognize and to accept the fact that a lease with the federal government must incorporate the provisions of a standard government contract (and thus will be more complex than a typical land lease for privately owned property).
- The mixing of retail and office uses in the same building has worked well. The private developer has undertaken the responsibility for the security and maintenance of both the retail and the public portions of the building.
- Programmed free entertainment and cultural events in The Pavilion have been an important element in terms of the public's perception of the project. The building's historic significance has also been a major factor in the project's success. In this regard, the developer believes that in order to succeed, an urban festival center must have more than a good location: it must have a unique setting (such as a historic structure or a waterfront location) and offer a blend of fashion, food, and the arts.
- The developer should prepare a strict leasing plan based on the results of a thorough market analysis—and should then stick to this plan. With an unanchored festival center such as The Pavilion, food-service tenants should typically occupy a major portion of the space.
- A project of this type requires considerable patience, time, and effort from the private developer. The lease negotiation process with the federal government lasted two years. In addition, approvals were required from multiple public and private agencies and commissions. The developer had to adjust to the inability of the government to provide immediate responses and to the government's limited experience in dealing on a "partnership" basis with private industry.
- In the renovation and conversion of older, historic structures, the development team must be prepared to comply with historic preservation guidelines and be able to adjust to unexpected conditions. For example, the original design for the balcony level called for welding a framing system to the existing columns, which were thought to be steel. However, the columns turned out to be cast iron, and welding would not work. Workers had to drill into the cast-iron columns and thread in a frame.

277

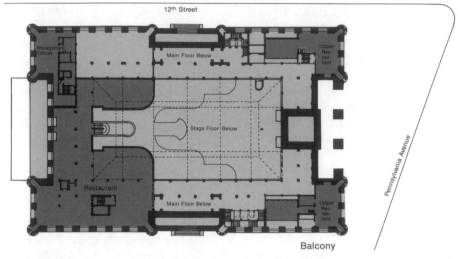

7-86

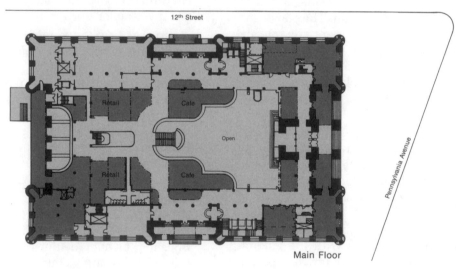

7-87

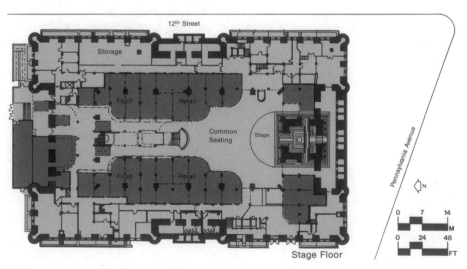

7-88

278

PROJECT DATA—THE PAVILION

Land Use Information:
Site Area: one city block
Gross Leasable Area (GLA): 52,939 square feet[1]
Parking Spaces: none[2]

Economic Information:
Site Acquisition Cost: N.A.[3]
Development Cost: $9.5 million[4]

Lease Information:
Sales: $500 per square foot
Rents: $28 per square foot[5]
Length of Leases: 5 to 15 years
Lease Provisions: triple net

Tenant Information:

Classification[6]	Number of Stores	Percent of Total Tenants	Square Feet of GLA	Percent of GLA
General Merchandise	–	–	–	–
Food	–	–	–	–
Food Service	19	42.2	38,497	72.7
Clothing	5	11.2	3,782	7.1
Shoes	1	2.2	493	.9
Home Furnishings	–	–	–	–
Home Appliances/Music	–	–	–	–
Building Materials/Garden	–	–	–	–
Automotive Supplies/Service Station	–	–	–	–
Hobby/Special Interest	–	–	–	–
Gifts/Specialty	19	42.2	9,667	18.3
Jewelry and Cosmetics	1	2.2	500	1.0
Liquor	–	–	–	–
Drugs	–	–	–	–
Other Retail	–	–	–	–
Personal Services	–	–	–	–
Recreation/Community	–	–	–	–
Financial	–	–	–	–
Offices (other than financial)	–	–	–	–
Total	45	100.0	52,939	100.0

Notes:

[1] GLA of The Pavilion. The Old Post Office Building also contains approximately 140,000 square feet of office space.

[2] While The Pavilion has no on-site parking, there are approximately 6,000 parking spaces within a four-block radius of the site.

[3] Evans Development Company has a 55-year lease with the federal government.

[4] Total hard costs and soft costs incurred by Evans Development Company in developing The Pavilion. Does not include cost of finishing tenant spaces. Federal funds supplied $30 million needed to renovate the remainder of the Old Post Office Building.

[5] Average minimum rent. Minimum rents range from $25 to $60 per square foot. Percentage rents range from 6 to 10 percent of gross sales.

[6] *Dollars & Cents of Shopping Centers: 1984* (Washington, D.C.: ULI–the Urban Land Institute, 1984), p. 271.

Developer:

Evans Development Company
World Trade Center, Suite 253
Baltimore, Maryland 21202

Architecture:

Benjamin Thompson & Associates
1 Story Street
Cambridge, Massachusetts 02138

Marketing:

Evans Marketing Group
1100 Pennsylvania Avenue, N.W.
Washington, D.C. 20004

General Contractor:

Turner Construction Company
Washington, D.C.

Construction Management:

Process Management, Inc.
Springfield, Massachusetts

MONTGOMERY VILLAGE OFF-PRICE CENTER
Gaithersburg, Maryland

7-90 Benches and planters with mature trees and shrubs create a comfortable pedestrian environment for shoppers.

One of the most important and rapidly evolving trends in retailing in the 1980s has been the emergence of off-price and factory outlet malls. While off-price retailing has its roots in discounting, the off-price center is vastly different from the discount center. Unlike the discount center, which is targeted to the lower-income, cost-conscious buyer to whom price is most important, the off-price center is aimed at the middle- and upper-middle-income buyer who is seeking quality merchandise at a price savings. In design and character, the off-price center of today is similar to the conventional shopping center and features coordinated signage and architectural design, landscaping, clean surroundings, and security.

The Montgomery Village Off-Price Center in Gaithersburg, Maryland (a suburb of Washington, D.C.), illustrates a number of the characteristics of today's off-price center. Targeted to an affluent, well-educated market, the center—containing 223,255 square feet of GLA—features an attractive, residentially scaled architectural design and a tenant mix that offers shoppers quality fashion merchandise and accessories at reduced prices, as well as services and convenience goods.

The center's first phase, completed in March 1983 and anchored by a 36,000-square-foot Safeway supermarket, contains 24 stores with a total of 117,458 square feet of GLA. Sales volumes for this phase during the first full year of operation averaged more than $278 per square foot. In response to this success, the developer has built a second phase with 105,797 square feet of GLA, which is anchored by a 25,000-square-foot Marshalls department store.

The strategy the developer used with the Montgomery Village Off-Price Center, as it has with its other off-price centers, was to acquire a site in a prime location within an established, affluent suburban trade area and then compete directly with nearby regional malls by offering shoppers the same quality merchandise and comfortable ambience. This approach has proven successful—attracting many national and regional off-price chains. Although rents are slightly higher than those in many off-price centers (which often select peripheral locations), tenants are willing to pay steeper rents for a location that draws heavier shopper traffic and results in higher sales volumes.

The Site

The center is approximately 20 miles northwest of downtown Washington, D.C., in the town of Gaithersburg in Montgomery County, Maryland. Situated at the southeast corner of Lost Knife Road and Odend'hal Avenue, the site is a short distance from a major east/west road (Montgomery Village Avenue) connecting with Interstate 270. Interstate 270 runs north to Frederick, Maryland, and south to Interstate 495 (the Capital Beltway), which provides access throughout the Washington, D.C., metropolitan area.

Set within the large planned community of Montgomery Village, the center is bordered on the west by a regional mall (Lakeforest Mall), on the north and east by townhouses and garden apartments, and on the south by multifamily residential and commercial development. The site slopes from west to east (with a drop of approximately 24 feet), and the developer had to detain stormwater runoff on site.

Planning and Architecture

The center has a linear configuration and Phase I comprises three buildings: a linear building approximately 660 feet long set along the site's northern boundary; a smaller linear building approximately 210 feet long located at the site's southeast corner; and a 3,500-square-foot freestanding structure situated along the site's southern boundary. The main building houses 14 tenants in stores ranging in size from 1,500 to 8,000 square feet (excluding the 36,000-square-foot anchor tenant). Store depths run from 110 to 150 feet and widths from 20 to 35 feet. The smaller linear building houses nine tenants in shops ranging in size from 1,000 to 2,400 square feet; the average tenant space is 20 feet wide by 60 feet deep.

The center's parking area contains 735 spaces (including 221 spaces for compact cars). Cars may enter and exit at four points, the main entrance being at the site's southern boundary. Parking was laid out to minimize walking distances for shoppers and to maximize visibility and pedestrian safety; more than one-half of the parking spaces are within 100 feet of storefronts. A separate service entrance at the rear of the main linear building accommodates truck deliveries. Landscaped islands are scattered throughout the parking area, and an attractive pylon sign at the southwest corner of the site identifies the center.

Buildings are contemporary in design and residential in scale and character (complementing the nearby residential development). The main building follows the natural contour of the site, stepping down from west to east. Buildings feature wood shake roofs with undulating rooflines that enhance the residential atmosphere and screen rooftop mechanical elements. Exteriors are of rough-sawn horizontal and vertical cedar siding stained in natural shades and of earth tone brick. Since these materials cover all sides of the buildings, the center at no point "turns its back" on the surrounding development. A variety of colored wood trims highlights storefronts, contrasting with the neutral tone facades and individualizing store-

7-91 Building exteriors feature wood shake roofs, undulating rooflines, cedar siding, and earth tone brick.

7-92 A continuous canopy covers walkways.

fronts. A continuous canopy supported by steel columns wrapped in face brick protects shoppers from the sun and rain. Walkways offering park benches and planters with mature trees and shrubs create a comfortable pedestrian environment for shoppers.

The development team has carefully controlled signage to assure consistency and compatibility with the center's architectural design theme, while also identifying tenants and avoiding rigid uniformity. All signs must be placed within a sign band of consistent height (despite the horizontal and vertical offsets of the buildings' rooflines). Tenants have some choice as to the size and color of signage.

The developer provides electric outlets, lighting, ready-to-paint drywall, acoustical ceilings, and concrete floors. However, tenants may also exercise a turnkey option. Individual heat pump units provide HVAC for each store.

Tenants

The developer selected tenants to attract primarily female shoppers from Gaithersburg and the northern half of Montgomery County, Maryland, an affluent suburban trade area. Leasing to several well-known women's apparel off-price retailers was a primary objective. Tenants have also been selected who will provide a wide array of merchandise so that shoppers are treated to the convenience of "one-stop" shopping. Thus, the tenant mix includes off-price retailers offering both soft and hard goods, as well as conventional retailers providing convenience goods and services (such as a bank, a sit-down restaurant, two fast food chains, an ice cream chain, a unisex hair salon, a liquor store, and a video center). Established national or regional chains have leased a major part of the space.

The Safeway supermarket, the anchor tenant for the center's first phase, stands at the eastern end of the main building. Since this building houses all of the off-price tenants, most shoppers drive or walk past these stores en route to the Safeway. Conventional retailers offering convenience goods and services (with the exception of Safeway) are located in the smaller building at the site's southeast corner, where they are easily seen and reached from adjacent roadways. Retailers of hard goods occupy the deepest tenant spaces (up to 150 feet deep).

Marketing

A developer-controlled marketing fund, with an annual budget of approximately $65,000, supports the promotion of the center. The marketing staff advises the tenants of the marketing plan for each year and holds meetings every two months to keep them in-

7-93   A 36,000-square-foot Safeway supermarket anchors the center's first phase.

7-94 Colored wood trims highlight storefronts.

formed of marketing activities. With the exception of the grand opening, marketing fund dollars have been directed toward radio, newspaper, and direct mail advertising rather than toward promotional events. Advertising is seasonal, with a major promotional campaign undertaken three times a year. Since the complex was one of the first off-price centers to open in the Washington, D.C., market, an important part of the initial promotion was to familiarize shoppers with off-price retailing.

The center's primary trade area (within a five-mile radius) had a 1983 estimated population of 94,033 and an estimated average household income of $42,434. The 1980 median property value within a five-mile radius was $104,048. Twenty-nine percent of the population within a three-mile radius had a household income of over $50,000, and over 41 percent had graduated from college.

Experience Gained

- The developer believes that off-price centers should be located in established, affluent suburban trade areas, not in remote locations. Sites adjacent to or near existing regional malls are often ideal locations.
- Centers should also be designed to have an appearance and ambience comparable to that of regional centers. They should be aesthetically attractive and offer amenities commonly found in a regional mall setting. High-quality architectural design and amenities will make shoppers comfortable and will assure them that the center provides quality merchandise. Today's shoppers expect such a setting, even in an off-price center.
- Since 70 to 75 percent of shoppers will be women, the tenant mix should be targeted to soft goods and women's apparel. Strong women's apparel tenants will contribute to the center's success. Roughly 70 percent of the tenants in the developer's off-price centers offer soft goods. Shoppers will also expect the convenience of service tenants (banks, food, food service) in an off-price center. Thus, mixing conventional and off-price

7-95 Parking was laid out to minimize walking distances for shoppers and to maximize visibility and pedestrian safety.

7-96 A pylon sign identifies the center.

merchants presents no problem, provided that *all* soft goods tenants are off-price (with conventional merchants limited to hard goods and service tenants).

- When off-price centers are new to a market area, they should be carefully promoted to educate the consumer. "Off-price" is an industry term that may be unfamiliar to or misunderstood by the consumer, and, thus, should be clearly defined when promoting the center. The word "discount" should not be used, since it tends to have a bad connotation among shoppers.

- As a general rule, it is recommended that space in an off-price center be leased primarily to experienced retailers. Because larger chains usually lease most of the space in an off-price center, turnover is minimal.

- The developer feels that land should not be purchased until a signed lease from the anchor tenant(s) is in hand. In addition, no more than 20 percent of the center's leasable space should be speculative.

- The center should be architecturally compatible with the surrounding community. The development team should work with community groups, both in the planning stages and during construction, to ensure that the center's design complements and enhances the surrounding area.

- It is important to provide a consistent sign band even if an undulating roofline is used. Signage controls ensure that signs identifying tenants will be consistent with the center's architectural design while being readily visible to shoppers.

- Sites with sloping terrain can be used to advantage in designing a shopping center by letting the building's lines form to the topography and by limiting the use of retaining walls.

- In order to create a safe, inviting environment after dark, it is important to light building facades, as well as pedestrian and parking areas.

- The use of mature trees rather than young seedlings to landscape the center—in spite of the additional cost—will give the center an inviting, established setting.

285

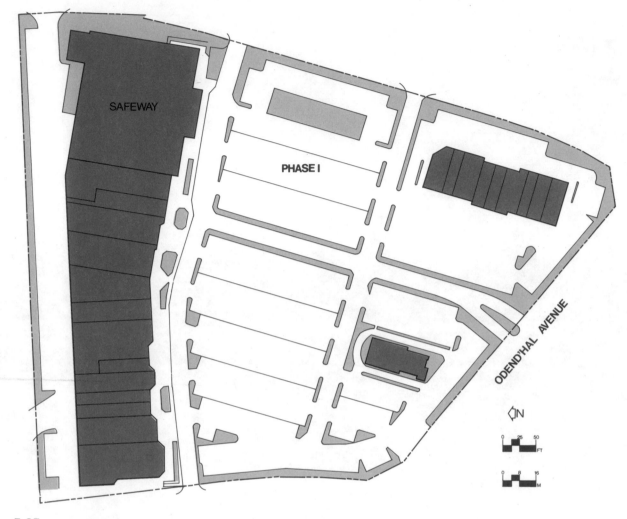

7-97

7-98 PROJECT DATA—MONTGOMERY VILLAGE OFF-PRICE CENTER

Land Use Information:[1]
Site Area: 11 acres (4.5 hectares)
Gross Building Area (GBA): 117,458 square feet
Gross Leasable Area (GLA): 117,458 square feet
Floor Area Ratio (FAR):[2] .24
Parking:
Total Spaces: 735
Index: 1 space per 100 square feet of sales area
      1 space per 300 square feet of storage area
Compact Spaces: 221

Land Use Plan:[1]

	Acres	Percent
Buildings	2.69	25
Landscaping	1.18	11
Parking	7.13	64
Total	11.00	100

Economic Information:[1]
Site Acquisition Cost: $2,310,000
Site Improvement Cost:

Excavation/Grading	$ 176,000
Sewer/Water	408,000
Paving	227,000
Curbs/Sidewalks	156,000
Landscaping	125,000
Total	$1,092,000

Construction Cost:

Superstructure	$2,191,000
HVAC	273,000
Electrical	464,000
Plumbing	151,000
Fees	59,000
Finishes	479,000
Graphics	29,000
Total	$3,646,000[3]

Operating Expenses:

Taxes	$	77,500
Insurance		10,700
Services		17,300
Maintenance		8,900
Janitorial		23,000
Utilities		9,300
Management		60,500
Miscellaneous		23,800[4]
Total	$	231,000

Lease Information:[1]

Sales: $278.25 per square foot[5]

Rents: $11.24 per square foot[6]

Term: 9 years (average)[5]

Lease Provisions: triple net; escalations vary (average of guaranteed increase in minimum rent of 15 percent every four years).

Tenant Information:[1]

Classification[7]	Number of Stores	Percent of Total Tenants	Square Feet of GLA	Percent of GLA
General Merchandise	—	—	—	—
Food	1	4.17	36,253	30.86
Food Service	4	16.67	8,808	7.50
Clothing	4	16.67	24,462	20.83
Shoes	2	8.33	5,002	4.26
Home Furnishings	3	12.50	10,244	8.72
Home Appliances/Music	—	—	—	—
Building Materials/Garden	—	—	—	—
Automotive Supplies/Service Station	1	4.17	7,391	6.29
Hobby/Special Interest	1	4.17	2,300	1.96
Gifts/Specialty	1	4.17	3,576	3.04
Jewelry and Cosmetics	1	4.17	7,631	6.50
Liquor	1	4.17	2,424	2.06
Drugs	—	—	—	—
Other Retail	2	8.33	4,736	4.03
Personal Services	2	8.33	2,741	2.33
Recreation/Community	—	—	—	—
Financial	1	4.17	1,890	1.61
Offices (other than financial)	—	—	—	—
Other	—	—	—	—
Total	24	100.00	117,458	100.00

Notes:

[1] Data for Phase I only.

[2] FAR equals GBA divided by total site area.

[3] $31 per square foot. Does not include cost of land or site improvements.

[4] Landlord's contribution to promotional fund.

[5] Excluding Safeway.

[6] Average minimum rent (including Safeway). Average percentage rent for soft goods tenants is 3 percent of gross sales.

[7] *Dollars & Cents of Shopping Centers: 1984* (Washington, D.C.: ULI–the Urban Land Institute, 1984), p. 271.

Developer:

Western Development Corporation
1204 Wisconsin Avenue, N.W.
Washington, D.C. 20007

Architecture/Planning:

Wah Yee Associates
26711 Northwestern Highway
Southfield, Michigan 48034

Landscape Architecture:

David Krause & Associates
199 West Brown Street
Birmingham, Michigan 48011

LIBERTY VILLAGE (Outlet Center)
Flemington, New Jersey

7-99   The center has a colonial village design theme.

The factory outlet center differs from the off-price center in two respects. First, as the term "factory outlet" suggests, a large proportion of the space is leased to factory outlets (manufacturers) rather than to off-price retailers. Second, the trade area of an outlet center typically is much larger than that of an off-price center. Unlike the off-price center, whose trade area is often similar in size to that of a community center, the outlet center generally is targeted to a large regional market and has strong support from tourists.

Liberty Village, located in Flemington, New Jersey, is a 120,668-square-foot (GLA) outlet center that offers shoppers a variety of quality merchandise at a price savings within a pleasant, well-designed shopping environment. It features a colonial village design theme as well as a tenant mix that is unique for an outlet center.

The center consists of nearly 108,000 square feet of new construction that has been integrated with 10 renovated buildings, originally constructed in 1972 as reproductions of colonial architecture. Tenants have been carefully selected to offer shoppers a department store mix of merchandise at outlet prices. Included are factory outlets, off-price stores, boutiques, food, and food service tenants.

The developer purchased the site for Liberty Village in 1980 and began construction in November 1981. The first building was occupied in May 1982. All space at Liberty Village was preleased and there is currently a waiting list.

The Site

The 12-acre site is ideally located for an outlet center. The town of Flemington is a historic community and the county seat of Hunterdon County, a predominantly rural county situated in the western portion of central New Jersey. More importantly, Flemington in recent years has acquired a reputation as one of the Northeast's major areas for factory outlets, with 37 outlet or off-price locations. The community is strategically positioned approximately 55 miles from New York City and 50 miles from Philadelphia and is easy to reach from major highways. Thus, it is within a 90-minute drive for 20 million people, yet distant enough from major retailers to avoid merchandising conflicts.

Liberty Village is located one block from Flemington's Main Street and is bordered on the north by Church Street, on the south by State Highway 12, on the east by Brown Street, and on the west by the tracks of the Black River and Western (BR&W) Railroad. The BR&W offers shoppers the novelty of traveling to Liberty Village on a restored steam railroad that provides service between Flemington and the historic and picturesque New Jersey towns of Ringoes and Lambertville. Many shoppers arrive at the center on bus tours. Liberty Village is also within a 10-minute walk of most of Flemington's other outlets, many of which are freestanding structures. Turntable Junction, a specialty center also designed in the style of a colonial village, is just across Church Street and contains 24 specialty boutiques and restaurants.

An abandoned foundry, as well as the 10 buildings renovated for the center, originally occupied the site. The terrain was basically flat—except for a small, low-lying, swampy area—and had little vegetation. Subsoils were stable; however, foundry refuse buried on the site caused some problems.

Planning and Design

The overall planning and design concept was to create an outlet center—distinct from other freestanding factory outlets and off-price stores in Flemington—that would offer shoppers a pleasant experience. The design concept, patterned after an early American colonial village, allowed the 10 existing historically detailed buildings on the site to be renovated and integrated with new construction while also being compatible with the colonial design of the adjacent Turntable Junction development. Materials used for the exteriors of the new buildings include wood clapboard siding, brick, and natural stone. Exteriors also feature pitch roofs, dormers, steeples, wood shutters, imitation chimneys, and colonial pastel colors.

All of the buildings are one story; mechanical equipment is housed in the attics. The developer's interior finishing included utilities, drywall, lighting, floor covering, and painting. Buildings were designed to have maximum flexibility in the use of space (electric, HVAC, and structural design allowed tenant spaces to range in size from 1,000 to 10,000 square feet) and were insulated in excess of building code requirements. In addition, the developer used prefabricated wood trusses throughout the center, which cut expenses and speeded up construction.

The new buildings have been carefully located on the site to avoid a typical shopping mall appearance and to screen from view the center's service area. They are linked by a brick paved and landscaped plaza complete with colonial-style street lamps, wooden benches and trash receptacles, and Belgian block curbs. Entrances to all stores are from this public plaza, which has been graded to accommodate the handicapped without the use of ramps.

The project was planned to separate vehicular and pedestrian traffic. A one-way loop roadway provides

7-100, 7-101   Building exteriors feature steeples, imitation chimneys, pitch roofs, dormers, and wood shutters.

vehicular access from the north, while Route 12 provides direct access from the south. Parking for shoppers is located in two areas near the site's southern and western boundaries, where it is removed from the buildings and the plaza yet is within convenient walking distance. Separate parking has been provided for employee and service vehicles as well as for buses. A detention pond on the low-lying portion of the site controls stormwater runoff. It is attractively landscaped and is a major "people-oriented" feature.

Tenants

The developer has sought nationally known, quality factory outlets as tenants for the complex. Although Liberty Village was originally envisioned as a center offering primarily tabletop goods, the developer soon decided to select a mix of tenants offering a department store variety of merchandise. Factory outlets occupy about 50 percent of the leasable space.

Even though the center does not have anchor tenants in the traditional sense, the many factory outlets and off-price stores serve as the major draws for the center, while the boutiques and food tenants provide a unique added attraction. The developer has been able to prelease all space without the aid of real estate brokers.

Marketing

Shoppers travel to the center from the New York and Philadelphia metropolitan areas, the entire state of New Jersey, eastern Pennsylvania, Long Island, and Connecticut. Some travel more than 100 miles one way. Shoppers are primarily well-educated, upper-middle-income professionals who are seeking quality merchandise at a price savings.

In promoting the center, the developer has had to avoid mentioning the names of factory outlets (to prevent confrontations with the manufacturers' major retail customers). Promotion, therefore, has focused on the center's unique character as well as on the attraction of Flemington as a major outlet area. Radio and newspaper advertising have been used. In addition, a consultant has been hired to organize bus tours to the center, and special events within the center are being planned. A mandatory cooperative advertising program for tenants was recently implemented, and informal tenants' meetings are held bimonthly to convey information and to respond to tenants' questions and concerns.

Experience Gained

- Location is crucial to the success of an outlet center. While the center must be close enough to major metropolitan areas to draw shoppers, it must be distant enough to avoid conflicts between the factory outlets and their major retail customers. As a rule of thumb, outlet centers should be located at least 50 miles from major retail stores in order to avoid such conflicts.

- The concept of creating a unique outlet center that combines factory outlets with off-price stores and boutiques in an attractive colonial village setting has proven particularly successful. Although the center's rents are higher than its competitors, tenants are enjoying high volumes of traffic from upper-middle-income shoppers.

- In order to succeed, an outlet center must function as a shopping destination that brings the serious shopper back repeatedly. Liberty Village's pleasant atmosphere and exceptional shopping values, together with the distinct character of the Flemington area, have made this possible.

- The project's departure from conventional retail development concepts, particularly its lack of anchor tenants, made it difficult for the developer to obtain a financing commitment (despite the pre-leasing of all space). To date, a syndication and a local bank have financed the project.

- Tenants' participation in the center's cooperative advertising program was not made mandatory until 50,000 square feet had been leased. In retrospect, the program should have been mandatory from the outset; it also should have been more ambitious, budgeted, and subsidized. This undoubtedly would have accelerated the attraction of tenants as well as shoppers.

- Although the center has no traditional anchor tenants, the ability of the developer to obtain a number of well-known, high-quality manufacturers as tenants from the start was important in quickly generating high volumes of shopper traffic and, therefore, in attracting other quality tenants.

- Unable to offer rents that were competitive with other freestanding factory outlet buildings in the area, the developer had to promote the entire concept of the center to tenants (that is, the center's unique ambience and location, its upper-middle-income shoppers, and its high volumes of shopper traffic).

- Good maintenance with a full-time staff has been important in conveying the image of an upscale outlet center.

- Roughly 60 percent of the center's sales volume occurs on weekends. The developer attributes

7-102, 7-103　Buildings are linked by a brick paved and landscaped plaza and have been carefully located to screen the center's service area from the view of shoppers.

this primarily to the increasing percentage of working women.

- The fact that many shoppers spend a full day at the center has not caused an unusually high demand for parking (because of the low turnover of parking spaces). Many shoppers arrive at the center by bus; also, a significant number of shoppers park their cars at other factory outlets in Flemington and walk from there to Liberty Village.

- The center originally had as tenants a number of artisans and craftsmen who produced limited quantities of high-priced, high-quality, handmade merchandise that was not particularly attractive to shoppers seeking bargains and service. Therefore, the artisans and craftsmen were replaced by a winery, a bakery, a chocolate maker, a farmer's stand, and similar tenants who sell to crowds, supply services, and are successful entrepreneurs.

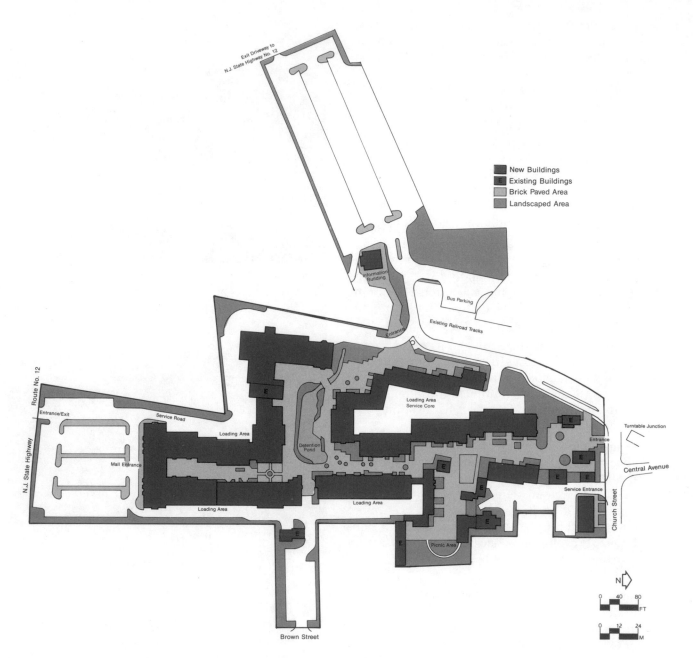

New Buildings
E Existing Buildings
Brick Paved Area
Landscaped Area

Exit Driveway to
N.J. State Highway No. 12

Information
Building

Bus Parking

Existing Railroad Tracks

Entrance

Route No. 12

Loading Area
Service Core

N.J. State Highway

Entrance/Exit

Service Road

Loading Area

Detention
Pond

Loading Area

Turntable Junction

Entrance

E

E

E

E

Mall Entrance

E

E

E

Central Avenue

E

Service Entrance

Loading Area

Loading Area

E

Church Street

E

E

E

Picnic Area

Brown Street

N

0 40 80
FT

0 12 24
M

7-104

PROJECT DATA—LIBERTY VILLAGE

Land Use Information:

Site Area: 11.95 acres (4.84 hectares)
Gross Building Area (GBA): 132,878 square feet[1]
Gross Leasable Area (GLA): 120,668 square feet
Floor Area Ratio (FAR):[2] .26
Parking Spaces: 500

Land Use Plan:

	Acres	Percent
Buildings	3.05	26.0
Parking	2.72	23.0
Open Space	6.18	51.0
Total	11.95	100.0

Economic Information:

Site Acquisition Cost: $3,643,794[3]
Site Improvement Cost: $6,767,046[4]
Construction Cost:[5]
New Construction: $42 to $46 per square foot
Renovation: $6.30 per square foot
Rents: $12.72 per square foot[6]
Sales: $150 to $160 per square foot[7]

Tenant Information:

Classification[8]	Number of Stores	Percent of Total Tenants	Square Feet of GLA	Percent of GLA
General Merchandise	3	5.7	6,651	5.9
Food	4	7.5	10,731	9.6
Food Service	1	1.9	1,174	1.1
Clothing	19	35.8	50,458	45.1
Shoes	2	3.7	3,599	3.2
Home Furnishings	3	5.7	4,674	4.2
Home Appliances/Music	5	9.4	11,993	10.7
Building Materials/Garden	–	–	–	–
Automotive Supplies/Service Station	–	–	–	–
Hobby/Special Interest	2	3.8	3,178	2.8
Gifts/Specialty	6	11.3	9,176	8.2
Jewelry and Cosmetics	3	5.7	5,112	4.6
Liquor	–	–	–	–
Drugs	–	–	–	–
Other Retail	–	–	–	–
Personal Services	–	–	–	–
Recreation/Community	1	1.9	726	.6
Financial	–	–	–	–
Offices (other than financial)	1	1.9	820	.7
Other	3	5.7	3,681	3.3
Total	53	100.0	111,973[9]	100.0

Notes:

[1] Includes 116,950 square feet of new construction and 15,928 square feet of renovation.
[2] FAR = GBA divided by total site area.
[3] $7 per square foot.
[4] $13 per square foot.
[5] Hard costs only. Soft costs were $5 per square foot.
[6] Average net rent. Does not include common area charges of $2.12 per square foot, real estate taxes of $1.25 per square foot, and a promotional charge of $1 per square foot. All leases include an escalator clause providing for an annual rent increase equal to 50 percent of the annual increase in the consumer price index.
[7] Estimate of average sales volume. Since most tenants do not pay percentage rents, more precise data on sales volumes are unavailable.
[8] *Dollars & Cents of Shopping Centers: 1984* (Washington, D.C.: ULI–the Urban Land Institute, 1984), p. 271.
[9] GLA leased as of May 1984.

Developer/Manager:

Liberty Village Associates
One Church Street, Box 161
Flemington, New Jersey 08822

Architecture:

Lehman Architectural Partnership
34 Woodland Road
Roseland, New Jersey 07068

Landscape Architecture:

Henry Kitz, Jr.
R.D.6
Flemington, New Jersey 08822

TOWN SQUARE (Mixed-Use Development)
St. Paul, Minnesota

7-106   The retail component of Town Square contains over 225,000 square feet of leasable space, including a 116,250-square-foot Donaldson's department store.

Town Square is a mixed-use development occupying a two-block area in the center of downtown St. Paul, Minnesota. Developed as a joint venture between the public and private sectors, the $100 million project serves as a focal point for St. Paul's downtown as well as a catalyst for the further revitalization of the city's retail and office core. It is an example of a successful large-scale, mixed-use development in a relatively small downtown area.

The project integrates a variety of public spaces and private development:

- over 225,000 square feet of GLA retail space with approximately 70 retail shops and restaurants on three levels (including a lower-level food court) and a two-story Donaldson's department store;
- two office towers of 27 and 25 stories (the North Central Tower and the Conwed Tower, respectively) offering more than 430,000 square feet of leasable office space;
- an enclosed city-owned park with a 90,000-square-foot rooftop garden;
- underground, on-site parking for 500 vehicles; and
- a 16-story, 250-room Radisson Plaza Hotel with two restaurants, an enclosed atrium, an indoor pool, a ballroom, meeting facilities, and two solar collection systems.

Town Square was started in June 1978 and completed in the winter of 1980, with the project's grand opening taking place in the fall of 1980. The first office tower (North Central Tower) began receiving tenants in July 1980, and the second office tower (Conwed Tower) welcomed its first tenant in January 1981. The project's retail space is being expanded by 150,000 square feet, which will be connected by skyway to Dayton's department store (located across the street from Town Square).

The Site

Set in St. Paul's central business district, the project is bordered on the north and south by Eighth and Sixth Streets and on the east and west by Minnesota and Cedar Streets. St. Paul, the state capital, is approximately a 15-minute drive from downtown Minneapolis. Within walking distance of the project are shopping districts, St. Paul's Civic Center complex, the state capital complex, the Minnesota Arts and Science Center, and three downtown hospitals and major businesses, including corporate headquarters for Burlington Northern, Economics Laboratory, and the 127-year-old St. Paul Companies. The city's skyway system, a 2.6-mile, second-level walkway, provides climate-controlled access to many of these and

other downtown areas. Town Square serves as the hub of the skyway, with access on every side.

The site can be easily reached from the east and west on Interstate 94 and from the north on Interstate 35E. It is approximately a 15-minute drive from the Minneapolis/St. Paul International Airport. Most of the major bus lines run within a one-block radius of the project.

The two-block site has a grade variance of 10 feet from the northwest corner to the southeast corner. A former river bed, the site was composed of a stratified mixture of tumblerock and unstable deposits, sitting atop two layers of subsurface water. These poor soil conditions called for nearly $1 million in site improvements.

Project History

Before Town Square was developed, one block of the two-block site had stood empty for several years. Known as the "super hole," it had been cleared by the St. Paul Housing and Redevelopment Authority for development. However, when the developer defaulted, the city converted the block into interim parking. The second block was underused and consisted primarily of deteriorated and vacant buildings.

Working together, the city and Operation '85, a group of downtown civic and business leaders, came up with the idea of Town Square. The city, backed by a strong commitment from St. Paul's business and civic leaders to revitalize the downtown area, aggressively sought private developers to implement the Town Square concept together with the city. Town Square was to be the cornerstone in the development of an economically healthy retail/commercial district in the core area of St. Paul. Two factors were of paramount importance: first, the project would be meeting a need for additional first-class office space in the downtown area; second, it would be an essential element in the revitalization of downtown St. Paul's depressed retail section. Because of competition from suburban shopping centers, as well as the poor merchandise mix in St. Paul's existing retail market, the city's retail core had declined dramatically throughout the 1960s and into the first half of the 1970s. Between 1958 and 1976, the city's central business district had lost $55 million, or 41 percent of its retail dollar volume, and about 200 retail establishments.

Development Financing and Strategy

Town Square represents a large-scale public and private partnership and financial commitment. The major developer, Oxford Development Group Limited,

7-107 A 25,000-square-foot food court is located on the lower (concourse) level.

Planning and Architecture

Town Square was designed to be a lively "people place," providing a variety of facilities, goods, and services, and acting as a focus for downtown and the city's skyway system. The project consists of a two-block-long, three-level base structure, which is topped by the two office towers, the hotel, and an indoor city park. The base structure contains the project's retail space, public malls, and servicing and parking facilities. Designed to be compact, it creates a close interaction of public space and private developments as well as a vibrant pedestrian environment. The lower level of the base structure, referred to as the "concourse," consists of a below-grade, 25,000-square-foot, 16-tenant food court featuring abundant landscaping, a waterfall, and sitting areas. The second or street level of the base structure contains a variety of retail shops and gives pedestrians access to the project from all four streets. The third or skyway level of the base structure connects to the downtown skyway system and contains retail shops as well as entrances to the office tower lobbies, the hotel, and Donaldson's department store. The office tower lobbies can be entered only from the street and skyway levels in the mall area; they have no direct access from the street itself, except for delivery entrances.

The project's public spaces culminate in the glass-enclosed Town Square Park, which is the size of a football field and was designed to serve a wide cross section of needs year-round. The park that sits atop the base structure features flowering plants and trees (selected and arranged to resemble regions of the

spent $67.5 million to develop the two office towers and the retail space. The Carlson Corporation and several prominent St. Paul businessmen jointly developed the $15 million Radisson Plaza Hotel, with part of the money coming from an $8.6 million mortgage financing package provided by six St. Paul banks and savings and loans. The city of St. Paul was responsible for land acquisition, relocation and demolition, utility relocations, and street and sidewalk improvements, as well as for the development of the project's public spaces—for example, the enclosed public park and the skyway bridges and concourses. A $4.8 million Urban Development Action Grant (UDAG) provided part of the $12 million cost to the city. The city obtained the remaining public funds through tax increment financing. Finally, using revenue bonds, the St. Paul Port Authority financed the $5.5 million underground parking garage, which was purchased later by Oxford.

Because of the many parties involved in the development of Town Square, members of the development team had to work together as closely as possible. To assure the necessary coordination and cooperation, a contract was prepared clearly defining the responsibilities of the various parties and specifically outlining the project's general objectives and requirements. In addition, because the project's public space was to be closely integrated with its retail and office space, the city and Oxford agreed to build a portion of the project under a joint construction management agreement.

7-108 Escalators and an octagonal glass elevator provide access between the three levels of retail space and the garden level.

United States), colorful banners, a children's play area, a performing arts amphitheater, wooden slat park benches, waterfalls, streams, pools, and a 750-watt sound system. The design of the park prevents it from seeming like a vacuum when it is not in use, while providing it with ample flexibility for group activities of varying sizes. Planners achieved both intimacy and flexibility by designing areas of varying size and character and defining them with elements such as landscaping and a series of manmade mounds. In addition to their visual interest, the mounds create meandering pathways and bridges and offer views of the park from high vantage points. The mounds are hollow and various service functions (kitchen, storage, manager's office, dressing rooms, and restrooms) are contained inside.

Escalators and an octagonal glass elevator provide access between the garden level and the three levels of retail space below. All four levels appear both unified and spacious through the use of abundant greenery, extensive skylights, large openings between levels, and a fountain that flows from the garden level down to the concourse.

Engineering

The project uses considerably less energy than a complex its size generally requires. Heat pumps use well water from St. Paul's aquifer to heat and cool the complex. The aquifer has a constant temperature of 55 degrees; it is estimated that a 35 percent energy savings is realized by using this deep-well, heat-exchange system. The hotel also has two separate solar

7-110   Visual unity and spaciousness are achieved through the use of large openings between levels, extensive skylights, and a fountain flowing from the garden level to the concourse level.

collection systems that were financed by a $414,000 grant from the U.S. Department of Energy. A hydronic solar system, consisting of flat solar collectors mounted on a 4,400-square-foot structure facing south, heats the hotel's domestic water. An air-to-air solar system, consisting of 2,900 square feet of vertical flat-plate-glass collectors, is used for heating corridors and stairwells in winter and is channeled to other systems to help heat domestic water in summer.

Market

The primary market for the retail portion of Town Square is composed of downtown workers (approximately 65,000 adults), downtown residents, and households within a five-mile radius. Another part of the primary market is made up of hotel guests and conventioneers. The secondary market includes the St. Paul suburban areas within a 15-mile radius. The center also draws shoppers from a number of western Wisconsin communities.

The city of St. Paul proper has a population of about 275,000, which has stayed substantially the same over the past several years. The greater St. Paul metropolitan area (comprising five counties) has a population of 866,500 and has shown strong growth, particularly in the southeastern segment.

Tenants

The mix of retail tenants is planned to attract hotel patrons and downtown office workers, as well as suburban shoppers. The emphasis is on food service and

7-109   Awnings were added over exterior entrances to give color and warmth and to integrate the project with the downtown setting.

7-111   Colorful banners are used throughout the mall.

fashion tenants. The 116,256-square-foot Donaldson's department store and the food court serve as the anchors for the project's retail component. Most retail tenant spaces (excluding food-service tenant spaces) range in size from 1,000 to 1,500 square feet.

Experience Gained

- The private/public partnership places great demands on the partners. The public agency must have the financial and leadership abilities to match those of the private developers, and the private developers cannot ignore the idiosyncrasies of municipal budgeting, approvals, and legislation.
- All involved parties must devise a "game plan" defining the responsibilities and objectives of the development. This plan becomes vital when aspects of the development overlap and affect each other.
- Public and private developers, the general contractor, and the architect should meet frequently to discuss the project's progress.
- The success of an integrated, mixed-use project of the magnitude of Town Square depends on the full cooperation of the public sector as well as the surrounding business community. The project must receive a citywide commitment giving it priority. The business community must back the project and be kept informed of its impact, as well as of its progress, setbacks, and complications. The recommendations of the business community should be solicited at appropriate times.

- Once a project of this complexity is under construction, the city and interested developers should work to keep up the momentum by examining future spin-off projects and opportunities. The public sector must be geared to repeat such projects, regarding them as part of an ongoing process of public and private partnerships.
- The major difficulties for both the public and private developers of Town Square stemmed from delayed decisions. Decisions on parking and public space came late, causing some formidable planning problems. All decisions concerning major project elements should be made at the outset.
- The eventual impact of a successful, large-scale, mixed-use development can often be underestimated. It is important to be prepared for an increase in the investment potential of property in the vicinity of the project. If properly conceived and executed, a center such as Town Square may create as much additional demand for new development as it absorbs.
- Design is crucial in large-scale, mixed-use projects. Much of the ultimate success of such a project depends on the detailed attention paid to amenities and public space.
- Although the performance of the retail component of Town Square had been satisfactory, averaging sales volumes of just under $200 per square foot during the project's first four years of operation, a number of changes were recently made to improve this performance. They included: (1) allowing more flexible criteria for storefront design and tenant identification signage in order to increase the design appeal of storefronts; (2) adding awnings over exterior entrances to the project in order to provide color and warmth and to better integrate the project with the downtown setting; (3) increasing lighting levels within the retail mall; (4) improving signs to direct visitors and shoppers to the retail areas; (5) adding permanent retail space in "dead" areas, such as the skyways; (6) extending a corridor on the skyway level to improve pedestrian circulation and accessibility; (7) increasing the seating capacity of the food court (from 150 seats to 350 seats); and (8) changing the tenant mix to provide a greater emphasis on fashion tenants.
- Because retail tenants on the skyway level tend to outperform those on the street level, rents are higher for space on the skyway level.
- Originally, 80 percent of the tables in the food court seating area accommodated four or more

people and 20 percent seated two people. This proved unsatisfactory, since most food court patrons are not part of a larger group. While increasing the seating capacity, the seating area was revised to provide a greater proportion of tables for two people.

● Since there are no direct entrances from the street to the office towers (except for delivery entrances), office workers must enter the tower lobbies through the retail mall. Direct access to the office tower lobbies should have been provided from both the street and the retail mall.

7-112   Concourse Level

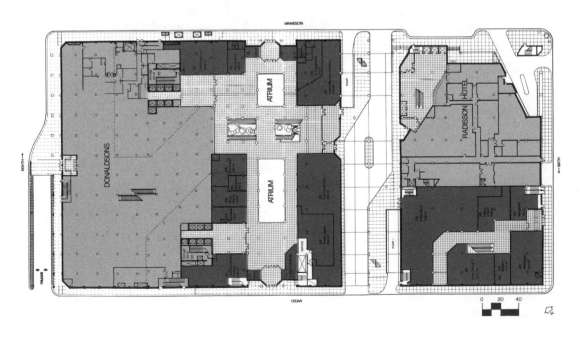

7-113   Street Level

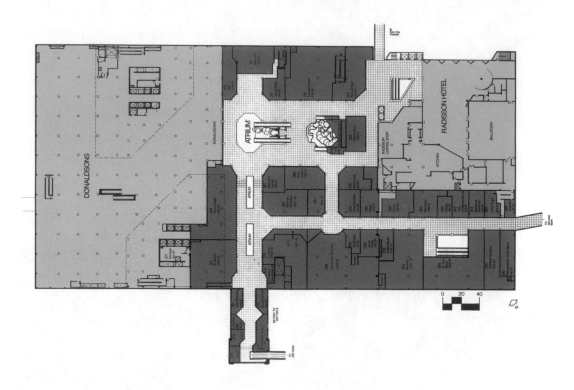

7-114   Skyway Level

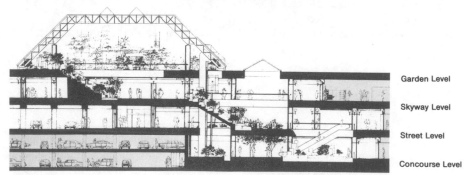

Garden Level

Skyway Level

Street Level

Concourse Level

7-115

7-116

PROJECT DATA—TOWN SQUARE

Land Use Information:
Site Area: 4.0 acres (1.62 hectares)
Gross Building Area (GBA in Square Feet):

Office	661,628
Retail	261,061
Hotel	210,000
Public Space (city)	89,342
Total	1,222,031

Gross Leasable Area (GLA in Square Feet):

Office	431,517
Retail	225,325
Total	656,842[1]

Floor Area Ratio (FAR):[2] 7.01
Parking Spaces: 500

Economic Information:
Total Project Cost:

Office and Retail Space	$ 67,500,000
Parking Garage	5,500,000
Hotel	15,000,000
Public Costs	12,000,000[3]
Total	$100,000,000

Lease Information:
Retail Sales: $190 per square foot[4]
Retail Rents: $25 per square foot[5]
Percentage Rents: 5 to 12 percent of gross sales[6]

Tenant Information:

Classification[7]	Number of Stores	Percent of Total Tenants	Square Feet of GLA	Percent of GLA	Percent of GLA in Regional Centers[7]
General Merchandise	—	—	—	—	14.1
Food	—	—		—	8.8
Food Service	16	22.5	25,115	23.0	7.0
Clothing	19	26.8	44,322	40.6	24.9
Shoes	5	7.0	7,124	6.5	6.8
Home Furnishings	—	—	—	—	1.8
Home Appliances/Music	—	—	—	—	2.9
Building Materials/Garden	—	—	—	—	1.6
Automotive Supplies/Service Station	—	—	—	—	1.0
Hobby/Special Interest	—	—	—	—	3.8
Gifts/Specialty	12	17.0	14,815	13.6	5.2
Jewelry and Cosmetics	4	5.6	2,318	2.1	2.8
Liquor	—	—	—	—	.4
Drugs	—	—	—	—	3.7
Other Retail	6	8.5	7,806	7.2	4.1
Personal Services	2	2.8	1,803	1.7	2.3
Recreation/Community	—	—	—	—	3.8
Financial	2	2.8	3,952	3.6	3.0
Offices (other than financial)	—	—	—	—	2.1
Other (vacancies)	5	7.0	1,814	1.7	—
Total	71	100.0	109,069[8]	100.0	100.0

Notes:

[1] GLA including 116,256-square-foot Donaldson's department store.

[2] FAR = GBA divided by total site area.

[3] Includes costs for land acquisition, relocation, and demolition, utility relocations, street and sidewalk improvements, skyway bridges and concourses, and public malls and park.

[4] Sales as of December 1983. The average volume for 1985 is expected to be $225 per square foot.

[5] Average minimum rent. Rents for small spaces are as high as $100 per square foot. Rent escalation is $2 per year over the next five years.

[6] Most tenants pay percentage rents of 7 to 8 percent of gross sales.

[7] *Dollars & Cents of Shopping Centers: 1984* (Washington, D.C.: ULI–the Urban Land Institute, 1984), p. 271.

[8] Total GLA excluding Donaldson's department store.

Developers:

Retail and Office:

Oxford Development Group Limited
400 Baker Building
Minneapolis, Minnesota 55402

Joint Venture/Carlson Companies
12755 Highway 55
Minneapolis, Minnesota 55441

Park/Public Space:

City of St. Paul
Department of Planning and Economic Development
25 West Fourth Street
St. Paul, Minnesota 55102

Architecture:

Retail, Office, and Park:

Skidmore, Owings & Merrill
Great West Plaza Tower I
1675 Broadway, Suite 400
Denver, Colorado 80202

Hotel:

BWBR Architects
400 Sibley Street
St. Paul, Minnesota 55101

Retail:

Windsor Faricy
28 West Fifth Street
Suite 375
St. Paul, Minnesota 55102

8.
Future Trends

The future of shopping centers will depend on the ability of centers to respond to consumer demand. The shopping center concept has been evolving ever since the first centers were built immediately following World War II. It is now a mature and distinctive land use and development concept, perhaps the most successful ever conceived.

The first edition of the Urban Land Institute's *Shopping Center Development Handbook,* published in 1977, identified the critical factors that would affect the future trends of shopping centers. To a great degree, those same factors—demographic and social changes, the economic environment, public policy, energy needs, and the availability of financing—will continue to determine the future of shopping centers.

In describing the trends expected, the first edition of the *Shopping Center Development Handbook* focused on three areas: renovation and expansion, the size and type of new types of shopping centers, and the movement toward new downtown shopping centers. To a larger extent, the perceived trends have materialized. Certainly the pace of rehabilitation and revitalization has grown dramatically. While new downtown retailing could be cited in only a few examples when the first edition was published, the list of downtown projects had grown to more than 100 by the beginning of 1984. The development of larger regional and super regional shopping centers has predictably slowed, as has the development of smaller regional centers in middle-sized markets.

However, predicting the future of a dynamic and volatile industry like shopping centers is difficult. The current pattern of segmentation into specialized shopping center types was not clearly foreseen. Likewise, some of the current challenges to traditional retailing, the boom in catalog sales, and the advent of electronic retailing concepts, were scarcely identified. Although these trends had begun to appear, the pace at which they would proceed was not anticipated. The shopping center industry has matured.

That is, the basic concepts of the shopping center are widely understood, and the foreseeable future can anticipate the refinement of shopping centers, including greater individualization of types and the integration of the shopping center with other land use activities.

The shopping center is no longer merely a physical place where retail sales occur. It has become an integral part of the social structure of most communities and will continue to expand in that role in the future. The interdependence of underlying and continually changing economic and social forces will be highly influential in shaping the future of shopping centers.

The industry has clearly demonstrated its ability to adapt to rapidly changing circumstances over the last 10 years and will undoubtedly continue to show this aptitude in the future. The shopping center has become an important part of the American lifestyle. There is little reason to expect that this will change.

Forces at Work

Demographic Changes

The United States appears to be heading toward zero population growth. The U.S. Census Bureau currently

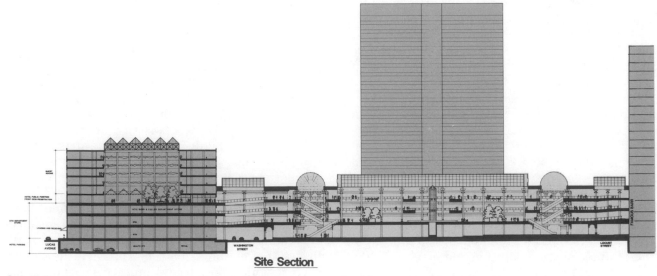

Site Section

8-1, 8-2   St. Louis Centre, St. Louis, Missouri, represents one example of the many new downtown shopping centers developed in recent years. A four-level, 330,000-square-foot (GLA) mall links two existing department stores.

predicts that population will peak at 309 million in the year 2050. Figure 8-3 illustrates both the growth in population during the past three decades and the expected growth during the 1980s. It also shows the rate of growth in percentages.[1] The projected growth rate for the 1980s is less than 1 percent.

For shopping centers the amount of growth is important because it determines the total demand for retail facilities. Shifts in the age structure of the population also affect this demand. The changing location of the U.S. population creates demand in new areas while reducing demand in others. Perhaps the most dramatic trend has been the population shift from the Northeast to the West and South. The other trend that suggests new opportunities for shopping center development has been the shift in population from major urban areas to rural areas.

Age Structure

The next decade will see the following patterns of age distribution:[2]

- The number of young adults between the ages of 25 and 34 will increase by approximately 6 million as the baby boom generation moves out of its early 20s into its late 20s and early 30s. This is the most mobile age group and will represent a strong force in creating housing demand and thus demand for new neighborhood and community retail centers in particular.

- The number of adults between the ages of 35 and 44 will increase by 12 million, almost five times the growth rate of this group in the 1970s. The retail market will feel the effects of this bulge in the middle-aged group. The design and merchandising of shopping centers will also have to reflect changing consumer preferences of a maturing population, which will be generally affluent and at the peak of its earning powers. The growth in the number of female professionals and dual career families will create new demand characteristics.

- The number of empty nesters, ranging in age from 45 to 54, actually decreased between 1970 and 1980 and is expected to increase by only about 2.5 million during the next decade. Since this group is no longer encumbered with the financial responsibilities of rearing a family, it has greater discretionary income and therefore will support the higher end of retailing and quality food service.

- New and preretirees, ages 54 to 64, will shrink in number during the 1980s by about 3 percent as the generation born during the Depression nears

8-3 DECLINING POPULATION GROWTH IN RECENT DECADES

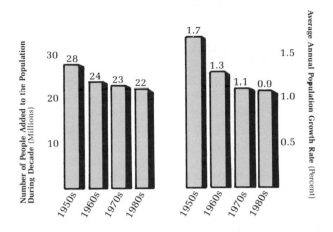

Sources: U.S. Bureau of the Census. *State and Metropolitan Data Book, 1982; Projections of the Population of the United States: 1982 to 2050 (Advance Report)*, Current Population Reports series P-25, No. 922.

retirement age. Also, the fact that retirement at age 65 is no longer the custom as it was in the past has affected the size of the retirement population. Supported by the law, a healthier older population so choosing may work beyond age 65.

- The retired and elderly population, age 65 and over, is increasing as a group more rapidly than the population as a whole. In the 1980s, the elderly population is expected to grow by about 25 percent or 6.3 million persons so that by 1990, 12.7 percent of the population will be in this age group, as compared to 11.3 percent in 1980. The characteristics of the elderly population will change. An increasingly large share of this population group will be female. Many more of the elderly will be better educated than their predecessors. They will be healthier, more active, and more independent. The percent of older people living in the suburbs will rise, even though they will continue to be underrepresented in the suburbs and overrepresented in nonmetropolitan areas. Fewer of this older group will wish to depend on the family unit, and will therefore seek to maintain fully independent and active lives. They will probably spend more of their time outside the home and will be looking for the community structure and retail facilities that meet their needs. They will have more discretionary in-

[1] See Urban Land Institute, *Development Review and Outlook 1983–1984* (Washington, D.C.: ULI–the Urban Land Institute, 1983), pp. 387–390. Data from U.S. Bureau of the Census, "Projections of the Population of the United States: 1982 to 2050" (Advance Report), Current Population Reports Series P-25, No. 922.

[2] Ibid., p. 387.

come: between 1970 and 1980, the average income for householders over 65 grew 25 percent faster than that for all U.S. households. Thus, the elderly will represent a powerful force in generating demand for shopping centers.

The shopping center industry will need to consider these factors carefully. During the baby boom, the post–high school group between the ages of 18 and 24 had a significant influence on the design and growth of shopping centers. However, this age group will be greatly eroded in the 1980s as the baby bust generation replaces the baby boom generation. Consequently, retail facilities such as fast food restaurants and youth-oriented clothing chains will be affected. The middle aging of the baby boom and the maturing of their parent groups will create new challenges for retailing that will be reflected in shopping centers.

Population Distribution

In the past, the mobility of the population has been a strong factor in propelling demand for new shopping centers. The pace at which Americans change their place of residence is slowing. This decline in mobility has a variety of probable causes, including the rise of the two-jobholder family (making moving more complicated), the rising cost of housing, the continued increase in homeownership (reducing mobility), and a pattern of overhousing in the purchase of the first home (reducing the need to move when a couple has children). The tendency of householders to stay in place and renovate existing housing to meet their changing needs will ensure a more stable long-term market for a retail facility. In the past, older neighborhoods tended to decline as people aged, causing an erosion of the retail markets. Today, more younger families or first-time buyers are purchasing and improving existing housing in older neighborhoods. This change in neighborhood demographics has created a demand for the renovation and expansion of shopping centers serving such revitalizing markets.

While overall population growth in the 1980s will reach new lows, some areas of the United States will continue to grow rapidly, creating an increased demand for new retail facilities. Other areas will experience essentially no population growth; still others will witness a net out-migration. The majority of the growth in the early 1980s was concentrated in three Sunbelt states—California, Texas, and Florida. In addition, several states that have relatively small and scattered populations are experiencing rapid percentage growth—Nevada, Alaska, Wyoming, Utah, Colorado, and Arizona. This growth pattern in the Sunbelt is expected to continue—as well as catch-up growth in some of the more desirable underpopulated

states—while the population in the Snowbelt and the mature Northeast will remain stable or decline.

Rural Urbanization

It is axiomatic that demand for new retail facilities is related to population growth. Thus, new shopping centers will tend to be concentrated in the high-growth Sunbelt areas: however, intraregional population movements will create new demand for shopping centers throughout the country. The most significant and unanticipated population trend that appeared in the 1970s and that may continue through the 1980s has been the deconcentration of population. The 1980 census showed a net migration into small towns and rural areas from the urban areas throughout the United States. Growth rates in suburbs, in small cities, in rural areas, and in less densely settled states and regions are likely to exceed the U.S. growth rate during the next decade. This movement began in the 1970s despite rising energy costs, which were thought to be a deterrent to deconcentration of the population. How strong the trend will be is uncertain. U.S. Census Bureau estimates in 1983 and 1984 suggest that the hitherto declining population in northeastern central cities is stabilizing, while closer-in suburbs are seeing increased growth, and suburbs farther out, as well as nonmetropolitan areas, are experiencing a slowdown in growth.

Conclusions—Demographic Changes

The following conclusions may be made regarding population distribution during the 1980s:

- Small cities will grow faster than average. There will be some exceptions, particularly in Sunbelt areas, but large cities will either experience slow growth or show losses in population and decreased density.
- Suburbs will continue to capture the major share of population growth throughout the 1980s and will outpace both central cities and rural areas. However, as it matures, the inner ring of suburbs of larger older cities may lose population.
- Nonmetropolitan area growth represents a new force in U.S. population distribution that will provide opportunities for additional retail facilities. Recent data, however, suggest a moderation in this trend.
- Migration to the Sunbelt will continue, resulting in greater opportunities in these areas for new development.

Social Changes

A variety of changes in American lifestyles have been noticeably occurring over the last half of the 1970s and will continue to represent the trend through the 1980s and beyond.

"Traditional" Families

At the beginning of the 1980s, about six out of every 10 households were composed of a married couple with or without children—a household composition that has historically been accepted as "traditional." Although it still makes up the largest category of households, the traditional household has been growing more slowly in number than all other household categories. While the number of families with one or two children at home is growing, those with three or more declined by 39 percent between 1970 and 1981. The four-person household will probably be the fastest growing household category during the 1980s as baby boom families have their second children. This is in contrast to the 1970s, when the fastest growing segment of the traditional household involved families without children.

However, the "traditional" family itself is changing. In the past, the structure of the traditional family has been husband as breadwinner, wife as homemaker, and children. If current trends continue, the traditional family of the 1980s will have two working parents (if not full-time, at least part-time), many of whom will be college-educated professionals. The young children of this new family will be more independent, and will likely attend preschools or day schools. The family will have a greater propensity to eat out, to eat prepared foods, and to require a more varied wardrobe. A greater percentage of personal services and entertainment activities, previously provided within the home, will be obtained from outside the home.

Single-Person Households

In 1970, 18 percent of all households comprised one person. By 1980, this figure had grown to 23 percent. Single-person households are the fastest growing segment of the housing market: four out of every 10 new households fall into this category. A forecast by Data Resources, Inc., based on an assumption of moderate economic growth, predicts that the number of single-person households will increase 19 percent from 1980 to 1985 and another 16 percent from 1985 to 1990.[3] By the end of 1985, 8.6 million elderly persons will be living alone, representing almost 40 percent of single-person households.

The rapid formation of single-person households suggests a variety of probable trends that will occur in the retail industry to support this pattern. Persons living alone tend to eat out more, travel more, spend more on personal services, make clothing purchases at the higher end of their income bracket, and spend more time outside the home. Shopping centers designed to serve this segment of the population will have to reflect all of these characteristics.

Families with One Parent

One-parent households represent a rapidly growing household category, the result primarily of rising divorce rates and children born to unmarried parents. The number of single-parent families grew from 6.7 million in 1970 to 11.4 million in 1982. While the rate of growth will slow, the absolute number of single-parent households will increase as the baby boom households age and as marriages fail. Typically, these households have below-average incomes. At the same time, they will have greater need of support from the community and from retail structures to provide services to meet their needs. The ability of shopping centers to provide these goods and services at affordable costs will be important.

Asian and Hispanic Population

Recent immigration and higher birth rates have resulted in dramatic increases in the Asian and Hispanic population in certain regions of the United States. For example, California's minority population will constitute over 50 percent of the state's population by the year 2000. For a variety of reasons, these population groups tend to be concentrated. They have special social characteristics and needs to which the shopping center industry has not responded directly; accommodating these needs presents a real and significant opportunity in the 1980s.

General Social Changes

Within the context of the various categories of household groups previously discussed, shopping centers in the 1980s and beyond obviously need to respond to the retailing and other community service needs of the changing lifestyles of households. A greater percentage of women in the workforce will of necessity cause shifts in shopping habits. More shopping will be done in the evenings, at noontime, on weekends, or at locations near work. The previous role women played as the dominant shoppers will likely change as parents reassign responsibilities for shopping to other members of the household.

The characteristics of the new households will also affect the demand for types of consumer goods and

---

[3] "Single Person Households by Age and Income: 1980–1995," *American Demographics*, April 1983, pp. 50–51.

services. The strong demand for restaurant and out-of-home entertainment will continue, just as will (most likely) the current enthusiasm for physical fitness and sports/recreational activities, even among the elderly.

Conclusions—Social Changes

All of the current or emerging social changes would appear to benefit the long-term vitality of shopping centers. The one exception may be the limited buying power among a rising number of families with one parent and perhaps among growing ethnic subgroups. What will be important for shopping center owners, developers, and managers to understand is the changing characteristics of the population within the service area of the particular retail facility. These characteristics will modify the tenant mix, center design, hours of operation, and other factors in order to maximize the value of the shopping center.

Economic Environment

Changes in the economy over the next decade are hard to predict. Although many suggestions are contradictory, none predict significant economic decline. The last decade has seen dramatic changes in interest rates affecting the real estate development sector of the economy. Shopping centers have fared as well as, and frequently better than, most other development types. While the superior performance of a shopping center depends directly on increasing sales per square foot, the basic financial structure of a center has been well conceived to avoid unprofitable operations. Obviously, however, excessive business failures among tenants will interrupt the flow of base rent income. Most operating expenses affected by inflation are passed on to tenants, and percentage rents assure the center of a proportioned share of inflation-driven sales.

In addition, shopping centers in general and regional shopping centers in particular benefit directly from growth in the gross national product. Such economic growth frees discretionary dollars, which can then be spent on the department store type of merchandise offered by regional centers.

Perhaps affecting individual centers even more than the general national economy will be the local economy. Some of the demographic and social changes discussed earlier may have significant economic implications for certain geographic areas of the country and individual market areas. Shopping center developers and managers will need to be more attuned during the 1980s to the "micro" characteristics of the local economy.

Raw land for a new suburban center may be relatively cheap compared with downtown land. However, after a shopping center has been developed on it, the site increases in value, as does the surrounding land. The land values of well-located shopping centers, particularly those of regional scale, will continue to increase over time. And the increased value will tend to encourage more intense use of the land.

Public Policy

During the 1970s, environmental controls were enacted, causing significant problems for shopping centers. However, today the need for certain environmental regulations is more universally understood, and shopping centers have, for the most part, adjusted to and accommodated them. Evidence suggests that these regulations will become no more stringent over the next decade, and some evidence suggests they will become more moderate.

Land Use Policy

The Carter administration endeavored to introduce a federal presence into communities making decisions concerning the location of new shopping centers. Rescinded at the beginning of the Reagan administration, this policy, which sought to deal with the competition between suburban shopping centers and downtown revitalization efforts, was unacceptable to a conservative administration. Nevertheless, the competition for retail dollars between new centers and existing retail areas (whether they be the downtowns of smaller cities or retail areas of suburbia other than shopping centers) will continue to be a local public policy issue in the 1980s. Fortunately, the attitude of shopping center developers toward the suitability of downtown sites for new retail facilities has changed significantly. Further, public support of such downtown projects is easier to obtain, thus making the cost of approvals significantly less than for a raw land site. Based on demographic and population distribution trends, the 1980s will undoubtedly see competitive proposals for retail development with which local public policies will intervene. In general, the weight of increased public regulation of all land uses has not fallen any more heavily on shopping centers than it has on other land uses.

However, there does appear to be a general public attitude that suburban activity centers, which frequently include a shopping center as the focus, need more thoughtful structuring. Such structuring, or rather restructuring, would intensify land use and introduce modes of transportation other than the automobile both to and within such activity areas. In other words, the public is anticipating that these low-density, automobile-oriented suburban activity areas (which include shopping centers, offices, higher-density residential uses, hotels, and other such uses) will evolve into urban centers almost or as complex as urban downtowns. It is reasonable to expect that public policy will seek to influence and shape this emerging land use trend. In relationship to this trend, shopping center development will encourage mixing of uses, alternatives to the automobile, and integrated vertical land use in mixed-use projects rather than disconnected horizontal multiuse projects. Achieving this will depend on the market support for such concepts. In the final analysis, rising land values and perceived economic returns from improvements will govern what will happen.

Taxation Policy

Taxation policy as it relates to real estate is uncertain. Observers in this field foresee a period of continuing tax policy changes that generally will be unfavorable to real estate. The ability of the real estate industry to communicate to the government the need for a favorable tax policy to support appropriate real estate development will be important to the shopping center industry. However, any tax changes that are made will probably be no more or less advantageous or disadvantageous to the shopping center industry than to any other segment of the development industry.

Energy

The first edition of the *Shopping Center Development Handbook* was written when the country was just coming out of the "energy crisis" resulting from the export embargo imposed by oil-producing countries in the Middle East. A quote from that edition nevertheless appears still to be valid: "Even if a curtailment in the supply of gasoline were to be introduced, reduction in automobile usage for other activities such as recreation, commuting, etc., will more likely occur before there is any significant reduction in shopping trips."[4]

Since 1977, however, because the supply of domestic fuel has increased and overall consumption has decreased (due to fuel conservation and economies in transportation), the country is less dependent on foreign oil. For the automobile industry, this has meant a recent shift in consumer attitudes. Consumers are inclined once more toward the purchase of larger, more convenient vehicles; they are no longer as preoccupied with maximum efficiency and minimum fuel consumption. And for shopping centers, this shift in

attitude means that small cars are less likely to dominate a center's parking facility. Thus, the preferred size of parking spaces in the future is indeterminate. Prognosticators continue to feel that a potential exists for shortages and rising fuel costs. The availability and cost of energy will obviously remain a concern in considering the development or management of shopping centers.

The three-year periods covered by the 1978, 1981, and 1984 *Dollars & Cents of Shopping Centers* provide ample evidence that both existing and new shopping centers are paying careful attention to ensuring or improving energy efficiency.[5] Both the 1978 and 1981 studies presented special data collected on actions being taken by shopping centers to recover rising energy costs and/or to modify center design and operations to reduce energy consumption. By 1982/1983, the Urban Land Institute's steering committee for *Dollars & Cents of Shopping Centers* had concluded that for the most part existing centers had been retrofitted and that developers of new centers were demonstrating through their projects a high awareness of energy costs. Therefore, the portion of the study dealing with energy was deleted from *Dollars & Cents of Shopping Centers: 1984*.

Financing Trends

In general, shopping centers will continue to be viewed as desirable investments. They provide not only diversification of risk, but also a high probability of mortgage amortization from continued income flow through lease devices that protect against inflation and pass-through increases in operating expenses and taxes. To predict how shopping centers will be financed during the next decade is to foretell a wide array of diverse financing packages. The changing financial environment has significantly altered old methods of financing. Developers are issuing bonds to take advantage of the extensive investment sales networks in the securities industry. Larger developers are considering the acquisition or creation of financial institutions. Interest rate volatility is tending to produce shorter loan maturities and a decline in long-term funds. As a result, some shopping center

---

[4] See Urban Land Institute, *Shopping Center Development Handbook* (Washington, D.C.: ULI–the Urban Land Institute, 1977), p. 254. Also see International Council of Shopping Centers, *Shopping Centers: The Next 15 Years* (New York: ICSC, 1975), p. 84; this publication was based on a conference for industry leaders conducted by ICSC in 1975.

[5] Urban Land Institute, *Dollars & Cents of Shopping Centers* (Washington, D.C.: ULI–the Urban Land Institute; 1984, pp. 320, 321; 1981, pp. 290, 293; 1978, pp. 260–263).

8-4 Originally opened in 1959, Lenox Square in Atlanta continues to undergo renovation and expansion. Shown here is Plaza Court, a dramatic three-level atrium added in 1981.

Future Development

The influences that will guide future shopping center development have already manifested themselves in current practice. Greater emphasis will be placed on maintaining the vitality and market of existing centers. As population growth slows, the demand for new large centers will decline, except where rapid growth is continuing in the Sunbelt areas of the country. An increasing number of smaller cities and the urbanization of the countryside will create demands for shopping centers to support this population redistribution and growth. Because of the changing demography of older suburban communities, many existing centers will have to be renovated and expanded. The rapid growth of office development in the core of many major cities has set the stage for the introduction of new retail facilities in downtowns. Having succeeded in urban areas, mixed-use development will likely be used more extensively in suburban activity nodes. As the shopping center industry matures, it will grow more adept at identifying and responding to demographic and social lifestyle changes with shopping center types tailored to meet the needs of a specific market.

Renovation, Revitalization, and Expansion

Having started in the 1950s, many of the earliest shopping centers, now at the age of 25 or 30, are in need of renovation, revitalization, and/or expansion. Even centers built in the late 1960s, when shopping center development was booming, are almost 15 years old. Two factors encourage rethinking an existing shopping center. One is a center's physical obsolescence. Even if it is well maintained, a 25-year-old center no longer presents itself as a contemporary retailing facility. Building design preferences and merchandising techniques have changed dramatically in the last 25 years. For example, the need for rent increases requires greater productivity from retailers. This can lead to downsizing of stores and therefore to conducting higher volumes of business within less space. Other principal reasons for revitalization are new market opportunities, the need to maintain a competitive advantage, and obsolete tenants whose leases are up for renewal.

No reliable monitoring system exists to measure the amount of renovation and expansion activity that is taking place. Trade magazines provide informative but incomplete reports. *Shopping Center World* conducted an analysis that indicated that 128 centers containing over 27 million square feet of GLA were

developers are using extended construction loans as the sole initial financing arrangement, with no permanent takeout commitment in place. Higher interest rates also make equity financing more important. Interest rates over 20 percent are a memory from the 1970s that should not be allowed to fade. Although public policy will seek to prevent their recurrence, uncertainties in the economy are themselves factors that will affect rates.

Finally, government programs, such as industrial development bonds (IDBs) (which have recently been constrained) and Urban Development Action Grants (UDAGs) or similar government financing vehicles offering lower interest rates, are being used to help finance new shopping centers. Syndication is also emerging as an increasingly strong financing vehicle.

All evidence implies that shopping centers will continue to be an attractive investment. For example, regional shopping centers, because of territorial control by department store anchors, afford more protection against competition than other types of real estate investments. Financing in the 1980s will be more diverse, more complex, and more creative than in the 1970s in order for development to proceed. Owners/developers have sold existing shopping centers to large financial institutions, to retirement funds, to organizations raising capital through the securities markets, and to foreign entities. New types of property management organizations are managing these centers. Such trends will more than likely be ongoing.

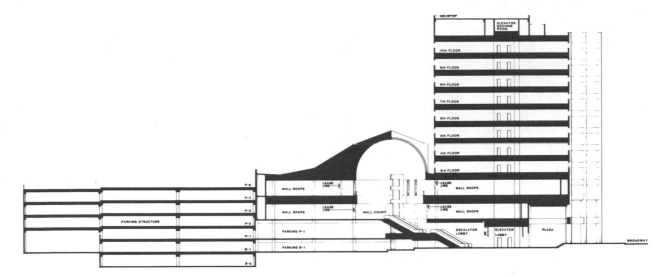

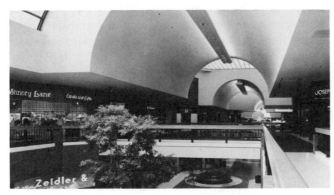

8-5, 8-6 Glendale Galleria, a two-level regional center built on 28 acres in downtown Glendale, California. The project contains 856,000 square feet of gross leasable area.

renovated/expanded in 1981, and 107 centers containing over 15.1 million square feet of GLA were renovated/expanded in 1982.[6] To understand the potential magnitude of this type of development, one must realize that approximately 13,000 centers are presently 15 or more years old and are therefore prime candidates for renovation, revitalization, or expansion. Even younger centers are being expanded when evidence shows that the market in which they are located will support additional mall shops and/or anchor tenants.

Downtown Retailing

Clearly the 1980s have already set a trend toward downtown retail growth. A 1983 study conducted by the Urban Land Institute identified over 100 downtown retail projects.[7] While these types of projects are highly visible and have significantly affected city revitalization, the absolute number of such centers that can be developed in any form is limited by the number of opportunities available. A simple tabula-

tion of these opportunities indicates that the number of new retail projects developing downtown will not be that great.[8]

Experience gained from early examples of downtown retailing has been valuable in defining, shaping, and executing subsequent downtown retail projects. Some of the earliest projects merely inserted a subur-

---

[6] Urban Land Institute, *Development Review and Outlook 1983–1984*, pp. 18–19, Figure 1-6. These numbers do not represent accurate totals for the United States. They are only the activity as reported in *Shopping Center World* and are therefore incomplete. However, no other more reliable source is available to assess the magnitude of expansion and renovation activity.

[7] J. Thomas Black, Libby Howland, and Stuart L. Rogel, *Downtown Retail Development: Conditions for Success and Project Profiles* (Washington, D.C.: ULI–the Urban Land Institute, 1983).

[8] Frank H. Spink, Jr., "Downtown Malls: Prospects, Design, Constraints," *Shopping Centers U.S.A.* (New Brunswick, New Jersey: Rutgers University, Center for Urban Policy Research, 1981).

8-7 Broadway Plaza, Los Angeles. Mixed-use developments that include significant retail components will represent a continuing trend in the 1980s and beyond.

ban shopping mall of one or more levels into the downtown fabric. Developers of recent projects are carefully shaping retail facilities, incorporating new construction with adaptive use of existing buildings as well as tying together existing anchor tenants through the use of carefully conceived mall elements. Two prominent examples of these approaches are The Grand Avenue in Milwaukee and Horton Plaza in San Diego.[9] Each center has its own special character, contributing to its success as a downtown retail project. No formula for success exists for developments such as these; to serve both as viable retail facilities and as elements in successful downtown revitalization, such projects will require the most sophisticated development skills.

Mixed-Use Development

Mixed-use developments that include a significant retail component represent a trend that will continue throughout the 1980s and beyond. Many downtown retail projects will likely be developed as part of a mixed-use development rather than as independent single-purpose retail facilities. Also, the same factors that are encouraging revitalization and expansion of existing suburban shopping centers will most likely encourage the conversion of many existing centers into mixed-use developments to which other income-producing uses are added during the process of renovating or expanding a shopping center. Further, the trend toward greater intensity of development in suburban activity nodes will encourage the creation of mixed-use and/or multiuse development in which retailing is only one component.

8-8   The trend toward segmentation and specialization of shopping centers has been rapidly evolving over the last 10 years and is expected to continue into the future. For example, the emergence of new anchor tenants (such as the home improvement store) has resulted in new special forms of community shopping centers.

Segmentation of Center Types

Perhaps the most significant trend that will continue into the 1980s will be the specialization of shopping facilities in order to serve more discretely defined market segments. Although obviously every shopping center will not become a special type, the trend toward segmentation has been rapidly evolving over the last 10 years and will continue into the future. As the shopping center industry has matured, it has become possible to shape the character of the tenants in a shopping center to meet more precisely the specific needs of prospective consumers. The earliest specialty centers had no anchor tenants; in fact, for some time, this trait defined a specialty center. However, the high-end fashion center represented the first clear strategy on the part of larger centers to target market segments. The festival mall, geared toward specialty food, food services, and tourists, was also a strategically developed concept. The off-price and outlet malls now being developed are seen by many as a whole new type of shopping center and by others as a temporary accommodation for tenants that are threatening to conventional retailers now but will likely be welcome later in more traditional centers. Only recently has specialization in community and neighborhood shopping centers begun to be recognized in the industry. Segmentation will represent a powerful concept when applied to revitalization and renovation activity: identifying an appropriate segment could be key to the successful execution of a renovation or expansion.

Challenges

Some striking changes in American family structure and lifestyles have affected and will continue to affect the shopping center industry, but to what extent is undetermined. One of the major events of the late 1970s and early 1980s has been the rapid expansion of catalog retailing. A shopper can buy almost any kind of goods through mail order catalogs without going to a shopping center. Another of the more challenging issues facing the shopping center industry in the 1980s will be electronic retailing and the impact it might have on more conventional shopping center development.[10] Conventional shopping centers will

[9] For further information on these projects, see Urban Land Institute, *Downtown Retail Development: Conditions for Success and Project Profiles.*

[10] William A. Gordon, "Electronic Retailing Trends and Implications," *Development Review and Outlook 1984–1985* (Washington, D.C.: ULI–the Urban Land Institute, 1984). Also see *Urban Land,* October 1984.

8-9　The Pavilion Outlet Center, Seattle. One of the most noted retail development phenomena of the 1980s has been the advent of off-price and outlet centers.

be challenged by electronic retailing's capacity to create computer networks that can not only identify available merchandise but can also offer quality specifications, comparative pricing, access to diversely located inventory, product customization, and other yet unthought of consumer advantages. This does not imply that electronic retailing will replace conventional retailing; it is a new form that must be understood and accommodated as it evolves. As a point of comparison, when the idea of teleconferencing was first introduced, many practitioners felt it would have

a significant impact on meeting activities and face-to-face exchanges. While teleconferencing is still in its infancy, it clearly will represent a new form of meeting and not necessarily a replacement for other existing meeting and conferencing activities. Many believe that it will simply increase the number of meetings and conferences that can occur cost effectively. Analysis of electronic retailing may reach a similar conclusion.

Retailing in general seems to be headed toward some rather dramatic restructuring in terms of traditional manufacturer/wholesaler/retailer/consumer relationships. Examples already exist of both manufacturers and distributors who have become retailers. Certainly one manifestation has been the growth in off-price retailing, a new type of discounting, which has in turn led to a new type of shopping center. Should such a restructuring take place, it will have a significant impact on how shopping centers are developed, organized, and managed.

Conclusions

The shopping center is a mature land use and real estate form, which the public has widely accepted as the best means of providing retailing to communities. The shopping center has evolved from a simple concept into a full community activity center, including not only retailing but also entertainment, services, and community facilities. Further, it is rapidly evolving into a component in a mixed-use development that integrates retailing and other land uses into an urban complex—even when set in suburban and exurban locations. Overall growth of the industry will slow as population growth slows. Fortunately, the industry has developed the sophistication both to understand and to respond to ever-changing demographic characteristics and lifestyles.

APPENDICES
AND
INDEX

APPENDIX A

Selected References

Books

Applebaum, William. *Shopping Center Strategy: A Case Study of the Planning, Location, and Development of the Del Monte Center, Monterey, California.* New York: International Council of Shopping Centers, 1978.

Dawson, John A. *Shopping Centers: A Bibliography.* CPL Bibliography #89. Chicago: Council of Planning Librarians (CPL), 1982.

Flynn, Robert J., ed. *Carpenter's Shopping Center Management: Principles and Practices.* 3d ed. New York: International Council of Shopping Centers, 1984.

Garrett, Robert L.; Hogan, Hunter A., Jr.; and Stratton, Robert M. *The Valuation of Shopping Centers.* Chicago: American Institute of Real Estate Appraisers, 1976.

Gruen, Victor, and Smith, Larry. *Centers for the Urban Environment: Survival of the Cities.* New York: Van Nostrand Reinhold, 1973.

Institute of Real Estate Management. *Managing the Shopping Center.* Chicago: IREM, 1983.

International Council of Shopping Centers. *Shopping Centers, 1988: Answers for the Next Decade.* New York: ICSC, 1979.

———. *Shopping Centers: The Next 15 Years.* New York: ICSC, 1975.

Levin, Michael S. *Measuring the Fiscal Impact of a Shopping Center on Its Community.* New York: International Council of Shopping Centers, 1975.

Lion, Edgar. *Shopping Centers: Planning, Development and Administration.* New York: John Wiley & Sons, 1976.

McKeever, J. Ross. *Shopping Center Zoning.* Technical Bulletin 69. Washington, D.C.: ULI–the Urban Land Institute, 1973.

Rams, Edwin M., ed. *Analysis and Valuation of Retail Location.* Reston, Virginia: Reston Publishing Company, 1976.

Real Estate Research Corporation. *Lessons for States and Cities: Implications for Public/Private Partnerships in Shopping Center Revitalization.* Chicago: RERC, 1982.

Redstone, Louis G. *New Dimensions in Shopping Centers and Stores.* New York: McGraw-Hill, 1973.

———. *The New Downtowns: Rebuilding Business Districts.* New York: McGraw-Hill, 1976.

Roca, Ruben A. *Market Research for Shopping Centers.* New York: International Council of Shopping Centers, 1980.

Sternlieb, George, and Hughes, James W., eds. *Shopping Centers: U.S.A.* New Brunswick, New Jersey: Rutgers University, Center for Urban Policy Research, 1981.

Touche Ross & Co. *Depreciable Lives of Shopping Centers.* New York: International Council of Shopping Centers, 1973.

Urban Land Institute. *Development Review and Outlook 1983–1984.* Washington, D.C.: ULI–the Urban Land Institute, 1983.

———. *Development Review and Outlook, 1984–1985.* Washington, D.C.: ULI–the Urban Land Institute, 1984.

———. *Parking Requirements for Shopping Centers: Summary Recommendations and Research Study Report.* Washington, D.C.: ULI–the Urban Land Institute, 1982.

———. *Standard Manual of Accounting for Shopping Center Operations.* Washington, D.C.: ULI–the Urban Land Institute, 1971.

Wenner, S. Albert. *Promotion and Marketing for Shopping Centers.* New York: International Council of Shopping Centers, 1980.

Periodicals

The Appraisal Journal (quarterly). American Institute of Real Estate Appraisers, 430 North Michigan Avenue, Chicago, Illinois 60611.

Chain Store Age Executive (monthly). Lebhar-Friedman, Inc., 425 Park Avenue, New York, New York 10022.

Directory of New and Expanding Centers (annual). International Council of Shopping Centers, 665 Fifth Avenue, New York, New York 10022.

Directory of Shopping Centers in the United States (annual, with quarterly updates). National Research Bureau, 310 South Michigan Avenue, Suite 1150, Chicago, Illinois 60604.

National Mall Monitor (bimonthly). National Mall Monitor, Suite 264, 2280 U.S. 19 S., Clearwater, Florida 33575.

Retail Expansion Plans (annual). International Council of Shopping Centers, 665 Fifth Avenue, New York, New York 10022.

Shopping Center World (monthly). Communication Channels, Inc., 6255 Barfield Road, Atlanta, Georgia 30328.

Shopping Centers Today (monthly). International Council of Shopping Centers, 665 Fifth Avenue, New York, New York 10022.

Stores (monthly). NRMA Enterprises, Inc., 100 West 31st Street, New York, New York 10001.

Survey of Buying Power (annual). Sales and Marketing Management, 633 Third Avenue, New York, New York 10017.

U.S. Bureau of the Census Reports
- Census of Retail Trade (Series RC) published every 5 years in years ending in 2 and 7.
- County Business Patterns (Series CBT)
- Current Business Reports (published monthly plus year-end report)
  1. Advance Monthly Retail Sales (Series CB)
  2. Monthly Wholesale Trade Sales and Inventory (Series BW)
  3. Monthly Retail Trade (Series BR)

Organizations

International Council of Shopping Centers
665 Fifth Avenue
New York, New York 10022   (212) 421-8181

National Retail Merchants Association, Inc.
100 West 31st Street
New York, New York 10001   (212) 244-8780

Urban Land Institute
1090 Vermont Ave., N.W.
Washington, D.C. 20005   (202) 289-8500

APPENDIX B

Data Checklist For Regional Center Market Analysis

Maps[1]
1. State or regional road map
2. General metropolitan area
3. City
4. Master plan
5. Central business district
6. Site topography
7. Site photography
8. Access improvement map
9. Population distribution dot map
10. Specialized functional area map (CBD, industry, etc.—specify)
11. Detailed downtown occupancy map (describe general area)

Economic Base Data
1. Composition
2. Growth trends
3. New employment sources
4. Community development program
5. Master plan data

Population Data
1. Latest data and projections used by planning commission
2. Latest data and projections used by real estate authority
3. Latest data regarding population distribution
4. Latest data regarding population growth trends
5. Latest population estimates based on building permits
6. Latest population estimates based on U.S. Post Office drop figures
7. Latest population estimates based on gas, electric, or water utility figures
8. Latest population estimates based on telephone utility figures
9. Latest population estimates based on special school surveys
10. Significant tourist population considerations
11. Significant racial and ethnic considerations
12. Special student population considerations
13. Detailed house count

Access Data
1. Existing road/street pattern
2. New and proposed roads/streets
3. Improvements of existing roads/streets
4. Special access considerations of the site
5. Traffic flow area
6. General parking situation
7. Downtown parking studies
8. Transit routes

The Site
1. Precise location (outline map)
2. Any physical problems (swamps, slopes, etc.; outline on map)
3. Detailed engineering studies of the site
4. Site size in acres
5. Site fragmentation if any
6. Site zoning
7. Zoning problems
8. Adjacent land uses
9. Adjacent zoning
10. Site easements or rights of way

Income Data
1. Major source of trade area income
2. Local surveys of income levels in the area
3. General income distribution pattern in the area
4. Income distribution in relationship to growth pattern
5. Estimated house values (specify areas)

Retail Expenditures
1. All local survey data from newspapers, planning groups
2. Tourist expenditures
3. Student expenditures

Competition
1. Convenience outlets serving the primary trade area
2. All major outlets for comparison goods serving the trade area (specify size limits for major stores)
3. All comparison goods outlets serving trade area
4. Downtown comparison goods stores, including major stores
5. Proposed shopping centers (located on map)
6. Proposed expansions of downtown major stores
7. Unusual local competition (discount houses, etc.)
8. Unusual merchandising of conventional facilities
9. Apparent expansion opportunities for existing centers
10. Qualitative appraisals where appropriate (specify)
11. Local opinions regarding store quality
12. "Expert" opinions regarding department store market shares

---

[1]Any map provided as a base map for graphics should depict the *entire* trading area of the location under consideration

Source: International Council of Shopping Centers, *Market Research for Shopping Centers* (New York: ICSC, 1980), pp. 40–42.

APPENDIX C

Tenant Classifications and Code Numbers

Categories from *Dollars & Cents of Shopping Centers: 1984*; code number from *Dollars & Cents: 1984*
and from the *Standard Industrial Classification (SIC) Manual*

TENANT CATEGORY	SIC CODE	$ & ¢ TENANT CLASS
General Merchandise		
Department Store	5311	A-01
Junior Department Store	5311	A-02
Variety Store	5311	A-03
Discount Department Store	5311	A-04
Showroom/Catalog Store	5399	A-05
Food		
Supermarket	5411	B-01
Convenience Market	5411	B-02
Meat, Poultry, and Fish	5423	B-03
Specialty Food	5499	B-04
Delicatessen	5411	B-05
Bakery	5463	B-06
Candy and Nuts	5441	B-07
Dairy Products	5451	B-08
Health Food	5499	B-09
Food Service		
Restaurant without Liquor	5812	C-01
Restaurant with Liquor	5812	C-02
Cafeteria	5812	C-03
Fast Food/Carryout	5812	C-04
Cocktail Lounge	5813	C-05
Doughnut Shop	5812	C-06
Ice Cream Parlor	5812	C-07
Pretzel Shop	5812	C-09
Cookie Shop	5812	C-10
Clothing		
Ladies' Specialty	5631	D-01
Ladies' Ready-to-Wear	5621	D-02
Bridal Shop	5621	D-03
Maternity	5621	D-04
Hosiery	5631	D-05
Childrens' Wear	5641	D-07
Menswear	5611	D-08
Family Wear	5651	D-09
Unisex/Jean Shop	5699	D-11
Leather Shop	5699	D-12
Uniform Shop	5699	D-13
Special Apparel—Unisex	5699	D-14
Shoes		
Family Shoes	5661	E-01
Ladies' Shoes	5661	E-02
Men's and Boys' Shoes	5661	E-03
Children's Shoes	5661	E-04
Athletic Footwear	5661/5941	E-05
Home Furnishings		
Furniture	5712	F-01
Lamps	5719	F-02
Floor Coverings	5713	F-03
Curtains and Drapes	5714	F-04
China and Glassware	5719	F-06
Fireplace Equipment	5719	F-07
Bath Shop	5719	F-08
Contemporary Home Accessories	5719	F-09
Cutlery	5719	F-10
Home Appliances/Music		
Appliances	5722	G-01
Radio, Video, Stereo	5732	G-02
Sewing Machines	5722	G-03
Records and Tapes	5733	G-04
Musical Instruments	5733	G-05
Gourmet Cookware	5719	G-06
Computer/Calculator (retail)	5999	G-07
Building Materials/Garden		
Paint and Wallpaper	5231	H-02
Hardware	5251	H-03
Home Improvements	5211	H-04
Automotive Supplies/Service Station		
Automotive (TB&A)	5531	K-01
Service Station	5541	K-03
Hobby/Special Interest		
Sporting Goods—General	5941	M-01
Hobby	5945	M-02
Art Gallery	5999	M-03
Cameras	5946	M-04
Toys	5945	M-05
Bike Shop	5941	M-06
Arts and Crafts	5999	M-07

TENANT CATEGORY	SIC CODE	$ & ¢ TENANT CLASS
Coin Shop	5999	M-08
Outfitters	5941	M-09
Game Store	5945	M-10
Gifts/Specialty		
Imports	5999	N-01
Luggage and Leather	5948	N-02
Cards and Gifts	5947	N-03
Candles	5999	N-04
Books and Stationery	5942/3	N-05
Decorative Accessories (including hardware and collectible gifts)	5947/5719	N-06
Jewelry and Cosmetics		
Credit Jewelry	5944	P-01
Costume Jewelry	5999	P-02
Jewelry	5944	P-03
Cosmetics	5999	P-04
Liquor		
Liquor and Wine	5921	Q-01
Wine and Cheese	5921/5451	Q-02
Drugs		
Super Drug (over 10,000 sq.ft.)	5912	R-01
Drugs	5912	R-02
Other Retail		
Fabric Shop	5949	S-01
Tobacco	5993	S-02
Pet Shop	5999	S-03
Flowers	5992	S-04
Plant Store	5992	S-05
Other Retail	5999	S-06
Telephone Store	5999	S-07
Eyeglasses—Optician	5999/8042	S-08
Personal Services		
Beauty	7231	T-01
Barber	7241	T-02
Shoe Repair	7251	T-03
Cleaner and Dyers	7212	T-04
Laundry	7212	T-05
Health Spa/Figure Salon	7299	T-06
Photographer	7221	T-07
Formal Wear/Rental	7299	T-08
Interior Decorator	7399	T-09
Travel Agent	4722	T-10
Key Shop	7699	T-11
Unisex Hair	7231/8299	T-12
Film Processing	7395	T-13
Photocopy/Fast Print	7332	T-14
Recreation/Community		
Post Office	7399	W-01
Music Studio and Dance	7911/8299	W-02
Bowling Alley	7933	W-03
Cinemas	7832	W-04
Ice/Roller Skating	7999	W-05
Community Hall	—	W-06
Arcade, Amusement	7993	W-07
Day Care and Nursery	8351	W-08
Financial		
Banks	602	X-01
Savings and Loan	612	X-02
Finance Company	6145	X-03
Brokerage	6211	X-05
Insurance	6411	X-06
Real Estate	6531	X-07
Automatic Teller Machine	6059	X-08
Offices (other than financial)		
Optometrist	8042	Y-01
Medical and Dental	8011/8021/ 8031	Y-02
Legal	8111	Y-03
Accounting	8931	Y-04
Employment Agency	7361	Y-06
Other Offices	—	Y-07
Other		
Vacant Space	—	Z-01
Miscellaneous Income	—	Z-02
Warehouse	—	Z-03

(Tenant class numbers not in sequence indicate classifications not repeated from previous *Dollars & Cents* studies.)

APPENDIX D

Sample Lease Agreement

Note: This document is presented to suggest the detail and complexity of typical lease agreements. Its use is neither endorsed nor recommended. Each shopping center developer must look to his own legal counsel to devise appropriate legal documents for the particular center under consideration.

CONTENTS

THIS LEASE AGREEMENT (hereinafter called "Lease") made as of the _____ day of _____ 19___ by and between: _____, (hereinafter called "Landlord"). having an office at _____, and _____

_____

_____

_____ (hereinafter called "Tenant").

WITNESSETH

FOR AND IN CONSIDERATION of the sum of One Dollar ($1.00) in hand paid by each of the parties to the other, and other good and valuable consideration, receipt and sufficiency of which is hereby acknowledged, the parties agree as follows:

DATA SHEET

(1) PREMISES: The area outlined in red on Exhibit A-2 hereto. For the purposes of this Lease, the Premises shall be deemed to contain _____ square feet.

(2) TERM: _____ years, _____ months, and _____ days commencing on _____ ("Commencement Date"), and ending at midnight _____ ("Termination Date").

(3) PERMITTED USE: The Premises shall be used by the Tenant solely for: _____

(4) TENANT NAME: Tenant shall operate and do business in the Premises and all signs and advertising shall be under the trade name _____

(5) ANNUAL MINIMUM RENT: $_____ (includes the amount set out in item 6 below), in monthly installments of $_____

(6) ANNUAL BASE ELECTRICAL COST: $_____ (included in the amount set out in item 5 above).

(7) PERCENTAGE RENT: _____

(8) RENTAL ADDRESS: All rentals and other payments that become due hereunder shall be payable to Landlord and sent to _____, or at such other place as Landlord may designate in writing to Tenant.

Each reference in this Lease to any of the data contained in this Data Sheet shall be construed to incorporate the data stated under that title.

ARTICLE 1: PREMISES

Landlord hereby demises and leases to Tenant and Tenant hereby rents and takes from Landlord, subject to and with the benefit of the terms, covenants, conditions, and provisions of this Lease, the Premises (extending to the center line of the party walls and to the exterior faces of all other walls) situated within the Shopping Center Tract. The Premises are as shown outlined on Exhibit A-2 together with the appurtenances specifically granted in this Lease, but reserving and excepting to Landlord the use of exterior walls (other than storefronts), the roof and the right to install, maintain, use, repair and replace pipes, ducts, conduits, wires, and appurtenant fixtures leading through the Premises in locations that will not materially interfere with Tenant's use thereof. The Premises are located on a tract(s) of land owned by Landlord as shown on Exhibit A-1 (hereinafter called "Shopping Center Tract"). The Shopping Center Tract, together with adjacent tracts of land owned or leased by others that have been or may be developed as department stores as shown on Exhibit A-1, shall constitute the "Shopping Center."

Tenant is also granted the right of nonexclusive use, in common with others, of the automobile parking areas and other Common Areas (as hereinafter defined) from time to time existing within the Shopping Center described in this Lease.

Tenant acknowledges that (1) Tenant has inspected the Premises and accepts the Premises in "as-is" condition, and (2) Landlord has made no warranties and/or representations regarding the conditions of the Premises.

After the Commencement Date of the Term, Landlord shall have the right, but not the obligation, to furnish to Tenant a written statement in recordable form specifying the actual as-built number of square feet of Rentable Floor Area in the Premises as certified to by Landlord's architect or engineer, the exact amount of the Annual Minimum Rent computed thereon, and, if there shall have been any change in Exhibits A-2 or A-3 with respect to the Premises, the same shall be modified to reflect such change. Such statement, when so executed by both Landlord and Tenant, shall be deemed to be incorporated in and become a part of this Lease.

ARTICLE 2: LANDLORD WARRANTIES, LEASE SUBORDINATION, AND ATTORNMENT

Landlord hereby warrants that it and no other person or corporation has the right to lease the Premises. So long as Tenant shall perform each and every covenant to be performed by Tenant hereunder, Tenant shall have peaceful and quiet use and possession of the Premises without hindrance on the part of Landlord, and Landlord shall warrant and defend Tenant in such peaceful and quiet use and possession under Landlord.

Tenant's rights under this Lease are and shall always be subordinate to the operation and effect of any mortgage, other security instrument, or ground lease now or hereafter placed upon the Shopping Center, or any part or parts thereof, by Landlord. This clause shall be self-operative, and no further instrument of subordination shall be required; provided, however, that at the request of Landlord, Tenant will execute and deliver any necessary or proper instruments or certificates acknowledging the priority of the mortgage, other security instruments, or ground lease to this Lease and the subordination of this Lease thereto. In the event of the enforcement by any mortgage of the remedies provided for by law or by such mortgage or other security instrument, Tenant shall, upon request of any person succeeding to the interest of such mortgagee as a result of such enforcement, automatically become the Tenant of said successor in interest, without change in the terms or other provisions of this Lease, provided, however, that said successor in interest shall not be bound by (i) any payment of rent or additional rent for more than one month in advance, except prepayments in the nature of security for the performance by Tenant of its obligations under this Lease, or (ii) any amendment or modification of this Lease made without the consent of such mortgagee or such successor in interest. In confirmation thereof, Tenant shall execute such further assurances as may be required.

Tenant agrees that, provided the mortgagee under any mortgagee or other security instrument as mentioned in the above paragraph shall have notified Tenant in writing (by the way of Notice of Assignment of Lease or otherwise) of its address, Tenant will give such mortgagee, by registered mail, a copy of any notice of default served upon Landlord. Tenant further agrees that if Landlord has failed to cure such default within the time provided for in this Lease, then the mortgagee shall have an additional thirty (30) days to cure such default or, if such default cannot be cured within that time, then such additional time as may be necessary if within such thirty (30) days the mortgagee has commenced and is diligently pursuing the remedies necessary to cure such default (including but not limited to commencement of foreclosure proceedings if necessary to effect such cure), in which event this Lease shall not be terminated while such remedies are being diligently pursued.

ARTICLE 3: TERM

TO HAVE AND TO HOLD for a Term beginning at the earlier of (a) the Commencement Date as set forth on the Data Sheet of this Lease Agreement and continuing until the Termination Date as set forth on said Data Sheet, or (b) the opening by Tenant of its business in the Premises, and continuing until said Termination Date, unless sooner terminated as hereinafter provided.

ARTICLE 4: IMPROVEMENTS

A. Performance of Landlord's Work. Landlord shall cause to be performed the work, if any, described in Exhibit B as "Landlord's Work," and if such Landlord's Work is done after the Commencement Date, then Landlord will coordinate its work with Tenant so as to minimize interference with Tenant. All such work shall be done in a good and workmanlike manner, employing good materials and conforming to all governmental requirements. Tenant agrees that Landlord may make any changes in Landlord's Work that may become reasonably necessary or advisable (other than substantial changes) without the written approval of Tenant.

B. Performance of Tenant's Work. Tenant agrees that it will, proceeding with all reasonable dispatch, perform the work described in Exhibit B as "Tenant's Work" in order to ready the Premises for opening as expeditiously as possible. No work shall be done or fixtures or equipment installed without (1) the express written approval of Landlord, or (2) in such manner as to interfere with Landlord or Landlord's other tenants. Tenant agrees to employ for such work one or more licensed, bonded, responsible contractors whose labor will work in harmony with other labor working in the Shopping Center, and to cause such contractors employed by Tenant to carry Workers' Compensation insurance in accordance with statutory requirements and comprehensive public liability insurance covering such contractors on or about the Premises and Shopping Center in amounts at least equal to the limits set forth in Article 18A: "Tenant's Insurance" and to submit certificates evidencing such coverage to Landlord, before the commencement of such Tenant's Work.

By entering the Premises to commence Tenant's Work, Tenant shall be deemed to have accepted the Premises and acknowledged that Landlord has completed Landlord's Work, if any, under Exhibit B, and to have agreed that the obligations of Landlord imposed hereunder have been fully performed to such date.

The provisions of this Section B of Article 4 also apply to any reconstruction, alterations, remodeling, or improvements performed by Tenant.

C. Leasehold Improvements. All leasehold improvements installed within the Premises by Tenant (including but not limited to light fixtures and carpeting) shall be the property of Tenant until Tenant shall vacate the Premises, at which time title to such leasehold improvements shall vest in Landlord. Tenant shall not change or alter the exterior of the Premises, including the portion thereof fronting on the enclosed mall, nor shall Tenant make any structural changes or alterations to the Premises or any part thereof without first obtaining the written consent of Landlord.

ARTICLE 5: PLANS

Tenant shall prepare at its sole cost and expense, and in full compliance with the provisions of Exhibits B and C hereof, complete plans and specifications for all Tenant's Work, whether original, reconstruction, remodeling, improvements, and/or alterations, including but not limited to storefront, signs, and/or advertising matter, and shall submit such plans and specifications in accordance with Exhibit B to Landlord, or Landlord's designated representative, for approval before commencement of any Tenant's work.

All such plans and specifications shall meet the requirements of this Lease and all applicable local, state, and federal regulations, rules, codes, and ordinances. Tenant shall not employ Landlord's general contractor or subcontractors without the express written consent of Landlord.

ARTICLE 6: USE

Tenant shall occupy the Premises upon the commencement of the Term, and thereafter will continuously conduct in 100 percent of the Premises only the business expressly set forth in the Data Sheet, for such hours of operation as shall be determined by Landlord. Tenant shall at all times conduct its business in a reputable manner as a quality retail establishment in accordance with the standards of the Shopping Center, and shall not conduct any fire, bankruptcy, going out of business, or auction sales, either real or fictitious. The Premises shall not be used in such manner that, in accordance with any requirement of law or of any public authority, Landlord shall be obliged on account of the purpose or manner of said use to make any addition or alteration to or in the building. All sales from vending machines, other than vending machines for the sole use of Tenant's employees, must be approved in advance in writing by Landlord.

Tenant will at all times during the Term of this Lease maintain displays of merchandise in the show windows of the Premises. All articles and the arrangement, style, color, and general appearance thereof, in the interior of the Premises that will be visible from the exterior therof, including, without limitation, window displays, advertising matter, signs, merchandise, and store fixtures, shall be maintained in keeping with the character and standards of the Shopping Center.

ARTICLE 7: RENT

Tenant convenants and agrees to pay to Landlord, without setoff, deduction, or demand, at the address set out in the heading of this Lease, or at such other place as Landlord may designate in writing to Tenant, rental at the following rates and times:

A. Annual Minimum Rent. Tenant shall pay annually during the Term of this Lease the sum specified on the Data Sheet as Annual Minimum Rent, which sum shall be payable in twelve (12) equal monthly installments, on or before the first day of each month, in advance. Should the Term of this Lease commence or terminate on a day other than the first day of a calendar month, the rental for such partial month shall be equal to the product obtained by multiplying the number of days of the Term included in the partial month by a fraction, the numerator of which is the Annual Minimum Rent and the demoninator of which is 360. No payment by Tenant or receipt by Landlord of a lesser amount than the monthly rent herein stipulated shall be deemed to be other than on account of the earliest stipulated rent, nor shall any endorsement or statement on any check or any letter accompanying any check or payment as rent be deemed an accord and satisfaction, and Landlord shall accept such check or payment without prejudice to Landlord's right to recover the balance of such rent or pursue any other remedy in the Lease provided.

B. Percentage Rent. Tenant shall pay during each Lease Year a sum computed by multiplying the percentage specified on the Data Sheet times the amount of Gross Sales made during such Lease Year which exceeds the amount of Gross Sales specified on the Data Sheet. Such Percentage Rent shall be paid in quarter-annual installments computed on all Gross Sales during such quarter-annual period in excess of one quarter (¼) of the amount of Gross Sales specified on the Data Sheet. Such quarter-annual installments shall be payable within fifteen (15) days after the expiration of each three (3) calendar month period of each Lease Year. In the event the total of the quarter-annual installments of Percentage Rent for any Lease Year does not equal the Percentage Rent computed on the total amount of Gross Sales for such Lease Year, then Tenant, at the time it submits the annual statement of Gross Sales pursuant to Article 9 hereof, shall pay Landlord any deficiency, or Landlord upon receipt of such annual statement shall issue to Tenant a credit invoice for such excess, as the case may be. Should the Term commence or terminate on a day other than February 1 or January 31, respectively, then the Percentage Rent for such Lease Year so commencing or terminating shall be equal to the product obtained by multiplying the percentage specified on the Data Sheet by the result obtained by subtracting from the Gross Sales for such Lease Year the sum determined by multiplying the amount of Gross Sales specified on the Data Sheet by a fraction, the numerator of which is the number of days within such Lease Year, and the denominator of which is 360.

In the event Tenant shall fail to open and operate for business on the date the Term commences, then, in order to compensate Landlord for its loss of Percentage Rent that might have been earned had the Tenant been open for business, Tenant agrees to pay Landlord for each day after the commencement date of the Term that Tenant fails to open and operate as required by Article 6 hereof, a sum equal to the amount obtained by dividing the Annual Minimum Rent by 360, such sum to be paid daily.

C. Other Charges. Tenant shall pay all other charges, sums, or amounts permitted to be imposed against it under any other Article of this Lease concurrently with the next succeeding installment of Annual Minimum Rent following notice of the same, unless a different time for such payment is specified in this Lease. Any monies paid or expense incurred by Landlord to correct violations of any of Tenant's obligations hereunder shall be additional rental.

ARTICLE 8: GROSS SALES

As used herein, the term "Gross Sales" shall mean the recognition of the entire amount of the actual sales price at the time of purchase, whether wholly or partially for cash or on credit, of all merchandise and services sold and all other receipts by sale, barter, or otherwise of all business conducted in or from the Premises including, without limiting the foregoing, all sales to employees or agents of Tenant, all orders taken in or from the Premises although said orders may be received by telephone or mail, or filled elsewhere, or procured from the Premises by house to house or other canvassing, all sales by any sublessee, licensee or concessionaire in or from the Premises, all without credit to Tenant for cash discounts (other than normal employee discounts) or uncollected or uncollectible credit accounts. Sales to customers on a layaway or lay-by basis shall be recognized within ninety (90) days of the layaway or lay-by transaction and in any event must be fully recognized when the merchandise leaves the Premises. The term "Gross Sales" shall also include, without limitation, all deposits not refunded to purchasers, all service charges for layaway or lay-by sales, and all commissions received for vending machines on the Premises for use by the general public and other cash receipts resulting from sales transactions on the Premises.

All sales are to be recorded on cash registers equipped with a transaction number control or recorded on sales checks which are numerically controlled. There shall be no adjustment to Gross Sales for cash shortages. There shall be excluded from Gross Sales any sum collected and paid out for any sales or excise tax based upon all taxable sales in this definition of Gross Sales as required by law whether now or hereafter in force, to be paid by Tenant or collected from its customers, to the extent that such taxes have been included in the Gross Sales price. The term "Gross Sales" shall not include the exchange or transfer of merchandise between the stores of Tenant, if any, where such exchange or transfers of merchandise are made solely for the convenient operation of the business of Tenant and not for the purpose of consummating a sale made in, from, or upon the Premises or for the purpose of depriving the Landlord of the benefit of a sale; the amount of returns to shippers or manufacturers, nor the amount of any cash or credit refunds accepted by the Tenant, nor sales of those fixtures which Tenant has the right to remove from the Premises after use thereof in the conduct of Tenant's business in the Premises. There shall also be excluded from the term "Gross Sales" all fees or service charges for delivery of merchandise and any specified "finance charge" applicable to credit transactions which is separately stated and is in addition to the purchase price.

For the purpose of this Article the term "Tenant" shall include all of Tenant's subtenants, licensees, and concessionaires.

ARTICLE 9: RECORDS AND REPORTS

Tenant shall and hereby agrees that it and its subtenants, licensees, and concessionaires will keep, in the Premises or at Tenant's headquarters, a permanent, accurate set of books and records, in accordance with generally accepted accounting methods and principles, of all sales of merchandise and all revenue derived from other departments of the business conducted in said Premises, whether included in Gross Sales or not, during each day of the Term hereof, and all supporting records including cash register tapes, sales checks, state sales and use tax reports, and business and occupation tax reports. Tenant further agrees that it and its subtenants will so keep, retain, and preserve these records for at least three (3) years after the expiration of each Lease Year.

Tenant further covenants and agrees (a) that not later than the fifteenth (15th) day of each calendar month it will deliver to Landlord an informal, unaudited statement signed by Tenant or by an authorized officer or agent of Tenant showing the Gross Sales made in the preceding calendar month; (b) that within fifteen (15) days after the expiration of each three (3) calendar month period of each Lease Year, it will deliver to Landlord a written statement signed by Tenant or by an authorized officer or agent of Tenant, showing the Gross Sales made in the preceding three (3) calendar month period; and (c) that not later than thirty (30) days after the close of each Lease Year, it will deliver to Landlord a statement of Gross Sales for the preceding Lease Year accompanied by the signed opinion of an independent Certified Public Accountant stating specifically that he has examined the report of Gross Sales of the preceding Lease Year, that his examination included such tests of Tenant's books and records as he considered necessary under the circumstances, and that such report presents fairly Gross Sales of the preceding Lease Year. If Tenant shall fail to deliver the foregoing to Landlord within said thirty (30) days, Landlord shall have the right thereafter to examine such books and records as may be necessary to certify the amount of Tenant's Gross Sales for such Lease Year, and Tenant shall promptly pay to Landlord the cost of such audit, or $500.00, whichever is greater. Tenant shall deliver the statements referred to hereinabove to Landlord at the same addresss as Rent is then being paid.

In the event Landlord is not satisfied with the annual statement of Gross Sales as submitted by Tenant and its subtenants, then and in that event, after ten (10) days' written notice, Landlord shall have the right to have its employees, mortgagees, or auditors make a special audit of Tenant's and its subtenant's books and records pertaining to Gross Sales. If such audit shall disclose a discrepancy of more than one percent (1%) of Gross Sales, Tenant shall promptly pay to Landlord the cost of said audit, or $500.00, whichever is greater, in addition to the deficiency in Percentage Rent, which shall be payable in any event. If such discrepancy is more than three percent (3%) of Gross Sales, or if Tenant shall fail to permit inspection and/or audit of its records, Landlord shall have the further remedy by not less than ten (10) days' notice to Tenant to declare this Lease terminated on account of Tenant's failure to properly report its Gross Sales. Landlord shall have the right to audit Tenant's books and records for a period of three (3) years after the close of each Lease Year.

ARTICLE 10: TAXES

A. Tenant shall pay to Landlord during the Term of this Lease its share of all taxes, assessments, and other governmental charges, general and special, ordinary and extraordinary, of any kind and nature whatsoever, including but not limited to assessments for public improvements or benefits against the land, building, or improvements comprising the Shopping Center Tract, which are payable to any lawful authority during each Lease Year (such taxes and assessments being hereinafter called "Taxes"). For the Lease Years in which this Lease commences and terminates, the provisions of this Article shall apply, and Tenant's liability for its share of the Taxes for such years shall be subject to a pro rata adjustment based on the number of days of said Lease Year during which the Term of this Lease is in effect. Should the United States government, the state in which the Shopping Center is located, or any political subdivision thereof, or any other authority possessing such jurisdiction and authority impose a tax, assessment, excise, and/or surcharge of any kind or nature upon, against, or with respect to (i) all or any part of the Rent (as such term is defined by such authority) to be paid by Tenant under this Lease, (ii) all or any part of the Rent (as such term is defined by such authority) to be received by Landlord under this Lease, or (iii) the parking areas or the number of parking spaces in the Shopping Center Tract, such tax, assessment, excise, and/or surcharge shall be deemed to constitute a part of the term "Taxes" as used herein.

Landlord and Tenant recognize the possibility of changes and/or limitations on the amount of Taxes that can be assessed on land, buildings, and improvements including the Shopping Center. Landlord and Tenant further recognize and acknowledge that as a result of any such changes in structure or limitations on amount, the amount of taxes and assessments of the type that have appeared on assessors' tax statements prior to the date hereof may decrease. Landlord and Tenant further recognize that there may be imposed new forms of taxes, assessments, charges, levies, or fees, or there may be an increase in certain existing taxes, assessments, charges, levies, or fees placed on or levied in connection with the ownership, leasing occupancy, or operation of the Shopping Center or the Premises. All such new or increased taxes, assessments, charges, levies, or fees which are in lieu of or imposed or increased as a result of or arising out of any changes in the structure of the current tax system or for the purpose of funding special assessment districts theretofore funded by Taxes, shall also be included within the meaning of Taxes.

B. Tenant's share of Taxes shall be equal to the product obtained by multiplying the Taxes by a fraction, the numerator of which shall be the number of square feet of the Premises, and the denominator of which shall be the total number of square feet of gross leased and occupied floor area (exclusive of any portion thereof used for a post office, child care nursery purposes, or center management offices) on the Shopping Center Tract. The gross leased and occupied floor area in effect for the whole of any Lease Year or portion thereof shall be the average of the gross leased and occupied floor area in effect on the first day of each calendar month in such Lease Year. Tenant's share of the Taxes shall be paid in monthly installments on or before the first day of each calendar month, in advance, in an amount estimated by Landlord; provided, that in the event Landlord is required under any mortgage covering the Shopping Center Tract to escrow Taxes, Landlord may, but shall not be obligated to, use the amount required to be so escrowed as a basis for its estimate of the monthly installments due from Tenant hereunder. Upon receipt of all tax bills and assessment bills attributable to any calendar year during the Term hereof, Landlord shall furnish Tenant with a written statement of the actual amount of Tenant's share of the Taxes for such calendar year. If the total amount of monthly installments paid by Tenant pursuant to this Article does not equal the sum due from Tenant as shown on such statement, Tenant shall pay to Landlord the deficiency upon receipt of such statement, or Landlord shall issue to Tenant at the time the statement is furnished a credit invoice for such excess, as the case may be. A copy of a tax bill or assessment bill submitted by Landlord to Tenant shall at all times be sufficient evidence of the amount of Taxes against the property to which such bill relates. Prior to or at the commencement of the Term of this Lease and from time to time thereafter throughout the Term hereof, Landlord shall notify Tenant in writing of Landlord's estimate of Tenant's monthly installments due hereunder. Landlord's and Tenant's obligations under this Article shall survive the expiration of this Lease.

C. Notwithstanding anything in this Article to the contrary, all costs and expenses incurred by Landlord during negotiations for or contests of the amount of Taxes shall be included within the term "Taxes." If a refund is obtained, Landlord shall issue a credit invoice for same, such portion to be based upon the percentage of the original Taxes paid by Tenant from which the refund was derived.

D. In addition to the foregoing, Tenant at all times shall be responsible for and shall pay, before delinquency, all taxes levied, assessed, or unpaid on any leasehold interest, any right of occupancy, any investment of Tenant in the Premises, or any personal property of any kind owned, installed, or used by Tenant including Tenant's leasehold improvements, or on Tenant's right to occupy the Premises.

ARTICLE 11: LEASE YEAR

The term "Lease Year" shall mean, in the case of the first Lease Year, that period from the commencement date of the Term to the first succeeding January 31; thereafter, "Lease Year" shall mean each successive twelve (12) calendar month period following the expiration of the first Lease Year, except that in the event of the termination of this Lease on any day other than on January 31, then the last Lease Year shall be the period from the end of the preceding Lease Year to such date of termination.

ARTICLE 12: TENANT'S SHARE OF COMMON EXPENSES

A. Tenant shall pay to Landlord, during the Term of this Lease, its share of the costs and expenses that may be incurred by Landlord in maintaining and operating the Common Area (as herein defined) and in maintaining and repairing the foundations, the exterior walls, the roof, and the downspouts and gutters of the buildings located within the Shopping Center Tract and the utility systems, lines, conduits, and appurtenances thereto serving said buildings. The share to be paid by Tenant shall be computed by subtracting from such costs and expenses any contribution or payment made to Landlord with respect thereto, by, through, or on behalf of any party that is not located on the Shopping Center Tract, for maintaining and operating the Common Area and other areas as set out above in this paragraph on their respective tracts, and then multiplying the remainder by a fraction, the numerator of which shall be the number of square feet of the Premises and the denominator of which shall be the total number of square feet of gross leased and occupied floor area (exclusive of any portion thereof used for a post office or child care nursery purposes or center management offices) on the Shopping Center Tract. The gross leased and occupied floor area in effect for the whole of any Lease Year or portion thereof shall be the average of the gross leased and occupied floor area in effect on the first day of each calendar month in such Lease Year. Tenant's share of such cost and expenses for each Lease Year shall be paid in monthly installments on the first day of each calendar month, in advance, in an amount estimated by Landlord from time to time. Within ninety (90) days after the end of each Lease Year, Landlord shall furnish Tenant with a statement of the actual amount of Tenant's share of such cost and expenses for such period. In the event the total of Tenant's monthly installments for any Lease Year does not equal Tenant's share as shown on such statement, then Tenant shall within thirty (30) days of receipt of such statement pay Landlord any deficiency, or Landlord upon receipt of such annual statement shall issue to Tenant a credit invoice for such excess, as the case may be.

B. The term "Common Area" means the entire areas designed from time to time by Landlord for common use or benefit for the occupants of the Shopping Center including, but not by way of limitation, parking lots (permanent and temporary), landscaped and vacant areas, passages for trucks and automobiles, areaways, roads, walks, enclosed mall, roof, curbs, corridors, courts and arcades, together with facilities such as washrooms, comfort rooms, lounges, drinking fountains, toilets, stairs, ramps, elevators, escalators, shelters, community rooms, porches, bus stations, and loading docks, with facilities appurtenant to each, and common utility facilities, water filtration and treatment facilities, including, but not limited to, treatment plant(s) and settling ponds whether located within or outside of the Shopping Center. Subject to reasonable, nondiscriminatory rules and regulations to be promulgated by Landlord, the Common Area is hereby made available to Tenant and its employees, agents, customers, and invitees for their reasonable nonexclusive use in common with other tenants, their employees, agents, customers, invitees, and Landlord for the purposes for which constructed. Landlord shall have the right to change the location and arrangement of parking areas and other Common Area; to enter into, modify, and terminate easements and other agreements pertaining to the use and maintenance of the Common Area; to construct surface or elevated parking areas and facilities; to establish and change the level of parking surfaces; to close all or any portion of the Common Area to such extent as may, in the opinion of Landlord's counsel, be necessary to prevent a dedication thereof or the accrual of any rights to any person or to the public therein; to close temporarily any or all portions of the Common Area; and to do and perform such other acts in and to said areas and improvements as, in the exercise of good business judgment, Landlord shall determine to be advisable with a view to the improvement of convenience and use thereof by tenants, their officers, agents, employees, and customers. Landlord may require the payment to it of a reasonable fee or charge by the public for the use of all or part of the Common Area, which may be by meter or otherwise, and in such event all fees or charges derived therefrom by Landlord shall be credited against Common Area costs and expenses.

Tenant and its employees shall park their cars only in those portions of the Common Area designated from time to time for that purpose by Landlord. Tenant shall furnish Landlord with state automobile license numbers assigned to Tenant's car or cars and cars of its employees within five (5) days after taking possession of Premises and shall thereafter notify Landlord of any changes within five (5) days after such changes occur. If Tenant or its employees fail to park their cars in the designated Area, Landlord shall have the right to charge Tenant Ten Dollars ($10.00) per day per car parked in any Common Area other than those designated.

C. Landlord shall operate and maintain the Common Area (as herein defined) and the foundations, the exterior walls, the roof, and the downspouts and gutters of the buildings located within the Shopping Center Tract and the utility systems, lines, conduits, and appurtenances thereto serving said buildings or shall cause the same to be operated and maintained in a manner deemed by Landlord reasonable, appropriate, and for the best interests of the occupants of the Shopping Center. Landlord shall have an annual audit made of the cost and expense of such operation and maintenance incurred during each Lease Year. Such cost and expense may include, but not be limited to, all sums incurred in connection with operating, repairing, lighting, cleaning, heating, air conditioning, ventilating, painting, insuring (including liability insurance for personal injury, death, and property liability, and insurance against fire, theft, or other casualties), removing snow, ice, debris, and surface water, sewer, striping, security police (including cost of uniforms, equipment, and all employment taxes and the costs of operating and maintaining vehicles), electronic intrusion and fire control devices and telephonic alert system devices, inspecting, traffic consultants and traffic regulation, directional signs, equipment depreciation, Workers' Compensation Insurance covering personnel, fidelity bonds for personnel, insurance against liability for defamation and claims of false arrest occurring in and about the Shopping Center, plate glass insurance, regulation of traffic, fees for permits and licenses, program services, management services and loudspeaker systems, all costs and expenses of plantings, rebuilding and replacing flowers, shrubbery, and planters, and all costs and expenses (other than those of a capital nature except as otherwise stated below) of operating, maintaining, repairing, and replacing paving, curbs, sidewalks, walkways, roadways, parking surfaces, landscaping, drainage, utilities, motor vehicles, machines and equipment, and lighting facilities, and the annual amortization of any capital improvement Landlord makes during the Term of this Lease in order to comply with safety or any other requirements of any federal, state, or local law or governmental regulation, and to the sum total of all of the above shall be added a sum equal to fifteen percent (15%) thereof for administration. Such costs and expenses shall not include any initial construction costs of a capital nature, except as otherwise stated above, nor profit or interest on Landlord's investment, but shall include the acquisition cost (rental fees and/or purchase price or, in lieu of purchase price, the annual depreciation allocable thereto) of machinery and equipment used in connection with said maintenance and operation. The annual audit shall be made available to Tenant for inspection.

ARTICLE 13: UTILITY SERVICES

A. Electricity, Water, and Sewer. Landlord agrees to cause mains, conduits, and other facilities to be provided (in accordance with the provisions of Article 4A hereof) which are capable of supplying electricity, water, and sewer service to the Premises or to nearby places. Tenant shall perform such work (in accordance with the provisions of Article 4B hereof) in order to complete the same within the Premises. Tenant, at its own expense and with equipment installed in accordance with specifications approved in writing by Landlord, shall heat or chill the water to meet its own requirement, if any. Tenant hereby acknowledges the limits of the design standard of the electrical service to be furnished to the Premises, and if additional capacity or wiring is required by Tenant, Tenant, after obtaining Landlord's approval with respect to the same, shall install such additional capacity or wiring at its own expense.

Tenant shall pay for all electricity, water, and sewer service used in the Premises. If Landlord shall elect to supply the service or services used, or if said services are invoiced to Tenant through Landlord, Tenant shall accept and use the same as tendered by Landlord and pay Landlord therefor, as additional rent at a rate equal to the greater of Landlord's actual costs for the furnishing of said services or at the rate charged for comparable services by local utilities or other local agencies furnishing said services. In the event Landlord finds it necessary or desirable to terminate furnishing any service it previously supplied, Landlord's sole obligation with respect to such services shall be to permit a local utility or similar agency to use those utility lines or conduits owned by Landlord and utilized for the furnishing of the discontinued service.

The sum as set out in item (6) on the Data Sheet shall hereinafter be referred to as the "Base Electrical Cost." At the expiration of each Lease Year, Landlord shall estimate the cost of the electricity that will be used in serving the Premises occupied by Tenant for the ensuing Lease Year. Should said cost for electricity as determined by Landlord for any ensuing Lease Year be more or less than the Base Electrical Cost, then Tenant's Annual Minimum Rent for such ensuing Lease Year shall be increased or decreased by the same amount.

However, should an increase or decrease in the Base Electrical Cost be occasioned by either (1) a change in the rates charged by the local public utility power company, or (2) an increase or decrease in the number of hours of use by Tenant, or (3) a change in the usage of the Premises, then on each such occasion a proportionate adjustment shall be made in Tenant's Annual Minimum Rent, upward or downward as the case may be, effective as of the first day of the ensuing calendar month.

B. Heating, Air Conditioning, and Ventilating. Landlord agrees at its own cost to construct, operate, and maintain a system designed to heat, air condition, and ventilate the Premises and other occupied areas, in accordance with the Description of Landlord's Work and Tenant's Work attached hereto as Exhibit B. Tenant shall perform such work and pay such amounts as are required of it under Exhibit B. Tenant agrees to accept and use such heating, air conditioning, and ventilation in the Premises and to pay for such use, as additional rent, its pro rata share of the costs and expenses during each Lease Year of operating the heating, air conditioning, and ventilating system, herein called "HVAC Charge," as hereinafter provided:

(1) Tentative HVAC Charge. Tenant's share of the HVAC Charge shall be paid in monthly installments on or before the first day of each calendar month, in advance, in an amount estimated by Landlord, based for the first year of the system's operation on anticipated costs and expenses. After such first year of operation, Landlord's estimate of Tentative HVAC Charge shall be based upon operational experience, taking into account reasonably anticipated increases or decreases, as the case may be. Should the Term of this Lease commence or terminate on a day other than the first day of a calendar month, the Tentative HVAC Charge for such partial month shall be equal to the product obtained by multiplying the number of days of the Term included in the partial month by a fraction, the numerator of which is the Tentative HVAC Charge and the denominator of which is thirty (30).

(2) Determination of HVAC Charge. Landlord shall have annual audits made of the HVAC Charge, and such audit reports shall be open to inspection by Tenant. The HVAC Charge for each Lease Year shall include all items of cost and expense that in usual accounting practice are treated as operating costs or expenses, including, but not limited to, fuel, water, electricity, supplies, wages and other compensation (including those of supervisory and management personnel), Workers' Compensation, payroll taxes, boiler, compressor, and other insurance and ordinary maintenance and repairs, to the sum total of which shall be added fifteen percent (15%) thereof, together with the reasonable imputed amortization of the cost to Landlord of constructing, erecting, and installing, including additions to, or replacements of, the heating, ventilation, and air conditioning equipment, and the resulting amount shall constitute the HVAC Charge. The HVAC Charge shall reflect all costs and expenses of full operation during hours when the Shopping Center is open, which hours shall be determined by Landlord, and all costs and expenses of operation on a reasonably curtailed basis, which shall be applicable to the service furnished generally to tenants and occupants during off-hours when the Shopping Center is not open.

(3) Tenant's share of the costs and expenses of operating the heating, ventilating, and air conditioning system shall be equal to the product obtained by multiplying the HVAC Charge by a fraction, the numerator of which is equal to the sum of Tenant's Tentative HVAC Charge during such Lease Year and the denominator is equal to the total of all Tentative HVAC Charges during such Lease Year invoiced to (i) tenants occupying retail space, and (ii) tenants occupying space used for post office or child care nursery purposes. Within ninety (90) days after the end of each Lease Year, Landlord shall furnish Tenant with a statement of the actual amount of Tenant's share of the HVAC Charge for such period. If the total of Tenant's Tentative HVAC Charge paid for any Lease Year does not equal Tenant's share as shown on such statement, Tenant

shall promptly pay Landlord the deficiency upon receipt of such statement, or Landlord shall issue to Tenant at the time such statement is furnished a credit invoice for such excess.

C. Discontinuance of Service. Landlord reserves the right with ten (10) days' prior written notice to Tenant to cut off and discontinue trash and rubbish removal, water, electricity, air conditioning, heating, ventilating, antenna service, and any or all other service without liability to Tenant, whenever and during any period in which bills for the same remain unpaid by Tenant. Any such action by Landlord pursuant to the immediately preceding sentence shall not be construed by Tenant or any other party interpreting this Lease as an eviction or disturbance of possession of Tenant or an election by Landlord to terminate this Lease on account of such nonpayment. Landlord may furnish or cause any of the above services to be furnished by an agent or independent contractor and Tenant will accept any pay for such services.

D. Interruption of Service. Landlord shall not be liable in damages or otherwise if the furnishing by Landlord or by any other supplier of any utility service or other service to the Premises shall be interrupted or impaired by fire, accident, riot, strike, act of God, the making of necessary repairs or improvements, or by any causes beyond Landlord's control.

E. Energy Shortage. Should it become necessary or desirable because of recommendations or directives of public authorities to reduce energy consumption within the Shopping Center, Tenant will reduce its energy consumption in accordance with reasonable, uniform, and nondiscriminatory standards established by Landlord.

ARTICLE 14: MERCHANTS' ASSOCIATION
Tenant will, upon commencement of the Term, promptly become a member of, participate fully in, and remain in good standing in the existing Shopping Center Merchants' Association organized to promote the activities of the Shopping Center, and will abide by the rules and regulations of such Association. Tenant agrees to pay to such Association such annual dues and/or special assessments as shall be fixed by the Association's Board of Directors payable in the manner prescribed by the Merchants' Association, but in no event shall Tenant pay an amount less than the amount paid by Tenant during the preceding Lease Year. In the event the Shopping Center Merchants' Association shall at the option of Landlord be disbanded, Tenant agrees to pay to Landlord, in lieu of dues to the Merchants' Association, a "Promotional Charge" equal to the amount payable by Tenant to the Merchants' Association during the last full year of its operation, to be used by Landlord for the advertising, promotion, public relations, and administrative expenses of the Shopping Center. The Promotional Charge payable by Tenant to Landlord will be subject to adjustment by a percentage equal to the percentage of increase or decrease from the "base period" (as hereinafter defined) of the Consumer Price Index (U.S. City Average) of the United States Bureau of Labor Statistics, or in the event such Index shall not be published, then such other index published by the United States government as may be selected by Landlord. The "base period" for the purposes of such adjustment shall be deemed to be the February of the year following disbanding of the Merchants' Association, and shall be adjusted every year thereafter.

ARTICLE 15: FIXTURES
All trade fixtures, merchandise, supplies, and movable apparatus owned by Tenant and installed in the Premises shall remain the property of Tenant and shall be removable from time to time and also at the expiration of the Term or any renewal or extension thereof, or other termination thereof, provided Tenant shall not at such time be in default under any covenant or agreement contained herein; and provided further that the Tenant repair any damage to the Premises caused by the removal of said fixtures; and, if in default, Landlord shall have a lien on said fixtures and apparatus as security against loss or damage resulting from any such default by Tenant, and said fixtures and apparatus shall not be removable by Tenant until such default is cured.

ARTICLE 16: CARE OF THE PREMISES
A. Tenant will (a) keep the inside and outside of all glass in the doors and windows of the Premises clean; (b) keep all exterior storefront surfaces of the Premises clean; (c) replace promptly, at its expense, any broken door closers and any cracked or broken glass on the Premises with glass of like kind and quality; (d) maintain the Premises at its expense in a clean, orderly and sanitary condition and free of insects, rodents, vermin, and other pests; (e) keep any garbage, trash, rubbish, or refuse removed at its expense on a regular basis and temporarily

stored in the Premises in accordance with local codes; provided, however, that Tenant will not store trash on the Premises so that it is visible to members of the public shopping in the Shopping Center; and further provided, however, that if Landlord shall decide at its sole option to provide trash removal service, Tenant shall pay Landlord monthly for such service at the prevailing competitive rate for such service as billed by Landlord; (f) keep all mechanical apparatus free of vibration and noise that may be transmitted beyond the Premises; (g) comply with all laws, ordinances, rules, and regulations of governmental authorities and all recommendations of the Insurance Services Office and/or Landlord's insurance carrier now or hereafter in effect; (h) light the show windows of the Premises and exterior signs until the closing of the Shopping Center and replace promptly all light bulbs and tubes when no longer serviceable; (i) store or stock in the Premises only such goods, wares, merchandise, or other property as shall be reasonably required in connection with Tenant's business on the Premises, and Tenant shall not use any portion of the Premises for storage or warehouse purposes beyond such needs; (j) use for office, clerical, or other nonselling purposes only such space in the Premises as is from time to time reasonably required for Tenant's business therein; and (k) conduct its business in all respects in a dignified manner in accordance with high standards of the store operation in the Shopping Center. Tenant will not, without the written consent of Landlord, place or maintain any merchandise or other articles in any vestibule or entry of the Premises, or outside of the Premises; use or permit the use of any musical instruments, loud speakers, phonographs, public address systems, flashing, moving and/or rotating lights, sound amplifiers, radio or television broadcasts within the Premises that are in any manner audible or visible outside the Premises; cause or permit odors to emanate or be dispelled from the Premises; except within the Premises, solicit business or distribute advertising material within the Shopping Center; permit the parking of delivery vehicles so that they interfere with the use of any driveway, walk, parking area, mall, or other Common Areas in the Shopping Center; receive or ship articles of any kind except through service facilities designated by Landlord; burn any papers, trash, or garbage of any kind in or about the Premises; use any portion of the Premises as living quarters, sleeping apartments, or lodging rooms; keep any live animals of any kind in, about, or upon the Premises; or use or permit to be used the Premises or any part thereof in any manner that will constitute an unreasonable annoyance to any occupant of the Shopping Center, or that will constitute a nuisance, or that will damage the reputation of the Shopping Center. Except as otherwise provided in this Article, the Premises, including but not limited to all items of Tenant's Work, shall at all times be kept in good order, condition, and repair of equal quality with the original work by Tenant at Tenant's own cost and expense and in accordance with all laws, directions, rules, and regulations of regulatory bodies or officials having jurisdiction in that regard. If Tenant refuses or neglects to commence repairs within ten (10) days after written demand, or fails to complete such repairs within a reasonable time thereafter, Landlord may make the repairs without liability to Tenant for any loss or damage that may accrue to Tenant's stock or business by reason thereof, and if Landlord makes such repair, Tenant shall pay to Landlord the costs thereof with interest from the date of commencement of such repairs.

B. Landlord shall keep or cause to be kept the foundations, the exterior walls, downspouts, and gutters of the building of which the Premises are a part and, to the extent Tenant or other tenants are not obligated to maintain the same, all utility systems, lines, conduits, and appurtenances thereto located within the Shopping Center in good repair, ordinary wear and tear excepted; provided, however, if the need for such repair is directly or indirectly attributable to or results from the business activity being conducted within the Premises, then, in such case, Tenant agrees to reimburse Landlord for all costs and expenses incurred by Landlord with respect to such repair. Landlord shall commence repairs it is required to do hereunder as soon as reasonably practicable after receiving written notice from Tenant of the necessity for such repairs, but in no event shall Landlord be required to make any other repairs.

C. Tenant will not paint or decorate any part of the exterior of the Premises, including storefronts, or any part of the interior visible from the exterior thereof, or paste any signs to any portion of the Premises, or display any signs attached to show windows or within three (3) feet of the mall lease line of the Premises without obtaining Landlord's written approval. Landlord shall have the right, at Landlord's sole discretion, to require Tenant to remove any sign visible from the Common Area that is not in keeping with the standards of the Shopping Center.

D. Tenant will repair promptly, at its expense, (i) any damage to the Premises or any other improvements within the Shopping Center caused by Tenant or anyone claiming by or through Tenant or (ii) caused by the installation or removal of Tenant's property, regardless of fault or by whom such damage shall be caused, unless caused by Landlord, its agents, employees, or contractors; if Tenant shall fail to make such repairs as aforesaid, Landlord may make the same and Tenant agrees to pay the cost thereof to Landlord.

E. Landlord shall have the exclusive right to use all or any part of the roof of the Premises or any additions thereto for any purpose; to erect additional stories or other structures over all or any part of the Premises; to erect in connection with the construction thereof temporary scaffolds and other aids to construction on the exterior of the Premises, provided that access to the Premises shall not be denied; and to install, maintain, use, repair, and replace within the Premises pipes, ducts, conduits, wires, and all other mechanical equipment serving other parts of the Shopping Center.

Landlord may make any use it desires of the side or rear walls of the Premises, provided that such use shall not encroach on the interior of the Premises.

ARTICLE 17: ADVERTISING

Tenant shall use as its advertised business address the name and address of the Shopping Center. Tenant's trade name set out in the Data Sheet shall not be changed without Landlord's prior written approval. Tenant agrees that Landlord's name or the name of the Shopping Center shall not be used in any confusing, detrimental, or misleading manner, and upon termination of this Lease, Tenant will cease to use Landlord's name or the name of the Shopping Center, or any part thereof, in any manner.

ARTICLE 18: INSURANCE

A. Tenant's Insurance

(i) Public Liability Insurance. Prior to entry into the Premises and during the Term hereof, Tenant shall keep in full force and effect, at its expense, a policy or policies of public liability insurance with respect to the Premises and the business of Tenant and any approved subtenant, licensee, or concessionaire, with companies licensed to do business in the state in which the Shopping Center is located in which both Tenant and Landlord shall be named insureds with limits of liability not less than: $2,000,000.00 for injury or death to one or more persons; and $1,000,000.00 with respect to damage to property, which will incude independent contractors coverage. Tenant shall furnish Landlord with certificates evidencing that such insurance is in effect, stating that Landlord shall be notified in writing thirty (30) days prior to cancellation, material change, or nonrenewal of insurance.

(ii) Boiler Insurance. If during the Term hereof Tenant receives Landlord's written approval to operate a pressure boiler or other pressure vessels in the Premises, Tenant will place and carry boiler insurance with companies licensed to do business in the state in which the Shopping Center is located in adequate amounts approved by Landlord, but not less than $100,000.00 property damage per occurrence, and will comply fully with all applicable laws, statutes, and regulations with reference to the operation and inspection of boilers and steam vessels. Tenant shall furnish Landlord with certificates or other evidence acceptable to Landlord that such insurance is in effect, which evidence shall state that Landlord shall be notified in writing thirty (30) days prior to cancellation, material change, or nonrenewal of insurance.

(iii) Workers' Compensation. If during the Term hereof, the nature of Tenant's operation is such as to place any or all of its employees under the coverage of state Workers' Compensation or similar statutes, Tenant shall also keep in force, at its expense, Workers' Compensation or similar insurance affording statutory coverage and containing statutory limits. Tenant shall also keep in force, at its expense, so called Employer's Liability Insurance affording employers liability protection with a limit of coverage of not less than $100,000.00. At the written request of Landlord, Tenant agrees to furnish to Landlord evidence of Workers' Compensation coverage.

(iv) During the Term hereof Tenant agrees to carry, at its expense, insurance for Fire and Extended Coverage, insuring for the full insurable value of Tenant's Work, Tenant's leasehold improvements, merchandise, trade fixtures, furnishings, operating equipment, and personal property, including wall coverings, carpeting, and drapes.

(v) If Tenant shall not comply with its covenants made in (i), (ii), (iii), and (iv) above, Landlord may obtain such insurance, and in such event Tenant agrees to pay the premium for such insurance.

B. Tenant will not do or suffer to be done, or keep or suffer to be kept, anything in, upon, or about the Premises that will contravene Landlord's policies insuring against loss or damage by fire or other hazards (including, without limitation, public liability) or that will prevent Landlord from procuring such policies in companies acceptable to Landlord. If anything done, omitted to be done, or suffered to be done by Tenant, or kept or suffered by Tenant to be kept, in, upon, or about the Premises shall cause the rate of fire or other insurance on the Premises or other property of Landlord in companies acceptable to Landlord to be increased beyond the minimum rate from time to time applicable to the Premises for the use permitted under this Lease or to any other property for the use or uses made thereof, Tenant will pay the amount of any increase.

C. Release. Anything in this Lease to the contrary notwithstanding, it is agreed that each party (the "Releasing Party") hereby release the other (the "Released Party") from liability which the Released Party would, but for this Article, have had to the Releasing Party during the Term of this Lease, resulting from the occurrence of any accident or occurrence or casualty to property which is (1) normally covered by a Fire and Extended Coverage policy (with a vandalism and malicious mischief endorsement attached) or by a sprinkler leakage, boiler and machinery, or water damage policy in the state in which the Shopping Center is located (irrespective of whether such coverage is being carried by the Releasing Party), or (2) covered by any other insurance against direct damage to property being carried by the Releasing Party at the time of such occurrence. Insofar as Tenant is the Releasing Party, it will also release from any such liability for damage to property the department stores and any ground lessor or mortgagee as if the department stores and ground lessor mortgagee were each a Released Party under this Article 18C.

ARTICLE 19: TENANT INDEMNITY

Tenant will indemnify Landlord and save it harmless from and against any and all claims, actions, damages, liability, and expense in connection with loss of life and/or personal injury arising from or out of the occupancy or use by Tenant of the Premises or any part thereof or any other part of Landlord's property, occasioned wholly or in part by any negligent act or omission of Tenant, its officers, agents, contractors, or employees.

ARTICLE 20: MECHANICS LIENS

Tenant agrees to pay promptly all sums of money in respect of any labor, services, materials, supplies, or equipment furnished or alleged to have been furnished to Tenant or anyone holding the Premises or any part thereof, through, or under Tenant in, at, or about the Premises, or furnished to Tenant's agents, employees, contractors, or subcontractors, which may be secured by any mechanics, materialsmen, suppliers, or other type of lien against the Premises or the Landlord's interest therein. In the event any such or similar lien shall be filed, Tenant shall, within twenty-four (24) hours of receipt thereof, give notice to Landlord of such lien, and Tenant shall, within ten (10) days after receiving notice of the filing of the lien, discharge such lien. Failure of Tenant to discharge the lien shall constitute a default under this Lease and in addition to any other right or remedy of Landlord, Landlord may but shall not be obligated to discharge the same of record by paying the amount claimed to be due, and the amount so paid by Landlord and all cost and expenses incurred by Landlord therewith, including reasonable attorneys' fees, shall be due and payable by Tenant to Landlord.

Tenant acknowledges that Landlord may have posted notice on the Shopping Center of nonresponsibility for liens under the laws of the state in which the Shopping Center is located, and Tenant covenants and agrees to so advise all contractors, materialsmen, suppliers, and other persons performing work or providing services and/or supplies to the Premises on behalf of Tenant.

ARTICLE 21: ASSIGNMENT OR SUBLETTING

Tenant agrees not to sell, assign, mortgage, pledge, franchise, or in any manner transfer this Lease or any estate or interest thereunder and not to sublet the Premises or any part or parts thereof and not to permit any licensee or concessionaire therein without the previous written consent of the Landlord in each instance first obtained. Consent by Landlord to one assignment of this Lease or to one subletting, sale, mortgage, pledge, or other transfer including licensing or the grant of a concession shall not be a waiver of Landlord's rights under this Article as to any subsequent similar action. This prohibition includes any subletting, assignment, or transfer which would otherwise occur by operation of law.

If, at any time during the Term of this Lease, Tenant or Tenant's guarantor, if any, is

(i) a corporation or a trust (whether or not having shares of beneficial interest) and there shall occur any

change in the identity of any of the persons then having power to participate in the election or appointment of the directors, trustees, or other persons exercising like functions and managing the affairs of Tenant; or

(ii) a partnership or association or otherwise not a natural person (and is not a corporation or a trust) and there shall occur any change in the identity of any of the persons who then are members of such partnership or association or who comprise Tenant;

Tenant shall so notify Landlord and Landlord may terminate this Lease by notice to Tenant given within ninety (90) days thereafter. This Section shall not apply if the Tenant or Tenant's guarantor, if any, named herein is a corporation and the outstanding voting stock thereof is listed on a recognized securities exchange or is wholly owned by another corporation whose outstanding voting stock is so listed.

Landlord's rights to assign this Lease are and shall remain unqualified. Upon any sale of the Premises, Landlord shall thereupon be entirely freed of all obligations of the Landlord hereunder and shall not be subject to any liability resulting from any act or omission or event occurring after such conveyance, except that any covenant or obligation of Landlord hereunder affecting land owned by Landlord shall continue for its term during such ownership, but no longer. Upon the sale or other transfer of Landlord's interest in this Lease, Tenant agrees to recognize and attorn to such transferee as Landlord, and Tenant further agrees to execute and deliver a recordable instrument setting forth the provisions of this paragraph.

Tenant agrees to pay to Landlord on demand reasonable attorneys fees incurred by Landlord in connection with Landlord giving its consent to any assignment or subletting by Tenant.

ARTICLE 22: EMINENT DOMAIN

A. If the whole or any part of the Premises shall be taken under the power of eminent domain, this Lease shall terminate as to the part so taken on the date ("taking date") Tenant is required to yield possession thereof to the condemning authority. Landlord shall make such repairs and alterations as may be necessary in order to restore the part not taken to useful condition. Effective with the taking date the Annual Minimum Rent and the amount of Gross Sales specified on the Data Sheet with respect to Percentage Rent shall be reduced in proportion to the amount of the Premises so taken, and the number of square feet of the Premises specified on the Data Sheet shall be reduced accordingly. If the amount of the Premises so taken substantially impairs the usefulness of the Premises for the use permitted in the Data Sheet, either party may, by notice to the other delivered at least sixty (60) days prior to the taking date, terminate this Lease as of the taking date.

B. If more than twenty percent (20%) of the Common Area or if any portion of the building in which the Premises are located shall be taken by eminent domain, Landlord may, by notice to Tenant delivered on or before the taking date, terminate this Lease as of the taking date.

C. The term "eminent domain" shall include the exercise of any similar governmental power and any purchase or other acquisition in lieu of condemnation. All compensation awarded for any taking of the fee and the leasehold shall belong to and be the property of Landlord provided, however, that Landlord shall not be entitled to any award made to Tenant for relocation or moving expenses.

ARTICLE 23: DAMAGE TO PREMISES

A. In the event the Premises are damaged or destroyed by fire, or other casualty insurable under a standard Fire and Extended Coverage policy, as issued from time to time in the state where the Shopping Center is located, Landlord shall, subject to being able to obtain all necessary permits and approvals therefor within 180 days of such casualty, and provided Landlord has not terminated this Lease pursuant to Article 23C hereof, commence to repair, reconstruct, and restore Landlord's work to the condition in which it was immediately prior to the happening of such casualty, except for the items Tenant is responsible to repair or replace pursuant to Article 23B hereof and prosecute the same diligently to completion. If the Premises are rendered partially or totally untenantable as a result of such casualty, then to the extent the Premises are rendered untenantable, the Annual Minimum Rent and the HVAC Charge shall be proportionately abated until Landlord has completed such repair, reconstruction, or restoration.

B. In the event Landlord is required or elects to repair, reconstruct, or restore Landlord's Work, Tenant agrees to repair or replace Tenant's Work, Tenant's leasehold improvements, its merchandise, trade fixtures, furnishings, operating equipment, and personal property, including wall coverings, carpeting, and drapes, as soon as possible after the occurrence of such casualty to at least a condition equal to that prior to its damage or destruction. In no event shall Landlord be liable for interruption to the business of

Tenant or for damage to or repair, reconstruction, or restoration of any items belonging to Tenant or within the Premises.

C. Landlord shall have the option to terminate this Lease upon giving written notice to Tenant of the exercise thereof within forty-five (45) days after the occurrence of an event described in Article 23A hereof, if:

(i) The event occurs within the last three (3) years of the Term; or

(ii) Twenty percent (20%) or more of the number of square feet located on the Shopping Center Tract designated by Landlord for occupancy by its tenants immediately prior to such event is rendered untenantable thereby.

D. If fifteen percent (15%) or more of the number of square feet located on the Shopping Center Tract designated by Landlord for occupancy by its tenants immediately prior to an event which is not insurable under a standard Fire and Extended Coverage policy as issued from time to time in the state where the Shopping Center is located, is rendered untenantable by such event, or if Landlord cannot obtain all necessary permits and approvals for the repair, reconstruction, and restoration of the Premises within the period permitted under Article 23A hereof, the Landlord shall have the option to terminate this Lease upon giving written notice to Tenant of the exercise thereof within forty-five (45) days after the occurrence of such uninsured event or lapse of time, as the case may be.

E. Upon any termination of this Lease under the provisions of this Article, the Rent imposed under this Lease shall be adjusted as of the date of such termination and the parties shall be released thereby without further obligation to the other party coincident with the surrender of possession of the Premises to the Landlord, except for items which have been theretofore accrued and are then unpaid, and except for obligations which are designated as surviving such termination.

ARTICLE 24: SURRENDER OF PREMISES

This Lease shall terminate at the end of the Term hereof without the necessity of any notice from either Landlord or Tenant to terminate the same, and Tenant hereby waives notice to vacate the Premises and agrees that Landlord shall be entitled to the benefit of all provisions of law respecting the summary recovery of possession of Premises from a tenant holding over to the same extent as if statutory notice had been given. For the period of six (6) months prior to the expiration of the Term, Landlord shall have the right to display on the exterior of the Premises (but not in any window or doorway thereof) the customary sign "For Rent", and during such period Landlord may show the Premises and all parts thereof to prospective tenants during normal business hours.

On the last day of the Term hereof, Tenant shall peaceably and quietly surrender the Premises, including, but not limited to, all leasehold improvements pursuant to the provisions of Article 4 hereof, broom-clean and in the same condition as the Premises were in upon delivery of possession thereto under this Lease; reasonable wear and tear excepted, and free of any and all liens and/or claims of right of possession by any person, firm, or corporation claiming through or under Tenant. Subject to the provisions of Article 15 hereof, on or before the last day of the Term, Tenant shall remove all trade fixtures from the Premises and repair any damage occasioned by any such removal. Property not so removed shall be deemed abandoned by Tenant, and Landlord, at Landlord's option, may retain all and any part of such property, and title thereto shall thereupon vest in Landlord, or Landlord may remove from the Premises and dispose of in any manner all or any of such property, in which latter event Tenant shall pay to Landlord upon demand the actual expense of such removal and disposition, and the repair of any and all damage to the Premises resulting from or caused by such removal. If the Premises be not surrendered at such time, Tenant shall indemnify Landlord against loss or liability resulting from delay by Tenant in so surrendering the Premises, including, without limitation, any claims made by any succeeding tenant founded on such delay. Tenant shall surrender all keys for the Premises to Landlord at the place then fixed for payment of Rent and shall inform Landlord of combinations on any locks and safes on the Premises. In the event Tenant shall fail to deliver the Premises to Landlord in the condition called for under this Article 24, Landlord shall have the right to cause any such deficiency to be corrected, and Tenant agrees to pay the cost thereof. The provisions of this Article 24 shall survive termination of this Lease.

ARTICLE 25: BANKRUPTCY OR INSOLVENCY

If any sale of Tenant's interest in the Premises created by this Lease shall be made under execution or similar legal process, or if Tenant shall be adjudicated as bankrupt or insolvent and such adjudication is not vacated within thirty (30) days, or if a receiver or trustee shall be appointed for Tenant's business or property and such appointment shall not be vacated within thirty (30) days, or if a corporate reorganization of Tenant or any arrangement with its creditors shall be approved by a court under the Federal Bankruptcy Act, or if Tenant shall make an assignment for the benefit of creditors, or if in any other manner Tenant's interest under this Lease shall pass to another by operation of law, Tenant shall be deemed to have breached a material covenant and Landlord may re-enter the Premises and declare this Lease and the tenancy hereby created terminated.

ARTICLE 26: DEFAULT OF TENANT

A. In the event Tenant shall:

(i) fail to pay Rent due under this Lease within ten (10) days after the same shall become due, or

(ii) fail to keep or perform any of the other terms, conditions, or covenants of the Lease to be kept or performed by Tenant for more than thirty (30) days after notice of such failure shall have been given to Tenant, or

(iii) vacate or abandon (not operating for business in the Premises for ten [10] consecutive days) the Premises, then the Landlord, besides other rights or remedies it may have, shall have the right to either (a) terminate this Lease upon the expiration of five (5) days after written notice of such intent is given to Tenant, in which event the Term hereof shall expire and terminate with the same force and effect as though the date set forth in said notice were the date originally set forth herein and fixed for the expiration of the Term, or (b) re-enter the Premises either by force or otherwise, dispossess Tenant and/or other occupants of the Premises, remove all property from the Premises and store the same in a public warehouse or elsewhere at the cost of and for the account of Tenant, and hold the Premises as hereinafter provided, without notice or resort to legal process and without being deemed guilty of trespass or becoming liable for any loss or damage which may be occasioned thereby, Tenant agreeing that no such re-entry or taking possession of the Premises by Landlord shall be construed as an election on Landlord's part to terminate this Lease, such right, however, being continuously reserved by Landlord.

B. In the event Landlord elects to re-enter the Premises, Landlord may, but shall not be obligated to, make such alterations and repairs as may be necessary in order to relet the Premises, and relet said Premises or any part thereof for such term or terms (which may extend beyond the Term of this Lease) and at such rental and upon such other terms and conditions as Landlord in its sole discretion may deem advisable. Upon each such reletting all rentals and other sums received by Landlord from such reletting shall be applied, first, to the payment of any indebtedness other than Rent due hereunder from Tenant to Landlord; second, to the payment of any costs and expenses of such reletting, including reasonable brokerage fees and attorneys' fees and of costs of such alterations and repairs; third, to the payment of Rent and other charges due and unpaid hereunder; and the residue, if any, shall be held by Landlord and applied in payment of future Rent as the same may become due and payable hereunder. If such rentals and other sums received from such reletting during any month be less than that to be paid during that month by Tenant hereunder, Tenant shall pay such deficiency to Landlord; if such rentals and sums shall be more, Tenant shall have no right to the excess. Such deficiency shall be calculated and paid monthly. Notwithstanding any such re-entry by Landlord, Landlord may at any time hereafter elect to terminate this Lease for such previous breach.

C. Should Landlord at any time terminate this Lease for any breach, in addition to any other remedies it may have, it may recover from Tenant all damages it may incur by reason of such breach, including the cost of recovering the Premises, reasonable attorneys' fees, and including the worth at the time of such termination of the excess, if any, of the amount of Rent reserved in this Lease for the remainder of the stated Term over the then reasonable rental value of the Premises for the remainder of the stated Term, all of which amounts shall be immediately due and payable from Tenant to Landlord. In determining the Annual Minimum Rent portion of the aggregate Rent which would be payable by Tenant hereunder, subsequent to default, the Annual Minimum Rent for each year of the unexpired Term shall be equal to the average Annual Minimum and Percentage Rents paid by Tenant from the commencement of the Term to the time of default, or during the preceding three (3) full calendar years, whichever period is shorter. The failure or refusal of Landlord to relet the Premises shall not affect Tenant's liability. The terms "entry" and "re-entry" are not limited to their technical meanings.

D. It is mutually agreed by and between Landlord and Tenant that the respective parties hereto shall and they hereby do waive trial by jury in any action, proceeding, or counterclaim brought by either of the parties hereto against the other (except for personal injury or property damage) on any matters whatsoever arising out of or in any way connected with this Lease, the relationship of Landlord and Tenant, Tenant's use or occupancy of said Premises, and any emergency statutory or any other statutory remedy. Tenant shall not interpose any counterclaim or counterclaims in a summary proceeding or other action based on termination or holdover.

E. Mention in this Lease of any particular remedy shall not preclude Landlord from any other remedy, in law or in equity. Tenant hereby expressly waives any and all rights of redemption granted by or under any present or future laws in the event of Tenant being evicted or dispossessed for any cause, or in the event of Landlord obtaining possession of Premises, by reason of the violation by Tenant of any of the covenants and conditions of this Lease or otherwise.

ARTICLE 27: CHANGES TO SHOPPING CENTER

Landlord hereby reserves the absolute right at any time and from time to time to: (a) make changes or revisions in the Site Plan as shown on Exhibit A, including but not limited to additions to, subtractions from, or rearrangements of the building areas and/or Common Areas (both interior and/or exterior) indicated on Exhibit A; (b) construct additional or other buildings or improvements in the Shopping Center Tract and to make alterations thereof or additions thereto and to build additional stores on any such building or buildings and to build adjoining same; and (c) to increase or decrease the land size of the Shopping Center and any land so added shall thereafter be subject to the terms of this Lease and shall be included in the term Shopping Center as used in this Lease and any land so withdrawn shall thereafter not be subject to the terms of this Lease and shall be excluded from the term Shopping Center as used in this Lease. In the event Landlord shall elect to construct any additonal buildings, all easement rights granted herein to Tenant shall automatically terminate as to the land upon which such additional buildings are constructed, and Landlord shall have the absolute right to redefine the Shopping Center Tract.

ARTICLE 28: NONINTERFERENCE

Tenant recognizes that the Shopping Center is open for business and that any construction work to be done in, at, or upon the Premises by Tenant may interfere with the operation of the Shopping Center. Therefore, Tenant agrees to use its best efforts during the performance of any construction work to cause no interference to the Shopping Center or any person, firm, or corporation doing business in the Shopping Center.

ARTICLE 29: EXPANSION OF TENANT'S PREMISES: RENT ADJUSTMENT

In the event of any expansion of the Premises, by the addition of a mezzanine floor or addition of other usable space so that the total number of square feet in the Premises is greater than that set out on the Data Sheet, adjustment shall be made in the application of the formulas for the computation of Tenant's additional rents payable under this Lease where such additional rent is calculated on the floor area in the Premises including payments under Article 10 (Taxes), Article 12 (Common Area), Article 13 (Utilities), and Article 14 (Merchants Association).

ARTICLE 30: NONLIABILITY

Save for its negligence, Landlord shall not be responsible or liable to Tenant for any loss or damage that may be occasioned by or through the acts or omissions of persons occupying adjoining premises or any part of the premises adjacent to or connected with the Premises or any part of the building of which the Premises are a part, or any persons transacting any business in the Shopping Center or present in the Shopping Center for any other purpose or for any loss or damage resulting to Tenant or its property from burst, stopping, or leaking water, sewer, sprinkler, or steam pipes or plumbing fixtures or from any failure of or defect in any electric line, circuit, or facility.

ARTICLE 31: INTEREST

Any amount due from Tenant to Landlord under this Lease which is not paid when due shall bear interest at the highest legal rate from the date due until paid; provided, however, the payment of such interest shall not excuse or cure the default upon which such interest accrued.

ARTICLE 32: EXPENSE OF ENFORCEMENT

If Landlord should prevail in any litigation by or against Tenant related to this Lease, or if Landlord should become a party to any litigation instituted by or against Tenant with respect to any third party, Landlord shall receive from Tenant all costs and reasonable attorneys' fees incurred in such litigation.

ARTICLE 33: HOLDING OVER

In the event Tenant remains in possession of the Premises after the expiration of this Lease and without the execution of a new lease, it shall be deemed to be occupying the Premises as a tenant from month to month, subject to all the conditions, provisions, and obligations of this Lease in so far as the same can be applicable to month-to-month tenancy cancellable by either party upon thirty (30) days' written notice to the other; provided, however, that during the month-to-month tenancy the Total Annual Minimum Rent shall be double the amount specified herein.

ARTICLE 34: RIGHTS OF PARTIES TO TERMINATE THIS LEASE

This Lease shall be binding from the date hereof until the commencement of the Term as provided herein and thereafter according to its terms; provided, however, that in consideration of the sums of money previously expended by Landlord in connection with the Shopping Center Tract, and the sum of One Dollar ($1.00) in hand paid by Landlord to Tenant, the receipt and sufficiency of which is hereby acknowledged, Landlord shall have the option to cancel this Lease if Tenant shall fail to open for business on or before the thirtieth (30th) day following Commencement Date by giving Tenant written notice. If this Lease is cancelled pursuant to such option, Tenant will execute an instrument in recordable form containing a release and surrender of all right, title, and interest in and to the Premises under this Lease or otherwise and Tenant appoints Landlord its attorney-in-fact to execute such a document.

ARTICLE 35: INSPECTION

Tenant will permit Landlord, its agents, employees, and contractors to enter all parts of the Premises to inspect the same and to enforce or carry out any provisions of this Lease.

ARTICLE 36: SHORT FORM

Tenant agrees that this Lease shall not be recorded without the prior written consent of Landlord.

ARTICLE 37: NONWAIVER

Landlord's failure to insist upon a strict performance of any covenant of this Lease or to exercise any option or right herein contained shall not be a waiver or relinquishment for the future of such covenant, right, or option, but the same shall remian in full force and effect.

ARTICLE 38: CAPTIONS

The captions and headings herein are for convenience and reference only.

ARTICLE 39: APPLICABLE LAW

This Lease shall be construed under the laws of the state in which the Shopping Center is located. If any provision of this Lease, or portion thereof, or the application thereof to any person or circumstance shall, to any extent, be invalid or unenforceable, the remainder of this Lease shall not be affected thereby and each provision of this Lease shall be valid and enforceable to the fullest extent permitted by law.

ARTICLE 40: SUCCESSORS

This Lease and the covenants and conditions herein contained shall inure to the benefit of and be binding upon Landlord, its heirs, executors, administrators, successors, and assigns, and shall be binding upon Tenant, its heirs, executors, administrators, successors, and assigns, and shall inure to the benefit of Tenant and only such assigns of Tenant to whom the assignment by Tenant has been consented to by Landlord.

ARTICLE 41: FORCE MAJEURE

The time within which any of the parties hereto shall be required to perform any act or acts under this Lease shall be extended to the extent that the performance of such act or acts shall be delayed by acts of God, fire, windstorm, flood, explosion, collapse of structures, riot, war, labor disputes, delays or restrictions by governmental bodies, inability to obtain or use necessary materials, or any cause beyond the reasonable control of such party, other than lack of monies or inability to procure monies to fulfill its commitments or obligations under this Lease (any such delay being called "unavoidable delay" in this Lease), provided, however, that the party entitled to such extension hereunder shall give prompt notice to the other party of the occurrence causing such delay. The provisions of this Article 41 shall not operate to excuse Tenant from prompt payment of Rent or any other payments required by the terms of this Lease.

ARTICLE 42: BROKERS

Each of the parties represents and warrants that there are no claims for brokerage commission or finder's fees in connection with the execution of this Lease, and agrees to indemnify the other against, and hold it harmless from, all liabilities arising from any such claim (incuding, without limitation, the cost of legal fees in connection therewith).

ARTICLE 43: NO PARTNERSHIP

Any intention to create a joint venture, partnership, or agency relation between the parties hereto is hereby expressly disclaimed. The provisions of this Lease in regard to the payment by Tenant and the acceptance by Landlord of a percentage of Gross Sales of Tenant and others is a reservation of Rent for the use of the Premises.

ARTICLE 44: AMENDMENTS IN WRITING

This Lease and the Exhibits attached hereto and forming a part hereof set forth all the covenants, promises, agreements, conditions, and understandings between Landlord and Tenant concerning the demised Premises, and there are no covenants, promises, agreements, conditions, or understandings, either oral or written, between them other than are herein set forth. Except as herein otherwise provided, no subsequent alteration, amendment, change, or addition to this Lease shall be binding upon Landlord or Tenant unless reduced to writing and signed by them.

ARTICLE 45: LIABILITY

If two or more individuals, corporations, partnerships, or other business associations (or any combination of two or more thereof) shall sign this Lease as Tenant, the liability of each such individual, corporation, partnership, or other business association to pay Rent and perform all other obligations hereunder shall be deemed to be joint and several. In like manner, if the Tenant named in this Lease shall be a partnership or other business association, the members of which are by virtue of statute or general law subject to personal liability, the liability of each such member shall be deemed to be joint and several.

If Landlord shall fail to perform any covenant, term, or condition of this Lease upon Landlord's part to be performed, and if as a consequence of such default any party claiming through, under, or by way of Tenant thereunder, including Tenant itself, shall recover a money judgment against Landlord, such judgment shall be satisfied only out of the proceeds of sale received upon execution of such judgment and levied thereon against the right, title, and interest of Landlord in the Shopping Center Tract, and Landlord shall not be liable for any deficiency. Such judgment and the satisfaction thereof out of the proceeds of sale received upon said execution and levy shall, in all events, be subject to all matters appearing of record prior to the entry or final date of the judgment.

ARTICLE 46: AUTHORITY

Tenant, if a corporation, warrants and represents to Landlord that Tenant's execution of this Lease is pursuant to a resolution of the Tenant's Board of Directors.

ARTICLE 47: COPIES

This Lease is executed in five (5) copies, any of which may be considered and used as an original copy.

ARTICLE 48: EXAMINATION

The submission of this Lease for examination does not constitute a reservation of or option for the Premises and this Lease becomes effective only upon execution and delivery thereof by Landlord and Tenant.

ARTICLE 49: ESTOPPEL

Tenant agrees that at any time and from time to time at reasonable intervals, within ten (10) days after written request by Landlord, Tenant will execute, acknowledge, and deliver to Landlord, Landlord's mortgagee, or other designated by Landlord, a certificate in a form as may from time to time be provided, ratifying this Lease and certifying (a) that Tenant has entered into occupancy of the Premises and the date of such entry if such is the case; (b) that the Lease is in full force and effect, and has not been assigned, modified, supplemented, or amended in any way (or, if there has been any assignment, modification, supplement, or amendment, identifying the same); (c) that this Lease represents the entire agreement beween Landlord and Tenant as to the subject matter hereof (or, if there has been an assignment, modification, supplement, or amendment, identifying the same); (d) the date of commencement and expiration of the Term; (e) that all conditions under this Lease to be performed by Landlord have been satisfied and all required contributions by Landlord to Tenant on account of Tenant's improvements have been received (and if not, what conditions remain unperformed); (f) that to the knowledge of the signer of such writing no default exists in the performance or observance of any covenant or condition in this Lease and there are no defenses or offsets against the enforcement of this Lease by Landlord or specifying each default, defense or offset of which the signer may have knowledge; (g) that no Annual Minimum Rent or other rental has been paid in advance and no security has been deposited with Landlord, and (h) the date to which Annual Minimum Rent and all other rentals have been paid under this Lease. Tenant hereby irrevocably appoints Landlord its attorney-in-fact to execute such a writing in the event Tenant shall fail to do so within ten (10) days of receipt of Landlord's request.

ARTICLE 50: NOTICES

Any notice desired or required to be given under this Lease shall be sent postage paid registered or certified mail return receipt requested, as to Landlord: _____ with a copy to: _____ and as to Tenant, to Tenant's address shown on page 1 of this Lease.

Either party may (1) by written notice designate a different address to which notices may be sent, and (2) by written notice designate not more than two (2) additional parties to whom copies of all notices must be sent.

STATE OF _____)
)ss.
COUNTY OF_____)

On this _____ day of _____, 19____, before me, a Notary Public within and for said County, personally appeared _____ and _____, to me personally known, who, being each by me duly sworn, did say that they were respectively the _____ and the _____ of _____, the corporation named in the foregoing instrument, and that the seal affixed to said instrument is the corporate seal of said corporation, and that said instrument was signed and sealed in behalf of said corporation by authority of its Board of Directors, and _____ and _____ acknowledged said instrument to be the free act and deed of said corporation.

Notary Public _____ County
My commission expires _____

STATE OF_____)
)ss.
COUNTY OF_____)

On this _____ day of _____ 19____, before me, a Notary Public within and for said County, personally appeared _____ and _____, to me personally known, who, being each by me duly sworn, did say that they were respectively the _____ and the _____ of _____, the corporation named in the foregoing instrument, and that the seal affixed to said instrument is the corporate seal of said corporation, and that said instrument was signed and sealed in behalf of said corporation by authority of its Board of Directors, and _____ and _____ acknowledged said instrument to be the free act and deed of said corporation.

Notary Public _____ County
My commission expires _____

EXHIBIT A
(not shown)
EXHIBIT B

GENERAL REQUIREMENTS

I. PREPARATION OF DRAWINGS

A. Tenant shall prepare, at Tenant's expense, Design Drawings, Working Drawings, Shop Drawings, Specifications, and Calculations as required in Exhibit C. All structural, mechanical, and electrical drawings shall be prepared and stamped by an engineer or architect licensed to do business within the state in which the Center is located.

B. Tenant shall secure Landlord's WRITTEN approval of all Design Drawings, Working Drawings, Shop Drawings, and Specifications in accordance with schedules and procedures outlined in Exhibit C prior to commencement of any construction.

II. PREPARATION FOR CONSTRUCTION

A. Materials and Warranties. Tenant shall use only new, first class materials in completion of Tenant's Work. All work and equipment shall be warranted for a minimum of one (1) year from installation.

B. Tenant Contractors

1. All contractors engaged by Tenant shall be bondable, licensed contractors, having good labor relations, and be capable of performing quality workmanship.

2. Tenant's contractors shall work in harmony with Landlord's and other contractors on the job and observe

the established rules and regulations appropriate for ethical and safe conduct on the site.

3. In the event that Tenant's contractor willfully violates the requirements of this Lease, Landlord may order Tenant's contractor to remove himself, his equipment, and his employees from Landlord's property.

C. Permits, Licenses, Codes. Tenant shall obtain all licenses and permits necessary to complete Tenant's Work. Tenant's Work shall conform to all applicable statutes, ordinances, regulations, and codes and to the requirements of all other regulatory authorities.

D. Modifications to Existing Facilities. Any modification to Landlord's existing facilities or building must receive the WRITTEN approval of Landlord, and all work shall be performed at Landlord's direction and at Tenant's expense.

III. COMMENCEMENT OF TENANT CONSTRUCTION

A. On-Site Meeting. A minimum of five (5) days prior to the commencement of Tenant construction, Tenant and Tenant's contractor shall meet with the Landlord's Tenant Coordinator in the Tenant's designated Premises. At that time, Tenant shall provide Landlord the following items:

1. Copy of Tenant's Building Permit.

2. Certificate setting forth name and address of Tenant's general, mechanical, electrical, and sprinkler contractor(s) involved in completion of Tenant's Work portion of Premises.

3. Certificate of Insurance as called for herein. Tenant's contractors shall not be permitted to commence any work until all required insurance has been obtained and certificates have been received by Landlord.

Tenant shall secure, pay for, and maintain or cause its contractor(s) to secure and maintain during preparation of Premises, the following insurance in the following amounts, which shall be endorsed in all policies to include Landlord and its beneficiaries and their employees and agents as insured parties, and which shall provide in all policies that Landlord shall be given ten (10) days' prior written notice of any alteration or termination of coverage, in amounts as set forth below:

Tenant's General Contractor and Subcontractor's Required Minimum Coverages and Limits of Liability.

a.) Workers' Compensation. Employer's Liability Insurance with limits of not less than $100,000.00 and where required by state law any insurance required by any Employee Benefit Acts or other statutes applicable where the work is to be performed as will protect the contractor and subcontractors from any and all liability under the aforementioned Act.

b.) Comprehensive General Liability Insurance (including Contractor's Protective Liability) in an amount not less than $3,000,000.00 for injury or death to any one or more persons, and $1,000,000.00 with respect to damage to property. Such insurance shall provide for explosion and collapse coverage and contractural liability coverage and shall insure the general contractor and/or subcontractors against any and all claims for personal injury, including death resulting therefrom, and damage to the property of others and arising from his operations under the Contract and whether such operations are performed by the general contractor, subcontractors, or any of their subcontractors or by anyone directly or indirectly employed by any of them.

c.) Comprehensive Automobile Liability Insurance, including the ownership, maintenance, and operation of any automotive equipment, owned, hired, and nonowned, in the following minimum amounts:

(i) Bodily injury, each person $1,000,000.00
(ii) Bodily injury, each occurrence................. $3,000,000.00
(iii) Property Damage, each occurrence................ $1,000,000.00

d.) Tenant's Protective Liability Insurance. Tenant shall provide Owner's Protective Liability Insurance as will insure Tenant against any and all liability to third parties for damage because of bodily injury liability (or death resulting therefrom) and property damage liability of others or a combination thereof which may arise from work in the completion of the premises, and any other liability for damages which the general contractor and/or subcontractors are required to insure under any provision herein. Said insurance shall be provided in minimum amounts as follows

(i) Bodily injury, each person $1,000,000.00
(ii) Bodily injury, each occurrence................. $3,000,000.00
(iii) Property Damage, each occurrence................ $1,000,000.00

e.) Tenant's Builders Risk Insurance. Tenant shall provide a completed Value Form "All Physical Loss" Builder's Risk coverage on its work in the Premises as it relates to the building within which the Premises is located, naming the interests of the Landlord, its general contractor, and all subcontractors, as their respective interest may appear, within a radius of 100 feet of the Premises.

B. Authorization for Access

1. Upon Tenant's compliance with applicable requirements as set forth within Section A above, Landlord shall issue Tenant a written letter of Authorization for Access to property. Tenant construction shall not be allowed to commence until requirements have been met and Authorization for Access issued.

2. Tenant, by occupying the designated space for construction, shall be deemed to have accepted the Premises; have acknowledged that Landlord has completed the work required of it pursuant to this Exhibit, and that the same are in the condition called for hereunder; and have agreed that Landlord is not then in default in any of its obligation under this Lease.

IV. TENANT CONSTRUCTION

A. Field Drawings. Tenant's Contractor shall maintain (in the Tenant's Premises), at all times during the Tenant's construction of the Premises, a set of Tenant Working Drawings bearing Landlord's stamped approval.

B. Landlord Inspection. The Premise will be inspected periodically by Landlord, for compliance with Landlord's requirements as set forth in this Lease and in accordance with Landlord Approved Working Drawings. Any unauthorized construction will be corrected at Tenant's expense.

C. Punch List. At the completion of the Premise, Tenant's representative and Tenant's contractor will meet with the Tenant Coordinator. They will conduct a final inspection and prepare a "punch list," which will enumerate any areas of construction fixturing or merchandising that are not in accordance with Tenant's Landlord Approved Drawings or Lease.

D. Occupancy Permit. Tenant shall secure its own Occupancy Permit before opening and forward a copy to Landlord.

V. GENERAL REQUIREMENTS

A. Proof of Payment. Tenant shall provide Landlord with proof of payment that all costs of construction of Tenant's Work have been paid. Such proof shall include Waiver of Lien and sworn statements from Tenant's contractors or such other proof as may be required by Landlord in special instances.

B. Conflicts. Where conflict between building codes, utility regulations, statutes, ordinances, or other regulatory authority requirements and Landlord's requirements, as set forth herein, exist the more stringent of the two shall govern.

C. Landlord Intrusion. Landlord, Tenant, or an authorized utility company, as the case may be, shall have the right, subject to Landlord's written approval, to run utility lines, pipes, conduits, or duct work, where necessary or desirable, through attic space, column space, or other parts of Premises, and to repair, alter, replace, or remove the same, all in a manner which does not interfere unnecessarily with Tenant's use thereof.

EXHIBIT C
DESIGN AND CONSTRUCTION CRITERIA

I. DRAWING CRITERIA

A. TENANT'S DESIGN DRAWING CRITERIA

1. Within thirty (30) days from either the date Tenant receives the Tenant Information Package or from the date Lease is executed, whichever is the latter, Tenant shall submit to Landlord for review and approval one (1) reproducible sepia transparency and two (2) blueline print sets of Design Drawings.

2. Tenant's Design Drawings shall include, but not be limited to, the following:

a.) Floor plan at 1/8" = 1'-0".

b.) Storefront elevations at 1/8" = 1'-0" scale including type of closure proposed.

c.) Sign Plan to include location, color, size, materials, etc.

d.) Longitudinal Section at 1/8" = 1'-0".

e.) Color photo of a similar store or color rendering.

f.) Storefront and Entrance Floor material samples.

3. Landlord shall return to Tenant one (1) set of prints of Design Drawings with suggested modifications and/or approval. If, upon receipt of approved Design Drawings bearing Landlord's comments, Tenant wishes to take exception thereto, Tenant may do so in writing by certified or registered mail addressed to Landlord within ten (10) days from date of receipt of Design Drawings. Unless such action is taken, it will be deemed that all comments made by Landlord on Design Drawings are acceptable and approved by Tenant.

4. If Design Drawings are returned to Tenant with comments, but not bearing approval of Landlord, said Design Drawings shall be immediately revised by Tenant and resubmitted to Landlord for approval within ten (10) days of their receipt by Tenant.

B. TENANT'S WORKING DRAWING CRITERIA

1. Within sixty (60) days from the date of receipt by Tenant of Landlord's approval of Tenant's Design Drawings or thirty (30) days prior to the commencement date of Tenant's Construction Days, whichever is the shorter, Tenant shall submit to Landlord for review and approval one (1) reproducible sepia set and two (2) blueline print sets of Working Drawings. Incomplete submissions will not be reviewed.

2. Tenant's Working Drawings shall include, but not be limited to, the following:

a.) Architectural Drawings.

1.) Key Plan showing location of Premises within the Shopping Center.
2.) Floor Plan at 1/8" = 1'-0" scale.
3.) Longitudinal Section at 1/8" = 1'-0" scale.
4.) Interior Elevations at 1/8" = 1'-0" scale.
5.) Storefront Plan, Section, Elevation at 1/4" = 1'-0" scale.
6.) Reflected Ceiling Plan at 1/8" = 1'-0" scale.
7.) Partition Wall Sections at 1/2" = 1'-0" scale.
8.) Store Fixtures & Furniture Plan at 1/8" = 1'-0" scale.
9.) Interior Color Finish Schedule.
10.) Specifications (if not on drawings).

b.) Electrical Drawings.

1.) Circuitry Plan at 1/8" = 1'-0" scale.
2.) Panelboard schedules.
3.) Riser Diagrams.
4.) Electrical Load Tabulations.
5.) Lighting Fixture Schedule indicating number of lamps per fixture, wattage, and type of each lamp.
6.) Specifications.

c.) Mechanical Drawings.

1.) HVAC Distribution Plan at 1/8" = 1'-0" scale.
2.) Mechanical/Electrical Data Tabulation Sheet.
3.) Plumbing Plan at 1/8" = 1'-0" scale.
4.) Specifications.

C. SIGN AND FIRE PROTECTION DRAWINGS

All submissions to include one (1) sepia transparency and two (2) blueline prints unless otherwise noted.

1. Sign Fabricator's Shop Drawings to be submitted by Tenant to Landlord prior to fabrication of sign; at a minimum scale of 1" = 1'-0" to include the following details:

a.) Dimensions clearly marked.

1.) Top of letter to soffit.
2.) Vertical edge of sign to vertical neutral strip.
3.) Height of letters above mall floor elevation.
4.) Letter projection from facia.

b.) Letters.

1.) Style and stroke.
2.) Face—indicate color, material, thickness.
3.) Returns—indicate color, material, thickness.

c.) Type of lighting.

d.) Electrical load.

e.) Brightness in foot—lamberts.

f.) Details at a minimum scale of 1 1/2" = 1'-0".

1.) Connection of sign letters and storefront.
2.) Mounting of transformer cabinet.
3.) Access to transformer cabinet.

2. Fire Protection Shop Drawings.

a.) Tenant's sprinkler subcontractor shall submit directly to Landlord's Fire Insurance Underwriter. Shop Drawings for approval. Submission shall include one (1) sepia transparency and two (2) blueline prints.

b.) Drawings shall include:

1.) Reflected Ceiling Plan with sprinkler head locations dimensioned at a minimum scale of 1/8" = 1'-0".
2.) Automatic Sprinkler details.
3.) Specifications.

II. ARCHITECTURAL CRITERIA

It is the desire of Landlord to give Tenant the greatest practical freedom in design, but such design must offer a pleasant, orderly appearance and must harmonize with the design of the Shopping Center itself and the design of the surrounding stores. All Tenant's work shall conform to the following standards.

A. STRUCTURAL

Landlord shall provide a two-level structural steel shell designed in accordance with governing building codes.

1. Framing. Columns shall be structural concrete.

2. Roof. Roof shall be insulated built-up bondable type by Landlord.

3. Any modification, revision, addition, or unusual loading to Landlord's structure shall be designed by Tenant's structural engineer and shall be subject to prior WRITTEN approval of Landlord.

B. FLOORS

1. Lower Level Floor. Landlord shall provide 4" slab on grade with troweled concrete surface. Should Tenant remove existing concrete tenant shall reinstall compacted back fill and 4" thick 3500 PSI/28 day concrete.

2. Upper Level Floor. Landlord shall provide structural slab designed for 100 lb. live load reducible based upon tributary area, with troweled finish surface. Upper level tenants shall make all floor penetrations necessary to facilitate tenant's utility connections and such penetrations must be sealed by Tenant in accordance wtih Landlord's standard project details. Penetration greater than twelve (12) inches square shall be framed in accordance with project details. Other penetrations by core drilling only.

3. Landlord has depressed Tenant slab ½". Tenant finish floor materials must be selected to cause Tenant's finish floor elevation to correspond exactly with Landlord's finish mall floor elevation.

4. Waterproofing. All kitchen, food handling, and restroom facilities areas on the upper level shall be waterproofed by Tenant in accordance with Landlord's standard project details.

5. Carpeting shall be used in all sales areas except in such instance where other equivalent types of floor covering materials are specifically approved by Landlord. Vinyl tile and vinyl asbestos tile are not considered acceptable finish materials.

6. Should an expansion joint occur in Premises, Tenant is responsible for the construction of the floor affected by that joint in a manner consistent with standard project details.

7. If Tenant elects to set base of Tenant's storefront back from lease line, Tenant shall furnish and install flooring material equal in quality and color to the mall flooring within area extending from lease line to such new storefront line, sliding or rolling grille line, or door track.

8. All exposed concrete within Premises must be sealed by Tenant.

C. PARTITIONS AND WALLS

1. Demising Partitions. Landlord shall provide exposed metal stud demising partitions between adjacent mercantile tenant spaces. Metal studs shall extend from Tenant's finished floor slab to underside of Landlord's overhead structural slab. Tenant shall install one layer of ⅝" fire code gypsum board, taped with spackled joints, tightly to the underside of superstructure slab above on Tenant's side of demising partitions and service corridor partitions. Calculations for the area of Demised Premises shall be made to the center of demising partitions.

2. Service Corridors. Landlord shall provide exposed concrete block or metal stud with gypsum board on Landlord's side of service corridor and exit core demising partitions. Demising partitions shall extend from finished floor slab to underside of Landlord's overhead structural slab. Calculations for area of Demised Premises shall be made to center of demising partitions and shall include that area required by code to accommodate a recessed door.

3. Service Door. Landlord shall provide 3'-0" × 7'-0" hollow metal door and frame for Premises adjacent to Landlord's service corridors and as governed by applicable building codes. Locksets will be mortise type and each door shall have not less than 1½ pair of butts. Service door and hardware shall be installed by Landlord at location designated by Landlord.

4. Interior Partitions. Tenant shall furnish and install all interior Tenant partitions from finished floor slab to the finished ceiling elevation. Interior partitions shall be metal stud or noncombustible wood stud construction covered both sides by one layer of fire code gypsum board.

5. Exterior Walls. Landlord shall provide concrete block and brick exterior walls. Calculations for area of Demised Premises shall be made to outside face of exterior walls.

6. Sales Area. Exposed concrete or block walls will not be permissible in sales area of Premises. Concrete or block walls not concealed by fixtures must be covered with gypsum board by Tenant. All wall finishes shall be furnished and installed by Tenant.

D. CEILINGS

1. Space Height. Landlord shall maintain minimum clear height of not less than 12'-6" from finished floor slab to overhead obstructions except in areas otherwise specifically noted to Tenant.

2. Maximum ceiling height will be 12'-0" unless otherwise specifically allowed by Landlord.

3. Exposed wood framing and combustible materials will not be allowed above Tenant's finished ceiling.

4. Should an expansion joint occur in the Premises, Tenant is responsible for the construction of the ceiling affected by that joint in a manner consistent with acceptable construction design practices.

5. Storage Area. If finished ceiling is to be omitted in Tenant's storage areas then the partition wall dividing remainder of Premises from storage area must be one-hour rated construction and extend from floor slab to underside of Landlord's overhead structure. However, if partition interferes with air flow through return air plenum space above ceiling, Tenant must provide an opening sized by Tenant's Engineer and approved by Landlord. Openings required for Tenant's return air in fire rated walls must be equipped with approved automatic fire dampers by Tenant.

6. Tenant shall provide and install access panels as required.

E. STOREFRONTS

1. Neutral Strips. Landlord shall provide vertical neutral strips at storefront lease line between Premises and adjacent tenant space, exit or service corridors, and/or department stores and a continuous horizontal neutral strip along storefront lease line at an elevation of 12'-0" from finished mall floor elevation.

2. Tenant shall be responsible for all storefront construction in an area extending horizontally on storefront lease line between Landlord's vertical neutral strips and vertically from Tenant's finished floor to underside of neutral strip provided by Landlord.

3. A minimum of 50% of Tenant's storefront shall be open for pedestrian circulation. Those Tenants having, in judgment of Landlord, an inordinate proportion of storefront to floor area will be considered exempt from this requirement. However, in no case will excessive blind wall sections be permitted.

4. No fixturing will be permitted within 2'-0" of storefront lease line. Fast food Tenants will be required to set fixtures back 4'-0" from storefront lease line.

5. No storefront or any part thereof shall project beyond lease lines describing Demised Premises with exception that signs may project beyond storefront lease line as described in Section F.

6. All storefront work requiring structural support, including sliding door tracks and housing boxes for grilles, shall be supported at their head sections by a welded structural steel framework which, in turn, shall be supported from the floor and laterally braced to the existing building structure. No portion of storefront shall be attached to or supported by Landlord's horizontal neutral strip or vertical neutral piers.

7. Aluminum storefront construction shall employ extruded anodized sections and/or sliding aluminum and glass doors, with pockets to receive sliding doors, open type rolling aluminum curtains, or ornamental metal grilles. All sliding door or rolling grille tracks must be recessed into their respective soffit or floor elements to maintain flush elevations.

8. All wood, if permitted by code, employed in conjunction with storefront work shall be kiln-dried, mill quality finish.

9. All glass used in conjunction with storefront work shall be tempered plate or laminated plate glass in accordance with applicable building code.

10. Tenant shall provide a ¾" × ¾" reveal at the storefront contiguous to and independent of Landlord's neutral strip and neutral piers.

11. Integral with the storefront design shall be a one-hour rated draft curtain extending downward twenty-four inches (24") from the finished ceiling elevation.

12. Base: All exterior base shall conform to mall material. No vinyl permitted.

F. SIGN CRITERIA

It is intended that the signing of the Premises be developed in an imaginative and varied manner. Although previous and current signing practices of tenants will be considered, all signs shall conform to the criteria set forth hereafter.

1. Exterior Signs

No exterior signs will be permitted unless Tenant's Premises as shown on exhibit A is in excess of 100,000 sq. ft.

2. Interior Signs

a.) Tenant shall be required to identify Premises by means of an illuminated sign furnished and installed by Tenant.

b.) Wording of Tenant's sign shall be limited to the Tenant name on page 1 of the lease.

c.) Tenant shall be limited to one sign (except at mall junctures).

d.) Tenant's sign shall conform to the following architectural and construction criteria.

1. Average height of sign letters shall not exceed fourteen inches (14").

2. Maximum height of any single letter shall not exceed eighteen inches (18").

3. Sign letters shall not project more than six inches (6") beyond sign fascia.

4. Maximum sign length shall not exceed ⅔ of length of sign fascia as determined by lease line and shall be no closer than thirty-six inches (36") to side lease line.

5. The top of any sign letter shall be no closer than eight inches (8") from the top of sign fascia.

6. The bottom of any sign letter shall be no closer than four inches (4") from bottom of sign fascia.

7. Sign illumination must be from source contained wholly within sign letters.

3. Logos and Graphics

a.) Multiple or repetitive signing on storefronts shall be permitted, if such signing is confined to one area only, exclusive of sign fascia, and is determined by Landlord to be part of an overall graphic design.

b.) The total logo or graphic area shall not exceed ten percent (10%) of the area of Tenant's storefront and shall be located at least thirty-six inches (36") from side lease line.

4. The following types of signs or sign components shall be PROHIBITED:

a.) Signs employing moving or flashing lights.

b.) Signs employing exposed raceways, ballast boxes, or transformers.

c.) Sign manufacturer's names, stamps, or decals.

d.) Signs employing luminous-vacuum formed type plastic letters.

e.) Signs employing unedged or uncapped plastic letters or letters with no returns and exposed fastenings.

f.) Painted, paper, or cardboard signs, stickers, or decals hung around, on, or behind storefront (including glass doors and/or windows).

g.) Signs purporting to identify leased department or concessionaires contained within the Premises.

h.) Surface mounted or suspended box or cabinet signs.

III. HEATING, VENTILATING, AND AIR CONDITIONING CRITERIA

Landlord shall provide a central air conditioning system to supply air to the Premises. It shall be the responsibility of the Tenant to design, furnish and install a complete internal ventilation and air conditioning distribution system in the Premises, including but not limited to all internal duct, diffusers, registers, grilles, variable air volume unit(s), wiring, and controls.

A. LANDLORD'S HVAC DESIGN CRITERIA

1. Heating

a.) Outside dry bulb temperature: −20 degrees F.

b.) Inside dry bulb temperature: Prevailing temperature of 68 degrees F dry bulb in merchandising areas and 60 degrees F dry bulb in service areas during occupied hours.

2. Cooling

a.) Outside dry bulb: 95 degrees F.

b.) Outside wet bulb: 75 degrees F.

c.) Inside dry bulb: Prevailing 75 degrees F dry bulb in merchandising areas.

d.) Inside relative humidity: 50%.

3. Total Electrical Heat Producing Load. Total heat gains from electrical equipment will be based upon the maximum light load allowed by Lease per Section IV plus a reasonable amount of miscellaneous equipment per specific business type.

4. Internal Sensible and Latent Heat Gains. Internal sensible and latent heat gains shall be based on 50 square feet of Premises per person.

5. Air Supply. Total cool air supply to Tenant's Premises shall be based on the total internal sensible heat load calculated from the Design Criteria established by paragraphs 2, 3, and 4 above and, where applicable, based on exposed outside wall "U" value of 0.20, a roof assembly "U" value of 0.12, and a supply air diffusion temperature difference of 20 degrees F (+/−) 3 degrees F.

B. LANDLORD'S CENTRAL SYSTEM

1. Cooling. Landlord shall provide large packaged roof-top air conditioning units (variable volume type) complete with air cooled refrigeration, condensing units, DX coils, supply fans, filters, all automatic dampers, and controls. These units shall furnish 60 degrees F (+/−) 3 degrees F supply air to Premises via common low pressure air distribution duct systems during occupied Shopping Center hours on a year-round basis. Landlord shall provide a supply duct outlet for each Premise at a point designated by Landlord.

2. Heating. Air conditioning units serving the mall common areas will provide heating to the mall common areas only.

3. Ventilation. Outside fresh air shall be provided at the central air-conditioning units with economizer cycle

and enthalpy controls and with not more than 5 CFM per person as required by code during occupied cycle.

4. Tenant Toilet Exhaust. Landlord will furnish a central toilet exhaust duct system at both levels including the fan(s).

5. Energy Shortage. Notwithstanding anything to the contrary contained herein, if Landlord is unable to obtain adequate gas, electricity, or alternate energy resources at reasonable rates, Landlord may increase the temperature of or decrease the amount of cooled air or decrease the temperature of or the amount of heated air furnished to the Premises.

C. TENANT'S SYSTEM

Description. Tenant shall design and install complete supply air distribution system within Premises from supply duct outlet(s) furnished and installed in Tenant's ceiling space by Landlord. Tenants shall furnish and install variable volume unit(s) complete with activator, control transformer and thermostats, insulated ductwork, supply diffusers, and associated wiring.

Variable Air Volume Units and Controls. Tenant shall furnish and install variable constant volume terminal units and controls in Tenant's Premises. Unit shall be no less than 20 gauge galvanized steel and shall contain a single motorized inlet damper, field adjustable with interchangeable mechanical constant volume regulator, one inch duo-density thermal acoustic fiberglass lining, and sound attenuating damper. Controls shall consist of a damper motor for 120 line voltage with integral 24 volt transformer and modulating room themostat for each terminal unit.

1. Reheating of conditioned air will not be permitted. Variable volume units shall be capable of modulating air supply to space to maintain space temperature. Cabinet heaters, duct heaters, or baseboard heaters in Tenant service areas or in Tenant areas with an exterior wall or roof exposure will be permitted to offset winter heat loss.

2. Return Air. All upper level tenants shall relieve air to ceiling space, which is return air plenum. All lower level tenants shall relieve air through the storefront to the mall.

3. Tenant Duct System Static Pressure Design. Tenant's air distribution system including ductwork, variable volume air control devices, diffusers, grilles, and registers shall be designed such that the static pressure loss in Tenant distribution system does not exceed 0.75" W.G.

4. Duct Work. Tenant's duct work shall be designed, furnished, and installed in strict accordance with the standards described in latest editions of ASHRAE Guide and Data Book and in latest editions of Duct Manual and Sheet Metal Construction for Ventilating and Air Conditioning Systems, published by SMACNA and/or local codes. Supply, return, and exhaust duct work, shall be galvanized steel except kitchen range exhaust duct work which shall be minimum 16 gauge welded steel and shall comply with local code requirements.

5. Diffusers, registers, grilles. Shall be of adjustable type for volume and direction control.

6. Thermostat. Shall be located in an accessible location and not obstructed by any merchandising or appliances nor shall it have light fixtures or other similar heat producing elements adjacent to it. Thermostat shall act to control variable volume units as well as any space heating devices used. Thermostat shall interlock with variable volume unit to be in minimum opening position when heat is being provided.

7. Ceiling Access Panels.Tenant shall provide access panels for service to Landlord's and/or Tenant's equipment and/or facilities, and all connections to Landlord's services and facilities above the ceiling level within the Premises at locations designated by Landlord.

8. Tenant Toilet Exhaust. Tenant shall design and provide exhaust from Tenant's toilet facilities per code requirements. Toilet exhaust duct from Premises shall be connected to Landlord's main toilet exhaust duct system at a location designated by Landlord.

9. Miscellaneous Exhaust System.

a.) All odor and moisture producing areas and high heat producing equipment and appliances must be exhausted by special mechanical exhaust systems to atmosphere. Special exhaust systems shall be designed to prevent odors, heat, and/or moisture from entering mall and Landlord's air conditioning system. Exhaust air quantities shall be in adequate amounts and shall be no less than required by code.

b.) Totally enclosed, highly illuminated show windows must be ventilated by means of positive air supply or exhaust. Such exhaust system may be discharged into false ceiling space, if and at such location as approved by Landlord.

c.) Special exhaust systems including fans, duct work, registers, grilles, controls, and accessories shall be provided by Tenant. Exhaust discharge openings directly to the exterior will not be allowed without permission of Landlord. In all cases, exhaust duct work shall connect directly to exhaust hoods, if provided, or registers or grilles mounted in ceiling in ventilated areas.

d.) Air quantities in excess of ten percent (10%) of total air supplied to the Premises, which are exhausted to atmosphere through Tenant's special exhaust system(s), require Landlord's approval.

10. Make-Up Air System. Tenant shall provide a complete make-up air system if Tenant requries exhaust air quantities in excess of ten percent (10%) of total air allowed to Premises upon approval of Landlord. Energy equipment and distribution system for make-up air shall be provided by Tenant.

11. Location of equipment serving special exhaust and make-up air systems and special heating and cooling systems shall be designated and/or approved by Landlord. Engineering designs showing structural loads added and all supports shall be furnished by Tenant. Routing of duct work serving special exhaust and make-up air systems shall be designated and/or approved by Landlord. Tenant's ducts passing through the roof shall have motorized shutoff damper(s).

12. Special cooling and heating equipment, such as required for refrigerated display cases, walk-in coolers, steam presses, etc. shall be provided by Tenant.

13. Sheet metal supply duct work shall be insulated with 1" thick, ½ lb. density insulation. Hot water piping for space heating shall be insulated with a minimum 1" thick insulation.

IV. ELECTRICAL CRITERIA

A. LANDLORD'S WORK

Landlord shall furnish and install empty electrical conduit from Landlord's distribution panel to a point within Tenant's Premises as designated by Landlord. Empty electrical conduit shall be sized to carry sufficient conductor capacity 480/277 volt, 3 phase, 4 wire for a total connected load equal to the maximum allowable light load per Tenant category in Section B plus a reasonable amount of miscellaneous equipment load.

B. MAXIMUM LIGHT LOAD

Tenant has been assigned a specific Tenant Category for the purpose of determining a maximum allowable light load for Premises. In no case shall Tenant's light load be allowed to exceed the maximum light load specified in the chart below.

Tenant Category	Maximum Light Load in Watts/Sq. Ft.
Clothing	5
Shoes	6
Jewelry, Gifts, Accessories	8
Restaurants	3
Fast Food/Specialty Food	5
Other	4
Hobby, Leisure	
Home Furnishing	
Miscellaneous	

C. TENANT'S WORK

Tenant, at its cost, shall provide all work which shall include, but not be limited to, furnishing and installing the following electrical equipment and services in the Premises in accordance with all governing codes.

1. Tenant shall furnish and install conductors and current-limiting rejection type fuses from Landlord's distribution panel to Premises, as well as all interior distribution equipment within Premises.

a.) Panelboard(s) with twenty percent (20%) spare capacity, transformers, conduits and branch wiring, outlet boxes, and final connection to electrical devices including equipment necessary to provide a complete and operating system.

b.) Lighting fixtures and lamps, time clocks, clocks, and signs.

c.) Security equipment with conduit and outlets if desired.

d.) Exit lights and emergency lighting as required by local codes and ordinances.

2. Electrical Material Standards for Tenant Premises.

a.) Electrical materials shall be new, shall meet National Electrical Code Standards, shall bear the Underwriter's Laboratories label, and shall be compatible with the general architectural design.

b.) All transformers shall be dry-type with low sound level, class H.

c.) All conductors shall be copper with color coded insulation. Feeders and branch circuit wiring in locations requiring insulation above 60 degrees C shall be THW or THWN or higher insulation. Branch circuit conductors shall not be smaller than No. 12 AWG. Communication, signal, and control wiring shall be sized in accordance with equipment manufacturer's recommendations.

d.) Panelboards shall be 480/277 or 208Y volt, 3 phase, 4 wire, solid neutral. Cabinets shall be constructed of code gauge sheet steel with hinged steel door and trim.

e.) Lighting fixtures shall bear Underwriter's label.

f.) Electric motors shall be designed to latest NEMA standards. Motors rated at ½ horse power and above shall be 3 phase.

g.) Bus bracing and AIC rating shall be greater than fault current value at point of application.

h.) Ballasts shall be energy saving type.

i.) Conduit shall be rigid, metallic EMT or flexible steel.

j.) Devices shall be specification grade.

k.) All conductors shall be terminated in proper terminals and shall be in conduit.

l.) Panelboard bussing shall be copper or plated aluminum.

V. PLUMBING CRITERIA

A. SANITARY SEWER

1. Lower Level. Landlord shall provide sanitary sewer branch line at locations designated by Landlord. Tenant shall design and install all sanitary waste facilities and extensions of service for Premises.

2. Upper Level. Landlord shall provide sanitary sewer branch lines at locations designated by Landlord. Tenant shall design and install all sanitary waste facilities and extensions of service for Premises. Tenant shall provide all required floor penetrations for connection to sanitary sewer tap provided by Landlord. All floor penetrations shall be completed in accordance with Landlord's standard design details and in such a manner to prevent permeations of odors or liquids to space below. All horizontal sanitary waste lines installed in attic space of lower level tenants shall be insulated to prevent condensation damage.

B. PLUMBING VENT RISER

Landlord shall penetrate roof membrane with vent risers and provide plugged vent branch connections at locations designated by Landlord. Tenant shall design and install all extensions of vent lines to Landlord's plugged connection. Tenant shall provide an additional plugged connection for future Tenant use at Landlord's vent riser location.

C. DOMESTIC WATER

1. Landlord shall provide cold water line in ceiling space of all levels. A valved connection shall be provided for each Premise at a point designated by Landlord.

2. If, in judgment of Landlord, Tenant is deemed to be a large consumer of water, Tenant shall be required to furnish and install water meter in an area easily accessible by Landlord and within the Tenant's Premises.

3. Tenant shall design and install all facilities and extensions of service for Premises.

4. If Tenant desires hot water, Tenant shall provide electric water heater.

D. PLUMBING DESIGN STANDARDS

1. Piping shall be supported from hangers at an adequate distance with adequate supporting hanger rods fastened to building framing whenever possible.

2. Water supplies to fixtures shall be valved at fixtures.

3. Tenant water closets shall be flush tank type.

4. Tenant shall provide floor drains in toilet areas, with back flow preventors at lower level only.

5. Tenant shall provide accessible clean-outs in toilet areas.

6. Water heaters shall be equipped with UL approved temperature and pressure relief valves.

7. Domestic hot water piping shall be insulated with minimum ¾" fiberglass insulation having an average thermal conductivity not exceeding .22 BTU in. per sq. ft. per degree F per hour at mean temperature of 75 degrees F.

E. GAS

1. Gas service from gas utility company shall be made available for Tenant's domestic use, other than water heating, at a point designated by Landlord.

2. Tenant shall design and install extensions of service from locations designated by Landlord to Premises in accordance with governing codes and subject to Landlord's written approval.

3. Gas Piping Requirements.

a.) Gas piping 1¼" and over shall be Schedule 40 black steel pipe with welded joints and fittings on all sizes.

b.) Gas piping 1" and under may be Schedule 40 black steel with screwed fittings if permitted by local code.

c.) Gas cocks and unions shall be installed ahead of each appliance.

F. INTERCEPTORS (GREASE AND HAIR)

1. Fast food and restaurant tenants shall provide grease interceptors in accordance with code requirements.

2. Beauty and barber shops shall provide and install hair interceptors in accordance with code requirements.

VI. TELEPHONE CRITERIA

Tenant shall make provisions for all telephone equipment within Premises as well as extensions of conductors to telephone equipment room.

VII. FIRE SPRINKLER CRITERIA

A. LANDLORD'S SYSTEM

1. Landlord shall furnish and install a bulk main distribution system with branch lines throughout each Tenant's Premises.

2. Landlord shall furnish and install sprinkler heads, on the branch lines, based on a standard grid throughout the entire Premises. Sufficient coverage will be provided for one sprinkler head per one hundred (100) square feet of Premise.

B. TENANT'S SYSTEM

1. Tenant shall alter the sprinkler system to include drops, heads, facilities for proper drainage, and any necessary test valves, orifices, or other equipment as may be required, all in accordance with Landlord's Fire Underwriter's approved drawings and specifications.

2. Before proceeding with any installation work, Tenant shall forward two (2) blue line prints of Tenant's Sprinkler Drawings bearing the Landlord's Fire Insurance Underwriter's stamp of approval to Landlord for Landlord's records.

3. Any damage caused by Tenant to Landlord's sprinkler system will be repaired by Landlord's contractor at Tenant's expense.

4. Tenant's sprinkler system shall be tested at water pressure of 200 psig for a period of two (2) hours in the presence of Landlord's representative.

5. Upon completion of the system, Tenant shall submit a written certificate to Landlord from the Underwriter stating that the system was inspected and approved.

VIII. MISCELLANEOUS

A. ROOF PENETRATIONS

All roof penetrations required by Tenant shall be performed by Landlord's roofing contractor at direction of Landlord. Tenant shall request, in writing, approval to penetrate roof. Upon approval of such request, Landlord will direct roofing contractor to proceed with installation, the direct cost of which shall be paid by Tenant.

B. STRUCTURAL REVISIONS

Any modification, revision, or addition to Landlord's structure when designed by Tenant shall be approved by Landlord. Tenant shall pay for all cost of such installation.

Structural supports, curbing, and flashing shall be in accordance with standard project details.

C. MECHANICAL, ELECTRICAL, OR HVAC REVISIONS

In the event Tenant's store design standards require mechanical, HVAC, or electrical revisions, Tenant shall request, in writing, approval to revise Landlord's systems. If approved by Landlord, Landlord shall make the necessary revisions to Landlord's Mechanical, HVAC, or Electrical System to accommodate Tenant's design. Tenant shall reimburse Landlord for all of Landlord's direct costs involved in modifying Landlord's systems.

D. TOILETS

Tenant must furnish and install toilets for employees in Premises exceeding three thousand (3,000) square feet.

E. TRASH REMOVAL

During construction, fixturing, and merchandise stocking of Tenant's Premises, Tenant shall provide trash removal service at areas designated by Landlord. It shall be the responsibility of Tenant and Tenant's Contractors to remove all trash and debris from Premises and to place them in containers supplied for that purpose. In the event Tenant's trash is allowed to accumulate for a 24 hour period or longer within Tenant's Premises or in arcades, mall, or service corridors adjacent to Premises, Landlord shall remove Tenant's or Tenant's contractor's trash at a charge of 1.5 times Landlord's cost.

APPENDIX E

Sample Merchants' Association Bylaws

Note: This sample set of merchants' association bylaws is presented to provide a general understanding of the organization of a typical merchants' association. It is not endorsed as a model. Rather, each association should develop documents appropriate to the particular center.

ARTICLE I

Purpose, Members, and Dues

Section 1. Purpose and General Statement: The purpose of the Association shall be to promote _____ (hereinafter referred to as the "Mall") through the sponsorship of commercial, cultural, educational, community, and other programs; and in furtherance of such purpose, to engage in and conduct promotional programs and publicity, special events, decorations, and cooperative advertising in the general interest and for the benefit of the Mall. The Association does not own any of the common areas of the Mall and the use of the same is in the absolute control of the landlord of the Mall. The rights and obligations of the tenants of the Mall that are members shall in no way be diminished or enhanced by their membership in the Association, and said rights and obligations shall be governed solely by the respective leases entered into with the landlord of the Mall. The Association shall be conducted as a nonprofit organization, and no part of the profits (if any) shall inure to the benefit of any member or be used for any other purpose.

Section 2. Members: Each and every business doing business in the Mall as a tenant, and any owner of property doing business in the Mall as a merchant, upon payment of dues shall be a member of the Association and as such shall be entitled to one vote. The owner of the Mall shall be a full member of the Association and in such capacity shall be entitled to one vote and shall have the right to attend and participate in all meetings of the members. Membership in the Association shall continue so long as the respective member (or associate member) continues to conduct business in the Mall as a merchant; provided, however, that membership in the Association may be terminated by a two-thirds vote of the Board of Directors upon the occurrence of either of the following events: (1) the member (or associate member) has failed to pay its dues when same have become due and payable; and (2) the member has failed to comply with the rules, regulations, resolutions, and Bylaws of the Association.

Section 3. Associate Membership: Associate membership is open to all persons or businesses doing business in the area adjacent to or contiguous with the Mall. Associate membership must be sponsored and approved by the owner of the Mall and be ratified by a majority vote of the Board of Directors, provided, however, that an associate member shall have no right to vote at Association members' meetings or become a member of the Board of Directors. Associate members shall pay $_____ to the Association in initial assessments (payable when approved for membership by the Board of Directors) as well as annual dues to the Association of $_____. In addition, associate members shall be subject to increases in dues in the same manner in which regular members shall be subject.

Section 4. Dues: An initial assessment and regular monthly dues shall be paid by the members of the Association as provided by Lease or other Agreement. Such monthly payments shall commence on the date provided by Lease or other Agreement and shall be subject to adjustments, increasing said monthly dues to the extent required by increases in the cost of promotional, public relations, and advertising services as provided in such Lease or other Agreement.

Section 5. Annual Meetings: The Association shall hold each year, during the second week within the month of March, an annual meeting of the members for the election of directors and the transaction of any business within the powers of the Association. Failure to hold an annual meeting at the designated time shall not, however, invalidate the corporate existence of the Association or affect otherwise valid corporate acts.

Section 6. Special Meetings: At any time in the interval between annual meetings, special meetings of the members may be called by the President or by the Board of Directors or by members having one-third of the votes entitled to be cast at such meeting.

Section 7. Place of Meetings: All meetings of the members shall be held at a place designated by the Board of Directors.

Section 8. Notice of Meetings: Not less than ten (10) days nor more than fifty (50) days before the date of every meeting of members, the Secretary-Treasurer shall give to each member written or printed notice stating the specific time and place of the meeting and, in the case of a special meeting, the purpose or purposes for which the meeting is called, either by mail or by presenting it to him personally or by leaving it at his place of business in the Shopping Center. If mailed, such notice shall be deemed to be given when deposited in the United States mail addressed to the member at his post office address as it appears on the records of the Association, with postage thereon prepaid. Notwithstanding the foregoing provision, a waiver of notice in writing, signed by the person or persons entitled to such notice and filed with the records of the meeting, whether before or after the holding thereof, or actual attendance at the meeting in person or by proxy, shall be deemed equivalent to the giving of such notice to such person. Any meeting of members, annual or special, may adjourn from time to time to reconvene at the same or some other place, and no notice need be given of any such adjourned meeting other than by announcement.

Section 9. Quorum: One-third of the members in good standing present, in person or by proxy, shall constitute a quorum. In the absence of a quorum, the members present or by proxy, by majority vote and without notice other than by announcement, may adjourn the meeting from time to time until a quorum shall attend. At any such adjourned meeting at which a quorum shall be present, any business may be transacted which might have been transacted at the meeting as originally notified.

Section 10. Votes Required: A majority of the votes cast at a meeting of members, duly called and at which a quorum is present, shall be sufficient to take or authorize action upon any matter which may properly come before the meeting, unless more than a majority of votes cast is required by statute or by these Bylaws.

Section 11. Proxies: Any member may vote either in person or by proxy or representative designated in writing by such member, provided, however, no person may serve as a proxy or representative for more than one (1) member.

Section 12. Voting: In all elections for directors every member of the Association shall have the right to vote, in person or by proxy or by representative. Votes may not be cumulated.

ARTICLE II

Board of Directors

Section 1. Powers: The business and affairs of the Association shall be managed by its Board of Directors. The Board of Directors may exercise all the powers of the Association, except such as are conferred upon or reserved to the members by statute, the Articles of Incorporation, or the Bylaws. The Board of Directors may enforce the rules, regulations, resolutions, and Bylaws of the Association by whatever means it deems appropriate, except such as are specifically prohibited by statute, Lease, or other Agreement, of the Bylaws of the Association. The Board of Directors shall keep full and fair accounts of its transactions.

Section 2. Number of Directors: The number of Directors of the Association shall be nine (9); all of whom shall be members (not associate members) of the Association; provided, however, that at all times the Mall management, _____, and the _____, department stores, shall be represented on the Board of Directors.

Section 3. Election of Directors: Directors shall be elected at each annual meeting of the members and shall hold office until the next annual meeting when the new Directors are elected. Notwithstanding the foregoing, at all times the Mall management, _____, and the _____, department stores, shall have their respective designated representatives on the Board of Directors. The first Board of Directors shall be elected at the Formation meeting held in February and shall hold office until the first annual meeting in March. Election of a director shall be by a majority vote of all members in good standing present at such meeting either in person or by proxy.

Section 4. Nominating Committee: A nominating committee of not less than three (3) representatives of active members of this Association shall be appointed by the President not less than thirty (30) days prior to the election, whose duty it shall be to nominate from the representatives of the active members of this Association as many members as may be voted on for members of the Board of Directors as there are vacancies to be filled. Said committee shall file a list of nominees recommended with the Secretary-Treasurer of this Association not later than fifteen (15) days before the election.

The Secretary-Treasurer of this Association shall mail to all members of this Association ten (10) days prior to the election a list of the nominees recommended by the nominating commitee.

All other nominations shall be submitted to the Secretary-Treasurer in writing with five (5) signatures of members in good standing at least three (3) days prior to the annual meeting. No nominations shall be accepted from the floor. If additional nominations are submitted, ballots will be prepared and voting will be by ballot. Members will vote for as many members as there are vacancies to be filled. Voting shall not be cumulative.

Section 5. Vacancies: Any vacancy, except those of Mall management, occurring in the Board of Directors for any cause shall be filled by a candidate receiving a majority of the votes of the remaining members of the Board of Directors. A director so elected shall hold office until the next annual meeting of members or until his successor is elected and qualifies.

Section 6. Regular Meetings: Regular meetings of the Board of Directors shall be held at least ten (10) times annually, but not more often than once each month, at such place or places as shall be designated by the Board.

Section 7. Special Meetings: Special meetings of the Board of Directors may be called at any time by the President or by a majority vote of the members of the Board of Directors. Such meetings shall be held at a place or places as shall be designated by the Board of Directors. The notice with respect to any such special meetings may, but need not, contain a statement of the purpose or purposes of such meeting.

Section 8. Members Attending Meetings: Any member in good standing of the Association shall be allowed to attend either regular or special meetings of the Board of Directors. The Board of Directors shall have the right, however, to move into executive session by a majority vote of the quorum at any duly constituted meeting.

Section 9. Notice of Meetings: Except as provided in Section 6, notice of the place, day, and hour of every regular and special meeting shall be given to each director two (2) days (or more) before the meeting, by delivering the same to him personally, or by sending the same to him by telegraph, or by leaving the same at his residence or usual place of business, or in the alternative, by mailing such notice three (3) days (or more) before the meeting, postage prepaid and addressed to him at his last known post office address, according to the records of the Association. Unless required by these Bylaws or by resolution of the Board of Directors, no notice of any meeting of the Board of Directors need state the business to be transacted thereat. No notice of any meeting of the Board of Directors need be given to any director who submits a signed waiver of notice before or after the meeting, or who attends and does not object thereat to the transaction of any business because of the lack of or tardy notice. Any meeting of the Board of Directors, regular or special, may adjourn from time to time to reconvene at the same or some other place, and no notice need be given of any such adjourned meeting other than by announcement of such meeting.

Section 10. Quorum: At all meetings of the Board of Directors, a majority of the entire Board of Directors shall constitute a quorum for the transaction of business. Except in cases in which it is by statute, by the Articles of Incorporation or by the Bylaws otherwise provided, the vote of a majority of such quorum at a duly constituted meeting shall be sufficient to elect and pass any measure. In the absence of a quorum, the directors present, by majority vote and without notice other than by announcement at such meeting, may adjourn the meeting from time to time until a quorum shall be present; any business may be transacted which might have been transacted at the meeting as originally scheduled.

Section 11. Removal of Directors: At any meeting of the members of the Association called for the purpose of removing any director, such director may be removed from office for cause or without cause, and another be elected in the place of the director removed by a majority of vote of members in good standing present at such meeting either in person or by proxy.

Section 12. Compensation: Directors, as such, shall not receive any stated compensation for their services, but by resolution of the Board, their expenses of attendance, if any, may be allowed for attendance at each regular or special meeting of the Board; provided, however, that nothing herein contained shall be construed to preclude any director from serving the Association in any other capacity and receiving compensation therefor.

ARTICLE III

Officers

Section 1. Executive Officers: The executive officers of this Association shall be a President, a Vice President, and a Secretary-Treasurer. The President and Vice President shall be active members or representatives of active members of this Association, elected by the Board of Directors from their own number at the first meeting after the annual election of directors, and they shall hold office for one (1) year and until their successors are elected. The Secretary-Treasurer shall be an employee of the Mall management and shall be appointed by the Mall management representative on the Board of Directors, and shall hold such position until his successor is appointed by the Mall management representative on the Board of Directors.

Section 2. President: It shall be the duty of the President to preside at all meetings of the Association and of the Board of Directors. He shall have general supervision over the affairs of this Association, subject to the direction and control of the Board of Directors. Standing committees shall be appointed by the President, with the consent and approval of the Board of Directors. Emergency or special committees may be appointed by the President.

Section 3. Vice President: In the absence of the President or in the event of his inability to act, the Vice President shall exercise all powers and perform all duties of the President.

Section 4. Secretary-Treasurer: The Secretary-Treasurer shall perform all the duties incident to the offices of a secretary and treasurer of a corporation, and such other duties as, from time to time, may be assigned to him by the Board of Directors or the President. The Secretary-Treasurer shall cause to be kept minutes of the meetings of the members and of the Board of Directors in books provided for that purpose; he shall see that all notices are duly given in accordance with the provisions of the Bylaws or as required by law; he shall be custodian of the records of the Association; he shall have charge of and be responsible for all funds, securities, receipts, and disbursements of the Association, and shall deposit, or cause to be deposited in the name of the Association, all monies or other valuable effects in such banks, trust companies, or other depositories as shall from time to time be selected by the Board of Directors; he shall render to the President and to the Board of Directors, whenever requested, an account of the financial condition of the Association. Within thirty (30) days of the annual election for Board of Directors, the Secretary-Treasurer shall tender to the new Board of Directors an audited statement of the accounts for the preceding fiscal year.

Section 5. Assistant Officers: The Board of Directors may appoint such assistant officers as it deems advisable, which assistant officers shall have such duties as from time to time may be assigned to them, or any one of them, by the Board of Directors or the President. Assistant officers shall be active members or representatives of the members of the Association.

Section 6. Removal: Any officer or agent of the Association may be removed by the Board of Directors whenever, in its judgment, the best interests of the Association will be served thereby.

Section 7. Compensation: Officers shall serve without salary; however, they shall be reimbursed for expenses incurred in the execution of their office, as approved by the Board of Directors.

ARTICLE IV

Sundry Provisions

Section 1. Fiscal Year: The fiscal year of the Association shall commence February 1st and terminate January 31st of the following year.

Section 2. Annual Reports: The Secretary-Treasurer shall cause to be prepared annually a full and correct statement of the affairs of the Association, including a balance sheet and a financial statement of the operations for the preceding fiscal year, which shall be submitted at the annual meeting of the members and mailed to all members, and filed within twenty (20) days thereafter at the principal office of the Association in the State of

————————.

Section 3. Disbursements: All checks, drafts, and orders for the payment of money, notes, and other evidences of indebtedness, issued in the name of the Association, shall, unless otherwise provided by resolution of the Board of Directors, be signed by any two (2) of the following three (3) officers: President, Vice President, or Secretary-Treasurer. These persons shall be bonded to the extent deemed necessary by the Board of Directors.

Section 4. Bonds: The Board of Directors may require any officer, agent, or employee of the Association to give bond to the Association, conditioned upon the faithful discharge of his duties, with one or more sureties and in such amount as may be satisfactory to the Board of Directors.

Section 5. Insurance: The Board of Directors shall purchase such insurance as it and the Mall management deem necessary to protect the Association and indemnify the owner of the Mall from any claims arising from the promotional or other activities of the Association.

Section 6. Dividends: No dividends shall be paid to any member of the Association.

Section 7. Meeting Agenda: No member may introduce at any meeting of members of the Board of Directors any topic for discussion not directly related to the purpose of the Association as defined in Article I, Section 1, of the Bylaws.

Section 8. Amendments: A unanimous vote of the members is required to adopt new Bylaws or to amend the following sections:

    Article I, Sections 1, 2, and 11
    Article II, Sections 2 and 3
    Article IV, Sections 1 and 7

All other sections may be amended at any annual meeting of the members by a majority of members present at such meeting either in person or by proxy, or at any special meeting called for that purpose.

APPENDIX F
Sample Zoning Ordinance Provisions

Note: Zoning for shopping centers can be handled in any of a variety of ways. In this sample the shopping center is treated as a conditional use, thus allowing for flexibility in the approval requirements for each center. These ordinance provisions are not endorsed as a model but rather are given as an example of one of several suitable methods.

8. Shopping Centers

The purpose of these regulations is to encourage the effective and timely development of land for commercial purposes in accordance with the objective and policies of the _____ Land Use Plan; to assure suitable design in order to protect the property values and the residential environment of adjacent neighborhoods; and to minimize traffic congestion on the public streets.

a. **Application**—In addition to the general application requirements provided in Subsection A of this Section, the applicant shall furnish the following information and exhibits to the Zoning Board of Appeals concerning his proposed development:

1) *Ownership*—All land in the proposed shopping center shall be held either in single ownership or in unified control and shall contain no public streets or alleys. A shopping center site cannot lie on two sides of a public street or alley.

2) *Existing Conditions*—

a) Boundary line of proposed shopping center, and the total acreage encompassed thereby;

b) The size and location of existing sewers, water mains, culverts, manholes, and other underground facilities within the tract.

3) *Proposed Conditions*—Preliminary sketches showing the following:

a) Location, general layout, and dimensions of principal and accessory buildings;

b) Traffic circulation within the confines of the shopping center;

c) Location, arrangement, and dimensions of automobile parking bays, aisles, and loading spaces;

d) Location and dimensions of vehicular drives, entrances, exits, and acceleration and deceleration lanes;

e) Location and dimensions of pedestrian entrances, exits, walks, and walkways;

f) Location, arrangement, and dimensions of truck loading and unloading spaces and docks;

g) Architectural sketches of the proposed buildings;

h) Drainage and sanitary systems.

4) *Market Analysis*—A market analysis, prepared and signed by a recognized independent market analyst acceptable to the Planning Commission, containing the following determination:

a) Trade area of proposed shopping center;

b) Population of the trade area, present and projected;

c) Effective buying power in the trade area, present and projected;

d) Net potential customer buying power for stores in the proposed shopping center, and on the basis of such buying power, the recommended store types and store floor area;

e) Residual amount of buying power and how it may be expected to be expended in existing business areas serving the proposed trade area.

5) *A statement of financial responsibility.*

b. **Procedure**—A public hearing shall be held in accordance with Article Six, Section V-A, and the Council shall pass a resolution accepting or rejecting the application. If the application is accepted, the Planning Commission shall have the administrative power and duty, in accordance with the requirements of this Ordinance, to review the preliminary and final site plans for proposed shopping centers and make a written report to the Council. The Council shall then act upon the accepted application in accordance with the provisions of Article Six, Section V-A. The Building and Zoning Officer shall grant no building permit or certificate of occupancy except for construction and occupancy in strict compliance with a conditional use permit and a final site plan approved by the Council. Such building permits must be requested within one (1) year of the date of approval of the conditional use permit.

1) *Preliminary Site Plan Submission*—A preliminary site plan for the development of such property shall be presented to the Planning Commission for review. The preliminary site plan shall show the following, together with appropriate dimensions:

a) Proposed name of the shopping center;

b) Location by legal description;

c) Names and addresses of applicant and designer who made the plan;

d) Scale of plan, 1″ to 100′;

e) Date;

f) North arrow;

g) Contours at two (2)-foot intervals;

h) Boundary line of proposed shopping center, indicated by a solid line, and the total acreage encompassed thereby;

i) Location, widths, and names of all existing or prior platted streets, railroad and utility rights-of-way, parks, and other public open spaces, permanent buildings and structures, houses or permanent easements, and section and municipal boundary lines, within five hundred (500) feet of the tract;

j) Existing sewers, water mains, culverts, and other underground facilities within the tract, indicating pipe sizes, grades, manholes, and location;

k) Location, arrangement, and dimensions of automobile parking space, width of aisles, width of bays, angle of parking;

l) Location, arrangement, and dimensions of truck loading and unloading spaces and docks;

m) Location and dimensions of vehicular drives, entrances, exits, and acceleration and deceleration lanes;

n) Location and dimensions of pedestrian entrances, exits, and walkways;

o) Drainage system and sanitary sewer;

p) Location, height, and materials of walls, fences, and screen plantings;

q) Ground cover, finished grades, slopes, banks, and ditches;

r) Location and general exterior dimensions of principal and accessory buildings;

s) Location, size, height, and orientation of all signs other than signs flat on building façades;

t) Preliminary architectural drawings for all buildings;

u) If it is proposed to restrict signs or to establish an association of merchants by means of lease provisions or covenants, the text of such provisions;

v) The stages, if any, to be followed in the construction of the shopping center;

w) A traffic flow chart showing circulation patterns within the confines of the shopping center.

2) *Action on Preliminary Site Plan*—Not more than sixty (60) days after receipt of the preliminary site plan, the Planning Commission shall determine whether the proposed shopping center would comply with all requirements of the ordinance, and on such basis, shall:

a) Approve the preliminary plan. The applicant may then proceed to file a final site plan; or,

b) Notify the applicant in writing how the plan must be amended to comply with the requirements of this Ordinance. The applicant may, within thirty (30) days thereafter or within such further period as may be agreed to by the Planning Commission, submit an amended preliminary plan containing the required changes. If an amended preliminary plan is not filed within the prescribed period, the original preliminary plan shall be considered disapproved. If an amended preliminary plan is filed within the prescribed period, the Planning Commission shall approve or disapprove the plan within thirty (30) days after the date of filing, or within such further period as may be agreed to by the applicant; or,

c) Notify the Council and the applicant in writing that the plan does not comply with the requirements of this Ordinance and is not susceptible to amendment. The applicant may then apply to the Council for a review of the decision of the Planning Commission.

3. *Final Site Plan Submission*—Within one (1) year after approval of the preliminary site plan, the applicant shall submit to the Planning Commission a final site plan of either (1) the entire shopping center, or (2) the first stage of such center that is to be constructed. Such plan shall be drawn to scale, shall include appropriate dimensions, shall contain all information required by the Ordinance for a preliminary plan, shall contain final architec-

tural drawings for all buildings included in the final site plan, and shall contain any additional information required by the Planning Commission at the time of the preliminary plan.

a) Stage Construction—If development of the shopping center is to be carried out in progressive stages, each stage shall be so planned that the requirements and intent of this Ordinance shall be fully complied with at the completion of each stage. No final plan for the initial stage of development of any shopping center shall be approved unless such stage comprises a total ground floor area of at least twenty-five thousand (25,000) squre feet and at least three (3) of the designated principal uses.

b) Action on Final Site Plan—Compliance with Preliminary Site Plan—Not more than thirty (30) days after receipt of a final site plan for a shopping center or for any stage thereof, the Planning Commission shall determine whether such final plan is in compliance with the preliminary plan as approved by the Commission. If the final plan is determined to be in compliance and if all applicable requirements of this Subsection are also complied with, the Commission shall recommend to the Council approval of the final plan. In all other instances, the Commission shall recommend disapproval of the final plan and shall so notify the applicant in writing. The applicant may then apply to the Council for a review of the decision of the Planning Commission. If the final plan is disapproved because of noncompliance with the preliminary plan, the final plan may thereafter be submitted to the Commission as an amended preliminary plan. The procedure for the consideration of such amended preliminary plan shall be the same as that for the consideration of an original preliminary plan.

c) Change of Final Site Plan—If the applicant wants to make any amendment to an approved final plan, a written request shall be submitted to the Commission. If, in the opinion of the Commission, a requested change is sufficiently substantial, the Commission shall require the submission of an amended final plan. The procedure for the consideration of such written request or of such amended final plan shall be the same as that for the consideration of a final plan.

c. **Standards for Development**—

1) *Permitted Uses*—Any use permitted in the CB zone except dwellings and dwelling units is permitted as a principal use of land in a shopping center.

2) *Site Area*—A shopping center shall be located on a zoning lot having an area of at least ten (10) acres.

3) *Floor Area Ratio*—The combined floor area ratio for all principal buildings, together with all accessory buildings, shall not exceed 0.35 on any zoning lot.

4) *Maximum Lot Coverage*—The total ground area, occupied by all principal buildings together with all accessory buildings, shall not exceed twenty-five (25) percent of the total area of the zoning lot.

5) *Building Setback Line*—Each zoning lot shall have a building setback from all street rights-of-way of at least eighty (80) feet. A strip twenty (20) feet deep along the front line shall be maintained as a landscaped buffer strip. The remaining area may be used for parking.

6) *Side and Rear Yards*—Each zoning lot shall have side and rear yards of at least fifty (50) feet in width. A strip twenty (20) feet in width or depth along side and rear lot lines shall be maintained as a landscaped buffer strip. The remainder of the area may be used for parking.

7) *Height Restriction*—No principal building shall exceed five (5) stories or fifty-five (55) feet in height; no accessory building or other structure shall exceed one (1) story or twenty (20) feet in height.

8) *Special Buffer Requirement Adjacent to Residential Areas*—Along any boundary line adjacent to a residential area, a buffer yard shall be provided which shall be at least one hundred (100) feet in depth, measured from the property line.

9) *Access and Traffic Control*—

a) Access Barrier—Each zoning lot, with its buildings, other structures, and parking and loading areas, shall be physically separated from each adjoining street by a curb or other suitable barrier against unchanneled motor vehicle ingress and egress. Such barrier shall be located at the edge of or within a twenty (20)-foot-deep strip along the property line. Except for the access ways permitted by (b) below, the barrier shall be continuous for the entire length of the property line.

b) *Access Ways*—Each zoning lot shall have not more than two (2) access ways to any one street unless unusual circumstances demonstrate the need for additional access points. Each access way shall comply with the following requirements:

The width of any access way leading to a public street shall not exceed twenty-five (25) feet at its intersection with the property line. Curb returns shall have a minimum radius of thirty (30) feet.

At its intersection with the property line, no part of any access way shall be nearer than one hundred (100) feet to the intersection of any two (2) street right-of-way lines, nor shall any such part be nearer than fifty (50) feet to any side or rear property line.

The location and number of access ways shall be so arranged that they will reduce traffic hazards as much as possible.

10) *Off-Street Parking Areas*—All off-street parking spaces and servicing drives shall be located within the boundaries of the property being developed as a shopping center. Off-street parking spaces shall be provided at the rate of at least three (3) square feet of parking area to one (1) square foot of gross floor area. Spaces provided behind the stores or shops shall not be considered usable by the public and shall not be considered in calculating the minimum space required; provided, however, that if the shopping center is so designed that all of the shops and stores face upon a central mall and all sections of the parking area are provided with adequate connecting internal drives, the location of parking areas may completely surround such shops and stores.

11) *Off-Street Loading Areas*—Each shop or store shall have a rear or side entrance that is accessible to a loading area and service drive. Service drives shall be a minimum of twenty-six (26) feet in width and shall be in addition to and not part of the drives or circulation system used by the vehicles of shoppers. The arrangement of truck loading and unloading facilities for each shop or store shall be such that in the process of loading or unloading no truck will block or extend into any other private or public drive or street used for vehicular circulation. Loading and delivery zones shall be clearly marked.

12) *Lighting*—All parking areas and access ways shall be floodlighted at night during business hours. All outside lighting shall be arranged and shielded to prevent glare or reflection, nuisance, inconvenience, or hazardous interference of any kind on adjoining streets or residential properties.

13) *Waste Pens*—Each building shall be provided with an enclosed waste pen of sufficient size to accommodate all trash and waste stored on the premises.

14) *Trash Burners and Incinerators*—There shall be no trash burner or incinerators, or any burning of trash or rubbish on the premises.

8.1 Regional Shopping Centers

These regulations are to apply to the development of shopping centers containing a wide range of retail business and accessory uses serving a trade area embracing a large segment of the community.

a. **Application**—In addition to the general application requirements provided in Subsection A of this Section, the applicant shall furnish the following information and exhibits to the Zoning Board of Appeals concerning his proposed development:

1) *Ownership*—All land in the proposed shopping center shall be held either in single ownership or in unified control and shall contain no public streets or alleys. A shopping center site cannot lie on two sides of a public street or alley.

2) *Existing Conditions*—

a) Boundary line of proposed shopping center, and the total acreage encompassed thereby;

b) The size and location of existing sewers, water mains, culverts, manholes, and other underground facilities within the tract.

3) *Proposed Conditions*—Preliminary sketches showing the following:

a) Location, general layout, and dimensions of principal and accessory buildings;

b) Traffic circulation within the confines of the shopping center;

c) Location, arrangement, and dimensions of automobile parking bays, aisles, and loading spaces;

d) Location and dimensions of vehicular drives, entrances, exits, and acceleration and deceleration lanes;

e) Location and dimensions of pedestrian entrances, exits, walks, and walkways;

f) Location, arrangement, and dimensions of truck loading and unloading spaces and docks;

g) Architectural sketches of the proposed buildings;

h) Drainage and sanitary systems.

4) *Market Analysis*—A market analysis, prepared and signed by a recognized independent market analyst acceptable to the Planning Commission, containing the following determination:

a) Trade area of proposed shopping center;

b) Population of the trade area, present and projected;

c) Effective buying power in the trade area, present and projected;

d) Net potential customer buying power for stores in the proposed shopping center, and on the basis of such buying power, the recommended store types and store floor area;

e) Residual amount of buying power and how it may be expected to be expended in existing business areas serving the proposed trade area.

5) A statement of financial responsibility.

b. **Procedure**—A public hearing shall be held in accordance with Article Six, Section V-A, and, in addition the Planning Commission shall review the application in accordance with the requirements of this Ordinance and shall prepare a written recommendation to the Council. The Council shall act upon the application in accordance with the provisions of Article Six, Section V-A. The Planning Commission shall have the further administrative power and duty to review the final plans for compliance with the standards of this Ordinance and the conditions set forth in the conditional use permit, and no building permit shall be issued except in compliance with such standards and conditions.

1) *Preliminary Site Plan Submission*—A preliminary site plan for the development of such property shall be presented to the Planning Commission for review. The preliminary site plan shall show the following, together with appropriate dimensions:

a) Proposed name of the shopping center;

b) Location by legal description;

c) Names and addresses of applicant and designer who made the plan;

d) Scale of plan, 1″ to 100′;

e) Date;

f) North arrow;

g) Contours at two (2)-foot intervals;

h) Boundary line of proposed shopping center, indicated by a solid line, and the total acreage encompassed thereby;

i) Location, widths, and names of all existing or prior platted streets, railroad and utility rights-of-way, parks, and other public open spaces, permanent buildings and structures, houses or permanent easements, and section and municipal boundary lines, within five hundred (500) feet of the tract;

j) Existing sewers, water mains, culverts, and other underground facilities within the tract, indicating pipe sizes, grades, manholes, and location;

k) Location, arrangement, and dimensions of automobile parking space, width of aisles, width of bays, angle of parking;

l) Location, arrangement, and dimensions of truck loading and unloading spaces and docks;

m) Location and dimensions of vehicular drives, entrances, exits, and acceleration and deceleration lanes;

n) Location and dimensions of pedestrian entrances, exits, and walkways;

o) Drainage system and sanitary sewer;

p) Location, height, and materials of walls, fences, and screen plantings;

q) Ground cover, finished grades, slopes, banks, and ditches;

r) Location and general exterior dimensions of principal and accessory buildings;

s) Location, size, height, and orientation of all signs other than signs flat on building facades;

t) Preliminary architectural drawings for all buildings;

u) If it is proposed to restrict signs or to establish an association of merchants by means of lease provisions or covenants, the text of such provisions;

v) The stages, if any, to be followed in the construction of the shopping center. The preliminary site plan shall show any areas reserved for future development even though specific plans for such areas have not been developed.

w) A traffic flow chart showing circulation patterns within the confines of the shopping center.

2) *Action on Preliminary Site Plan*—Not more than sixty (60) days after receipt of the preliminary site plan, the Planning Commission shall determine whether the proposed shopping center would comply with all requirements of this Ordinance, and on such basis, shall:

a) Approve the preliminary plan and recommend to the Council that the conditional use permit be granted stating any special conditions which should in the opinion of the Planning Commission be a part of such permit. Such recommendation shall cover height of buildings, staging of construction, and the development of reserved areas shown on the preliminary site plan. The applicant may then proceed to file a final site plan; or,

b) Notify the applicant in writing how the plan must be amended to comply with the requirements of this Ordinance. The applicant may, within thirty (30) days thereafter or within such further period as may be agreed to by the Planning Commission, submit an amended preliminary plan containing the required changes. If an amended preliminary plan is not filed within the prescribed period, the original preliminary plan shall be considered disapproved. If an amended preliminary plan is filed within the prescribed period, the Planning Commission shall approve or disapprove the plan within thirty (30) days after the date of filing, or within such further period as may be agreed to by the applicant; or,

c) Notify the Council and the applicant in writing that the plan does not comply with the requirements of this Ordinance and is not susceptible to amendment. The applicant may then apply to the Council for a review of the decision of the Planning Commission.

3) *Final Site Plan Submission*—Within one (1) year after approval of the preliminary site plan, the applicant shall submit to the Planning Commission a final site plan of either (1) the entire shopping center, or (2) the first stage of such center that is to be constructed. Such plan shall be drawn to scale, shall include appropriate dimensions, shall contain all information required by this Ordinance for a preliminary plan, shall contain final architectural drawings for all buildings included in the final site plan, and shall contain any additional information required by the Planning Commission at the time of the preliminary plan.

a) Stage Construction—If development of the shopping center is to be carried out in progressive stages, each stage shall be so planned that the requirements and intent of this Ordinance shall be fully complied with at the completion of each stage. No final plan for the initial stage of development of any shopping center shall be approved unless such stage comprises a total ground floor area of at least twenty-five thousand (25,000) square feet and at least three (3) of the designated principal uses.

b) Action on Final Site Plan—Compliance with Preliminary Site Plan—Not more than thirty (30) days after receipt of a final site plan for a shopping center or for any stage thereof, the Planning Commission shall determine whether such final plan is in compliance with the preliminary plan as approved by the Commission. If the final plan is determined to be in compliance and if all applicable requirements of this Subsection are also complied with or if the Planning Commission shall determine that modifications, if any, and the proposed development of the reserve areas, if any, contained in the final site plan are in harmony with the general purposes and intent of the approved preliminary plan, and not in conflict with the comprehensive plan for development, the Commission shall so notify the Council. The applicant may then apply for a Building Permit. In all other instances, the Commission shall recommend disapproval of the final plan and shall so notify the applicant in writing. The applicant may then apply to the Council for a review of the decision of the Planning Commission. If the final plan is disapproved because of noncompliance with the preliminary plan, the final plan may thereafter be submitted to the Commission as an amended preliminary plan. The procedure for the consideration of such amended preliminary plan shall be the same as that for the consideration of an original preliminary plan.

c) Change of Final Site Plan—If the applicant wants to make any amendment to an approved final plan, a written request shall be submitted to the Commission. If, in the opinion of the Commission, a requested change is sufficiently substantial, the Commission shall require the submission of an amended final plan. The procedure for the consideration of such written request or of such amended final plan shall be the same as that for the consideration of a final plan.

c. **Standards for Development**—

1) *Permitted Uses*—Any use permitted in the CB zone is permitted as a principal use of land in a shopping center except that the Planning Commission shall have the power to recommend and the Council to approve as part of the conditional use permit uses which are not permitted in the CB zone and in addition shall have the power to exclude certain specific uses not compatible with a regional shopping center.

2) *Site and Floor Area*—A Regional Shopping Center shall contain 500,000 square feet of gross leasable area and

be located on a zoning lot of at least 50 acres.

3) *Floor Area Ratio*—The combined floor area ratio for all buildings shall not exceed 0.50 on any zoning lot.

4) *Maximum Lot Coverage*—The total ground area. occupied by all principal buildings together with all accessory buildings, shall not exceed twenty-five (25) percent of the total area of the zoning lot.

5) *Building Setback Line*—Each zoning lot shall have a building setback from all street rights-of-way of at least eighty (80) feet. A strip fifty (50) feet deep along the front line shall be maintained as a landscaped buffer strip. The remaining area may be used for parking.

6) *Side and Rear Yards*—Each zoning lot shall have side and rear yards of at least fifty (50) feet in width. A strip twenty (20) feet in width or depth along side and rear lot lines shall be maintained as a landscaped buffer strip. The remainder of the area may be used for parking.

7) *Height Restriction*—The height of any building in the Regional Shopping Center shall not exceed the limit as specified in the conditional use permit recommended by the Planning Commission and approved by the Council.

8) *Special Buffer Requirement Adjacent to Residential Areas*—Along any boundary line adjacent to a residential area, a buffer yard shall be provided which shall be at least one hundred (100) feet in depth, measured from the property line.

9) *Access and Traffic Control*—

a) *Access Barrier*—Each zoning lot, with its buildings, other structures, and parking and loading areas, shall be physically separated from each adjoining street by a curb or other suitable barrier against unchanneled motor vehicle ingress and egress. Such barrier shall be located at the edge of or within a twenty (20)-foot-deep strip along the property line. Except for the access ways permitted by (b) below, the barrier shall be continuous for the entire length of the property line.

b) *Access Ways*—Each zoning lot shall have not more than two (2) access ways to any one street unless unusual circumstances demonstrate the need for additional access points. Each access way shall comply with the following requirements:

The width of any access way leading to a public street which exceeds 25 feet shall have a median between the entrance and exit lanes. Curb returns shall have a minimum radius of thirty (30) feet.

At its intersection with the property line, no part of any access way shall be nearer than one hundred (100) feet to the intersection of any two (2) street right-of-way lines. nor shall any such part be nearer than fifty (50) feet to any side or rear property line.

The location and number of access ways shall be so arranged that they will reduce traffic hazards as much as possible.

10) *Off-Street Parking Areas*—All off-street parking spaces and servicing drives shall be located within the boundaries of the property being developed as a shopping center. Off-street parking spaces shall be provided at the rate of at least two (2) square feet of parking area to one (1) square foot of gross floor area. Spaces provided behind the stores or shops shall not be considered usable by the public and shall not be considered in calculating the minimum space required; provided, however, that if the shopping center is so designed that all of the shops and stores face upon a central mall and all sections of the parking area are provided with adequate connecting internal drives, the location of parking areas may completely surround such shops and stores.

11) *Off-Street Loading Areas*—Each shop or store shall have a rear or side entrance that is accessible to a service entrance. Further, any loading dock shall be enclosed within the building. The arrangement of truck loading and unloading facilities for each shop or store shall be such that in the process of loading or unloading no truck will block or extend into any drive or street used for vehicular circulation. Loading and delivery zones shall be clearly marked.

12) *Lighting*—All parking areas and access ways shall be floodlighted at night during business hours. All outside lighting shall be arranged and shielded to prevent glare or reflection, nuisance, inconvenience, or hazardous intereference of any kind on adjoining streets or residential properties.

13) *Waste Pens*—Each building shall be provided with an enclosed waste pen of sufficient size to accommodate all trash and waste stored on the premises.

14) *Trash Burners and Incinerators*—There shall be no trash burner or incinerators, or any burning of trash or rubbish on the premises.

Metric Conversion Table

Meters	=	feet × 0.305
Kilometers	=	miles × 1.609
Square Meters	=	square feet × 0.093
Square Kilometers	=	square miles × 2.590
Cubic Meters	=	cubic feet × 0.028
Cubic Meters	=	cubic yards × 0.765
Hectares	=	acres × 0.405
(a hectare is 10,000 square meters)		

INDEX